Homo Juridicus

Homo Juridicus

Culture as a Normative Order

Isaak I. Dore

Professor of Law
St. Louis University School of Law

Visiting Professor
Université de Toulouse Capitole Faculté de Droit, France

Carolina Academic Press
Durham, North Carolina

Library of Congress Cataloging-in-Publication Data

Names: Dore, Isaak I. (Isaak Ismail), 1950- author.
Title: Homo juridicus : culture as a normative order / Isaak I. Dore.
Description: Durham, North Carolina : Carolina Academic Press, 2016. |
Includes bibliographical references and index.
Identifiers: LCCN 2016012276 | ISBN 9781611636970 (alk. paper)
Subjects: LCSH: Law and anthropology. | Law--Philosophy.
Classification: LCC K487.A57 D67 2016 | DDC 340/.115--dc23
LC record available at http://lccn.loc.gov/2016012276

Carolina Academic Press, LLC
700 Kent Street
Durham, North Carolina 27701
Telephone (919) 489-7486
Fax (919) 493-5668
www.cap-press.com

Printed in the United States of America

For Joël Monéger

Contents

Copyright Acknowledgments and Permissions

Ruth Benedict, Patterns of Culture 45–50, 56 (1934). Excerpts from Patterns of Culture by Ruth Benedict. Copyright 1934 by Ruth Benedict; copyright renewed (c) 1961 by Ruth Valentine. Reprinted by permission of Houghton Mifflin Harcourt Publishing Company. All rights reserved.

Paul Schiff Berman, *An Anthropological Approach to Modern Forfeiture Law: The Symbolic Function of Legal Actions Against Objects*, 11 Yale J. L. & Human. 1, 23–26, 18–19, 37–38, 44–45 (1999). Copyright (1999) The Yale Law Journal Company, Inc. All rights reserved.

John M. Conley & William M. O'Barr, Just Words: Law, Language, and Power 32–37 (2d ed. 2005). Reprinted by permission of University of Chicago Press.

Janet L. Dolgin, David S. Kemnitzer & David M. Schneider, *Introduction*, *in* Symbolic Anthropology: A Reader in the Study of Symbols and Meanings 33–43 (Janet L. Dolgin, David S. Kemnitzer & David M. Schneider eds., 1977). Permission granted by Janet Dolgin.

Emile Durkheim, Rules of the Sociological Method. Reprinted with the permission of Free Press, a Division of Simon & Schuster, Inc. (edited by George E.G. Catlin, and translated by Sarah A. Solovay and John H. Mueller. Copyright © 1938 by George E.G. Catlin, renewed © 1966 by Sarah A. Solovay, John H. Mueller, and George E.G. Catlin. All rights reserved.

Emile Durkheim, Suicide: A Study in Sociology. Reprinted with permission of Free Press, a Division of Simon & Schuster, Inc. Translated by John A. Spaulding and George Simpson. Copyright © 1951 by The Free Press; copyright renewed © 1979 by The Free Press. All rights reserved.

Friedrich Engels, The Origin of the Family, Private Property and the State 153–160 (Resistance Books, 2004). Reprinted by permission of LW books.

Clifford Geertz, *Thick Description: Toward an Interpretive Theory of Culture*, *in* Clifford Geertz, The Interpretation of Cultures: Selected Essays 5–12 (1973). Reprinted by permission of Copyright Clearance Center.

Carol J. Greenhouse, Barbara Yngvesson & David M. Engel, Law and Community in Three American Towns 118–121, 124–127, 188 (1994) Cornell University Press.

Marvin Harris, Cultural Materialism: The Struggle for a Science of Culture 36, 38–39, 45, 51–57 (1979) copyright (1979) by Rowman & Littlefield. All rights reserved. For the life of this edition only.

MARVIN HARRIS, THE RISE OF ANTHROPOLOGICAL THEORY: A HISTORY OF THEORIES OF CULTURE 326–335 (updated ed., 2001). Copyright (2001) by Rowman & Littlefield. For the life of this edition, English print only.

A.L. KROEBER, ANTHROPOLOGY: RACE, LANGUAGE, CULTURE, PSYCHOLOGY, PREHISTORY 5–11 (New ed., 1948). Reprinted by permission of the Kroeber family.

CLAUDE LÉVI-STRAUSS, STRUCTURAL ANTHROPOLOGY 18–21, 33–34, 37–41 (Claire Jacobson & Brooke Grundfest Schoepf trans., 1963). Reprinted by permission of Copyright Clearance Center.

Bronislaw Malinowski, *The Group and the Individual in Functional Analysis*, 44 AM. J. SOCIOL. 938, 938–941, 961–964 (1939). Reprinted with permission of University of Chicago Press.

BRONISLAW MALINOWSKI, THE DYNAMICS OF CULTURE CHANGE: AN INQUIRY INTO RACE RELATIONS IN AFRICA 44–46 (1949). Reprinted by permission of Yale University Press.

UGO MATTEI AND LAURA NADER, PLUNDER—WHEN THE RULE OF LAW IS ILLEGAL 82–86, 104–07, 110 (2008). Reprinted by permission of Wiley Global Permissions.

MARGARET MEAD, COMING OF AGE IN SAMOA: A PSYCHOLOGICAL STUDY OF PRIMITIVE YOUTH FOR WESTERN CIVILIZATION 196–201, 206–207 copyright (1928) 49, 55, 61, 73 by Margaret Mead. Reprinted by permission of Harper Collins Publishers.

Laura Nader, *Controlling Processes: Tracing the Dynamic Components of Power*, 38 CURRENT ANTHROPOLOGIST, No. 5, 713–15 (Dec. 1997). Reprinted by permission of University of Chicago Press.

Laura Nader, *The Anthropological Study of Law*, 67 AM. ANTHROPOL. 3, 23–25 (1965). Permission granted by Professor Laura Nader.

Laura Nader, *The Crown, the Colonists, and the Course of Zapotec Law*, *in* HISTORY AND POWER IN THE STUDY OF LAW: NEW DIRECTIONS IN LEGAL ANTHROPOLOGY 320, 332–342 (June Starr & Jane F. Collier eds., 1989) Cornell University Press.

A.R. RADCLIFFE-BROWN, STRUCTURE AND FUNCTION IN PRIMITIVE SOCIETY 178–185, 197–199, 212–219 (1952). Reprinted by permission of Simon and Schuster Publishing Co.

A.R. RADCLIFFE-BROWN, METHOD IN SOCIAL ANTHROPOLOGY 324–328, 397–400 (1958). Reprinted with permission of University of Chicago Press.

ROBERT PAUL RESCH, ALTHUSSER AND THE RENEWAL OF MARXIST SOCIAL THEORY 23–24, 26–27 (1992). Copyright (1992) by University of California Press. All rights reserved.

JAMES P. SPRADLEY, YOU OWE YOURSELF A DRUNK: AN ETHNOLOGY OF URBAN NOMADS 180–184, 190–192 (1970). Reprinted by permission of Waveland Press, Inc. Long Grove, IL: Waveland Press, Inc., © (1970) Reissued in 2000. All rights reserved.

JAMES SPRADLEY & DAVID W. MCCURDY, CONFORMITY AND CONFLICT: READINGS IN CULTURAL ANTHROPOLOGY 321–325 (11th ed., 2003). Permission granted by Anne Sutherland.

JULIAN H. STEWARD, THEORY OF CULTURE CHANGE 30, 36–42 (1963). Reprinted by permission of University of Illinois Press.

VICTOR TURNER, THE RITUAL PROCESS: STRUCTURE AND ANTI-STRUCTURE 100–04 (1969). Reprinted by permission of Transaction Publishers Inc.

Stephen A. Tyler, *Introduction*, *in* COGNITIVE ANTHROPOLOGY 1, 3–6 (Stephen A. Tyler ed., 1969). Reprinted by permission of Copyright Clearance Center.

Leslie A. White, THE SCIENCE OF CULTURE 364–391 (1949). Copyright (1949) by American Museum of Natural History. All rights reserved.

Acknowledgments

I wish to thank a number of colleagues and friends who have contributed to this project. Laura Underkuffler, J. DuPratt White Professor of Law at Cornell Law School, provided constant support and encouragement over the years to my fanciful pursuits of the study of law in various interdisciplinary contexts, including this latest escapade. Cécile le Gallou of Toulouse Law School and Distinguished Visiting Professor at St. Louis University School of Law (Spring 2015) provided invaluable comments and suggestions. Cécile also took on the daunting task of preparing a version of this book in French, for which I am deeply honored. I also thank Dean Hugues Kenfack of Toulouse Law School for his support and encouragement in the preparation of this book. I would also like to thank Peter Wogan, Professor of Anthropology (and Chairman of the Department) at Willamette University for his helpful comments and unwavering support from the very inception of this project.

Special thanks go to that august group of scholars (*les juridico-gourmands*) at the University of Orléans, France, where this book was the subject of a seminar and where I received many helpful suggestions. There are too many group members for me to thank them individually, but I would like to recognize the special help of Nathalie Dion, Catherine Thibierge (the leading light of L'école d'Orléans), and Cyril Sintez, all seasoned scholars in the fields of *l'épistemologie juridique* and *la normativité*, in which fields this book hopes to make a modest contribution.

This project would not have come to see the light of day without the help of many other individuals. First, I remain eternally grateful to Laura Poole and Lea Popielinski for their excellent editorial advice. Laura's help went beyond the call of duty in many ways.

My deepest thanks go to Stephanie Haley, my wonderful assistant and friend who has helped me in so many ways over the past 35 years. Steph (as we fondly call her) singlehandedly prepared the manuscript for publication from start to finish.

I also thank my excellent team of research assistants who have cycled through law school and gone on to bigger and better things. Jared Hausmann provided outstanding research assistance. He found obscure materials and sent them to me by tracking me down through my various peregrinations. He also provided valuable help by checking the materials for the entire book. I also thank Andrew Kaiser and Kyrstin Beasley for help with proofing and checking citations. My sincere thanks to Claire Kates who (even while studying abroad) provided tremendous help with checking citations, proofing, and preparing the index and Teacher's Manual.

A final word of thanks for the outstanding research support from LeAnn Noland, Erika Cohen, and Kathleen Casey of St. Louis University Law Library.

Prologue

The Metaphysics of Culture I

Plato, the acknowledged inventor of the science of metaphysics, had a reason for his invention. As I have explained elsewhere,[i] he was seeking a middle ground between the radically rigid skepticism of the Heraclitean doctrine of Flux and the equally rigid doctrine of Parmenides claiming that reality was permanent, unchanging and uncreated. While Plato's reasons for his invention are important, of equal or even greater note is the power of its symbolism. As for his symbolism, we must first note that symbols are creatures of the imagination, and second, as such, they impose no limits on the creative abilities of the mind. Third, this power of the mind is shown by the fact that it can create any symbol it wants and assign to it any signification or meaning it chooses. Indeed "man is an animal suspended in webs of significance that he himself has spun."[ii] The totality of these webs of meaning constitute culture, and they include symbols and norms, legal and nonlegal.

We shall return to Plato's metaphysics and its relation to culture as a normative order. Of immediate concern is how normativity operates as part of what Geertz calls our "webs of significance." Is Man a juridical animal? If so, to what extent? These questions constitute the central theme of this book, as captured by its first subtitle (on which more later). We use the term "juridical" in the broad sense of denoting legal as well as other relations that promote normative order and are of "significance" à la Geertz. From this broad perspective we may rephrase the above two questions as follows: To what extent are human relations governed by law? Can we do without law? What, indeed, is law? To what extent are human relations governed by normative forces other than law?

These questions require the empirical study of human relations in the broadest variety of normative contexts. This study is thus necessarily *relational*. It deals with the totality of relations between human beings belonging to particular sociocultural formations. Just as it is impossible to imagine a culture in which there are no human relations, it is also a truism that human relations are more orderly than chaotic, structured rather than unstructured; and they occur within certain frameworks of understanding. These understandings regulate behavior in several ways and acquire a *force* proportional to their ability to persuade, incite, seduce, influence, direct, restrain, repress or control particular behavioral acts in particular cultural contexts. Herein lies the essence of "normative force" or "normativity." Of course the word

---

i. For further detail see Isaak Dore, The Epistemological Foundations of Law, 48, 58–60, 123–39 (2007).

ii. Clifford Geertz, *Thick Description: Toward an Interpretive Theory of Culture* in The Interpretation of Cultures: Selected Essay by Clifford Geertz 3 at 5 (1973).

"force" includes the idea of coercion. It can, but need not necessarily, mean physical force. Thus when we encounter the numerous references in this book to "normative force" we must bear in mind that we are (more often than not) not referring to physical coercion but rather to the many nuanced ways in which human relations are *determined*. The idea of normativity in culture, then, evokes the totality of force relations that constitute it.[iii]

Just as "force" includes physical coercion but goes beyond it, so the idea of normativity includes "law" but goes beyond it. For purposes of this book, a law is the clearest example of a "norm" that has regulative force. But there are many nonlegal norms of the same genre. Thus again we use the word "norm" in the broadest relational sense. Indeed, "law" and "norm" are interchangeable notions in conditions of culture. This approach to culture in essence broadens Jacques Derrida's thesis regarding the "force" of law which he proposed at his famous lecture at Cardozo Law School in 1989, with the qualification that my notion of *force* is empirical rather than "mystical."[iv]

The twin notions of norms and normativity are treated in this book as not only relational but also dynamic. This raises the *problématique* of stability as well as instability, structure as well as antistructure in sociocultural formations. In sum, this book studies culture in normative as well as dynamic relational contexts, with law as just one of its many symbols.

Plato's doctrine of the Forms is a dazzling example of the power of the mind (or imagination, which in this case, is the same thing) to develop a symbol with a "significance" or meaning. Plato conjured up out of thin air a magnificent world of suprasensible reality that should serve as a beacon of perfection for the sensible world. If the Platonic Form was a "representation" (to use Durkheimian terminology) of perfection, it also contained (as did its Durkheimian analog) the implicit epistemological claim that it was knowable. Put differently, the Platonic Form was: 1. A symbol. 2. It was full of meaning. 3. It was an object of knowledge, and 4. Its meaning was knowable. All tokens of culture have these properties.

But we must take a temporary detour from the philosophical meaning of Plato's metaphysic in favor of its symbolic aspects, *i.e.*, its shared meaning. Here we make a direct transition into the social function of the Form *qua* symbol. In anthropological parlance anything that has a shared meaning can be a symbol, and the Platonic Form certainly satisfies this definitional requirement, as well as the condition that a symbol is a creature of the mind.

Plato's metaphysic is also a particularly apposite example for a book dedicated to exploring the normative foundations of culture. This is because Man (the only animal of culture) is largely a metaphysical entity—a proposition that is at the same time self-evident and counterintuitive. It is counterintuitive because one might (understandably) ask how can a human being as a living breathing animal, having a physical

iii. *See generally* Catherine Thibierge (dir) et al, La force normative: naissance d'un concept (2009).

iv. Jacques Derrida, *Force of Law: The "Mystical Foundation of Authority,"* 11 Cardozo L. Rev. 920 (1989–1990). *See also*, Nicolas Emeric and Sintez Cyril "Par-delà le concept de force dans la philosophie de Jacques Derrida" in Catherine Thibierge, La force normative, *supra* note iii.

existence, and also having certain definite bio-physiological needs be described as "meta" physical? It is of course absurd to deny the materio-physical aspects of human existence. But humans do not lead a purely brute animal existence; which brings us to the self-evident nature of the proposition. It is self-evident for two reasons. First, culture (of which law is a component) is a metaphysical construct because at its irreducible core lies a system of meanings ("webs of significance"). Second these meanings are *shared by* human beings *qua* human beings given the cognitive abilities of the human brain. Thus in addition to their physical universe, humans necessarily inhabit a nonphysical or metaphysical cultural universe which radically sets them apart from other sentient beings.

Plato's metaphor shows that humans can, do and perhaps should inhabit the suprasensible world simultaneously with their phenomenal world. This is not unlike the Kantian distinction between phenomena and noumena (*i.e.*, the causal world of sense perception or experience, and the "intelligible" world of "understanding") and his assertion that humankind inhabits both universes at the same time.[v] The French philosopher Alain Supiot makes a similar point when he asserts that human beings inhabit not only "a universe of things but also a universe of signs".[vi]

The universe of signs represents the metaphysical dimension, and as noted above, it depends on the limitless power of the imagination. The juridical and normative aspects of human existence belong to this dimension and contrast with the materio-physical dimension. The latter is conventionally understood to refer to the finite physical/material or economic aspects of the human condition, captured as *Homo Economicus*. The metaphysical dimension is infinite and includes, but is not limited to, the juridico-normative dimension. It is this dimension that is captured by the term *Homo Juridicus* in this book. Unlike Supiot's notion, my notion of *Homo Juridicus* is shorn of its religious (particularly Christian) underpinnings and does not rest on the view of man as *Imago Dei*. Supiot claims that under the Western liberal tradition, inherited from the Enlightenment, the concept of the juridical subject is based on certain indemonstrable propositions positing humans as rational and autonomous beings. This concept of rationality and autonomy has Christian foundations viewing humans as rational, autonomous and free and having been created in the image of God.

> It is by transforming each of us into a *homo juridicus* that, in the West, the biological and symbolic dimensions that make up our being have been linked together. The law connects our infinite mental universe with our finite physical existence and in so doing fulfills the anthropological function of instituting us as rational beings.[vii]

My view of *Homo Juridicus* is based on ethnographic data providing an empirical foundation for the concept. It is this data that must be evaluated critically by us. The contours of this critical evaluation, I suggest, ought to track the following criss-

---

v. Dore, *supra* note i, at 432–33.

vi. ALAIN SUPIOT, HOMO JURIDICUS: ON THE ANTHROPOLOGICAL FUNCTION OF LAW vii (Saskia Brown trans., 2007).

vii. *Id.* at ix.

crossing themes: How convincing is the claim by the classical evolutionists discussed in Chapter 1 that *ubi societas ibi ius, i.e.*, that law and normativity are "universal" institutions of human society? What is the *significance* or *meaning* underlying this alleged universality? Is it empirical, symbolic, metaphorical or metaphysical?

How persuasive is the historical particularist claim of the Boasian school (discussed in Chapter 2) that cultural normativity must be studied on its own terms empirically, and that there is no "one-size-fits-all" model for it? In the same vein, how credible is the claim by certain particularists that all norms are products of culture?; that the individual does not create culture but culture creates the individual?

If a symbol can only be understood in terms of its *raison d'être* and social meaning, what social meaning do legal and nonlegal norms have? How persuasive is the claim of Edward Sapir that the social significance of law is best understood by studying the logical and linguistic aspects of legal thought? Is law a creature of the mind, and if so, how is it harnessed by humankind as a social tool? What is its relationship to social order, freedom, oppression, and so on? And what are we to make of the claim of the "culture and personality" school (represented by Ruth Benedict and Margaret Mead) that cultural normativity is connected to individual personality and psychology? That culture is simply individual personality writ large? These themes are also examined in Chapter 2.

I treat culture as occupying a large part of our metaphysical universe, and if law is only a part of the webs of culture within which we find ourselves "suspended," how does law interact with other components of culture? Here we enter the "structural" and "functional" aspects of normativity, taken up in Chapter 3. This chapter examines various methodological approaches to functionalism and presents case studies based thereon, so that the reader can evaluate critically how the phenomenon of normativity can be best understood. It will be seen that such evaluation involves the examination of the epistemic reliability of these various methodologies and their progeny. Among the important epistemological questions discussed in Chapter 3 is Durkheim's methodological aim of studying law as a "social fact" *i.e.*, something that is capable of scientific study in the same way as any natural or physical fact, as well as A.R. Radcliffe-Brown's claimed discovery of the "sociological laws" of human evolution.

Chapters 4 and 5 are respectively devoted to Marxism and Neo-Marxism. The radical anthropology of Karl Marx and Frederick Engels advances a new theory of cultural and normative evolution, claiming it to be scientifically based, and asserting a certain form of determinism and universalism. The methodological approaches of structural Marxism as well as other 21st century variants of cultural Marxism and their case studies will be examined. Again the reader will be invited to compare and contrast critically the epistemic reliability of these methodologies and their claims with those of their predecessors. To the extent that Marxism as a general doctrine unites our physical universe with our "universe of signs" it has created a fertile area of debate, if not controversy. Finally, Marvin Harris's Neo-Marxist theory of cultural materialism and the materialist approaches of Leslie White and Julian Steward also raise provocative epistemological questions as to the place of normativity within the universe of signs.

Chapters 6 and 7 respectively present an "emic" perspective of law and normativity, in contrast with the "etic" posture of the two preceding chapters. The emic approach is closely associated with "cognitivism," a school of thought that seeks to understand the cultural universe from an internalist perspective. It's use of the various methods of linguistics, ethnoscience and componential analysis to construct a "cultural grammar" of each subject culture raises further epistemological questions for debate, as does the claim that it can construct a "cognitive map" of any subject culture. Again, the classic question of cultural autonomy versus individual autonomy arises in the context of whether the individual "map reader" is also a "map maker," and, regardless of how one answers the question, what knowledge does the map produce and how epistemically reliable is it?

As part of the emics of legal and normative cognitivism, Chapter 6 also examines what the poor, the homeless and ordinary working-class Americans think and feel about justice in their own country, and their view of the religious right's alliance with the power structure and the perpetuation of hierarchy. In the same vein, Chapter 7 is devoted to two important subschools within the overall cognitive enterprise, namely, interpretivism and symbolism. The former tackles once again the internalist perspective, challenging the view that the ethnographer should "go native" in order to capture the internal point of view a native culture. The interpretivist school raises new questions of epistemology as does its methodology of "thick description."[viii] Finally, the use of symbols, their social function and their relationship to legal and nonlegal norms shows how significant symbols are as part of our universe of signs. Given that symbols are creatures of the mind, that they are as limitless as the power that produces them, it will not surprise the reader that they can be invented for just about any reason we choose, just as Plato invented his symbolic world to suit his particular philosophical project. However, most symbols are not invented for philosophical reasons yet serve socially useful purposes, both legal and nonlegal.

Chapter 8 is a natural transition from the preceding one in that the foregoing theories of interpretation set the context for postmodern anthropological theory. This final chapter examines the critical spirit of postmodernism towards cultural normativity; its relationship to power and domination both nationally and internationally, as well as the clash of cultures. This is particularly well illustrated by the use of the cultural defense doctrine when a member of a cultural minority is indicted under the criminal law of a dominant culture for violating the fundamental cultural mores of the latter.

Naturally, the foregoing are only some of the thematic highlights of the book. Its interdisciplinary approach captures a wide range of themes cutting across several disciplines of social science such as law, anthropology, sociology, psychology, linguistics and philosophy. For these you must plow forward, and, as they say here in France, I wish you "bonne continuation"!

---

viii. Geertz, *supra* note ii at 3.

Homo Juridicus

Chapter 1

Cultural Normativity in Evolutionary Context

"Anthropology" is a term of Greek origin. It is derived from "anthropos," meaning man, and "logos," meaning study or knowledge.[1] Anthropology, then, is the study of human beings as a species, as individuals, and as social beings.

As a field of knowledge, anthropology has become more and more specialized. The most basic division is between *physical anthropologists* and *cultural anthropologists*. Physical anthropologists, who are fewer in number than cultural anthropologists, generally study humans from a biological perspective—that is, how the human species has evolved, who its primitive relatives are, and how they have adapted.[2] Cultural anthropology focuses on social, cognitive, linguistic, normative and historical studies of cultural groups through examinations of their customs, myths, institutions, and social relationships.

As anthropologists have striven to understand "culture" and how it is manifested and regulated among the various peoples of the world, and as cultural anthropologists have over time become increasingly dissatisfied with the parameters of study developed by earlier anthropologists, cultural anthropology has evolved into many schools of thought. In an attempt to frame more workable cultural theories and better methods of obtaining cultural information, each new generation of anthropologists has taken the cultural information it has received and recast it into new theoretical molds, claiming that each new theory is a better or more accurate representation of the "truth."

These developments have confirmed the classical Western approach to studying cultural phenomena as narrow and ethnocentric—a bias that has become particularly obvious in relation to the institution of law. The Western approach views law as a large but static edifice of rules regulating social interaction through established norms. Legislators enact rules, which the executive branch enforces. When a rule is broken, the judiciary steps in to judge the facts and assign a proper remedy as necessary. Thus, rules—and institutions that create and enforce them—form the core of the Western idea of law.

With the emergence of new schools of thought grew the realization that institutions of social control, including law, can exist in many forms. For example, the

---

1. Pospíšil, Leopold, J., Anthropology and Science, 50.

2. Roger M. Keesing and Felix M. Keesing (hereinafter Keesing and Keesing), *New Perspectives in Cultural Anthropology*, 7 (1971). *See also*, 1 Victor Barnouw, An Introduction to Anthropology: Physical Anthropology and Archeology, and Victor Barnouw, An Introduction to Anthropology, Ethnology 2 (1971).

effectiveness of law does not depend on whether it is created, written, and enforced by formal Western-style law-making and law-enforcing institutions. These new, more flexible approaches involved gathering empirical data that ultimately led to broader and more flexible notions of normativity in cultural institutions. The data was usually in the form of ethnographic studies of various societies and cultures. These studies provided a more inclusive perspective of the meaning of social behavior and a more comprehensive understanding of how normative order exists beyond the boundaries of Western theory.

What follows is a historical snapshot of the various schools of thought in cultural anthropology, beginning with the classical evolutionists of the seventeenth and eighteenth centuries. The synopsis shows how the quest for understanding cultural continuity and regularity evolved as each school challenged, discarded, and built on the methods and contributions of previous schools. It also shows how the classical Western idea of law has become relegated to the status of one among many equally legitimate notions of law.

Classical Evolutionism

Although the emergence of anthropological theory as a discipline dates back to the late seventeenth and eighteenth centuries, its inspirational roots are much older. As a science of culture, anthropological theory was inspired by contact among different cultures. Such contact became possible only with the development of improved methods of communication and transportation, which in turn were responses to other, greater socioeconomic and historical forces. This intercultural interaction led to recordings of these contacts and thus to their accumulation and diffusion. A variety of enterprising individuals—including historians, traders, missionaries, and travelers dating back to the times of the ancient Greeks—compiled these records. Among them were the accounts assembled by the great Greek historian and traveler Herodotus (484–425 BCE) and the Roman historian Tacitus (ca. CE 55–120). Records of intercultural contact were also kept in ancient China and India. Others were gathered during the Age of Discovery (early fifteenth–late sixteenth centuries) with the development of new trade routes and the search of external markets, the spread of colonialism, and the travels of European Jesuit missionaries who sought to "civilize" the non-Christian world.[3]

These accounts, which served as crude ethnographies of the customs of different cultures, were not always accurate. Indeed, although they included some empirical data based on direct observation and reasoning, considerable information was received secondhand and involved exaggeration, speculation, and guesswork. However, by the middle of the nineteenth century, anthropology had become firmly established as an academic discipline as its pioneers began to formulate their theories. These first professional anthropologists, known as the classical evolutionists, used

3. *See* 2 Barnouw, *supra* note 2, at 23 *et seq.*; Roger Bastide, Applied Anthropology (Harper Torchbook Edition, 1973) 10 *et seq.*

the cultural accounts written by the Jesuits and others as data and tried to assimilate it into theoretical frameworks. They came to be known as "evolutionists" because of their preoccupation with theoretical models that explained the evolution of various phases of culture. These scholars employed the comparative method, a process by which modern groups and institutions were "arranged in a sequence of increasing antiquity."[4] They assumed that older (including extinct) cultures were the key to understanding contemporary social and normative arrangements, that is, in some measure the latter resembled the former.

Because most classical evolutionists did not collect their own empirical data on the cultures they studied, modern scholars refer to them as "armchair anthropologists." Their lack of ethnographic research experience proved problematic. Because the comparative method was wholly dependent on field data, it was obvious that misuse or inaccurate use of the data would yield faulty results.[5] Aware of these pitfalls, yet unable to verify the accuracy of their data, these early evolutionists concentrated on simply compiling large numbers of cases.[6] This left the classical evolutionists vulnerable to attacks on their credibility—including charges that they used data only when it conformed to a certain theory.[7] Although the work of these early evolutionists is not highly valued today, the theories embedded in their works continue to be studied by contemporary anthropologists to evaluate and improve on modern anthropology. The following sections introduce the normative theories of three of the most influential of these early evolutionists: Herbert Spencer, Edward B. Tylor, and Lewis Henry Morgan.[8]

Spencer: Social Structure and Evolution

British scholar Herbert Spencer (1820–1903) was among the first of the professional anthropologists to study social classifications.[9] Because Spencer had an academic background in biology, his theories concerning social structure and evolution were influenced by his knowledge of organic systems. He began working on his theories of evolution before Charles Darwin, who held his ideas in great esteem.[10] It was Spencer, not Darwin, who popularized "evolution" as a term and who coined the phrase "survival of the fittest."[11] Indeed, because of Spencer's major contributions

4. Marvin Harris, The Rise of Anthropological Theory: A History of Theories of Culture 151 (1968).

5. *Id.* at 156.

6. *Id.* at 156–57.

7. *Id.* at 157.

8. *See generally* 1–2 Edward B. Tylor, Primitive Culture: Researches into the Development of Mythology, Philosophy, Religion, Language, Art, And Custom, (3d ed. 1891); Herbert Spencer published a multivolume series under the title of Descriptive Sociology (1873–1934); Lewis Henry Morgan, Ancient Society (foreword by Elisabeth Tooker, 1985).

9. *See* Harris, *supra* note 4, at 159.

10. *Id.* at 129.

11. *Id.* at 128.

to biological theory at the time when Darwin's ideas became popular, it has been asserted that the biocultural theories known as "social Darwinism" should really be called "Spencerism."[12]

The sociocultural roots of Spencer's and Darwin's evolutionism are too complex to be described in this introduction. Suffice it to note that both were reacting to other mid-nineteenth-century writers and thinkers. Spencer, in particular, was reacting to Charles Lyell's criticisms of Jean-Baptiste Lamarck, who believed in an immutable law of nature that ensured the creation of ever more perfect bioforms over time. This belief included a "faith in the perfectability of mankind."[13] Lyell, in rejecting Lamarck, sided with Malthus's pessimistic view that humankind, far from being destined for progress and perfection, was doomed to misery.[14] Lyell rejected Lamarck's evolutionism, contending instead that new bioforms and their superior normative orders only emerged in time and space to replace older ones because they were preadapted by their Creator.

Both Spencer and Darwin rejected Lyell's anti-evolutionism. Spencer was a strong believer in the universality of causation, under which everything has its assignable cause of a comprehensible kind.[15] Scientific progress is thus not only possible but also inevitable and can be explained by laws of increasing generality. It has been asserted that Spencer's belief in causation led him to embrace his evolutionary theory because it posited that social normativity is explainable in terms of cause and effect. Social and moral rules are created willfully because they are useful. This aspect of his theory of causation was criticized by other thinkers, such as Emile Durkheim. As I discuss in Chapter 3, Durkheim, Franz Boas, and others argued that causality is different from will and purpose. For example, the will or purpose to bring about an effective social institution does not necessarily lead to its existence. Under this critique, Spencer's principle of causality only explained the nonvolitional conditions of social life, that is, those conditions that were indispensable and without which social life would not exist. Durkheim would therefore propose a common spirit, social consensus, or tradition, rather than a "cause," to explain the existence of moral rules and institutions.[16]

Given Spencer's belief in the universality of causation, it was not surprising that he believed the universe followed one continuous and progressive scheme of development—as did nature, culture, and law. Social cohesion and normative order were thus established causally. The more developed the society, the greater the cohesion and harmony within the normative order, and the lower the need for coercion.[17] His evo-

---

12. *Id.* at 129.

13. *Id.* at 114. *See generally*, C. Lyell, Principles of Geology (8th ed. 1850); and J.B. Lamarck, Hydrogeology (A. V. Carozzi, trans., 1964).

14. *See generally*, Thomas R. Malthus, An Essay on the Principle of Population (1803). 2 Herbert Spencer: An Autobiography 6 (1904).

15. C. Elvin Hatch, Theories of Man and Culture 16 (1973).

16. *Id.* at 189, 208–09.

17. *Id.* at 168–69. This too was an aspect of Spencer's thought rejected by Durkheim. The latter attributed developed social relations and cohesion to a collective consciousness that transcended individual interests.

lutionary classification thus placed the more developed society at the apex, with the simplest or "lowest social aggregates" at the opposite end of his classificatory scheme:

> If organization consists in such a construction of the whole that its parts can carry on mutually dependent actions, then in proportion as organization is high there must go a dependence of each part upon the rest so great that separation is fatal; and conversely. This truth is equally well shown in the individual organism and in the social organism.
>
> The lowest animal-aggregates are so constituted that each portion, similar to every other in appearance, carries on similar actions, and here spontaneous or artificial separation interferes scarcely at all with the life of either separated portion ... The like happens for the like reason with the lowest social aggregates ... With highly organized aggregates of either kind it is very different. We cannot cut a mammal in two without causing immediate death ... [When] a civilized society is so divided that part of it is left without a central controlling agency it may presently evolve one, yet there is meanwhile much risk of dissolution, and before reorganization is efficient, a long period of disorder and weakness must be passed through.[18]

Contrasting his approach with that of Auguste Comte, Spencer asserted that his aim was to give a coherent account of the progress of the external world. By contrast, Comte's aim (according to Spencer) was to give an account of the genesis of human knowledge and conceptions of nature.[19] He characterized Comte's end as subjective (insofar as it was concerned with human conceptions), whereas he characterized his own inquiry as objective (insofar as its aim was to interpret the genesis of the phenomena that constitute nature itself).[20]

Spencer's materialism started with the premise that the phenomenal world evolved in accordance with its own natural laws and that "there can be no complete acceptance of sociology as a science, so long as the belief in a social order not conforming to natural law, survives."[21] The implication is that each society evolves its own normative structures during a given period of time, as need arises. Thus the "average opinion in every age and country is a function of social structure in that age and country."[22] For this reason, Spencer counsels against legislative intervention in social life, because (as he warns in the following excerpt) such intervention could disrupt the natural processes (*e.g.*, "generalizations of Biology") whereby society purifies itself and achieves its own normative equilibrium.

---

18. Herbert Spencer, The Evolution of Society: Selections from Herbert Spencer's Principles of Sociology 24–25 (Robert Carneiro et al., 1967), hereinafter Spencer, The Evolution of Society.

19. 2 Spencer, Autobiography, *supra* note 14, at 488–89.

20. *Id.*

21. Herbert Spencer, The Study of Sociology 360 (1961).

22. *Id.* at 356.

Herbert Spencer, The Study of Sociology 341–49 (1891).

It may be fully admitted that individual altruism, left to itself, will work advantageously—wherever, at least, it does not go to the extent of helping the unworthy to multiply. But an unquestionable injury is done by agencies which undertake in a wholesale way to foster good-for-nothings: impeding that natural process of elimination by which society purifies itself. For not only by such agencies is this preservation of the worst at the expense of the best carried further than it would else be, but there is scarcely any of that compensation which accompanies individual altruism. A mechanical-working State-apparatus, distributing money drawn from grumbling rate-payers, produces little or no moralizing effect on the capables to make up for multiplication of the incapables. Here, however, it is needless to dwell on the perplexing questions hence arising. My purpose is simply to show that a rational policy must recognize certain generalizations of Biology; and to insist that only when familiarity with these generalizations, as everywhere exemplified by living beings, has woven them into the conceptions of things, is there gained a strong conviction that disregard of them must cause enormous mischiefs.

The biological truths and their corollaries, thus presented as bases for sociological conclusions, are introductory to a more general biological truth including them, which underlies all rational legislation. I refer to the truth that every species of organism, not excepting the human, is always adapting itself, both directly and indirectly, to its conditions of existence . . .

While, however, every society, and every stage of it, presents conditions more or less special, to which the natures of citizens adapt themselves; there are certain general conditions which, in every society, have to be fulfilled to a considerable extent before it can hold together, and which have to be fulfilled completely before social life can be complete. For each citizen so to behave as not to deduct from the aggregate welfare, he must perform such function, or share of function, as is of value equivalent at least to what he consumes; and both in discharging his function and in pursuing his pleasure, he must leave others similarly free to discharge their functions and to pursue their pleasures . . .

Now, under one of its chief aspects, civilization is a process of developing a nature capable of fulfilling these all-essential conditions; and, neglecting their superfluities, laws and the appliances for enforcing them, are expressions and embodiments of these all-essential conditions. On the one hand, those severe systems of slavery, and serfdom, and chastisements for vagabondage, which characterize the less-developed social types, stand for the necessity that the citizen shall be self-supporting. On the other hand, the punishments for murder, assault, theft, etc., and the penalties on breach of contract, stand for the necessity that the citizen shall neither directly injure other citizens, nor shall injure them indirectly, by taking or intercepting the returns their activities bring. And it needs no detail to show that one fundamental trait in social progress, is an increase of industrial energy, leading men to achieve self-maintenance without being coerced in the harsh ways once general; that another fundamental trait is the gradual establishment of such a nature in men that, while pursuing their respective ends, they injure and impede one another in smaller degrees; and that a concomitant trait is the growth of governmental restraints which more effectually check the remaining aggressiveness.

Along with the proofs thus furnished that the biological law of adaptation, holding of all other species, holds of the human species, and that the change undergone by the human species since societies began to develop, has been an adaptation to the conditions implied by harmonious social life, we receive the lesson that the one thing needful is maintenance of these conditions . . . These are conclusions from which there is no escape, if Man is subject to the laws of life in common with living things in general . . .

Thus, that which sundry precepts of the current religion embody—that which ethical systems, intuitive or utilitarian, equally urge, is that which Biology also, generalizing the laws of life, dictates. All other requisites are unimportant compared with this primary requisite, that each shall so live as neither to burden his fellows nor to injure his fellows. And all other appliances for influencing men's actions and natures, are unimportant compared with those serving to maintain and increase the conformity to this primary requisite. But unhappily, legislators and philanthropists, busy with schemes which hinder adaptation instead of aiding it, neglect those arrangements by which adaptation is effected . . .

Neither the limits of this chapter, nor its purpose, permit exposition of all the truths which Biology yields as data for Sociology. Enough has been said in proof of that which was to be shown—the need for studying biological science as a preparation for studying the science of society.

The effect to be looked for from it, is that of giving strength and clearness to convictions otherwise feeble and vague. Sundry of the doctrines I have presented under their biological aspects, are doctrines admitted in considerable degrees. Such acquaintance with the laws of life as they have gathered incidentally, leads many to suspect that appliances for preserving the physically-feeble, bring results that are not wholly good. Others there are who get glimpses of evils caused by fostering the reckless and the stupid. But their suspicions and qualms fail to determine their conduct, because the *inevitableness* of the bad consequences has not been made clear: there lacks the effect of biological knowledge. When countless illustrations have shown them that all strength, all faculty, all fitness, presented by every living thing, has arisen partly by a growth of each power consequent on exercise of it, and partly by the more frequent survival and greater multiplication of the better-endowed individuals, entailing gradual disappearance of the worse-endowed—when it is seen that all advance, bodily and mental, has been achieved through this process, and that suspension of it must cause

> arrest, while reversal of it would bring universal decay—when it is seen that the mischiefs entailed by disregard of these truths, though they may be slow, are certain; there comes a conviction that social policy must be conformed to them, and that to ignore them is madness . . .

Legal and Social Differentiation

Spencer's views about the division of labor in society, as well as other aspects of human endeavor including legal differentiation, show the same evolutionary approach that is evident in his approach to biology in general. Spencer viewed the division of labor as serving an evolving normative function, moving from the initial rudimentary phase toward ever-increasing stages of complexity. The early or rudimentary division of labor is in the form of basic categories such as warriors, hunters, and toolmakers, all of which fulfill specific social needs.[23] As society grows, like the body of a biological organism, its parts acquire more and more specialized functions. Thus the previously homogeneous parts become dissimilar yet continue to work together in a complimentary relationship and depend on each other; in this process they form an "aggregate" composition.

> This division of labor, first dwelt on by political economists as a social phenomenon, and thereupon recognized by biologists as a phenomenon of living bodies, which they called the 'physiological division of labor,' is that which in the society, as in the animal, makes it a living whole. The consensus of functions becomes closer as evolution advances. In low aggregates, both individual and social, the actions of the parts are but little dependent on one another, whereas in developed aggregates of both kinds that combination of actions which constitutes the life of the whole makes possible the component actions which constitutes the lives of the parts . . . where parts are little differentiated they can readily perform one another's functions, but where much differentiated they can perform one another's functions very imperfectly or not at all.[24]

The same analogy is used with regard to the evolution of social administration. Just as the human body evolves and becomes organically and functionally more complex, so human society becomes more complex as each individual or group of people specializes in various activities, up to a point when an individual rises to a position of prominence. This individual (who is supported by others in subordinate positions) acts as the "nerve center" that coordinates and controls the behavior of all individuals in society, using established rules and regulations.[25] Yet although Spencer clearly acknowledges that such persons of prominence do emerge and can channel

23. Spencer, The Evolution of Society, *supra* note 18, at 4–5. 1 Herbert Spencer, Essays: Scientific, Political and Speculative 19 (1891).

24. Spencer, The Evolution of Society, *supra* note 18, at 25.

25. "The change from the homogeneous to the heterogeneous is displayed in the progress of civilization as a whole, as well as of every nation." 1 Herbert Spencer, Essays: Scientific, Political and Speculative 19 (1891).

or influence behavior either through sheer charisma or brute despotism, in his view these leaders are ultimately the creatures of the societies they govern, and their roles are more or less predetermined by society itself.

> Those who regard the histories of societies as the histories of their great men, and think that these great men shape the fates of their societies, overlook the truth that such great men are the products of their societies. Without certain antecedents—without a certain average national character, they could neither have been generated nor could have had the culture which formed them. If their society is to some extent re-molded by them, they were, both before and after birth, molded by their society—were the results of all those influences which fostered the ancestral character they inherited, and gave their own early bias, their creed, morals, knowledge, aspirations. So that such social changes as are immediately traceable to individuals of unusual power, are still remotely traceable to the social causes which produced these individuals; and hence, from the highest point of view, such social changes also, are parts of the general developmental process.[26]

Spencer paid considerable attention to the evolution of law and legal systems throughout the world, citing many examples of what he called "rude" and "developed" societies. Referring to the former also as "the primitive horde," he asserted that normative regulation in such societies (*e.g.*, the Sandwich Islanders, the Samoans, the Bechuanas, the Karens, and the Ancient Egyptians) was largely handed down through a variety of sources, including myth, superstition, customary traditions, and ancestral worship. In support of the latter two were invoked ancestors both distinguished and undistinguished, to discover "the dictates of the dead to the living."[27] Also invoked by sorcerers whenever occasion demanded were deities or their ghosts; in this way, the spirits of the gods and the deceased would be kept constantly at hand.[28]

Spencer identified four predominant sources of customary norms in primitive societies:

> As laws originate partly in the customs inherited from the undistinguished dead, partly in the special injunctions of the distinguished dead, partly in the average will of the undistinguished living, and partly in the will of the distinguished living, the feelings responding to them, allied though different, are mingled in proportions that vary under diverse circumstances.[29]

Legitimation of norms is sought through "ghost theory," that is, appeal to deities and spirits. This serves three purposes: first, as norm signifier; second, as rule legitimizer; and third, as promoter of stability through fear: "possessing a supposed supernatural

26. *Id.* at 268–69.

27. 2 Herbert Spencer, The Principles of Sociology 518 (1898).

28. 3 *id.* at 222–26.

29. 2 *id.* at 531.

sanction, its rules have a rigidity enabling them to restrain in greater degrees than could any rules having an origin recognized as natural."[30] Because both elements bolster the authority of the rules so identified, they are binding on the people as well as their rulers. Given this special origin, obedience to the law is of cardinal importance. Thus, acts of disobedience are instantly punished, often with brutal and disproportionate consequences.[31]

In the excerpt that follows, Spencer outlines normative regulation (and its sources) in primitive societies.

3 Herbert Spencer, The Principles of Sociology 261–64 (1898).

§ 693. In the preceding division of this work, . . . it was shown that in early societies such regulation of conduct as is effected by custom, and afterwards by that hardened form of custom called law, originates in the expressed or implied wills of ancestors—primarily those of the undistinguished dead, and secondarily those of the distinguished dead. Regard for the wishes of deceased relatives greatly influences actions among ourselves, and it influences them far more among savage and semi-civilized peoples; because such peoples think that the spirits of the deceased are either constantly at hand or occasionally return, and in either case will, if made angry, punish the survivors by disease or misfortune. When, in the course of social development, there arise chiefs of unusual power, or conquering kings, the belief that their ghosts will wreak terrible vengeance on those who disregard their injunctions becomes a still more potent controlling agency; so that to regulation of conduct by customs inherited from ancestors at large, and ordinarily enforced by the living ruler, there comes to be added regulation by the transmitted commands of the dead ruler.

Hence originates that early conception of law which long continues with slowly increasing modification, and which, in our day, still survives in those who hold that Right means "that which is ordered"—firstly, by a revelation from God, and secondly by god-appointed or god-approved kings. For the theological view implies that governments in general exist by divine permission, and that their dictates have consequently a divine sanction. In the absence of a utilitarian justification, which only gradually emerges in the minds of thinking men, there of course exists for law no other justification than that of being supernaturally derived—first of all directly and afterwards indirectly.

It follows, therefore, that primitive law, formed out of transmitted injunctions, partly of ancestry at large and partly of the distinguished ancestor or deceased ruler, comes usually to be enunciated by those who were in contact with the ruler—those who, first of all as attendants communicated his com-

30. *Id.* at 519.

31. *Id.*

mands to his subjects, and who afterwards, ministering to his apotheosized ghost, (became some of them) his priests. Naturally these last, carrying on the worship of him in successive generations, grow into exponents of his will; both as depositaries of his original commands and as mouth-pieces through whom the commands of his spirit are communicated. By necessity, then, the primitive priests are distinguished as those who above all others know what the law is, and as those to whom, therefore, all questions about transgressions are referred—the judges.

§ 694. In small rude societies judicial systems have not arisen, and hence there is little evidence. Still we read that among the Guiana Indians the Pe-i-men are at once priests, sorcerers, doctors, and judges. Concerning the Kalmucks, who are more advanced, Pallas tells us that the highest judicial council consisted partly of priests and also that one of the high-priests of the community was head-judge.

Though among the semi-civilized Negro races of Africa, theological development has usually not gone far enough to establish the cult of a great god or gods, yet among them may be traced the belief that conduct is to be regulated by the wills of supernatural beings, who are originally the ghosts of the distinguished dead; and in pursuance of this belief the ministrants of such ghosts come to be the oracles. Thus Lander tells us that "in Badagry the fetish-priests are the sole judges of the people." Cameron describes a sitting of a Mganga, chief medicine-man at Kowédi. After the chief's wife had made presents and received replies to her inquiries others inquired.

Questions were "put by the public, some of which were quickly disposed of, while others evidently raised knotty points, resulting in much gesticulation and oratory. When the Waganga [apparently the plural of Mganga] pretended they could not find an answer the idols were consulted, and one of the fetish men who was a clever ventriloquist made the necessary reply, the poor dupes believing it to be spoken by the idol."

§ 695. Of ancient historic evidence readers will at once recall that which the Hebrews yield.

There is in the Bible clear proof that the ideas of law and of divine will were equivalents . . .

Of course we may expect that Egypt with its long history furnishes good evidence, and we find it. Here are relative facts from three authorities—Bunsen, Brugsch, and Erman.

"That the oldest laws were ascribed to Hermes, implies however nothing more than that the first germ of the Civil law sprung from the Sacred Books, and that it was based in part upon the religious tenets which they contained."

Mentu-hotep, a priest and official of the 12th dyn., on his tomb, "prides himself on having been 'a man learned in the law, a legislator.'"

"The chief judge was always of highest degree; if he was not one of the king's own sons, he was chief priest of one of the great gods, an hereditary prince."

> "All the judges of higher rank served Ma'at, the goddess of Truth, as priests and the chief judge wore a small figure of this goddess as a badge round his neck."
>
> A court which held a sitting in the 46 of Ramses II, consisted of 9 priests (prophets and priests) and one lay member, the registrar. But in another case (Ramses IX) the lay element preponderated.
>
> Which last statement implies a step towards differentiation of the secular from the sacred in legal administration.

Spencer points out that in these early societies there is little by way of differentiation of functions in the administration of justice, with the ruler serving as both judge and executioner.[32] Specialized functions do crystallize, however, but only as society evolves into a more complex form through increased industrialization. In the foregoing excerpt, Spencer notes one such differentiation in ancient Egypt, which he points out as having a "long history" and which he presumably regarded as relatively more developed than the other social groupings he considered. This differentiation saw the move from religious to secular law (see end of excerpt).

The emergence of secular law marks a higher stage in normative evolution. At this stage, small societies merge into large ones and "with the consequent increase of its business, entailing delegation of functions, there goes, in the judicial organization as in other organizations, a progressive differentiation."[33] The industrial era boosts the emergence of an industrial class that becomes politically important, and the judiciary eventually becomes officered by it. Its leaders become specialists in the law, setting themselves apart from their predecessors.[34] This phase is different from the prior phase in one fundamental respect: while the prior normative order was characterized by the principle of compulsion, regulating *status* and maintaining inequality, the new order is characterized by cooperation, fulfillment of *contracts*, and formal equality of men's rights.[35]

The following excerpt summarizes the transition from the old to the newer normative form.

2 Herbert Spencer, The Principles of Sociology 535–37 (1896).

> Maintenance of the unchangeable rules of conduct thus originating, which is requisite for social stability during those stages in which the type of nature is yet but little fitted for harmonious social cooperation, pre-supposes implicit obedience; and hence disobedience becomes the blackest crime. Treason and rebellion, whether against the divine or the human ruler bring penalties exceeding all others in severity. The breaking of a law is punished not because

32. *Id.* at 503.

33. 2 Spencer, Principles of Sociology, *supra* note 27, at 505.

34. *Id.* at 512.

35. *Id.* at 536.

of the intrinsic criminality of the act committed, but because of the implied insubordination. And the disregard of governmental authority continues, through subsequent stages, to constitute, in legal theory, the primary element in a transgression.

In societies that become large and complex, there arise forms of activity and intercourse not provided for in the sacred code; and in respect of these the ruler is free to make regulations. As such regulations accumulate there comes into existence a body of laws of known human origin; and though this acquires an authority due to reverence for the men who made it and the generations which approved it, yet it has not the sacredness of the god-descended body of laws: human law differentiates from divine law. But in societies which remain predominantly militant, these two bodies of laws continue similar in the respect that they have a personally-derived authority. The avowed reason for obeying them is that they express the will of a divine ruler, or the will of a human ruler, or, occasionally, the will of an irresponsible oligarchy.

But with the progress of industrialism and growth of a free population which gradually acquires political power, the humanly-derived law begins to sub-divide; and that part which originates in the *consensus* of individual interests, begins to dominate over the part which originates in the authority of the ruler. So long as the social type is one organized on the principle of compulsory cooperation, law, having to maintain this compulsory cooperation, must be primarily concerned in regulating *status*, maintaining inequality, enforcing authority; and can but secondarily consider the individual interests of those forming the mass. But in proportion as the principle of voluntary cooperation more and more characterizes the social type, fulfilment of contracts and implied assertion of equality in men's rights, become the fundamental requirements, and the *consensus* of individual interests the chief source of law: such authority as law otherwise derived continues to have, being recognized as secondary, and insisted upon only because maintenance of law for its own sake indirectly furthers the general welfare.

Finally, we see that the systems of laws belonging to these successive stages, are severally accompanied by the sentiments and theories appropriate to them; and that the theories at present current, adapted to the existing compromise between militancy and industrialism, are steps towards the ultimate theory, in conformity with which law will have no other justification than that gained by it as maintainer of the conditions to complete life in the associated state.

The last sentence of the excerpt concludes with the view that the law's legitimacy is self-generated once the transition from a regime of status to a regime of contract is complete. Under the previous regime, the laws established by aggregate feeling are enforced by making revenge for wrongs "a socially-imposed duty."[36] Failure to take

36. *Id.* at 525.

revenge is a disgrace. The rude justice of balancing a loss by the infliction of an equal (or greater) injury was achieved without regard to whether the responsible party or someone else suffered. Punishments could be vicariously inflicted through vengeful action against the responsible party's family or tribe.[37] Under the regime of contract the new consensus is that of protecting all individual interests equally, without regard to personality. The equalization of injuries through retaliation is no longer allowed, and all transgressors are dealt with equally by the law.

Conclusion

Spencer made a significant contribution to the study of norms and normativity in a cultural context. He was a prolific writer as well as an astute observer. He identified certain basic truisms about societal evolution and legal systems. Even if his analogies between living organisms and social units may seem quaint in the modern era, his observations as to the fact that normative orders evolved cannot be denied. Similarly, his observations of the *progressive* nature of human evolution rings largely true, as does his conclusion that the division of labor and legal differentiation go hand in hand with increased industrialization.

Spencer also contributed a vocabulary to the field of anthropology that influenced later anthropologists; this terminology, together with his thought, laid much of the foundation for the early twentieth-century structural functionalists. Words such as "function," "structure," and "superorganic," which were embedded throughout his work, reappeared in the theoretical writings of Alfred Kroeber, Edward Sapir, Emile Durkheim, A. R. Radcliffe-Brown, and Bronislaw Malinowski.[38]

Tylor: Comparative Cross-Cultural Ethnography

Sir Edward B. Tylor (1832–1917), who has often been called "the Father of Ethnology," was, like Spencer, a British scholar. Tylor, along with L. H. Morgan (discussed next), is viewed as a unilineal anthropologist because of his hypothesis that all humans have traveled down a "substantially uniform" evolutionary path—beginning at the "primitive" or "savage" level, evolving into barbarism, and culminating at the height of civilization with nineteenth-century Western society.

> [T]he institutions of man are as distinctly stratified as the earth on which he lives. They succeed each other in series substantially uniform over the globe, independent of what seem the comparatively superficial differences of race and language, but shaped by similar human nature acting through successively changed conditions in savage, barbaric, and civilised life.[39]

---

37. *Id.* at 529.

38. Bohannan and Glazer, High Points in Anthropology 5–6 (1988).

39. Edward B. Tylor, *On a Method of Investigating the Development of Institutions; Applied to Laws of Marriage and Descent*, 18 Journal of the Royal Anthropological Institute 245, 269 (1889).

Tylor's Grand Project of Ethnography

Tylor believed that the laws of cause and effect so commonly accepted in the natural sciences could also be applied to human society and the science of culture.[40] Respectively invoking Pythagoras, Aristotle, and Leibnitz, he asserts that there is an objectively understandable normative order in the cosmos, that "nature is not full of incoherent episodes, like a bad tragedy," and "that nature never acts by leaps and nothing happens without sufficient reason."[41] Indeed, for Tylor, just as certain uniformities pervade nature, so analogous uniformities pervade human civilization, and they are due to uniform causes. These uniform causes and their uniform consequences mark the various phases of cultural evolution; each phase is the outcome of prior normative processes and shapes future evolutionary changes. The study of these phenomena—namely, the uniform cause-effect relationships of how the past influences the present, and how the present influences the future—constitute together the grand project of ethnography, as explained by Tylor in the following excerpt.

1 E.B. Tylor, Primitive Culture 1–7 (1871).

> Culture or Civilization, taken in its wide ethnographic sense, is that complex whole which includes knowledge, belief, art, morals, law, custom, and any other capabilities and habits acquired by man as a member of society. The condition of culture among the various societies of mankind, in so far as it is capable of being investigated on general principles, is a subject apt for the study of laws of human thought and action. On the one hand, the uniformity which so largely pervades civilization may be ascribed, in great measure, to the uniform action of uniform causes: while on the other hand its various grades may be regarded as stages of development or evolution, each the outcome of previous history, and about to do its proper part in shaping the history of the future. To the investigation of these two great principles in several departments of ethnography, with especial consideration of the civilization of the lower tribes as related to the civilization of the higher nations, the present volumes are devoted.
>
> Our modern investigators in the sciences of inorganic nature are foremost to recognize, both within and without their special fields of work, the unity of nature, the fixity of its laws, the definite sequence of cause and effect through which every fact depends on what has gone before it, and acts upon what is to come after it. They grasp firmly the Pythagorean doctrine of pervading order in the universal Kosmos. They affirm, with Aristotle, that nature is not full of incoherent episodes, like a bad tragedy. They agree with Leibnitz in what he calls 'my axiom, that nature never acts by leaps (la nature n'agit jamais par saut),' as well as in his 'great principle, commonly little employed, that nothing happens without sufficient reason.' Nor again, in studying the

40. E.B. Tylor, The Origins of Culture 1–7 (1898).

41. *Id.* at 2.

structure and habits of plants and animals, or in investigating the lower functions even of man, are these leading ideas unacknowledged.... None will deny that, as each man knows by the evidence of his own consciousness, definite and natural cause does, to a great extent, determine human action. Then, keeping aside from considerations of extra-natural interference and causeless spontaneity, let us take this admitted existence of natural cause and effect as our standing-ground, and travel on it so far as it will bear us. It is on this same basis that physical science pursues, with ever-increasing success, its quest of laws of nature. Nor need this restriction hamper the scientific study of human life, in which the real difficulties are the practical ones of enormous complexity of evidence, and imperfection of methods of observation....

'One event is always the son of another, and we must never forget the parentage,' was a remark made by a Bechuana chief to Casalis the African missionary.... The philosophy of history at large, explaining the past and predicting the future phenomena of man's life in the world by reference to general laws, is in fact a subject with which, in the present state of knowledge, even genius aided by wide research seems but hardly able to cope. Yet there are departments of it which, though difficult enough, seem comparatively accessible. If the field of enquiry be narrowed from History as a whole to that branch of it which is here called Culture, the history, not of tribes or nations, but of the condition of knowledge, religion, art, custom, and the like among them, the task of investigation proves to lie within far more moderate compass.... The evidence is no longer so wildly heterogeneous, but may be more simply classified and compared, while the power of getting rid of extraneous matter, and treating each issue on its own proper set of facts, makes close reasoning on the whole more available than in general history. This may appear from a brief preliminary examination of the problem, how the phenomena of Culture may be classified and arranged, stage by stage, in a probable order of evolution.

Surveyed in a broad view, the character and habit of mankind at once display that similarity and consistency of phenomena which led the Italian proverb-maker to declare that 'all the world is one country,' 'tutto il mondo è paese.' To general likeness in human nature on the one hand, and to general likeness in the circumstances of life on the other, this similarity and consistency may no doubt be traced, and they may be studied with especial fitness in comparing races near the same grade of civilization. Little respect need be had in such comparisons for date in history or for place on the map; the ancient Swiss lake-dweller may be set beside the mediaeval Aztec, and the Ojibwa of North America beside the Zulu of South Africa. As Dr. Johnson contemptuously said when he had read about Patagonians and South Sea Islanders in Hawkesworth's Voyages, 'one set of savages is like another.' How true a generalization this really is, any Ethnological Museum may show. Examine for instance the edged and pointed instruments in such a collection; the inventory includes hatchet, adze, chisel, knife, saw, scraper, awl, needle,

> spear and arrow-head, and of these most or all belong with only differences of detail to races the most various. So it is with savage occupations; the wood-chopping, fishing with net and line, shooting and spearing game, fire-making, cooking, twisting cord and plaiting baskets, repeat themselves with wonderful uniformity in the museum shelves which illustrate the life of the lower races from Kamchatka to Tierra del Fuego, and from Dahome to Hawaii. Even when it comes to comparing barbarous hordes with civilized nations, the consideration thrusts itself upon our minds, how far item after item of the life of the lower races passes into analogous proceedings of the higher, in forms not too far changed to be recognized, and sometimes hardly changed at all. Look at the modern European peasant using his hatchet and his hoe, see his food boiling or roasting over the log-fire, observe the exact place which beer holds in his calculation of happiness, hear his tale of the ghost in the nearest haunted house, and of the farmer's niece who was bewitched with knots in her inside till she fell into fits and died. If we choose out in this way things which have altered little in a long course of centuries, we may draw a picture where there shall be scarce a hand's breadth difference between an English ploughman and a negro of Central Africa. These pages will be so crowded with evidence of such correspondence among mankind, that there is no need to dwell upon its details here but it may be used at once to override a problem which would complicate the argument, namely, the question of race. For the present purpose it appears both possible and desirable to eliminate considerations of hereditary varieties or races of man, and to treat mankind as homogeneous in nature, though placed in different grades of civilization. The details of the enquiry will, I think, prove that stages of culture may be compared without taking into account how far tribes who use the same implement, follow the same custom, or believe the same myth, may differ in their bodily configuration and the colour of their skin and hair.
>
> A first step in the study of civilization is to dissect it into details, and to classify these in their proper groups. Thus, in examining weapons, they are to be classed under spear, club, sling, bow and arrow, and so forth; among textile arts are to be ranged matting, netting, and several grades of making and weaving threads; myths are divided under such headings as myths of sunrise and sunset, eclipse-myths, earthquake-myths, local myths which account for the names of places by some fanciful tale, . . .

In addition to expounding on the dual grand project of ethnography, in the excerpt Tylor argues that there are broad uniformities in the human project itself ("general likeness in human nature," "general likeness in the circumstances of life"). This enables general laws of human social development to be developed *cross-culturally*, that is, these laws are not dependent on race or ethnicity of human societies but on their grades of civilization.

Tylor's position that some groups of peoples were not as "evolved" as those within his own western British culture was not based on any overt theory of racial superiority. Indeed, he believed it to be "both possible and desirable to eliminate considerations of hereditary varieties or races of man, and to treat mankind as homogeneous in nature."[42] Differences between groups were to be explained not by race or other physical attributes but by their "grades" of evolution.[43] However, Tylor did believe that some groups of people (such as Western Europeans) had superior intellect and thinking capability that exceeded that of other (non–Western European) groups.[44] "There seems to be in mankind inbred temperament and inbred capacity of mind," he wrote.[45] According to Tylor, this innate temperament explained why some races took giant steps forward toward "civilization," while others have "stood still or fallen back."[46] Thus we see a trace of racial determinism or evolutionary racism that most major late nineteenth-century thinkers could not avoid.

In his major two-volume work, *Primitive Culture* (1871), Tylor published the first working definition of "culture" in an anthropological context, defining it "in its wide ethnographic sense, [as] that complex whole which includes knowledge, belief, art, morals, law, custom, and any other capabilities and habits acquired by man as a member of society."[47] As a general definition of culture, which appears at the beginning of the first excerpt (above), it is still acceptable in modern anthropology.[48]

Primitive Culture presents in systematic form many of the normative theories Tylor developed over a six-year period. Two of the most important were the concepts of survivals and animism. He defined "survivals" as "processes, customs, opinions, and so forth which have been carried on by force of habit into a new state of society different from that in which they had their original home."[49] He believed that an anthropologist should be able to reconstruct a past culture by studying which survivals existed within that culture and how they were changed, modified, rejected, or revived in the newer normative order.[50] The excerpt that follows contains a brief explanation of the concept of survivals and its importance to his grand project of rational ethnography.

1 Edward B. Tylor, Primitive Culture 14–20 (2d ed., 1871).

> Among evidence aiding us to trace the course which the civilization of the world has actually followed, is that great class of facts to denote which I have

42. 1 Tylor, Primitive Culture, *supra* note 8, at 7.

43. *Id.*

44. Tylor, Anthropology: An Introduction to the Study of Man and Civilization 74–75 (1881); hereinafter "Anthropology."

45. *Id.* at 74.

46. *Id.*

47. 1 Tylor, Primitive Culture, *supra* note 8, at 1.

48. Marvin Harris, Culture, People, Nature: An Introduction to General Anthropology 122 (5th ed.) (1988); Keesing and Keesing, *supra* note 2, at 20.

49. 1 Tylor, Primitive Culture, *supra* note 8, at 16.

50. *Id.* at 16–17, 70 *et seq.*

found it convenient to introduce the term "survivals." These are processes, customs, opinions, and so forth which have been carried on by force of habit into a new state of society different from that in which they had their original home, and they thus remain as proofs and examples of an older condition of culture out of which a newer has been evolved. Thus, I know an old Somersetshire woman whose hand-loom dates from the time before the introduction of the "flying shuttle" which new-fangled appliance she has never even learnt to use, and I have seen her throw her shuttle from hand to hand in true classic fashion; this old woman is not a century behind her times, but she is a case of survival. Such examples often lead us back to the habits of hundreds and even thousands of years ago. The ordeal of the Key and Bible, still in use, is a survival; the Midsummer bonfire is a survival; the Breton peasants' All Souls' supper for the spirits of the dead is a survival. The simple keeping up of ancient habits is only one part of the transition from old into new and changing times. The serious business of ancient society may be seen to sink into the sport of later generations, and its serious belief to linger on in nursery folk-lore, while superseded habits of old-work life may be modified into new-world forms still powerful for good and evil. Sometimes old thoughts and practices will burst out afresh to the amazement of a world that thought them long since dead or dying; here survival passes into revival, as has lately happened in so remarkable a way in the history of modern spiritualism, a subject full of instruction from the ethnographer's point of view. The study of the principles of survival has, indeed, no small practical importance, for most of what we call superstition is included within survival, and in this way lies open to the attack of its deadliest enemy, a reasonable explanation. Insignificant, moreover, as multitudes of the facts of survival are in themselves, their study is so effective for tracing the course of the historical development through which alone it is possible to understand their meaning, that it becomes a vital point of ethnographic research to gain the clearest possible insight into their nature. This importance must justify the detail here devoted to an examination of survival, on the evidence of such games, popular sayings, customs, superstitions and the like, as may serve well to bring into view the manner of its operation....

In carrying on the great task of rational ethnography, the investigation of the causes which have produced the phenomena of culture, and the laws to which they are subordinate, it is desirable to work out as systematically as possible a scheme of evolution of this culture along its many lines.... By comparing the various stages of civilization among races known to history with the aid of archaeological inference from the remains of pre-historic tribes, it seems possible to judge in a rough way of an early general condition of man, which from our point of view is to be regarded as a primitive condition, whatever yet earlier state may in reality have lain behind it. This hypothetical primitive condition corresponds in a considerable degree to that of modern savage tribes, who, in spite of their difference and distance,

> have in common certain elements of civilization, which seem remains of an early state of the human race at large. If this hypothesis be true, then, notwithstanding the continual interference of degeneration, the main tendency of culture from primaeval up to modern times has been from savagery towards civilization.... Survival in Culture, placing all along the course of advancing civilization way-marks full of meaning to those who can decipher their signs, even now sets up in our midst primaeval monuments of barbaric thought and life. Its investigation tells strongly in favour of the view that the European may find among the Greenlanders or Maoris many a trait for reconstructing the picture of his own primitive ancestors. Next comes the problem of the Origin of Language. Obscure as many parts of this problem still remain, its clearer positions lie open to the investigation whether speech took its origin among mankind in the savage state, and the result of the enquiry is that, consistently with all known evidence, this may have been the case. From the examination of the Art of Counting a far more definite consequence is shown. It may be confidently asserted, that not only is this important art found in a rudimentary state among savage tribes, but that satisfactory evidence proves numeration to have been developed by rational invention from this low stage up to that in which we ourselves possess it....

"Animism" was Tylor's label for what he characterized as the most basic religious beliefs of "lower races" in souls and spirits.[51] Animism was an evolutionary tool that Tylor believed could be used by an anthropologist to locate the place of a culture in an evolutionary framework.[52] To complement his general classificatory scheme in which a culture was either savage, barbarian, or civilized, he developed a three-tiered scheme for religious evolution: animism (the lowest form of religion), polytheism, and monotheism (the religious pinnacle).

Primitive Culture explained Tylor's use of the comparative method, the approach by which he formulated theories about cultural evolution. Under the comparative method and with the help of archeology, Tylor and other classical evolutionists compared the various historical phases of civilization to determine an early general condition of humans (which they called the "primitive condition").[53] Because they believed that the normative characteristics of the primitive tribes were similar to those of "modern savage tribes," they asserted that studying the culture of these modern savage tribes would lead them to an understanding of cultural evolution (hence the conclusion that "the main tendency of culture from primeval up to modern times has been from savagery towards civilization").[54]

51. *Id.* at 23.

52. *Id. See also id.* at 357.

53. *Id.* at 21.

54. *Id.*

Law and Morality in Evolutionary Context

Tylor believed that the study of these evolutionary phases ("successively changed conditions") was the key to developing a general science of humans and civilization, including social and legal environment. With regard to the latter, just as every scientific endeavor required a grasp of its founding principles, so did legal science:

> So the law-student plunges at once into the intricacies of legal systems which have grown up through the struggles, the reforms, and even the blunders of thousands of years; yet he might have made his way clearer by seeing how laws begin in their simplest forms, framed to meet the needs of savage and barbaric tribes. It is needless to make a list of all the branches of education in knowledge and art; there is not one which may not be the easier and better learnt for knowing its history and place in the general science of Man.[55]

Tylor cites areas of English law (*e.g.*, the theory of primogeniture) that can only be understood by tracing their origins to the Middle Ages. One of the tasks of ethnography in the legal and moral spheres, according to Tylor in the following excerpt, is to bridge the gap between past and present law.

Edward B. Tylor, The Origins of Culture 534–35 (1871).

> The two vast united provinces of Morals and Law have been as yet too imperfectly treated on a general ethnographic scheme, to warrant distinct statement of results. Yet thus much may be confidently said, that where the ground has been even superficially explored, every glimpse reveals treasures of knowledge. It is already evident that enquirers who systematically trace each department of moral and legal institutions from the savage through the barbaric and into the civilized condition of mankind, thereby introduce into the scientific investigations of these subjects an indispensable element which merely theoretical writers are apt unscrupulously to dispense with. The law or maxim which a people at some particular stage of its history might have made fresh, according to the information and circumstances of the period, is one thing. The law or maxim which did in fact become current among them by inheritance from an earlier stage, only more or less modified to make it compatible with the new conditions, is another and far different thing. Ethnography is required to bridge over the gap between the two, a very chasm where the arguments of moralists and legists are continually falling in, to crawl out maimed and helpless. Within modern grades of civilization this historical method is now becoming more and more accepted. It will not be denied that English law has acquired, by modified inheritance from past ages, a theory of primogeniture and a theory of real estate which are so far from being products of our own times that we must go back to the middle

55. Tylor, Anthropology, *supra* note 44, at vi.

> ages for anything like a satisfactory explanation of them; . . . But the point to be pressed here is, that the development and survival of law are processes that did not first come into action within the range of written codes of comparatively cultured nations. Admitted that civilized law requires its key from barbaric law; it must be borne in mind that the barbarian lawgiver too was guided in judgment not so much by first principles, as by a reverent and often stupidly reverent adherence to the tradition of earlier and yet ruder ages.
>
> Nor can these principles be set aside in the scientific study of moral sentiment and usage. When the ethical systems of mankind, from the lowest savagery upward, have been analyzed and arranged in their stages of evolution, then ethical science, no longer vitiated by too exclusive application to particular phases of morality taken unreasonably as representing morality in general, will put its methods to fair trial on the long and intricate world-history of right and wrong.

It is thus obvious to Tylor that law is one of many social norms, and it must be studied in historical context just as "all the branches of education in knowledge and art" must be. It is, then, part of the "general science of Man."[56] He laments that law and morals have not been properly studied within a general ethnographic scheme. The task of ethnography is to trace the origin of legal and moral institutions as far back as possible (*i.e.*, from the savage condition of man to his civilized state). Indeed, for Tylor, barbaric law provides the key to civilized law, because when it is so traced a variety of norms and their reasons will become evident, even if some of these reasons show only a blind faith in custom ("stupidly reverent adherence to the tradition of earlier and yet ruder years"; see excerpt above). Notwithstanding this adherence, Tylor argues, humankind will improve its sense of right and wrong by learning from the past. Such study will also show how humankind's sense of what is right and wrong *evolves* over time.

Tylor gives numerous examples of universally shared mores and belief systems that evolve over time, including the sense of what is right and wrong. These beliefs find expression in statements such as "Thou shall not kill" and "Thou shalt not steal," the belief that crimes must be punished, the distinction between real and personal property, the rudimentary origins of language, and the rudiments of social regulation and government.[57] According to Tylor, these normative beliefs evolved as the society in which they existed evolved. Yet he cautions against "measuring other people's corn by one's own bushel,"[58] namely, the tendency to judge customs and mores of "older" stages of culture by "modern" standards. Tylor asserts the principle of the "sacredness of human life" is shared by all societies, primitive as well as modern; however, the observance of this principle is not the same in all societies. For example, the aged are cared for in different ways by different cultures. Advances in civilization show the evolution of a growing sense of the sacredness of human life, so that any attempt to

56. *Id.*

57. *Id.* at 410–30.

58. *Id.* at 410.

cut short the life of an aging person (even one whose life is burdensome and painful) is looked on with horror.

The principle of the sacredness of human life is naturally linked to another universal, namely, the prohibition of homicide.[59] Here again, the rule is implemented in different, even contradictory ways. For example, in some cultures killing someone (outside of one's tribe) is a mark of valor, because it is founded on the tribes' sense of self-preservation: "[t]heir existence depends on holding their own in deadly strife with neighboring tribes, and thus they put a premium on the warrior's proof of valour in fight against the enemy."[60] Clearly then, if the anthropologist is to identify and understand the norms that exist in a given culture, the exceptions thereto, and the reasons therefor, he will not hastily dismiss the exception(s) as canceling out the rule.

The fourth universal identified by Tylor is the principle that the wrongdoer must be punished. Again, the methods of punishment vary from tribe to tribe, from fines to imprisonment to blows or even death.[61] In older cultures, the absence of a central authority resulted in each being a judge in his own cause. This was the old practice of vengeance, which did not depend on its proportionality vis-à-vis the crime, nor did it depend on from whom it was extracted. Tylor points out that the primitive law of vengeance in some instances permitted violence against the criminal's entire family.[62] At the same time, it served the purpose of keeping the peace, the core purpose of all criminal law. With social advances, the law of vengeance gives way to just compensation to redress wrongs in the same way the Roman *lex talionis* (retaliation) is commuted to money damages.[63] Finally, the state takes over the function of suppressing harmful conduct and its law takes the place of private vengeance. Thus:

Vengeance and blood feuds
(yield to)
Retaliation
(which yields to)
Compensation
(coexisting with)
State prosecution of harmful conduct
(leading to)
Prohibition or outlawing of vengeance
(leading to)
Law taking the place of private vengeance
State punishes crimes

59. *Id.* at 411–13.

60. *Id.* at 412–13.

61. Tylor, Anthropology, *supra* note 44, at 414.

62. *Id.* at 414–15.

63. *Id.* at 415–16.

The process culminates with the state seeking to punish the criminal for the ends of public justice: "The state now replaces, by the justice of legal tribunals, the barbaric expedients of private vengeance and private war."[64]

Tylor's purpose in studying these normative transitions is to show that there are uniformities notwithstanding the flux. In the foregoing example, the notion that wrongdoers must be punished is common to all societies, primitive as well as advanced. The previous example was the sacredness of human life, and before that the sense of right and wrong.

Another important universal is the origin and function of language. Regarding the origin of language, Tylor detects universally common roots in all cultures. Language, at its origin, is the primal collection of grunts designed to vocalize simple thoughts provoked by the material world around us.[65] As society becomes more complex, so does its language, so that imitative sounds become linked to the expression of complex emotions and thoughts. Tylor identifies common traits of linguistic origin and evolution in societies as far-flung and diverse as the Siamese, the Zulu, the Karen, the Buddhists, the English, the French, and so on.

Edward B. Tylor, The Origins of Culture 200–01 (1871).

> From the earliest times of language to our own day, it is unlikely that men ever quite ceased to be conscious that some of their words were derived from imitation of the common sounds heard about them. In our own modern English, for instance, results of such imitation are evident; flies *buzz*, bees *hum*, snakes *hiss*, a cracker or a bottle of ginger-beer *pops*, a cannon or a bittern *booms*. In the words for animals and for musical instruments in the various languages of the world, the imitation of their cries and tones is often to be plainly heard, as in the names of the *hoopoe*, the *ai-ai* sloth, the *kaka* parrot, the Eastern *tomtom*, which is a drum, the African *ulule*, which is a flute, the Siamese *khong-bong*, which is a wooden harmonicon, and in like manner through a host of other words. But these evident cases are far from representing the whole effects of imitation on the growth of language. They form, indeed, the easy entrance to a philological region, which becomes less penetrable the farther it is explored.
>
> The operations of which we see the results before us in the actual languages of the world seem to have been somewhat as follows. Men have imitated their own emotional utterances or interjections, the cries of animals, the tones of musical instruments, the sounds of shouting, howling, stamping, breaking, tearing, scraping, with others which are all day coming to their ears, and out of these imitations many current words indisputably have their

64. *Id.* at 419.

65. 1 Tylor, Primitive Culture, *supra* note 8, at 200–01. *See also* Alfred Russel Wallace, *Primitive Culture: Researches into the Development of Mythology, Philosophy, Religion, Art and Custom*, 42 Academy 69, 70 (1872) (book review, of Tylor's Primitive Culture).

> source. But these words, as we find them in use, differ often widely, often beyond all recognition, from the original sounds they sprang from. In the first place, man's voice can only make a very rude copy of most sounds his ear receives....

Two other universal norms worth noting are the law of property and government itself. Under the former, Tylor asserts that all cultures, old and new, subscribe to the principle of ownership of material goods and distinguish between personal and real property.[66] Real property included the idea of common land and family freehold, whereas personal property included individual ownership in movables. As with the other universals, we find variables including different practices of inheritance, yet the conceptual underpinnings of the two types of property remain the same.

Finally, Tylor attaches great importance to the "rudiments of government," which he asserts is a universal phenomenon in all cultures. He did not accept the view that early cultures were lawless. The fact that they flourished for successive generations instead of disintegrating and dying off convinced Tylor that their early condition could not have been lawless or anarchic. As he explains in the next excerpt, societies are made up of family units, with their corresponding marital and kinship ties.[67] These include the parent–child relationship, the spousal relationship, relationships of property, inheritance, and so on.[68] These promote social cohesion and maintain normative order ("mutual forbearance, helpfulness, and trust of all").[69]

Painting with a broad brush, Tylor asserted that the methods and mechanisms of these various norms may vary, with the "rude tribes" having perhaps only a headman or chief, or that a larger grouping of families may constitute a clan with a patriarch or hereditary chief. Clans grew through amalgamation or military conquest. Nations emerged, as did the need for public order maintained either by military force or by constitutional government in the form of a kingdom or republic. The latter, as more sophisticated forms of government, require specialized organs such as popular assemblies and/or legislative and judicial bodies.[70]

E.B. Tylor, Anthropology: An Introduction to the Study of Man and Civilization 402–08 (1881).

> Mankind can never have lived as a mere struggling crowd, each for himself. Society is always made up of families or households bound together by kindly ties, controlled by rules of marriage and the duties of parent and child. Yet the forms of these rules and duties have been very various. Mar-

66. Tylor, Anthropology, *supra* note 44, at 419.

67. "Marriage has been here spoken of first, because upon it depends the family, on which the whole framework of society is founded." *Id.* at 404.

68. *See id.* at 404–05.

69. *Id.* at 405 (*see* excerpt below).

70. *Id.* at 436–38.

riages may be shifting and temporary pairing, or unions where the husband may have several wives, and the wife several husbands. It is often hard to understand the family group and its ties in the rude and ancient world. Thus it seems to us a matter of course to reckon family descent in the male line, and this is now put in the clearest way by the son taking the father's surname. But in lower stages of civilization, on both sides of the globe, many tribes take the contrary idea as a matter of course. In most Australian tribes the children belong to the mother's clan, not the father's; so that in native wars father and son constantly meet as natural enemies. . . . In the savage and barbaric world there prevails widely the rule called by McLennan exogamy or marrying-out, which forbids a man to take a wife of his own clan—an act which is considered criminal, and may even be punished with death. It is a strange contrast to the popular idea that savage life has no rules, when we find Australian tribes where every man is bound to marry into the particular clan which is, so to speak, the wife-clan to his own. Among the Iroquois of North America the children took the clan-name or totem of the mother; so if she were of the Bear clan, her son would be a Bear, and accordingly he might not marry a Bear girl, but might take a Deer or Heron. Such laws appear also among higher nations who reckon descent in the male line. . . . Though the family and tribe rules of the savage and the barbaric world are too intricate to be fully discussed here, there are some instructive points to which attention should be called. Marriage is in early stages of society a civil contract. . . . Among peoples of higher culture more formal promises and ceremonies come in, with feasts and gatherings of kinsfolk; and then, as in other important matters of life, the priest is called in to give divine blessing and sanction to the union. Where this is done, a wedding has come to be very different from what it was in the rough times of marriage by capture, such as might be seen in our own day among fierce forest tribes in Brazil, where the warriors would make forays on distant villages and by main force bring home wifes. . . . Within a few generations the same old habit was kept up in Wales, where the bridegroom and his friends, mounted and armed as for war, carried off the bride; and in Ireland they used even to hurl spears at the bride's people, though at such a distance that no one was hurt, . . .

Marriage has been here spoken of first, because upon it depends the family, on which the whole framework of society is founded. What has been said of the ruder kinds of family union among savages and barbarians shows that there cannot be expected from them the excellence of those well-ordered households to which civilized society owes so much of its goodness and prosperity. Yet even among the rudest clans of men, unless depraved by vice or misery and falling to pieces, a standard of family morals is known and lived by. Their habits, judged by our notions, are hard and coarse, yet the family tie of sympathy and common interest is already formed, and the foundations of moral duty already laid, in the mother's patient tenderness, the father's desperate valour in defence of home, their daily care for the little ones, the affection of brothers and sisters, and the mutual forbearance, helpfulness, and trust of all. From the family this extends to a wider circle. The natural way in which a tribe is formed is from a family or group, which in time increases and divides into many households, still recognising one another as kindred, and this kinship is so thoroughly felt to be the tie of the whole tribe, that, even when there has been a mixture of tribes, a common ancestor is often invented to make an imaginary bond of union. Thus *kindred* and *kindness* go together—two words whose common derivation expresses in the happiest way one of the main principles of social life.

Among the lessons to be learned from the life of rude tribes is, how society can go on without the policeman to keep order. It is plain that even the lowest men cannot live quite by what the Germans call "faustrecht," or "fist-right," and we call "club law." The strong savage does not rush into his weaker neighbour's hut and take possession, driving the owner out into the forest with a stone-headed javelin sent flying after him. Without some control beyond the mere right of the stronger, the tribe would break up in a week, whereas in fact savage tribes last on for ages. . . . It is clear that low barbarians may live among themselves under a fairly high moral standard, and this is the more instructive because it shows what may be called natural morality. . . . But the reality is quite as instructive, that the laws of virtue and happiness may be found at work in simple forms among tribes who make hatchets of sharpened stones and rub sticks together to kindle fire. Their life, seen at its best, shows with unusual clearness the great principle of moral science, that morality and happiness belong together—in fact that morality is the method of happiness.

It must not be supposed that in any state of civilization a man's conduct depends altogether on his own moral sense of right and wrong. Controlling forces of society are at work even among savages, only in more rudimentary ways than among ourselves. Public opinion is already a great power, and the way in which it acts is particularly to be noticed. Whereas the individual man is too apt to look to his own personal interest and the benefit of his near friends, these private motives fall away when many minds come together, and public opinion with a larger selfishness takes up the public good, encouraging the individual to set aside his private wishes and give up his property or even his life for the commonwealth. The assembled tribe can crush the mean and cowardly with their scorn, or give that reward of glory for which the high-spirited will risk goods and life . . .

Conclusion

The foregoing materials show that Tylor firmly believed in the basic unity of humankind (*tutto il mondo è paese*). His ethnographic project was to develop general laws about normative systems that were applicable to humanity as a whole, without reference to racial or ethnic concerns. These laws were to be developed by studying humankind's past, which he thought was the key to understanding the present. The lessons thus learned and the laws so drawn, he believed, would enable humans to plan a better life for the future, as he explains in the following excerpt.

Edward B. Tylor, Anthropology: An Introduction to the Study of Man and Civilization 438–40 (1881).

Here this sketch of anthropology may close. The examination of man's age on the earth, his bodily structure and varieties of race and language, has led us on to enquire into his intellectual and social history. In his many-sided life there may be clearly traced a development, which, not withstanding long periods of stoppage and frequent falling back, has on the whole adapted modern civilized man for a far higher and happier career than his ruder ancestors. In this development, the preceding chapters have shown a difference between low and high nations, which it only remains to put before the reader as a practical moral to the tale of civilization. It is true that both among savage and civilized peoples progress in culture takes place, but not under the same conditions. The savage by no means goes through life with the intention of gathering more knowledge and framing better laws than his fathers. On the contrary, his tendency is to consider his ancestors as having handed down to him the perfection of wisdom, which it would be impiety to make the least alteration in. Hence among the lower races there is obstinate resistance to the most desirable reforms, and progress can only force its way with a slowness and difficulty which we of this century can hardly imagine. Looking at the condition of the rude man, it may be seen that his aversion to change was not always unreasonable, and indeed may often have arisen from a true instinct. With his ignorance of any life but his own, he would be rash to break loose from the old tried machinery of society, to plunge into revolutionary change, which might destroy the present good without putting better in its place. Had the experience of ancient men been larger, they would have seen their way to faster steps in culture. But we civilized moderns have just that wider knowledge which the rude ancients wanted. Acquainted with events and their consequences far and wide over the world, we are able to direct our own course with more confidence toward improvement. In a word, mankind is passing from the age of unconscious to that of conscious progress. Readers who have come thus far need not be told in many words of what the facts must have already brought to their minds—that the study of man and civilization is not only a matter of scientific interest, but at once passes into the practical business of life. We have in it the means of understanding our own lives and our place in the world, vaguely and imperfectly it is true, but at any rate more clearly than any former generation. The knowledge of man's course of life, from the remote past to the present, will not only help us to forecast the future, but may guide us in our duty of leaving the world better than we found it.

Morgan: Classifications of Unilinear Anthropology

Linkage of Normative Structure and Economic Progress

Lewis Henry Morgan (1818–1881) is considered the father of American anthropology because of the extensive fieldwork he conducted—in particular, his ethnography of the Iroquois, his development of a classificatory system of kinship, and his contribution to anthropological evolutionary theory in general. The latter claimed (as explained later) that humanity passes through three phases of normative evolution: savagery, barbarism, and civilization.

After years of working with the Seneca, Morgan published the first scientific ethnography of a Native American culture, *The League of the Iroquois* (1851). From 1859 to 1862, his interest in Native Americans carried him into middle America and Canada; he conducted extensive research in Wisconsin, Kansas, Nebraska, the Hudson Bay, and the Rocky Mountains. He concluded (erroneously) that all North American Native cultures had the same kinship system.[71] In 1859, Morgan asserted (also erroneously) that the same kinship system existed in India as well.[72] Subsequently, with the aid of the Smithsonian Institution, he drafted a list of questions concerning kinship structures in culture, which he distributed worldwide. He compiled the forty-eight responses he received and published the results in his book *Systems of Consanguinity and Affinity in the Human Family.*[73]

Morgan's complex classification of various types of kinship orders is not of immediate relevance here, but it is important to note that he theorized that the various kinship systems represented corresponding family types, which in turn evolved in conjunction with various stages of economic progress. Thus, the first family type was the consanguine family characterized by marriage between brothers and sisters (own and collateral) in the pre-savage phase.[74] Morgan held out Malayan society as an example of a society that had had such a customary past.[75] This was the first of a five-stage sequence of the evolution of family types, the last (and the most economically and normatively developed) stage being that of "the monogamian family."

The second phase, exemplified by Hawaiian society, was that of "the punaluan family" founded on the intermarriage of several sisters (own and collateral) with one another's husbands and intermarriage of several brothers (own and collateral) to one another's wives. Here the brothers did not marry their sisters (own or collateral), nor did the sisters marry their brothers (own and collateral).[76] The third stage was what Morgan called "the syndyasmian or pairing family," characterized by the

---

71. Harris, *supra* note 4, at 178–79.

72. *Id.* at 190.

73. *See* Lewis Henry Morgan, Systems of Consanguinity and Affinity in the Human Family (1871).

74. "It belongs to a condition of society out of which the least advance portion of the human race have emerged." Morgan, Ancient Society, *supra* note 8, at 401.

75. *Id.* at 27, 385.

76. *Id.* at 27, 424 *et seq.*

formal pairing of male and female without exclusive cohabitation.[77] In other words, such cohabitation was at the pleasure of the parties, and separation was always an option. Morgan found evidence of this among the Iroquois and other Native American tribes, although he stressed that Iroquois marriages were monogamous and generally stable.[78] The fourth stage was that of the patriarchal family involving one man marrying several wives (polygamy).[79] The last phase was the monogamian family in which one man marries one wife with exclusive cohabitation. This is the modern family of civilized society, according to Morgan.[80] These kinship terminologies and their family archetypes are discussed in Part III of *Ancient Society* under the heading "Growth of the Idea of Family."

Closely related to this normative approach to family is Part IV, titled "Growth of the Idea of Property." This too was an evolutionary normative phenomenon, according to Morgan.[81] The nuclear family emerged with the "rise of property . . . the settlement of its rights, and above all, with the established certainty of its transmission to lineal descendants."[82] The family became organized in relation to rights and privileges associated with property. Thus social structure became normatively linked to the economy.[83] Morgan thus viewed the growth of property as going hand in hand with technological progress. The products of inventors and discoveries in turn also required rules of property.

The linkage between normative structure and economy and the rudimentary lifestyle of the Native American tribes led Morgan to conclude that the latter were incapable of conceptualizing (let alone using) Western notions of property ownership. The following excerpt explains this in more detail.

Lewis Henry Morgan, Houses and House-Life of the American Aborigines 79–82 (1881).

"Usages and Customs With Respect to Land and Food"

> Among the Iroquois the tribal domain was held and owned by the tribe in common. Individual ownership, with the right to sell and convey in fee-simple to any other person, was entirely unknown among them. It required the experience and development of the two succeeding ethnical periods to bring mankind to such a knowledge of property in land as its individual ownership with the power of alienation in fee-simple implies. No person in Indian life could obtain the absolute title to land, since it was vested by custom in the tribe as one body; and they had no conception of what is im-

77. *Id.* at 27–28, 453 *et seq.*

78. *Id.* at xxii.

79. *Id.* at xxii, 453 *et seq.*

80. Morgan, Ancient Society, *supra* note 8, at 27, 468 *et seq.*

81. *Id.* at 525 *et seq.*

82. Morgan, Systems of Consanguinity, *supra* note 73, at 492.

83. *See* Jerry D. Moore, Visions of Culture: An Introduction to Anthropological Theories and Theorists 24 (2d ed. 2004).

plied by a legal title in severalty with power to sell and convey the fee. But he could reduce unoccupied land to possession by cultivation, and so long as he thus used it he had a possessory right to its enjoyment which would be recognized and respected by his tribe. Gardens planting-lots, apartments in a long-house, and, at a later day, orchards of fruit were thus held by persons and by families. Such possessory right was all that was needed for their full enjoyment and for the protection of their interest in them. A person might transfer or donate his rights to other persons of the same tribe, and they also passed by inherence, under established customs, to his gentile kin. This was substantially the Indian system in respect to the ownership of lands and apartments in houses among the Indian tribes within the areas of the United States and British America in the Lower Status of barbarism. In later times, when the State or National Government acquired Indian lands and made compensation therefore, payment for the lands went to the tribe, and for improvements to the individual who had the possessory right. At the Tonawanda Reservation of the Seneca-Iroquois, a portion of the lands are divided into separate farms, which are fenced and occupied in severalty, while the remainder are owned by the tribe in common. When a young man marries and has no land on which to subsist, the chiefs may allot him a portion of these reserved lands. The title to all these lands, occupied and unoccupied, remains in the tribe in common. Individuals may sell or rent their possessory rights to each other, or rent them to a white man. No white man can now acquire a title from an Indian to Indian lands in any part of the United States. A person could transfer his possessions to another, but apartments in a house must remain to his gentile kindred. In the time of James II the right to acquire lands was vested in the Crown exclusively as a royal prerogative, to which prerogative our State and National Governments succeeded. . . .

And here I may be allowed a brief digression, to notice a recent opinion of the late Secretary of the Interior, Hon. Carl Schurz, shared in to some extent by the National Government, in relation to the division of our Indian reservations into lots or tracts, and their conveyance in severalty to the Indians themselves, with power of alienation to white men after a short period, say twenty-five years. It is to be hoped that this policy will never be adopted by any National Administration, as it is fraught with nothing but mischief to the Indian tribes. The Indian is still, as he always has been, and will remain for many years to come, entirely incapable of meeting the white man, with safety to himself, in the field of trade and of resisting the arts and inducements which would be brought to bear upon him. He is incapable of steadily attaching that value to the ownership of land which its importance deserves, or of knowing how far the best interests of himself and family are involved in its continued possession. The result of individual Indian ownership, with power to sell, would unquestionably be, that in a very short time he would divest himself of every foot of land and fall into poverty. The case of the Shawnee tribe of Kansas affords a perfect illustration of this pernicious policy. The Shawnees were removed to Kansas under the Jackson policy, so called, and occupied a splendid reservation on the Kansas River, where they were told they were to make their home forever. But after a few years of undisturbed possession, our people, in the natural flow of population, reached Kansas, where they found the Shawnees in possession of the best part of what has since been the State of Kansas. Our people at once wanted these Indian lands, and they determined to root out the Shawnees in the interest of civilization and progress. They accomplished this result in the most speedy and scientific manner, using as their proposed lever this identical plan since adopted by Mr. Schurz. First, the government was induced to re-purchase a part of the reservation on the ground that they had more land than they needed for cultivation; and, secondly, the government induced the Indians to have the remainder divided up into farms and conveyed to heads of families in severalty, with power of alienation. In 1859, when this scheme was being worked out, I visited Kansas, and found the Shawnee's cultivating and improving their farms, some of which embraced a thousand acres, and owning them, too, like other farmers. When next in Kansas, ten years later, the work was done. There was not a Shawnee in Kansas, but American farmers were in possession of all these lands. It was this individual ownership with power to sell that had done the work.

In managing the affairs of our Indian tribes, we must apply a little common sense to their condition. In their brains they are in the same stage of growth and development with our remote forefathers when they learned to domesticate animals, and, came to rely upon a meat and milk subsistence. The next condition of advancement at which the Indian would naturally reach is the pastoral, the raising of flocks and herds of domestic animals. The Indian has taught himself to raise the horse in herds, and some of the tribes raise sheep and goats. A few of them raise cattle. If the government could assist them in this until they were started, they would soon become expert herdsmen; would make a proper use of the unoccupied prairie area in the interior of the continent as well as of the reservations, and would become prosperous and abundant in their resources.

Morgan's Classifications for a Unilinear Evolutionary Trajectory

Morgan conjectured that humanity's initial survival depended on the ability to provide for oneself the basic means of subsistence (which he called "arts of subsistence"). Being able to provide oneself with the crudest arts of subsistence, early humans were able to survive, and then flourish as they worked their way up the ladder of civilization. Not having control over the means of subsistence, a person survived on "fruits and nuts" in the earliest times.[84] In time, so the speculation goes, humans felt motivated (if not forced) to manipulate their environment to produce more to meet the needs of the expanding family. During this early phase, which Morgan dubbed the period of "savagery," humans had two principal sources of food at their disposal.

84. Morgan, Ancient Society, *supra* note 8, at 10.

Three other sources became available in the subsequent "barbaric" period, as seen in Table 1.1. It is explained in greater detail in the excerpt from his book *Ancient Society*.

In 1877, Morgan published *Ancient Society*, his best-known work, in which he developed his normative scheme concerning the three principal stages through which humans passed: savagery, barbarism, and civilization. He described each of these "ethnical periods" and their subdivisions in great detail, including the tribes he believed were influential participants within a given period, the familial structure of those tribes, the technology common to each particular stage, and the technology that prompted advancement to the higher stage.[85] Subscribing to the view that technological advancement was the driving force for normative progress, he described the stages and their corresponding technological innovations as seen in Table 1.1.

Table 1.1
Morgan's Stages of Evolution and Their Technological Innovations

Stage	Technological Innovation
I. Lower Status of Savagery	Infancy of the human race; rudimentary subsistence on "fruit and nuts"
II. Middle Status of Savagery	Fish subsistence; knowledge of the use of fire
III. Upper Status of Savagery	Invention of the bow and arrow
IV. Lower Status of Barbarism	Invention of the art of pottery
V. Middle Status of Barbarism	Domestication of animals in the Eastern Hemisphere, and cultivation of maize and plants by irrigation with the use of adobe-brick and stone in the Western Hemisphere
VI. Upper Status of Barbarism	Invention of the process of smelting iron ore, with the use of iron tools
VII. Status of Civilization	Invention of a phonetic alphabet, with the use of writing[86]

Lewis Henry Morgan, Ancient Society 3–6, 9–13, 16–17 (1877).

The latest investigations respecting the early condition of the human race, are tending to the conclusion that mankind commenced their career at the bottom of the scale and worked their way up from savagery to civilization through the slow accumulations of experimental knowledge.

As it is undeniable that portions of the human family have existed in a state of savagery, other portions in a state of barbarism, and still other portions in a state of civilization, it seems equally so that these three distinct conditions are connected with each other in a natural as well as necessary

85. *See id.* at 3–18.

86. *Source:* Morgan, Ancient Society, *supra* note 8, at 10–12.

sequence of progress. Moreover, that this sequence has been historically true of the entire human family, up to the status attained by each branch respectively, is rendered probable by the conditions under which all progress occurs, and by the known advancement of several branches of the family through two or more of these conditions.

An attempt will be made in the following pages to bring forward additional evidence of the rudeness of the early condition of mankind, of the gradual evolution of their mental and moral powers through experience, and of their protracted struggle with opposing obstacles while winning their way to civilization. It will be drawn, in part, from the great sequence of inventions and discoveries which stretches along the entire pathway of human progress; but chiefly from domestic institutions, which express the growth of certain ideas and passions.

As we re-ascend along the several lines of progress toward the primitive ages of mankind, and eliminate one after the other, in the order in which they appeared, inventions and discoveries on the one hand, and institutions on the other, we are enabled to perceive that the former stand to each other in progressive, and the latter in unfolding relations. While the former class have had a connection, more or less direct, the latter have been developed from a few primary germs of thought. Modern institutions plant their roots in the period of barbarism, into which their germs were transmitted from the previous period of savagery. They have had a lineal descent through the ages, with the streams of the blood, as well as a logical development ...

The period of savagery, of the early part of which very little is known, may be divided, provisionally, into three sub-periods. These may be named respectively the *Older,* the *Middle,* and the *Later* period of savagery; and the condition of society in each, respectively, may be distinguished as the *Lower,* the *Middle,* and the *Upper Status* of savagery.

In like manner, the period of barbarism divides naturally into three sub-periods, which will be called, respectively, the *Older,* the *Middle,* and the *Later* period of barbarism; and the condition of society in each, respectively, will be distinguished as the *Lower,* the *Middle,* and the *Upper Status* of barbarism.

It is difficult, if not impossible, to find such tests of progress to mark the commencement of these several periods as will be found absolute in their application, and without exceptions upon all the continents. Neither is it necessary, for the purpose in hand, that exceptions should not exist. It will be sufficient if the principal tribes of mankind can be classified, according to the degree of their relative progress, into conditions which can be recognized as distinct.

I. *Lower Status of Savagery.*

This period commenced with the infancy of the human race, and may be said to have ended with the acquisition of a fish subsistence and of a knowledge of the use of fire. Mankind were then living in their original restricted habitat, and subsisting upon fruits and nuts. The commencement of articulate speech belongs to this period. No exemplification of tribes of mankind in this condition remained to the historical period.

II. *Middle Status of Savagery.*
It commenced with the acquisition of a fish subsistence and a knowledge of the use of fire, and ended with the invention of the bow and arrow. Mankind, while in this condition, spread from their original habitat over the greater portion of the earth's surface. Among tribes still existing it will leave in the Middle Status of savagery, for example, the Australians and the greater part of the Polynesians when discovered. It will be sufficient to give one or more exemplifications of each status.

III. *Upper Status of Savagery.*
It commenced with the invention of the bow and arrow, and ended with the invention of the art of pottery. It leaves in the Upper Status of Savagery the Athapascan tribes of the Hudson's Bay Territory, the tribes of the valley of the Columbia, and certain coast tribes of North and South America; but with relation to the time of their discovery. This closes the period of Savagery.

IV. *Lower Status of Barbarism.*
The invention or practice of the art of pottery, all things considered, is probably the most effective and conclusive test that can be selected to fix a boundary line, necessarily arbitrary, between savagery and barbarism. The distinctness of the two conditions has long been recognized, but no criterion of progress out of the former into the latter has hitherto been brought forward. All such tribes, then, as never attained to the art of pottery will be classed as savages, and those possessing this art but who never attained a phonetic alphabet and the use of writing will be classed as barbarians.

The first sub-period of barbarism commenced with the manufacture of pottery, whether by original invention or adoption. In finding its termination, and the commencement of the Middle Status, a difficulty is encountered in the unequal endowments of the two hemispheres, which began to be influential upon human affairs after the period of savagery had passed. It may be met, however, by the adoption of equivalents. In the Eastern hemisphere, the domestication of animals, and in the Western, the cultivation of maize and plants by irrigation, together with the use of adobe-brick and stone in house building have been selected as sufficient evidence of progress to work a transition out of the Lower and into the Middle Status of barbarism. It leaves, for example, in the Lower Status, the Indian tribes of the United States east of the Missouri River, and such tribes of Europe and Asia as practiced the art of pottery, but were without domestic animals.

V. *Middle Status of Barbarism.*
It commenced with the domestication of animals in the Eastern hemisphere, and in the Western with cultivation by irrigation and with the use of adobe-brick and stone in architecture, as shown. Its termination may be fixed with

the invention of the process of smelting iron ore. This places in the Middle Status, for example, the Village Indians of New Mexico, Mexico, Central America and Peru, and such tribes in the Eastern hemisphere as possessed domestic animals, but were without a knowledge of iron. The ancient Britons, although familiar with the use of iron, fairly belong in this connection. The vicinity of more advanced continental tribes had advanced the arts of life among them far beyond the state of development of their domestic institutions.

VI. *Upper Status of Barbarism.*
It commenced with the manufacture of iron, and ended with the invention of a phonetic alphabet, and the use of writing in literary composition. Here civilization begins. This leaves in the Upper Status, for example, the Grecian tribes of the Homeric age, the Italian tribes shortly before the founding of Rome, and the Germanic tribes of the time of Caesar.

VII. *Status of Civilization.*
It commenced, as stated, with the use of a phonetic alphabet and the production of literary records, and divides into *Ancient* and *Modern.* As an equivalent, hieroglyphical writing upon stone may be admitted.

RECAPITULATION.

Periods.	Conditions.
I. Older Period of Savagery,	I. Lower Status of Savagery,
II. Middle Period of Savagery,	II. Middle Status of Savagery,
III. Later Period of Savagery,	III. Upper Status of Savagery,
IV. Older Period of Barbarism,	IV. Lower Status of Barbarism,
V. Middle Period of Barbarism,	V. Middle Status of Barbarism,
VI. Later Period of Barbarism,	VI. Upper Status of Barbarism,

VII. Status of Civilization.

I. *Lower Status of Savagery, From the Infancy of the Human Race to the commencement of the next Period.*
II. *Middle Status of Savagery, From the acquisition of a fish subsistence and a knowledge of the use of fire, to etc.*
III. *Upper Status of Savagery, From the Invention of the Bow and Arrow, to etc.*
IV. *Lower Status of Barbarism, From the Invention of the Art of Pottery, to etc.*
V. *Middle Status of Barbarism, From the Domestication of animals on the Eastern hemisphere, and in the Western from the cultivation of maize and plants by Irrigation, with the use of adobe-brick and stone, to etc.*

VI. *Upper Status of Barbarism, From the Invention of the process of Smelting Iron Ore, with the use of iron tools, to etc.*
VII. *Status of Civilization, From the Invention of a Phonetic Alphabet, with the use of writing, to the present time. . . .*

Another advantage of fixing definite ethnical periods is the direction of special investigation to those tribes and nations which afford the best exemplification of each status, with the view of making each both standard and illustrative. Some tribes and families have been left in geographical isolation to work out the problems of progress by original mental effort, and have, consequently, retained their arts and institutions pure and homogeneous; while those of other tribes and nations have been adulterated through external influence. Thus, while Africa was and is an ethnical chaos of savagery and barbarism, Australia and Polynesia were in savagery, pure and simple, with the arts and institutions belonging to that condition. In like manner, the Indian family of America, unlike any other existing family, exemplified the condition of mankind in three successive ethnical periods. In the undisturbed possession of a great continent, of common descent, and with homogeneous institutions, they illustrated, when discovered, each of these conditions, and especially those of the Lower and of the Middle Status of barbarism, more elaborately and completely than any other portion of mankind. The far northern Indians and some of the coast tribes of North and South America were in the Upper Status of savagery; the partially Village Indians east of the Mississippi were in the Lower Status of barbarism, and the Village Indians of North and South America were in the Middle Status. Such an opportunity to recover full and minute information of the course of human experience and progress in developing their arts and institutions through these successive conditions has not been offered within the historical period. It must be added that it has been indifferently improved. Our greatest deficiencies relate to the last period named.

Differences in the culture of the same period in the Eastern and Western hemispheres undoubtedly existed in consequence of the unequal endowments of the continents; but the condition of society in the corresponding status must have been, in the main, substantially similar.

The ancestors of the Grecian Roman and German tribes passed through the stages we have indicated, in the midst of the last of which the light of history fell upon them. Their differentiation from the undistinguishable mass of barbarians did not occur, probably, earlier than the commencement of the Middle Period of barbarism. The experience of these tribes has been lost, with the exception of so much as is represented by the institutions inventions and discoveries which they brought with them, and possessed when they first came under historical observation. The Grecian and Latin tribes of the Homeric and Romulian periods afford the highest exemplification

> of the Upper Status of barbarism. Their institutions were likewise pure and homogeneous, and their experience stands directly connected with the final achievement of civilization. . . .

Evolution of Government and Law in Morgan's Classifications

Perhaps his training as a lawyer motivated Morgan to study the "Growth of the Idea of Government," to which he devotes Part II of the book, by far its longest segment. His thesis is the same: systems of government developed from the simple to the complex as technological innovations improved humanity's material well-being and social welfare. It is thus obvious that what began as an inquiry into kinship systems and how they affected family relationships blossomed into a worldview on the development of humanity itself. This global perspective on human evolution is what Morgan set out to explain in *Ancient Society*, as introduced in the book's preface:

> Throughout the latter part of the period of savagery, and the entire period of barbarism, mankind in general were organized in gentes, phratries and tribes. These organizations prevailed throughout the entire ancient world upon all the continents, and were the instrumentalities by means of which ancient society was organized and held together. Their structure, and relations as members of an organic series, and the rights, privileges and obligations of the members of the gens, and the members of the phratry and tribe, illustrate the growth of the idea of government in the human mind. The principal institutions of mankind originated in savagery, were developed in barbarism, and are maturing in civilization.[87]

Morgan devotes considerable attention in this part of the book to globally applicable notions of political, social, and legal normativity. As the foregoing passage explains, the first and most ancient normative order was founded on gentes, phratries, and tribes. The most modern form, by contrast, was based on the concept of property and territoriality.[88] The former model was based on purely personal relationships (*societas*), whereas the latter was based on relations to territory such as the township/municipality, county or the state (*civitas*).[89]

The ancient model represented the system of consanguinity in which the gens is a social grouping related by blood, not marriage, with all descendants having a common ancestor.[90] The gens could evolve into phratries (clans) binding two or more such groups. Such evolution planted the seeds for the emergence of property rights and political offices. When several such clans coalesced into a single social unit with a single dialect, it became a tribe with a unified government and a defined territory. The fusion of tribes led to the creation of a nation. Thus, Morgan argued that government was a major evolutionary achievement because it represented the normative culmina-

---

87. Morgan, Ancient Society, *supra* note 8, at xxx.

88. *Id.* at 6, 62.

89. *Id.* at 300.

90. *Id.* at 63–64.

tion of an evolutionary phase that moved from "promiscuous horde to brother-sister group families, from group families to gens, and then progressively through stages of phratry, tribe, and nation."[91]

I have already presented how more sophisticated property rights were said to have developed with material and economic progress that regulated lineal inheritance and ownership of (for example) discoveries and inventions, such as the fruits of agriculture in the middle stages of barbarism.[92] According to Morgan, the social institutions of a clan-based kinship system provided the impetus for the emergence of legal rights, property, and political office. State ownership and individual ownership emerged by the end of the upper stages of barbarism and became stable features of civilization.

In summary, central to Morgan's ideas about the emergence of government and law is the concept of property. The law of property secured rights to inventions and discoveries, as well as the inheritance of land, wealth, and goods. Property and its concepts were directly linked by Morgan to humanity's material progress.[93] During the phase of savagery, property rights did not really exist and property was not inherited because it was usually buried with its owner on the owner's death. In the lower status of barbarism, property was more important in that it was distributed among the gens on death, but without specific inheritance by spouses.[94] However, by the middle status of barbarism, which was characterized by the emergence of agriculture, rights to land emerged at the individual and communal levels.[95] The end of the upper stages of barbarism ushered in two early forms of land tenure, namely, state ownership and individual ownership. These matured into well-established normative institutions as the phase of civilization was consolidated.[96]

Morgan's thesis of the connection between technology and the evolution of property relations and government was based on the (unverified) supposition that different normative organizations were derived from earlier simpler forms.[97] He was convinced that apart from the lower status of savagery (for which there was no remaining evidence and which therefore had to be a matter of pure conjecture), many social and legal institutions within barbarous and even savage systems were discernible in one form or another in contemporary human society.[98] "The history of the human race is one in source, one in experience, and one in progress."[99] Given this belief, Morgan concluded that the history and experience of Native American tribes mirrored "the history and experience of our own remote ancestors when in corresponding condi-

---

91. Moore, Visions of Culture, *supra* note 83, at 28.

92. Morgan, Ancient Society, *supra* note 8, 525 at 532, 535. *See* section above titled "Linkage of Normative Structure and Economic Progress."

93. Morgan, Ancient Society, *supra* note 8, at 525–26.

94. *Id.* at 530–31.

95. *Id.* at 532–38.

96. *Id.* at 552.

97. Moore, Visions of Culture, *supra* note 83, at 28.

98. Morgan, Ancient Society, *supra* note 8, at 7.

99. *Id.* at xxx.

tions."[100] The origins of social and normative institutions such as the family, property, government, and law must therefore everywhere be the same.[101]

Conclusion

Morgan's classificatory scheme cannot withstand empirical scrutiny and is tainted by the same racism that influenced Spencer and Tylor. Indeed, Morgan was making highly speculative assumptions about marriage, kinship, and descent.[102] His conception of property, including his argument that the "barbarous nations" were ignorant of the concept of property (not to mention inherited property) may have been simply an ethnocentric projection of his own attachments to the prevailing capitalist ethic of his day.[103] The reader may wish to review Morgan's claims in the excerpt titled "Houses and House-Life of the American Aborigines." Toward the end of the excerpt, Morgan, in reference to the Indian tribes, asserts: "In their brains they are in the same stage of growth and development with our remote forefathers." In *Ancient Society*, he says that the Indians were "possessed of inferior mental endowments."[104] Thus ethnocentrism, bias, guesswork, and racism have provided fertile ground for attacking Morgan's conclusions.

Even so, Morgan's conceptualization of progress due to technological and economic factors has general acceptance even today. It had a strong influence on the thoughts of Karl Marx and Friedrich Engels. In fact, Engels's *Origin of the Family, Private Property and the State* draws on some of Morgan's ideas. His ethnical periods also have appeal today as at least a classification of ideal types, that is, a typology of culture. This typology claimed that the normative phases of "savagery," "barbarism," and "civilization" represented their corresponding stages of progress measured by four sets of cultural achievements: namely, arts of subsistence through inventions and discoveries, organization of the family, the idea of government, and the idea of rights to property. In addition, Morgan was the first scholar to emphasize the importance of kinship and develop a comprehensive classificatory system that was meant to be applicable cross-culturally. He was the first to show the connection between kinship orders and political systems.

---

100. *Id.* at xxxi. The Indian tribes represented the lower and middle stages of barbarism. Some tribes of North and South America were in the upper status of savagery. By contrast, Australian and Polynesian tribes were in savagery "pure and simple," while Africa was in "an ethnical chaos of savagery and barbarism." On the other hand, the Greek of the "Homeric and Remulian periods," who had pure and homogeneous institutions, exemplified the upper status of barbarism, and were thus close to achieving civilization. All these societies mirrored each other's experiences at different epochs. *Id.* at 16–17.

101. Similarly, declared Morgan, "So essentially identical are the arts institutions and mode of life in the same status in all the continents, that the archaic form of the principal domestic institutions of the Greeks and Romans must even now be sought in the corresponding institutions of the American aborigines." *Id.* at 17.

102. MEYER FORTES, KINSHIP AND THE SOCIAL ORDER: THE LEGACY OF LEWIS HENRY MORGAN 32 (1969).

103. MOORE, VISIONS OF CULTURE, *supra* note 83, at 24–25.

104. MORGAN, ANCIENT SOCIETY, *supra* note 8, at 40.

Nevertheless, what is quite apparent from the writings of Spencer, Tylor, and Morgan is that all three claimed to be laying down universally applicable principles of evolution. Spencer's belief in the universality of causation assumes that the universe followed a single and continuous scheme of development. Tylor's and Morgan's schemes also posit unilineal and uniform evolutionary stages for all civilizations. A more tolerant form of relativism, collectively known as the Boasian school, introduced the demise and replacement of evolutionism. A critical retrospective of this approach appears in the next excerpt, wherein French sociologist Roger Bastide (1898–1974) presents a blistering critique of the evolutionary model. His critique is highly persuasive, but it must be remembered that evolutionism was a product of its times. It emerged during the era of European empire building and colonial domination. Its evangelizing mission was part and parcel of an overall political and philosophical paradigm of nineteenth- and twentieth-century political Europe.

Bastide charges that early European contact with indigenous populations was filled with cultural conceit, racism, and ethnocentrism. These attitudes motivated rash and biased judgments (based on a mix of "empiricism and guesswork") that showed a complete lack of understanding of the sociocultural matrixes of indigenous peoples. They also engendered attitudes of superiority to the point that Europeans attempted to transplant their culture into non-European populations in an effort to convert, assimilate, or "acculturate" the latter. Thus "applied anthropology" was born, masquerading as the science of human evolution. But it failed in its mission, prompting critics such as Lucien Lévy-Bruhl and Boas to reexamine and redefine anthropological science. This newer approach to anthropology is taken up in the materials following the excerpt by Bastide in Chapter 2.

Roger Bastide, Applied Anthropology 10–14 (Alice L. Morson trans., 1971).

> It may be said that from the very first contacts between European and indigenous populations—or at least from the moment when groups rather than individuals confronted each other (groups of traders or of missionaries) a strategy began to be elaborated by the dominant groups, filled with cultural conceit, to change the mentality, transform the behaviour, and reorganise the social structure of the dominated groups, in terms of interests which were external to the latter. It would be incorrect then, to assume that what the Anglo-Saxons call 'controlled acculturation' and the French, 'planned acculturation' is a recent development. It dates from the very beginnings of inter-ethnic relations.
>
> For the traders, it was a question of creating new needs by means of gifts-giving so as to create new markets for European industrial goods, and by means of the 'swap' (predecessor to the slave trade) to drain off exotic goods toward distant metropolises. For the missionaries, it was a matter of wresting the souls of the natives from the 'shadows' of paganism, to make them receive the Christian faith. One need only read, for example, the *Réductions* of the

Jesuits of South America to become aware of this drive for planning—pushed to its extremes. For in order better to change the Amerindian societies, they isolated them, wrenching them from all the influences of their environment and their past, and turning them into a sort of boarding school or college, in which a whole ethnic group was under the control of a handful of pedagogues. The missionaries did not embark without plans, conscious designs, and a developed strategy.

However, we cannot speak of applied social anthropology in that era. First of all, quite justifiably, because at that time a scientific anthropology did not yet exist. The plans developed in Rome, Madrid or Lisbon had to be revised and modified after contact with the realities, that is, with the spontaneous, unforeseeable reactions of the men they wished to evangelise. Throughout this first stage, which may be qualified as pre-scientific, there existed a mixture of reasoning, guess-work and empiricism. . . .

Scientific anthropology was born only in the second half of the nineteenth century, when the first ethnological school appeared, that of evolutionism. It is not our concern here to show what evolutionism was. Suffice it to say that all peoples pass through the same states of development from 'savagery' to 'barbarism' and from 'barbarism' to 'civilisation'. The only thing we need emphasize is that evolutionism posed both a problem and a duty to the Western conscience. The problem: if all peoples must pass through the same stages of development, how is it that certain among them have stopped along the way or, at least, only advance along the common path with a greater or lesser delay? The duty: if the goal of this evolution—entrance into civilisation—is not everywhere assured, then is not it the role of the whites, who already enjoy the benefits of that civilisation, to help their inferior brothers to achieve it more quickly? And if so, what means should be taken to awaken them and place them on the road to progress? But now, this search for means can go beyond pure empiricism, for there exists a science that explains why and how a population passes from one stage to another. A historicizing ethnology lets us understand the lessons of the past, informs us concerning the true processes and paths of our own evolution, which can from then on be applied to the acculturation of peoples still in states of 'barbarism' or 'savagery'. As anthropology becomes a science, by a counter-stroke, applied anthropology is born. . . .

But the failure of this first applied anthropology disillusioned those who had promoted it. Conversion was most often only superficial and Christian concepts were reinterpreted in terms of traditional beliefs. Schools failed to change people profoundly; society took back its children at the end of class to undo the white masters' teaching. The 'man of progress', civilisation's delegate to the 'barbarians' or 'savages', had believed that it sufficed to acquaint them with the values he believed superior to arouse the enthusiasm and fervour of their masses. But he quickly recognised his powerlessness, spoke of 'inveterate laziness', and 'congenital inferiority' or of 'diabolical powers' unleashed against the word of God. True, an 'elite' was formed everywhere which believed in Western values and assimilated them, but this elite ungratefully then turned against its teachers.

II. The Problem of Cultural Relativism

We may take the work of Levy-Bruhl as evidence of this failure. Emphasising the result of the contradistinction between prelogical and logical mentality, he saw conversion from one to the other, if not as impossible, at least as especially difficult. Scholars of the period were not taken in, and if the reaction of some anthropologists was so impassioned, it was precisely because they saw in Levy-Bruhl's work a condemnation either of the missionary endeavour (Allier) or of the colonialists' work of assimilative education. In the United States, Boas, who had denounced evolutionism, just as vigorously denounced as false the idea of a prelogical mentality. But with Boas, we come to a second stage of the history of anthropology, that of the triumph of cultural anthropology, to which we must turn for a moment.

Certainly reason is one and the same among all men, regardless of their skin colour, or the texture of their hair. But it reveals itself through different sorts of cultural endeavour. We are not to judge the value of these varieties; there are no superior or inferior cultures. There are only *different* cultures. Evolutionism's chief mistake was to judge other civilisations by reference to our own, and thus to fall into the sin of ethnocentrism. Undoubtedly the Australian aborigines when they were discovered may well have still been in the Stone Age, but they offered the observer a social wealth and complexity superior to our own. Obviously, Eastern civilisations did not reach as high a level of technological development as did those of the West, but they did, on the other hand, reach a higher level of spiritual development and metaphysical knowledge than ours.

Chapter 2

Cultural Normativity in Relativist Context

As seen at the end of the previous chapter, evolutionary theory came under attack at the dawn of the twentieth century. Its claims to be a science of the laws of human evolution were criticized largely due to the lack of empirical evidence for such "laws." Yet the search persisted for foundational principles that would give an epistemologically reliable account of human society, its normative organization, and its evolution. Another goal of this quest was to develop a methodology that would provide "better," "truer," or more epistemically reliable accounts of human society. Anthropology thus claimed its place as a "science"; it was now only a question of which methods would be used to gather knowledge.

The new method proclaimed at the dawn of the twentieth century was the historical method. Its goal was to show the world as it actually is. Central to this approach was rejecting the assumption that uniformities in ethnological and normative phenomena were the result of similarly uniform laws or causes. The new argument was that such uniformities could evolve in a multitude of ways and processes. The task of the new scientific methodology was to study these processes in their *own* historical contexts. Thus was born the new "Boasian school," whose chief protagonist was Franz Boas.

The Boasian School

Boas: Historicism, Particularism, and Ethnographic Research

Methodological Critique

In 1896, German-born U.S. anthropologist Franz Boas (1858–1942) launched the first serious attack against the classical evolutionists' comparative methodology. He rejected the generalizations in which cultures showing similar traits were proclaimed to have similar origins and would therefore follow the same evolutionary track.

> It must . . . be clearly understood that anthropological research which compares similar cultural phenomena from various parts of the world, in order to discover the uniform history of their development, makes the assumption that the same ethnological phenomenon has everywhere developed in the same manner. Here lies the flaw in the argument of the new method, for no

> such proof can be given. Even the most cursory review shows that the same phenomena may develop in a multitude of ways.[1]

Boas believed that the comparative method's "fundamental assumption . . . cannot be accepted as true in all cases" because "We cannot say that the occurrence of the same phenomenon is always due to the same causes."[2] He maintained that the comparative method should be replaced with a more scientific approach. His answer to this need was the historical method.

> The comparative method and the historical method, if I may use these terms, have been struggling for supremacy for a long time, but we may hope that each will soon find its appropriate place and function. The historical method has reached a sounder basis by abandoning the misleading principle of assuming connections wherever similarities of culture were found. The comparative method, notwithstanding all that has been said and written in its praise, has been remarkably barren of definite results, and I believe it will not become fruitful until we renounce the vain endeavor to construct a uniform systematic history of the evolution of culture, and until we begin to make our comparisons on the broader and sounder basis which I ventured to outline. Up to this time we have too much reveled in more or less ingenious vagaries. The solid work is still all before us.[3]

Boas believed that without a historical reconstruction of a people being studied, their culture would appear static. Although he did not suggest that the study of history should be the aim of anthropology (as it was for nineteenth-century evolutionary anthropologists who used history to develop evolutionary frameworks into which all cultures could be "fit"), he argued that cultures were products of historical processes and that cultural evolution did not depend on racial aptitude. Rather, he argued that because every cultural assemblage of a people was based within the unique history of that people, tracing the historical progression of a particular culture would explain the significant and distinctive normative characteristics of its particular adherents.[4]

Boas may be regarded as the founder of cultural relativism or particularism, in that his approach encouraged recognition of the equality and the uniqueness of different cultures even as it discouraged notions of determinism based on racial, biological, or geographical origins. For example, as he argues in the following excerpt, similarities between cultures that are attributed to geographical conditions are in fact not due to geography but to social intercourse between cultures—the phenomenon known as the diffusion of culture. He cites examples of how products from the Baltic were found in Mediterranean countries, and of how works of art moved from the eastern Mediterranean to Sweden. He attributed such diffusionary trends to intermarriage, war, slav-

1. Franz Boas, *The Limitations of the Comparative Method of Anthropology*, 4 Science 901, 903 (1896).

2. *Id.* at 904.

3. *Id.* at 908.

4. Franz Boas, The Mind of Primitive Man 1–17 (1911).

ery, and trade. Moreover, Boas rejected as ethnocentric and inaccurate evolutionary schemes that classified some cultures as "primitive" and others as "civilized."[5] In *The Mind of Primitive Man*, he disqualifies race as an explanation for cultural variation and charges that anthropologists who proclaimed the superiority of the "white race" made the unwarranted assumptions not only that social and normative progress is due to exceptional aptitude but also that the European race has the highest aptitude.[6]

Thus Boas replaces evolutionary determinism with a form of cultural determinism.[7] Culture is not created, it is learned. Nor is culture the product of mental processes of human beings; instead, it is the product of the combination of the physical and psychical character of man as well as the influence of his surroundings and environment. The latter included the physical conditions of a country as well as its prevalence of defenses and epidemics, migrations and contact with other cultures, and heredity among its people.[8] Cultural traits, which are transmitted over time, modify and adapt to fit new social contexts. Man's behavior and beliefs are thus the reflections of his own cultural characteristics and traditions.[9] A trait is just another example of cultural normativity, in that it embodies a guide or standard underlying behavior occurring on a more or less regular basis.

Thus, any cultural trait (and the entire culture itself) has a rich history and cannot be explained without extensive historical study and fact-gathering.[10] Long-term fieldwork was therefore essential in Boas's view. He insisted that all cross-cultural comparisons and accounts of cultural traits be supported by empirical data acquired during long periods of primary field research within the relevant cultural setting. In the following excerpt, he offers a cogent critique of evolutionary approaches to culture and explains his own preferred methodology.

Franz Boas, *Limitations of the Comparative Method of Anthropology*, 4 Science 901, 901–908 (1896).

The Bobbs-Merrill Reprint Series in Anthropology, A-476 pp. 901–908.

Modern Anthropology has discovered the fact that human society has grown and developed everywhere in such a manner that its forms, its opinions and its actions have many fundamental traits in common. This momentous discovery implies that laws exist which govern the development of

5. Franz Boas, *The History of Anthropology*, 20 Science 513, 516 (1904); Roger M. Keesing & Felix M. Keesing, New Perspectives in Cultural Anthropology 382 (1971).

6. Boas, The Mind of Primitive Man, *supra* note 4, at 17.

7. Elvin Hatch, Theory of Man and Culture 49 (1973); *See also* Keesing & Keesing, *supra* note 5, at 382.

8. Franz Boas, *The Principles of Ethnological Classification* (1887), *in* A Franz Boas Reader: The Shaping of American Anthropology 1883–1911 61, 64 (George W. Stocking ed., 1974); Boas, The Mind of Primitive Man, *supra* note 4, at 11–13, 40, 48, 76–77.

9. Hatch, *supra* note 7, at 49.

10. Marvin Harris, The Rise of Anthropological Theory, 258 (updated ed. 2001); Hatch, *supra* note 7, at 57.

society, that they are applicable to our society as well as to those of past times and of distant lands; that their knowledge will be a means of understanding the causes furthering and retarding civilization; and that, guided by this knowledge, we may hope to govern our actions so that the greatest benefit to mankind will accrue from them. Since this discovery has been clearly formulated, anthropology has begun to receive that liberal share of public interest which was withheld from it as long as it was believed that it could do no more than record the curious customs and beliefs of strange peoples; or, at best, trace their relationships, and thus elucidate the early migrations of the races of man and the affinities of peoples.

While early investigators concentrated their attention upon this purely historical problem, the tide has now completely turned, so that there are even anthropologists who declare that such investigations belong to the historian, and that anthropological studies must be confined to researches on the laws that govern the growth of society.

A radical change of method has accompanied this change of views. While formerly identities or similarities of culture were considered incontrovertible proof of historical connection, or even of common origin, the new school declines to consider them as such, but interprets them as results of the uniform working of the human mind. . . .

When studying the culture of any one tribe, more or less close analogs of single traits of such a culture may be found among a great diversity of peoples. Instances of such analoga have been collected to a vast extent by Tylor, Spencer, Bastian, Andree, Post and many others, so that it is not necessary to give here any detailed proof of this fact. The idea of a future life, the one underlying shamanism; inventions such as fire and the bow; certain elementary features of grammatical structure—these will suggest the classes of phenomena to which I refer. It follows from these observations that when we find an analogon of single traits of culture among distant peoples, the presumption is not that there has been a common historical source, but that they have arisen independently. . . .

In treating this, the most difficult problem of anthropology, the point of view is taken that if an ethnological phenomenon has developed independently in a number of places its development has been the same everywhere; or, expressed in a different form, that the same ethnological phenomena are always due to the same causes. This leads to the still wider generalization that the sameness of ethnological phenomena found in diverse regions is proof that the human mind obeys the same laws everywhere. It is obvious that if different historical developments could lead to the same results, that then this generalization would not be tenable. Their existence would present to us an entirely different problem, namely, how it is that the developments of culture so often lead to the same results. It must, therefore, be clearly understood that anthropological research which compares similar cultural phenomena from various parts of the world, in order to discover the uniform history of their development, makes the assumption that the same ethnological phenomenon has everywhere developed in the same manner. Here lies the flaw in the argument of the new method, for no such proof can be given. Even the most cursory review shows that the same phenomena may develop in a multitude of ways. . . .

Another example may not be amiss: The use of masks is found among a great number of peoples. The origin of the custom of wearing masks is by no means clear in all cases, but a few typical forms of their use may easily be distinguished. They are used for deceiving spirits as to the identity of the wearer. The spirit of a disease who intends to attack the person does not recognize him when he wears a mask, and the mask serves in this manner as a protection. In other cases the mask represents a spirit which is personified by the wearer, who in this shape frightens away other hostile spirits. Still other masks are commemorative. The wearer personifies a deceased person whose memory is to be recalled. Masks are also used in theatrical performances illustrating mythological incidents.

These few data suffice to show that the same ethnical phenomenon may develop from different sources. The simpler the observed fact, the more likely it is that it may have developed from one source here, from another there.

Thus we recognize that the fundamental assumption which is so often made by modern anthropologists cannot be accepted as true in all cases. We cannot say that the occurrence of the same phenomenon is always due to the same causes, and that thus it is proved that the human mind obeys the same laws everywhere. We must demand that the causes from which it developed be investigated and that comparisons be restricted to those phenomena which have been proved to be effects of the same causes. . . . In short, before extended comparisons are made, the comparability of the material must be proved.

The comparative studies of which I am speaking here attempt to explain customs and ideas of remarkable similarity which are found here and there. But they pursue also the more ambitious scheme of discovering the law, and the history of the evolution of human society. The fact that many fundamental features of culture are universal, or at least occur in many isolated places, interpreted by the assumption that the same features must always have developed from the same causes, leads to the conclusion that there is one grand system according to which mankind has developed everywhere; that all the occurring variations are no more than minor details in this grand uniform evolution. It is clear that this theory has for its logical basis the assumption that the same phenomena are always due to the same causes. . . .

We have seen that the facts do not favor the assumption of which we are speaking at all; that they much rather point in the opposite direction. Therefore we must also consider all the ingenious attempts at constructions of a grand system of the evolution of society as of very doubtful value, unless at the same time proof is given that the same phenomena could not develop by any other method. Until this is done, the presumption is always in favor of a variety of courses which historical growth may have taken.

It will be well to restate at this place one of the principal aims of anthropological research. We agreed that certain laws exist which govern the growth of human culture, and it is our endeavor to discover these laws. The object of our investigation is to find the *processes* by which certain stages of culture have developed. The customs and beliefs themselves are not the ultimate objects of research. We desire to learn the reasons why such customs and beliefs exist—in other words, we wish to discover the history of their development. The method which is at present most frequently applied in investigations of this character compares the variations under which the customs or beliefs occur and endeavors to find the common psychological cause that underlies all of them. I have stated that this method is open to a very fundamental objection.

We have another method, which in many respects is much safer. A detailed study of customs in their bearings to the total culture of the tribe practicing them, and in connection with an investigation of their geographical distribution among neighboring tribes, afford us almost always a means of determining with considerable accuracy the historical causes that led to the formation of the customs in question and to the psychological processes that were at work in their development. The results of inquiries conducted by this method may be three-fold. They may reveal the environmental conditions which have created or modified cultural elements; they may clear up psychological factors which are at work in shaping the culture; or they may bring before our eyes the effects that historical connections have had upon the growth of the culture.

We have in this method a means of reconstructing the history of the growth of ideas with much greater accuracy than the generalizations of the comparative method will permit. The latter must always proceed from a hypothetical mode of development, the probability of which may be weighed more or less accurately by means of observed data. But so far I have not yet seen any extended attempt to prove the correctness of a theory by testing it at the hand of developments with whose histories we are familiar. This method of starting with a hypothesis is infinitely inferior to the one in which by truly inductive processes the actual history of definite phenomena is derived. The latter is no other than the much ridiculed historical method. Its way of proceeding is, of course, no longer that of former times when slight similarities of culture were considered proofs of relationships, but it duly recognizes the results obtained by comparative studies. Its application is based first of all, on a well-defined, small geographical territory, and its comparisons are not extended beyond the limits of the cultural area that forms the basis of the study. Only when definite results have been obtained in regard to this area is it permissible to extend the horizon beyond its limits, but the greatest care must be taken not to proceed too hastily in this, as else the fundamental proposition which I formulated before might be overlooked, viz: that when we find an analogy of single traits of culture among distant peoples the presumption is not that there has been a common historical source, but that they have arisen independently. . . . Not one observed fact can be brought forward in support of this hypothesis which cannot be much better explained by the well known facts of diffusion of culture; for archaeology as well as ethnography teach us that intercourse between neighboring tribes has always existed and has extended over enormous areas. In the Old World the products of the Baltic found their way to the Mediterranean and the works of art of the eastern Mediterranean reached Sweden. In America the shells of the ocean found their way into the innermost parts of the continent and the obsidians of the West were carried to Ohio. Inter-marriages, war, slavery, trade, have been so many sources of constant introduction of foreign cultural elements, so that an assimilation of culture must have taken place over continuous areas. . . .

The immediate results of the historical method are, therefore, histories of the cultures of diverse tribes which have been the subject of study. I fully agree with those anthropologists who claim that this is not the ultimate aim of our science, because the general laws, although implied in such a description, cannot be clearly formulated nor their relative value appreciated without a thorough comparison of the manner in which they assert themselves in different cultures. But I insist that the application of this method is the indispensable condition of sound progress. The psychological problem is contained in the results of the historical inquiry. When we have cleared up the history of a single culture and understand the effects of environment and the psychological conditions that are reflected in it we have made a step forward as we can then investigate in how far the same causes or other causes were at work in the development of other cultures. Thus by comparing histories of growth general laws may be found. This method is much safer than the comparative method, as it is usually practiced, because instead of a hypothesis on the mode of development actual history forms the basis of our deductions. . . .

The great and important function of the historical method of anthropology is thus seen to lie in its ability to discover the processes which in definite cases led to the development of certain customs. If anthropology desires to establish the laws governing the growth of culture it must not confine itself to comparing the results of the growth alone, but whenever such is feasible it must compare the processes of growth, and these can be discovered by means of studies of the cultures of small geographical areas.

Thus we have seen that the comparative method can hope to reach the grand results for which it is striving only when it bases its investigations on the historical results of researches which are devoted to laying clear the complex relations of each individual culture. The comparative method and the historical method, if I may use these terms, have been struggling for supremacy for a long time, but we may hope that each will soon find its appro-

> priate place and function. The historical method has reached a sounder basis by abandoning the misleading principle of assuming connections wherever similarities of culture were found. The comparative method, notwithstanding all that has been said and written in its praise, has been remarkably barren of definite results, and I believe it will not become fruitful until we renounce the vain endeavor to construct a uniform systematic history of the evolution of culture, and until we begin to make our comparisons on the broader and sounder basis which I ventured to outline. Up to this time we have too much reveled in more or less ingenious vagaries. The solid work is still all before us.

Boas ends the excerpt with this challenge: "The solid work is still before us." The next section examines the nature of this challenge and the type of ethnographic studies that he had in mind when he issued it. He was convinced that if such studies were systematically pursued, they would decisively refute the evolutionary model.

Refutation of the Evolutionary Model

Under Boasian theory, the origin of cultural normativities are external to the human mind and are autonomous. Indeed, Boas viewed such autonomous evolution as essentially following the Darwinian theories of adaptation and natural selection.[11] Evolution is thus driven by a set of diverse procedures, methods, and mechanisms (rather than conscious designs) that produce their respective variations in culture. These processes were diffusion, assimilation, migration, and unfettered invention.[12]

Boas also broke ranks with Lewis Henry Morgan on the issue of kinship. The latter had argued that matrilineal systems led to patrilineal ones,[13] but Boas claimed his studies of the Kwakiutl exhibited mixed features of the patrilineal and matrilineal systems.[14] The following excerpt, which exemplifies these mixed patrilineal and matrilineal features of Kwakiutl society, also emphasizes the uniqueness of this particular culture.

---

11. Franz Boas, *The Relation of Darwin to Anthropology, notes for a lecture*, Boas Papers B/B 61.5, American Philosophical Society. *See also* Herbert S. Lewis, "Boas, Darwin, Science and Anthropology," 42 Current Anthropology No. 3 at 387 (2001) (quoting Boas's express reference to the ideas of "the immortal Darwin which have helped to make anthropology what it is at the present time").

12. *See* for example, Franz Boas, *Mythology and Folk-Tales of the North American Indians*, 4 J. Am. Folklore 374, 381–387, 390, 393 (1914) (arguing that the similarities in folklore were the result of the dissemination of stories and ideas between different groups).

13. Lewis Henry Morgan, Ancient Society 349–50 (orig. 1877). Classics of Anthropology, with Foreword by Elizabeth Tooker (1985).

14. Franz Boas, Kwakiutl Ethnography 51–53 (Helen Codere ed., 1966); *See also* Boas, The Mind of Primitive Man, *supra* note 4, at 185: "If we do not make the assumption that the same phenomena have everywhere developed in the same way, then we may just as well conclude that paternal families have in some cases arisen from maternal institutions, in other cases in other ways."

Franz Boas, Kwakiutl Ethnography 51–52 (Helen Codere ed., 1966).

"Social Organization—The System Of Relationship"

It might seem that the numayma as here described are analogous to the sibs, clans, or gentes of other tribes, but their peculiar constitution makes terms inapplicable. The numayma is neither strictly patrilineal nor lineal, and within certain limits, a child may be assigned to any one the lines from which he or she is descended, by bequest even to unrelated lines.

The significance of the numayma in the life of the people becomes clear when we describe how names and the seats (rank) pertaining to them are obtained.

Names are obtained first of all by inheritance, the right to a name being counted in the line of primogeniture, not necessarily in the male line, for if the first-born child happens to be a girl, rank is supposed to be transmitted through her (Boas, 1925a, 103–7).

According to several statements, the girl retains this position even if she has younger brothers. "If the eldest one of the children of the one whose office is to give away property is a girl, she takes it, although she is a woman. Often the younger brother of the eldest sister tries to take away from his sister the office of giving away property, but the chiefs do not agree because it never goes to the next one to the eldest" (Boas, 1925a, 91). Here the term ts!a'ya, younger brother, is used although ordinarily a woman's brother is called *wEq!wa'* without reference to relative age.

In another passage, it is stated that "when a *L!a'qwalal,* dies, his eldest son will take his place, even if the eldest is a woman, although he may have many younger brothers" (Boas, 1921, 1107). The grammatical form of the sentence shows that the father's younger brothers are meant. A third passage refers in the same way to the younger brothers of the deceased: "Although the late *Do'qwayes* had a younger brother, *PE'ngwid,* he could not take the place of his late elder brother, because *Do'qwayes* had a daughter" (Boas, 1921, 1087). Some of the younger men of the present generation maintain that when there is a younger brother, he will succeed, not the first-born daughter.

The family histories indicate that there is no full agreement in regard to this custom. In fact, in one family history it is said that a certain chief was unfortunate, for his first-born child was a girl (Boas, 1921, 866). In this case, the line of descent is carried on in the male line. Difficulties in carrying through the rule of primogeniture in case the eldest child is a girl arise also owing to religious customs, because women cannot hold hereditary offices connected with the winter ceremonial (Boas, 1925a, 63). It is clear that the concept of patrilineal descent pervades this system, for when a woman is designated to carry on the line of primogeniture, she receives a man's name and with that man's status, but her position is transmitted to her eldest son as soon as he is grown up. It is interesting that notwithstanding the strong

> stress upon patrilineal descent, the question "whose child are you or is he" is always answered with the name of the mother.
>
> The strength of the feeling for patrilineal descent is expressed by the fact that not only is residence patrilocal, but that a woman married to a man of another tribe, not of a numayma of the same tribe, is called a "woman married out seaward" and that children are always called "children of [the father's tribe]," never children of the mother's tribe. An exception to this are children of a first-born daughter of a chief, who bears a man's name belonging to the tribe.

Boas used these observations to argue against the doctrine of unilinear evolution. In addition, he urged the U.S. Natural History Museum staff to arrange artifacts according to the function they performed in a given environment, as opposed to their place in a supposed evolutionary scheme.[15] His point was that similar artifacts might have been used not at similar times but in similar environments by different groups. Such differences, he argued, showed that although like causes may indeed have like normative effects, like effects may not necessarily have like causes.[16] His critique of the evolutionists maintains that their sweeping generalizations were due to a lack of comparable data. He claims the evolutionists focused only on the similarity of ethnic phenomena while disregarding individual instances of variation, and as soon as one examines these variations, it becomes apparent that "the sameness of ethnic phenomena is more superficial than complete."[17] Boas cites as examples beliefs in souls and in "totemism" (the feeling of being related supernaturally to certain species of animals or classes of objects). Such beliefs, although superficially similar, are in fact so varied that psychological laws covering all of them cannot be deduced.[18]

In a similar vein, and contrary to Edward B. Tylor, Boas argued that no historical evidence existed to suggest that language development among cultures took similar evolutionary paths. He argued that sounds perceived as different might be similar in meaning, like the various shades of a generally recognized color. An outsider may not understand some sounds in a community's language because elements of a culture are meaningful in that culture's terms, even though they may be meaningless in another culture.[19] This situation provides another example of particularism or relativism in Boasian theory, also widely known as "historical particularism."[20]

Despite his particularism, however, Boas does not attempt to deny that certain cultural traits are universal. In *The Mind of Primitive Man* he devotes an entire chapter to the "universality of cultural traits."[21] He advances what he calls "the theory of the

15. Regna Darnell, And Along Came Boas: Continuity and Revolution in Americanist Anthropology 124 (2000).

16. Boas, The Mind of Primitive Man, *supra* note 4, at 182–196.

17. *Id.* at 188.

18. *Id.* at 190–91.

19. *Id.* at 194.

20. Harris, *supra* note 10, at 250.

21. Boas, The Mind of Primitive Man, *supra* note 4, at 155.

similarity of the mental functions in all races" according to which emotions, intellect, and willpower are shared by all races, and similar thought patterns and actions related thereto also appear in similar (if not identical) form.[22] Examples are beliefs in souls, the underworld, a world (or worlds) up above, grammatical structures using three pronouns (one each for the speaker, the person addressed, and the person spoken of), and the distinction between single and plural forms.[23] Boas is quick to declare that when the anthropologist finds such analogies of single traits of culture among diverse cultures, the presumption must not be that these traits have a common historical source but that they have risen *independently*, for a variety of reasons and causes.[24] Some of these causes may be commonly shared by the diverse cultures under study, but this is not necessarily so and remains a matter for empirical investigation.

The excerpt that follows identifies at least three such common causes: geographical environment, custom, and mental processes. Boas concludes that none of these is decisive or the sole cause of a particular trait.

As he explains, the evolutionists' assumption that similar ethnic phenomena are due to the same causes can be tested in three ways: (1) evidence from the earliest period of human history, (2) survivals in contemporary civilization, and (3) archeology. Boas concludes that these three "historical proofs" do not support the evolutionists' theory and goes on to cite the emergence of pottery, metallurgy, agriculture, and the domestication of animals as just some of the many examples that disprove the evolutionist assumption.

Franz Boas, The Mind of Primitive Man 158–59, 182–85 (1911).

> These examples will suggest the classes of phenomena to which I refer. It follows from these observations that when we find analogues of single traits of culture among distinct peoples, the presumption is, not that there has been a common historical source, but that they have arisen independently; and the theory suggests itself that a common cause accounts for the constant recurrence of these phenomena among the most varied members of mankind, no matter to what race they may belong. . . .
>
> Some investigators—like Ratzel, and in older times Karl Ritter and Guyot—have laid particular stress upon the influence of geographical environment upon the life of man, and emphasize those similarities which appear in similar types of environment.
>
> Others believe that many of the customs, beliefs, and inventions common to people who live in regions far apart are an old heritage derived from the earliest times, when mankind was still confined to a small part of the earth's surface.

22. *Id.* at 155–56.

23. *Id.* at 156–57.

24. *Id.* at 158.

Still others have tried to isolate the most generalized forms of similar ethnic phenomena. Bastian, the most important representative of this group of investigators, has called these forms "elementary ideas," and has tried to show that they are unexplainable.

Psychologists finally have endeavored to explain the similarities by an analysis of mental processes.

It seems necessary to discuss these four methods of approach a little more fully. . . .

In the absence of historical data in regard to the earliest history of primitive man the world over, we have only three sources of historical proof of this assumption,—the evidence contained in the earliest history of the civilized people of the Old World, survivals in modern civilization, and archaeology. The last-named is the only method by means of which we can approach the problem in regard to people that have no history.

While it is certainly true that analogues can be found between the types of culture represented by primitive people and those conditions which prevailed among the ancestors of the present civilized peoples at the dawn of history, and that these analogues are supported by the evidence furnished by survivals, the evidence of archaeology does not support the complete generalization. The theory of parallel development, if it is to have any significance, would require that among all branches of mankind the steps of invention should have followed, at least approximately, in the same order, and that no important gaps should be found. The facts, so far as known at the present time, are entirely contrary to this view. We find, for instance, large areas of the world inhabited by people well advanced in the arts of life, but who have never made the discovery of pottery, one of the essential steps in the advance of civilization. Pottery is not found in the extreme southern parts of Africa, in Australia, in northeastern Siberia, in the whole northwestern part of North America, and in the extreme south of South America. . . .

The same may be said in regard to the use of metals. The invention of metallurgy, which marks so important an advance of European civilization, does not appear associated with analogous levels of development in other parts of the world. Similar remarks may be made in regard to the development of agriculture and of the domestication of animals. People whom in a general way we ought to class as on the same level of culture may some possess the art of agriculture, others may have domesticated animals, while still others may rely upon the bounty of the sea or upon the natural vegetable products of their home. As soon as we begin to investigate the industrial achievements of different types belonging to different races, parallelism of industrial development does not seem to exist in any degree of detail. . . .

Thus it does not seem to be certain that every people in an advanced stage of civilization must have passed through all the stages of development, which we may gather by an investigation of all the types of culture which occur all over the world.

> A still more serious objection is based on another observation. The validity of the general sameness of the evolution of mankind is based on the assumption that the same cultural features must always have developed from the same causes, and that all variations are only minor details of the grand uniform type of evolution. In other words, its logical basis is the assumption that the same ethnical phenomena are always due to the same causes. Thus the inference in regard to the sequence of maternal and paternal institutions, to which I referred before, is based on the generalization that because in a few cases paternal families have developed from maternal ones, therefore all paternal families have developed in the same way. If we do not make the assumption that the same phenomena have everywhere developed in the same way, then we may just as well conclude that paternal families have in some cases arisen from maternal institutions, in other cases in other ways.
>
> In the same way it is inferred that because many conceptions of the future life have evidently developed from dreams and hallucinations, all notions of this character have had the same origin. This is true only if it can be shown that no other causes could possibly lead to the same ideas. . . .

Particularism in Law and Morality

It is interesting to compare the approach to law and morality of Boas with that of Tylor.[25] Both remarkable parallelism and distinct difference are found between the thoughts of the two. The parallelism is that both viewed legal and moral norms as evolving over time. The difference is that Tylor viewed morality as a universal pattern showing the essential unity of humankind, and thus bolstered his thesis that all of humanity evolved in similar ways. By contrast, Boas emphasized the particularity of legal and moral normative orders.

Similarly to Tylor, Boas begins by stating that moral standards used to assess the value of particular acts evolve "with increasing civilization."[26] With regard to the preservation of human life as a moral value, a subject also treated by Tylor, Boas maintains that it was not of importance to primitive humans, whose societies were characterized by limited altruism.[27] But the value of human life, as well as altruism generally, increased as society progressed. However, as Boas points out in the following excerpt, there is a lack of comparable data as to the motives that underlie rules against murder and the exceptions thereto. Here again, in an approach similar to that of Tylor, Boas identifies different motives under which the taking of human life may be tolerated (*e.g.*, revenge, self-defense, sacrifice). A Tylorian approach emphasizes the *fact* of the existence of the general rule against murder (subject to certain exceptions) as evidence of a universal pattern. A Boasian approach, by contrast, demands an empirical inquiry of diverse psychological motivations and cites this diversity as a reason against drawing sweeping normative generalizations. Perhaps, after all,

---

25. *See* Chapter 1, section titled "Law and Morality in Evolutionary Context."

26. Boas, The Mind of Primitive Man, *supra* note 4, at 191.

27. *Id.*

Boas and Tylor are not very far apart in recognizing difference, at least in relation to law and morality. Tylor does make a bow toward particularism by warning against "measuring other people's corn by one's own bushel."[28]

Franz Boas, The Mind of Primitive Man 191–192 (1911).

> Another example may not be amiss. In a general review of moral standards we observe that with increasing civilization a gradual change in the valuation of actions takes place. Among primitive man, human life has little value, and is sacrificed on the slightest provocation. The social group among whose members any altruistic obligations are binding is exceedingly small; and outside of the group any action that may result in personal gain is not only permitted, but even approved; and from this starting-point we find an ever-increasing valuation of human life and an extension of the size of the group among whose members altruistic obligations are binding. The modern relations of nations show that this evolution has not yet reached its final stage. It might seem, therefore, that a study of the social conscience in relation to crimes like murder might be of psychological value, and lead to important results, clearing up the origin of ethical values; but I think here the same objections may be raised as before; namely, the lack of comparable motives. The person who slays an enemy in revenge for wrongs done, a youth who kills his father before he gets decrepit in order to enable him to continue a vigorous life in the world to come, a father who kills his child as a sacrifice for the welfare of his people, act from such entirely different motives, that psychologically a comparison of their activities does not seem permissible. It would seem much more proper to compare the murder of an enemy in revenge with destruction of his property for the same purpose, or to compare the sacrifice of a child on behalf of the tribe with any other action performed on account of strong altruistic motives, than to base our comparison on the common concept of murder (Westermarck).
>
> These few data may suffice to show that the same ethnic phenomenon may develop from different sources; and we may infer that the simpler the observed fact, the more likely it is that it may have developed from one source here, from another there.

None of Boas's writings adhere to any particular theoretical framework. He did not have any design or normative typology into which he could classify his cultural data.[29] His purpose was to refute the evolutionary model and encourage rigorous empiricism in ethnographic fieldwork. His students and followers—including such prominent anthropologists as Clark Wissler, Alfred Kroeber, Robert Lowie, Edward Sapir, Ralph Linton, Ruth Benedict, Margaret Mead, and Leslie Spier—took up the task

28. Edward B. Tylor, Anthropology 410 (1898).

29. Keesing & Keesing, *supra* note 5, at 382.

of embarking on the fieldwork demanded by Boas as well as formulating theoretical frameworks for such fieldwork. Introduced next are the pertinent contributions of these anthropologists, followed by excerpts of their own writings that explain their respective approaches and achievements.

Wissler: Culture Area and Universals

Boas's particularism at the dawn of the twentieth century and his avoidance of the grandiose theoretical schemes of mid-nineteenth-century evolutionists, had a lasting influence on anthropology. His particularism taught that culture developed independently of free will; far from being the product of individual choice, culture channeled and constrained individual choice and thus functioned as the essential determinant of individual behavior.

Evolutionary schemes gradually came to be replaced by geographical categories or "culture areas." The concept of culture area could accommodate the strictures of the Boasian approach in that it was susceptible to ethnographic fieldwork, it could be studied in specific historical contexts, and it portrayed both the autonomy of a given culture and its independence from individual will. Among the early twentieth-century pioneers of this concept was Clark Wissler, for whom a culture area defined groups of people both living in the same geographic location and sharing similar cultural traits.[30] Within each culture area was a "culture center" wherein particular traits originated and whence they spread.[31] The outer limits of this spread was the margin or boundary at which the previously common normative traits became so diffused that they mixed with elements of other cultures and thus lost many of the characteristics they had possessed within the cultural center.[32]

In Wissler's tabulation of universal cultural traits (*see* the section titled "Normative Uniformities in Culture: The Universal Pattern" and the accompanying excerpt), the second ("Material Traits") includes "food habits." With regard to the peoples inhabiting the eastern half of the United States and parts of Canada, Wissler notes that the chief subsistence crop was maize. He notes that the cultivation of this crop spread to Mexico, prompting his conclusion that "(since) we have no reason to doubt a historical connection between the two areas, . . . we may treat them as parts of the same whole."[33] This, then, is an example of a culture area.

Central to the idea of a culture area is the presence of certain traits or "trait complexes." The latter are a series of recurrent activities related to the pursuit of particular human endeavors that range from food production and use of a particular technology to blood sacrifice, sun worship, totemism, and so on. For example, regarding food production, all activities leading to maize production and consumption are a "maize

---

30. Clark Wissler, Man and Culture 55–56 (1923).

31. *Id.* at 61–2.

32. *Id.* at 57.

33. Clark Wissler, The American Indian: An Introduction to the Anthropology of the New World 12 (2d ed., 1922). *See generally id.* at 12–41. On the spread of the trait of spinning and twisting of fiber into thread, *see id.* at 44 *et seq.*

complex."[34] Similarly, the Ojibwe tribe cultivated wild rice for consumption. Thus the "wild rice complex" was their cultural trait.

Nevertheless, Wissler's concept of culture area remains nebulous in that it does not specify whether a single trait can constitute a culture area or whether a culture must exhibit traits in all the nine categories of his tabulation. Furthermore (as seen in the next two excerpts), Wissler uses phrases such as "culture area," "culture center," "culture type," "cultural scheme," "culture complexes," "trait complexes," and "universal pattern," sometimes interchangeably and at other times with subtle variations in meaning. Such terms and labels promote confusion rather than conceptual clarity. Not surprisingly, Wissler's concepts have encountered strong criticism. I return to this point later, but first I present the key concept in his own words.

Clark Wissler, Man and Culture 47–58, 61–64, 66–67, 71 (1923).

The Content of Culture

The field-worker in anthropology begins his study of tribal culture by concentrating upon one or two points. Thus, he may set out to see how fire is kindled, observing that it is made by boring one stick into another, but that these simple looking implements are fashioned according to a specific pattern and that the procedure is likewise fixed as in any handicraft. Yet, it is not enough to say that fire is kindled by wood friction; the individuality of the implements and the accompanying procedures must be recorded and representative objects collected. Thus, the fire-making implement, accompanied by photographs and field notes, becomes the objective record of a unit of observation. Such is, for practical purposes at least, a unit of the tribal culture and is spoken of as a *trait.* This term is also applied to mannerisms and to concepts of whatever kind. Thus the custom of a man marrying his wife's sisters may be observed and, if so, is set down as a trait of the tribal culture. It follows then that a tribal culture is characterized by the enumeration of its observable traits and that the culture of one tribe is distinguished from that of another by differences in these traits. . . .

The Culture Complex

We are now confronted with a more serious problem. If we mean by *trait* a unit in the tribal culture, then we must discover the nature and characteristics of this unit. When potatoes are shoveled into a bushel measure, we may correctly speak of them as a bushel of potatoes, by which we imply that each potato is a complete and independent unit in itself. Some students of culture seem to have regarded traits as similar independent units, to be scooped up in the tribal measure and dealt with as a mere collection. Yet,

34. Clark Wissler, *Aboriginal Maize Culture as a Typical Culture-Complex*, 21 Am. J. Sociol. 656, 658 (1916). Wissler asserts that "the white colonist took over the entire material complex of maize culture" of the Indians.

when one carefully scrutinizes a trait, he finds, not a clear-cut unit, but a kind of complex. For example, the Ojibway Indians in the vicinity of Lake Superior were observed to use wild rice for food and this was correctly set down as a trait of their culture. Yet, each member of the tribe did not snatch his rice food directly from the plant as do the birds, but received it as the end of a cycle of activities in which he, as an individual, played a varying part. Thus, though the plant is wild, some care was given the plots where it grew; later, the plants were tied in bunches to discourage rice-eating birds, then the rice was gathered, cured, hulled, winnowed, stored, cooked, and eaten. Incidentally, some of it was exchanged and some given away. The many processes involved required techniques of various complexities and special appliances. But that is not all, for intimately bound up in the whole are property rights, labor obligations, etiquette, methods of keeping time, and a number of special religious observances, prohibitions, and taboos. It is thus plain that if we arrive at an adequate notion of the wild rice trait, we must see it as a complex of many processes, all of which bear a functional relation to the end to be achieved. The name usually given to such a chain of activities is the *trait-complex,* or in this instance, the *wild rice complex.*

Some of the best known trait-complexes are, head hunting, totemism, couvade, tobacco, maize, wheat, dog traction, the horse, use of milk, the wheel, exogamy, sun worship, and blood sacrifice....

The Culture Type

At the outset, we spoke of our own culture as belonging to the Euro-American type because, by the comparative method, we discovered that the cultures of some tribal, or national, units were very much alike in trait content. In other words, we find it convenient to ignore political boundaries and to classify the cultures of the world according to their content; for as we have shown, what are essentially the same trait-complexes may be found in a number of cultures. The milking of cows, for example, the milk-butter-cheese complex, is found in Euro-American cultures and a number of Asiatic cultures, but strange to say, some of the latter have a cattle-complex that excludes the use of milk. Many Negro peoples of Africa use milk but so little are some of them addicted to butter and cheese that they may be said to have a mere milk complex....

The Culture Area

Our definition of the culture type should be understood as a method of classification by which cultures themselves can be grouped, but ... the culture type has its geography, since it appears that a trait-complex is not to be found scattered at random up and down a continent, but localized, or in clusters. From what has gone before; it follows that the segregation of cultures of the same type will form a geographical area, characterized by the type. Anthropological research in the New World has revealed a number of these areas. For example, .. the United States and Canada comprise nine areas as follows:

the Plains Plateau, California, North Pacific Coast, Eskimo, Mackenzie, Eastern Woodland, Southeastern and Southwestern areas. We observe, for one thing, that these areas are geographical and, to a certain extent, characterize the territories covered, the significance of which we shall consider later. Further, each area embraces a large number of tribal units and consequently an equal number of tribal cultures; but these many tribal cultures belong to one type, so that the culture area defines the range of the culture type....

Now the fact is that the drawing of precise boundaries to the range of a culture type is beset by the difficulties inherent in all variable phenomena, for it will sometimes prove difficult to decide to which of two or more culture areas a given marginal tribe belongs. Thus, if we take any aboriginal area in America, and tabulate the tribal distribution of traits, we find that those upon the margins lack some of the trait-complexes common to the central group of tribes. However, it does not follow that these marginal tribes possess a lesser number of trait-complexes, because they manifest additional traits not found at the center and whose true home is in the adjoining culture area. In other words, the tribal cultures lying at the boundary between two distinct culture areas are mixtures, or markedly divergent from the respective culture types. Again, the trait-complexes, as previously noted, will appear on the margins in attenuated form, that is, they will have lost many of the elements they possess at the center. So if we seek the type specimen of tribal culture, we must look to the geographical center of the area.

To define one of these areas satisfactorily, then, one must proceed by a suitable statistical method and tabulate the trait-complexes for the successive tribes. With this list before him, he will have little difficulty in fixing a satisfactory boundary to the area, for it matters little to which of the two adjoining areas the most marginal tribal culture is assigned....

THE CULTURE CENTER

...([C]ulture centers) were the sources from which sprang new cultures. This may be correct, but we must not take it for granted. Our observations so far produce facts of distribution only, but, when confronted with such an all-prevailing type of distribution as we found in the culture area, interpretations automatically come to mind. For example, .. several patterns of stone in the central section and spread thence outward in all directions. If so, then the central part of the culture area may be regarded as the point of dispersal, or the center of influence. Our problem, then, is to prove or disprove the correctness of this assumption, or to find evidence to support the inference that trait-complexes do move in this way. Fortunately, we find such proof from an unexpected quarter. In the pottery distribution noted, Nelson discovered that the radii of distribution varied as the time. Thus, the traits confined to the small central section were of recent origin, while those reaching the outer zones were the oldest. This he was able to prove absolutely since at the center he found stratified deposits, one style of pottery above the other, the time-relations for which were obvious. There can thus be no doubt whatever as to the order in which these different pottery traits came into existence. But this sequence in the vertical section, as it were, is also the horizontal sequence, or the sequence of distribution....

The Adhesion of Trait-Complexes

A review of the preceding sections indicates that each trait-complex has a continuous distribution radiating from a center. This can be set down as one of the basic, verifiable characteristics of culture traits. Further, we observed that these trait-complex centers often coincide resulting in an accumulation of traits in a circumscribed territory, to which we gave the name *culture area*. These two things should not be confused; the former is an expression of culture processes, whereas the latter appears to be a mere accumulation in a locality. One of our problems, therefore, is to discover the nature of this accumulative association of traits. Since we found tribal cultures to be such collections of traits, and classified these cultures by the traits they have in common, the question arises as to the nature of a culture. Is it a mere accidental conglomeration, or is there some functional relation between the several trait-complexes? Thus, when we enumerate the trait-complexes manifested by a tribal unit and speak of them collectively as a culture, we are merely asserting that we conceive them to be related one to the other only in that they pertain to the same tribal unit; so, unless we find some basis for their association other than mere presence in a group, these trait-complexes are without functional relations to each other. In our discussion of the trait-complex, we found its components associated because they had logical and functional relations, necessary or assumed so by the tribe, as the case may be. In the wild rice complex, for example, a sequence of processes was necessary to produce the food ready for eating. Yet, while it is obvious that rice could not be served unless it was gathered, it is not at all clear that this process must be accompanied by specific ceremonies. Apparently these could be dispensed with without disturbing the remainder of the complex. It appears, therefore, that while some traits in the complex are indispensable, others are not. A review of any trait will make this clear, as for example, the milk complex; some cultures know butter and cheese; some have all but these traits; some milk cows, others goats, camels, horses, or reindeer. Again, maize is now cultivated in Europe and America; in the former, it is used for feeding cattle and horses, but in America it is also a popular human food. In Africa kaffir corn is a great staple, but in America it is fed to live-stock. So, in general, if one follows out the full distribution of a trait-complex, he meets with an attenuation as he leaves its center....

It appears, then, that the association of trait-complexes is due to causes wholly external to themselves, a subject to which we shall return under another head. One of our problems, then, is to observe what complexes are associated. This is a matter that can be approached by the methods of empirical science. The first attempt of this kind was made by Tylor in 1888 by correlating trait distributions, one with the other. Thus, if one wrote at the head of a column the name of a trait-complex, say maize, and at the head of another, pottery, he could then take up the names of the tribes in order, writing them under each head when the trait in question was present. As we have stated, the result would be that many of the names in the first column would also appear in the second: If this were merely a matter of accident, each tribal name would have an even chance of falling in the second column; but if the correspondences between the two columns were found to be greater than could be allowed for accident, then we must seek another explanation. Tylor first tried this method out with specific social traits, such as the many curious rules and prohibitions governing the social intercourse of men and women. Thus among some cultures the son-in-law must not look upon the face of his wife's mother, much less speak to her. First, Tylor made an inventory of the cultures in which the custom is found, and out of some 359 cultures listed, found it in thirty-six. He then followed through the same lists the custom of the son-in-law to reside with the parents of the wife, finding that in fourteen cultures, the husband not only lived permanently with his wife's parents, but also kept out of their sight. A mere chance relation would account for about half as many cases. The point is, then, that the number of times the custom of avoiding the wife's mother is found in a culture, where it is the rule for the husband to reside at the home of the wife's parents, is twice as great as it should be were it merely a matter of chance. In this manner Tylor tried out a large number of marriage and social customs, finding that their coincidences, or their presence in a culture, was something more than an accident. To such associations of trait-complexes Tylor gave the name *adhesions* and a very good name it is; for limiting its meaning to the "state of sticking to one another," when brought into contact under favorable conditions, we have an adequate characteristic of the phenomenon.

So to discover *adhesions* one must proceed to work out the distributions of complexes among the successive tribal cultures and then correlate these distributions. In this way one may discover what trait-complexes are associated. Practically everyone who seriously studies the distribution of culture phenomena uses this method, but the quality of the work depends upon its precision. . . .

We could, if necessary, take up the other adhesions noted and account for them now as mere logical, necessary relations, or again, as historic coincidences. But something yet remains: why do so many trait-complexes occur in agricultural areas and not among hunters? This we shall take up later, for the answer lies outside the trait-complex involved. In short, a tribal culture is a collection of trait-complexes, developed and acquired in the course of tribal life; so the association of one with the other can be fully accounted for when we learn the events brought them into these relations.

Wissler's concept of culture areas is not without its critics—among them Carter Woods, who strongly criticizes Wissler's method,[35] including the assertion that it is never clear in which area Wissler classified certain tribes. Indeed, by eliminating every tribe in relation to which there is insufficient data, Wissler designates only a minority of the tribes of an area as representing the entire area.[36] He is then said to draw generalizations from the few tribes for the whole region. Furthermore, he is alleged to wrongly include culturally diverse tribes in the same category or classification, for example, the Fox and the Iroquois, the Pueblo and the nomadic tribes of the Southwest, and the wide variety of tribes in the Plains.[37] Woods puts forward region-specific ethnographic data to support his argument that the high homogeneity that would be expected from the leveling effect of the diffusion process in a geographic area is found in only a minor portion of the total number of tribes within a culture area.[38] Thus Wissler's regions are said to have been too widely drawn to possess a relatively uniform total culture. Woods concludes by citing none other than Boas:

> The assumption that the generalized characteristics of the culture are present in any one of the constituent social groups may give an entirely erroneous picture of the integration of cultural values . . . The description of a typical tribe gives a safer insight into integrated culture than the description of a culture area. On the other hand, an analysis of culture area as defined from various points of view, material culture, social organization and beliefs, gives us an insight into the conditions that helped to shape each individual culture.[39]

Normative Uniformities in Culture: The Universal Pattern

Wissler differed with the Boasian approach in one significant way: he distanced himself from the extreme relativism of that approach, believing instead that there were some things that all people in all cultures had in common. He called this commonality "the universal pattern." We must then ask if this means that all of humanity shares certain common traits, if the content of culture is identical everywhere, or whether it is better to say that certain traits serve as the lowest common denominators in all cultures. Wissler embraces the latter hypothesis, as discussed next.

According to Wissler, every human grouping that can properly be called a culture has nine common traits: speech (language, writing systems, etc.), material traits (food habits, shelter, transportation, dress, etc.), art (carving, painting, music, etc.),

---

35. Carter A. Woods, *A Criticism of Wissler's North American Culture Areas*, 36 AM. ANTHROPOL. 517 (1934).

36. *Id.* at 520.

37. *Id.* at 519–21.

38. *Id.* at 521; *See also*, George Peter Murdock, *Clark Wissler, 1870–1947*, 50 AM. ANTHROPOL. 292, 294 (1948). "The conception of regional centers of cultural elaboration from which diffusion spreads like ripples equally in all directions is now generally recognized as over simple . . ."

39. Woods, *supra* note 35, at 523 (quoting Franz Boas, *Anthropology*, *in* 2 ENCYCLOPEDIA OF THE SOCIAL SCIENCES 73, 105–106 (1930)).

mythology and scientific knowledge, religion, family and social systems, property, government, and war.[40]

> Wherever a group of men and women are congregated, there one will find the essential activities upon which all these complexes are built. It is because the same relations in communication, thought, and tools everywhere prevail that the cultures of the world have the same form and manifest the same process. This is what is meant by the universal pattern.[41]

In the following excerpt, Wissler admits that these nine cultural traits are "conventional and arbitrary"[42] and also contradicts himself by stating that they have an empirical foundation that no anthropologist can deny.

Clark Wissler, Man and Culture 74–97 (1923).

The Universal Pattern

The Culture Scheme

1. Speech
   Languages, writing systems, etc.
2. Material Traits
   a. Food habits
   b. Shelter
   c. Transportation and travel
   d. Dress
   e. Utensils, tools, etc.
   f. Weapons
   g. Occupations and industries
3. Art. Carving, painting, drawing, music, etc.
4. Mythology and Scientific Knowledge.
5. Religious Practices
   a. Ritualistic forms
   b. Treatment of the sick
   c. Treatment of the dead
6. Family and Social Systems
   a. The forms of marriage
   b. Methods of reckoning relationship
   c. Inher*itance*
   d. Social control
   e. Sports and games
7. Property
   a. Real and personal

40. Wissler, Man and Culture, *supra* note 30, at 74.

41. *Id.* at 97.

42. *Id.* at 79.

   b. Standards of value and exchange
   c. Trade
8. Government
   a. Political forms
   b. Judicial and legal procedures
9. War

... This outline can be greatly elaborated, if the reader gives his constructive imagination full play. It is, however, full enough for our purposes.

Now, if we take up our own culture and fit the details into this scheme, we see how readily they fall under these heads. So do the old cultures of Rome, Greece, etc. But these and our own are so intimately connected in origin that we should suspect the pattern of one to fit all. On the other hand, there are lowly, simple, crude peoples, like the Australians, who are said to have no culture. If we take literally many of the statements made by contemptuous writers on the subject, this would end the matter; but the facts are otherwise, for turning to the literature of the subject and taking first the main headings in our outline, we find all represented in the supposedly simple life of the Australian. Thus, even among very primitive peoples there are cultures which readily fall under the heads enumerated above.

Now someone may object, on the ground that even though this be true, the content under each head is so meager as to be contemptible and remind us that the Australian, for instance, went without clothes of any kind, and that, here at once, our pattern fails to fit. Yes, it is true that the Australian was not over-burdened with clothing, but it is not true that he was devoid of *dress*, or that he did not put great store upon it. Ornaments there were in considerable numbers and the septum of the nose was often pierced to carry a wooden button, a practice analogous to the ear-piercing of our own people. In short, he had something to place under this head. If, again, we are told that so crude a savage could have no religion, the answer is not far to seek. Go to a library, take down the books of Spencer and Gillen, there you will find a complex of religious practices that almost defies understanding....

So far we have dealt with categories of classification rather than with concrete trait-complexes, but, when passed in review, we find many of these complexes identical for all cultures. Thus, all the historic cultures, however primitive, knew fire. They also knew its value in the preparation of food. In every case they knew, or formerly knew, how to chip stone. The principle of the knife was known and the fundamental idea of the drill. Likewise, the art of twisting string, or the making of cord; as to weaving, there was not one that did not understand the fundamental step. The fact that some of them went no further is not to the point. Still other technical processes could be enumerated, but the reader can add to the list at his leisure. The point is that there are certain groups of technical traits that belong to all cultures. We can go even farther, for there were common beliefs. The belief in a soul or spiritual counterpart of some kind, that defies death, is universal....

> Now we have, as it were, set up a few categories which, taken together, seem to cover the entire range of culture content. Thus, under speech we may include language, sign-talk, gesture, and all forms of writing, and so far as we now see, something under this category will be found in every culture....
>
> It appears, then, that for the different cultures these categories show a wide range in content. Further, since under each category we find the familiar trait-complexes, all more or less interlocking, we may properly speak of the pattern as made up of *culture complexes*: speech, art, religion, etc.... The very existence of a universal pattern implies a fair degree of rigidity in limitations and asserts that every culture is predestined to keep within these bounds....
>
> CULTURE COMPLEXES
>
> We may now inquire as to the significance of the nine topical heads in the foregoing outline of the pattern. As we have said, they are conventional and arbitrary, and yet they are the results of experience, for everyone who draws up a scheme to cover the culture of a people will arrive at similar divisions; so there must be some basis to these topical heads. Moreover, when critically examined, we see them as basic concepts of human activity. For example, the term *war* stands for something instantly recognized, nor can an anthropologist conceive of any existing culture, however primitive, in which the idea is not equally definite.... Yet, in the main, the nine heads in our outline do express the fundamental and embracing concepts of culture ...
>
> In a similar way we could show a distinction in each of the culture complexes, but the reader can be spared the tedium of it, for it appears that the whole series of culture complexes can be resolved into supplementary constructs (tools, etc.) and the neuro-muscular mechanism of man. Hence, one need not be surprised that such a bewildering maze as civilization turns out to be a matter of bulk rather than of complexity, for we find in it everywhere the familiar trait-complexes, each fashioned upon the same general lines. And what is even more significant, wherever a group of men and women are congregated, there one will find the essential activities upon which all these complexes are built. It is because the same relations in communication, thought, and tools everywhere prevail that the cultures of the world have the same form and manifest the same processes. This is what is meant by the universal pattern.

Law as a Universal Pattern

In Wissler's tabulation of the nine universal traits, "Family and Social Systems" (the sixth heading) is of special significance to law because it expressly mentions social control. As a universal need, social discipline manifests in a variety of ways, according to Wissler (*e.g.*, judicial control, blood revenge, and public ridicule).[43] He also notes the existence of basic notions of property, including the distinction be-

---

43. WISSLER, THE AMERICAN INDIAN, *supra* note 33, at 177; *see* particularly the example of public ridicule in Greenland.

tween real and personal property.[44] Another prominent method of instilling social discipline is through the symbolism of certain myths and rituals, such as when an inanimate object is ascribed animate features. Wissler studied this practice among the Crow and Blackfoot tribes, who from early childhood were taught to demonize water and use it as a disciplinary tool.[45]

Wissler also studied Native Americans to understand the nature of their government, their judiciaries, and their establishment of normative order. Such study, he hoped, would further show the existence of normative patterns that would have analogs in other societies. The results of his studies of the normative order of the Oglala Sioux were widely cited. This society elected a council of seven elder chiefs to govern it.[46] This council then appointed four younger councilors to whom they delegated the power to maintain "general welfare; to see that good hunting is provided, helpful campsites selected, etc."[47] These four then elected four additional officers (the *wakicum*), who were given executive powers. They had a special tipi at the center of the camp to symbolize the seat of government. They were assisted by a group of subordinates including two officers (the *akicita*).

All civil and economic affairs of the camp fell under the authority of the *wakicum*. They issued orders that were enforced by the *akicita*, the latter being a complex institution vested with police, prosecutorial, and judicial functions. This is the institution that enforced existing customs and administered justice, including offenses against the tribe (but not private wrongs). Enforcement took place through formal and informal means: public ridicule, gossip, revenge, retaliation, public ostracism, reparation, or orders from the *akicita* to destroy the offender's tipi, robes, and implements; kill his dogs and horses; and drive him out of camp or, in rare cases, administer capital punishment. The accused had a right of appeal to the council.[48]

The foregoing summary of the Oglala Sioux social and legal order first negates the prevailing perception in certain circles at the time that early Native tribal societies had been "a semi-civilized and barbarous people . . . in a hopeless state of anarchy without [legal] protections and sanctions."[49] But second, and perhaps more important, the account of their particular legal systems is a good example of the particularism of the Boasian approach. For example, the council had jurisdiction to punish crimes against the tribe, but not those against the family. In the latter instance it was up to

44. *Id.* at 183–185.

45. *See generally* David McAllester, *Water as a Disciplinary Agent among the Crow and the Blackfoot*, 43, AM. ANTHROPOL. 593 (1941); Clark Wissler & D.C. Duvall, *Mythology of the Blackfoot Indians*, 2 ANTHROPOL. PAP. AM. MUS. NAT. HIST. 1, 74–79, 128–129 (1908). *See also* Carl Wissler, *Ceremonial Bundles of the Blackfoot Indians*, 7 ANTHROPOL. PAP. AM. MUS. NAT. HIST. 65, 220–27 (1912) (on Blackfoot ceremonies and rituals concerning tipis). *See also*, WISSLER, THE AMERICAN INDIAN, *supra* note 33, at 6 (on the taboo against eating fish and other water animals).

46. Clark Wissler, *Societies and Ceremonial Associations in the Oglala Division of the Teton-Dakota*, 11 ANTHROPOL. PAP. AM. MUS. NAT. HIST. 3 at 7 (1912).

47. *Id.*

48. George D. Watson, Jr., *The Oglala Sioux Tribal Court: From Termination to Self-Determination*, 3 GREAT PLAINS RESEARCH 61, 66 (1933).

49. *Id.* at 64 (quoting Ezra A. Hayt, *Report of the Indian Commission* 105 (1879)).

the family to avenge the wrong. Thus their law was responsive to the then-prevalent cultural mores of the tribe. Wissler's goals are to emphasize the fact of social discipline through law and show that law was responsive to the particular needs of that particular community, rather than to advocate a stable set of legal norms that were universally applicable.

In the excerpt below, Wissler examines law in tribal society.

Clark Wissler, *Societies and Ceremonial Associations in the Oglala Division of the Teton-Dakota*

ANTHROPOL. PAP. AM. MUS. NAT. HIST. 1, 7–11 (1912).

The Oglala were formerly, it is said, composed of four divisions (Oglala, Kiaksai, Oyukhpe and Wazazies). When reservations were established, two of these divisions were placed under the Pine Ridge Agency. . . .

The two former Pine Ridge divisions are now known as the Red-cloud camp (Oglala) and the Kiaksai. As far as our information goes, it appears that the former had by far the more complex organization and in the main prevailed when the reservation was established. It was in this camp that the chiefs society originated. As will be fully explained later, this was an organization comprising the majority of the efficient older men of forty years or more. It elected its own members. Independent of its organization, it elected seven chiefs (wic'asa itac'a^{n}) to govern the people. These chiefs were elected for life. Since it was customary for vacancies to be filled by the election of a worthy son or relative these offices were partially hereditary. These seven chiefs did not actually participate in the daily government but delegated powers to younger or more virile men, by the appointment of four councilors to serve for life, though they could resign at any time. These may or may not be members of the chiefs society but the seven chiefs are not eligible to the office. They are spoken of as the "owners of the tribe," but more particularly as the "shirt wearers" since upon investment in office they are given a special form of hair-fringed shirt. These shirts are spoken of as "owned by the tribe." Their owners are the supreme councilors and executives. They are charged with the general welfare; to see that good hunting is provided, healthful campsites selected, etc. Thus, though theoretically deputies, these four men are the real power in the government.

The seven chiefs, often assisted by the four shirt wearers and the whole chiefs society, elect four officers (wakic'u^{n}) to organize and control the camp. All except the four shirt wearers are eligible to this office. These men serve for about one year. It seems to have been the custom to re-elect two or three of them so as to have experienced men in office. In former times, the tendency was for the people to scatter out in winter, but early in the spring the camp circle was formed and its government organized. This was initiated by the selection of the wakicun.

The wakicun are after all the true executives, the shirt men standing as councilors. A tipi was set up in the center of the camp circle as the office of the wakicun in which they occupied "the seats of honor." The shirt men as well as the seven chiefs had seats there as councilors, but did not sit continuously like the wakicun. As soon as invested in office the wakicun appointed two young men to act as orderlies, see that fuel and food were provided, etc. They appointed a herald to promulgate their orders. They also selected two head akicita (akic'ita itaca'^{n}). . . .

The Indians define the word akicita as "those who see that there is general order in camp when traveling from one place to another; those who attend to the duties of overseeing the buffalo hunt so that no one may chase the buffalo singly; those who see that all can charge the buffalo at once or split up the party so that when one chases buffalo one way, the other band closes in; and those who supervise the chase to get better results. They also see that no one kills another, but in case one does, they either kill him or destroy all his property, kill his horses, destroy his tipi, etc." Thus, though in general literature the term akicita is rendered as "soldiers," its approximate equivalent seems to be police or marshals. . . .

Returning to a consideration of the scheme of government, it is clear that all the civil and economic affairs of the camp are in the hands of the wakicun. On all these matters, they are free to instruct and can enforce their orders through the akicita. They decide when to break camp, where to go and again select the new site. Hunting must be carried on when and as they direct. They also see that every person receives a fair share of the meat and is provided with enough robes to make the winter endurable. They settle disputes, judge and compound crimes, and make rules to ensure proper decorum in camp. However, our informants all felt their chief function to have been the regulation of the hunt, or the conservation of the food supply.

So far, we have been sketching the government of the Red-cloud division. The Kiaksai, had, according to our informants, the wakicun and their akicita but no shirt wearers. Instead of seven chiefs they had six who themselves exercised the functions of the four shirt men. There was no chiefs society, but all the older men of the camp were considered as a general council with power to appoint six chiefs. Otherwise, the operation of the government was about the same as in the Red-cloud division.

The Institution of Marriage

Among Wissler's tabulation of the nine universal traits that constitute his culture scheme are "the family" and "the forms of marriage." He adopts the following definition of Edward Westermarck as a good working definition of marriage: "A relation of one or more men to one or more women which is recognized by the custom or law and involves certain rights and duties to both in the case of the parties entering the union and in the case of the children born of it."[50] Wissler asserts that marriage as defined above "appears everywhere," that is, in all cultures. He also counsels against viewing marriage through the cultural laws of the West, pointing out that many

50. Clark Wissler, An Introduction to Social Anthropology 183 (1929).

cultures have many different forms of marriage. In one type, one may expect the wife to be the social companion of the husband, yet in other societies men do not follow this custom and do not even eat with their wives.[51] Some cultures practice monogamy; others polygamy; and yet others support polyandry. Yet "each of these forms of marriage is found somewhere among primitive peoples and is described in ethnographic literature."[52]

Wissler sidesteps the old debate as to whether there was a period in human history where the institution of marriage did not exist and was characterized by a state of total promiscuity (as argued by Morgan)[53] by simply citing the lack of available data.[54] But Wissler does note that "modern anthropologists" (that is, those of his time) do not accept this thesis of promiscuity.[55] Regardless of the data, however, Wissler's Boasian particularistic tendencies are well in evidence when he says that the forms of marriage vary from culture to culture, depending on social and economic conditions.

Clark Wissler, An Introduction to Social Anthropology 183–187, 194–195 (1929).

Marriage

> Many other curious deviations from our idea of marriage are to be found in the descriptive literature of social anthropology, but marriage, in the minimum sense of the definition (of Westermarck) appears everywhere, and so is a reality in the social sense, or is an aspect of culture. . . . Each of these forms of marriage is found somewhere among primitive peoples . . . [N]o form of marriage tends to be more frequent among hunting peoples than among agriculturists. Pastoral people, however, lead in the practice of polygamy. Hobhouse states the outcome of his study as follows:
>
> We find monogamy here and there in every grade of culture except the pastoral, and the most that can be properly said is that there is more of it . . . under the conditions of the jungle or forest life. On the explanation of this fact our authorities throw very little light. Probably the forces making for monogamy throughout the uncivilised world are two. One is the relative number of the sexes, as to which, in the absence of a census, we have no trustworthy information. The other is economic. First, poverty is against polygamy, as is seen on the reverse side by the constant gain of general over occasional polygamy as we advance on the industrial scale. Secondly, the special conditions of the forest life, perhaps in particular the close association of family groups, and the related practice of assigning a specific cousin as a partner tells in favour of monogamy. . . .

---

51. *Id.*

52. *Id.* at 184.

53. *See* Chapter 1, *supra* section on "Evolution of Government and Law in Morgan's Classifications."

54. Wissler, An Introduction to Social Anthropology, *supra* note 50, at 187.

55. *Id.* at 185.

We may approach the question in a similar way by noting the relative number of tribes observing each form of marriage. Thus, if a world census were taken as to the forms of marriage tolerated, we would find a large majority favoring polygyny; on the other hand, monogamy, polyandry, and group marriage constitute the minority, but of these monogamy leads. The literature on tribal practices is often confusing, for monogamy is tolerated everywhere. A polygynous people do not forbid monogamous marriages, they merely leave a man free to take more wives, if he can or so desires. On the other hand, a polygynous tribe will frown upon polyandry and group marriage. The forms of marriage then are not exclusive, and a tribe can be characterized by the unions it forbids rather than by the prevalent type. In seeking the original form of marriage, some authorities seize upon the fact that monogamy is tolerated among all peoples as evidence of its greater antiquity. This peculiarity, they say, is because monogamy was the natural original form of marriage preceding the development of social institutions. But this is not sufficient proof, because it seems equally probable that monogamy may have developed out of polygyny as a more satisfactory social adjustment.

Morgan, on the other hand, regarded marriage as having been preceded by a state of no marriage, which he designated as a state of promiscuity. This has logical justification, but considered biologically, there is little support for it. The chief objection is that promiscuity among humans seems to reduce the birth rate, or at least, the child survival rate, below the level necessary for the tribe to exist. A high degree of certainty cannot be accorded this statement, but in so far as reliable data are available, everything points to such a biological limitation on promiscuity. We now know that no tribes have been observed living in complete promiscuity and everywhere we find some form or marriage required and standardized notions of incest maintained.

Returning to the forms of marriage, it is admitted that a man usually marries one woman at a time and so is monogamous at the outset. Yet, this kind of logical interpretation is not important when we consider the form of marriage recognized by the tribe as its ideal. As we have said, the majority of peoples appear to take polygyny as their ideal. Our knowledge of the large anthropoids, the gorilla and the chimpanzee, is as yet too incomplete to give a clear statement of their mating habits, but since they are the most like man in their behavior, we may anticipate some important inferences when they have been more carefully observed. In the meantime, we must leave the matter undecided, though, as it stands, polygyny has the better of the argument.

Summary

Viewing marriage as a socially sanctioned relation between men and women, a wide range of custom is noted. The primary bond is between one man and one woman, which may be exclusive or multiple. The classification of form of

> marriage is usually based upon the distinction between a single relation and a multiple one; in monogamy both the man and the woman are married but one at a time, in polygyny only the woman is so restricted, etc. Every possible combination on this principle seems to be found in practice somewhere, thus exhausting the possibilities. Monogamy, the simplest form of marriage, occurs everywhere even among people allowing polyandry. Under all forms of culture it is regarded as proper, though not always as ideal. On the whole, however, the number of tribes known to practice monogamy exclusively is far less than those regarding polygyny as the preferred form of marriage. Biological factors may influence the form of marriage by a kind of natural selection, because if marriage customs are unfavorable to the bearing and rearing of children, the group cannot survive. The sex ration in the population may also have an influence. . . . The assigned causes for divorce are similar to those in contemporary society. Lack of affection and temperamental clashes appear even in the most primitive tribes, suggesting that it is the emotional tie that plays a large role in stabilizing the marriage relation and the economic and social conditions are relatively less important.

These excerpts reveal why Wissler views marriage as a universal institution. Because it plays a vital role in the continuation of the human race, it is granted a prestigious position by all anthropologists. The cultural implications of defining marriage are once again at play, especially in the United States, where same-sex marriage has been legalized. This change in the legal definition of marriage was due to the fact that the cultural view (or definition) of marriage has evolved into a more inclusive and less exclusive concept of monogamy.

Cultural Particularism as a Bridge to Tolerance and Peace

Wissler's particularism has a comparativist slant: one can best appreciate one's own culture only when it is compared with others.[56] Just as appreciations of individuality and self-identity are achieved when each person compares him- or herself to others, so it is with culture. Where and when one culture differentiates with another (or others) marks the drawing of political boundaries.[57] To this statement, which is generally true, Wissler points out important exceptions, as illustrated by the Native American tribes of the Great Plains (possibly tribal societies in Africa, Australia, and northern Asia as well) within which cultural unity did not coincide with political unity. Thus among the primitive tribes the cultural unit can be much larger, so that many hostile states may live under the sway of a single culture.[58] Language is similarly tied to tribal culture, rather than to political boundaries: "We find that the [primitive] type of culture shows the same disregard for linguistic differences as for political boundaries. This would, of course, follow, since the boundaries of language

---

56. Wissler, Man and Culture, *supra* note 30, at 12.

57. *Id.* at 13.

58. *Id.* at 18.

and states tend to coincide, and if culture ignores one, it must also ignore the other . . . In short, . . . when tribal connections are broken, they are not so long maintained without some change in speech."[59]

The point of such painstaking comparative particularism is that one should not rush into hasty generalizations. Just as Oglala Sioux law was responsive to the needs of that society, cultural traits such as linguistic and political boundaries vary with the nature and type of society under study.

Casting a critical eye at the institution of slavery, Wissler identifies it as a cultural phenomenon,[60] a way of the "Old World" including Athens, Crete, Egypt, and Chaldea. He chides historians for "dodging" the question of the origin of slavery and for treating the phenomenon as somehow an inevitable phase through which humankind had to pass. But where the historian failed, the anthropologist succeeded by demonstrating that slavery was a cultural phenomenon, that as such it was not inevitable, particularly when viewed in comparative context with more recent tribal societies in which slavery was unknown.[61] Indeed, slavery was only one passing culture in one part of the world; other cultural traits (such as the use of fire, ideas concerning spirits) were much older. Thus, when one looks at slavery as part of the history of culture as a whole, it can be seen as one particular phase in particular parts of the world. According to Wissler, it was with the advent of Christianity, the Enlightenment, and the French and American Revolutions that the doctrine of the rights of the individual brought about the demise of slavery as an institution.[62]

Wissler points out that the individual rights doctrine, particularly in the aftermath of World War I, triggered a new self-awareness, which in turn triggered a desire for a "self-realized society" and a new "culture consciousness."[63] This involved a quest for culture rights, whereby each threatened European nation began thinking of protecting its culture. The challenge, according to Wissler, has been to understand the various culture processes of each nation. Indeed, due to an almost universal ignorance of culture process, political leaders have failed to exercise their responsibilities.[64]

Wissler's plea is for a greater understanding of culture and culture processes, for only then can social conditions be improved and peaceful settlement of cultural differences take place. Here again one sees the Boasian influence in favor of particularism, relativism, and tolerance.[65] Nonetheless, he warns that the centers of culture areas are prone to militarism as groups nearest the center vie for domination. In the following excerpt, Wissler gives examples of militarism and expansion among the

---

59. *Id.* at 19.

60. *Id.* at 331.

61. Wissler, Man and Culture, *supra* note 30, at 331.

62. *Id.* at 332–33.

63. *Id.* at 334.

64. *Id.*

65. International cross-cultural contacts must take place "upon an assumed equality of worth." Politicians are chided for ignoring this maxim. *Id.* at 338. Wissler accuses the leaders of the American and French Revolution for overzealously promoting their revolutions abroad. *Id.* at 339.

Iroquois, the Hawaiian Islanders, and certain tribes in Africa. He does not exempt Europe and North America from this tendency but criticizes the U.S. statesmen of his day for being as ignorant of their cultural processes as they are "of what goes on in Mars."[66] His thesis is that once political leaders understand cultural processes, they will be less inclined to militarism and war and more tolerant of cultural differences.

Clark Wissler, Man and Culture 340–41 (1923).

> *The setting in a culture area is especially favorable to the usurpation of power by one of the tribal or national groups near the center*; hence, if war is to be avoided in the Euro-American area, means must be found to discourage militarist ambitions among the strongest nations. For instance, when the Atlantic seaboard was being colonized, the French and English came into conflict with the Iroquoian Federation, an association of Indian tribes then rapidly building up a military machine. According to tradition the five original tribal groups living side by side, fought each other for ascendancy until some great genius reflecting upon this situation developed the idea of a league and from this evolved the famous pact of the so-called Five, and later, Six Nations. But this league entered at once upon wars of conquest, and levied tribute in men and goods upon the surrounding tribes, in the manner of all military powers. Elsewhere, at a number of such marginal centers of Indian culture the colonists found analogous struggles developing, but this is in no wise different from what was happening in other parts of the world. Thus, in the Hawaiian Islands, there were originally a number of independent tribes, but eventually these all came under the control of two strong war-like leaders, one of whom was conquered by the other. In Africa also, we see the rise of native negro kingdoms by the same steps. In every case the primary struggle is between the few groups nearest the culture type for the area. Even the late World War was such a struggle, and though the attempt was made to bind the few largest nations in a pact to keep the peace, one of them refused to be bound and since this was the strongest nation numerically and materially, the conditions are extra-favorable to another struggle for military supremacy. So the great problem in Euro-American culture is to meet this situation without becoming in the end a prey to militarism. It is for the United States, in particular, to ponder deeply over the laws of culture and the ultimate consequences of the positions now being taken by her statesmen, who for the most part are as ignorant of these principles as of what goes on in Mars. Yet even with the clearest insight and the most rational of procedures, the avoidance of such a fate will be no light task, since we observe that everywhere in the world the tendency has been for culture areas to develop dominant centers and then to become the seats of militarism. However, there is reason to believe that

66. Wissler, Man and Culture, *supra* note 30, at 341.

once the leaders of our great nations become fully aware of these facts, they will be less inclined to hazard all in the fortunes of war.

Kroeber: Culture as a "Superorganic" Phenomenon

Alfred Louis Kroeber (1876–1960) was one of Boas's earlier students. He also conceived of culture as *sui generis* and autonomous. In the Boasian tradition, he espoused historical particularism and rejected causation as a factor in the study of cultural manifestations. In 1923 Kroeber published an essay (summarized and excerpted below) in which he attempted to explain the discipline of anthropology, its methods, and its goals.

Just as Immanuel Kant had claimed to have effected a Copernican revolution by propounding the theory that objects conform to the mind (and not the other way around),[67] so Kroeber could have made an analogous claim that culture creates society.[68] Was Kroeber the new Copernicus of anthropology? What was his concept of anthropology? What was unique about his approach? What follows outlines Kroeber's approach to anthropology and the uniqueness of this approach.

To begin, it must be noted that according to Kroeber, anthropology concerns itself with both the organic *and* normative factors of human life, whereas other sciences deal with only one or the other.[69] Although the two are entangled, Kroeber insists that they are conceptually distinct. For example, heredity (an organic or biological concept) can almost imperceptibly merge with the normative sociocultural realm. This happens when heredity is displaced by tradition or environment (nurture rather than nature).[70] When nurture takes over, biology cannot provide the explanation because nurture or tradition are nonbiological phenomena. Thus, according to Kroeber, one of the distinctive tasks of anthropology, is "the interpretation of those phenomena into which both innate organic factors and 'social' or acquired factors enter."[71] In referring to social factors Kroeber had in mind normative or sociocultural phenomena that were nonorganic. Although anthropology accepts the teachings of natural sciences such as biology, anatomy, and physiology as they apply to humanity, sociocultural phenomena (*i.e.*, norms) cannot be studied in the same way. The latter cannot be subjected to experimentation, simplification, and verification in a laboratory.[72] This is because they are events, in real time in diverse societies, that involve their insti-

---

67. Isaak Dore, The Epistemological Foundations of Law 19, 402, 403 (2007).

68. A.L. Kroeber, Anthropology: Race, Language, Culture, Psychology, Prehistory at 8 *et seq.* (New ed., 1948).

69. *Id.* at 1–2.

70. For example, one's race or color of skin is determined by heredity, but the customs and traditions of a race evolve over time due to various social, historical, and environmental factors in which heredity has no role to play.

71. *Id.* at 3.

72. *Id. See also*, A.L. Kroeber, Introduction, *in* The Nature of Culture 1 (1952).

tutions, customs, and beliefs. Studies of these come not in the form of laws (as in natural science) but as generalizations.[73]

Kroeber illustrates with the example of the evolution of birds and reptiles (and humans) over millions of years. He emphasizes that this was an organic phenomenon and represented the "transformation" of the species, whereas the evolution of man-made technology (such as the invention of the airplane) was a mere "accretion to the stock of existing civilization rather than a transformation."[74] If this fundamental distinction is not observed, social scientists are likely to lapse into the error of thinking that only organic causes matter. An example of this error is the pursuit of eugenics with the goal of preserving a particular race or nationality or even civilization itself. Such a pursuit is predicated on the false belief that organic/hereditary forces are all that count for human betterment when supra-heredity or "superorganic" forces are, in fact, far more powerful.[75] Thus Kroeber dismisses the eugenics movement as a misconceived and futile attempt to seek "a biological short cut to a moral end."[76]

Kroeber argues that Charles Darwin's theory of evolution was misapplied by the evolutionists who tried to explain human civilization by naively assuming that their (European) civilization was at the apex, with others arranged in descending order. Kroeber accuses these evolutionists of simply assuming that the normative phenomena that were the most different from those of European society represented the earliest forms of society. Thus if European society was monogamous, the earliest human societies were supposed to have been indiscriminately promiscuous. Because the Europeans recognized patrilineal descent, the earliest societies had to be matrilineal (since paternity was assumed to have been uncertain).[77] Kroeber dismisses all of these speculations as "newspaper science," guesswork,[78] and the results of the incorrect transfer of biological/organic concepts into the realm of human history and culture (*i.e.*, an oversimplified view of human progress).[79]

---

73. Kroeber, Anthropology, *supra* note 68 at 4.

74. *Id.* at 5.

75. *Id.* at 5–6.

76. "Of all the comminglings of the cultural with the vital, that which has crystallized under the name of the eugenics movement is the most widely known and of directest appeal. As a constructive program for national progress, eugenics is a confusion of the purposes to breed better men and to give men better ideals; an organic device to attain the social; a biological short cut to a moral end. It contains the inherent impossibility of all short cuts. It is more refined but no less vain than the short cut which the savage follows, when, to avoid the trouble and danger of killing his foe in the body, he pierces, in safety and amid objurgations uttered in the convenience of his own home, a miniature image addressed by the name of the enemy. Eugenics, so far as it is more than an endeavor at social hygiene in a new field, is a fallacy; a mirage like the philosopher's stone, the elixir of life, the ring of Solomon, or the material efficacy of prayer. There is little to argue about it. If social phenomena are only or mainly organic, eugenics is right, and there is nothing more to be said. If the social is something more than organic, eugenics is an error of unclear thought." A.L. Kroeber, *The Superorganic* (1917), *in* The Nature of Culture, *supra* note 72, at 22, 38.

77. Kroeber, Anthropology, *supra* note 68, at 6.

78. *Id.* at 7.

79. Theories of racial superiority are similarly dismissed by Kroeber as being organically founded: "And yet, it must be maintained that little really satisfactory evidence has been produced to support

Even the doyen of the evolutionists, Herbert Spencer himself, does not escape Kroeber's wrath. Kroeber acknowledges his debt to Spencer, who coined the term "superorganic"—a term Kroeber borrowed. At the same time, he criticizes Spencer for treating evolution as a biological phenomenon and failing to recognize its essentially nonorganic character.

> It would seem probable that the greatest of the champions of acquired heredity, Herbert Spencer, was led to his stand by a similar motive. The precise method by which organic evolution takes place is after all essentially a biological problem, and not a philosophical one. Spencer, however, like Comte, was a sociologist as much as a philosopher. That he should have contested so stubbornly what in itself is a technical question of biology, is hardly intelligible except on the supposition that he felt the question to bear vitally on his principles; and that, in spite of his happy coinage of the term which has been prefixed as title to the present essay, he did not adequately conceive of human society as holding a specific content that is non-organic.[80]

As seen, for Kroeber, the word "social" had a wide meaning that captured everything that transcended the organic aspects of individual life but was unique to humans and did not apply to other animals. These nonorganic or superorganic elements mark the boundaries of the normative realm and include the faculty of speech and the abilities to symbolize, abstract, and generalize. These supposedly unique human capabilities combine to produce learning, knowledge, and practices that are transmitted from generation to generation.[81] Thus, "the mass of learned and transmitted motor reactions, habits, techniques, ideas, and values—and the behavior they induce—is what constitutes *culture*."[82] Every individual is under the sway of these transmitted ways of life, and lives his or her life accordingly. Every culture has its own superorganic transmission system so that life in each culture is different when compared with life in another culture (an axiom well in keeping with Boasian particularism). Culture, therefore, has a very powerful influence on human behavior. Its normative processes are very different from, say, heredity. As Kroeber wryly observes, "No religion, no

---

the assumption that the differences which one nation shows from another—let alone the superiority of one people to another—are racially inherent, that is organically founded. It does not matter how distinguished the minds are that have held such differences to be hereditary—they have in the main only taken their conviction for granted. The sociologist or anthropologist can, and occasionally does, turn the case inside out with equal justification; and he then sees every event, every inequality, the whole course of human history, confirming his thesis that the distinctions between one group of men and another, past and present, are due to social influences and not to organic causes." Kroeber, *The Superorganic*, *supra* note 76, at 33–34.

80. *Id.* at 37–38.

81. *See also* Kroeber, Anthropology, *supra* note 68, at 257.

82. *Id.* at 8 (emphasis in original).

tool, no idea was ever produced by heredity."[83] Hence, he reaches the conclusion that "human societies are more determined by culture than the reverse."[84]

Whereas this conclusion could be viewed as Kroeber's analog to the Kantian claim of effecting a Copernican revolution, he invokes Copernicus more modestly. His point is that as serious ethnography got under way, anthropologists became aware of the vast "universe" of culture and realized that contemporary European civilization was just one of many. This nudged European anthropologists away from their "unconscious ethnocentricity towards relativity."[85] This, Kroeber claims, is analogous to the change from a geocentric to a heliocentric view in astronomy.

A.L. Kroeber, Anthropology: Race, Language, Culture, Psychology, Prehistory 5–11 (New ed., 1948).

> In their more elementary aspects the two strands of the organic or hereditary and the sociocultural or "environmental" run through all human life. They are distinct as mechanisms, and their products are distinct. Thus a comparison of the acquisition of the power of flight respectively by birds in their organic development out of the ancestral reptile stem millions of years ago, and by men as a result of cultural progress in the field of invention during the past generation, reveals at once the profound differences of process that inhere in the ambiguous concept of "evolution." The bird gave up a pair of walking limbs to acquire wings. It added a new faculty by transforming part of an old one. The sum total of its parts or organs was not greater than before. The change was transmitted only to the blood descendants of the altered individuals. The reptile line went on as it had been before, or if it altered, did so for causes unconnected with the evolution of the birds. The airplane, on the contrary, gave men a new faculty without diminishing or even impairing any of those they had previously possessed. It led to no visible bodily changes, no alterations of mental capacity. The invention has been transmitted to individuals and groups not derived by descent from the inventors; in fact, it has already influenced the fortunes of all of us. Theoretically, the invention is transmissible to ancestors if they happen to be still living. In sum, it represents an accretion to the stock of existing civilization rather than a transformation.
>
> Once the broad implications of the distinction which this example illustrates have been grasped, many common errors are guarded against. The program of eugenics, for instance, loses much of its force. There is certainly much to be said in favor of intelligence and discrimination in mating, as in everything else. There is need for the acquisition of more exact knowledge on human heredity. But, in the main, the claims sometimes made that eugenics is necessary to preserve civilization from dissolution, or to maintain the flour-

83. *Id.*

84. Paul A. Erickson & Liam D. Murphy, Readings for a History of Anthropological Theory 138 (3d ed., 2010).

85. Kroeber, Anthropology, *supra* note 68, at 11.

ishing of this or that nationality, rest on the fallacy of recognizing only organic causes as operative, when sociocultural as well as organic ones are active—when indeed the super-hereditary factors may be much the more powerful ones. So, in what are mis-called race problems, the average thought of the day still reasons confusedly between sociocultural and organic causes and effects. Anthropology is not yet in a position always to state just where the boundary lies between the contributing organic causes and the superorganic or "socio-cultural" causes of such phenomena. But it does hold to their fundamental distinctness and to the importance of their distinction, if true understanding is the aim. Without sure grasp of this principle, many of the arguments and conclusions in the present volume will lose their significance. . . .

What has greatly influenced some of the earlier anthropology, mainly to its damage, has been not Darwinism, but the vague idea of progress, to the organic aspect of which Darwin happened incidentally to give such support and apparent substance that the whole group of evolutionistic ideas, sound and unsound, has luxuriated rankly ever since. It became common practice in the older anthropology to "explain" any part of human civilization by arranging its several forms in an evolutionary sequence from lowest to highest and allowing each successive stage to flow spontaneously, without specific cause, from the preceding one. At bottom this logical procedure was astonishingly naïve. In these schemes we of our land and day stood at the summit of the ascent. Whatever seemed most different from our customs was therefore reckoned as earliest, and other phenomena were disposed wherever they would best contribute to the straight evenness of the climb upward. The relative occurrence of phenomena in time and space was disregarded in favor of their logical fitting into a plan. It was argued that since we hold to definitely monogamous marriage, the beginnings of human sexual union probably lay in the opposite condition of indiscriminate promiscuity. Since we accord precedence to descent from the father, and generally know him, early society must have reckoned descent from the mother and no one knew his own father. We abhor incest; therefore the most primitive men normally married their sisters. These are fair samples of the conclusions or assumptions of the classic evolutionistic school of anthropology. . . . Today they are long since threadbare; they have descended to the level of newspaper science or have become matter for idle amateur guessing. They are evidence of a tendency toward the easy smugness of feeling oneself superior to all the past. These ways of thought are mentioned here only as an example of the beclouding that results from bad transference of biologically legitimate concepts into the realm of the history of human society and culture, or viewing these as unfolding according to a simple scheme of progress.

6. *Society and Culture*

The relation between what is biological and what is sociocultural has just been said to be a sort of central pivot of anthropology, from which the range of the subject then extends outward on both sides, into the organic and into the more-than-organic. It is now necessary to consider the more precise relation of society and culture within the "organic-plus." In man, social and cultural phenomena normally occur associated much as the joint sociocultural phenomena co-occur with the organic ones. Nevertheless, the social and the cultural aspects within the larger sociocultural field can nearly always be distinguished. . . .

But in a much wider sense the word "social" is also used, loosely, for whatever transcends the biological individual: for what we have so far designated as more-than-organic or sociocultural. . . .

It so happens that man is an essentially unique animal in that he possesses speech faculty and the faculty of symbolizing, abstracting, or generalizing. Through these two associated faculties he is able to communicate his acquired learning, his knowledge and accomplishments, to his fellows and his descendants—in fact, even to his ancestors, if they happen to be still alive and are willing to listen to him. So he transmits much of his ideas, habits, and achievements to succeeding generations of men. This is something that no other animal can do, at least not to any significant degree. . . .

Now the mass of learned and transmitted motor reactions, habits, techniques, ideas, and values—and the behavior they induce—is what constitutes culture. Culture is the special and exclusive product of men, and is their distinctive quality in the cosmos.

Not only is culture a unique phenomenon, but it can be said to have a large degree of influence. Of course culture can appear and go on only in and through men, men in some kind of societies; without these it could not come into being nor maintain itself. But, given a culture, the human beings that come under its influence behave and operate quite differently from the way they would behave under another culture, and still more differently from the way they would act under no culture. In the latter case they would be merely animals in their behavior. They are human beings precisely because they are animals plus a culture. Somehow human beings began long ago to produce culture and have continued ever since to produce it. In that sense culture derives wholly from men. But the other side of the picture is that every human being is influenced by other men who in turn have been influenced by still others in the direction of maintaining and developing certain ideas, institutions, and standards. And a shorthand way of expressing this is to say that they are all influenced by the culture they grow up in; in fact, in a broad way, they are dependent on it for most of the specific things they do in their lives. Culture is therefore a powerful force in human behavior—in both individual and social behavior. Any given form of culture, whether of the Eskimo or of our contemporary Western civilization, has behind it a long history of other forms of culture by which it was conditioned and from which it derives. And in turn each culture is changing and shaping the forms of culture that will succeed it and which therefore more or less depend on it. Culture thus is a factor that produces enormous effects, and as such we study it. . . .

And, as has been pointed out, the process of transmission, a process of acquisition by learning by which culture is perpetuated and operates on new generations, is quite different from the process by which heredity—another indubitable force—operates on them. Equally distinct are the results. No religion, no tool, no idea was ever produced by heredity.

Culture, then, is all those things about man that are more than just biological or organic, and are also more than merely psychological. It presupposes bodies and personalities, as it presupposes men associated in groups, and it rests upon them; but culture is something more than a sum of psychosomatic qualities and actions. It is more than these in that its phenomena cannot be wholly understood in terms of biology and psychology. Neither of these sciences claims to be able to explain why there are axes and property laws and etiquettes and prayers in the world, why they function and perpetuate as they do, and least of all why these cultural things take the particular and highly variable forms or expressions under which they appear. Culture thus is at one and the same time the totality of products of social men, and a tremendous force affecting all human beings, socially and individually. And in this special but broad sense, culture is universal for man. . . .

Culture, on the contrary, whatever else it may also be—such as a tremendous influence on human behavior—is always first of all the product of men in groups: a set of ideas, attitudes, and habits—"rules" if one will—evolved by men to help them in their conduct of life. . . .

Now while some of the interest of anthropology in its earlier stages was in the exotic and the out-of-the-way, yet even this antiquarian motivation ultimately contributed to a broader result. Anthropologists became aware of the diversity of culture. They began to see the tremendous range of its variations. From that, they commenced to envisage it as a totality, as no historian of one period or of a single people was ever likely to do, nor any analyst of his own type of civilization alone. They became aware of culture as a "universe," or vast field, in which we of today and our own civilization occupy only one place of many. The result was a widening of a fundamental point of view, a departure from unconscious ethnocentricity toward relativity. This shift from naïve self-centeredness in one's own time and spot to a broader view based on objective comparison is somewhat like the change from the original geocentric assumption of astronomy to the Copernican interpretation of the solar system and the subsequent still greater widening to a universe of galaxies.

The Assimilative, Composite, and Autonomous Qualities of Culture

Kroeber observes that in contrast to the organic process, the sociocultural process shows a high degree of "cultural assimilativeness."[86] At the organic level, different species of animal cannot interbreed, whereas a fair amount of blending occurs across

86. Kroeber, Anthropology, *supra* note 68, at 259.

different cultures. Again, this blending occurs in the normative realm. This blending (presumably of such cultural phenomena as languages, religions, food, habits, clothing styles, laws, and styles of government) is due to what Kroeber considers to be the "compositeness" of cultures,[87] their openness to receptivity and adaptability. Indeed, according to Kroeber, the culture of today is "received" and or adapted from the culture of yesterday. This is what gives culture its longevity. Cultural longevity, in turn, creates social and normative stability. A culture that frequently changed its religions, food habits, laws of property, ethics, type of government, and so on would render itself greatly unstable and breed insecurity among its adherents.[88] Kroeber also asserts (see next excerpt) that the receptive abilities of culture are far stronger than its innovative abilities. Reception of cultural phenomena of the type mentioned above is not only from within (*i.e.*, intergenerational transmissions) but also from without, through the phenomenon of diffusion (intercultural transmissions).[89] The most common causes of diffusion have to do with technological innovation; others include proselytizing religious, political, or social ideas.

In his "Eighteen Professions" Kroeber portrays culture as something above and beyond the individual. The following three aphorisms are illustrative:

(1) Civilization, though carried by men and existing through them, is an entity in itself.
(2) History is not concerned with the agencies producing civilization, but with civilization as such. The causes are the business of the psychologist.
(3) The personal or individual has no historical value. [90]

Kroeber elaborated the idea that the individual was of "no historical value," which to some degree advanced Boas's conviction that culture develops independently of free will, in his essay "The Superorganic," published two years after "Professions."[91] While acknowledging Spencer's invention of the term "superorganic,"[92] Kroeber adopted it to describe something different: the completely autonomous nature of culture. He characterized culture as superorganic because he identified it not only as a mental phenomenon rather than a hereditary one but also as existing on a separate plane from the organic characteristics that compose it. Kroeber also believed that civilization was not "mental action itself," because "it is carried by men, without being in them."[93] As a result, individuals do not carry any historical worth; instead, they are a part of culture that they pass from generation to generation.

87. *Id.* at 256.

88. *Id.* at 257.

89. *Id.*

90. A.L. Kroeber, *Eighteen Professions*, 17 AM. ANTHROPOL. 283, 283–284 (1915). Other aphorisms include "The absolute equality and identity of all human races . . . must be assumed by the historian." "The so-called savage is no transition between the animal and the scientifically educated man. . . . All men are totally civilized . . . There is no higher or lower in civilization for the historian." *Id.* at 285–86.

91. Kroeber, *The Superorganic*, *supra* note 76, at 22.

92. *Id.* at 37.

93. *Id.* at 38.

> Gunpowder, textile arts, machinery, laws, telephones are not themselves transmitted from man to man or from generation to generation, at least not permanently. It is the perception, the knowledge and understanding of them, their *ideas* in the Platonic sense, that are passed along. Everything social can have existence only through mentality.[94]

Thus history was determined not by individuals but by cultural forces that operated independently of individuals. Indeed, Kroeber labored to show that patterns of art, philosophy, religion, and technological advances evolved this way. He embarked on two detailed studies of women's dress fashions to prove that even something as personal as how one dressed was dictated by something external to the individual. In his own words, his study of dress fashions was an attempt to "find pattern in so fluidly capricious a thing as dress fashion, and to express quantitatively and objectively something of the qualitative behavior of change in the pattern."[95]

Kroeber believed that cultural norms and their associated patterns of behavior, if studied historically, could be charted as "growth curves." These he studied in his extraordinarily voluminous book, *Configurations of Culture Growth*, published in 1944. In this work, he studied the major civilizations of the world, including ancient Egypt, Mesopotamia, India, Japan, Greece, Rome, China, and the modern West. His hope was to detect standard cycles of growth and decline by cross-cultural comparisons of historically different patterns. He detected spurts of growth and stagnation in the cultures he studied but was unable to find any predictable or standard cycles. He was so faithful to empiricism that he was game enough to say: "I see no evidence of any true law in the phenomena dealt with; and nothing cyclical, regularly repetitive, or necessary."[96]

Despite his inability to find general cycles of growth patterns in *Configurations*, Kroeber continued to study the growth of civilization, characterizing each civilization with a number of normative patterns, the similarities of which made up a particular style or "super-style"[97] and proposing that such styles be compared.

A.L. Kroeber, Anthropology: Race, Language, Culture, Psychology, Prehistory 256–259 (1948).

113. Compositness of Culture

> One general characteristic of culture is what may be called its openness, its receptivity. The culture of today is always largely received from yesterday: that is what tradition or transmission means; it is a passing or sending along, a "handing-through" from one generation to another. Even in times of the most radical change and innovation there are probably several times

94. *Id.*

95. The studies were titled "Order in Changes of Fashion" and "Three Centuries of Womens' Dress Fashions: A Quantitative Analysis." *See* A.L. Kroeber, *Introduction: History and Process of Civilization*, *in* The Nature of Culture, *supra* note 72, at 329.

96. A.L. Kroeber, Configurations of Culture Growth 761 (1944).

97. A.L. Kroeber, An Anthropologist Looks at History 71–77 (1963).

as many items of culture being transmitted from the past as there are being newly devised.... It means also, put in term of process of dynamics, that on the whole the passive or receptive faculties of culture tend to be considerably stronger than its active or innovating faculties. This is something that seems to be pretty deeply ingrained in the nature of culture because it is deeply ingrained in the nature of man, something without which it would lose its continuity, and there with its stability. And most participants in most cultures—most human beings, in short—seem to want a pretty high degree of social stability on account of the security and repose it gives them. A culture that was so unstable and novelty-mongering that it could continually reverse its religion, government, social classification, property, food habits, manners, and ethics, or could basically alter them within each lifetime—such a culture can be imagined. But it would scarcely seem attractive to live under, to most men and women; and it would presumably not survive very long in comparison or competition with more stable cultures, through lacking the necessary continuity....

Now allied to this receptivity of its own past is a receptivity that every culture shows toward cultural material worked out by other cultures. Such acceptance of foreign elements and systems of course constitutes a geographical spread; and the designation most in use for it is diffusion" (§ 171). Such spreads occasionally are rapid, but often they require a considerable time interval. Accordingly, much of what is acquired by diffusion from outside also has its origin in the past, much as what a culture receives by internal handing-on of traditions; but the characteristic of diffusion, the emphasis of the process, is on transmission in *space*. The amount of diffusion which is constantly going on between cultures that have contacts is impressive, and the amount of cultural material or content of foreign origin which gradually accumulates within any one culture may fairly be said to be normally greater than what is originated within it. Also, an integrating process, ... brings it about that as soon as a culture has accepted a new item, it tends to lose interest in the foreignness of origin of this item, as against the fact that the item is now functioning within the culture. One might say that once acceptance is made, the source is played down and forgotten as soon as possible. So it comes about that a large proportion of every culture was not spontaneously developed by it, but was introduced from outside and fitted into it, after which the people of the culture were no longer much concerned about the fact of introduction. Probably the greater part of every culture has percolated into it....

There are several reasons. A steel knife or ax just is physically more effective than a stone one; a motortruck more so than a freight wagon. In other words, in the sphere of practical, mechanical things, there are objective superiorities, and the invention of a superior artifact in one culture anywhere tends to start the process of its adoption by other cultures as soon as they learn about it. Then, whatever comes from a society that is stronger, wealthier, cleverer, or has greater prestige comes with a favorable recommendation.

> Missionization may accentuate this process; and there often is conscious missionization for products and brands, for political and social ideas, as well as for religions. Finally, man is an animal who has a great faculty for getting bored, and many things are taken up just because they are new and different. Some of these will be dropped again for the same reason; but others will stick. There probably are still other factors at work; but those mentioned may suffice to make it reasonable that there should be so much cultural receptivity, diffusion, assimilation, and compositeness.

Kroeber's aims as an anthropologist were to show that culture was not "caused" by individual choice and to emphasize its nonorganic driving forces. He did this through his "Professions," his notion of the superorganic, his study of dress fashions, and in his major work, *Configurations*. It must be noted that Kroeber's notions of human culture as superorganic generated much criticism from scholars such as Sapir, Benedict, and even Boas himself.[98] Their critiques led Kroeber in a later work to "recant" any "overstatements" he may have made concerning his concept of the superorganic,[99] but did not make what he conceded particularly clear.[100] The latter events are recounted by Marvin Harris in the following excerpt.

Marvin Harris, The Rise of Anthropological Theory: A History of Theories of Culture 326–335 (updated ed., 2001).

The Superorganic

> In all essentials save one, Kroeber's "professions" faithfully mirror Boas' influence. The exception is found in number six, "The personal or individual has no historical value, save as illustration."
>
> Whereas Boas' idiography led him increasingly in the direction of interactive problems of personality and culture, Kroeber took the culture concept in the opposite direction and argued for the complete subordination of the individual to his cultural milieu. It was this de-emphasis of the individual, elaborated at greater length in "The Superorganic" .., which convinced everybody that Kroeber had departed from the Boasian fold. . . .
>
> In "The Superorganic," Kroeber made extensive appeal to the "principle of the simultaneity of invention" to show that history was determined by cultural patterns, not by individuals. . . . Kroeber went on to claim that the subordination of the individual to the culture pattern held true in all cultures, that everywhere the individual (to return to Hegel) was the mere agent of culturological forces: . . .

---

98. Ruth Benedict, Patterns of Culture 231 (1934); David Bidney, *On the Concept of Culture and Some Cultural Fallacies*, 46 Am. Anthropol. 30, 42 (1944); Franz Boas, Anthropology and Modern Life 245 (1928).

99. A.L. Kroeber, *White's View of Culture*, *in* The Nature of Culture, *supra* note 72, at 112.

100. *See* text at note 104, *infra*.

The Controversy with Sapir

. . . Sapir argued that it would require a belief in "social determinism amounting to religion" to accept Kroeber's viewpoint. Although he admitted that the "average historian" tended to exaggerate the determining influence of specific personalities, this was no reason to eliminate the individual from all consideration as a cultural factor. Sapir then threw out a challenge which goes a long way toward explaining the main thread of Kroeber's career. Kroeber was finding his superorganic forces by a kind of trick:

> Shrewdly enough Dr. Kroeber chooses his examples from the realm of inventions and scientific theories. Here it is relatively easy to justify a sweeping social determinism in view of a certain general inevitability in the course of the acquirement of knowledge. This inevitability, however, does not altogether reside, as Dr. Kroeber seems to imply, in a social "force" but, to a very large extent, in the fixity, conceptually speaking, of the objective world. This fixity forms the sharpest of predetermined grooves for the unfolding of man's knowledge. Had he occupied himself more with the religious, philosophic, aesthetic, and crudely volitional activities and tendencies of man, I believe that Dr. Kroeber's case for the non-cultural significance of the individual would have been a far more difficult one to make. . . . One has only to think seriously of what such personalities as Aristotle, Jesus, Mahomet, Shakespeare, Goethe, Beethoven mean in the history of culture to hesitate to commit oneself to a completely non-individualistic interpretation of history . . .

Patterns

Kroeber spent the rest of his career doing something very similar to what Sapir had said could not be done: showing how patterns of art, religion, philosophy, as well as of technology and science, waxed and waned, acquired their characteristic content and kept rolling majestically along, quite independently of particular individuals. Among American Indians as well as the ancient Greeks, it is the cultural pattern which summons forth geniuses in appropriate numbers, whenever the time is ripe, be they Edisons or Christs.

As a matter of fact, it was Kroeber's special delight to pick out aspects of culture which seemed most vulnerable to the effect of individual fancy and to demonstrate the existence of patterns unknown to the culture carriers. His study of dress fashions, going back to an inspiration first felt in 1909, was an impressive accomplishment along these lines. . . .

Even his "guru" became alarmed and felt obliged to call for a purge of the mystical patterns that Kroeber claimed were the decisive forces of history: "It has been claimed," wrote Boas, "that human culture is something superorganic, that it follows laws that are not willed by any individual participating in the culture, but that are inherent in the culture itself. . . ." This was too much for Boas' no-nonsense empiricism: "It seems hardly necessary to consider culture a mystic entity that exists outside the society of its individual carriers, and that moves by its own force" . . .

Configurations

Kroeber's fascination with the superorganic culminated in the publication of the singularly monumental *Configurations of Culture Growth* (1944). His wife, Theodora, has said that this book was the product of seven years of labor, during which "every summer, every holiday and free hour" .. were devoted to it. It was intended as a magnum opus. The task he assigned himself was no less than that of discovering "the common features in the growth" of philology, sculpture, painting, drama, literature, and music in Egypt, Mesopotamia, India, Japan, Greece, Rome, Europe, and China. Although he "cheerfully renounces search for causes" .., he does ask the question, have civilizations been alike or unlike in producing their "highest manifestations"?

Despite the prodigious research effort expended upon this task, *Configurations* was a failure. Kroeber was able to discover no similarities whatsoever in the abstract growth curves of different civilizations.... Kroeber could find nothing but unpredictable culture growths: "In reviewing the ground covered, I wish to say at the outset that I see no evidence of any true law in the phenomena dealt with; nothing cyclical, regularly repetitive, or necessary"...

But beyond this reaffirmation of the value of the superorganic concept on exclusively heuristic grounds, Kroeber made certain epistemological concessions to his critics which produced harmony at the expense of enlightenment: "I take this opportunity of formally and publicly recanting," wrote Kroeber, "any extravagances and overstatements of which I may have been guilty through overardor of conviction, in my 'Superorganic.'"...

As part of this same recantation, Kroeber modified the stand he had taken concerning the relationship between culture and individual behavior. Acknowledging a debt to Bidney, he proposed that Aristotle's distinction between "efficient" and "formal" cause is relevant. Individuals are the efficient causes; culture is the formal cause. But Kroeber further assures us that a formal cause is nothing like the kind of cause with which science is concerned. And indeed it is not. For the only meaning to be derived from Kroeber's proposal that culture is a "formal" cause, in the context of his explicit hostility to historical determinism, is that culture is culture. His new position follows: "So far as the latter (mechanical-scientific causes) are concerned, the prospect seems to me that they will continue to reside in the psychic or psychosomatic level": But this corresponds exactly to Boas' final conclusion concerning the possibility of formulating cultural laws. The futility of the entire exchange between Bidney, White, and Kroeber is its most salient feature. As far as the epistemological problem of the nature of culture is concerned, Kroeber's retreat to an Aristotelian *deus ex machina* merely intensified the lack of clarity which had characterized his earlier enthusiasm for the superorganic. His "recantation" helped not one bit to set the matter straight and indeed was nothing more than an unnecessary and irrelevant reassurance that he did not believe in ghosts....

> Kroeber's inclination during the last two decades of his life was to deal with the question of growths of civilizations without bothering with the encyclopedic inventories which had given *Configurations* its saving claim as an inductive product. Instead, the free play of intuition characteristic of the more lurid judgments in *Configurations* was now explicitly defended. Each civilization is to be characterized by a multiplicity of patterns whose common denominators added up to its particular style or "super-style." Kroeber himself suggested the comparison between these "super-styles" and the kind of pattern portraits which Ruth Benedict had achieved. The comparisons reveal the fundamental connectedness of Benedict and Kroeber within the historical particularistic tradition. Although Benedict's patterns are described in a psychological idiom, this is a superficial difference. As far as Kroeber was concerned, the only important distinction between his approach and Benedict's was that his portraits were to be dynamic, covering the early as well as mature phases of style growths . . . His styles are like organic growths, unfolding through time in an irreversible but inexplicable process.

Kroeber's Improved Definition of Culture

By 1952, Kroeber was ready to propose a more comprehensive definition of culture as a normative order, one that incorporated his later thoughts on the subject. Previously he was mainly concerned with the distinction between the organic, nonorganic, and superorganic aspects of culture and with proving his thesis that culture creates society and not vice versa. His early definition of culture ("the mass of learned and transmitted motor reactions, habits, techniques, ideas, and values") says nothing about patterns, fashions, configurations, styles, superstyles, or growth curves. In his book "The Nature of Culture," he gives a much more expanded definition:

> Qualities of culture are: (1) It is transmitted and continued not by the genetic mechanism of heredity but by interconditioning of zygotes. (2) Whatever its origins in our through individuals, culture quickly tends to become suprapersonal and anonymous. (3) It falls into patterns, or regularities of form and style and significance. (4) It embodies values, which may be formulated (overtly, as mores) or felt (implicitly, as in folkways) by the society carrying the culture, and which it is part of the business of the anthropologist to characterize and define.[101]

This definition retains his view of culture as superorganic and impersonal, expressed here with the terms "supra-personal and anonymous." In point 3 he refers to a number of normativities; *i.e.*, "patterns," "regularities of form," and "style," which subsumed his later concepts of patterns, configurations, styles, and superstyles.

---

101. A.L. Kroeber, *Culture, Events and Individuals* (1946), *in* The Nature of Culture, *supra* note 72, at 104, 104.

As already discussed, in this book he recants whatever "extravagancies" and "overstatements" he may have proposed in "The Superorganic."[102] Now viewing this concept as "unnecessary and productive of new difficulties," he declared that he never expressly claimed that culture was "separate, autonomous, and (having) wholly self-sufficient forces."[103]

> I have been under fire, long ago from Boas and Benedict for mysticism, and subsequently from Bidney for idealism, in reifying culture. White has cited several such criticisms. I take this opportunity of formally and publicly recanting any extravagances and over statements of which I may have been guilty through overardor of conviction in my "Superorganic" . . . As of 1948, it seems to me both unnecessary and productive of new difficulties, if, in order to account for the phenomena of culture, one assumes any entity, substance, kind of being, or set of separate, autonomous, and wholly self-sufficient forces. I do not find that I have ever explicitly declared my belief in such. But I do find that I have been ambiguous, and that I have written a number of passages which might be so construed and which quite probably do contain implications in this direction. I am grateful to my critics in proportion as they have been specific in indicating such implications.[104]

Perhaps to mollify his critics, Kroeber tried to move away from the idea of direct internal causes in culture by adopting the Aristotelian concept of "formal causes."[105] This doctrine addresses the interrelationship between "material," "formal," "efficient," and "final" causes.[106] Aristotle proposed that any particular thing is the way it is as the accumulated result of these four causes. Materiality being largely self-explanatory, the formal cause can be explained as generally the process whereby the thing in question attains a determinate pattern or character. The efficient cause is the agent or agency that started or unleashed the process of such determination. As for Kroeber, apart from saying that the causes of normativities within culture are not "mechanistic" and therefore do not have cause-and-effect relationships, his invocation of Aristotle seems to urge the study of the *relationships* between cultural patterns, not their causes. Harris, according to the excerpt above, is not persuaded that this approach will either mollify Kroeber's critics or move far enough away from the concept of superorganic and internal causes to provide a clear and intelligible methodology for the study of cultural patterns.

Here is Kroeber's invocation of Aristotle:

> Every anthropologist or historian concerned with culture realizes that cultural situations make more sense, reveal more meaning, in proportion as we know more of their cultural antecedents, or, generically, more total cultural

102. *See* text at notes 99–100 *supra*. A.L. Kroeber, *White's View of Culture*, *supra* note 99, at 110, 112.

103. *Id.*

104. *Id.*

105. *Id.* at 114.

106. For further discussion *see* Dore, *supra* note 67, at 195.

context. In other words, cultural forms or patterns gain in intelligibility as they are set in relation to other cultural patterns. This interrelating of forms is evidently like the consideration of Aristotelian "formal causes." Of course, they are not "causes" at all in the sense of modern mechanistic science, whose concern is with efficient causes (if with any). And if Aristotelian terminology be objected to in 1948, I shall be happy to adopt whatever more appropriate new term may be coined or proposed.

I am convinced that this primacy of patterns and pattern relation must be accepted in our intellectual operations with cultural data, possibly not forever, but at any rate in the present development of our learning and science. It is easy to cry for dynamic mechanisms, but they have been very hard to find. What the mechanisms or efficient causes residing in persons have explained in culture is perhaps some of its vague recurrences, its hazily defined common denominators. All the characterized qualities of culture, all its variations and specificities, remain essentially unexplained by dynamic psychic mechanisms. Historians, though their material consists of a mixture of culture, persons, and events, increasingly realize the inadequacy of specific causal explanations, and more and more are content to present sequences of significant forms.[107]

Conclusion

The pioneers of the Boasian school rejected unilineal evolutionism and advocated a comparative approach that would be much more amenable to acknowledging cultural and normative diversity. Ultimately, however, this new approach claimed the same privileged access to "truth" that Spencer, Tylor, and Morgan had claimed. Boas's and Kroeber's claim that culture was "autonomous" was a generalized claim applicable to all cultures. Kroeber also developed the notions of culture as a superorganic phenomenon and of growth curves which he claimed could be detected in different cultures at different times. Similarly, Wissler's universal pattern claimed that there were certain normativities shared by all people in all cultures.

Sapir: Linguistics and Anthropology

Edward Sapir (1884–1939), another of Boas's early students, disagreed with Kroeber's cultural determinism. As seen in the excerpt by Harris, Sapir asserted that Kroeber's nonindividualist interpretation of history could not explain the important contributions to religion, philosophy, and aesthetics made by particular individuals.[108] His main contributions involved the relationship between linguistics and anthropology. To him, language was the main vehicle for cultural expression; thus, it was a valuable guide to the scientific study of any culture. Not only is "the network of cultural patterns of a civilization . . . indexed in the language which expresses that

---

107. Kroeber, *White's View of Culture*, *supra* note 99, at 114.

108. Edward Sapir, *Do We Need a "Superorganic?*, 19 Am. Anthropol. 441, 442–43 (1917).

civilization," but "human beings do not live in an objective world . . . but are very much at the mercy of the particular language which has become the medium of expression of their society."[109]

Sapir's thesis is that language expresses ideas; insofar as the latter lead to innovations, the former can be used to study the history of inventions and reconstruct the history of ancient or primitive cultures. Language can similarly be useful to the sociologist studying social attitudes and social style[110] and to the psychologist studying symbolism in behavior.[111]

Sapir posited that just as language has its own grammatical pattern(s), behavior has an unconscious normative patterning. Similarly, he saw both language and behavior as symbolic because he identified them as being based on shared meanings, ideas, and feelings. Thus he believed that Kroeber's notion of an objective superorganic normativity was misconceived. To Sapir, human beings do not live in an objective world, and culture is not an objective entity. Rather, culture is the interactions of particular individuals who abstract from these interactions specific meanings at a purely subjective level.[112] From this unique form of linguistic determinism Sapir derived the idea that culture is an aggregate pattern of meanings, ideas, and actions or "configurations" (a term later developed by Benedict).

Linguistics as a Science of Cultural Normativity

Sapir's linguistic determinism emphasized the connection not only among linguistics and anthropology and cultural history but also between linguistics and sociology, psychology, philosophy, and, more remotely, physics and physiology. He asserts that the normative patterns of culture of every civilization are "indexed" in its language.[113] These patterns are made intelligible through the symbols of language and in this sense describe social reality.[114] In other words, the phenomenal world that surrounds us is not an objective world that precedes all attempts to describe it through language. Rather, language unveils the world to us and conditions our thinking about social processes and problems. The "real world," then, is constructed by the language habits of a particular society. This conclusion is harmonious with Boasian particularism,

109. Edward Sapir, *The Status of Linguistics as a Science*, 5 LANGUAGE 207, 209 (1929). For the epoque in which he was writing, this statement was very avant-garde. It anticipates a major current of intellectual thought in the West almost half a century later.

110. *Id.* at 210.

111. *Id.* at 211–12. *See generally,* Edward Sapir, *Cultural Anthropology and Psychiatry*, 27 J. ABNORM. SOC. PSYCH. 229 (1932), *reprinted in* SELECTED WRITINGS OF EDWARD SAPIR IN LANGUAGE, CULTURE AND PERSONALITY 509 (David G. Mandelbaum ed., 1949). Sapir also claims, in somewhat sweeping terms, that linguistics can be of assistance to the philosopher as well as the natural scientist. Sapir, *The Status of Linguistics as Science*, *supra* note 109, at 212–13.

112. Sapir, *Cultural Anthropology and Psychiatry*, *supra* note 111, at 236.

113. Sapir, *The Status of Linguistics as a Science*, *supra* note 109, at 209.

114. *Id.*; *See generally*, EDWARD SAPIR, THE PSYCHOLOGY OF CULTURE: A COURSE OF LECTURES 180–200 (Judith T. Irvine ed., 2002); 4 EDWARD SAPIR, THE COLLECTED WORKS OF EDWARD SAPIR: ETHNOLOGY (Regna Darnell & Judith Irvine ed., 1994); J.C. Smith, *The Unique Nature of the Concepts of Western Law*, 46 CAN. B.R. 191, 194 (1968).

in that each culture through its own language has its own perception of reality. No wonder then, that "No two languages are even sufficiently similar to be considered as representing the same social reality."[115]

According to Sapir, the words of a language are actually social patterns that dispose us to certain acts of understanding. Thus a narrative, story, or poem is not a collection of random words; instead, these words have meanings and significance that reflect the life of the community within which they are expressed. Even a set of lines drawn without design on a piece of paper may be understood under certain linguistic categories as "straight," "curved," "crooked," and so on. The language habits of a culture thus predisposes its members to particular interpretative acts of understanding.

Sapir did not regard language merely as a symbolic guide to culture. Rather, he stated that language helps explain the phenomenon of diffusion of inventions and ideas and thus can help in the "reconstruction" of primitive cultures.[116] A particular accent or mode of pronunciation, form of speech, or turn of phrase (including slang expressions), as well as technical jargon, all function as symbols that are revelatory of social differentiation on the basis of region, class, occupation, and so on. These symbols are meaningless unless they are contextualized within their proper linguistic settings.

Sapir wrote that acts, like words, can be symbols—they are meaningful in that they express certain understandings. For example, shaking a fist at someone expresses hostility without actual physical contact. Knocking on a door communicates the expectation that the person behind the door will open it. Sapir called such acts "language acts";[117] They are primary in that their meaning is immediately clear. Other symbols that do not involve acts or verbalization become so complex that they are not directly connected with a meaning. Examples of these "secondary" or "referential" symbols include the colors on a flag, which symbolize a certain country. As society becomes more complex, so do its symbols. The more complex the symbol, the less directly its meaning is linked to a set of words or acts. Thus a complex culture will have symbols that perform many tasks in "cross-functional" patterns; contextualizing a single act, which may represent several distinct configurations of meanings, may be difficult. According to Sapir, here is where linguistics can facilitate the understanding of complex configurative patterns: unlike the interactions of nonlinguistic patterns, the patterning of language itself is fairly self-contained.[118] Through this facilitation, linguistics can populate a truly scientific study of the configurative patterns of normativity in culture.

115. Sapir, *The Status of Linguistics as a Science*, *supra* note 109, at 209.

116. *Id.* at 210.

117. *Id.* at 211.

118. *Id.* at 212.

Edward Sapir, *The Status of Linguistics as a Science*, 4 Language 207, 209–14 (1928).

Language is becoming increasingly valuable as a guide to the scientific study of a given culture. In a sense, the network of cultural patterns of a civilization is indexed in the language which expresses that civilization. It is an illusion to think that we can understand the significant outlines of a culture through sheer observation and without the guide of the linguistic symbolism which makes these outlines significant and intelligible to society. Some day the attempt to master a primitive culture without the help of the language of its society will seem as amateurish as the labors of a historian who cannot handle the original documents of the civilization which he is describing.

Language is a guide to "social reality". Though language is not ordinarily thought of as of essential interest to the students of social science, it powerfully conditions all our thinking about social problems and processes. Human beings do not live in the objective world alone, nor alone in the world of social activity as ordinarily understood, but are very much at the mercy of the particular language which has become the medium of expression for their society.... The fact of the matter is that the "real world" is to a large extent unconsciously built up on the language habits of the group. No two languages are ever sufficiently similar to be considered as representing the same social reality. The worlds in which different societies live are distinct worlds, not merely the same world with different labels attached.

The understanding of a simple poem, for instance, involves not merely an understanding of the single words in their average significance, but a full comprehension of the whole life of the community as it is mirrored in the words, or as it is suggested by their overtones. Even comparatively simple acts of perception are very much more at the mercy of the social patterns called words than we might suppose. If one draws some dozen lines, for instance, of different shapes, one perceives them as divisible into such categories as "straight", "crooked", "curved", "zigzag" because of the classificatory suggestiveness of the linguistic terms themselves. We see and hear and otherwise experience very largely as we do because the language habits of our community predispose certain choices of interpretation....

From this standpoint we may think of language as the *symbolic guide to culture*. In another sense too linguistics is of great assistance in the study of cultural phenomena. Many cultural objects and ideas have been diffused in connection with their terminology, so that a study of the distribution of culturally significant terms often throws unexpected light on the history of inventions and ideas. This type of research, already fruitful in European and Asiatic culture history, is destined to be of great assistance in the reconstruction of primitive cultures....

Correctness of speech or what might be called "social style" in speech is of far more than aesthetic or grammatical interest. Peculiar modes of pronunciation, characteristic turns of phrase, slangy forms of speech, occupational terminologies of all sorts—these are so many symbols of the manifold ways in which society arranges itself and are of crucial importance for the understanding of the development of individual and social attitudes. Yet it will not be possible for a social student to evaluate such phenomena unless he has very clear notions of the linguistic background against which social symbolisms of a linguistic sort are to be estimated. . . .

All activities may be thought of as either definitely functional in the immediate sense, or as symbolic, or as a blend of the two. Thus, if I shove open a door in order to enter a house, the significance of the act lies precisely in its allowing me to make an easy entry. But if I "knock at the door", a little reflection shows that the knock in itself does not open the door for me. It serves merely as a sign that somebody is to come to open it for me. To knock on the door is a substitute for the more primitive act of shoving it open of one's own accord. We have here the rudiments of what might be called language. A vast number of acts are language acts in this crude sense. That is, they are not of importance to us because of the work they immediately do, but because they serve as mediating signs of other more important acts. A primitive sign has some objective resemblance to what it takes the place of or points to. Thus, knocking at the door has a definite relation to intended activity upon the door itself. Some signs become abbreviated forms of functional activities which can be used for reference. Thus, shaking one's fist at a person is an abbreviated and relatively harmless way of actually punching him. . . .

Symbols of this sort are primary in that the resemblance of the symbol to what it stands for is still fairly evident. As time goes on, symbols become so completely changed in form as to lose all outward connection with what they stand for. Thus, there is no resemblance between a piece of bunting colored red, white, and blue, and the United States of America,—itself a complex and not easily definable notion. The flag may therefore be looked upon as a secondary or referential symbol. . . .

In ordinary life the basic symbolisms of behavior are densely overlaid by cross-functional patterns of a bewildering variety. It is because every isolated act in human behavior is the meeting point of many distinct configurations that it is so difficult for most of us to arrive at the notion of contextual and non-contextual form in behavior. Linguistics would seem to have a very peculiar value for configurative studies because the patterning of language is to a very appreciable extent self-contained and not significantly at the mercy of intercrossing patterns of a non-linguistic type. . . .

Behind the apparent lawlessness of social phenomena there is a regularity of configuration and tendency which is just as real as the regularity of physical processes in a mechanical world, though it is a regularity of infinitely less apparent rigidity and of another mode of apprehension on our part. . . . Better than any other social science, linguistics shows by its data and methods, necessarily more easily defined than the data and methods of any other type of discipline dealing with socialized behavior, the possibility of a truly scientific study of society . . .

The Unconscious Patterning of Behavior: Implications for Law

To summarize, Sapir's thought was focused on understanding configurations of cultural patterns and he identified linguistics as the key to the truly scientific study of these patterns. He posited that symbols (*e.g.*, flags) have socially understood meanings, as do symbolic acts (language acts) such as shaking a fist. Sapir also thought that gestures and postures have society-wide meanings that transcend individual psychology. Both symbols and gestures can have primary and secondary functions. An example of a primary act would be food consumption, its function being to satisfy a basic organic need. The connection between hunger and food consumption is direct and self-evident. A secondary function is demonstrated by an act or symbol that is not directly or obviously connected to what it stands for, an example being the colors of a flag representing a country.

Every cultural pattern is thus defined by a function as well as by a form.[119] If the function is primary, it may be easily (even intuitively) understood. However (as in the case of a complex symbol) the functional aspect of behavior may become transformed and acquire a newer or deeper significance. Thus individual behavior must be studied to show how it reflects deep-seated cultural patterns that the individual does not so much know but feels. In this sense we have the "unconscious patterning of behavior in society."[120] The individual is simply following the outlines of socially understood and accepted normative demarcations and significances of his or her culture. There is, in other words, no mysterious force such as Kroeber's superorganic; only the individual, who is unaware of these demarcations. Take the simple act of breathing. Its primary function is the intake of life-sustaining oxygen. In certain contexts, for example, when performing yoga, meditation or a particular religious chant, breathing in a particular way has social meaning because it is consciously associated with health or spirituality. These special social contexts symbolize nothing other than socialized modes or patterns of behavior.[121]

The more complex the social context, the more complex and less easily understood the form of behavior. For example, a person will readily know how to act in particular social contexts, but will be unable to articulate the precise rule under which his conduct is subsumed. This inability, according to Sapir, applies to all societies generally: at some level one intuitively knows the rule, but cannot deliberately articulate it in symbolic words. This line of Sapir's thought has great significance for social regulation through law. Here, law is not codified or formally promulgated by someone whose competence to make law is officially recognized. Instead, the unconsciously learned

119. Edward Sapir, *The Unconscious Patterning of Behavior in Society*, *in* E.S. DUMMER, THE UNCONSCIOUS: A SYMPOSIUM (1927), *reprinted in* SELECTED WRITINGS, *supra* note 111, at 544, 547.

120. *Id.* at 548.

121. *Id.* at 546.

patterns of culture perform the same primary function as formal law; namely, the regulation of individual conduct in public/social contexts.

We may ask whether unconsciously learned normative patterns or formal law is the more powerful source of social regulation. It seems fair to say that the former are antecedent to law and that the latter plays a supplementary as well as a clarificatory function. Sapir points out instances in which the functional aspects of behavior are transformed into a complex cultural pattern—at these times, legal rules that are deliberately promulgated may demystify or simplify this complexity. In some senses, cultural forces that control us even unconsciously give us a greater sense of security. Indeed, he says, "any attempt to subject the higher forms of social behavior to purely conscious control must result in disaster."[122] Insofar as law is a deliberate form of "conscious control," its limitations are obvious under Sapir's doctrine of the unconscious force of culture patterns. One then wonders whether breaking the law, or unlawful conduct generally, is symptomatic of the limitations of the legal system, or whether only persistent instances of violations that are statistically significant should be regarded as such symptoms. For Sapir, the fact that conscious control may "result in disaster" indicates a moral lesson: "It is almost as though a misguided enthusiast exchanged his thousands of dollars of accumulated credit at the bank for a few glittering coins of manifest, though little, worth."[123] The analogy in the context of law is that the "accumulated credit" are the rich and complex patterns of culture and the worthless "glittering coins" are rules of law. Whereas its presentation is deliberately exaggerated, it does seem to be a logical extension of Sapir's idea that society courts disaster if it attempts to institute "conscious control" of the higher forms of social behavior. Although he does not explicitly define law as a form of conscious control, this does seem to be a reasonable inference.

Edward Sapir, *The Unconscious Patterning of Behavior in Society, in* E.S. Dummer, The Unconscious: A Symposium (1927), *reprinted in* Selected Writings of Edward Sapir in Language, Culture and Personality 544, 546–559 (David G. Mandelbaum ed., 1949).

All cultural behavior is patterned. This is merely a way of saying that many things that an individual does and thinks and feels may be looked upon not merely from the standpoint of the forms of behavior that are proper to himself as a biological organism but from the standpoint of a generalized mode of conduct that is imputed to society rather than to the individual, though the personal genesis of conduct is of precisely the same nature, whether we choose to call the conduct individual or social. It is impossible to say what an individual is doing unless we have tacitly accepted the essentially arbitrary

122. *Id.* at 549.

123. *Id.*

modes of interpretation that social tradition is constantly suggesting to us from the very moment of our birth. . . .

Forms and significances which seem obvious to an outsider will be denied outright by those who carry out the patterns; outlines and implications that are perfectly clear to these may be absent to the eye of the onlooker. It is the failure to understand the necessity of grasping the native patterning which is responsible for so much unimaginative and misconceiving description of procedures that we have not been brought up with. It becomes actually possible to interpret as base what is inspired by the noblest and even holiest of motives, and to see altruism or beauty where nothing of the kind is either felt or intended.

Ordinarily a cultural pattern is to be defined both in terms of function and of form, the two concepts being inseparably intertwined in practice, however convenient it may be to dissociate them in theory. Many functions of behavior are primary in the sense that an individual organic need, such as the satisfaction of hunger, is being fulfilled, but often the functional side of behavior is either entirely transformed or, at the least, takes on a new increment of significance. In this way new functional interpretations are constantly being developed for forms set by tradition. Often the true functions of behavior are unknown and a merely rationalized function may be imputed to it. Because of the readiness with which forms of human conduct lose or modify their original functions or take on entirely new ones, it becomes necessary to see social behavior from a formal as well as from a functional point of view. . . .

Now it is a commonplace of observation that the reasoning intelligence seeks to attach itself rather to the functions than to the forms of conduct. For every thousand individuals who can tell with some show of reason why they sing or use words in connected speech or handle money, there is barely one who can adequately define the essential outlines of these modes of behavior. No doubt certain forms will be imputed to such behavior if attention is drawn to it, but experience shows that the forms discovered may be very seriously at variance with those actually followed and discoverable on closer study. In other words, the patterns of social behavior are not necessarily discovered by simple observation, though they may be adhered to with tyrannical consistency in the actual conduct of life. If we can show that normal human beings, both in confessedly social behavior and often in supposedly individual behavior, are reacting in accordance with deep-seated cultural patterns, and if, further, we can show that these patterns are not so much known as felt, not so much capable of conscious description as of naïve practice, then we have the right to speak of the "unconscious patterning of behavior in society." The unconscious nature of this patterning consists not in some mysterious function of a racial or social mind reflected in the minds of the individual members of society, but merely in a typical unawareness on the part of the individual of outlines and demarcations and significances of conduct which he is all the time implicitly following. . . .

Why are the forms of social behavior not adequately known by the normal individual? How is that we can speak, if only metaphorically, of a social unconscious? I believe that the answer to this question rests in the fact that the relations between the elements of experience which serve to give them their form and significance are more powerfully "felt" or "intuited" than consciously perceived. It is a matter of common knowledge that it is relatively easy to fix the attention on some arbitrarily selected element of experience, such as a sensation or an emotion, but that it is far from easy to become conscious of the exact place which such an element holds in the total constellations of behavior. It is easy for an Australian native, for instance, to say by what kinship term he calls so and so or whether or not he may undertake such and such relations with a given individual. It is exceedingly difficult for him to give a general rule of which these specific examples of behavior are but illustrations, though all the while he acts as though the rule were perfectly well known to him. *In a sense it is well known to him.* But this knowledge is not capable of conscious manipulation in terms of word symbols. It is, rather, a very delicately nuanced feeling of subtle relations, both experienced and possible. To this kind of knowledge may be applied the term "intuition," which, when so defined, need have no mystic connotations whatever. It is strange how frequently one has the illusion of free knowledge, in the light of which one may manipulate conduct at will, only to discover in the test that one is being impelled by strict loyalty to forms of behavior that one can feel with the utmost nicety but can state only in the vaguest and most approximate fashion. It would seem that we act all the more securely for our unawareness of the patterns that control us. It may well be that, owing to the limitations of the conscious life, any attempt to subject even the higher forms of social behavior to purely conscious control must result in disaster. Perhaps there is a far-reaching moral in the fact that even a child may speak the most difficult language with idiomatic ease but that it takes an unusually analytical type of mind to define the mere elements of that incredibly subtle linguistic mechanism which is but a plaything of the child's unconscious. Is it not possible that the contemporary mind, in its restless attempt to drag all the forms of behavior into consciousness and to apply the results of its fragmentary or experimental analysis to the guidance of conduct, is really throwing away a greater wealth for the sake of a lesser and more dazzling one? It is almost as though a misguided enthusiast exchanged his thousands of dollars of accumulated credit at the bank for a few glittering coins of manifest, though little, worth....

No matter where we turn in the field of social behavior, men and women do what they do, and cannot help but do, not merely because they are built thus and so, or possess such and such differences of personality, or must needs adapt to their immediate environment in such and such a way in order to survive at all, but very largely because they have found it easiest and aesthetically most satisfactory to pattern their conduct in accordance with

> more or less clearly organized forms of behavior which no one is individually responsible for, which are not clearly grasped in their true nature, and which one might almost say are as self-evidently imputed to the nature of things as the three dimensions are imputed to space. It is sometimes necessary to become conscious of the forms of social behavior in order to bring about a more serviceable adaptation to changed conditions, but I believe it can be laid down as a principle of far-reaching application that in the normal business of life, it is useless and even mischievous for the individual to carry the conscious analysis of his cultural patterns around with him. That should be left to the student whose business it is to understand these patterns. A healthy unconsciousness of the forms of socialized behavior to which we are subject is as necessary to society as is the mind's ignorance, or better unawareness, of the workings of the viscera to the health of the body. In great works of the imagination form is significant only in so far as we feel ourselves to be in its grip. It is unimpressive when divulged in the explicit terms of this or that simple or complex arrangement of known elements. So, too, in social behavior, it is not the overt forms that rise readily to the surface of attention that are most worth our while. We must learn to take joy in the larger freedom of loyalty to thousands of subtle patterns of behavior that we can never hope to understand in explicit terms. Complete analysis and the conscious control that comes with a complete analysis are at best but the medicine of society, not its food. We must never allow ourselves to substitute the starveling calories of knowledge for the meat and bread of historical experience. This historic experience may be theoretically knowable, but it dare never be fully known in the conduct of daily life.

In a different context, Sapir suggests that the law itself is one of the higher social forms. He states that the "understandings and procedures which constitute the law of the land" are "patterns . . . (which) are compulsive for the vast majority of human beings."[124] In addition to law, Sapir includes in this category of higher forms symbols of love, affection, hostility, emotionally charged words, and fundamental economic arrangements.[125] Law is included in this category, but he is careful to say that not all laws are unconsciously obeyed. He asserts that compliance with law is a matter of *degree*.[126] "The degree of compulsiveness is no simple relation to the official, as contrasted with the inner or psychological, significance of these patterns."[127] By this Sapir means that the compulsive force of law varies with the degree to which the individual himself feels personally compelled by his conscience. For example, an offensive word may be of no consequence legally, but it may have such strong cultural significance that an individual will feel compelled to not use the word in speech. Sapir believed that these varying degrees of compulsiveness in law and culture as a whole must be

124. Sapir, *Cultural Anthropology and Psychiatry*, *supra* note 111, at 517.

125. *Id.*

126. *Id.*

127. *Id.*

studied in the context of "the ceaseless eternally shifting, balancing of concretely definable motivations of particular people at particular times and in particular places."[128] In addition to legal and nonlegal normative patterns at the general level, he wrote about patterns at the subgroup level (*e.g.*, in trade, industry, politics) where specialized laws and patterns govern.[129] Subgroups must be included in the study of culture, because their members feel compelled to adhere to their special norms, for which outsiders would have no regard.

If there is a moral conclusion to be drawn from the foregoing presentation of Sapir's thought, it is that laws which are not of compelling significance to one's inner conscience may be disregarded or disobeyed. Sapir's exacting empiricism seems to require the (difficult if not impossible) study of such inner motivations to determine or even predict what kinds of laws will succeed and what kinds will fail.[130]

Indeed, Sapir warns that the unconscious patterning of cultural behavior may give the lawmaker the impression that these patterns are self-determining, or that they somehow evolve in accordance with a process that is just as unstoppable as it is natural.[131] He further warned that this impression may wrongly lead to the belief that cultural patterns and law develop not because they are representative of a culture but because they are preordained to follow a specific order or pattern within that culture. Thus conscious legislative patterning would not result in creating law for the people but in "creating" people for the law. However, if "the shifting balances of concretely definable motivations" are taken into account by the lawmaker, law would be created for the people and not the other way around. Thus morally controversial laws, such as those supporting lynching or the death penalty, are to be studied from the internal rather than an external point of view.[132] To understand the popularity of lynch laws in some parts of the United States, Sapir urged the close examination of "the psychological tissue of (its) rural life."[133] The implication here—that laws develop not in terms of right or wrong from a moral standpoint but in terms of cultural wants, needs, and preferences—once again illustrates the particularism of the Boasian school.

---

128. Edward Sapir, *Psychiatric and Cultural Pitfalls in the Business of Getting a Living*, 9 MENTAL HEALTH 237 (1939), *reprinted in* SELECTED WRITINGS, *supra* note 111, at 578, 578.

129. Sapir, *Cultural Anthropology and Psychiatry*, *supra* note 111, at 517.

130. Sapir, *Psychiatric and Cultural Pitfalls*, *supra* note 128, at 578.

131. *See* text at note 128 *supra* (referring to the constantly shifting motivations of people according to time and place).

132. Sapir, *Psychiatric and Cultural Pitfalls*, *supra* note 128, at 589. *See also* REGNA DARNELL, EDWARD SAPIR, LINGUIST, ANTHROPOLOGIST, HUMANIST 102–120 (2010) (arguing that culture patterns are internal to culture). For the argument that Western concepts of law should not be used to analyze non-Western legal systems, *see* Smith, *supra* note 114, at 193.

133. Sapir, *Psychiatric and Cultural Pitfalls*, *supra* note 128, at 589.

Edward Sapir, *Cultural Anthropology and Psychiatry*, 27 J. Abnorm. Soc. Psych. 229 (1932), *reprinted in* Selected Writings of Edward Sapir in Language, Culture and Personality 509, 516–18 (David G. Mandelbaum, ed., 1949).

Clearly, not all cultural traits are of equal importance for the development of personality, for not all of them are equally diffused as integral elements in the idea-systems of different individuals. Some modes of behavior and attitude are pervasive and compelling beyond the power of even the most isolated individual to withstand or reject. Such patterns would be, for example, the symbolisms of affection or hostility; the overtones of emotionally significant words; certain fundamental implications and many details of the economic order; much, but by no means all, of those understandings and procedures which constitute the law of the land. Patterns of this kind are compulsive for the vast majority of human beings but the degree of compulsiveness is in no simple relation to the official, as contrasted with the inner or psychological, significance of these patterns. Thus, the use of an offensive word may be of negligible importance from a legal standpoint but may, psychologically considered, have an attracting or repelling potency that far transcends the significance of so serious a behavior pattern as, say, embezzlement or the nature of one's scientific thinking. A culture as a whole cannot be said to be adequately known for purposes of personality study until the varying degrees of compulsiveness which attach to its many aspects and implications are rather definitely understood. No doubt there are cultural patterns which tend to be universal, not only in form but in psychological significance, but it is very easy to be mistaken in those matters and to impute equivalences of meaning which do not truly exist.

There are still other cultural patterns which are real and compelling only for special individuals or groups of individuals and are as good as non-existent for the rest of the group. Such, for instance, are the ideas, attitudes, and modes of behavior which belong to specialized trades. We are all aware of the reality of such private or limited worlds of meaning. The dairy-man, the movie actress, the laboratory physicist, the party whip, have obviously built up worlds which are anonymous or opaque to each other or, at best, stand to each other in a relation of blanket acceptance. There is much tacit mythology in such hugely complex societies as our own which makes it possible for the personal significance of subcultures to be overlooked. For each individual, the commonly accepted fund of meanings and values tends to be powerfully specialized or emphasized or contradicted by types of experience and modes of interpretation that are far from being the property of all men. If we consider that these specialized cultural participations are partly the result of contact with limited traditions and techniques, partly the result of identification with such biologically and socially imposed groups as the

> family or the class in school or the club, we can begin to see how inevitable it is that the true psychological locus of a culture is *the individual* or *a specifically enumerated list of individuals,* not an economically or politically or socially defined group of individuals. "Individual," however, here means not simply a biologically defined organism maintaining itself through physical impacts and symbolic substitutes of such impacts, but that total world of form, meaning, and implication of symbolic behavior which a given individual partly knows and directs, partly intuits and yields to, partly is ignorant of and is swayed by.

The Role of the Individual and Personality in Culture: The Controversy between Sapir and Kroeber

Although Sapir views the individual as following culturally imposed patterns of behavior with "tyrannical consistency," largely unaware that he is doing so, there is no mysterious superorganic force that causes this unconscious conformity. Only occasionally is it necessary to become conscious, "to bring about a more serviceable adaptation to changed conditions" (as in the last paragraph of the foregoing excerpt). Beyond such intermittent bursts of necessary awareness, Sapir celebrates the relative indeterminacy of normative forces ("We must take joy in the larger freedom of loyalty to thousands of subtle patterns of behavior that we can never hope to understand in explicit terms"). Kroeber, of course, did portray the superorganic as a nonorganic force of unknown origin. But even he, in the end, seemed to implicitly consider the origin of the superorganic to be culture-based. Thus Sapir and Kroeber may not have been all that far apart, especially since both asserted (1) that individual will is superseded by the force of culture and (2) that the embodiments of this force are normative patterns of culture.

Whereas Kroeber boldly stated that "the individual has no historical value,"[134] Sapir argued that "it is only through a minute and sympathetic study of individual behavior . . . in a state of society, that it will ultimately be possible to say things about society itself and culture that are more than fairly convenient abstractions."[135] He believed that individuals have varying temperaments and backgrounds and interact and affect each other in ways that are best understood by psychiatrists, rather than anthropologists and sociologists. The argument, in essence, is that culture cannot be defined impersonally.[136]

> Surely, if the social scientist is interested in effective consistencies, in tendencies, and in values, he must not dodge the task of studying the effects produced by individuals of varying temperaments and backgrounds on each other. Anthropology, sociology, indeed social science in general, is noto-

134. *See* text at note 90 *supra.*

135. Edward Sapir, *Why Cultural Anthropology Needs the Psychiatrist*, 1 Psychiatry 7 (1938), *reprinted in* Selected Writings, *supra* note 111, at 569, 576. *See also* Sapir, *Cultural Anthropology and Psychiatry, supra* note 111, at 514–18.

136. Sapir, *Why Cultural Anthropology Needs a Psychiatrist, supra* note 135, at 576.

> riously weak in the discovery of effective consistencies. This weakness, it seems, is not unrelated to a fatal fallacy with regard to the objective reality of social and cultural patterns defined impersonally.
>
> Causation implies continuity, as does personality itself. The social scientist's world of reality is generally expressed in discontinuous terms. An effective philosophy of causation in the realm of social phenomena seems impossible so long as these phenomena are judged to have a valid existence and sequence in their own right. It is only when they are translated into the underlying facts of behavior from which they have never been divorced in reality that one can hope to advance to an understanding of causes. The test can be made easily enough. We have no difficulty in understanding how a given human being's experiences tend to produce certain results in the further conduct of his life. Our knowledge is far too fragmentary to allow us to understand fully, but there is never a serious difficulty in principle in imputing to the stream of his experiences that causative quality which we take for granted in the physical universe. To the extent that we can similarly speak of causative sequences in social phenomena, what we are really doing is to pyramid, as skilfully and as rapidly as possible, the sorts of cause and effect relations that we are familiar with in individual experience, imputing these to a social reality which has been constructed out of our need for a maximally economical expression of typically human events. It will be the future task of the psychiatrist to read cause and effect in human history. He cannot do it now because his theory of personality is too weak and because he tends to accept with too little criticism the impersonal mode of social and cultural analysis which anthropology has made fashionable.[137]

Like Kroeber, Sapir believed that cultural patterns do have the force as described above. However, he also believed that in the aggregate culture patterns are "merely abstracted configurations of ideas and action patterns, which have endlessly different meanings for various individuals in the group and which . . . must be set in relation to each other in a complex configuration of evaluations."[138] This is the juncture at which the concept of personality becomes relevant in the understanding of culture patterns. In stark contrast to Kroeber, Sapir asserts that personality is not "a mysterious entity resisting the historically given culture but rather a distinctive configuration of experience which . . . as it accretes more and more symbols to itself, creates finally that cultural microcosm of which official 'culture' is little more than a metaphorically and mechanically expanded copy."[139]

---

137. *Id.* at 576–77.

138. Edward Sapir, *The Emergence of the Concept of Personality, in A Study of Cultures*, 5 J. Soc. Psychol. 408 (1934), *reprinted in* Selected Writings, *supra* note 111, at 590, 593–94. *See also* Edward Sapir, Culture Language, and Personality 164–71 (David G. Mandelbaum ed., 1957).

139. Sapir, *The Emergence of the Concept of Personality*, *supra* note 138, at 595.

Edward Sapir, *The Emergence of the Concept of Personality in a Study of Cultures*, 5 J. Soc. Psychol. 408 (1934), *reprinted in* Selected Writings of Edward Sapir in Language, Culture, and Personality 590, 594–97 (David G. Mandelbaum ed., 1949).

The more fully one tries to understand a culture, the more it seems to take on the characteristics of a personality organization. Patterns first present themselves according to a purely formalized and logically developed scheme. More careful explorations invariably reveal the fact that numerous threads of symbolism or implication connect patterns or parts of patterns with others of an entirely different formal aspect. Behind the simple diagrammatic forms of culture is concealed a peculiar network of relationships, which, in their totality, carve out entirely new forms that stand in no simple relation to the obvious cultural table of contents. Thus, a word, a gesture, a genealogy, a type of religious belief may unexpectedly join hands in a common symbolism of status definition. If it were the aim of the study of culture merely to list and describe comprehensively the vast number of supposedly self-contained patterns of behavior which are handed on from generation to generation by social processes, such as inquiry as we have suggested into the more intimate structure of culture would hardly be necessary. Trouble arises only when the formulations of the culture student are requisitioned without revision or criticism for an understanding of the most significant aspects of human behavior. When this is done, insoluble difficulties necessarily appear, for behavior is not a recomposition of abstracted patterns, each of which can be more or less successfully studied as a historically continuous and geographically distributed entity in itself, but the very matrix out of which the abstractions have been made in the first place. All this means, of course, that if we are justified in speaking of the growth of culture at all, it must be in the spirit, not of a composite history made up of the private histories of particular patterns, but in the spirit of the development of a personality. The complete, impersonalized "culture" of the anthropologist can really be little more than an assembly or mass of loosely overlapping idea and action systems which, through verbal habit, can be made to assume the appearance of a closed system of behavior. What tends to be forgotten is that the functioning of such a system, if it can be said to have any ascertainable function at all, is due to the specific functioning and interplays of the idea and action systems which have actually grown up in the minds of given individuals. In spite of the often assorted impersonality of culture, the humble truth remains that vast reaches of culture, far from being in any real sense "carried" by a community or a group as such, are discoverable only as the peculiar property of certain individuals, who cannot but give these cultural goods the impress of their own personality. With the disappearance of such key individuals, the

> tight, "objectified" culture loosens up at once and is eventually seen to be a convenient fiction of thought.
>
> When the cultural anthropologist has finished his necessary preliminary researches into the overt forms of culture and has gained from them an objectivity of reference by working out their forms, time sequences, and geographical distribution, there emerges for him the more difficult and significant task of interpreting the culture which he has isolated in terms of its relevance for the understanding of the personalities of the very individuals from whom he has obtained his information. As he changes his informant, his culture necessarily changes. There is no reason why the culturalist should be afraid of the concept of personality, which must not, however, be thought of, as one inevitably does at the beginning of his thinking, as a mysterious entity resisting the historically given culture but rather as a distinctive configuration of experience which tends always to form a psychologically significant unit and which, as it accretes more and more symbols to itself, creates finally that cultural microcosm of which official "culture" is little more than a metaphorically and mechanically expanded copy.... In short, the application of the personality point of view tends to minimize the bizarre or exotic in alien cultures and to reveal to us more and more clearly the broad human base on which all culture has developed. The profound commonplace that all cultures start from the needs of a common humanity is believed in by all anthropologists, but it is not demonstrated by their writings.
>
> An excellent test of the fruitfulness of the study of culture in close conjunction with a study of personality would be provided by studies in the field of child development. It is strange how little ethnology has concerned itself with the intimate genetic problem of the acquirement of culture by the child.... We may suggest as a difficult but crucial problem of investigation the following: Study the child minutely and carefully from birth until, say the age of ten with a view to seeing the order in which cultural patterns and parts of patterns appear in his psychic world; study the relevance of these patterns for the development of his personality; and, at the end of the suggested period, see how much of the total official culture of the group can be said to have a significant existence for him. Moreover, what degree of systematization, conscious or unconscious, in the complicating patterns and symbolisms of culture will have been reached by this child? This is a difficult problem, to be sure, but it is not an impossible one. Sooner or later it will have to be attacked by the genetic psychologists. I venture to predict that the concept of culture which will then emerge, fragmentary and confused as it will undoubtedly be, will turn out to have a tougher, more vital, importance for social thinking than the tidy tables of contents attached to this or that group which we have been in the habit of calling "cultures."

Herein lies the basic difference of opinion between Sapir and Kroeber. The role of the individual and personality is critical to cultural normativity according to Sapir.

He argues that Kroeber "greatly overshoots the mark in his complete elimination of the peculiar influence of individuals on the course of history."[140] He also critiques Kroeber's stance in that "it requires a social determinism amounting to a religion to deny to individuals all directive power, all culture-molding influence."[141]

In emphasizing the difference between organic and nonorganic societal changes, Kroeber cited the invention of the airplane as an example of the latter. But Sapir criticizes Kroeber for "shrewdly" choosing scientific inventions because the latter are an inexorable part of human history and thus imply a sense of inevitability in the acquisition of knowledge; Kroeber has wrongly harnessed this sense of inevitability to justify his social determinism.[142] In other words, even if such inevitability exists in the scientific or objective world, according to Sapir it does not reside in the social world. Had Kroeber focused on religious, philosophic, aesthetic, and volitional activities of man, according to Sapir, he would have had more difficulty making these claims. Sapir asserts that if individual creativity and influence is denied, it would be impossible to account for the emergence of cultural giants such as Aristotle, Jesus, Mohammed, Shakespeare, Goethe, Beethoven, et al.

Edward Sapir, *Do We Need a "Superorganic"?* 19 Am. Anthropol. 441, 442–44 (1917).

> It seems to me that it requires a social determinism amounting to a religion to deny to individuals all directive power, all culture-moulding influence.... Shrewdly enough, Dr. Kroeber chooses his examples from the realm of inventions and scientific theories. Here it is relatively easy to justify a sweeping social determinism in view of a certain general inevitability in the course of the acquirement of knowledge. This inevitability, however, does not altogether reside, as Dr. Kroeber seems to imply, in a social "force" but, to a very large extent, in the fixity, conceptually speaking, of the objective world. This fixity forms the sharpest of predetermined grooves for the unfolding of man's knowledge. Had he occupied himself more with the religious, philosophic, aesthetic, and crudely volitional activities and tendencies of man, I believe that Dr. Kroeber's case for the non-cultural significance of the individual would have been a far more difficult one to make. No matter how much we minimize exaggerated claims, I fail to see how we can deny a determining and, in some cases, even extraordinarily determining cultural influence to a large number of outstanding personalities.... One has only to think seriously of what such personalities as Aristotle, Jesus, Mahomet, Shakespeare, Goethe, Beethoven mean in the history of culture to hesitate to commit oneself to a completely non-individualistic interpretation of history. I do not believe for a moment that such personalities are merely the cat's-paws

140. Sapir, *Do We Need a "Superorganic"?*, *supra* note 108, at 441.

141. *Id.* at 442.

142. *Id.*

> of general cultural drifts.... The second point in Dr. Kroeber's essay that I find myself compelled to take exception to concerns his interpretation of the nature of social phenomena. If I understand him rightly, he predicates a certain social "force" whose gradual unfolding is manifested in the sequence of socially significant phenomena we call history. The social is builded out of the organic, but is not entirely resolvable into it, hence it implies the presence of an unknown principle which transcends the organic, just as the organic, while similarly builded out of the inorganic, is not resolvable into it but harbors a new and distinctive force that works itself out in organic phenomena. I consider the analogy a false one. Moreover, I do not believe that Dr. Kroeber has rightly seized upon the true nature of the opposition between history and non-historical science.
>
> The analogy is a false one because, while the organic can be demonstrated to consist objectively of the inorganic plus an increment of obscure origin and nature, the social is merely a certain philosophically arbitrary but humanly immensely significant *selection* out of the total mass of phenomena ideally resolvable into inorganic, organic, and psychic processes. The social is but a name for those reactions or types of reaction that depend for their perpetuation on a cumulative technique of transference, that known as social inheritance. This technique, however, does not depend for its operation on any specifically new "force," but, as far as we can tell at present, merely implies a heightening of psychic factors.

As we saw in the previous section on Kroeber, he acknowledged several of his critics by name in his somewhat ambiguous public "recanting" of his Superorganic thesis, and he clearly understood that his critics were accusing him of wrongly conceiving culture to be autonomous and having its own internal causes.[143] In that acknowledgment he did not mention Sapir, possibly because Sapir's criticism was more about excluding the influence of the individual and personality in cultural patterns. Kroeber specifically replied to this criticism in his essays in *The Nature of Culture*, published in 1952. Here he claims that there is an unresolved "contradiction" between the earlier body of Sapir's culturo-linguistic work and his later assertions that culture can be meaningfully studied only in terms of "individual psychiatric personality."[144] He also makes the surprising claim that this later emphasis was advanced by Sapir because the latter had become personally frustrated by his preoccupation with cultural and linguistic forms.[145] Kroeber adds that this new emphasis on individual psychiatric personality was an "emotional" and "near-tragic" development rather than a robust intellectual advance on Sapir's part:

> A contradiction remains unresolved between the body of Sapir's actual culturo-linguistic work and the several programmatic papers of his later

143. *See* text accompanying note 102–104 *supra*.

144. A.L. Kroeber, *Causes in Culture* (1947), *in* The Nature of Culture, *supra* note 72, at 108.

145. *Id.*

> years in which he seemed to assert that culture is fully meaningful only in terms of individual psychiatric personality. This view can possibly be explained as a personal reaction to a sense of ego frustration finally induced in him by years of preoccupation with cultural and linguistic forms; though he also continued to find internal satisfaction with such activity, which he continued as long as he lived....
>
> Malinowski was far less troubled by his inconsistency of exalting culture as *sui generis* and a completely interrelated system, and at the same time as derivable from and reducible to the needs and derived imperatives of physiology and psychology. It would seem that Malinowski's inconsistency was intellectual and nondisturbing; Sapir's, emotional and near-tragic.[146]

Kroeber, who accuses Sapir of taking an anticultural approach by advocating the use of psychiatry to develop an adequate theory of personality, remains dubious that such a theory would be possible. He goes so far as to make a personal thrust against Sapir, namely, that his interest in personality and psychiatry must be viewed against the backdrop of a "partly regretted career":[147]

> In his last years, Edward Sapir sometimes preached but did not himself seriously practice an almost anticultural attitude. He proclaimed that society and culture as such are barren abstractions, and that cause and effect in human history will ultimately be read by a psychiatry which shall have freed itself from the influence of anthropology and anthropological analysis of culture and shall also have evolved an adequate theory of personality. This seems somehow almost as if it were a personal disappointment reaction in Sapir. It is certainly an aspiration rather than a present or realizable program. As a program it is oriented in reverse from Sapir's own lifework with languages, in which, in common with all linguists, he dealt with relations of forms and essentially eschewed both personalities and specific causality.... Now there is little doubt that the active causes of history must reside chiefly in persons. There is also no doubt that the causality must therefore be infinitely manifold. But how any psychiatry or psychology could really evolve "a theory of personality" that would reduce these myriad times myriad causes into a system or organization—with or especially without the aid of cultural analysis—seems a complete mystery. The idea sounds like a wish-fulfilment expression set against the backdrop of a partly regretted career. Its historic significance is presumably connected with the personality-and-culture movement.[148]

---

146. *Id.*

147. A.L. Kroeber, *The History and Present Orientation of Cultural Anthropology* (1950), *in* The Nature of Culture, *supra* note 72, at 144, 148.

148. *Id.* at 147–48.

Benedict: Cultural Integration and Configurationalism

Benedict's Methodology

Ruth Benedict (1887–1948), another of Boas's students schooled in the cultural relativist tradition, was quite familiar with Sapir and his work on the patterning of culture. She advanced the notion that a culture should be studied in terms of its unique, consistent patterns of thought and action.[149] Consistencies in these patterns, according to Benedict, is what leads to normative integration of cultural traits and emotional patterns. Thus each culture, like each individual, has its own temperament, psychological profile, or "configuration." Hence Benedict's claim that "a culture, like an individual, is a more or less consistent pattern of thought and action."[150]

Her best-known examples of configurationalism are her profiles of the Pueblo, whom she characterized as "Apollonian" (*i.e.*, extroverted, tending to stress cooperation, moderation, and anti-individualism) and the Plains tribes, whose ethos she described as "Dionysian" (*i.e.*, introverted, aggressive, and individualistic).[151] These studies show that Benedict's notion of cultural configuration boils down to a search for a unifying emotional pattern for each society.

Benedict's justification of her choice of tribal societies was rather similar to the evolutionist justification of the study of primitive society. She believed that the study of simple societies was the key to understanding more complex ones, such as her own. She cites Darwin in support of this method:

> The understanding we need of our own cultural processes can most economically be arrived at by a détour. When the historical relations of human beings and their immediate forbears in the animal kingdom were too involved to use in establishing the fact of biological evolution, Darwin made use instead of the structure of beetles, and the process, which in the complex physical organization of the human is confused, in the simpler material was transparent in its cogency (*sic*). It is the same in the study of cultural mechanisms. We need all the enlightenment we can obtain from the study of thought and behaviour as it is organized in the less completed groups.[152]

Although this search may be criticized for its oversimplification and extreme reductionism,[153] in fairness it must be noted that Benedict was the first anthropologist to advocate the systemic study of the emotional side of cultural life. Thus a particular practice or ritual that may appear irrational or even repulsive to an outside observer appears far from erratic to an inside observer.[154] Neither did she totally ignore inte-

---

149. Benedict, *supra* note 98, at 46.

150. *Id.*

151. *Id.* at 79. For further discussion of these prototypes *see* text at notes 165–184 *infra*.

152. *Id.* at 56.

153. Bohannan & Glazer, High Points in Anthropology at 175 (2d ed. 1988).

154. Benedict, *supra* note 98, at 46.

grative trends at the nonemotional level. She explains the above-quoted statement by urging the study of all normative traits in relation to each other:

> The significance of cultural behavior is not exhausted when we have clearly understood that it is local and man-made and hugely variable. It tends also to be integrated. A culture, like an individual, is a more or less consistent pattern of thought and action. Within each culture there come into being characteristic purposes not necessarily shared by other types of society. In obedience to these purposes, each people further and further consolidates its experience, and in proportion to the urgency of these drives the heterogeneous items of behavior take more and more congruous shape. Taken up by a well-integrated culture, the most ill-assorted acts become characteristic of its peculiar goals, often by the most unlikely metamorphoses.[155]

This view of the individuality of culture also shows the progression from—indeed, a rejection of—the universal standard of rationality imposed by the early evolutionists (*e.g.*, Tylor) on all societies. Benedict's writings contained the plea to depart from "post-mortem dissections and reconstructions" by "armchair students" of anthropology.[156] She argued that the traits and emotions of each culture were unique and merited individualized study so that their underlying meanings could be appreciated; thus, the same standard of rationality could not be applied to all cultures. This approach also advanced the Boasian particularist agenda.

One other aspect of Benedict's conception of culture needs to be noted: its autonomy. Here Benedict's view is not unlike Kroeber's conception of culture as *sui generis*. This similarity is made clear in her description of the relationship between culture and personality. Culture has a strong formative influence on personality and constrains individual will, because of the strong emotional attachment to custom.[157]

> The life-history of the individual is first and foremost an accommodation to the patterns and standards traditionally handed down in his community. From the moment of his birth the customs into which he is born shape his experience and behavior. By the time he can talk, he is the little creature of his culture, and by the time he is grown and able to take part in its activities, its habits are his habits, its beliefs his beliefs, its impossibilities his impossibilities. Every child that is born into his group will share them with him.[158]

Nonetheless, in contrast to Kroeber, Benedict maintains that the phenomenon of normative integration "is not in the least mystical."[159] Instead, its process of consolidation is similar to the emergence and consolidations of styles in art or architecture. Just as the latter can be studied, so can the former. Thus, the central goal of Benedict's

---

155. *Id.*

156. *Id.* at 48.

157. Hatch, *supra* note 7, at 89.

158. Benedict, *supra* note 98, at 2–3.

159. *Id.* at 47.

methodology was to understand human thought and behavior through culturally integrated patterns. As such the theory not only rejected universalism in favor of cultural relativism, it also adopted an approach that was nonevolutionary, noncomparative, and nonbiological.[160]

Ruth Benedict, Patterns of Culture 45–50, 56 (1934).

The Integration of Culture

The diversity of cultures can be endlessly documented. A field of human behaviour may be ignored in some societies until it barely exists; it may even be in some cases unimagined. Or it may almost monopolize the whole organized behaviour of the society, and the most alien situations be manipulated only in its terms. Traits having no intrinsic relation one with the other, and historically independent, merge and become inextricable, providing the occasion for behaviour that has no counterpart in regions that do not make these identifications.... The significance of cultural behaviour is not exhausted when we have clearly understood that it is local and man-made and hugely variable. It tends also to be integrated. A culture, like an individual, is a more or less consistent pattern of thought and action. Within each culture there come into being characteristic purposes not necessarily shared by other types of society. In obedience to these purposes, each people further and further consolidates its experience, and in proportion to the urgency of these drives the heterogeneous items of behaviour take more and more congruous shape. Taken up by a well-integrated culture, the most ill-assorted acts become characteristic of its peculiar goals, often by the most unlikely metamorphoses. The form that these acts take we can understand only by understanding first the emotional and intellectual mainsprings of that society.

Such patterning of culture cannot be ignored as if it were an unimportant detail. The whole, as modern science is insisting in many fields, is not merely the sum of all its parts, but the result of a unique arrangement and inter-relation of the parts that has brought about a new entity. Gunpowder is not merely the sum of sulphur and charcoal and saltpeter, and no amount of knowledge even of all three of its elements in all the forms they take in the natural world will demonstrate the nature of gunpowder. New potentialities have come into being in the resulting compound that were not present in its elements, and its mode of behaviour is indefinitely changed from that of any of its elements in other combinations.

Cultures, likewise, are more than the sum of their traits. We may know all about the distribution of a tribe's form of marriage, ritual dances, and puberty initiations, and yet understand nothing of the culture as a whole which has used these elements to its own purpose. This purpose selects from among

160. Bohannan & Glazer, *supra* note 153, at 175.

the possible traits in the surrounding regions those which it can use, and discards those which it cannot. Other traits it recasts into conformity with its demands. The process of course need never be conscious during its whole course, but to overlook it in the study of the patterns of human behaviour is to renounce the possibility of intelligent interpretation.

This integration of cultures is not in the least mystical. It is the same process by which a style in art comes into being and persists. Gothic architecture, beginning in what was hardly more than a preference for altitude and light, became, by the operation of some canon of taste that developed within its technique, the unique and homogeneous art of the thirteenth century. It discarded elements that were incongruous, modified others to its purposes, and invented others that accorded with its taste. When we describe the process historically, we inevitably use animistic forms of expression as if there were choice and purpose in the growth of this great art form. But this is due to the difficulty in our language forms. There was no conscious choice, and no purpose. What was at first no more than a slight bias in local forms and techniques expressed itself more and more forcibly, integrated itself in more and more definite standards, and eventuated in Gothic art.

What has happened in the great art styles happens also in cultures as a whole. All the miscellaneous behaviour directed toward getting a living, mating, warring, and worshipping the gods, is made over into consistent patterns in accordance with unconscious canons of choice that develop within the culture. Some cultures, like some periods of art, fail of such integration, and about many others we know too little to understand the motives that actuate them. But cultures at every level of complexity, even the simplest, have achieved it. Such cultures are more or less successful attainments of integrated behaviour, and the marvel is that there can be so many of these possible configurations.

Anthropological work has been overwhelmingly devoted to the analysis of culture traits, however, rather than to the study of cultures as articulated wholes. This has been due in great measure to the nature of earlier ethnological descriptions. The classical anthropologists did not write out of first-hand knowledge of primitive people. They were armchair students who had at their disposal the anecdotes of travellers and missionaries and the formal and schematic accounts of the early ethnologists. It was possible to trace from these details the distribution of the custom of knocking out teeth, or of divination by entrails, but it was not possible to see how these traits were embedded in different tribes in characteristic configurations that gave form and meaning to the procedures....

There is as great an unreality in similar studies of culture. If we are interested in cultural processes, the only way in which we can know the significance of the selected detail of behaviour is against the background of the motives and emotions and values that are institutionalized in that culture.

> The first essential, so it seems today, is to study the living culture, to know its habits of thought and the functions of its institutions, and such knowledge cannot come out of post-mortem dissections and reconstructions.
>
> The necessity for functional studies of culture has been stressed over and over again by Malinowski. He criticizes the usual diffusion studies as post-mortem dissections of organisms we might rather study in their living and functioning vitality. One of the best and earliest of the full-length pictures of a primitive people which have made modern ethnology possible is Malinowski's extended account of the Trobriand Islanders of Melanesia. Malinowski, however, in his ethnological generalizations is content to emphasize that traits have a living context in the culture of which they are a part, that they function. He then generalizes the Trobriand traits—the importance of reciprocal obligations, the local character of magic, the Trobriand domestic family—as valid for the primitive world instead of recognizing the Trobriand configuration as one of many observed types, each with its characteristic arrangements in the economic, the religious, and the domestic sphere....
>
> The understanding we need of our own cultural processes can most economically be arrived at by a detour. When the historical relations of human beings and their immediate forbears in the animal kingdom were too involved to use in establishing the fact of biological evolution, Darwin made use instead of the structure of beetles, and the process, which in the complex physical organization of the human is confused, in the simpler material was transparent in its cogency (*sic*). It is the same in the study of cultural mechanisms. We need all the enlightenment we can obtain from the study of thought and behaviour as it is organized in the less complicated groups.

Identification of Normative Patterns: Three Case Studies

Even the casual observer would agree that humanity is made up of diverse peoples, each grouped into social units defined by territory, race, boundary, and so on, within which they practice their own traditions, religions, and ways of life. Given the range of these diverse ways of life, Benedict asserted that no single way could be said to be *the* way of life for any human society. Kroeber had already made this important advance through his claim of a "Copernican revolution."[161] In short, no single culture could embrace all of these diverse ways of life, just as no language can employ every grunt or sound possible in the human vocal apparatus.[162]

Fundamental to Benedict's approach was the assumption that each culture represents only a small fraction of the totality of possible human behaviors and practices (i.e., "patterns"). These normativities are to be captured by the anthropologist and described in a way not colored or biased by his own culture. As cultural patterns are studied and compared, it becomes obvious that they can be diametrically opposed

161. *See* text accompanying notes 67, 84–85 *supra*.

162. Peter Crawford, *Patterns of Culture*, *in* MASTERPLOTS II: WOMEN'S LITERATURE SERIES 5 at 1779 (1995) (Frank N. Magill ed.).

such that what is acceptable in one culture may be unacceptable in another. This conclusion again emphasizes the particularist/relativist approach to culture. However, what is unique about Benedict's method is the projection of Sapir's approach to the individual and personality onto culture itself. As seen in the previous section, one of Sapir's main concerns was to affirm the importance of individuality that would transcend culture. Benedict carried Sapir's project a step further by conceiving culture as "personality writ large."[163] Indeed, one could improve on Mead's term by saying that Benedict's goal was to study culture as "personality writ large conceived psychologistically."

Benedict claimed that "a culture, like an individual, is a more or less consistent pattern of thought and action."[164] Under this view, each culture is a distinctive and incommensurable psychological type in which a society may coalesce and flourish. In her book *Patterns of Culture*, with which her approach is famously associated, the two main prototypes she presented were borrowed from Friedrich Nietzsche, namely, the Apollonian and Dionysian types. To understand Benedict's use of these categories, it is necessary to see how Nietzsche himself used them.

Nietzsche's Prototypes

Nietzsche advanced the theory that Greek drama was built around two archetypes of philosophic thought, represented by the deities Apollo and Dionysus. The former represented normative order, harmony, beauty, restraint, and neatness of boundaries, whereas the latter stood for the opposite notions of disorder, excess, and the collapsing of boundaries. Apollonian art thus presented the empirical world as beautiful and orderly; it also glorified the individual, and life itself, in a general sense.[165] Dionysian art, by contrast, presented the world as tumultuous and always in flux, to the point of overwhelming and tragically destroying the individual. Nietzsche argued that the genius of Greek culture was its ability to maintain a proper balance between these two forms of artistic expression in drama—that is, until Socrates arrived with his keen rationalist philosophy. Nietzsche asserted that Socrates's philosophy threw a "wet blanket" over the Dionysian aspect of Greek tragedy[166] and criticized Socrates for singularly orienting Western philosophy toward an excessively Apollonian or rationalist point of view.[167] In particular, he rejected the unflinching Socratic view that reason alone can penetrate all distortions of reality and present the world as it really is.[168] According to Nietzsche, reason can never penetrate reality, nor can it ever yield immutable principles of knowledge.

---

163. Margaret Mead, An Anthropologist at Work: Writings of Ruth Benedict 202 (1966).

164. Benedict, *supra* note 98, at 46.

165. Maudemarie Clark, *Language and Deconstruction: Nietzsche, de Man, and Postmodernism*, *in* Nietzsche as Postmodernist: Essays Pro and Contra 76 (Clayton Koelb ed., 1990).

166. Richard D. Chessick, A Brief Introduction to the Genius of Nietzsche 31 (1983).

167. Friedrich Nietzsche, Twilight of the Idols 41 (R.J. Hollingdale trans., Penguin Books ed., 1990).

168. *Id. See also* Friedrich Nietzsche, The Birth of Tragedy 18, 52 (Walter Kaufmann trans., Vintage Books ed., 1967).

The Dionysian model in Greek tragedy allowed for a fusion between audience and actors whereby the audience chanted as part of the chorus and lost its sense of isolation from the rest of the players.[169] As discussed elsewhere in this book, the ideas of fusion between subject and object, between reader and text, and between observation and participation are prominent themes of postmodern thought; Benedict (as well as Nietzsche) is associated with these trends of progressive thought (including feminism in Benedict's case).[170]

The Prototypes in Patterns of Culture

Benedict adopted the Nietzschean archetypes and applied them to primitive cultures. Her closest analogy to the Dionysian type in Native American culture was "drunkenness, and . . . the illuminations of frenzy."[171] By contrast, she asserted that the Apollonian tendency in Native culture manifests itself in outlawing such activities and taking "control over all disruptive psychological states."[172] She informs her readers that in Native American culture generally, ecstatic experiences and visions are cornerstones of the whole religious structure. Such experiences (*i.e.*, ecstasy, orgy, visions, comas) can be externally induced through the ingestion of intoxicants or drugs or they can be self-induced through fasting, torture (*i.e.*, self-torture), or dance.[173] For example, among the Pima, intoxication was the visible expression or "mirroring" of religion and a highly symbolic form of its exaltation. It showed "the patterning of its mingling of clouded vision and of insight."[174]

Benedict selected two Native tribes in North America, the Pueblo and the Kwakiutl, and one New Guinea tribe, the Dobu. She sought in each a consistent pattern of thought and action (or worldview) that permeated the consciousness of its individual members, was unique to that culture, and was not shared by the other cultures.

"Pueblo" is a blanket term for the tribes of the Southwest, including the Navajo, Pima/Papago, and Zuni. She found that the Pueblo fit the Apollonian model because they rejected all forms of excess in favor of "an *ethos* distinguished by sobriety, and by its distrust of excess."[175] Consequently all their social arrangements, from religious rites to marital norms, were very low-key and modest. They had a religion of fertility without orgy.[176] All ceremonies strictly followed tradition, with no use of drugs or

---

169. Bernd Magnus & Kathleen M. Higgins, *Nietzsche's Works and Their Themes, in* The Cambridge Companion to Nietzsche 22–3 (Bernd Magnus and Kathleen M. Higgins eds., 1996).

170. *See* Crawford, *supra* note 162, at 1780.

171. Benedict, *supra* note 98, at 79. Ruth Benedict, *Psychological Types in Cultures of the Southwest, in* Mead, An Anthropologist at Work, *supra* note 163, at 248, 249.

172. Benedict, *Psychological Types, supra* note 171, at 249.

173. *Id.* at 250. *See generally*, Ruth Benedict, *The Vision in Plains Culture*, 24 Am. Anthropol. 1, 3 (1922).

174. Benedict, *Psychological Types, supra* note 171, at 250.

175. *Id.* at 249.

176. *Id. See also* Ruth Benedict, *An Introduction to Zuni Mythology, in* Mead, An Anthropologist at Work, *supra* note 163, at 226, 231 (stating that Zuni marriages were monogamous).

other signs of the pursuit of trance or ecstasy.[177] For example, the *datura*, a particularly powerful intoxicant that can induce a coma lasting up to four days, is used among the Mohave, the Yokuts, and the Serrano. Its recreational use is prohibited by the Zuni. If it is used at all by them, it is to promote the Apollonian goals of sobriety or to catch a thief. In the latter instance, a small dose of the *datura* is administered by a priest under close supervision with the goal of loosening a tongue. After that the person is given an emetic four times and washed with yucca suds to cleanse him of traces of the *datura*. Thus neither this intoxicant nor any other drug is used to achieve visions. In fact, Benedict notes the absence of the vision complex among the peoples of the Southwest as a remarkable example of their resistance to the Dionysian tendencies of the neighboring tribes.[178] Similarly, whereas fasting is used in the surrounding cultures as a way of inculcating visions, Benedict gives the practice of fasting in the Southwest an Apollonian interpretation. The practice is used for ceremonial cleanliness but never as a "power-giving experience" in the Dionysian sense.[179]

By contrast, the Kwakiutl of the Pacific Northwest were the opposite of the Zuni, according to Benedict; they fell into the Dionysian model in that they indulged themselves in ecstasy and excess.

> In their religious ceremonies the final thing they strove for was ecstasy. The chief dancer, at least at the high point of his performance, should lose normal control of himself and be rapt into another state of existence. He should froth at the mouth, tremble violently and abnormally, do deeds which would be terrible in a normal state. Some dancers were tethered by four ropes held by attendants, so that they might not do irreparable damage in their frenzy.[180]

The worth of the individual was measured or indexed by the extent to which he could display conspicuous consumption and self-glorification through wealth. Wanton destruction of material possessions was a way of proving wealth, as was the ability to pay exorbitant sums for bribes.[181]

Unlike the Zuni, the Kwakiutl sought states of vision, frenzy, and ecstasy through fasting as well as a variety of intense dances such as the Bear Dance, the Kwakiutl Cannibal Dance, and the Ghost Dance:[182]

> The cannibal dance of the Kwakiutl is a typically Dionysian ritual. It is not only that it is conceived as a dramatization of a condition of ecstasy which the main participant must dance to its climax before he can be restored to normal life; every ritualistic arrangement is designed—I do not mean

177. Benedict, *supra* note 98, at 59, 62–63. The Zuni were a highly "ceremonious" people; thus all their cults regarding masked gods, healing, the sun, the dead, and warfare showed strict respect to form and ceremony. *Id.* at 59.

178. Benedict, *Psychological Types*, *supra* note 171, at 253.

179. *Id.* at 254.

180. Benedict, *supra* note 98, at 175–76.

181. *Id.* at 193.

182. Benedict, *Psychological Types*, *supra* note 171, at 254, 258–59.

consciously—to heighten the sense of the anti-natural act. A long period of fasting and isolation precedes the rite, the dance itself is a crouching, ecstatic pursuit of the prepared body held outstretched toward him by a woman attendant. With the required ritualistic bites the anti-natural climax is conceived to be attained, and prolonged vomiting and fasting and isolation follows.[183]

Benedict saw the third group, the Dobu, as falling under neither of the Nietzschean dichotomies. Instead, they are described as "dangerous" and "treacherous,"[184] with a world outlook characterized by paranoia, suspicion, and ill will that paints everyone as a potential enemy, including one's spouse. Self-protection mandated the practice of sorcery, the focus of all Dobuan social institutions on the prevention of enemy attacks, and the enactment of revenge should an attack occur.[185]

Apart from these three psychological prototypes, Benedict employed a fourth ("abnormality") that, in her view, was represented by the West European model. She recognized all four types as different and that the practices of any one of them do not necessarily coincide with those of any of the others. There is thus nothing inevitable about the social institutions of a given culture. For example, marriage may have very different cultural functions among the Dobu when compared with its functions among the Zuni or in Western Europe. Benedict argued that Western institutions are neither basic nor essential for humanity but instead are the product of "compulsive" drives, just as different drives produce different normativities in other cultures.[186]

This conclusion leads to Benedict's concept of abnormality. Whatever is taboo in a culture or excluded by it is labeled abnormal. For example, homosexuality is accepted in some cultures but is problematic in the West. This is because the latter has a narrow focus that subsumes all activities, from procreation to death, under "the will to power" (a Nietzschean term). Therefore, according to Benedict, the natural behavioral instincts of individuals is restricted in the West and hence the taboo of homosexuality. By contrast, individuals who are considered "normal" have "a license which they may almost endlessly exploit."[187] This statement may be considered a warning from Benedict about the dangers of majoritarian rule.

Conclusion

Benedict's writings identified four prototypes of culture: the two Nietzschean polar opposites, the Dobu, and the Western type (she acknowledges the latter but does not further describe it). Benedict does not exclude the possibility that other pro-

183. *Id.* at 258–59.

184. Benedict, *supra* note 98, 131.

185. *Id.* at 161, 169–72. In summing up the life of the average Dobuan, Benedict concludes that "all existence appears to him as a cut throat struggle in which deadly antagonists are pitted against one another in a contest for each one of the goods of life. Suspicion and cruelty are his weapons in the strife and he gives no mercy, as he asks none." *Id.* at 172.

186. Crawford, *supra* note 162, at 1780.

187. Benedict, *supra* note 98, 274 at 276.

totypes may exist, but she does expressly say that not every culture will show such highly integrated normative profiles as the ones she discussed. "All cultures .. have not shaped their thousand items of behavior to a balanced and rhythmic pattern ... lack of integration seems to be as characteristic of certain cultures as extreme integration is of others."[188]

The statement is ambiguous; it may mean that anthropology may not have much explanatory power in certain cultures that are marked by the absence of configuratory patterns. Even in those cultures like the Kwakiutl or the Zuni, where integrated patterns were found, Benedict may have done more to describe than to explain those patterns. It is not clear in her writings *why* the Zuni are Apollonian or *why* the Kwakiutl came to acquire their Dionysian predispositions. In the end, she merely states that each culture chooses its own distinctive patterns: "In its least flattering light, one might sum it up as the observation that some cultures are different and others are similar."[189]

Benedict's factual reportings in *Patterns of Culture* about the Kwakiutl and the Pueblo have provoked intense criticisms. For example, it has been charged that she had tended to "underestimate the orgiastic potentiality of Zuni character,"[190] understated the role of alcohol in Zuni society, and understated the intensity of certain initiation ceremonies—for example, the initiation of boys who were severely whipped until they bled.[191] Although these criticisms may be legitimate, it may be unfair to expect from Benedict an explanatory theory to account for particular normativities. Her goal was never to develop a metatheory of explanation in the causal sense, only to describe these particularities in culture-specific contexts. Furthermore, in characterizing the Southwest Pueblos as Apollonian, she expressly qualified her label by pointing out that they did not fit that model in every sense. She used this category primarily to differentiate Pueblo culture from that of other Native Americans:

> The Southwest Pueblos are Apollonian. Not all of Nietzsche's discussion of the contrast between Apollonian and Dionysian applies to the contrast between the Pueblos and the surrounding peoples. The fragments I have quoted are faithful descriptions, but there were refinements of the types in Greece that do not occur among the Indians of the Southwest, and among these latter, again, there are refinements that did not occur in Greece. It is with no thought of equating the civilization of Greece with that of aboriginal America that I use, in describing the cultural configurations of the latter, terms borrowed from the culture of Greece. I use them because they are categories that bring clearly to the fore the major qualities that differentiate Pueblo culture from those of other American Indians, not because all the attitudes that are found in Greece are found also in aboriginal America.[192]

188. *Id.* at 223.

189. HARRIS, *supra* note 10, at 403.

190. *Id.* at 405 (quoting E.C. PARSONS, PUEBLO INDIAN RELIGION 879 (1939)).

191. *Id.* at 405–06.

192. BENEDICT, *supra* note 98, at 79.

Benedict on Law and Culture

Benedict was a strong supporter of Sapir's approach to ethnography, particularly his interest in culture and individual personality. (This interest is shown clearly in his approach to law, as seen earlier.[193]) Sapir's key ideas on normative regulation may be summarized as follows:

1. A large part of social regulation is self-regulating and that it is largely in the form of the "unconscious patterning of behavior";
2. This form of unconscious regulation is antecedent to law, the latter being a conscious or deliberate attempt to regulate society;
3. Too much conscious regulation could lead to "disaster";
4. The compulsive force of law is proportionate to the individual's internal convictions of its rightness;
5. There are no preordained rules or patterns that are natural and/or inevitable;
6. There are no preordained rules of right and wrong, as illustrated by lynch laws, which in his time were popular albeit morally questionable.

Sapir's influence on Benedict in matters of social regulation is apparent; her notion of law and its regulatory consequences is similar to Sapir's as well. She viewed law negatively, to the point of calling it an "arrogant" institution, and subscribed to the idea that there are no legal or moral absolutes in the sense that they are natural or preordained. She also subscribed to the idea that modes of behavior should be evaluated in terms of their popularity and function, not on the basis of what can be objectively categorized as right and wrong. In addition, she supported the relativistic agenda of Boasian historical particularism.

Benedict carries forward Sapir's idea of compulsion in law to a more general, society-wide level by asserting that the dominant traits of any civilization (including Western civilization) are "compulsive" not in terms of being "basic or essential in human behavior, but rather in the degree to which they are social and overgrown in our own culture."[194] She makes the same remark when contrasting the Dobuan ethos of treachery and fear with the Kwakiutl ethos of revenge and humiliation. She reminds us nothing in these two lifestyles is inevitable;[195] they have their own compulsive forces embedded in culture. As for differing cultural perceptions, Benedict cites homosexuality and trance as two examples.[196] With regard to homosexuality, she points out that "even a mild homosexual" is regarded as abnormal in Western culture.[197] Whereas in ancient Greek culture homosexuality was an "honourable es-

193. *See supra* section on Sapir titled "The Unconscious Patterning of Behavior: Implications for Law."

194. Benedict, *supra* note 98, at 250.

195. *Id.*

196. *See id.* at 262–65.

197. *Id.* at 262.

tate" (citing Plato's *Republic*),[198] and among Native Americans homosexuals are often regarded as "exceptionally able."[199]

> When the homosexual response is regarded as a perversion, however, the invert is immediately exposed to all the conflicts to which aberrants are always exposed. His guilt, his sense of inadequacy, his failures, are consequences of the disrepute which social tradition visits upon him, and few people can achieve a satisfactory life unsupported by the standards of their society. The adjustments that society demands of them would strain any man's vitality, and the consequences of this conflict we identify with their homosexuality.[200]

In certain Western cultures homosexuals face a number of legal difficulties with regard to marriage, adoption, job security, housing, and so on. We must then wonder what Benedict's ultimate goals were in citing these examples from Native and Western culture. One is clearly her plea for the recognition of the relativity of cultural values. Another is her suggestion that there are no absolute normative standards by which to judge conduct as right or wrong. Perhaps another, which is implicit in the above-quoted passage, is a plea for tolerance within cultures for behaviors that are considered to be deviant or abnormal.

Benedict also laments what she calls a "dualism" in nineteenth-century thought that placed "society" on the one hand and the "individual" on the other, in mutually antagonistic positions.[201] Many political revolutionaries, as well as proponents of freedom in politics and in law, have invoked this dualism. Benedict's rejection of it is based in her denial of a fundamental schism between society and the individual. She blames "the regulative activities of society" for the antagonism the average person feels toward his society and identifies the law as the primary source of such regulation, which means that in her view, law restricts freedom and its absence is to be equated with freedom.[202] However, Benedict also identified these perceptions as belonging to only the average person and not reflective of the true picture; indeed, she argues that such perceptions are naive when projected at the national/philosophical level.[203] This naiveté is the result of her convictions that social regulation (including regulation through law) is only "incidental" and that "law is not equivalent to social order."[204] In simpler cultures that are homogeneous, Benedict believes that customs and habits will supersede any need for formal legal authority. She cites a Native American legend according to which in the early days, tribes had no fights over fishing areas or hunting grounds because there was no law apportioning these resources.

---

198. *Id.* at 262–63.

199. Benedict, *supra* note 98, at 263.

200. *Id.* at 265.

201. *Id.* at 251.

202. *Id.* at 252.

203. *Id.*

204. Benedict, *supra* note 98, at 252.

Thus, "everybody did what was right."[205] In other words, there was no control imposed from without, and fishing and hunting practices were mutually internalized by the inhabitants themselves.

Benedict ends with the proposition that even in Western society law is only a "crude" tool and that it is often necessary to check its "arrogant" tendencies.[206]

Conclusion

Both Sapir and Benedict consider law to play a limited role in society, agree that it has potential to do mischief, and note that cultural patterns are antecedent to law and play a much more important role than law in regulating individual behavior. Perhaps one contrast between them is that Benedict's analysis appears to create a new antagonistic "dualism." She replaces the dualism between society and individual with that of the individual and law. If the law is representative of the denial of freedom, then this denial must necessarily result in an antagonism between the individual and law. (By contrast, an approach based on the writings of Sapir and Wissler may place less emphasis on the antagonism and more on a codependent, if not a symbiotic relationship, between the individual, the law, and culture. Here they would be inextricably linked and would invariably affect one another.)[207]

Finally, Benedict's discussion of abnormality illustrates the relativity of legal values. Their evolution is fluid; they evolve as transgressions or progressions, depending on the culture frame as well as the time frame.[208]

Mead: Culture and Personality

The contributions of Kroeber, Sapir, and Benedict represent a clear movement away from nineteenth-century notions of causality and evolution. In its earlier variants, represented particularly by Sapir and Benedict, this new movement tended to interpret culture in psychological terms. Thus emerged the approach known as *culture and personality*.[209] Benedict adhered to this approach, as already discussed. Margaret Mead, a student of Benedict who was significantly influenced by her, also advocated this approach. The culture and personality approach was designed to relate cultural beliefs and normative practices to individual personality and vice versa.[210] Perhaps more than any other adherent, Mead emphasized that the study of the individual would lead to a better understanding of culture and society as a whole.[211] She believed that studying the individual should include early childhood development and socio-

205. *Id.*

206. *Id.* at 253.

207. Erickson & Murphy, *supra* note 84, at 147–48.

208. Sapir made a similar point regarding breathing etiquette. *See* text at note 121, *supra*.

209. Harris, *supra* note 10, at 393, 401, 403 *et seq.*

210. *Id.* at 398.

211. Keesing & Keesing, *supra* note 5, at 395.

cultural practices that had a formative effect on personality.[212] Cultural differences and similarities could then be explained as a consequence of such personality similarities and differences. However, most proponents of this approach (including Mead) did not explain why specific practices and experiences molding particular personality types occur only in certain cultures and not in others.

Mead was a scholar of prodigious output who carried out numerous ethnographic studies. Discussed here are her two best-known case studies involving, in all, four primitive cultures.

Normative Conditioning in Adolescence: Samoa

Mead set about the task of investigating the reliability of theories that claimed that physical or bodily changes during adolescence were responsible for the changing psychological dispositions noted during this period.[213] Her goal was to refute such theories through anthropological research. She argued that the social environment played a great role in psychological attitudes and that neither race nor human nature could be said to be responsible for such basic emotions as love, anger, and fear under different social conditions, as well as more complex phenomena such as rebellion against authority.[214] Concerning the latter, Mead poses the basic question of her research: "Were these difficulties due to being adolescent or to being adolescent in America?"[215]

According to Mead, the only way to answer this question was for the anthropologist to go to a different and more simple culture in another part of the world and study the conditions there. This belief is very similar to the belief not only of her mentor Benedict but also of the early evolutionists, who saw primitive cultures as holding the key to understanding cultural development in more complex societies.[216] The culture chosen by Mead was Samoa, a South Pacific island chain inhabited by a Polynesian people. In studying her target population, adolescent girls, Mead expanded on Benedict's theories of normative patterning by exploring the ease with which behavioral patterns—particularly at the adolescent stage—can be conditioned by one culture in ways that can be contrasted with parallel phases of adolescence in other cultures.

One of Mead's most famous studies on the subject was titled *Coming of Age in Samoa*, in which she compared adolescent girls in Samoa with their counterparts

---

212. *See* MARGARET MEAD, GROWING UP IN NEW GUINEA: A COMPARATIVE STUDY OF PRIMITIVE EDUCATION 6, 135, 205 (Appollo ed., 1962).

213. MARGARET MEAD, COMING OF AGE IN SAMOA—A PSYCHOLOGICAL STUDY OF PRIMITIVE YOUTH FOR WESTERN CIVILIZATION 3 (1928).

214. *Id.* at 4.

215. *Id.* at 5.

216. Similarly in her book SEX AND TEMPERAMENT IN THREE PRIMITIVE SOCIETIES, Mead states: "I have studied this problem in simple societies because here we have the drama of civilization writ small, a social microcosm alike in kind, but different in size and magnitude, from the complex social structures of peoples who like our own, depend upon a written tradition." xvi–xvii (Routledge & Kegan Paul, 1977).

in the United States. Three of her objectives in embarking on this exercise were proving that differences between the two groups were due to cultural influences rather than biological differences, that there was no uniform or universal pattern of cultural determinism, and that there was definitely a "biopsychological plasticity in human affairs sufficient to permit the cultural conditioning of adolescent behavioral patterns."[217]

> Can we think of adolescence as a time in the life history of every girl child which carries with it symptoms of conflict and stress as surely as it implies a change in the girl's body?
>
> Following the Samoan girls through every aspect of their lives we have tried to answer this question, and we found throughout that we had to answer it in the negative. . . .
>
> If it is proved that adolescence is not necessarily a specially difficult period in a girl's life—and proved it is if we can find any society in which that is so—then what accounts for the presence of storm and stress in American adolescents? First, we may say quite simply, that there must be something in the two civilizations to account for the difference.[218]

In the excerpt that follows, Mead identifies three differences between Western and Samoan civilization. These mainly concern characteristics that she identified as peculiarly Samoan, the primitive structure of their society, and the absence of neurosis.[219] As to the first, Mead focuses largely on the low intensity of the Samoan lifestyle, in a land in which "no one plays for high stakes," where conflicts are easily resolved, where life is generally peaceful and harmonious, and whose people have "conventionalized" the "lack of deep feeling."[220] As to the second, Mead reports that children of primitive societies have relatively uncomplicated choices compared to their counterparts in modern societies, where they must navigate an array of choices about religion, morality, sex, marriage, diet, political doctrine, and more. By contrast, the Samoan children had one religion, engaged in sexual experimentation freely, and seemed to face few (if any) difficult ethical choices. With regard to the third difference, the absence of neurosis, Mead believes that this is due to the "gentler" upbringing of Samoan children by loving parents and extended families and greater overall tolerance for the handicapped in Samoan society.[221]

---

217. Harris, *supra* note 10, at 408.

218. Mead, Coming of Age in Samoa, *supra* note 213, at 196–97.

219. *Id.* at 198.

220. *Id.* at 199–200.

221. *Id.* at 207–09.

Margaret Mead, Coming of Age in Samoa: A Psychological Study of Primitive Youth for Western Civilization 196–201, 206–207 (1928).

Is adolescence a period of mental and emotional distress for the growing girl as inevitably as teething is a period of misery for the small baby? Can we think of adolescence as a time in the life history of every girl child which carries with it symptoms of conflict and stress as surely as it implies a change in the girl's body?

Following the Samoan girls through every aspect of their lives we have tried to answer this question, and we found throughout that we had to answer it in the negative....

If it is proved that adolescence is not necessarily a specially difficult period in a girl's life—and proved it is if we can find any society in which that is so—then what accounts for the presence of storm and stress in American adolescents? First, we may say quite simply, that there must be something in the two civilisations to account for the difference. If the same process takes a different form in two different environments, we cannot make any explanations in terms of the process, for that is the same in both cases. But the social environment is very different and it is to it that we must look for an explanation. What is there in Samoa which is absent in America, what is there in America, which is absent in Samoa, which will account for this difference?

Such a question has enormous implications and any attempt to answer it will be subject to many possibilities of error. But if we narrow our question to the way in which aspects of Samoan life which irremediably affect the life of the adolescent girl differ from the forces which influence our growing girls, it is possible to try to answer it.

The background of these differences is a broad one, with two important components; one is due to characteristics which are Samoan, the other to characteristics which are primitive.

The Samoan background which makes growing up so easy, so simple a matter, is the general casualness of the whole society. For Samoa is a place where no one plays for very high stakes, no one pays very heavy prices, no one suffers for his convictions or fights to the death for special ends. Disagreements between parent and child are settled by the child's moving across the street, between a man and his village by the man's removal to the next village, between a husband and his wife's seducer by a few fine mats....

In this casual attitude toward life, in this avoidance of conflict, of poignant situations, Samoan contrasts strongly not only with America but also with most primitive civilisations. And however much we may deplore such an attitude and feel that important personalities and great art are not born in so shallow a society, we must recognise that here is a strong factor in the painless development from childhood to womanhood.... So, high up in our list of explanations we must place the lack of deep feeling which the Samoans have conventionalised until it is the very framework of all their attitudes toward life.

And next there is the most striking way in which all isolated primitive civilisation and many modern ones differ from our own, in the number of choices which are permitted to each individual. Our children grow up to find a world of choices dazzling their unaccustomed eyes. In religion they may be Catholics, Protestants, Christian Scientists, Spiritualists, Agnostics, Atheists, or even pay not attention at all to religion. This is an unthinkable situation in any primitive society not exposed to foreign influence. There is one set of gods, one accepted religious practice, and if a man does not believe, his only recourse is to believe less than his fellows; he may scoff but there is no new faith to which he may turn. . . .

Similarly, our children are faced with half a dozen standards of morality: a double sex standard for men and women, a single standard for men and women, and groups which advocate that the single standard should be freedom while others argue that the single standard should be absolute monogamy. Trial marriage, companionate marriage, contract marriage—all these possible solutions of a social impasse are paraded before the growing children while the actual conditions in their own communities and the moving pictures and magazines inform them of mass violations of every code, violations which march under no banners of social reform.

The Samoan child faces no such dilemma. Sex is a natural, pleasurable thing; the freedom with which it may be indulged in is limited by just one consideration, social status. . . .

And in making the comparison there is a third consideration, the lack of neuroses among the Samoans, the great number of neuroses among ourselves. We must examine the factors in the early education of the Samoan children which have fitted them for a normal, un-neurotic development. . . .

The implications of this observation are double. Samoa's lack of difficult situations, of conflicting choice, of situations in which fear or pain or anxiety are sharpened to a knife edge will probably account for a large part of the absence of psychological maladjustment. Just as a low-grade moron would not be hopelessly handicapped in Samoa, although he would be a public charge in a large American city, so individuals with slight nervous instability have a much more favourable chance in Samoa than in America. . . .

With the exception of the few cases . . . adolescence represented no period of crisis or stress, but was instead an orderly developing of a set of slowly maturing interests and activities. The girls' minds were perplexed by no conflicts, troubled by no philosophical queries, beset by no remote ambitions. To live as a girl with many lovers as long as possible and then to marry in one's own village, near one's own relatives and to have many children, these were uniform and satisfying ambitions.

Social Misfits, Delinquency, and Law in Samoa

The last paragraph in the excerpt seems to portray Samoa as a virtual paradise for the adolescent girl, who experiences "no period of crisis or stress" and whose mind is "perplexed by no conflicts." However, the paragraph begins with the qualifier "With the exception of the few cases." Let us examine these few cases and query the way they deviated from the normal, peaceful life of a Samoan adolescent. Before she discusses the exceptional cases of delinquency, Mead notes that in less serious situations social discipline is imposed from within the family, where "violent outbursts of wrath and summary chastisements do occur but consistent and prolonged disciplinary measures are absent, and a display of temper is likely to be speedily followed by conciliatory measures."[222] The influence of Christian missionaries, especially the pastor, was also a disciplinary force. But these observations concerned conflict between a girl ("the deviant") and her elders.[223] Conflict between young people of the same age group, within the same family, was solved by breaking up the age group and removing the child "with the weakest claim on the household." She did not explain the criteria for such a decision. "The fact that the age-group gang breaks up before adolescence and is never resumed except in a highly formal manner, coupled with the decided preference for household rather than group solidarity, accounts for the scarcity of conflict."[224]

Thus, first-level discipline is the concern of the Samoan household, not a wider group of islanders. Indeed, the little group-level intervention she observed led Mead to the conclusion that no public delicts existed in Samoa and therefore no public or institutionalized mechanisms had been designed to deal with them. "The absence of any important institutionalised relationship to the community is perhaps the strongest cause for lack of conflict here."[225] In her observation, the community itself makes "no demands upon the young girls except for the occasional ceremonial service."[226] From such statements one gleans the impression that in Samoa, the norms of good behavior are somehow autonomous and largely internalized; that the occasional deviant is dealt with quite effectively within the household, sometimes with help from the pastor; and that there is little, if any, formal law in the Western sense.

The "exceptional cases," then, fall into the category of what Mead calls "delinquents"[227] who violate "group standards."[228] Delinquency in this context is defined not just in terms of the act or behavior alone, but in terms of the "attitude" underlying the behavior. The psychologistic element, which was so much in evidence in the writings of Sapir and Benedict, is emphasized here as well. In the following excerpt, Mead elaborates on her concept of delinquency, gives some examples, and identifies

---

222. *Id.* at 158–59.

223. MEAD, COMING OF AGE IN SAMOA, *supra* note 213, at 169–170.

224. *Id.* at 159.

225. *Id.* at 159–60.

226. *Id.* at 160.

227. *Id.* at 171.

228. MEAD, COMING OF AGE IN SAMOA, *supra* note 213, at 172.

Samoan delinquency as the equivalent to behavior that in Western culture would be prohibited by formal law.

Margaret Mead, Coming of Age in Samoa: A Psychological Study of Primitive Youth for Western Civilisation 172–173 (1928).

> I am using the term delinquent to describe the individual who is maladjusted to the demands of her civilisation, and who comes definitely into conflict with her group, not because she adheres to a different standard, but because she violates the group standards which are also her own.
>
> A Samoan family or a Samoan community might easily come to conceive the conduct and standards of Sona and Lita as anti-social and undesirable. Each was following a plan of life which would not lead to marriage and children. Such a choice on the part of the females of any human community is, of course, likely to be frowned upon. The girls who, responding to the same stimuli, follow Sona's and Lita's example in the future will also run this risk.
>
> But were there really delinquent girls in this little primitive village, girls who were incapable of developing new standards and incapable of adjusting themselves to the old ones? My group included two girls who might be so described, one girl who was just reaching puberty, the other a girl two years past puberty. Their delinquency was not a new phenomenon, but in both cases dated back several years. The members of their respective groups unhesitatingly pronounced them "bad girls," their age mates avoided them, and their relatives regretted them. As the Samoan village had no legal machinery for dealing with such cases, these are the nearest parallels which it is possible to draw with our "delinquent girl," substituting definite conflict with unorganized group disapproval for the conflict with the law which defines delinquency in our society.

Here Mead identifies two girls as delinquents. The first girl was "quarrelsome, insubordinate, impertinent. She contended every point, objected to every request, shirked her work, fought with her sisters, mocked her mother, [and] went about the village with a chip on her shoulder."[229] After being sent to live with the pastor and soon being expelled from his household, she was sent from home to home but led a very troubled life—to the point that no other home would accept her.[230] Mead reports: "When I left, she was living, idle, sullen, and defiant in her long-suffering mother's house."[231] One can only conclude that this girl's rehabilitation was a failure, if a rare one.

---

229. *Id.* at 174.

230. *Id.* at 177.

231. *Id.* at 178.

The second girl was a compulsive thief since early childhood, and who also behaved "like a boy." After observing her being shunned by all children, Mead predicted that she would "sink lower and lower in the village esteem and especially in the opinion of her own sex from whom she so passionately desires recognition and affection."[232]

Mead attributed the delinquency of both girls partly to their personalities and partly to their social environment. Both girls were, in her opinion, "victims of lack of affection."[233]

> So it would appear that their delinquency was produced by the combination of two sets of causal factors, unusual emotional needs and unusual home condition. Less affectionate children in the same environments, or the same children in more favourable surroundings, probably would never have become as definitely outcast as these.[234]

Conclusion

Mead's observations about the cases of deviance and delinquency were meant to show that a simple and small tribal order is marked by the absence of formal law. This absence was not meant to suggest that binding rules of social conduct were entirely absent. Instead, she observed a high degree of harmony and an absence of social turmoil because such rules are internalized by the population at large. We may think of this as "law" by another name; otherwise there would be no cases of deviance or delinquency (this is a rare case of the exception proving the rule). Mead also notes the household and missionary influence, including church and pastor, as sources of social discipline. The institution of exile to break up group gangs seems rather like an institutionalized social mechanism although Mead does not characterize it as such.

In keeping with Sapir and Benedict, Mead emphasizes the attitudinal (or psychological) element in the compulsive force of law. To the extent that there is overall normative harmony, members have more or less mutually shared internal convictions motivating conduct. When these are at odds with group sentiment, they mark the boundary between social obeisance and deviance and/or delinquency. Finally, also consistent with the beliefs of Sapir and Benedict, Mead views behavior patterns as the product of individual personality and the sociocultural environment. Thus in the case of the two delinquents, Mead concluded that the element lacking in their social environment was "affection," which led her to claim that had Lita and Mala been brought up in more favorable surroundings they would not have become delinquents.

Mead's *Coming of Age in Samoa* received much of the same criticism as Benedict's theory of configurationalism.[235] She was charged with formulating sweeping gen-

---

232. *Id.* at 180.

233. Mead, Coming of Age in Samoa, *supra* note 213, at 180.

234. *Id.*

235. Keesing & Keesing, *supra* note 5, at 396.

eralizations and emphasizing only major characteristics.[236] Nor have doubts about her ethnographic conclusions subsided. In fact, more than fifty years after the book was published, another anthropologist, Derek Freeman, wrote a scathing critique of Mead's methodology and ethnological data. Freeman's book, *Margaret Mead and Samoa*, confirmed for many that several of her main conclusions about Samoan culture were fatally flawed.[237]

Despite the controversy that has surrounded *Coming of Age in Samoa* and Benedict's *Patterns of Culture*, these works had an indisputably profound effect on anthropologists as well as nonanthropologists in the twentieth century. "The artful presentation of cultural differences to a wide professional and lay public by Mead and Benedict must be reckoned among the important events in the history of American intellectual thought."[238]

Standardization of Sex Temperament in Primitive Society: Three Cases Studies

In another major case study, Mead investigated three primitive societies in Papua New Guinea to see what temperament each society had toward gender-based differences among its people, and how these temperaments came about. The three societies were the Arapesh, Mundugumor, and Tchambuli (now Chambri). As explained shortly, Mead's data convinced her that the varying temperaments about gender and sexuality in these societies were exclusively the result of cultural conditioning.

Mead explains at the outset that every society distinguishes among genders as well as among gender roles. In some societies, differentiation is expressed in dress and occupation without regard to temperamental differences. In others, difference manifests itself in temperament[239] (*i.e.*, certain temperaments are "masculine" and others "feminine"). Focusing on temperament as a psychologistic trait, Mead set out to examine the particular trait of a "dominating nature." She explains that she will

> examine the "masculine" woman and the "feminine" man as they occur in these different tribes, to inquire whether it is always a woman of dominating nature who is conceived of as masculine, or a man who is gentle, submissive, or fond of children or embroidery who is conceived as feminine.[240]

Mead does not explain why she chose this particular trait as opposed to another or others for her study.[241] The only explanation given is that she will study "the patterning of sex-behaviour from the standpoint of temperament, with the cultural assumptions

---

236. Harris, *supra* note 10, at 410.

237. Derek Freeman, Margaret Mead and Samoa: The Making and Unmaking of an Anthropological Myth 95, 111 *et seq.* (1983).

238. Harris, *supra* note 10, at 409.

239. Mead, Sex and Temperament, *supra* note 216, at xix–xx.

240. *Id.* at iv.

241. She does however identify other traits such as bravery, aggressiveness, objectivity and malleability. *Id.* at xxi.

that certain temperamental attitudes are 'naturally' masculine and others 'naturally' feminine."[242] Her assumption was that each tribe would have a clear conception of what males and females are naturally like and use this as the norm to condemn the individuals who deviate from it.[243] Instead she discovered that temperaments she would have considered to be inherent to one gender were mere variations of the human temperament itself and that they could be found in the other gender as well. In summarizing her findings in each of the three societies, Mead says:

> In one, both men and women act as we expect women to act—in a mild parental responsive way; in the second, both act as we expect men to act—in a fierce initiating fashion; and in the third, the men act according to our stereotype for women—are catty, wear curls and go shopping, while the women are energetic, managerial, unadorned partners.[244]

Her point is the same one that Benedict made in *Patterns of Culture*: all cultures choose from a range of behavior patterns accompanied by underlying psychological attitudes (temperaments, in Mead's terminology) that are available to the human race. Mead's ethnographic data of the three tribes showed to her how completely a culture may impose, on either gender, patterns that are appropriate to only one segment of the human race.[245]

The following excerpt explains the standardization of sex temperament in the three societies as the consequence of cultural conditioning.

Margaret Mead, Sex and Temperament in Three Primitive Societies 279–80 (Routledge & Kegan Paul 1977).

> We have now considered in detail the approved personalities of each sex among three primitive peoples. We found the Arapesh—both men and women—displaying a personality that, out of our historically limited preoccupations, we would call maternal in its parental aspects, and feminine in its sexual aspects. We found men, as well as women, trained to be co-operative, unaggressive, responsive to the needs and demands of others. We found no idea that sex was a powerful driving force either for men or for women. In marked contrast to these attitudes, we found among the Mundugumor that both men and women developed as ruthless, aggressive, positively sexed individuals, with the maternal cherishing aspects of personality at a minimum. Both men and women approximated to a personality type that we in our culture would find only in an undisciplined and very violent male. Neither the Arapesh nor the Mundugumor profit by a contrast between the

242. *Id.* at xxi.

243. *Id.* at xxi.

244. Mead, Sex and Temperament, *supra* note 216, at iv.

245. *Id.*

> sexes; the Arapesh ideal is the mild, responsive man married to the mild, responsive woman; the Mundugumor ideal is the violent aggressive man married to the violent aggressive woman. In the third tribe, the Tchambuli, we found a genuine reversal of the sex-attitudes of our own culture, with the woman the dominant, impersonal, managing partner, the man the less responsible and the emotionally dependent person. These three situations suggest, then, a very definite conclusion. If those temperamental attitudes which we have traditionally regarded as feminine—such as passivity, responsiveness, and a willingness to cherish children—can so easily be set up as the masculine pattern in one tribe, and in another be outlawed for the majority of women as well as for the majority of men, we no longer have any basis for regarding such aspects of behaviour as sex-linked. And this conclusion becomes even stronger when we consider the actual reversal in Tchambuli of the position of dominance of the two sexes, in spite of the existence of formal patrilineal institutions.
>
> The material suggests that we may say that many, if not all, of the personality traits which we have called masculine or feminine are as lightly linked to sex as are the clothing, the manners, and the form of head-dress that a society at a given period assigns to either sex. When we consider the behaviour of the typical Arapesh man or woman as contrasted with the behaviour of the typical Mundugumor man or woman, the evidence is overwhelmingly in favour of the strength of social conditioning. In no other way can we account for the almost complete uniformity with which Arapesh children develop into contented, passive, secure persons, while Mundugmor children develop as characteristically into violent, aggressive, insecure persons. Only to the impact of the whole of the integrated culture upon the growing child can we lay the formation of the contrasting types. There is no other explanation of race, or diet, or selection that can be adduced to explain them. We are forced to conclude that human nature is almost unbelievably malleable, responding accurately and contrastingly to contrasting cultural conditions. The differences between individuals who are members of different cultures, like the differences between individuals within a culture, are almost entirely to be laid to differences in conditioning, especially during early childhood, and the form of this conditioning is culturally determined. Standardized personality differences between the sexes are of this order, cultural creations to which each generation, male and female, is trained to conform. There remains, however, the problem of the origin of these socially standardized differences.

Having presented her findings, Mead asks what Benedict did not, namely, why the temperaments are as they are. The last sentence of the excerpt poses the question of their origin; in subsequent pages, Mead grapples with the question but does not advance any causal explanation or theory. Instead she concentrates on refuting the notion that these temperaments could have a cause other than cultural conditioning, which she refers to as "the intricate, elaborate, and unfailing fashion in which culture is able to shape each new-born child to the culture image."[246] In its least flattering sense, her conclusion mimics the tautology that "culture patterns originate in culture" or that "some cultures are similar, others are different."[247]

Nevertheless, like her mentor Benedict, Mead is rightly associated with twentieth-century progressive thought, particularly feminism. The thesis that male-female stereotypes are culturally conditioned, not hereditary or the products of biological or genetic factors, is consistent with Mead's (debatable) conclusion that the United States has been more successful than Europe in jettisoning "male domination."[248]

246. *Id.* at 282.

247. *See* Harris's caustic comment on Benedict, text at note 189 *supra*.

248. Mead, Sex and Temperament, *supra* note 216, at 310.

Chapter 3

Structural Functionalism and Normativity

The structural functionalist school was founded in Britain in the first half of the twentieth century. The intellectual backdrop for this movement was the scientific revolution inspired by Albert Einstein's theory of relativity.[1] As a result, it placed great emphasis on the "interrelations of elements of experience" and "combinations of elements comprising whole systems."[2]

> In the philosophy of science, for example, A.N. Whitehead (as in his *Science of the Modern World* 1926) called the new approach "organismic." Others have called it "holistic," "integrative," "functional" in the sense that all parts of a system *do* something, that is, have a significant *function* in relation to the whole.[3]

As applied to anthropology, the functional method sought to explain the recurrent functions of customs and institutions, rather than the origins or causes of cultures or the differences and similarities among them. The functional method involved the general assumption that social systems were normatively integrated, stable, and made up of parts that fit harmoniously in an equilibrium that changed little over time.[4] This assumption was inspired by, if not founded on, the concept of social solidarity of the French sociologist Emile Durkheim,[5] who is also credited with providing the framework that produced the phrase "structural-functional."[6]

> Alfred Reginald Radcliffe-Brown, the principal theoretician of this movement, was quite explicit about Durkheim's role. On the one hand he hailed Durkheim's definition of "function" as "the first systematic formulation of the concept [as] applying to the strictly scientific study of society" . . . On the other, he explicitly rejected definitions of function which did not relate to "social structure," a concept which can be shown to derive its main inspiration from Durkheim's emphasis upon social solidarity. The combination of

1. Roger M. Keesing & Felix M. Keesing, New Perspectives in Cultural Anthropology 388 (1971).

2. *Id.*

3. *Id.*

4. Mark Abrahamson, Functionalism 6 (1978).

5. Marvin Harris, The Rise of Anthropological Theory: A History of Theories of Culture 515 (updated ed., 2001).

6. *Id.*

"function" with "social structure" gave rise to the awkward but descriptive label, "structural-functional."[7]

Under this approach, every society was regarded as a functionally integrated whole—that is, a complete normative structure. The functional method studied the interrelationships between the social groupings that composed the whole and were organized along territorial, kinship, political, and other lines.[8] Emulating the methods and aspirations of the physical sciences, the functionalists set for themselves the task of providing scientific explanations for cultural differences and similarities, that is, generalizations that were verifiable on the basis of data gathered through improved standards of fieldwork and organized ethnographic frameworks.[9]

Explored here are the contributions of three dominant figures of the structural-functionalist school: Emile Durkheim, Bronislaw Malinowski, and A. R. Radcliffe-Brown.

Durkheim: Social Solidarity and the Collective Consciousness

As noted above, the functionalists believed that society has a systemic order, that it is highly integrated by a web of interrelated units making up the whole, with social solidarity as the glue that holds the units together and promotes overall normative order.[10] Discussed first is Durkheim's concept of social solidarity, followed by a description of his functionalist methodology.

In his famous 1893 book, *The Division of Labor*, Durkheim divided social solidarity into two evolutionary categories: mechanical and organic. The former refers to primitive society without a highly developed division of labor. In a society characterized by mechanical solidarity, segments are more or less homogeneous and consequently lack a strong collective consciousness.[11] He further posited that the absence of a binding collective consciousness could give rise to despotism because "Where individuals are in simple dependence upon the collective type, they quite naturally become dependent upon the central authority in which it is incarnated."[12]

Durkheim believed that as a society evolved and developed a more sophisticated system of division of labor, mechanical solidarity would transform itself into the second stage, organic solidarity,[13] which he defined as a society of highly specialized and differentiated individuals dependent for survival on one another and upon

---

7. *Id.* (quoting A.R. Radcliffe-Brown, Structure and Function in Primitive Society 178 (1952)).

8. Radcliffe-Brown, Structure and Function, *supra* note 7, at 190–93.

9. *Id.* at 178–79, 187. Harris, *supra* note 5, at 522.

10. Emile Durkheim, The Division of Labor in Society 63–64, 174 (George Simpson trans., 1933); Paul Bohannan & Mark Glazer, High Points in Anthropology 233 (2d ed., 1988).

11. Durkheim, Division of Labor (Simpson, trans.), *supra* note 10, at 181.

12. *Id.* at 180.

13. *Id.* at 174–81.

the collective consciousness.[14] These individuals would have specific roles in society, resulting directly from the relatively higher development of their division of labor. As a consequence of their new societal position, individuals in this type of society would not be grouped together by lineage, as in societies characterized by mechanical solidarity, but instead would be grouped around occupation.[15]

Durkheim saw no necessary correlation between overall happiness and advances in the division of labor.[16] In his view, the division of labor emerged as a normative arrangement for reducing competition.[17]

> In the same city, different occupations can co-exist without being obliged mutually to destroy one another, for they pursue different objects . . . Each of them can attain his end without preventing the others from obtaining theirs . . . Since they perform different services, they can perform them parallelly.[18]

Different and/or parallel functions not only are a healthy manifestation of the division of labor, but the latter becomes the "essential condition" of social solidarity.[19]

Social Solidarity and Social Determinism in Evolutionary Context

A society in which the totality of beliefs and sentiments are more or less common to all its members (*i.e.*, a collective type of society) is characterized by a form of solidarity that Durkheim called "mechanical."[20] A society in which social solidarity is the result of relations between different specialized functions (by which he meant division of labor) will have what he called "organic" solidarity. Following is a more detailed explanation of these two uniquely Durkheimian notions in an evolutionary context.

In the collective type, members share a greater number of sentiments in common than they hold individually. The degree of mechanical solidarity is proportional to the intensity with which group ideas and sentiments dominate over personal ones. When they dominate completely, this form of solidarity is at its maximum. In this type of society, individual consciousness is completely overwhelmed and "individuality is nil."[21] The individual is just a part of a "horde" or of homogeneous segmentary clans so similar to one another that group sentiments leave no room for individualism.[22] Durkheim emphasized that the social tendencies in such a society move together only

---

14. *Id.*
15. *Id.* at 182.
16. Durkheim, Division of Labor (Simpson trans.), *supra* note 10, at 250.
17. *Id.* at 266–67.
18. *Id.* at 267.
19. *Id.* at 400.
20. *Id.* at 130.
21. Durkheim, Division of Labor (Simpson trans.), *supra* note 10, at 130.
22. *Id.* at 174.

to the extent that they cannot move individually. Hence the term "mechanical," which invokes an analogy with the cohesion of the elements of inanimate bodies (*i.e.*, in which any kind of thought process is definitely ruled out). According to this view, just as a person may do as he wishes with a thing he possesses, so society may do as it wishes with any individual member. "The individual conscience is simply a reflection of the collective type and follows all of its movements as the possessed object follows those of its owner."[23] In societies of this type, personal rights are not distinguished from property rights. They are in the phase of "communism" because the special cohesion of this type "swallows up the individual within the group."[24]

A society in which there is a division of labor is the opposite of the collective type. Individuals resemble each other in the latter, whereas the former presumes their difference. The collective type is possible only insofar as the individual is subsumed by society, whereas a society with division of labor is possible only if each individual has his own sphere of autonomy and personality.[25] Here society cedes greater freedom to the individual to perform specialized tasks that it cannot itself discharge. Each specialist then depends on other specialists for his or her well-being. There is a functional coordination and integration of the professions that make up society as a whole. The greater the coordination and integration, the greater the cohesion and solidarity. However, the dependence of individuals on society increases with the growing division of labor. Conversely, the more specialized the individual, the more personal his or her activity.[26] This tension results in a certain harmony between the state and the individual that enables greater possibilities of collective movement as each person acquires the freedom of personal movement. Durkheim analogously uses the term "organic" to describe this kind of solidarity: as each organ of an animal has its own physiognomy and performs its part, the unity of the organism as a whole increases. In other words: "[As] the unity of the organism increases the more marked the individuality of its parts . . . By virtue of this analog we propose to call the solidarity which is due to the division of labor, organic."[27]

Durkheim's social typology, which is evolutionary in nature, adopts the view that mechanical and organic solidarity are subsequent evolutionary phases. He refers to this progression as "a law of history,"[28] by which the division of labor and its corresponding form of solidarity mark the dawn of "civilization."[29] Unlike Lewis Henry Morgan's multistaged evolutionary scale, Durkheim proposed a system of phases, of which organic solidarity (civilization) is apparently the last. Nor did he view the achievement of civilization as a matter of social planning or consciously designed

23. Emile Durkheim: Selections from his Work 42, at 44 (George Simpson ed., 1963).

24. Emile Durkheim, The Division of Labor in Society 130 (W.D. Halls trans., 1984).

25. Durkheim, Division of Labor (Simpson trans.), *supra* note 10, at 131.

26. *Id.*

27. Durkheim: Selections from his work, *supra* note 23, at 44.

28. Durkheim, Division of Labor (Halls trans.), *supra* note 24, at 126.

29. Durkheim, Division of Labor (Simpson trans.), *supra* note 10, at 336.

social engineering, much less a utilitarian construct. Instead, he described it simply as the natural and inevitable consequence of the increase of social "density."

> Civilization too is an inexorable result of the changes occurring in the volume and in the density of societies. The development of science, art, and economic activity derives from human necessity. Men cannot exist without them under the new conditions into which they are thrust. When the number of individuals involved in social relations grows larger, they can survive only by increased specialization, by increased labor, by great refinement of their capacities. From this wholesale excitation there must come a higher degree of culture. Looked at in this way, civilization emerges not as a goal urging peoples on by its attractiveness to them, not as a thing of value foreseen and longed for, of which they seek to appropriate as much as possible by every means possible, but civilization emerges as the effect of a cause, as the inevitable result of a fixed situation. It is not the lodestar leading on historical development, the end which men seek to get closer to in order to be happier or morally better. Neither happiness nor morality necessarily increases with life's intensity. Men proceed because they have to; the speed of their procession depends upon the greater or lesser strength of the pressure they exert on one another, strength itself dependent upon their numbers.
>
> But the above must not be taken to mean that civilization serves no purpose but rather that the services it renders are not the cause of its progress. It develops because it cannot fail to develop. Once on its way this development is found to be generally useful or at least utilizable. It fulfills needs aroused simultaneously with it since these needs depend upon the same causes. But this adjustment to needs occurs after the fact. Moreover, we must not overlook the fact that the benefits thus rendered by civilization are not clear-cut wealth, not a growth in our capital stock of happiness, but are merely reparation for the losses it causes. This hyperactivity in general existence tires and weakens our nervous system so that we need reparation sufficient to recoup our losses, that is, we need more varied and sophisticated types of satisfaction. Accordingly it becomes even clearer that civilization cannot realistically be made the aim and purpose of the division of labor. Rather is civilization merely a backlash. Civilization can explain neither the existence nor the advances of the division of labor since no inherent and absolute value inheres in it. Rather, on the contrary, civilization has a basis for existence only to the extent that the division of labor is itself found to be indispensable.[30]

The first idea in this passage concerns the familiar evolutionist view that population growth spurs technological innovation. The latter is a matter of "human necessity," a self-evident truth requiring no empirical proof. Second is the idea that when certain conditions of social morphology are ripe (*e.g.*, population density, its distribution in the structure of society, and its effect on the environment), specialization

30. DURKHEIM: SELECTIONS FROM HIS WORKS, *supra* note 23, at 51–52.

necessarily emerges among members of the group, to the point that "they can survive only by increased specialization." Third, as specialization becomes entrenched there emerges "a higher degree of culture" that is synonymous with civilization. Fourth, the achievement of civilized normative order is not a utilitarian endeavor—one that is desire-dependent—but the "inexorable" result of social forces.

One may ask whether, when Durkheim asserts that civilization is the "effect of a cause," he is asserting a binary cause–effect relationship between social forces and culture. Was he claiming that social forces that demand individual specializations are caused by civilization, or was he making the opposite claim that specializations (at the individual level) are the driving force of culture? If the latter, perhaps it amounts to a Copernican reversal of the traditional evolutionist as well as the historical particularist view of the relationship between culture patterns (*i.e.*, civilization) and individual behavior (*i.e.*, specialization). If so, he would of course be diverging from the cultural determinism of Franz Boas, Alfred Kroeber, Edward Sapir, Ruth Benedict, and Margaret Mead, who believed that unconscious pressure of culture determines individual behavior.

In fact, Durkheim did not intend such a reversal. His reference to "a higher *degree* of culture" refers to technological and evolutionary factors and not to culture at all ("culture" here meaning progress in educational, artistic, aesthetic, and other achievements normally associated with culture). His concept of civilization is similarly a measure of social morphology that includes improved material conditions of life. In the foregoing passage, Durkheim states clearly that the new solidarity characteristic of civilization is the "effect" of the interactions inherent to the state of specialization that in and of themselves become necessary for survival. Specialization must be understood in its broadest economic sense, to include means of production as well as the relations among production, distribution, and consumption.

Durkheim used the descriptive phrases "organic solidarity," "mechanical solidarity," and "civilization" to denote distinct evolutionary phases of human society. Within these phases, he acknowledged—in the Boasian tradition—that "Men proceed because they have to." In the next section, we see that the discipline of sociology explains normative rules of behavior ("social facts") in civilized society as independent of individual will, and views such rules as factors that constrain, control, and even coerce individual behavior. In the above passage, in particular with this statement, Durkheim returns to the historical/particularist fold by affirming his belief in the absence of individual choice and asserting that the social psyche is not only independent of the individual psyche but has a coercive force, although of unknown origin. Nevertheless, he also felt that the reward for such conformity and coercion is greater individual fulfillment, even as they allow society to flourish as an organic whole.

Durkheim also emphasized culture and collective emotions in his view of the role of the state, whose "foremost function is . . . to defend the common consciousness from all its enemies."[31] He felt as well that even as the state guards the common consciousness, it may slip into a tyrannical or despotic role to which the individual

31. Durkheim, Division of Labor (Halls trans.), *supra* note 24, at 42.

acquiesces without much (if any) resistance. Here we see an obvious similarity to the ideas of Sapir, Benedict, and Mead about the unconscious patterning of behavior through submission to superior culture forces. In the end, however, Durkheim felt that due to action at the individual and subgroup levels, as well the division of labor, individual diversity would have greater play, to the point of becoming a "right" against collective tyranny.[32] Indeed, he wrote that "governmental absolutism" does not arise from the congenital nature of society per se, but from "individual, transitory, and contingent conditions."[33] Thus he couples a good measure of idealism to his social determinism. Even though people submit to the state, the latter is not an inherently pathological institution. Ultimately society in a strong state with the optimal division of labor will flourish.

Society and Law

Law plays an indispensable role in Durkheim's social morphology; he advanced three bold metatheses about its role.[34] The first was that law is the "external symbol" of social solidarity; as such, it serves as an index of social development. The second was that as society evolves from the collective type to one with specializations (*i.e.*, from mechanical to organic forms of solidarity), the law evolves from a "repressive" nature to a "restitutive" condition. The third thesis used the idea of sanction in law; for example, punishments inflicted by law are designed to preserve the common consciousness of society. We have already seen the governmental corollary in the quotation above, in which Durkheim linked the prime function of the state to the preservation and protection of "the common consciousness." By giving law an identical function, he made it the central political instrument of the state—which would thereby discharge its mission.

Durkheim did not engage research that can be called ethnographic in the modern sense, but he did study the development of the laws of ancient Greece and Egypt, the Law of the Twelve Tables of Rome (*Lex Duodecim Tabularum*), the biblical law of the Pentateuch, the laws of the Manu, the Salic law of the Franks, and ancient Jewish law. These extensive studies led him to conclude that the stage of social development determined the extent to which law was repressive or restitutive.[35]

Durkheim's three metatheses, though very much intertwined in the body of his thought, are not expressly laid out *seriatim* in his writings. Nevertheless, they serve as useful analytical devices to anchor his doctrine of law. To explain this doctrine and

---

32. Emile Durkheim, Professional Ethics and Civic Morals 61–62 (Cornelia Brookfield trans., 1958), *reprinted in* Emile Durkheim: Sociologist of Modernity at 181 (Mustafa Emirbayer ed., 2003). See *also* Emile Durkheim: *Two Laws of Penal Evolution*, *in* Emile Durkheim: On Institutional Analysis (Mark Traugott ed., trans., 1978), *reprinted in* Emile Durkheim: Sociologist of Modernity 171 (Mustafa Emirbayer ed., 2003).

33. Durkheim, *Two Laws*, Sociologist of Modernity, *supra* note 32, at 172.

34. Steven Lukes & Andrew Scull, *Introduction*, *in* Durkheim and the Law 1, 1 (Steven Lukes & Andrew Scull eds., 1983).

35. *See, e.g.*, Durkheim, Division of Labor (Halls trans.), *supra* note 24, at 35, 94–95, 109–15.

its three grand conceptions, it is first necessary to restate Durkheim's psychosociological conception of crime; this undergirds all three theses, especially the third. In short, an act is a crime if it offends the collective consciousness.[36] According to him, this simple definition is frequently misunderstood as referring not to the essential characteristic of crime but to one of its consequences or "repercussions." In other words, since crime offends general sentiments, it is often thought that the criminal nature of the act defines these sentiments, rather than vice versa. Durkheim's point in terms of law was that if the act defines the general sentiments, then the act itself remains undefined and thus cannot be considered criminal. He therefore reverses the binary opposition between crime and sentiment. Instead of asserting that an act offends general sentiments because it is criminal, he maintains that the act is criminal because it offends the sentiments: "We do not condemn it because it is a crime, but it is a crime because we condemn it."[37] Not only is it the psychosociological element embedded in the general consciousness that defines crime, the existence of crime paradoxically ends up strengthening solidarity because crime compels social bonding through the condemnation of antisocial behavior.[38]

Durkheim deliberately eschews any attempt to minutely define solidarity or consciousness. Instead, he is content with the notion that the latter is made up of primary "sentiments," "dispositions," and "tendencies" that are normative in nature and are strongly felt and internalized community-wide. All values, including what is good or bad, are derived from these social dispositions. Thus we do not like something because it is good; rather, it is good because we like it. The clear implication is that there are no universal or objective goods, since such notions are relative to the society in which they take hold and can change. It follows that there are no norms that are universal; they exist only to pursue the particular values of particular societies. In the excerpt that follows, Durkheim explains this point as well as his binary reversal of the opposition between crime and sentiment pertaining to his three theses, particularly the third (the law punishes conduct that offends the common consciousness).

Emile Durkheim, The Division of Labor in Society 47–49 (W.D. Halls trans. 1984) *reprinted in* Durkheim and the Law 47–49 (Steven Lukes & Andrew Scull eds., 1983).

[W]e may state that an act is criminal when it offends the strong, well-defined states of the collective consciousness.

Normally, this proposition is scarcely disputed, although we give it a meaning very different from the one it should have. It is taken as if it expressed, not the essential characteristic of crime, but one of its repercussions. We well know that crime offends very general sentiments, but ones

36. *Id.* at 39.

37. *Id.* at 40.

38. *Id.* at 58, 63.

which are strongly held. But it is believed that their generality and strength spring from the criminal nature of the act, which consequently still remains wholly to be defined. It is not disputed that any criminal act excites universal disapproval, but it is taken for granted that this results from its criminal nature. Yet one is then hard put to it to state what is the nature of this criminality. Is it in a particularly serious form of immorality? I would concur, but this is to answer a question by posing another, by substituting one term for another. For what immorality *is* is precisely what we want to know—and particularly that special form of immorality which society represses by an organized system of punishments, and which constitutes criminality. Clearly it can only derive from one of several characteristics common to all varieties of crime. Now the only characteristic to satisfy that condition refers to the opposition that exists between crime of any kind and certain collective sentiments. It is thus this opposition which, far from deriving from the crime, constitutes the crime. In other words, we should not say that an act offends the common consciousness because it is criminal, but that it is criminal because it offends that consciousness. We do not condemn it because it is a crime, but it is a crime because we condemn it. As regards the intrinsic nature of these feelings, we cannot specify what that is. They have very diverse objects, so that they cannot be encompassed within a single formula. They cannot be said to relate to the vital interests of society or to a minimum of justice. All such definitions are inadequate. But by the mere fact that a sentiment, whatever may be its origin and purpose, is found in every consciousness endowed with a certain degree of strength and precision, every act which disturbs it is a crime. Present-day psychology is increasingly turning back to Spinoza's idea that things are good because we like them, rather than that we like them because they are good. What is primary is the tendency and disposition: pleasure and pain are only facts derived from this. The same holds good for social life. An act is socially evil because it is rejected by society. But, it will be contended, are there no collective sentiments which arise from the pleasure or pain which society feels when it comes into contact with their objects? This is doubtless true, but all such sentiments do not originate in this way. Many, if not the majority, derive from utterly different causes. Anything which obliges our activity to take on a definite form can give rise to habits which result in dispositions which then have to be satisfied. Moreover, these dispositions alone are truly basic ones. The others are only special forms of them, and are more determinate. Thus to find charm in a particular object, collective sensibility must already have been so constituted as to be able to appreciate it. If the corresponding sentiments are abolished, an act most disastrous for society will not only be able to be tolerated, but honoured and held up as an example. Of itself pleasure is incapable of creating a disposition out of nothing; it can only link those dispositions which already exist to a particular end, provided that end is in accord with their original nature.

The other two components of his meta–legal thesis are, first, that the law serves as an index of social development, and second that as society evolves (according to the "law of history") from mechanical to organic forms of solidarity, so the law evolves from its prior repressive nature to a restitutive condition. Durkheim begins his first thesis with the premise that social solidarity is a "moral phenomenon which by itself is not amenable to exact observation and especially not to measurement."[39] Due to this absence of a criterion internal to solidarity, which would allow its measurement, Durkheim substitutes the external criterion of law. He regards law as a "visible symbol" of solidarity, and therefore uses it as his key methodological tool to examine solidarity empirically.[40] He also considers law to be the eternally true reflection of solidarity because *ubi societas ibi ius*. Thus law is one of those inevitable effects of a cause (in this case, social solidarity).

Because law reproduces the main forms of solidarity, the first step in Durkheim's methodology involves the classification of different types of law to investigate the different types of solidarity they reflect. This step merges with the second, which is based on the idea of sanction in law. Because every legal rule contains a sanction whose severity is a reflection of the importance attached to the rule by the public consciousness, Durkheim proposes to classify rules of law according to the nature of the sanctions they embody. Accordingly, he identifies two types of sanctions: repressive and restitutory. The former impose some pain or injury on the perpetrator, whereas the latter are aimed at restoring the *status quo ante*. Penal and religious law fall under the first category; civil, commercial, procedural, administrative, and constitutional law fall under the second.[41]

Penal laws mandate the infliction of pain in the name of the group. Such treatment is based on an emotional reaction that causes the offender to suffer for the sake of suffering, which thereby assuages intense group feelings.[42] Such feelings, which are the source of the unity and identity of the group, are to be found in the collective type whose predominant form of solidarity is mechanical. In such a society, far from destroying the bonds of solidarity, crime has the consequence of actually strengthening them. Thus Durkheim holds to the somewhat controversial view that a certain measure of crime is normal for a healthy society.[43]

Restitutive law is found in secular societies with specialized functions characterized by the division of labor.[44] But there is not a complete absence of penal law in

39. *Id.* at 24.

40. Law is a "visible symbol" in that it reflects the two forms of solidarity as well as their corresponding collective emotions.

41. Durkheim, Division of Labor (Halls trans.), *supra* note 24, at 29.

42. For examples of some particularly gruesome and cruel punishments, *see*, Emile Durkheim, *Two Laws of Penal Evolution*, 4 Année Sociologique 65 (T. Anthony Jones & Andrew Scull trans., 1901), *reprinted in* Durkheim and the Law, *supra* note 34 at 102, 108.

43. Emile Durkheim, Rules of the Sociological Method 67 (8th ed., Sarah A. Solovay & John H. Mueller trans., George Catlin ed., 1938).

44. Durkheim, *Two Laws in* Durkheim and The Law, *supra* note 34, at 39–57.

such societies; instead, "there are . . . administrative and governmental functions where certain relationships are regulated by repressive law, because of the special character marking the organ of the common consciousness."[45] These are exceptional cases, however. In the following passage, Durkheim compares restitutive and repressive law:

> The very nature of the restitutory sanction is sufficient to show that the social solidarity to which that law corresponds is of a completely different kind.
>
> The distinguishing mark of this sanction is that it is not expiatory but comes down to a mere *restoration of the "status quo ante."* Suffering proportioned to his offence is not inflicted upon him who has broken the law or has failed to realize it; he is merely condemned to submit to it. If certain acts have already been performed, the judge restores them to what they should be. He pronounces what the law is, but does not talk of punishment. Damages awarded have no penal character: they are simply the means of putting back the clock so as to restore the past, so far as possible, to its normal state.[46]

Here, Durkheim describes the evolution of society from repressive to restitutive law (from quantitative to qualitative punishment) as accompanied by a corresponding diminution in the intensity and religiosity of group feelings.[47] Public wrongs are deemphasized in favor of private wrongs.[48] Indeed, rules whose sanction is restitutory and designed to redress private wrongs are not part of the collective consciousness; moreover, the more the law is restitutory the more independent it becomes of this consciousness.[49] This independence is reinforced by the fact that restitutory law demands specialized bodies, tribunals, and courts staffed by officials with special training.

However, Durkheim also insists that such legal evolution is not the result of political theory, values, or beliefs. Instead it is promoted by changes in the organizational structure of societies over long historical periods—changes over which individuals have no control. Thus, social forces dictate change. This conclusion is consistent with Durkheim's psychosociological belief that society lays down the law through the bodies that represent it.[50] Thus the resolution of a dispute between two private parties, such as a divorce, is the result of a social intervention rather than mere arbitration.[51] Although marriage is a private contract, neither party to it can terminate it at will without resort to the law. Even more fundamentally, the contract of marriage itself

---

45. Durkheim, Division of Labor (Hall trans.), *supra* note 24, at 82.

46. *Id.* at 68 (emphasis in original).

47. Durkheim, *Two Laws*, *supra* note 42 at 116.

48. *Id.* at 122.

49. Durkheim, Division of Labor (Halls trans.), *supra* note 24, at 69.

50. *Id.* at 70. *See also* Emile Durkheim, *Review of Gaston Richard's "Essai Sur l'Origine de l'Idée de Droit,"* 35 Revue Philosophique 290 (Andrew Scull trans., 1893), *reprinted in* Durkheim and the Law, *supra* note 34, at 148–49 (explaining that peaceful settlement of disputes ("arbitration") in civilized systems is inspired by the collective conscience of society at large).

51. Durkheim, Division of Labor (Halls trans.), *supra* note 24, at 70.

presupposes a social structure of the family, about which there is nothing contractual. By this logic, marriage rests on the family, not the family on marriage. This reversal of a binary opposition is reminiscent of Durkheim's reversal of the binary opposition between crime and sentiment.[52] Both were intended to emphasize the psychosociological foundations of human institutions.

> There may be, for instance, two families, A. and B.; a woman leaves A. to go off with a man of B. and becomes in some respects an integral part of this group. A change has been brought about in the scale of the families. If this change occurs peacefully, with the consent of the two families concerned, we then get, in more or less rudimentary form, the marriage contract. Hence it follows that marriage, being of necessity a contract, pre-supposes an existing structure of the family that has nothing contractual about it. This is one proof the more that marriage rests on the family and not the family on marriage.[53]

Durkheim emphasizes the same psychosociological foundations of myriad other rules and institutions of administrative law and contract law generally. He defines a contract as a "juridical moral bond" that creates "a relation *conceived by the public consciousness* as existing between two subjects, individual or collective, or between these subjects and a thing, and by virtue of which, one of the parties in question has at least a certain right over the other."[54]

Notably, in Durkheim's view, law not only plays a central role in the civilized normative order but is in fact an "index" of its sophistication:

> In the end this law plays a part analogous in society to that of the nervous system in the organism. That system, in effect, has the task of regulating the various bodily functions in such a way that they work harmoniously together. Thus it expresses in a very natural way the degree of concentration that the organism has reached as a result of the physiological division of labour. Therefore we can at the different levels of the animal scale ascertain the measure of that concentration according to the development of the nervous system. Likewise this means that we can ascertain the measure of concentration that a society has reached through the social division of labour, according to the development of co-operative law with its restitutory sanctions.[55]

Law, Social Solidarity, and Morality

Because Durkheim believed that social solidarity is a "moral phenomenon which by itself is not amenable to exact observation,"[56] he examined law as the "external visible symbol" of solidarity to study social solidarity and concluded that there is

---

52. *See* text at note 37 *supra*.

53. Durkheim, Professional Ethics, *supra* note 32, at 177.

54. *Id.* at 176 (emphasis added).

55. Durkheim, Division of Labor (Halls trans.), *supra* note 24, at 83.

56. *See* text at note 39 *supra*.

a necessary connection between law and morality. Moreover, he believed that the "higher degree of culture" (synonymous with civilization) is achieved through increased specialization, and that these conditions are not brought about due to utilitarian considerations but rather the "inexorable" progress of humanity according to the laws of history.[57]

According to Durkheim, morality is also not the product of any kind of utilitarian calculus. Moral rules are not designed to satisfy individual wants and desires or maximize the happiness of the greatest number of people in society. Neither is morality other-oriented in the sense of acting for the good of others, although he does argue that acts benefiting particular others would necessarily exclude the rest of the members of society. Therefore, morality can only be conceived as impersonal duties owed to society at large, although in discharging these duties particular others may benefit in certain circumstances. In short, only those rules that promote and protect social solidarity can be called moral.[58]

According to Durkheim, morality is made up of a totality of general precepts from which specific moral norms are derived. There are no metaphysical abstractions from which morality is derived; rather, morality reflects the ethos of particular societies. Therefore, given the existence of "so vast and varied a world," no *a priori* universal philosophical system is possible.[59] This conclusion reflects the particularist/relativist approach of Durkheimian sociology.

In this view, morality develops within a society because certain general precepts of acting and thinking become popular and then crystallize into moral rules that largely reflect solidarity and foster a sense of belongingness or attachment of the individual to his group.[60] As they mark the boundary between what is individual and what is social, they acquire a normative force and prestige of their own and "impose themselves on (us) by virtue of their authority."[61] These ways of acting, which have an official imprimatur, are transmitted through education, writings, and repeated behavior. This public and official recognition is key, but recognition alone is not sufficient. The morality must be operative; it is thus a product of experience. It is studied *ex post facto* and is not a product of an *a priori* scheme: "Morality does not have to be constructed from fundamentals . . . we only have to supervise its workings."[62] Of course morality would not be operational without the prior understanding by the individual, as a rational and autonomous being, of its precepts.[63]

---

57. *See* text at note 30 *supra*.

58. Emile Durkheim, Moral Education: A Study in the Theory and Application of the Sociology of Education 58–59 (Everett K. Wilson & Herman Schnurer trans., 1961).

59. Roger Cotterrell, Emile Durkheim: Law in a Moral Domain 56 (1999) (quoting Emile Durkheim, *Définition du fait moral* (1893)).

60. Durkheim, Moral Education, *supra* note 58, at 117 (asserting that "we understand the *raison d'être* of moral rules, from the moment that we conform voluntarily to them").

61. *Id.* at 116.

62. Emile Durkheim, *Review: Levy-Bruhl, La morale et la science des moeurs, in* Durkheim: Essays on Morals and Education 29, 32 (W.S.F. Pickering ed., H.L. Sutcliffe trans., 1979).

63. Durkheim, Moral Education, *supra* note 58, at 116, 118.

Durkheim advanced a concept of the collective consciousness, which he viewed as being made up of a complex set of collective beliefs, ideas, understandings, interpretations and perceptions, or "representations."[64] All normative institutions of society (family, marriage, property, money, etc.) reflect these collective representations. Morality is concerned with duties of the individual within the context of these collective representations, and law provides the concrete criteria for these duties. Otherwise, morality would remain an abstraction. Durkheim's approach to the phenomenon of law and morality is well illustrated by his reference to a contract as a "juridical moral bond." To him, it is first and foremost a moral bond, but the law steps in to add specific juridical criteria (*e.g.*, contract formation, dissolution, breach) and its sanctions are official, organized, and predictable. Similarly, law provides the criteria for dissolving marriage, inheritance of property, uses of money, and so on.[65] Thus he believed that morality, conceived in terms of operative duties, is most efficacious when it is embodied in law but also has the broader function of sharpening the locus of individuals' social identity. Morality thus has a broader scope than law and is more diffuse as well.

Nevertheless, Durkheim insisted, both morality and law are social realities. His functional methodology sought to explain their fundamental connection: "This is why morality as a social fact, revealed by sociological inquiry, finds substantial expression in law."[66] When there is a fundamental schism between law and social morality, as when a dictatorial government imposes laws that are inconsistent with the basic tenets of the morality of its society, such a regime will not last long.[67] National systems must also conform with basic tenets of international solidarity; when they do not, they may pay the ultimate price of war and defeat.

Durkheim did not believe that giving expression to morality is the law's sole mission. He saw law as a political instrument of the government that, as such, can be used in nonmoral regulatory contexts. In these contexts the law could end up overregulating or not regulating well. An example of poor regulation witnessed by Durkheim involved inadequate governmental regulation of the economy during an age of industrial innovation and economic expansion. The rapid expansion and conflict between capital and labor created economic dislocation as well as an abnormal division of labor.[68] He concluded from this experience that law can perpetuate such "anomie" (*i.e.*, by forcing an abnormal division of labor) instead of curing it. The task of the state would then be law reform to create a more harmonious division of labor

---

64. Emile Durkheim, *Individual and Collective Representations*, *in* Emile Durkheim, Sociology and Philosophy at 2 (D.F. Pocock trans., 1953). Cotterrell, *supra* note 59, at 54 (citing Emile Durkheim, The Rules of the Sociological Method and Selected Texts on Sociology and Its Method 247 (W.D. Halls trans., 1982)).

65. Cotterrell, *supra* note 59, at 54–55 (citing Durkheim, *Définition du fait moral*, *supra* note 59, at 277).

66. Cotterrell, *supra* note 59, at 56.

67. Emile Durkheim, Professional Ethics, *supra* note 32, at 87.

68. Durkheim, Division of Labor (Simpson trans.), *supra* note 10, at 354, 366.

and to promote social solidarity that in turn would essentially moderate competition instead of exacerbating it.[69]

Durkheim also assigned legal and moral rules the role of social intervention in case of deviance, in the form of sanctions. Legal sanctions are official and organized, as discussed already. A legal sanction, in short, is "the consequence of an act that does not result from the content of the act, but from the violation by that act of a pre-established rule."[70] Because social facts take the form of constraints, moral sanctions function as the external constraints of moral rules (a conclusion that further affirms his conviction that every moral rule is a social fact). It must be emphasized that in Durkheim's definition, sanctions are triggered not by the content of a rule but by its breach, and that a sanction can be negative (*e.g.*, punishment) or positive (*e.g.*, praise or honor).[71]

Durkheim's conflation of moral and legal, and his equation of positive and negative sanctions, creates difficulties. For example, sanctions that are strictly legal rarely, if ever, trigger praise or honor. He further leaves his readers with the impression that morality is diffused throughout the consciousness and that law, although reflective of morality, has a somewhat narrower scope. Thus his boundary between moral and legal rules is very nebulous. Perhaps this was not important for Durkheim's purposes, as explained by Roger Cotterrell:

> Durkheim's identification of moral rules is far from rigorous. But perhaps it is sufficient for his purposes. His category of moral rules ranges from the fundamental to the seemingly trivial. The word *moeurs*, which he often uses, refers to manners and customs as well as morals. Perhaps for his purposes there is no need to distinguish sociologically the various categories of social rules mentioned above. All, in one way or another, are constraining social facts. All have sociological significance as sanctioned rules of conduct. This conclusion would explain why, when he does wish to identify clearly a category of moral rules that he sees as socially most significant and imperative—given that they attract special social processes for their sanctioning—he has no hesitation to identifying them as *law*. Law and morality are 'too intimately related to be radically separated'; they are 'inseparable and arise from one and the same science'. So morality in the broadest sense—as mores or *moeurs*—can be thought of as a vast spectrum. It ranges from the most insignificant expectations about social interaction to the most insistent and enduring, the most fiercely defended, the most publicly sanctioned.
>
> As we should expect, legal rules, for Durkheim, differ from other moral rules only in degree. While most jurists are anxious to mark out a distinct realm of law apart from morality, Durkheim's sociological purposes are quite

69. *Id.* at 365.

70. Emile Durkheim, *The Determination of Moral Facts*, in DURKHEIM, SOCIOLOGY AND PHILOSOPHY, *supra* note 64, at 43.

71. *Id.*, at 43–44.

different. Law is a particular way in which the sanctioning of moral rules may be carried out. Legal sanctions are not distinguished by their intrinsic character. They are, indeed, sometimes 'purely moral', as where they entail 'deprivation of certain rights, such as infamy among the Romans, dishonour among the Greeks, civic degradation, etc.'. Nor are they necessarily harsher than moral sanctions. Durkheim sees penal rules as 'notable for their clarity and precision, whilst purely moral rules are generally somewhat fluid in character' but he attaches little weight to this generalisation.

The real difference is in the way sanctions are administered. Moral sanctions are *diffuse*—administered . . . by everybody without distinction'. By contrast, legal sanctions are *organised*—'applied only through the medium of a definite body'. Law has 'specially authorised representatives' charged with the task of enforcement. Its rules 'are instituted by definite organs and under a definite form and . . . the whole system which the law uses to realise its precepts is regulated and organized.'[72]

The Functionalist Method

Durkheim explained that social solidarity was reflected by a common consciousness ("conscience collective") that pervaded all segments of society and blended with individual consciousness to form a composite of ideals shared by all members of society.

> The totality of beliefs and sentiments common to average citizens of the same society forms a determinate system which has its own life; one may call it the *collective* or *common conscience* . . . It is, in effect, independent of the particular conditions in which individuals are placed; they pass on and it remains . . . Moreover, it does not change with each generation, but, on the contrary, it connects successive generations with one another. It is, thus, an entirely different thing from particular consciences, although it can be realized only through them.[73]

This passage captures perhaps the single most important theme of Durkheim's methodology: that the independent existence of social phenomena cannot be reduced to individual will.[74] Thus every social fact is to be understood in terms of its function—that is, what it contributes to the needs of collective life. Social causation can be understood only in this sense, but it also shows the irreducibility of the collective

72. COTTERRELL, *supra* note 59, at 60 (quoting Durkheim).

73. DURKHEIM, DIVISION OF LABOR (Simpson trans.), *supra* note 10, at 79–80. This translation uses the term "common conscience" instead of the term "common consciousness" which is a better translation of the French "conscience collective."

74. This view also represents a rejection by Durkheim of Spencer's notion that social harmony is the product of individual will and cooperation. *See* ELVIN HATCH, THEORIES OF MAN AND CULTURE 168–69 (1973). *See below* the excerpt from Durkheim's *Rules of the Sociological Method.*

consciousness—which, not unlike the concept of culture in the Boasian tradition, is *sui generis.*

A fundamental tenet of Durkheim's methodology is that what is social is susceptible to scientific examination. A social fact is an objective thing that is analogous to a material entity in that both have objective existence. Thus a social fact or a category of facts would consist of ways of acting, thinking, and feeling that are external to the individual and have a coercive power such that they control him.[75] To simplify, one could call a category of fact an "institution."[76] Durkheim saw society as made up of a variety of institutions. At the most general level is political society, which can be broken down into subgroups or institutions such as law, religious denominations, literary associations, political parties, occupational associations, all of them "instituted by the collectivity."[77] Each institution is normative in nature in that it has its own ways of acting and thinking that control the individuals who belong to it. Thus the proper domain of sociology is the objective and therefore scientific study of the psychosocial aspects of these institutions.

By this logic, certain social manners of acting and thinking ("currents of opinion") become well established through repetition or habit. When they are so crystallized, they mark the boundary between social and individual behavior[78] and acquire a reality of their own (*i.e.*, as objective social facts capable of being scientifically studied in isolation from the individual events that reflect them). Legal and moral rules are originated when the institutions that crystallize from currents of opinion, and their associated attitudes and behaviors, are transmitted by education and become fixed in writing and repeated behavior.[79] Durkheim recognized many other institutions and currents of opinion that influence, for example, birthrates, suicides, marriages.[80] Regardless of the results of crystallization, its hallmark is the coercive power of social facts.

> A social fact is to be recognized by the power of external coercion which it exercises or is capable of exercising over individuals, and the presence of this power may be recognized in its turn either by the existence of some specific sanction or by the resistance offered against every individual effort that tends to violate it.[81]

This statement can easily stand as a general definition of law, but Durkheim had a broader reach in mind. He was referring to all legal and nonlegal customs, practices, and attitudes at the collective level, for example, literary styles. Here we are reminded of the dress styles in Kroeber's claim that fashions are dictated by currents of popular

75. Durkheim, Rules (Solovay & Mueller trans.), *supra* note 43, at 3.

76. *Id.* at lvi.

77. *Id.*

78. *Id.* at 7.

79. *Id.*

80. Durkheim, Rules (Solovay & Mueller trans.), *supra* note 43, at 8.

81. *Id.* at 10.

opinion, as well as his superorganic, which has strong affinities with the Durkheimian notion of a supra-individual psychosocial coercive force of unknown origin.[82] Durkheim also distinguishes between direct and indirect constraints. In terms of the definition just quoted, he viewed "law, morals, beliefs, customs, and even fashions"[83] as enforced by "some direct reaction of society." Examples of indirect constraints are those that are enforced by economic associations, such as trade groups and professional organizations. The difference between a direct and indirect constraint is that the former is exercised in the name of society (presumably the state), whereas the latter is enforced by a subgroup. What is common to both types is that their norms are (1) of general application and (2) enforced externally. Thus, a social fact arises when any norm whose *raison d'être* is external to individual consciousness becomes general. In other words:

> A social fact is every way of acting, fixed or not, capable of exercising on the individual an external constraint; or again, every way of acting which is general throughout a given society, while at the same time existing in its own right independent of its individual manifestations.[84]

Although this definition may seem cumbersome, it captures the essential elements of a social norm, namely, that it is a standard of social behavior, a general norm, external to the individual, a constraint on behavior, and coercive in nature.

The definition is not without its difficulties. For example, one wonders how a norm or standard as a conceptual construct can also be a fact whose existence is studied by the sociologist. After all, the concept of norm is a mental construct and as such it cannot have a concrete material existence. A second difficulty is that sociology is ultimately a science of human behavior; as such, it is necessarily rooted in the substratum of individual behavior and individual consciousness. To build a science that is external to this substratum requires the sociologist to operate in a social vacuum.

Durkheim anticipated such criticisms and sought to refute them. With regard to the first objection, his response is essentially that knowledge in general is not based on material objects alone; one can have knowledge about nonmaterial things. He cited many objects of knowledge that for their conception require data from outside the mind, for example, from observations and experiments involving visible and invisible objects: "We assert not that social facts are material things but that they are things by the same right as material things, although they differ from them in type."[85] Durkheim recognized that such nonmaterial facts are as much a feature of reality as material ones and knowledge of them does not require any metaphysical conceptions or speculations. The sociologist studying such phenomena must realize, as does the physicist or chemist, that he is ignorant about the phenomena under study and must

82. See *supra* Chapter 2, text at note 95.

83. Durkheim, Rules (Solovay & Mueller trans.), *supra* note 43, at 10.

84. *Id.* at 13.

85. *Id.* at xliii. *See also id.* at 14 *et seq.*

investigate them with an open mind, ready for whatever surprises or disappointments may lie ahead.[86]

With regard to the second critique—that social phenomena are internal to individual consciousness and not external to it—Durkheim's response is that matters of internal consciousness are the domain of psychology, whereas collective consciousness has its own peculiar nature and must be studied in and of itself. He argues that it is easy to fall into the trap of collapsing this fundamental distinction when one thinks of certain individual habits, because habits "dominate us and impose beliefs and practices upon us."[87] However, he specified that habits rule us from within, whereas social beliefs and practices act on us from without. He concluded that in this way the influence of social beliefs differs fundamentally from the effect of habit.

For Durkheim, a social fact is to be understood in terms of the function it fulfills, rather than in terms of its end or purpose. The function in turn reveals the link between societal needs at the general level and the social fact in question, without regard to whether this correspondence is intentional. In any case, he believed that all intentionalist inquiries are too subjective to allow scientific treatment.[88]

Emile Durkheim, Rules of the Sociological Method 1, 3–4, 6–8, 10, 13, xliii, xlv, xlvii, lii–liii, lv (8th ed., Sara A. Solovay & John H. Mueller trans., George E. Catlin ed., 1938).

What Is A Social Fact?

> ... [The social realm] ... is a category of facts with very distinctive characteristics: it consists of ways of acting, thinking, and feeling, external to the individual, and endowed with a power of coercion, by reason of which they control him ... And this term fits them quite well, for it is clear that, since their source is not in the individual, their substratum can be no other than society, either the political society as a whole or some one of the partial groups it includes, such as religious denominations, political, literary, and occupational associations, etc. On the other hand, this term "social" applies to them exclusively, for it has a distinct meaning only if it designates exclusively the phenomena which are not included in any of the categories of facts that have already been established and classified. These ways of thinking and acting therefore constitute the proper domain of sociology. It is true that, when we define them with this word "constraint," we risk shocking the zealous partisans of absolute individualism. For those who profess the complete autonomy of the individual, man's dignity is diminished whenever he is made to feel that he is not completely self-determinant. It is generally accepted today, however, that most of our ideas and our tendencies are not developed

86. *Id.* at xlv, 45.

87. *Id.* at lv.

88. Durkheim, Rules (Solovay & Mueller trans.), *supra* note 43, at 95.

by ourselves but come to us from without. How can they become a part of us except by imposing themselves upon us? This is the whole meaning of our definition. And it is generally accepted, moreover, that social constraint is not necessarily incompatible with the individual personality . . .

[S]ociological phenomena cannot be defined by their universality. A thought which we find in every individual consciousness, a movement repeated by all individuals, is not thereby a social fact . . . Indeed, certain of these social manners of acting and thinking acquire, by reason of their repetition, a certain rigidity which on its own account crystallizes them, so to speak, and isolates them from the particular events which reflect them. They thus acquire a body, a tangible form, and constitute a reality in their own right, quite distinct from the individual facts which produce it. Collective habits are inherent not only in the successive acts which they determine but, by a privilege of which we find no example in the biological realm, they are given permanent expression in a formula which is repeated from mouth to mouth, transmitted by education, and fixed even in writing. Such is the origin and nature of legal and moral rules, popular aphorisms and proverbs, articles of faith wherein religious or political groups condense their beliefs, standards of taste established by literary schools, etc. . . .

Currents of opinion, with an intensity varying according to the time and place, impel certain groups either to more marriages, for example, or to more suicides, or to a higher or lower birth-rate, etc. These currents are plainly social facts . . .

We thus arrive at the point where we can formulate and delimit in a precise way the domain of sociology. It comprises only a limited group of phenomena. A social fact is to be recognized by the power of external coercion which it exercises or is capable of exercising over individuals, and the presence of this power may be recognized in its turn either by the existence of some specific sanction or by the resistance offered against every individual effort that tends to violate it. One can, however, define it also by its diffusion within the group, provided that, in conformity with our previous remarks, one takes care to add a second and essential characteristic that its own existence is independent of the individual forms it assumes in its diffusion. This last criterion is perhaps, in certain cases, easier to apply than the preceding one. In fact, the constraint is easy to ascertain when it expresses itself externally by some direct reaction of society, as is the case in law, morals, beliefs, customs, and even fashions. But when it is only indirect, like the constraint which an economic organization exercises, it cannot always be so easily detected. Generality combined with externality may, then, be easier to establish. Moreover, this second definition is but another form of the first; for if a mode of behavior whose existence is external to individual consciousness becomes general, this can only be brought about by its being imposed upon them . . .

Our definition will then include the whole relevant range of facts if we say: *A social fact is every way of acting, fixed or not, capable of exercising on the individual an external constraint; or again, every way of acting which is general throughout a given society, while at the same time existing in its own right independent of its individual manifestations . . .*

The proposition which states that social facts are to be treated as things—the proposition at the very basis of our method—is one of those which have provoked most contradiction. It has been considered not only paradoxical but ridiculous for us to compare the realities of the social world with those of the external world. But our critics have curiously misinterpreted the meaning and import of this analogy, for it was not our intention to reduce the higher to the lower forms of being, but merely to claim for the higher forms a degree of reality at least equal to that which is readily granted to the lower. We assert not that social facts are material things but that they are things by the same right as material things, although they differ from them in type . . .

Things include all objects of knowledge that cannot be conceived by purely mental activity, those that require for their conception data from outside the mind, from observations and experiments, those which are built up from the more external and immediately accessible characteristics to the less visible and more profound. To treat the facts of a certain order as things is not, then, to place them in a certain category of reality but to assume a certain mental attitude toward them on the principle that when approaching their study we are absolutely ignorant of their nature, and that their characteristic properties, like the unknown causes on which they depend, cannot be discovered by even the most careful introspection. . . .

Our principle, then, implies no metaphysical conception, no speculation about the fundamental nature of beings. What it demands is that the sociologist put himself in the same state of mind as the physicist, chemist, or physiologist when he probes into a still un-explored region of the scientific domain. When he penetrates the social world, he must be aware that he is penetrating the unknown; he must feel himself in the presence of facts whose laws are as unsuspected as were those of life before the era of biology; he must be prepared for discoveries which will surprise and disturb him. . . .

Another proposition has been argued no less vehemently than the preceding one, namely, that social phenomena are external to individuals. . . . [B]ut because society is composed only of individuals, the common-sense view still holds that sociology is a superstructure built upon the substratum of the individual consciousness and that otherwise it would be suspended in a social vacuum. . . .

In no case can sociology simply borrow from psychology any one of its principles in order to apply it, as such, to social facts. Collective thought, in its form as in its matter, must be studied in its entirety, in and for itself, with an understanding of its peculiar nature. How much it resembles the thought of individuals must be left for future investigation. It is a problem which is rather within the jurisdiction of general philosophy and abstract logic than in the science of social facts. . . .

> . . . [W]e gave definition of social facts as ways of acting or thinking with the peculiar characteristic of exercising a coercive influence on individual consciousness. Confusion has arisen on this score which requires comment. . . .
>
> The peculiar characteristics of social constraint is that it is due, not to the rigidity of certain molecular arrangements, but to the prestige with which certain representatives are invested. It is true that habits, either physical or social, have in certain respects this same feature. They dominate us and impose beliefs and practices upon us. But they rule us from within, for they are in every case an integral part of our self. On the contrary, social beliefs and practices act on us from without; thus the difference exerted by them differs fundamentally from the effects of habit.

Suicide: A Case Study in Functional Methodology

In the foregoing excerpt, Durkheim asserts that "currents of opinion, with an intensity varying according to time and place, impel certain groups either to more marriages . . . or to more suicides" and that "these currents are plainly social facts." As we have seen, he believed that a social fact is a way of acting that is general and exists independently of any individual manifestation. He devoted considerable attention to suicide as a social fact, and his conclusions are illustrative of his methodology.

Suicide would seem to be a private act committed by desperate people for subjective reasons, yet Durkheim shows that it is a subject of sociology and thus amenable to objective study. He classified and explained different types of suicide as caused by different social causes or "suicidogenetic currents,"[89] and further asserted that in contemporary society, "the rising tide of suicide originates in a pathological state just now accompanying the march of civilization."[90] His diagnosis of a pathological societal condition suggested possibilities of social reform.[91] His study of suicide also illuminates his general concepts of social integration and normative regulation, as well as some particular ones (*e.g.*, egoism, altruism, *anomie*, and fatalism) that I address only to the extent necessary to explain the methodological aspects of this suicide case study.

Durkheim identifies three institutions that affect social cohesion: religion, family, and politics. He claims that these also affect the incidence of suicide. Taking the religious factor, he notes that in the Protestant countries of Prussia, Saxony, and Denmark, the greatest numbers of suicides were found among Protestants and Catholics and the lowest numbers were among Jews. He assigns this finding to his perception that Protestantism permits greater individual freedom.

---

89. Emile Durkheim, Suicide: A Study in Sociology 366 (John A. Spaulding & George Simpson trans., 1951).

90. *Id.* at 368.

91. Sociologist of Modernity, *supra* note 32, at 31.

Regarding the family, Durkheim identifies "density" as key. If a family group is relatively small, "common sentiments and memories cannot be very intense; for there are not enough consciences in which they can be represented and reinforced by sharing them."[92] In such a group there are no powerful traditions that unite or even survive it. In other words, societies with such low levels of family integration are unstable and cannot survive long. They therefore have correspondingly higher suicide rates than families that are denser and more closely knit through common sentiments, and are thus more durable. In the political realm, Durkheim notes that great political upheavals, revolutions, and wars can rouse collective faith and stimulate patriotism that can serve as bulwarks against social threats and thereby discourage suicide.[93]

Durkheim's case study of suicide showed the phenomenon to be inversely linked to the level of social integration. The greater the integration, the more readily its cohesive force will deter suicide. Conversely, the weaker the level of integration, the greater the instances of individualism and "egoism" leading to suicide.[94] He concluded that individualism and egoism are the human consequences of the lack of social integration, an opinion he explains through his dichotomy of the "social man" and the "physical man." Social man lives in a highly integrated society with strong common sentiments and solidarity, where he flourishes because life is socially and individually fulfilling. If this integration is absent, lacking, or lost, social life loses "all objective foundation," and only the physical man is left to endure a solitary, unfulfilling existence.[95] Such a society consists of "an artificial combination of illusory images, a phantasmagoria vanishing at the least reflection; that is, nothing that can be a goal for our action."[96]

A person in this condition is "bereft of reasons for existence." However, Durkheim is quick to point out that such despair does not occur only in a single individual but is tied to the "national temperament" that estimates the value of existence and life itself. Sadness, detachment, and alienation form a collective trend or "current" that drives individuals to suicide.

Durkheim contrasts this form of egoistic suicide with what he calls altruistic suicide, which he believed to occur mainly in primitive societies and be manifestly coercive. Examples would be suicide due to old age or sickness, suicide of widows, and suicides of followers or servants on the death of their chiefs.[97] He characterized egoistic suicide as, at best, suggested or counseled, and altruistic suicide as a matter of duty. He also observed that egoistic suicide is due to excessive individuation, whereas altruistic suicide is due to rudimentary individuation.

---

92. Durkheim, Suicide, *supra* note 89, at 202.

93. *Id.* at 203.

94. *Id.* at 209.

95. *Id.* at 213.

96. *Id.*

97. Durkheim, Suicide, *supra* note 89, at 219.

The third type, anomic suicide,[98] was seen by Durkheim as the result of industrial and commercial factors. He laments the decline of religious cohesion and the decline of governmental regulation of economic life associated with the laissez-faire capitalism of his day and characterizes the condition of economic life of this period as one of "moral anarchy."[99] He asserts that the never-ending quest for increasing productivity and access to markets without proper social regulation leads to social disharmony, worker alienation, and suicide. In his major work, *The Division of Labor in Society*, he includes an entire chapter, "The Anomic Division of Labor," to a discussion of how nonregulation creates an asymmetrical division of labor and disharmony in social relations. Commentators credit Durkheim with launching a severe critique of the ideology of industrial society.[100]

Just as Durkheim placed egoistic suicide in opposition to altruistic suicide, he designated *fatalistic suicide* as the opposite of anomic. Fatalistic suicide results from overregulation, in contrast to anomic suicide, which is a result of too little regulation. Fatalism itself results from oppressive discipline that violently chokes freedom and initiative.

The following excerpt from *Suicide* presents Durkheim's main thesis on the causal connection between religious, domestic, and political integration and suicide and how suicide is evidence of an alienating and therefore a pathological trend in contemporary civilization.

Emile Durkheim, Suicide: A Study in Sociology 208–10, 213–14, 366–68 (John A. Spaulding & George Simpson trans., 1951).

We have thus successively set up three following propositions:

Suicide varies inversely with the degree of integration of religious society.
Suicide varies inversely with the degree of integration of domestic society.
Suicide varies inversely with the degree of integration of political society.

This grouping shows that whereas these different societies have a moderating influence upon suicide, this is due not to special characteristics of each but to a characteristic common to all.... The cause can only be found in a single quality possessed by all these social groups, though perhaps to varying degrees. The only quality satisfying this condition is that they are all strongly integrated social groups. So we reach the general conclusion: suicide varies inversely with the degree of integration of the social groups of which the individual forms a part.

---

98. *Id.* at 258.

99. Durkheim, Professional Ethics, *supra* note 32, at 15.

100. Cotterrell, *supra* note 59, at 183 (citing Phillippe Besnard, *Anomie and Fatalism in Durkheim's Theory of Regulation*, *in* Emile Durkheim: Sociologist and Moralist 163, 180 (S.P. Turner ed., 1993)).

But society cannot disintegrate without the individual simultaneously detaching himself from social life, without his own goals becoming preponderant over those of the community, in a word without his personality tending to surmount the collective personality. The more weakened the groups to which he belongs, the less he depends on them, the more he consequently depends only on himself and recognizes no other rules of conduct than what are founded on his private interests. If we agree to call this state egoism, in which the individual ego asserts itself to excess in the face of the social ego and at its expense, we may call egoistic the special type of suicide springing from excessive individualism. . . .

. . . What is there then in individualism that explains this result?

If, . . . as has often been said, man is double, that is because social man superimposes himself upon physical man. Social man necessarily pre-supposes a society which he expresses and serves. If this dissolves, if we no longer feel it in existence and action about and above us, whatever is social in us is deprived of all objective foundation. All that remains is an artificial combination of illusory images, a phantasmagoria vanishing at the least reflection; that is, nothing which can be a goal for our action. Yet this social man is the essence of civilized man; he is the masterpiece of existence. Thus we are bereft of reasons for existence; for the only life to which we could cling no longer corresponds to anything actual; the only existence still based upon reality no longer meets our needs. Because we have been initiated into a higher existence, the one which satisfies an animal or a child can satisfy us no more and the other itself fades and leaves us helpless. So there is nothing more for our efforts to lay hold of, and we feel them lose themselves in emptiness. . . .

But this is not all. This detachment occurs not only in single individuals. One of the constitutive elements of every national temperament consists of a certain way of estimating the value of existence. There is a collective as well as an individual humor inclining peoples to sadness or cheerfulness, making them see things in bright or somber lights. . . . As these currents are collective, they have, by virtue of their origin, an authority which they impose upon the individual and they drive him more vigorously on the way to which he is already inclined by the state of moral distress directly aroused in him by the disintegration of society. Thus, at the very moment that, with excessive zeal, he frees himself from the social environment, he still submits to its influence. However individualized a man may be, there is always something collective remaining—the very depression and melancholy resulting from this same exaggerated individualism. He effects communication through sadness when he no longer has anything else with which to achieve it. . . .

But it does not follow from the fact that a suicidogenetic current of a certain strength must be considered as a phenomenon of normal sociology, that every current of the same sort is necessarily of the same character. If the spirit of renunciation, the love of progress, the taste for individuation

> have their place in every kind of society, and cannot exist without becoming generators of suicide at certain points, it is further necessary for them to have this property only in a certain measure, varying with various peoples. It is only justified if it does not pass certain limits. Likewise, the collective penchant for sadness is only wholesome as long as it is not preponderant. So the above remarks have not settled the question whether the present status of suicide among civilized nations is or is not normal. We need further to consider whether its tremendous aggravation during the past century is not pathological in origin....
>
> ... [T]his aggravation springs not from the intrinsic nature of progress but from the special conditions under which it occurs in our day, and nothing assures us that these conditions are normal. For we must not be dazzled by the brilliant development of sciences, the arts and industry of which we are the witnesses; this development is altogether certainly taking place in the midst of a morbid effervescence, the grievous repercussions of which each one of us feels. It is then very possible and even probable that the rising tide of suicide originates in a pathological state just now accompanying the march of civilization without being its necessary condition.

Given the emphasis on the collective consciousness, it is not surprising that even so private and personal an act as taking one's own life is viewed through the collective lens. Furthermore, Durkheim's very definition of a social fact shows an uncompromising focus on societal rather than personal or individual sentiments. Durkheim thus espouses a form of cultural determinism and particularism not unlike that of the Boasian school.

In the next section, I discuss the implications such determinism has for functional methodology, the epistemic reliability of the functional method, and whether it bears out the Durkheimian claim of determinism.

Functional Methodology and Cultural/Social Determinism

For Durkheim, the collective consciousness has a source other than individual will. Boas similarly maintained that culture is something the individual simply learns rather than creates. We have seen how this view contrasts with the utilitarianism of Spencer and Tylor. Durkheim in particular showed no concern for the utilitarian measure of the greatest benefit of the greatest number, for to do so would have risked an inadmissible reductionism. Thus he saw no relevance in, for example, debates over whether social solidarity was politically useful or whether the *sui generis* nature of the collective consciousness promoted a socially useful purpose.

> To show how a fact is useful is not to explain how it originated or why it is what it is. The uses which it serves presuppose the specific properties characterizing it but do not create them. The need we have of things cannot give them existence, nor can it confer their specific nature upon them. It is to causes of another sort that they owe their existence. The idea we have of

> their utility may indeed motivate us to put these forces to work and to elicit from them their characteristic effects, but it will not enable us to produce these effects out of nothing.[101]

Utilitarianism was, for Durkheim, a signpost to individualism and reductionism—something to be avoided at all costs. Accordingly, as the next excerpt shows, the object of study had to be something that transcends the individual: "When the individual has been eliminated," Durkheim maintained, "society alone remains. We must, then, seek the explanation of social life in the nature of society itself."[102] In his view, society as a whole acquires or gives birth to a psychic individuality distinct from that of any individual member.

> It is, then, in the nature of this collective individuality, not in that of the associated units, that we must seek the immediate and determining causes of the facts appearing therein. The group thinks, feels, and acts quite differently from the way in which its members would were they isolated. If, then, we begin with the individual, we shall be able to understand nothing of what takes place in the group.[103]

Having rejected the *laissez-faire* utilitarianism of Spencer, Durkheim goes on to reject the contractarian notions of social organization of Thomas Hobbes and Jean-Jacques Rousseau by asserting that it is "contradictory" to say that the individual is himself the creator of a machine that will dominate and constrain him. To say that such domination is the product of some social contract may disguise the contradiction but does not eliminate it. According to Durkheim, constraint is simply a superior social force that is natural and to which the individual simply "bows." This superior social force may be symbolized in the form of a religion (which the individual freely accepts)[104] or it may be represented by a scientific theory (in which case it is an epistemological verity). In either case, these superior constraints (*i.e.*, the totality of social constraints) are freely accepted by the individual because the forces (in their totality) are not just physical. They are intellectual and moral as well, and the individual realizes that by accepting them his "social being" is much richer, more complex, and more stable than his "individual being." With this proposition, Durkheim achieved a reversal reminiscent of Marx's inversion of the Hegelian dialectic. Just as Marx argued that being determines consciousness and not vice versa, Durkheim asserted that sociocultural conditions determined individual consciousness: "The determining cause of a social fact should be sought among the social facts preceding it and not among the states of the individual consciousness."[105]

---

101. Durkheim, Rules (Solovay & J.H. Mueller trans.), *supra* note 43, at 90.

102. *Id.* at 102.

103. *Id.* at 103–4.

104. *See* Emile Durkheim The Elementary Forms of the Religious Life 418–19 (Joseph W. Swain trans., 1915) (arguing that the categories of religion, *e.g.*, god, soul, spirit, totem, are nothing but inventions to explain the unseen but felt power of the collective consciousness).

105. Durkheim, Rules (Solovay & Mueller trans.), *supra* note 43, at 110. *See* excerpt below.

Dichotomy between the social and the individual aspects of life is fundamental to Durkheim's functional methodology. The function of a social fact (*e.g.*, a ritual) is social and cannot do anything other than produce "socially useful effects."[106] In doing so it may (and usually does) serve the individual, but the latter is not its cause. Thus it follows for Durkheim that the function of a social fact is meaningful only insofar as it serves an end that is social rather than individual. So determined was Durkheim to maintain this rigid dichotomy that he insisted even if all individuals in society engaged in a certain act, that did not create a social fact because the underlying motivations for that act would be internal to the individuals. By contrast, the superior coercive forces to which the individual "bows" have an external source—the collective consciousness. For Durkheim, only "the collective aspects of the beliefs, tendencies and practices of a group" (in short, the social psychology) could characterize truly social phenomena.[107]

Durkheim saw culture as thus superimposing itself on and transcending individual wants; indeed, the individual must discipline himself within the parameters of the collective life because the latter is really alien to his natural self and needs. Thus, in his view, the "principle of association"[108] (that is, association of an individual to the group) is a social imperative, not a matter of choice. For its part, he saw group life as reflected in many forms (*e.g.*, symbolism and ritual) and also believed that such reflections of collective life in turn transfigure the world by superimposing special meaning and value on it. Although these meanings and values bind the group by a sense that group activity is directed by some external force, ritualistic practices are ultimately nothing more than a representation of social forces. What makes them seemingly external is that they acquire an autonomy and permanence independent of the individual. Thus, for Durkheim, symbolism and ritual serve not only as mechanisms to reinforce respect for collective life, but also as forms of social control.[109] Whereas other social thinkers, such as Boas, would not look beyond a symbol or ritual for meaning but would simply describe it as learned custom or habit, Durkheim considered behavior to be far more complex and the key to understanding the functioning of society. As he did so, he claimed that his functional methodology was epistemically reliable in that it yielded empirically verifiable truths, or knowledge, about society as it actually is.

Emile Durkheim, The Rules of Sociological Method 89–91, 101–7, 109–13, 121–24 (8th ed., Sara A. Solovay & John H. Mueller trans., George E.G. Catlin ed., 1938).

Most sociologists think they have accounted for phenomena once they have shown how they are useful, what role they play, reasoning as if facts existed

106. *Id.*

107. *Id.* at 7.

108. *Id.* at 104.

109. *Id.* at 122–24.

only from the point of view of this role and with no other determining cause than the sentiment, clear or confused, of the services they are called to render. That is why they think they have said all that is necessary, to render them intelligible, when they have established the reality of these services and have shown what social needs they satisfy. . . .

But this method confuses two very different questions. To show how a fact is useful is not to explain how it originated or why it is what it is. The uses which it serves presuppose the specific properties characterizing it but do not create them. The need we have of things cannot give them existence, nor can it confer their specific nature upon them. It is to causes of another sort that they owe their existence. . . . To give a government the authority necessary for it, it is not enough to feel the need for this authority; we must have recourse to the only sources from which all authority is derived. We must, namely, establish traditions, a common spirit, etc.; and for this it is necessary again to go back along the chain of causes and effects until we find a point where the action of man may be effectively brought to bear. . . .

If the authority before which the individual bows when he acts, feels, or thinks socially governs him to this extent, it does so because it is a product of social forces which transcend him and for which he, consequently, cannot account. The external impulse to which he submits cannot come from him, nor can it be explained by what happens within him. . . .

When the individual has been eliminated, society alone remains. We must, then, seek the explanation of social life in the nature of society itself. It is quite evident that, since it infinitely surpasses the individual in time as well as in space, it is in a position to impose upon him ways of acting and thinking which it has consecrated with its prestige. This pressure, which is the distinctive property of social facts, is the pressure which the totality exerts on the individuals. . . .

By reason of this principle, society is not a mere sum of individuals. Rather, the system formed by their association represents a specific reality which has its own characteristics. Of course, nothing collective can be produced if individual consciousnesses are not assumed; but this necessary condition is by itself insufficient. These consciousnesses must be combined in a certain way; social life results from this combination and is, consequently, explained by it. Individual minds, forming groups by mingling and fusing, give birth to a being, psychological if you will, but constituting a psychic individuality of a new sort. It is, then, in the nature of this collective individuality, not in that of the associated units, that we must seek the immediate and determining causes of the facts appearing therein. The group thinks, feels, and acts quite differently from the way in which its members would were they isolated. If, then, we begin with the individual, we shall be able to understand nothing of what takes place in the group. In a word, there is between psychology and sociology the same break in continuity as between biology and the physicochemical sciences. Consequently, every time that a social phenomenon is directly explained by a psychological phenomenon, we may be sure that the explanation is false. . . .

As a consequence of my birth, I am obliged to associate with a given group. It may be said that later, as an adult, I acquiesce in this obligation by the very fact that I continue to live in my country. But what difference does that make? This "acquiescence" is still imperative. Pressure accepted and submitted to with good grace is still pressure. . . .

We have shown, then, that the source of all that is obligatory is outside the individual. . . .

Finally, if social evolution really had its origin in the psychological constitution of man, its origin seems to be completely obscure. For we would then have to admit that its motivating force is some inner spring of human nature. But what could this be? Is it the sort of instinct Comte speaks of, which impels man more and more to express his nature? But that is begging the question and explaining progress by an innate "tendency toward progress"—a metaphysical entity of the very existence of which there is no demonstration. Even the highest animal species are not at all activated by the need to progress, and among human societies there are many which are content to remain indefinitely stationary.

Or is this motivating force, as Spencer seems to believe, the urge for greater happiness which the increasingly complex forms of civilization are designed to satisfy more and more completely? We would then have to establish the fact that happiness increases with civilization, and we have elsewhere described all the difficulties to which this hypothesis gives rise. But further, even if one or the other of these two postulates were admissible, historical development would not thereby be rendered intelligible, for the explanation which would result from it would be purely teleological. We have shown above that social facts, like all natural phenomena, are not explained by the simple consideration that they serve some end. . . .

We arrive, therefore, at the following principle: *The determining cause of a social fact should be sought among the social facts preceding it and not among the states of the individual consciousness.* Moreover, we see quite readily that all the foregoing applies to the determination of the function as well as the cause of social phenomena. The function of a social fact cannot but be social, i.e., it consists of the production of socially useful effects. To be sure, it may and does happen that it also serves the individual. But this happy result is not its immediate cause. We can then complete the preceding proposition by saying: *The function of a social fact ought always to be sought in its relation to some social end. . . .*

Psychological training, more than biological training, constitutes, then, a valuable lesson for the sociologist; but it will not be useful to him except on condition that he emancipates himself from it after having received profit from its lessons, and then goes beyond it by special sociological training. He must abandon psychology as the center of his operations, as the point of departure for his excursions into the sociological world to which they must always return. He must establish himself in the very heart of social facts, in order to observe them directly, while asking the science of the individual mind for a general preparation only and, when needed, for useful suggestions.

A certain conception of society and collective life emerges from the group of rules just established. But first let us set forth the contrary theories which divide opinion on this point. For some, such as Hobbes and Rousseau, there is a break in continuity between the individual and society. Man is thus naturally refractory to the common life; he can only resign himself to it when forced. Social ends are not simply the meeting-point of individual ends; they are, rather, contrary to them. Thus, to induce the individual to pursue them, it is necessary to constrain him; and the social task consists par excellence in the institution and organization of this constraint. . . .

Neither Hobbes nor Rousseau seems to have realized how contradictory it is to admit that the individual is himself the author of a machine which has for its essential role his domination and constraint. At least, it seemed to them sufficient for the elimination of this contradiction that it be disguised in the eyes of those who are its victims, by the clever artifice of the social contract.

It is from a quite different idea that the philosophers of natural law, the economists, and, more recently, Spencer have taken their inspiration. For them social life is essentially spontaneous and society is a natural phenomenon. But, if they confer this character upon it, it is not because they find in it a specific nature but merely because they find its basis in the nature of the individual. No more than the aforementioned thinkers do they see in it a system of things existing separately, by reason of causes peculiar to itself. But, whereas the former conceived of it only as a conventional arrangement which is attached by no bond to reality and is supported in mid-air, so to speak, Spencer and the economists give as its bases the fundamental instincts of human nature. Man is naturally inclined to the political, domestic, and religious life, to commerce, etc.; and it is from these natural drives that social organization is derived. Consequently, wherever it is normal, it has no need to impose itself. When it has recourse to constraint, it is because it is not what it ought to be or because the circumstances are abnormal. In principle, we have only to leave individual forces to develop freely and they will tend to organize themselves socially. Neither one of these doctrines is ours. To be sure, we do make constraint the characteristic of all social facts. But this constraint does not result from more or less learned machinations, destined to conceal from men the traps in which they have caught themselves. It is due simply to the fact that the individual finds himself in the presence of a force which is superior to him and before which he bows; but this force is an entirely natural one. It is not derived from a conventional arrangement which human will has added bodily to natural reality;

it issues from innermost reality; it is the necessary product of given causes. Also, recourse to artifice is unnecessary to get the individual to submit to them of his entire free will; it is sufficient to make him become aware of his state of natural dependence and inferiority, whether he forms a tangible and symbolic representation of it through religion or whether he arrives at an adequate and definite notion of it through science. Since the superiority of society to him is not simply physical but intellectual and moral, it has nothing to fear from a critical examination. By making man understand by how much the social being is richer, more complex, and more permanent than the individual being, reflection can only reveal to him the intelligible reasons for the subordination demanded of him and for the sentiments of attachment and respect which habit has fixed in his heart.

It would be only a singularly superficial criticism, therefore, that would attack our concept of social constraint by restating the theories of Hobbes and Machiavelli. But if, contrary to these philosophers, we say that social life is natural, our reason is not that we find its source in the nature of the individual. It is natural rather because it springs directly from the collective being which is, itself, a being in its own right, and because it results from special cultivation which individual consciousnesses undergo in their association with each other, an association from which a new form of existence is evolved. If, then, we agree with certain scholars that social reality appears to the individual under the aspect of constraint, we admit with the others that it is a spontaneous product of reality. The tie which binds together these two elements, so contradictory in appearance, is the fact that this reality from which it emanates extends beyond the individual. We mean to say that these words, "constraint" and "spontaneity," have not in our terminology the meaning Hobbes gives to the former and Spencer to the latter.

Conclusion

The breadth and depth of Durkheim's scholarship is as impressive as it was ambitious. He sought to elevate sociology to the level of a scientific study with the goal of unveiling eternal verities about the human condition in general and social evolution in particular. To that end he advanced a unique functionalist methodology. Nevertheless, his claim that social facts have objective existence in the same way that material things do has been controversial. His claim that law can be studied objectively has been particularly controversial. In our time, it has become commonly accepted that there is little objectivity in law and judicial behavior in relation to law and that legal reasoning is far from objective.[110]

Equally controversial was his attempt to trace the two configurations of culture (and their collective emotions) back to their sociostructural or morphological bases. His dualist typology of repressive/mechanical and restitutive/organic solidarity has

110. Isaak Dore, The Epistemological Foundations of Law, Ch. 12–13 (2007).

been described as overly broad and accused of "crushing" all preindustrial societies into a single category.[111] His claim that the evolution of society from primitive law to Roman law to modern industrial society showed a uniform decline of repressive law has also been challenged. Indeed, it has been asserted that such evolution has taken restitutive law to repressive law![112]

The turn of the twentieth century was a critical if not revolutionary period for social thought and social theory. The evolutionary theories of Spencer and Tylor were rejected in favor of the historical particularist model, championed by Boas. This shift paved the way for the emergence of the structural-functionalist school, which demanded a more rigorous methodology for studying social facts. Durkheim was the founding father of this school.

Although Boas and Durkheim used different methodologies, their ideas had many similarities:

- *Cultural determinism.* Boas and Durkheim were cultural determinists. They believed in not only the autonomy of culture but also its power to transform personality. According to them, the individual learns culture instead of creating it.
- *Cultural relativism.* The particularist model of the Boasian school suggests that all cultures are at the same time equal and yet unique and different from each other. This hypothesis is consistent with Durkheim's notion that culture is *sui generis*, and that any particular social fact has meaning only when studied in relation to the society within which it exists and to whose functioning it contributes.
- *Rejection of utilitarianism.* The rejection of both Boas and Durkheim of the reductionism of the evolutionary models of Spencer and Tylor required a rejection of the individual as a causal force in culture. Boas and Durkheim held the view that the individual is not a calculating animal acting in self-interest.
- *The primacy of emotion.* Boas and Durkheim attached great significance to the subjective element in personality: the latter was not only transformed by culture, but emotion itself was grounded in culture, and vice versa. Whereas Boas found the emotional strength of cultural traits through association and repetition, Durkheim found this strength in his collective consciousness, which acquired a moral authority of its own. This authority bound and constrained individual choice. Similarly, for Boas, the individual and his personality is *tabula rasa* at birth. It is molded by culture, as are his beliefs and emotions.

There are also differences in the views of Boas and Durkheim:

---

111. Lukes & Scull, *supra* note 34, at 10.

112. Cotterrell, *supra* note 59, at 85 (citing Leon Sheleff, *From Restitutive Law to Repressive Law: Durkheim's The Division of Labour in Society Revisited*, 16 Eur. J. Sociol. 16, 19–20 (1975); Leon Sheleff, Social Cohesion and Legal Coercion: A Critique of Weber, Durkheim and Marx 137 (1997)).

- *Social control.* Durkheim believed that culture is superimposed and transcends the individual, who therefore must surpass his own natural wants and desires and discipline himself within the parameters of the collective life. The latter thus has a disciplinary and coercive effect on the individual because the dictates of collective life are alien to his natural self and needs. Thus, for Durkheim, social control mechanisms are an essential part of the social structure, and are normative in nature, whereas for Boas their importance is secondary.
- *Group behavior and customs.* Particular forms of group activities, especially those associated with group symbols (*e.g.*, a clan totem or a flag) and rituals (*e.g.*, religious ceremonies) had greater significance for Durkheim. He viewed these as both representations and reinforcements of the collective life that showed the force of culture—a force almost external to society itself—which, in combination with the emotional element, engendered respect for the collective life and operated as a normative mechanism of social control. Boas, by contrast, would not have looked beyond the symbol or ritual practice for meaning. Thus, he would simply describe such practices as customs or habits that are learned, whereas Durkheim found behavior far more complex. For example, he posited that the desecration of a clan symbol would provoke a reaction far more serious than that resulting from a mere breach of custom, because symbols have great meaning and are objects of deep respect.
- *Functionalism.* The most important difference between Durkheim and Boas is their respective methodologies. Durkheim, who insisted on studying society as an integrated whole, set out a method to explain how each social fact contributed to the function of the whole. Otherwise, he warned, societies and cultures would be reduced to individual thoughts and motives. Boas did not concern himself with the function of any particular social institution. His method was descriptive, because his concern was to codify cultural traits as they became assimilated or modified to suit particular cultures.

Malinowski: Functionalism and Culture Studies

Bronislaw Malinowski (1884–1942) was another pioneer of the functionalist method. Like Durkheim, Malinowski avoided evolutionary schemes and emphasized the study of recurrent functions of customs and institutions in society as a whole, rather than their origins. He asserted that evolutionary schemes about the origins and differences between cultures were bound to be speculative because there was no direct observation of or recorded data on social phenomena. As the two following excerpts of his writings demonstrate, only rigorous observation and written records about particular customs and institutions could explain their social functions. Once the functions of an institution were understood, its origins would be understood. For these reasons, the functionalist method demanded rigorous and extensive fieldwork involving the complete immersion of the scientist/observer in the customs, thoughts, languages, and ways of life of the culture being studied.

Malinowski's Functional Methodology

Malinowski asserts that certain basic material facts about human nature and human existence, in short the human condition, impose "a certain determinism" on human behavior. In other words, humans can only survive by meeting certain basic minimum needs of subsistence (*e.g.*, food, clothing, shelter). Because these basic physiological needs are predetermined, human behavior in meeting these needs is also predetermined. But the human condition shows that people do more than just survive; they live in groups and communities. Both aspects of the human condition necessarily entail certain "vital sequences" in the form of cultural processes (or institutions) that are built around each sequence. The example of the family institution is one such vital sequence of human existence.

> Human nature imposes on all forms of behavior, however complex and highly organized, a certain determinism. This consists of a number of vital sequences, indispensable to the healthy run of the organism and to the community as a whole, which must be incorporated in each traditional system of organized behavior. These vital sequences constitute crystallizing points for a number of cultural processes, products and complex arrangements which are built around each sequence.[113]

Here Malinowski shows (as did Sapir; *see* Chapter 2) that even the basic physiological needs of breathing and eating take on complex meanings of etiquette in cultural contexts. Breathing in a sociocultural setting is not just the mere intake of oxygen for survival; its social nature is indicated by the fact that in certain cultures the noisy exhalation of breath in close quarters is considered impolite, or the noisy intake of breath is a sign of respect. Eating is similarly more than the mere satisfaction of a physiological impulse. It is an activity in which humans partake in a variety of ways, each having their own rules of commensalism, etiquettes, symbolism, and other culturally significant meanings.[114]

> In short it would be idle to disregard the fact that the impulse leading to the simplest physiological performance is as highly plastic and determined by tradition as it is ineluctable in the long run, because it is determined by physiological necessities. We see also why simple physiological impulses can not exist under conditions of culture.[115]

Malinowski's functional methodology thus focuses on the individual organism under conditions of culture.[116] In doing so it adopts two axioms: (1) every culture must satisfy the biological system of needs, and (2) every cultural achievement that

113. Bronislaw Malinowski, A Scientific Theory of Culture and Other Essays 85 (1944).

114. Bronislaw Malinowski, The Dynamics of Culture Change: An Inquiry into Race Relations in Africa 43 (1949).

115. Malinowski, Theory, *supra* note 113, at 87.

116. Bronislaw Malinowski, *The Group and the Individual in Functional Analysis*, 44 Am. J. Sociol. 938, at 939 *et seq.* (1939).

implies the use of artifacts and symbolism is an instrumental enhancement of human anatomy and refers directly or indirectly to the satisfaction of a bodily need.[117] These maxims, which depict humans as biological entities, dictate the study of basic biological and material needs not only to survive as an individual but also as a member of the group. Because no person exists in total isolation, his or her membership in and association within the wider group are basic conditions of human existence. Thus it is within the group, according to Malinowski, that a person's biological needs are transformed into cultural responses. These responses are imperatives because without them, people cannot subsist within the group. These imperatives satisfy needs and, as humans flourish, give rise to bigger and more complex "derived" needs for which more cultural and normative institutions arise.[118] This relationship between group, imperative, need, and institution cause each culture to become a functionally and normatively integrated whole. According to Malinowski, the task of the ethnographer is to study a culture from within, in particular the integrative functions of the cultural institutions in a society as a whole.

The excerpt that follows explains the functional method's two axioms as well as Malinowski's notion of derived needs. It contains a brief explanation of the (cultural and normative) imperatives that arise from basic needs in conditions of culture.

Bronislaw Malinowski, A Scientific Theory of Culture and Other Essays 171–73 (1944).

Here I would like to suggest that we must take our stand on two axioms: first and foremost, that every culture must satisfy the biological system of needs, such as those dictated by metabolism, reproduction, the physiological conditions of temperature, protection from moisture, wind, and the direct impact of damaging forces of climate and weather, safety from dangerous animals or human beings, occasional relaxation, the exercise of the muscular and nervous system in movement, and the regulation of growth. The second axiom in the science of culture is that every cultural achievement that implies the use of artifacts and symbolism is an instrumental enhancement of human anatomy, and refers directly or indirectly to the satisfaction of a bodily need. If we were to start with an evolutionary consideration, we could show that as soon as the human anatomy is supplemented by a stick or a stone, a flame or a covering wrap, the use of such artifacts, tools, and commodities not only satisfies a bodily need, but also establishes derived needs. The animal organism which creates a change in temperature by the use of shelter, permanent or temporary, of fire, protective or warming, of clothing or blanketing, becomes dependent on those items of the environment, on their skillful production and use, and on the cooperation which may be necessary in the handling of the material.

---

117. Malinowski, Theory, *supra* note 113, at 171.

118. *Id.* at 120, 171.

> A new type of need, closely linked to the biological one and dependent upon it, but obviously implying new types of determinism, arises with the beginning of any cultural activity. The animal, which passes from nourishment obtained directly from environmental contact to food collected, preserved, and prepared, will starve if at any stage the cultural processes break down. New needs of an economic character have to be registered side by side with the purely biological necessity of nutrition. As soon as the gratification of sex impulses becomes transformed into permanent cohabitation, and the rearing of infants leads to a permanent household, new conditions are imposed, each of them as necessary to the preservation of the group as is any phase of the purely biological process.
>
> Were we to look at any community, more or less primitive, or even fully civilized, we would see that everywhere there exists a tribal commissariat determined primarily by the nutritive needs of human metabolism, but in itself establishing new needs, technological, economic, legal, and even magical, religious or ethical. And again, since reproduction in the human species does not take place by simple mating, because it is linked up with the necessity for prolonged nurture, education, and the first molding into citizenship, it imposes a whole set of additional determinants, that is, needs, which are satisfied by a regulated courtship, by the taboos of incest and exogamy, by preferential marriage arrangement; and as regards parenthood and kinship, by the system of counting descent, with all which that implies in cooperative, legal, and ethical relations. The minimum conditions of bodily survival, as regards inclemencies of the weather, are again satisfied by dress and habitation. The need of safety leads to physical arrangements within the house, as well as within human settlements as a whole, and also to the organization of neighborhood groups.
>
> If we were to enumerate briefly the derived imperatives imposed by the cultural satisfaction of biological needs, we would see that the constant renewal of apparatus is a necessity to which the economic system of a tribe is a response. Again, human cooperation implies norms of conduct sanctioned by authority, physical force, or social contract. Here we have the response of various systems of control, primitive or developed. The renewal of the human personnel in every component institution, and in the cultural group as a whole, implies not only reproduction, but also systems of education. The organization of force and compulsion in the support of authority and defense is functionally related to the political organization within each institution and also later on in specific groupings, which we have defined as political units, or the prototype of the political state.

The "derived imperatives" briefly mentioned are more fully discussed below.

Functional Study of Sociocultural Institutions

Malinowski believed that there are certain "universal institutional types"[119]—a view reminiscent of the evolutionist doctrines of Tylor and Morgan, who maintained that all societies go through universal phases and have parallel normative institutions. Of course, Malinowski does not expressly subscribe to any particular universalistic scheme of evolution. Nonetheless, his idea that all cultures have similar institutions is not inconsistent with evolutionary doctrine. Indeed, his "List of Universal Institutional Types" is implicitly based on an unarticulated evolutionary scheme.

His concept of institution is based on three core ideas. First, the institution is a cultural response conditioned by humanity's material environment; second, it is an organized system of purposeful activities.[120] These purposeful activities and their underlying values constitute the institution's "charter."[121] The institution has its own personnel with a chain of command and division of functions, duties, and privileges. The third component of an institution is "the technical acquired skills, habits, legal norms, and ethical commands which are accepted by the members or imposed upon them."[122] The normative nature of all institutions is made especially clear by the second and third prongs.

Here is Malinowski's diagram of an institution.[123]

```
              CHARTER
             /       \
      PERSONNEL     NORMS
             \       /
       MATERIAL APPARATUS
                 |
             ACTIVITIES
                 |
              FUNCTION
```

To summarize his functional definition, an "institution" is a specific group of individuals who are united for a purpose, follow certain rules of behavior, and operate together within a given environment to satisfy particular needs. Every institution contributes toward the integral working of society as a whole, and in doing so satisfies individual needs. The following is a more detailed definition:

119. *Id.* at 62. *See id.* at 62–66. The list includes the family, territorial communities (neighborhoods, municipalities and provinces) totemic groups, secret societies, occupational/professional institutions, rank and status groups, and political authority.

120. *Id.* at 52–53.

121. *Id.*

122. Malinowski, Theory, *supra* note 113, at 52.

123. *Id.* at 53.

> We can define an institution as: a group of people united for the pursuit of a simple or complex activity; always in possession of a material endowment and a technical outfit; organized on a definite legal or customary charter, linguistically formulated on myth, legend, rule, and maxim; and trained or prepared for the carrying out of its task.[124]

One example of a "cultural universal" is the institution of family.[125] The family supplies members of the society through procreation, trains them, and protects them from birth. The fact that the individual is taken care of in this way by the family institution is only one aspect of family life. Other areas of study would include sexual relationships, emotional connections, and lifestyles of members beyond the immediate domestic circle. Malinowski regards family institutions as some among many instrumental and integrative imperatives that are fundamentally cultural in nature.[126] As the individual lives within his culture; is protected, nourished, and thrives in it; the family also trains and molds him.

Other institutions in Malinowski's scheme similarly emerge as integrative cultural imperatives to satisfy individual needs: church, totemic clan, magical and shamanistic groups, economic institutions, educational institutions, political institutions, and of course legal institutions.[127] The latter two are of special interest because they fall under his concept of a "universal institution," which he calls "authority." An authority exists in every culture, according to Malinowski. In simple societies, it resides in a subdivision of a tribe and is the "prototype state" of modern times.[128] All of these institutions, however, are integrated around a specific purpose or function. Similarly, the integrative aspects of culture as a whole are carried out according to certain processes, practices, and rituals. These rituals, which depend on the nature of the institution, may be religious, magical, artistic, ceremonial, recreational, symbolic, didactic, or technical. Again, they are to be studied from an internal rather than an external perspective.

Although rituals exist to serve the needs of the individual, their routines of operation are also normative in nature because they impose a measure of control or even constraints on individual behavior. However, in a warning reminiscent of Durkheim's admonition that the law should not stray too far from the social solidarity it is meant to protect, Malinowski notes that there must be a good balance between individual interest and institutional controls. If this balance is upset or wrongly set, there could be social anarchy or even tyranny and brutal oppression. The consequence of the latter would be the killing of individual initiative; such a society would be unable

---

124. Malinowski, Dynamics, *supra* note 114, at 50.

125. Malinowski, Theory, *supra* note 113, at 55.

126. Malinowski, Dynamics, *supra* note 114, at 50.

127. Malinowski, Theory, *supra* note 113, at 58–59.

128. *Id.* at 61. *See also* Malinowski, Dynamics, *supra* note 114, at 44–45.

to develop or preserve its cultural heritage. Durkheim similarly prognosticated that such a society could not last long.[129]

Bronislaw Malinowski, *The Group and the Individual in Functional Analysis*, 44 Am. J. Sociol. 938, 938–941, 961–964 (1939).

Functionalism differs from other sociological theories more definitely, perhaps, in its conception and definition of the individual than in any other respect. The functionalist includes in his analysis not merely the emotional as well as the intellectual side of mental processes, but also insists that man in his full biological reality has to be drawn into our analysis of culture. The bodily needs and environmental influences, and the cultural reactions to them, have thus to be studied side by side.

The field worker observes human beings acting within an environmental setting, natural and artificial; influenced by it, and in turn transforming it in co-operation with each other. He studies how men and women are motivated in their mutual relations by feelings of attraction and repulsion, by co-operative duties and privileges, by profits drawn and sacrifices made. The invisible network of social bonds, of which the organization of the group is made up, is defined by charters and codes—technological, legal, customary, and moral—to which every individual is differentially submitted, and which integrate the group into a whole. Since all rules and all tribal tradition are expressions in words—that is, symbols—the understanding of social organization implies an analysis of symbolism and language. Empirically speaking the field worker has to collect texts, statements, and opinions, side by side with the observation of behavior and the study of material culture.

In this brief preamble we have already insisted that the individual must be studied as a biological reality. We have indicated that the physical word must be part of our analysis, both as the natural milieu and as the body of tools and commodities produced by man. We have pointed out that individuals never cope with, or move within, their environment in isolation, but in organized groups, and that organization is expressed in traditional charters, which are symbolic in essence.

II. *The Individual Organism Under Conditions of Culture*

Taking man as a biological entity it is clear that certain minima of conditions can be laid down which are indispensable to the personal welfare of the individual and to the continuation of the group. All human beings have to be nourished, they have to reproduce, and they require the maintenance of certain physical conditions: ventilation, temperature within a definite range, a sheltered and dry place to rest, and safety from the hostile forces of nature,

129. *See* text at note 67 *supra*.

of animals; and of man. The physiological working of each individual organism implies the intake of food and of oxygen, occasional movement, and relaxation in sleep and recreation. The process of growth in man necessitates protection and guidance in its early stages and, later on, specific training.

We have listed here some of the essential conditions to which cultural activity, whether individual or collective, has instrumentally to conform. It is well to recall that these are only minimum conditions—the very manner in which they are satisfied in culture imposes certain additional requirements. These constitute new needs, which in turn have to be satisfied. The primary—that is, the biological—wants of the human organism are not satisfied naturally by direct contact of the individual organism with the physical environment. Not only does the individual depend on the group in whatever he achieves and whatever he obtains, but the group and all its individual members depend on the development of a material outfit, which in its essence is an addition to the human anatomy, and which entails corresponding modifications of human physiology. . . .

Indeed, functionalism is, in its essence, the theory of transformation of organic—that is, individual—needs into derived cultural necessities and imperatives. Society by the collective wielding of the conditioning apparatus molds the individual into a cultural personality. The individual, with his physiological needs and psychological processes, is the ultimate source and aim of all tradition, activities, and organized behavior.

The word "society" is used here in the sense of a co-ordinated set of differentiated groups. The juxtaposition and opposition of "the individual" and "the society," as an indifferentiated mass, is always fictitious and therefore fallacious.

From the structural approach we have found that social organization must always be analyzed into institutions—that is, definite groups of men united by a charter, following rules of conduct, operating together a shaped portion of the environment, and working for the satisfaction of definite needs. This latter defines the function of an institution.

Here, once more, we see that every institution contributes, on the one hand, toward the integral working of the community as a whole, but it also satisfies the derived and basic needs of the individual. Thus the family is indispensable to society in supplying its members, training them, and safeguarding their early stages. At the same time to consider the role of the family without reference to individuals in their sex drive, in their personal affections, as between husband and wife, parents and children, or to study the early stages of life-history of the individual outside the domestic circle would be absurd. The local group, as the organization for the joint use of an apportioned territory, as the means of collective defense, and as the medium for the primary division of labor, works as a part of society and as one of its indispensable organs. At the same time, every one of the benefits just listed is enjoyed by every individual member. His role and membership in that group have to be stated from the point of view of psychology, education, and also of the physiological benefits derived by each from the joint activities. The tribe and state carries out a collective policy in war and peace, in conquest and intertribal or international trade; but the very existence of tribe or state depends on the quality of citizenship, which is an individual fact and which consists in the contributions toward, and the benefits derived from, the participation of the individual in group life. . . .

We have seen that, starting from the individual organism and its requirements, and studying the cultural satisfaction thereof, we come upon instrumental and integrative imperatives. In every culture there corresponds to these such types of organized activities as economics, education, political organization, and legal system; and again organized religion and magic, as well as artistic and recreational activities.

If space would allow we could show that, since every one of these integrative pursuits is carried on by a group, whether this be family, clan, or congregation; since dogma, mythology, and sacred history provide its charters; since every ritual implies a liturgical apparatus; and since the activities are integrated around a definite purpose or function, the communion with the supernatural—we would find that the integrative aspects of culture are again carried on in institutions, religious, magical, artistic, ceremonial, and recreational. The church, the congregation, the totemic clan, the magical or shamanistic corporations, as well as sporting teams and organizations of musicians, dancers, and actors, are examples of such institutions. . . .

Culture remains sound and capable of further development only in so far as a definite balance between individual interest and social control can be maintained. If this balance be upset or wrongly poised, we have at one end anarchy, and at the other brutal dictatorship. The present world is threatened in its various parts and through different agencies both with anarchy and with the brutal oppression in which the interests of the state, managed by small gangs with dictatorial powers, are made completely to overrule the elementary rights and interests of the individual. The theoretical discussion of the relation between the individual and the group has thus in our present world not merely an academic but also a deep philosophical and ethical significance. It cannot be too often repeated that any culture which kills individual initiative, and relegates the interests of most of its members to complete insignificance at the expense of a gang-managed totalitarian state, will not be able to develop or even to preserve its cultural patrimony.

Basic Human Needs and Their Cultural Imperatives

Malinowski theorized that institutions arise as cultural responses to individual needs. As for what those needs are, and how they are defined, he answers the latter question as follows:

> By need, then, I understand the system of conditions in the human organism, in the cultural setting, and in the relation of both to the natural environment, which are sufficient and necessary for the survival of group and organism. A need therefore is the limiting set of facts. Habits and their motivations, the learned responses and the foundations of organization, must be so arranged as to allow the basic needs to be satisfied.[130]

As to the first question, Malinowski proposed a "Theory of Needs." Following is a representative set, together with their cultural responses.[131]

Basic Needs	Cultural Responses
1. Metabolism	1. Commissariat
2. Reproduction	2. Kinship
3. Bodily comforts	3. Shelter
4. Safety	4. Protection
5. Movement	5. Activities
6. Growth	6. Training
7. Health	7. Hygiene

Malinowski emphasizes that there is no "point-for-point" correspondence between a cultural institution and a basic need.[132] A cultural institution may serve more than one need, and an ethnographer will see a "chained series of institutions, related to each other within each chain but also, one and all, appearing virtually under every single heading."[133] Apart from this important observation, the table of needs and cultural responses seems largely self-explanatory. Even so, examining some of the entries may be helpful.

With the first basic need, metabolism, Malinowski has in mind "the processes of food intake, digestion, the collateral secretions, the absorption of nutritive substances, . . . rejection of waste matter."[134] The cultural response to this would be the creation of an organizational and normative framework that would first guarantee the supply of food, so that certain digestive processes can be carried out; and second, to ensure the appropriate sanitary arrangements for the end process.[135] The institution charged with this task is what Malinowski called a tribal or national "commissariat," an institution analogous to a bureaucratic (often military) office charged with drawing up plans and rules for growing, preparation, consumption, and distribution of food and with the authority to enforce these plans and rules.[136] Malinowski sees food

130. Malinowski, Theory, *supra* note 113, at 90.

131. *Id.* at 91.

132. *Id.* at 110.

133. *Id.*

134. *Id.* at 91.

135. Malinowski, Theory, *supra* note 113, at 92.

136. *Id.* at 96. *See* excerpt above.

production, distribution, and consumption, as well as the tasks of the commissariat, as a set of "organized behavior systems." A community that has reached a high degree of density will require a complex and highly organized commissariat devising and imposing ever more complex laws, regulations, and sanctions for procuring and distributing food, including laws about ownership of the means of production.[137] In general, he concludes (as do many of his predecessors) that the more complex the society, the more complex its law. Thus the commissariat will have extensive laws regulating behavior in a variety of ways to keep the chain of activities running smoothly. These regulations could be general (*e.g.*, governing the planting of seeds) or perhaps detailed and intrusive (*e.g.*, regulating "biting, chewing and swallowing"). Furthermore, all regulations would be backed by the coercive authority of the state.[138]

Another institution is the household (or family) within which food preparation and consumption occur.[139] The household or family is part of the universal chain of interrelated institutions responsive to the basic metabolic needs of the individual. Any break in the chain would have an adverse effect on a community's nutritive needs.

In sum, Malinowski finds no fewer than four "instrumental imperatives," required to support the basic metabolic need: educational systems (necessary to train individuals in the above tasks), economic arrangements (regulating production and distribution), legal systems (to enforce rules), and the state (functioning as the overall political structure and possessing coercive powers).

Malinowski justifies the second basic need, reproduction, on the grounds that no culture can survive in which reproduction (*i.e.*, mating, pregnancy, and childbirth) is not supported by the institution of "legally-founded parenthood."[140] Accordingly, the parallel institutions of courtship, the household, and marriage itself emerge in service of this basic need. The fact that all of these institutions have their own customs, expectations, laws, and rituals, shows that even the most private of relationships raise public (*i.e.*, legal) issues because the traditions involved are rooted in the group at large, particularly in kinfolk.

Malinowski viewed kinship as a highly complex institution,[141] governed by law, and as providing the aegis for the institutions to function. Legal systems define kinship structure in terms of parenthood, ancestry, descent, inheritance, ownership of property, and a host of other related matters, which means that the law would also define forms of marriage and establish sanctions for its validity, duration, and dissolution. These related matters are also in dynamic interrelationship with the various institutions that support reproduction.

> In short we can say, first and foremost, that the understanding of cultural responses to the need of propagation requires a consecutive, substantial

137. *Id.* at 98.

138. *Id.*

139. *Id.* at 96–97.

140. Malinowski, Theory, *supra* note 113, at 99.

141. Malinowski, Dynamics, *supra* note 114, at 50.

> analysis of its component institutions, from courtship to the most extensive kinship differentiation of the tribe. Since all these institutions are related, no ethnographic account of them, nor yet a theoretical treatment, can be satisfactory, unless the relationship, as well as each partial institution, is fully described and analyzed. We have shown that over and above the determinants of biology—in its minimum form the vital sequence of attraction, conjugation, impregnation, gestation, and childbirth—there enter, with the full force of ineluctable cultural determinism, the elements of economic, educational, legal, and political determinism.[142]

The foregoing discussion of just the first two entries in Malinowski's theory of needs and their cultural responses clearly demonstrates the normative character of the latter. Therefore, the remainder of his enumerated needs and their cultural responses are not discussed. We may safely assume the normative nature of these responses as well.

The discussion also distinctly reveals the normative determinism in Malinowski's approach (*i.e.*, the idea that cultural forces exist beyond the control of the individual yet regulate his behavior in many intrusive if not coercive ways). The regulation of individual behavior by cultural forces external to the individual is a prominent theme of the historical particularists discussed in Chapter 2, and Malinowski's notion of socially imposed meanings on certain private acts is also reminiscent of this approach (as with the discussion about breathing and socially imposed meaning).

Malinowski's determinism makes the unique point that because humans' basic physiological needs are predetermined, they supply "the limiting set of facts" as to what they must and must not do.[143] The basic metabolic need requires, for example, "the intake of oxygen" and eating.[144] However, people cannot choose not to breathe or eat without ensuring their demise. This is physiological determinism, not to be confused with cultural determinism as the umbrella under which Malinowski included economic, educational, legal, and political (*i.e.*, normative) determinisms.

The next excerpt, which nicely summarizes the previous two sections, explains in particular the material bases of institutional growth and how the material exigencies of life entail four "instrumental imperatives": an economic system, a legal system, a political system, and an educational system. These are universal to every culture, for without them no culture can survive. First is the economic system, which is a system of rules that govern production, consumption, distribution, ownership, division of labor, wealth, and value. An economic system is a universal feature of all organized human life, but it is nevertheless a derived imperative. Second is a legal system, a derived imperative that channels cooperative as well as competitive behavior. It consists of rules that are enabling as well as constraining in nature, both being necessary for collective existence. The third imperative, authority, may be vested in the head of the family, elders, clan or subclan, or a magical or totemic group. This institution works

142. Malinowski, Theory, *supra* note 113, at 103.

143. *Id.* at 90.

144. *Id.* at 77.

with the legal system to maintain and/or defend the common cultural enterprise or to enforce it through sanctions when necessary. This authority exists under the aegis of an overall political organization. The fourth universal cultural imperative is an educational system, whose function is to maintain the continuity of cultural patrimony from one generation to the next.

The functional method focuses on how the instrumental imperatives operate in their respective domains and how they contribute to the vibrancy of life in their particular conditions of culture.

Bronislaw Malinowski, The Dynamics of Culture Change: An Inquiry into Race Relations in Africa 44–46 (1949).

> We have started from the axiom that culture is an instrumental reality, an apparatus for the satisfaction of fundamental needs, that is, organic survival, environmental adaptation, and continuity in the biological sense. To this we have added the empirical corollary that, under conditions of culture, the satisfaction of organic needs is achieved in an indirect, round-about manner. Man uses tools; covers himself with clothes, and shelters himself in caves or huts, windshields or tents. He uses fire for warmth and for cooking. In this, he transforms his anatomical endowments in all his contacts with the physical milieu. He does this not alone but organized into groups. Organization means the tradition of skills, of knowledge, and of values.
>
> Our argument thus leads us to the conclusion that the cultural satisfaction of primary biological needs imposes upon man secondary or derived imperatives. Thus, the whole body of material apparatus must be produced, maintained, distributed, used and valued. Some economic organization, however rudimentary, is indispensible to every human society. It consists in a system of traditional rules, of technique, of property, and of the way of using and consuming objects. The functional approach to the comparative study of cultures thus postulates that the study of systems of production, distribution, and consumption must be carried out, even in the most primitive societies. It must be primarily directed toward the establishment of such concepts as property, especially property in land, division of labor, incentives, wealth, and value. Value as the main motive of organized human effort, as the principle by which human beings are made to cooperate, to produce, to maintain wealth, and to surround it with religious and sentimental beliefs, must exist even at the most primitive stages of development.
>
> In this, we have defined the economic aspect in the comparative study of cultures. We have laid down the principle that some form or other of economic system is a universal feature of all organized human life, since it corresponds to a universal, albeit derived, imperative.
>
> Another derived, yet universal, aspect of all culture is the one which might be described as normative. Man achieves his mastery over the environment

and his competitors through cooperation. Cooperation means life in common. Both cooperation and life in common imply sacrifices and joint effort, subordination of private interests to mutual gain—in short, the existence of rules, of authority, and of constraint. Cooperative existence in groups, however simple and small, offers temptations as regards the sex impulse, as regards the use of food and the possession of wealth, the satisfaction of ambition, and the display of power. Rank, leadership, authority, and hierarchy are social distinctions which must have existed under the earliest forms of civilization, although at such levels they may be largely associated with age, sex, and the position in the family. The functional approach to the normative problems does not allow us to be misled by the absence of formal and institutionalized types of legislation, jurisdiction, or codification. Legislation, effective sanctions, and the administration of tribal rules are often carried out as by-products of other activities.

Authority may be often vested in the head of the family, the elders of a clan, or in the leader of a magical team or a totemic group. The codification of tribal rules is embodied in those principles of mutual behavior referring to marriage and parenthood, to economic pursuits, and ritual rules. These, although perhaps not always explicitly codified, are invariably known to all the members of a society. Litigation may take the form of a more or less friendly discussion, but since law, however primitive, never can work automatically, implying as it does constraint and readjustment, there exist even in the simplest forms of culture types of debate and quarrel, mutual recrimination, and readjustment by those in authority—all of which correspond to the judicial process in more highly developed cultures. Furthermore, an analysis of norms of conduct would reveal that even in primitive communities norms can be classified into rules of law, into custom, into ethics, and into manners. Those rules which define the constitution of the family, the nature of marriage, of descent, of kinship, and of the constitution of political authority, land tenure, and property are the genuine rules of primitive law. Their knowledge is as important for the administrator as it is interesting for the theoretical student. The normative or legal aspect of the community is thus the second derived imperative of culture, and in the satisfaction of this imperative we shall have to search for the mechanisms of codification, judicial process, and sanction in every human community.

The very existence of law implies the use of constraint and authority as its ultimate sanction. In all groups there is another reason why some form of organized force must be forthcoming. This is connected with intertribal relations. Security in the tenure of tribal territory, possibilities of aggression, and the need of collective defense constitute what might be called the derived imperative of political organization.

There is one more imperative imposed by culture upon all human groups. Since culture is the cumulative achievement of generations, there must be ways and means by which this common heritage is handed over from one

> generation to another. The need of such systems we may call the educational imperative. Here again, the functional approach leads us to investigate through the exact study of early life histories how the family and the group of playmates, the initiation ceremonies, and apprenticeship, how the entry into club, clan, village, community, and the tribe are accompanied by training and teaching, by the inculcation of technique rules of craftsmanship, the principles of knowledge, social norms, and moral maxims.

Applied Functionalism: Case Studies in Magic

Just as Durkheim applied the functional method to study suicide, which seems an unlikely topic of functional analysis, Malinowski also chose an unusual topic for the application of his functional methodology: magic. His theory of needs teaches that humans are thrust into the world under circumstances that in their totality constitute what may be called the human condition. The latter includes a human being as a biological entity who copes with physical and environmental conditions in order to satisfy basic needs. One does so using such knowledge as one has acquired to meet those needs to the maximum extent possible. This knowledge includes mastery of at least the basic scientific principles for the exploitation and manipulation of the environment (*e.g.*, developing tools and weapons for hunting and fishing, learning the uses of fire, building shelters). This knowledge, which may be rudimentary, is nonetheless based on certain objective and scientific truths.

Precisely because knowledge is rudimentary and therefore finite, people resort to magic as a "complementary" aid.[145] Magic is the belief that "by spell and rite results can be obtained."[146] People must resort to magic, according to Malinowski, because objective or empirical knowledge fail them. Many environmental phenomena—rain, sunshine, wind, heat, cold, disease, illness, life, death—are beyond human control. Not being able to deal with or manipulate these factors scientifically, primitive people deal with them magically. By this logic, the more a vital interest cannot be controlled scientifically, the greater the temptation to resort to magic.[147]

Malinowski tried to determine exactly what magic is in the conception of the native mind: a supernatural power or perhaps a natural force that is somehow captured by the magician or sorcerer and put to beneficial use. He concluded that it is instead a way of claiming one's own intrinsic power over nature. This notion, he observed, is apparent in all native folklore.[148] As such, the power of magic is viewed as being in the possession of anthropomorphic beings, such as the magician, sorcerer, or witch—a conception further reinforced by the fact that magic is harnessed

---

145. Malinowski, Theory, *supra* note 113, at 198.

146. *Id.*

147. Bronislaw Malinowski, Argonauts of the Western Pacific, 395–96 (1922). *See also*, Malinowski, Dynamics, *supra* note 114, at 48 (pointing out that magic is not used for activities and goals that are within human control, *e.g.*, in making a fire, or in cooking or cleaning).

148. Malinowski, Argonauts, *supra* note 147, at 401.

by humans for humans, to obtain practical human goals.[149] Malinowski recognized no abstract explanations or speculations about the origin of magic, humans, or even the origin of the cosmos of which humanity is a part.

One important case study of magic by Malinowski was of the social institution of *kula*, which was engaged in by inhabitants of the Trobriand Islands in the Western Pacific. *Kula* was a particular form of ceremonial trade on the high seas, using canoes. Malinowski describes in great detail how this activity was heavily regimented by magical rites and ceremonies beginning with a rite to expel evil spirits from the wood of the trees felled for building each canoe. Pulling logs and the critical stages of building the canoes (*e.g.*, lashing, caulking, and painting) were accompanied by more special ceremonies, and many other rituals were performed as the canoes set sail. The details of these are less important than the fact that all preparations and ceremonies were attended by others, which inculcated a joint spirit of cooperation and common enterprise.[150]

Malinowski also investigated fishing, another vital activity and an important means of livelihood in which the use of magic was very much in evidence. Where fishing was abundant, a good catch was usually ensured under all weather conditions and thus no magic was used. However, when expeditions for ocean fishing were organized by the islanders, fear of various uncertainties and dangers led them to perform extensive magical rites.[151] Similarly, heavy reliance on magic appears in agricultural endeavors, including gardening.[152]

Here the function of magic was not so much that it would necessarily produce desired outcomes but that it would supply emotional satisfaction, because everything humanly possible had been done to obtain desirable outcomes. Such emotional satisfaction, according to Malinowski, generates optimism, positive attitudes, and an esprit de corps. He thus saw magic as purposive in nature, with a "positive pragmatic function,"[153] not just an arbitrary and meaningless effort resorted to by primitives for no reason.

Bronislaw Malinowski, A Scientific Theory of Culture and Other Essays 198–200 (1944).

> Knowledge, indeed scientific knowledge is always man's primary guide in his relations with the environment. It is his steady standby in all vital concerns. Without knowledge and without strict adherence to knowledge, no culture could survive. . . .

---

149. *Id.*

150. *Id.* at 415–18. *See also* Malinowski, Dynamics, *supra* note 114, at 48–49.

151. Bronislaw Malinowski, Coral Gardens and Their Magic: A Study of the Methods of Tilling the Soil and of Agricultural Rites in the Trobriand Islands 17 (1935).

152. *Id.* at 62–63.

153. Malinowski, Theory, *supra* note 113, at 199. *See also* Malinowski, Dynamics, *supra* note 114, at 48–49.

Magic, as the belief that by spell and rite results can be obtained, enters as a complementary factor. It always appears in those phases of human action where knowledge fails man. Primitive man cannot manipulate the weather. Experience teaches him that rain and sunshine, wind, heat and cold, cannot be produced by his own hands, however much he might think about or observe such phenomena. He therefore deals with them magically.

Primitive man has but the most elementary knowledge of conditions of human health and illness. Emotionally and pragmatically he strongly resents the occurrence of disease. A mystical theory that the malice of other men can produce illness is strongly suggested by man's psychology and by his social relations. In many ways the explanations given by the theory of witchcraft and sorcery are serviceable, in that they translate the inexorable decrees of destiny into manipulation of human malice. The sick man, primitive or civilized, wants to feel that something can be done. He craves for miracles, and the conviction that what has been produced by a malicious sorcerer can be counteracted by a more powerful and friendly witch-doctor, may even assist the organism to resist illness through the belief that something effective is being done.

Magic, including sorcery, has thus its practical as well as social characteristics, which allow us to explain its persistence. Psychologically, magic in all its forms implies the optimistic attitude that through rite and spell something is being achieved in taming chance and restoring luck. The form of rite and spell closely corresponds to this positive, pragmatic function. It is always the enactment of the desired end in word and act. We can here reformulate Frazer's theory: it is not the association of ideas, that like produces like or that contact persists, but the affirmation and enactment of desired ends and results, which form the psychological basis of magic. Socially, magic as the spiritual counterpart of leadership helps to integrate the acting group through discipline and the introduction of order. In agriculture the magician becomes the leader, not so much because of the superstitious reverence which he inspires, but because he gives the workers the guarantee that if they obey his taboos and his injunctions, his magic will add a quota of supernatural benefits to . . . their efforts. The magic of war again, inspiring the fighters with belief in victory, makes their courage more effective and allows leadership to be followed with fuller enthusiasm.

Functionalism and Fieldwork

The foregoing materials show that Malinowski's functional method was designed to give an insider's perspective of the institutions of culture. Indeed, in his famous monograph *Argonauts of the Western Pacific*, he explains in detail the "proper conditions of ethnographic work." These consist of "cutting oneself off from the company of other white men, and remaining in as close contact with the natives as possible, which really can only be achieved by camping right in their villages."[154] Thus he urged the ethnographer to operate under conditions of complete immersion in the customs, language, and ways of life of the culture under study. He did precisely this with the inhabitants of the Trobriand Islands in the Western Pacific, as he recounts in the next passage:

> Soon after I had established myself in Omarakana (Trobriand Islands), I began to take part, in a way, in the village life, to look forward to the important or festive events, to take personal interest in the gossip and the developments of the small village occurrences; to wake up every morning to a day, presenting itself to me more or less as it does to the native. I would get out from under my mosquito net, to find around me the village life beginning to stir, or the people well advanced in their working day according to the hour and also to the season, for they get up and begin their labours early or late, as work presses. As I went on my morning walk through the village, I could see intimate details of family life, of toilet, cooking, taking of meals; I could see the arrangements for the day's work, people starting on their errands, or groups of men and women busy at some manufacturing tasks . . . Quarrels, jokes, family scenes, events usually trivial, sometimes dramatic but always significant, formed the atmosphere of my daily life, as well as of theirs. It must be remembered that as the natives saw me constantly every day, they ceased to be interested or alarmed, or made self-conscious by my presence, and I ceased to be a disturbing element in the tribal life which I was to study . . . In fact, as they knew that I would thrust my nose into everything, even where a well-mannered native would not dream of intruding, they finished by regarding me as part and parcel of their life, a necessary evil or nuisance, mitigated by donations of tobacco . . . Also, over and over again, I committed breaches of etiquette, which the natives, familiar enough with me, were not slow in pointing out. I had to learn how to behave, and to a certain extent, I acquired "the feeling" for native good and bad manners. With this, and with the capacity of enjoying their company and sharing some of their games and amusements, I began to feel that I was indeed in touch with the natives, and this is certainly the preliminary condition of being able to carry on successful field work.[155]

Under these conditions Malinowski became intimately familiar with the psychological dispositions of the natives on topics such a love, ambition, vanity, sharing, food production, and sexual mores, as well as the ceremonial and magical aspects of the *kula* and the use of magic and sorcery in other areas of native life.

> One of the first conditions of acceptable Ethnographic work certainly is that it should deal with the totality of all social, cultural, and psychological as-

---

154. MALINOWSKI, ARGONAUTS, *supra* note 147, at 6.

155. *Id.* at 7–8.

> pects of the community, for they are so interwoven that not one can be understood without taking into consideration all the others. The reader of this monograph will clearly see that, though its main theme is economic—for it deals with commercial enterprise, exchange and trade—constant reference has to be made to social organisation, the power of magic, to mythology and folklore, and indeed to all other aspects as well as the main one.[156]

The picture that emerges from these writings contrasts with the determinism of Boas and Durkheim, however. According to Malinowski, culture is consistent with the nature of humanity. Thus there is no need for an individual to surpass himself and adapt himself to the coercive dictates of culture. Indeed, it has been observed that "Malinowski's monistic view of behavior resembled Tylorian reductionism more than Boasian determinism."[157] Malinowski's fieldwork further led him to conclude that many of an individual's inborn tendencies and motivations, such as ambition, vanity, "love of accumulation for its own sake,"[158] "love of give and take for its own sake,"[159] the "fundamental human impulse to display, to share, to bestow,"[160] are given expression in cultural life. These conclusions not only show a certain unity between humankind's nature and culture but also explode a number of myths about primitive life, such as the views that primitive people are "lazy" or "indolent" and incapable of collaborative work.[161] For example, Malinowski describes situations in which a farmer or gardener overproduces a crop to earn social distinction and prestige, because he is then able to distribute the excess to feed and support relatives.[162] In the context of the *kula* exchange, however, the quest for prestige can breed a competitive spirit as well as a desire to avoid humiliation:

> It is obvious that, however much a man may want to give a good equivalent for the object received . . . , he may not be able to do so. And then, as there is always a keen competition to be the most generous giver, a man who has received less than he gave will not keep the grievance to himself, but will brag about his own generosity and compare it to his partner's meanness; the other resents it, and the quarrel is ready to break out.[163]

An instructive example of the desire among the Trobrianders to gain prestige and avoid humiliation is cited by Malinowski in the context of adherence to custom, including sexual mores. He describes the Trobrianders' attitude to sexual aberrations as follows:

---

156. *Id.* at xvi.

157. Hatch, *supra* note 74, at 277.

158. Malinowski, Argonauts, *supra* note 147, at 173.

159. *Id.*

160. *Id.* at 175.

161. *Id.* at 60–61, 156 *et seq.*

162. *Id.* at 61.

163. Malinowski, Argonauts, *supra* note 147, at 97–98.

> To ask a man seriously whether he had indulged in such practices would deeply wound his vanity and self-regard, as well as shock his natural inclination. Vanity would be especially wounded, by the implication that he must be unable to procure the full natural enjoyment of his impulse if he has to resort to such substitutes. The Trobriander's contempt for any perversion is similar to his contempt for the man . . . who suffers hunger because there is nothing in his yamhouse.[164]

Here we see an example not only of a unity between culture and individual motivations but also of a systemic harmony between individual inclination and morality at large, which binds society as a whole. Malinowski cites many other situations to show that individual inclinations or emotions have an even "greater sway over custom than has reason."[165]

Bronislaw Malinowski, Argonauts of The Western Pacific: An Account of Native Enterprise and Adventure in the Archipelagoes of Melanesian New Guinea x–xiii, xvi–xvii, 6–9, 11–15, 21–25, 60–61, 97–98 (1922).

> One of the first conditions of acceptable Ethnographic work certainly is that it should deal with the totality of all social, cultural and psychological aspects of the community, for they are so interwoven that not one can be understood without taking into consideration all the others. The reader of this monograph will clearly see that though its main theme is economic—for it deals with commercial enterprise, exchange and trade—constant reference has to be made to social organisation, the power of magic, to mythology and folklore, and indeed to all other aspects as well as the main one.
>
> The geographical area of which the book treats is limited to the Archipelagoes lying off the eastern end of New Guinea. Even within this, the main field of research was in one district, that of the Trobriand Islands. This, however, has been studied minutely. I have lived in that one archipelago for about two years, in the course of three expeditions to New Guinea, during which time I naturally acquired a thorough knowledge of the language. I did my work entirely alone, living for the greater part of the time right in the villages. I therefore had constantly the daily life of the natives before my eyes, while accidental, dramatic occurrences, deaths, quarrels, village brawls, public and ceremonial events, could not escape my notice. . . .
>
> *Proper conditions for ethnographic work.* These, as said, consist mainly in cutting oneself off from the company of other white men, and remaining

---

164. Bronislaw Malinowski, The Sexual Life of Savages in Northwestern Melanesia 469–70 (1929).

165. Malinowski, Argonauts, *supra* note 147, at 345.

in as close contact with the natives as possible, which really can only be achieved by camping right in their villages....

But the Ethnographer has not only to spread his nets in the right place, and wait for what will fall into them. He must be an active huntsman, and drive his quarry into them and follow it up to its most inaccessible lairs.... Good training in theory, and acquaintance with its latest results, is not identical with being burdened with "preconceived ideas." If a man sets out on an expedition, determined to prove certain hypotheses, if he is incapable of changing his views constantly and casting them off ungrudgingly under the pressure of evidence, needless to say his work will be worthless. But the more problems he brings with him into the field, the more he is in the habit of moulding his theories according to facts, and of seeing facts in their bearing upon theory, the better he is equipped for the work. Preconceived ideas are pernicious in any scientific work, but foreshadowed problems are the main endowment of a scientific thinker, and these problems are first revealed to the observer by his theoretical studies....

Having settled this very general rule, let us descend to more detailed consideration of method. The Ethnographer has in the field, according to what has just been said, the duty before him of drawing up all the rules and regularities of tribal life; all that is permanent and fixed; of giving an anatomy of their culture, of depicting the constitution of their society. But these things, though crystallised and set, are nowhere *formulated*.... After this is realised an expedient has to be found to overcome this difficulty. This expedient for an Ethnographer consists in collecting concrete data of evidence. and drawing the general inferences for himself.

Though we cannot ask a native about abstract, general rules, we can always enquire how a given case would be treated. Thus for instance, in asking how they would treat crime, or punish it, it would be vain to put to a native a sweeping question such as, "How do you treat and punish a criminal?" for even words could not be found to express it in native, or in pidgin. But an imaginary case, or still better, a real occurrence, will stimulate a native to express his opinion and to supply plentiful information....

To return to our example, a number of definite cases discussed will reveal to the Ethnographer the social machinery for punishment. This is one part, one aspect of tribal authority. Imagine further that by a similar method of inference from definite data, he arrives at understanding leadership in war, in economic enterprise, in tribal festivities—there he has at once all the data necessary to answer the questions about tribal government and social authority. In actual field work, the comparison of such data, the attempt to piece them together, will often reveal rifts and gaps in the information which lead on to further investigations....

The collecting of concrete data over a wide range of facts is thus one of the main points of field method....

. . . [A]n Ethnographer, who wishes to be trusted, must show clearly and concisely, in a tabularised form, which are his own direct observations, and which the indirect information that form the bases of his account. . . .

Again, in this type of work, it is good for the Ethnographer sometimes to put aside camera, note book and pencil, and to join in himself in what is going on. He can take part in the natives' games, he can follow them on their visits and walks, sit down and listen and share in their conversations. . . . I have carried away a distinct feeling that their behaviour, their manner of being, in all sorts of tribal transactions, became more transparent and easily understandable than it had been before.

Finally, let us pass to the third and last aim of scientific field-work, to the last type of phenomenon which ought to be recorded in order to give a full and adequate picture of native culture. Besides the firm outline of tribal constitution and crystallised cultural items which form the skeleton, besides the data of daily life and ordinary behaviour, which are, so to speak, its flesh and blood, there is still to be recorded the spirit—the natives' views and opinions and utterances. For, in every act of tribal life, there is, first, the routine prescribed by custom and tradition, then there is the manner in which it is carried out, and lastly there is the commentary to it, contained in the natives' mind. A man who submits to various customary obligations, who follows a traditional course of action, does it impelled by certain motives, to the accompaniment of certain feelings, guided by certain ideas. These ideas, feelings, and impulses are moulded and conditioned by the culture in which we find them, and are therefore an ethnic peculiarity of the given society. An attempt must be made therefore, to study and record them. . . .

So, the third commandment of field-work runs: Find out the typical ways of thinking and feeling, corresponding to the institutions and culture of a given community, and formulate the results in the most convincing manner. What will be the method of procedure? . . . As my knowledge of the language progressed, I put down more and more in Kiriwinian, till at last I found myself writing exclusively in that language, rapidly taking notes, word for word, of each statement. . . .

Our considerations thus indicate that the goal of ethnographic field-work must be approached through three avenues:

1. *The organisation of the tribe, and the anatomy of its culture* must be recorded in firm, clear outline. The method of *concrete, statistical documentation* is the means through which such an outline has to be given.
2. Within this frame, the *imponderabilia of actual life,* and the *type of behaviour* have to be filled in. They have to be collected through minute, detailed observations, in the form of some sort of ethnographic diary, made possible by close contact with native life.

3. A collection of ethnographic statements, characteristic narratives, typical utterances, items of folk-lore and magical formulae has to be given as a *corpus inscriptionum*, as documents of native mentality.

These three lines of approach lead to the final goal, of which an Ethnographer should never lose sight. This goal is, briefly, to grasp the native's point of view, his relation to life, to realise *his* vision of *his* world. . . .

A good garden worker in the Trobriands derives a direct prestige from the amount of labour he can do, and the size of garden he can till. The title *tokwaybagula,* which means good "or efficient gardener," is bestowed with discrimination, and borne with pride. Several of my friends, renowned as *tokwaybagula*, would boast to me how long they worked, how much ground they tilled, and would compare their efforts with those of less efficient men. When the labour, some of which is done communally, is being actually carried out, a good deal of competition goes on. Men vie with one another in their speed, in their thoroughness, and in the weights they can lift, when bringing big poles to the garden, or in carrying away the harvested yams.

The most important point about this is, however, that all, or almost all the fruits of his work, and certainly any surplus which he can achieve by extra effort, goes not to the man himself, but to his relatives-in-law. . . .

[Having described his methodology, Malinowski describes the social significance of the *Kula* as follows:]

This social code, such as we find it among the natives of the Kula is, however, far from weakening the natural desirability of possession; on the contrary, it lays down that to possess is to be great, and that wealth is the indispensable appanage of social rank and attribute of personal virtue. But the important point is that with them to possess is to give—and here the natives differ from us notably. A man who owns a thing is naturally expected to share it, to distribute it, to be its trustee and dispenser. And the higher the rank the greater the obligation. A chief will naturally be expected to give food to any stranger, visitor, even loiterer from another end of the village. He will be expected to share any of the betel-nut or tobacco he has about him. So that a man of rank will have to hide away any surplus of these articles which he wants to preserve for his further use. In the Eastern end of New Guinea a type of large basket, with three layers, manufactured in the Trobriands, was specially popular among people of consequence, because one could hide away ones small treasures in the lower compartments. Thus the main symptom of being powerful is to be wealthy, and of wealth is to be generous. Meanness, indeed, is the most despised vice, and the only thing about which the natives have strong moral views, while generosity is the essence of goodness.

This moral injunction and ensuing habit of generosity, superficially observed and misinterpreted, is responsible for another wide-spread misconception, that of the *primitive communism of savages.* This, quite as much as

> the diametrically opposed figment of the acquisitive and ruthlessly tenacious native, is definitely erroneous, . . .
>
> Thus the fundamental principle of the natives' moral code in this matter makes a man do his fair share in Kula transaction and the more important he is, the more will he desire to shine by his generosity. *Noblesse oblige* is in reality the social norm regulating their conduct. . . . But it is very important to realise that there is no actual haggling, no tendency to do a man out of his share. The giver is quite as keen as the receiver that the gift should be generous, though for different reasons. Then, of course, there is the important consideration that a man who is fair and generous in the Kula will attract a larger stream to himself than a mean one.
>
> The two main principles, namely, first that the Kula is a gift repaid after an interval of time by a counter-gift, and not a bartering; and second, that the equivalent rests with the giver, and cannot be enforced, nor can there be any haggling or going back on the exchange—these underlie all the transactions.

Functionalism and Law

Yet another myth Malinowski tried to lay to rest was the belief that primitive humans were "completely dominated by the group—the horde, the clan or the tribe—that he obeys the commands of his community . . . with a slavish, fascinated, passive obedience."[166] In his classic work, *Crime and Custom in Savage Society*, he showed that respect for law and the rights of others was not an automatic reflex among the Trobrianders but was based on the principle of reciprocity.[167] He writes elsewhere that

> in the Trobriands I had found that people keep to what custom—or, more correctly, law—bids them to do because they know that not far ahead there looms the occasion when in the name of the same law they will be entitled to demand the counter-service.[168]

This principle was not an isolated occurrence here and there, but was quite pervasive in social life, from the private (personal) level to the public:

> The serial balancing of services, the reciprocal interlocking of claims, which makes up the personal bond of husband and wife, of chief and subject, of economic partners, supplies the real compulsion for their respective contributions to the joint work or enterprise.[169]

The passage refers to the principle of reciprocity as being applicable to husband and wife, chief and subject, and economic partners. With these broad references, Malinowski asserted the pervasiveness of reciprocity in Trobriand society. The principle

166. Bronislaw Malinowski, Crime and Custom in Savage Society 3–4 (1926).

167. *Id.* at 25–26, 39–49.

168. Bronislaw Malinowski, *Introduction, in* Ian Hogbin, Law and Order in Polynesia xli (1934).

169. *Id.* at xxxv.

had legal status because it sanctioned a mutuality of claims and expectations among all members of society. The principle was evidenced by "definite rules, . . . arranged into well-balanced claims of reciprocal services."[170] Even the chief, who had all the outward trappings of authority, respected and was bound by "legal fetters."[171]

These views directly oppose the Durkheimian notion of repressive solidarity, in which group sentiment is so dominant that the individual acts in slavish obedience to it. Malinowski boldly asserted that this is "a mistaken view," "a myth."[172] He later names Durkheim as one who holds such "exaggerated views."[173] In relation to the Trobrianders, Malinowski maintains that "*law* covers the whole culture and the entire tribal constitution of these natives,"[174] and there is thus a complex legal regime of marriage, as well as family law and kinship law. There are independent legal regimes for the constitution of a village community, the position of the headman as chief of his district, and the privileges and duties of the public magician.[175] The latter has an important social role in that he uses "black magic" to persuade individuals to observe tribal law. Such exhortations and the obedience they evoke in turn prevent violence and help maintain equilibrium and normative order.[176]

With these claims, Malinowski propounds an anthropological definition of law. Legal rules as found among the Trobrianders are differentiated from nonlegal rules in that (1) they contain jural opposites in the form of a right of one person and a corresponding obligation of another; (2) they have binding force, in the sense they are enforced by the sanctions of a definite social machinery; and (3) they are based on mutual dependence and reciprocal services.[177]

Again in contrast to Durkheim, Malinowski asserted that primitive law does not consist exclusively or even mainly of negative prohibitions and is not exclusively or even chiefly composed of criminal law.[178] In support of this assertion he cites examples of positive law (or "civil law") among the Trobrianders; punishment does not always result from breaching such laws, but compliance with them is rewarded. Indeed, compliance is not so much due to rewards or punishments but to personal sentiments such as loyalty, friendship, and ambition.[179]

Finally, Malinowski emphasizes that Melanesian law is not embodied in a formal legal system that is independent and self-contained but is integrated into the social fabric of reciprocal expectations.

---

170. Malinowski, Crime, *supra* note 166, at 46.

171. *Id.*

172. *Id.* at 48.

173. *Id.* at 55.

174. *Id.* at 49, emphasis in original.

175. Malinowski, Crime, *supra* note 166, at 76.

176. *Id.* at 85–86.

177. *Id.* at 55.

178. *Id.* at 56.

179. *Id.* at 58.

Bronislaw Malinowski, Crime and Custom in Savage Society 55–59 (1951).

An Anthropological Definition of Law

The rules of law stand out from the rest in that they are felt and regarded as the obligations of one person and the rightful claims of another. They are sanctioned not by a mere psychological motive, but by a definite social machinery of binding force, based, as we know, upon mutual dependence, and realized in the equivalent arrangement of reciprocal services, as well as in the combination of such claims into strands of multiple relationship. The ceremonial manner in which most transactions are carried out, which entails public control and criticism, adds still more to their binding force.

We may therefore finally dismiss the view that 'group-sentiment' or 'collective responsibility' is the only or even the main force which ensures adhesion to custom and which makes it binding or legal. *Esprit de corps*, solidarity, pride in one's community and clan exist undoubtedly among the Melanesians—no social order could be maintained without them in any culture high or low. I only want to enter a caution against such exaggerated views as those of Rivers, Sidney Hartland, Durkheim, and others . . .

It results also from the account here given that primitive law does not consist exclusively or even chiefly of negative injunctions, nor is all savage law criminal law . . .

[These] views are fully endorsed by the great French sociologists Durkheim and Mauss, who add besides one more clause: that responsibility, revenge, in fact all legal reactions are founded in the psychology of the group and not of the individual . . .

In our own province we so far met with positive commandments only, the breach of which is penalized but not punished, and the machinery of which can by no procrustean methods be stretched beyond the line which separates *civil* from *criminal* law. If we have to provide the rules described in these articles with some modern, hence necessarily inappropriate label,—they must be called the body of 'civil law' of the Trobriand Islanders.

'Civil law,' the positive law governing all the phases of tribal life, consists then of a body of binding obligations, regarded as a right by one party and acknowledged as a duty by the other, kept in force by a specific mechanism of reciprocity and publicity inherent in the structure of their society. These rules of civil law are elastic and possess a certain latitude. They offer not only penalties for failure, but also premiums for an overdose of fulfillment. Their stringency is ensured through the rational appreciation of cause and effect by the natives, combined with a number of social and personal sentiments such as ambition, vanity, pride, desire of self-enhancement by display, and also attachment, friendship, devotion and loyalty to the kin.

It scarcely needs to be added that 'law' and 'legal phenomena,' as we have discovered, described and defined them in a part of Melanesia, do not consist in any independent institutions. Law represents rather an aspect of their tribal life, one side of their structure, than any independent, self-contained social arrangements. Law dwells not in a special system of decrees which foresee and define possible forms of non-fulfillment and provide appropriate barriers and remedies. Law is the specific result of the configuration of obligations, which makes it impossible for the native to shirk his responsibility without suffering for it in the future.

The Contrast with Durkheim

Durkheim's approach to law, which was discussed in the first part of this chapter,[180] contained three metatheses: (1) law is the external symbol of social solidarity, and as such, serves as an index of social development; (2) the evolution of society from the collective type to one with specialized division of labor is accompanied by a parallel movement from mechanical and repressive solidarity to organic and restitutive solidarity; and (3) because punishment is designed to protect the common consciousness, the nature of a legal rule is to be understood according to the nature of the sanction it embodies. Durkheim proposed two categories of sanction: repressive and restitutive. The former are prevalent in societies of the collective type, the latter in specialized societies. Repressive law is a reflexive collective reaction to protect group sentiments, whereas restitutive law—which he also called "civil law"—is largely detached from group sentiments. Repressive law is penal or religious in nature and inflicts pain for the sake of pain, avenging and mollifying the intensity of group feelings in the process.

The contrast with Malinowski cannot be more obvious. First, Durkheim's concept of civil law applies to the developed specialized societies and not to societies of the collective type. This is more than a semantic difference; Malinowski expressly declares civil law to exist in Melanesian society. Second, according to Malinowski, "primitive law does not consist exclusively or even chiefly of negative injunctions, nor is all savage law criminal law."[181] As we saw in the excerpt, he also rejects Durkheim's view that primitive law extracts revenge based "in the psychology of the group and not the individual." Malinowski affirms the role of individual sentiments as well, including rational calculation, altruism, pride, and loyalty—not to mention the expectation of reciprocity at the personal or individual level. Suicide is also an important sanction, according to Malinowski, because the individual lawbreaker *qua individual* pays the ultimate price through self-enforcement.[182] Durkheim's study of suicide characterizes it as a pathological phenomenon caused by capitalism and the alienation of the individual from society. Malinowski's view, by contrast, indicates that far from being alienated from society, the individual demonstrates solidarity with society by paying the ultimate price.

---

180. *See* section on "Society and Law," *supra*.

181. MALINOWSKI, CRIME, *supra* note 166, at 56 (excerpt above).

182. *Id.* at 94 *et seq.*

Malinowski summarized the Durkheimian approach as follows:

> In modern anthropological jurisprudence, it is universally assumed that all custom is law to the savage and that he has no law but his custom. All custom again is obeyed automatically and rigidly by sheer inertia. There is no civil law or its equivalent in savage societies. The only relevant facts are the occasional breaches in defiance of custom—the crimes. There is no mechanism of enforcement of the primitive rules of conduct except the punishment of flagrant crime.[183]

In rejecting this view, Malinowski claims that his ethnographic research showed many specific legal methods and procedures of dispute resolution among the Trobrianders. He identified four such procedures, ranging from formal legal to informal social types.[184] They include litigants meeting in public to exchange recriminations and the use of magical curses.[185] He also rejects the idea that primitive people obey rules instinctively, unwittingly, or spontaneously.[186] Indeed, according to Malinowski, a functional approach to law shows that it imposes nonspontaneous compulsory behavior through a wide variety of formal and informal sanctions. Their purpose is to ensure cooperation based on mutual concessions on a reciprocal basis in the service of common ends.[187]

In sum, although Malinowski did not deny the role of custom and tribal sentiment in regulating behavior, he asserted a vast parallel domain of law whose chief characteristics are reciprocity, systematic incidence, publicity, and ambition.[188] These constitute what he calls the "minimum definition of law."

> The binding forces of Melanesian civil law are to be found in the concatenation of the obligations, in the fact that they are arranged into chains of mutual services, a give and take extending over long periods of time and covering wide aspects of interest and activity. To this there is added the conspicuous and ceremonial manner in which most of the legal obligations have to be discharged. This binds people by an appeal to their vanity and self-regard, to their love of self-enhancement by display. Thus the binding force of these rules is due to the natural mental trend of self-interest, ambition and vanity, set into play by a special social mechanism into which the obligatory actions are framed.[189]

Malinowski's expanded or "maximal" definition should be added as well, because his concept of primitive law shows a considerable degree of subtlety and *souplesse.*

---

183. *Id.* at 63.

184. *Id.* at 60–61.

185. *Id.* at 60.

186. Malinowski, Crime, *supra* note 166, at 79–83.

187. *Id.* at 64.

188. *Id.* at 68.

189. *Id.* at 67.

> The most important fact from our point of view in this struggle of social principles is that it forces us to re-cast completely the traditional conception of law and order in savage communities. We have to abandon now definitely the idea of an inert, solid 'crust' or 'cake' of custom rigidly pressing from outside upon the whole surface of tribal life. Law and order arise out of the very processes which they govern. But they are not rigid, nor due to any inertia or permanent mould. They obtain on the contrary as the result of a constant struggle not merely of human passions against the law, but of legal principles with one another. The struggle, however, is not a free fight: it is subject to definite conditions, can take place only within certain limits and only on the condition that it remains under the surface of publicity. Once an open challenge has been entered, the precedence of strict law over legalized usage or over an encroaching principle of law is established and the orthodox hierarchy of legal systems controls the issue.
>
> For as we have seen the conflict takes place between strict law and legalized usage, and it is possible because the former has the strength of more definite tradition behind it, while the latter draws force from personal inclinations and actual power. There exist thus within the body of law not only different types such as quasi-civil and quasi-criminal, or the law of economic transactions, of political relations, etc., but there can be distinguished degrees of orthodoxy, stringency, and validity, placing the rules into a hierarchy from the main law of Mother-right, totemism, and rank down to the clandestine evasions and the traditional means of defying law and abetting crime.[190]

Malinowski, Boas, and Durkheim: Some General Conclusions

Malinowski demanded and practiced empiricism on a scale that has seldom been matched. He rejected speculative evolutionary schemes as to the origin and causes of cultural uniformities and differences. Along with Spencer and Tylor, he believed that the individual was motivated by natural inclinations. But this similarity among the three is, on closer scrutiny, superficial. Malinowski gave motives, inclinations, and emotions prominence so that they could be understood as having greater sway than reason over custom. Spencer and Tyler, by contrast, portrayed humans as rational creatures rather than emotional ones. Malinowski's concept of the individual-in-culture is far more nuanced and complex because he expressly recognized the emotional *and* rational components of individual behavior.

Malinowski saw symbiosis between the individual and culture and therefore did not espouse the brands of cultural determinism advocated by Boas and Durkheim. He saw no cleft between culture and human nature. Yet his thorough abandonment of speculative theories led him to espouse and practice a functionalist methodology not unlike Durkheim's, which set him apart from the Boasian school. Whereas the

190. *Id.* at 122–123.

latter saw the individual merely learning culture and not creating it, which gave the person only a passive role in culture, Malinowski viewed the individual as having an active, goal-oriented role. The Boasian school would be content to describe as custom a taboo or ritual, but Malinowski and Durkheim viewed these as complex actions to be studied in terms of their larger normative as well as personal implications.

Boas's particularism is another point of contrast with Malinowski. To Boas, each culture is unique and has its own history and character. Insofar as man is a product of culture, under the Boasian approach the individuals of each society exhibit distinct personalities. To Malinowski, all men are basically alike. Trobrianders, for example, are driven by motives of wealth maximization and avoidance of onerous obligations (when the risks are low enough), just like their counterparts in the West.

The views of Durkheim and Malinowski may be contrasted on the question of conformity to custom and the existence of civil and repressive law. For Durkheim, social solidarity becomes the foundation of normative order from which the collective consciousness emerges. This emergence is reflected by an emotional commitment to the demands of a collective life that transcends humanity's animal nature. Malinowski's concept of the unity between culture and human nature represents a very different idea: humans are not shackled and repressed by custom. Instead, social life and custom are what enable the realization of a person's inborn feelings and inclinations. Malinowski presented a far more dynamic relationship of humanity and culture and rejected Durkheim's claim that primitive law is repressive and criminal in nature. In this context, he goes so far as to say that primitive society, as exemplified by the Trobrianders, has a richly textured and multilayered legal system, or "civil law." For Durkheim, civil law exists only in the more developed specialized societies.

The Durkheimian and Boasian views assign a fairly passive role to the individual because he is molded, if not constrained by, cultural forces from which there is no escape. Malinowski's view of the goal-oriented individual shows an active role. Moreover, he believed that the individual can and does escape social rules whenever the risks are low enough and/or he can get away with it.[191]

There is some narrow convergence between the views of Malinowski and Durkheim on the question of cultural constraints. Both accept this notion, but for Durkheim, these constraints are imposed from above and are therefore external to the individual, who simply must succumb to the moral authority of the rules of collective life. Malinowski, by contrast, views social constraints, including suicide (as a sanction) as internal to the individual. The drive to avoid humiliation, to gain renown, and so on are all internal impulses that motivate conformity with social rules.

A final comparison between Malinowski and the Boasian tradition stems from Malinowski's attention to detail and his rigorous fieldwork standards. In accordance with his functionalist approach, every social fact had to be viewed as a part and in the context of the larger whole. Not only did he thereby explode certain myths about primitive life and preconceived notions as to the "nature" of primitive humans, he maintained that placing a particular custom in its proper cultural context gave mean-

191. Malinowski, Sexual Life of Savages, *supra* note 164, at 509–10.

ing to it and revealed something about social organization. The notion of cultural configurations of the Boasian school makes a similar point, as Benedict did when her study of cultural patterning led her to develop the theory of cultural integration (which involved a mosaic of cultural and emotional configurations). By this logic, consistencies in cultural patterns tend to have an integrative force in society and cultural events should never be studied in isolation. Benedict gives the example of one such event, the Hopi snake dance, which, when regarded in isolation, appeared to be absurd and irrational to an outside observer, but when placed in its proper cultural context was recognized as having a distinct integrative role. Similarly, Malinowski cited the example of polygamy among the Trobrianders, which in context is a basis of the political order but to an outsider may seem morally offensive.

Malinowski's methodology enabled him to claim to have identified certain "objective" characteristics and conditions of social life. One such characteristic is normative institutionalization. Thus within culture, which comprises a network of interrelated institutions, each one is an organized system of purposeful activities. For example, a clan, tribe, or family would have (a) its own charter or constitution, rules, beliefs, myths; (b) people; (c) laws; (d) material apparatus; (e) activities; and (f) functions. Individual needs, which are served by institutions, are another characteristic.[192] Among the primary needs identified by Malinowski are metabolism, reproduction, bodily comforts, safety, movement, growth, and health. Other needs, such as law, education, and economic and political organization, are "derived" or "instrumental." An integrative cultural framework of knowledge, art, religion, and so on is required to meet these needs, according to Malinowski.

Radcliffe-Brown: Functionalism and Social Structure

A. R. Radcliffe-Brown (1881–1955) was another leading member of the functionalist movement, although he rejected this label.[193] Emphasizing fieldwork, like Malinowski, he studied tribal organization in Australia, Africa, and the Andaman Islands in the Indian Ocean. He moved away from the concept of culture and individual to the concept of society, particularly its structure and continuity. He strongly rejected Malinowski's approach of studying the biopsychological needs of individuals,[194] to the point of calling himself an "antifunctionalist."

Malinowski had been very specific in defining needs in terms of seven biological imperatives of survival.[195] Radcliffe-Brown rejected the biological approach to human needs and substituted "necessary conditions of existence" within society. As explored in detail, the principal focus of this broader formulation was the conditions that make

192. Some needs are "primary," others are "derived or "instrumental." The third and final set are needs for mental and moral "integration." For further reading, *see* Malinowski, *The Group and Individual in Functional Analysis*, *supra* note 116.

193. A.R. Radcliffe-Brown, *Functionalism: A Protest*, 51 AM. ANTHROPOL., 320, 321 (1949).

194. *Id.* at 322.

195. *See* text at notes 131 *supra*.

it possible for society to exist as an ongoing normative order, which Radcliffe-Brown called "social structure."

Radcliffe-Brown was quite scathing in his rejection of Malinowski's functionalism. Not only did he scorn the concept of biological needs as "a falsehood invented by the authors for some reason of their own," he also asserted that the word "need" was "tainted with ambiguity."[196] With regard to the word "functionalism," he makes the following caustic remark:

> It is worth while to point out that names ending in—*ism* do not apply to scientific theories, but do apply to philosophical doctrines. There are such things as socialism and utilitarianism, and also Platonism, Hegelianism and Marxism. Chemists work on the basis of the atomic theory, but no one calls their theory "atomism" though this may be an appropriate name for the philosophy of Democritus. By calling his doctrine "functionalism" Malinowski seems to have wished to emphasize that it was the product of one mind, like any philosophical doctrine, not, like a scientific theory, the product of the co-operative thinking of a succession of scientists. Might it not prevent confusion if it were renamed Malinowskianism?[197]

If "functionalism" cannot be used as a descriptive term for Radcliffe-Brown's methodology, perhaps the best choice is "structural-functional." Two reasons may be given. First, the fundamental theoretical premise of his methodology is based on Durkheim's concept of social solidarity. As we shall see, Durkheimian notions of functionalism (*i.e.*, solidarity and group sentiment) are also quite prominent in Radcliffe-Brown's methodology. Second, because Radcliffe-Brown's approach to function is inextricably tied to the idea of social structure, "structural-functional" or "functional-structural" are natural choices.[198]

Early Durkheimian Influences

Embracing a fundamental theoretical premise of Durkheim's methodology, Radcliffe-Brown concentrated on studying society as an integral whole.

> Individual human beings . . . are connected by a definite set of social relations into an integrated whole. The continuity of the social structure, like that of an organic structure, is not destroyed by changes in the units. Individuals may leave the society, by death or otherwise; others may enter it. The continuity of structure is maintained by the process of social life, which consists of the activities and interactions of the individual human beings and of the organized groups into which they are united. The social life of the community is here defined as the *functioning* of the social structure. The *function* of any

196. Radcliffe-Brown, *Functionalism*, *supra* note 193, at 321.

197. *Id.* at 322–23.

198. Harris, *supra* note 5, at 515.

> recurrent activity, such as the punishment of a crime, or a funeral ceremony, is the part it plays in the social life as a whole and therefore the contribution it makes to the maintenance of the structural continuity.
>
> The concept of function as here defined thus involves the notion of a *structure* consisting of a *set of relations* amongst *unit entities*, the *continuity* of the structure being maintained by a *life-process* made up of the *activities* of the constituent units.
>
> If, with these concepts in mind, we set out on a systematic investigation of the nature of human society and of social life, we find presented to us three sets of problems. First, the problems of social morphology—what kinds of social structures are there, what are their similarities and differences, how are they to be classified? Second, the problems of social physiology—how do social structures function? Third, the problems of development—how do new types of social structure come into existence?[199]

The conclusions he reached from his fieldwork show the influence of Durkheim's concept of the collective consciousness and social solidarity. For example, Radcliffe-Brown's research on the Andaman Islanders concluded that the function and purpose of many of their gatherings for feasting, dancing, ceremonies, and rituals were to enhance social integration and contribute to the maintenance of normative order and social structure.[200] Here, he explains his general theory of the social function of rites and ceremonies:

> Thirty-seven years ago (1908), in a fellowship thesis on the Andaman Islanders (which did not appear in print till 1922), I formulated briefly a general theory of the social function of rites and ceremonies . . . Stated in the simplest possible terms the theory is that an orderly social life amongst human beings depends upon the presence in the minds of the members of a society of certain sentiments, which control the behaviour of the individual in his relation to others. Rites can be seen to be the regulated symbolic expressions of certain sentiments. Rites can therefore be shown to have a specific social function, when, and to the extent that, they have for their effect to regulate, maintain and transmit from one generation to another sentiments on which the constitution of the society depends. I ventured to suggest as a general formula that religion is everywhere an expression in one form or another of a sense of dependence on a power outside ourselves, a power which we may speak of as a spiritual or moral power.[201]

The reference to group sentiments is certainly reminiscent of Durkheim's notion of collective consciousness, and Radcliffe-Brown's treatment of symbolic behavior also parallels Durkheim's analysis that symbolism permits the reaffirmation of group

---

199. Radcliffe-Brown, Structure and Function, *supra* note 7, at 180.

200. Keesing & Keesing, *supra* note 1, at 390.

201. Radcliffe-Brown, Structure and Function, *supra* note 7, at 157.

solidarity. Finally, his reference to a "dependence on a power outside of ourselves" is remarkably similar to Durkheim's view that group symbols and rituals reinforce collective life in a way that seemed to be under the sway of a powerful force external to society. Indeed, Radcliffe-Brown held the view that taboos are external restraints, enjoined from without, which also have social value as a constraint on behavior and in the reinforcement of group values. Both thinkers accepted the idea that social life required the existence of obligatory norms, which the individual could not ignore. Therefore, both believed that sanctions imposed for infractions of norms are integral elements in the functioning of social institutions.[202]

Of course these views contrast with the Boasian tradition, in which social life was viewed as a natural condition (*i.e.*, without "obligatory" norms) for the individual. Where Radcliffe-Brown and Durkheim would treat a taboo as an external constraint, Boas would classify it simply as a habit; on the concept of sanctions, Radcliffe-Brown based social cohesion on enforceable norms, whereas for Boas the application of a sanction was merely an internal reflex.[203]

These similarities in the thought of Durkheim and Radcliffe-Brown must not obscure the varying nuances, indeed, the differences, in their thoughts. Durkheim's idea of the collective consciousness was not verifiable within the phenomenal world; the very notion of consciousness suggests something intangible. For Radcliffe-Brown, social structure has a physical existence. Therefore, the contribution of institutions (*i.e.*, their function) must be assessed in relation to the phenomenal features of society. These features, in turn, are the actual network of social relations, their cohesion, and their stability. Furthermore, Durkheim's desire to avoid reductionism prevented him from examining whether and to what extent social institutions were useful to individual well-being. Radcliffe-Brown, by contrast, accepted and acknowledged the utilitarian function of institutions, namely, the promotion of stability and cohesion.[204] The utilitarian aspect of his approach implicitly deems the autonomy of the collective consciousness to be irrelevant and posits that beliefs and values acquire a life of their own. Radcliffe-Brown's methodology treats as valuable only those beliefs that have a functional significance and ignores those that do not.[205]

The following excerpt shows Durkheim's influence on Radcliffe-Brown's methodology for studying function.

A.R. Radcliffe-Brown, Structure and Function in Primitive Society 178–185 (1952).

> The concept of function applied to human societies is based on an analogy between social life and organic life. The recognition of the analogy and of some of its implications is not new. In the nineteenth century the analogy,

202. Hatch, *supra* note 74, at 233.

203. *Id.* at 233–34.

204. *Id.* at 228–31.

205. *Id.* at 230.

the concept of function, and the word itself appear frequently in social philosophy and sociology. So far as I know the first systematic formulation of the concept as applying to the strictly scientific study of society was that of Emile Durkheim in 1895. *(Régles de la Méthode Sociologique.)*

Durkheim's definition is that the 'function' of a social institution is the correspondence between it and the needs *(besoins* in French) of the social organism. This definition requires some elaboration. In the first place, to avoid possible ambiguity and in particular the possibility of a teleological interpretation, I would like to substitute for the term 'needs' the term 'necessary conditions of existence', or, if the term 'need' is used, it is to be understood only in this sense. It may be here noted, as a point to be returned to, that any attempt to apply this concept of function in social science involves the assumption that there *are* necessary conditions of existence for human societies just as there are for animal organisms, and that they can be discovered by the proper kind of scientific enquiry.

For the further elucidation of the concept it is convenient to use the analogy between social life and organic life. Like all analogies it has to be used with care. An animal organism is an agglomeration of cells and interstitial fluids arranged in relation to one another not as an aggregate but as an integrated living whole. For the biochemist, it is a complexly integrated system of complex molecules. The system of relations by which these units are related is the organic structure. As the terms are here used the organism is *not* itself the structure; it is a collection of units (cells or molecules) arranged in a structure, i.e. in a set of relations; the organism *has* a structure. . . .

To turn from organic life to social life, if we examine such a community as an African or Australian tribe we can recognise the existence of a social structure. Individual human beings, the essential units in this instance, are connected by a definite set of social relations into an integrated whole. The continuity of the social structure, like that of an organic structure, is not destroyed by changes in the units. Individuals may leave the society, by death or otherwise; others may enter it. The continuity of structure is maintained by the process of social life, which consists of the activities and interactions of the individual human beings and of the organised groups into which they are united. The social life of the community is here defined as the *functioning* of the social structure. The *function* of any recurrent activity, such as the punishment of a crime, or a funeral ceremony, is the part it plays in the social life as a whole and therefore the contribution it makes to the maintenance of the structural continuity.

The concept of function as here defined thus involves the notion of a *structure* consisting of a *set of relations* amongst *unit entities,* the *continuity* of the structure being maintained by a *life-process* made up of the *activities* of the constituent units.

If, with these concepts in mind, we set out on a systematic investigation of the nature of human society and of social life, we find presented to us three sets of problems. First, the problems of social morphology—what kinds of social structures are there, what are their similarities and differences, how are they to be classified? Second, the problems of social physiology—how do social structures function? Third, the problems of development—how do new types of social structure come into existence?

Two important points where the analogy between organism and society breaks down must be noted. In an animal organism it is possible to observe the organic structure to some extent independently of its functioning. It is therefore possible to make a morphology which is independent of physiology. But in human society the social structure as a whole can only be *observed* in its functioning. Some of the features of social structure, such as the geographical distribution of individuals and groups can be directly observed, but most of the social relations which in their totality constitute the structure, such as relations of father and son, buyer and seller, ruler and subject, cannot be observed except in the social activities in which the relations are functioning. It follows that a social morphology cannot be established independently of a social physiology.

The second point is that an animal organism does not, in the course of its life, change its structural type. A pig does not become a hippopotamus. (The development of the animal from germination to maturity is not a change of type since the process in all its stages is typical for the species.) On the other hand a society in the course of its history can and does change its structural type without any breach of continuity.

By the definition here offered 'function' is the contribution which a partial activity makes to the total activity of which it is a part. The function of a particular social usage is the contribution it makes to the total social life as the functioning of the total social system. Such a view implies that a social system (the total social structure of a society together with the totality of social usages in which that structure appears and on which it depends for its continued existence) has a certain kind of unity, which we may speak of as a functional unity. We may define it as a condition in which all parts of the social system work together with a sufficient degree of harmony or internal consistency, i.e. without producing persistent conflicts which can neither be resolved nor regulated. . . .

The concept of function as defined above constitutes a 'working hypothesis' by which a number of problems are formulated for investigation. No scientific enquiry is possible without some such formulation of working hypotheses. Two remarks are necessary here. One is that the hypothesis does not require the dogmatic assertion that everything in the life of every community has a function. It only requires the assumption that it *may* have one, and that we are justified in seeking to discover it. The second is that what appears to be the same social usage in two societies may have different functions in the two. Thus the practice of celibacy in the Roman Catholic Church of today has very different functions from those of celibacy in the early Christian Church. In other words, in order to define a social usage, and therefore in order to make valid comparisons between the usages of different peoples or periods, it is necessary to consider not merely the form of the usage but also its function. On this basis, for example, belief in a Supreme Being in a simple society is something different from such a belief in a modern civilised community.

The acceptance of the functional hypothesis or point of view outlined above results in the recognition of a vast number of problems for the solution of which there are required wide comparative studies of societies of many diverse types and also intensive studies of as many single societies as possible. In field studies of the simpler peoples it leads, first of all, to a direct study of the social life of the community as the functioning of a social structure, and of this there are several examples in recent literature. Since the function of a social activity is to be found by examining its effects upon individuals, these are studied, either in the average individual or in both average and exceptional individuals. Further, the hypothesis leads to attempts to investigate directly the functional consistency or unity of a social system and to determine as far as possible in each instance the nature of that unity. Such field studies will obviously be different in many ways from studies carried out from other points of view, *e.g.*, the ethnological point of view that lays emphasis on diffusion. We do not have to say that one point of view is better than another, but only that they are different, and any particular piece of work should be judged in reference to what it aims to do....

The Concept of Structure

According to Radcliffe-Brown, a structural system is made up of groups such as the family or clan, each of which has its own internal relationships (*e.g.*, mother and child, father and child, husband and wife). The second component of a structural system is individuals, who also have person-to-person relationships among themselves. The totality of these relations, which constitutes the social structure of a given group, is based on the expectation that all individuals and groups will behave in a certain way. There thus emerge entire series of socially recognized norms and patterns of conduct pertaining to specific aspects of social life. Each such set of norms is referred to by Radcliffe-Brown as an "institution." "Social structure therefore has to be described by the institutions which define the proper or expected conduct of persons in their various relationships."[206]

He observes that institutions, which have a relatively higher degree of continuity than groups, survive regardless of turnover among the individuals who populate them, and posits that this durability appears because social relations are based on patterns of behavior that are more or less constant. Radcliffe-Brown thus concludes

206. A.R. Radcliffe-Brown, Method in Social Anthropology 175 (1958).

that the structural features of social life consist of the totality of continuing institutional relationships.[207]

The next excerpt explains Radcliffe-Brown's notion of social structure.

A.R. Radcliffe-Brown, Method in Social Anthropology 174–177 (1958).

To arrive at a description of a structural system we have not only to consider social groups, such as the family, the clan and the horde, in western Australia, with the internal structure of the group and the relations between the groups, and also social classes, but we have to examine the whole set of socially fixed relationships of person to person, as in the Australian kinship system. The social reality of groups and classes consists in the way in which they affect the interactions of persons, as belonging to the same or different groups or classes. From this point of view the structure of a region at a particular time consists of the whole set of social relationships in which the persons of that region are involved.

In any of the relationships of which the social structure consists there is an expectation that a person will conform to certain rules or patterns of behavior. The term *institution* is used to refer to this, (an institution being an established or socially recognised system of norms or patterns of conduct referring to some aspect of social life.) The family institutions of a society are the patterns of behavior to which the members of the family are expected to conform in their conduct in relation to one another. There are patterns or norms of conduct for a father towards his children, for a wife to a husband and vice versa, for child to parent, for brother to brother or sister. These institutions are accepted in a particular society, of which they are the institutions, as fixing, with a certain measure of flexibility, the *proper* conduct of a person in a certain relationship. They define for a person how he is expected to behave, and also how he may expect others to behave. Not every one always behaves as he ought, as he is expected to; minor or major deviations are frequent in any society; to deal with these there are *sanctions* of various kinds. Social structure therefore has to be described by the institutions which define the proper or expected conduct of persons in their various relationships. The structural features of social life of a particular region consists of all those continuing arrangements of persons in institutional relationships which are exhibited in the actions and interactions that in their totality make up the social life.

A question that needs to be mentioned, though it can only be dealt with very briefly, is that of structural continuity. We may first consider the continuity of social groups. A group such as a nation, a tribe, or a clan may have a

207. *Id.*

continuous existence although its membership is continually changing, since it loses members by death and gains new members by birth . . .

The same sort of continuity can be observed in social classes. In a Polynesian society the class of chiefs is continuous since when a chief dies he is replaced, in some instances by his eldest son. An occupational or professional class may have the same kind of continuity; as doctors or lawyers die or retire their places are taken by new recruits to the profession. . . .

Thus, as social structure is an arrangement of persons in institutionalised roles and relationships, structural continuity is the continuity of such arrangements . . . Structural continuity in human societies is dynamic in this sense, the matter being individual human beings, the form being the way in which they are connected by institutional relationships.

An aspect that has to be considered is the fact that individuals change their position in social structure during the course of life. A man may change his nationality, or leave one church to join another. What is everywhere present is the process by which a human being begins life as an infant and grows into an adult; the social position of a person changes, either gradually, or by institutionally defined stages, as from a boy he becomes a young man and finally an elder. In some African societies a very important structural feature is a system of age-grades, an individual passing from one grade to the next in accordance with the institutional pattern.

Social structure, therefore, is to be defined as the continuing arrangement of persons in relationships defined or controlled by institutions, i.e., socially established norms or patterns of behavior.

The Structural-Functional Methodology of Radcliffe-Brown

Perhaps the best starting point to explain the functional aspect of Radcliffe-Brown's methodology is his analogy between the social and animal organism. Just as an animal organism is made up of cells and fluids arranged in relation to one another to make up the aggregate whole, society is made up of a complex network of relations among individuals—relations that are just as real as the genetic components of organisms or the atomic particles of matter.[208] A living organism exists not simply because it has certain cells, molecules, and fluids but because of the structure in which these components are united. Similarly, Radcliffe-Brown explains, social phenomena in human society are present not because society has individuals, but because they are the result of the social structure by which they are united.[209] What unites individuals within a certain structure are the social values they seek to pursue in common.[210]

The totality of these social relations constitute the structure of society and ensures its continued existence. In other words, under this structural-functional methodology,

---

208. Radcliffe-Brown, Structure and Function, *supra* note 7, at 190.

209. *Id.* at 190–91.

210. *Id.* at 200.

the function of any social institution is the role it plays in promoting the social values sustaining the structural continuity of society as a whole.[211] The identification of the particular social relations that have this function is what Radcliffe-Brown calls "social morphology";[212] the related study of how these social institutions function is "social physiology."[213] In fact, he deems the two to be so closely related that one cannot be studied without the other.

Radcliffe-Brown predicates the study of recurrent social practices that contribute to structural continuity on four assumptions: (1) that the social organism has a certain functional unity, (2) that all social structures work in harmony, (3) that they are at least internally consistent even if not totally harmonious, and (4) that they do not produce conflicts that cannot be resolved or regulated. His methodology does not ignore practices at the individual level. However, the individual is studied only under conditions of culture (*i.e.*, the manner and extent to which his life and behavior is molded by society).

In the above excerpt from *Structure and Function in Primitive Society*, Radcliffe-Brown clearly states that not every social practice contributes to the structural unity and continuity of society and that the task of social morphology is to ferret out only those social structures that do so. He also emphasizes that the same practice may have different functions in different societies. This approach is nonhistorical in many ways. He is particularly hostile to what he calls "conjectural history," a critical if not derogatory reference to the attempts of the evolutionists as well as the historical particularists to study culture by historical reconstruction. According to him, the latter approach is the domain of ethnology, whereas the domain of social anthropology is the study of discoverable laws for the development of human society, as illustrated by the study of primitive cultures.[214] He claims that the proposed methodology is more epistemically reliable because it is "scientific." Indeed, Radcliffe-Brown believes social anthropology to be on par with the natural sciences: "I conceive of social anthropology as the theoretical natural science of human society, that is, the investigation of social phenomena by methods essentially similar to those used in the physical and biological science."[215]

In the words of one of his students: "Radcliffe-Brown's signal contribution is ... derived ... from his emphasis on a strictly nonhistorical, sharply scientific method in anthropology. The objective of social anthropology is the formulation of general propositions as to society."[216]

---

211. *Id.*

212. A.R. Radcliffe-Brown, A Natural Science of Society 56 (1957).

213. Radcliffe-Brown, Method, *supra* note 206, at 40.

214. Radcliffe-Brown, *The Comparative Method in Social Anthropology*, *in* The Social Anthropology of Radcliffe-Brown 54 (Adam Kuper ed., 1977).

215. Radcliffe-Brown, Structure and Function, *supra* note 7, at 189.

216. Robert Redfield, *Introduction*, *in* Social Anthropology of North American Tribes xi (Fred Eggan ed., 1962).

Boas and Durkheim similarly claimed that a rendering of a scientifically reliable method can describe human society as it really is.[217] Whereas Boas's particularism demanded extensive fieldwork in specific societies, Radcliffe-Brown's goal was more ambitious in that he sought to discover through fieldwork general laws (which he called "sociological laws") that are applicable to humanity as a whole.[218] Such laws would be applicable cross-culturally because they would describe regularities between comparative morphology and physiology (*i.e.*, between the structures and functions being classified and compared).[219]

Thus Radcliffe-Brown's scientific quest was to formulate verified laws about a "concrete reality" that consists of the actually existing relations among individuals, groups, and associations. These relations are observable, according to Radcliffe-Brown, whereas culture is not. Because culture cannot be observed, he dismissed it as a "vague abstraction."[220]

Structure, Function, and the "Laws" of Sociology

For Radcliffe-Brown, the function of a social institution is defined by the extent to which it meets or satisfies one or more of the conditions necessary for a society to survive. Thus certain universal conditions must be met by every society to continue its existence.[221] Any such condition that is identified (*i.e.*, when it is established that all human societies must meet a particular condition in order to survive) he called a "sociological law."[222] One necessary condition would be the functional consistency among the constituent parts of the total social structure (*i.e.*, consistency in relations between individuals, between individuals and groups, between the groups themselves, and between individuals and groups on one hand and society on the other). Radcliffe-Brown treated consistency as a relative notion, not one that signified perfect harmony. A measure of inconsistency or even flux and dynamism would be tolerable as long as they did not threaten to overthrow the social structure itself.[223] Thus functional consistency is the first of three sociological laws.[224]

The second sociological law is a system of justice and legal institutions that mediate the internal inconsistencies that do exist, so as to protect the integrity of the structure (*i.e.*, society). The legal system defines rights and duties in relation to persons and things to ensure a smooth and harmonious network of relations between individu-

---

217. Radcliffe-Brown, Method, *supra* note 206, at 167. *See* text at notes 84–88 *supra*, discussing Durkheim's scientific approach to social facts. *See* also Chapter 2 for Boas's refutation of the evolutionary model.

218. Radcliffe-Brown, *Comparative Method*, *supra* note 214, at 4, 54, 68.

219. Radcliffe-Brown, Structure and Function, *supra* note 7, at 195.

220. *Id.* at 190.

221. *Id.* at 43.

222. *Id.*

223. *Id.* at 192.

224. Radcliffe-Brown, A Natural Science, *supra* note 212, at 124–28.

als and groups of individuals and between society and citizens (*i.e.*, consistently) in accordance with the first law.

The third sociological law defining a necessary condition for society, the law of continuity,[225] incorporates the self-evident proposition that society as a corporate entity must have a degree of permanence that transcends its individuals as well as some of its social structures. People will die and new ones will be born; some social institutions will undergo modification or fall into desuetude; yet society as a corporate entity endures and continues to exercise joint rights over its territory and its citizens. These rights are rights *in rem* (*i.e.*, rights over persons "as against the world").[226] Society may also have rights *in personam* (*i.e.*, the citizens may owe duties to society). A right *in rem* would be operating clan-based societies in which the killing of a clan member gives rise to the right to exact vengeance or indemnification in favor of the clan. This principle applies with equal force in a primitive clan-based society as in the modern system of sovereign states, in which states frequently make claims on behalf of their nationals against other states on the international plane.

The notion of corporate rights *in rem* suggests a fourth sociological law, although Radcliffe-Brown did not explicitly characterize it as such. He did refer to it as one of the "fundamental social necessities" and as a "sociological cause."[227] A fifth sociological law implicit in Radcliffe-Brown's writings is the need to define unilineal succession through a matrilineal or patrilineal system. If this definition is not clearly established, as was the case with the "hordes" of the Andaman Islanders whom Radcliffe-Brown studied extensively, the resulting social structure is "loose and indefinite," which makes it contrary to the first and particularly to the third law.[228]

Radcliffe-Brown is not just unclear about the last two necessities or "laws," he compounds the lack of clarity by identifying only two laws in his summary of the necessary conditions of existence of a society with unilineal succession.

> The sociological laws, i.e. the necessary conditions of existence of a society, that have been suggested as underlying the customs of unilineal (patrilineal or matrilineal) succession are:
>
> 1. The need for a formulation of rights over persons and things sufficiently precise in their general recognition as to avoid as far as possible unresolved conflicts.
> 2. The need for continuity of the social structure as a system of relations between persons, such relations being definable in terms of rights and duties.[229]

---

225. Radcliffe-Brown, Structure and Function, *supra* note 7, at 45. *See also*, Radcliffe-Brown, A Natural Science, *supra* note 212, at 55.

226. Radcliffe-Brown, Structure and Function, *supra* note 7, at 32–33.

227. *Id.* at 46.

228. *Id.*

229. *Id.* at 47.

The first entry apparently collapses the first two of his sociological laws, because they are so intertwined. Thus, only if "rights over persons and things" are clearly defined and unresolvable conflicts are minimized can there be functional consistency among the constituent parts of the social structure as a whole.

It must be noted that the very notion of society as a functioning whole whose existence and operation are subject to scientifically verifiable laws is diametrically opposed to the "shreds and patches" theory of culture.[230] This theory is primarily associated with Robert H. Lowie, who asserted that culture traits accumulate purely by historical accident. He famously referred to culture as "that planless hodge-podge, that thing of shreds and patches called civilization."[231] After noting that the idea of diffusion may have led to the conception of cultural traits as accidental, Radcliffe-Brown explicitly rejects this conception as incompatible with his structural-functionalism.[232]

Case Studies in Applied Structural-Functionalism

With the foregoing universalisms in mind, we may inquire whether applied structural functionalism yields insight about institutions within social structures; whether it can give truly scientific accounts of social phenomena on par with those of natural science, as claimed by Radcliffe-Brown; and whether these accounts reveal the universalisms subsumed by his sociological laws. The first case study is on the social function of ceremonial rituals among the Andaman Islanders. The second is the function of legends in the same community. Following these are four general institutional physiologies: of economic systems, law (modern and primitive), and justice. The latter studies are not strictly case studies because they were not undertaken with reference to any particular society, although Radcliffe-Brown did regard Andaman custom as a form of law. These physiologies are nevertheless a good illustration of applied structural functionalism describing institutions that Radcliffe-Brown asserts are universal.

The Function of Ceremony among the Andamanese

Radcliffe-Brown rejects the comparative method under which isolated customs from different cultures are compared with a view to finding similarities.[233] Structural functionalism methodology requires that "the institutions of *one* society or social type are studied together so as to exhibit their intimate relations as parts of an organic system."[234]

Radcliffe-Brown's study of ceremonial customs among the Andaman islanders led him to conclude that the function of customs was to keep a certain system of sen-

230. *Id.* at 186.

231. R.H. Lowie, Primitive Society 441 (1920).

232. Radcliffe-Brown, Structure and Function, *supra* note 7, at 186.

233. A.R. Radcliffe-Brown, The Andaman Islanders 324 (1948).

234. *Id.* (emphasis added).

timents alive in their minds. The "ceremonial" implied a complex system of beliefs about a certain power or force that was essentially moral in nature. The force, which was omnipresent, was believed by the islanders to be the source of all that was good and evil in human experience, although the force itself was neither good nor evil. It was at once revered and feared, and rituals had to be performed to keep its evil potentialities at bay.

In Radcliffe-Brown's assessment, the force translated into a moral obligation, internalized by the islanders, to set aside egoistic desires in favor of the requirements of social custom.[235] The islanders reported feeling this force from within as well as without, which to him meant that the moral sense inculcated thereby compelled behavior among them that was also demanded by social opinion from without, despite the internal conflicts experienced by individuals over following selfish desire at the expense of social custom.[236]

The ceremony of dance, in which all the islanders took part, aroused intense collective emotions of belonging and togetherness. Other ceremonies in which the whole community participated augmented the power of their society as a whole, while at the same time instilling a sense of harmony in the individual with that society. In this way, the islander experienced the moral force of society from outside his or her own self, albeit the self might sometimes conflict with society.[237]

Whereas Radcliffe-Brown defined a social institution as settled expectations of behavior in pursuit of common social values, the islander experienced the moral force of society through everything that has social value. One commodity that has obvious social value is food. The islanders rejoiced collectively when the harvest was plentiful or a hunt was successful; such celebrations, sometimes in the form of initiation ceremonies, reinforced common bonds between individuals as well as between the person and the group at large.[238] By the same token, when food was scarce the entire community would feel thwarted and restrained; thus, just as rejoicing strengthens social euphoria under conditions of plenty, weakness and suffering make for social dysphoria under conditions of scarcity. Radcliffe-Brown observed that other environmental conditions of social value (*e.g.*, the weather) play the same role in affecting group sentiments through the "ceremonial," whether the effect was positive or negative.

> But it is really through the ceremonial that this is mainly brought about. It is in the initiation ceremonies that the moral force of the society acting through foods is chiefly felt, and the same experience is repeated in a less intense form in the rite of painting the body after food. It is similarly through the protective use of the materials used for weapons and through the various ritual prohibitions connected with them that the moral force of the society acting

235. *Id.* at 325.

236. *Id.*

237. *Id.* at 325–26.

238. Radcliffe-Brown, Andaman Islanders, *supra* note 233, at 326–27.

> through them is chiefly felt. The argument has been that it is by means of the ceremonial that the individual is made to feel the social value of the various things with which the ceremonial is concerned. Putting this in other words we can now define the ceremonial as the means by which the individual is made to feel the moral force of the society acting upon him either directly, or in some instances indirectly through those things that have important effects on the social life. By its action upon the individual the ceremonial develops and maintains in existence in his mind an organised system of dispositions by which the social life, in the particular form it takes in the Andamans, is made possible, using for the purpose of maintaining the social cohesion all the instinctive tendencies of human nature, modifying and combining them according to its needs.[239]

The ceremonial is also used to curb, modify, or enhance certain instincts inherent to human nature, such as fear. According to Radcliffe-Brown, every individual since early childhood is made to feel through ceremonies that he lives in a world full of dangers and that the only way to avoid these is to conform to social custom. He therefore identified four distinct characteristics of the ceremonial: (1) it involves collective action, (2) it is required by custom, (3) it is performed on occasions of changes in the course of social life, and (4) it expresses collective sentiments about such change.[240]

The Function of Legends among the Andamanese

Radcliffe-Brown recognized that legends, like ceremonies, express group sentiments.[241] These sentiments again reflect experience with objects that have social value (*i.e.*, whatever improves welfare has an effect on the sentiments of the individual). Because the social values of each society depend on the way each society is constituted, he considered it important to study the legends of the Andamanese with reference to the ways of life of the islanders. His analysis of these legends indicates first that they serve as symbolic, if crude, methods of evaluating human conduct. For example, according to one legend, the bad temper of an ancestor resulted in a cyclone that caused great harm; according to another legend, the young people who ignored the rules of an initiation ceremony were turned into stone.[242] Thus each legend has a lesson or moral that embodies a proper standard of conduct.

Second, Andaman legends express the social value of past events as reflected either by tradition, the ways by which the islanders win their sustenance, or as expressed in customs.[243] The latter have a hallowed status insofar as they codify rules of behavior of the ancestors who are seen to have led perfect, orderly lives. In one's current life, therefore, all that the individual must do is conform to the

---

239. *Id.* at 327.

240. *Id.* at 328.

241. *Id.* at 396.

242. *Id.* at 398.

243. Radcliffe-Brown, Andaman Islanders, *supra* note 233, at 398.

tried-and-true norms of the past. Third, the legends of the islanders embody the social value of natural phenomena, from geographical and territorial landmarks to seasonal changes and the local flora and fauna.

Radcliffe-Brown's heavy emphasis on adherence to tradition and custom was intended to show that ceremonials as well as legends can be regarded as forms of law,[244] because they represent a world of order in the same way that law does. He did not represent the Andaman conception of law as distinguishing law from morality in the Western sense; instead, he presented their determining criterion of behavior as right versus wrong. This distinction is simply postulated as preexisting and preceding all human action, and right behavior is postulated as presumptively conducive to all that is of social value. Thus, the right way is the one that has been followed since time immemorial; any other way is wrong and therefore contrary to law.

Radcliffe-Brown appears to see among the Andamanese an attitude to law that is reminiscent of ancient Stoic philosophy. This is the belief that the cosmos has an absolutely uniform order.[245] Because the ancestors had knowledge of it, current behavior should emulate that of the ancestors on pain of minor to serious consequences. In short, the natural order of the universe must be synonymous with the moral order of society.

In the following excerpt Radcliffe-Brown explains how ceremonies, rituals, and legends maintain social cohesion by adherence to customary law.

A.R. Radcliffe-Brown, Method in Social Anthropology 324–328, 397–400 (1958).

> I have tried to show that the ceremonial customs are the means by which the society acts upon its individual members and keeps alive in their minds a certain system of sentiments. Without the ceremonial those sentiments would not exist, and without them the social organisation in its actual form could not exist....
>
> In the attempt to exhibit the meaning of the ceremonial I have shown that it implies a complex system of beliefs about what I have called power, and have stated those beliefs in more or less precise terms....
>
> With this qualification, then, the ceremonial of the Andaman Islands may be said to involve the assumption of a power of a peculiar kind, and we have been able to formulate certain principles which, although the native is quite incapable of stating them as principles, are revealed in the ceremonial. This power, though in itself neither good nor evil is the source of all good and all evil in human life. It is present in the society itself and in everything that can affect in important ways the social life. All occasions of special contact with it are dangerous, i.e., are subject to ritual precautions... It is, in a few words, the moral power of the society acting upon the individual directly

244. *Id.* at 399.

245. *Id.*

or indirectly and felt by him in innumerable ways throughout the whole course of his life . . .

The moral force of the society is also felt, in a quite different way, in all states of intense collective emotion, of which the dance affords a good example. I have shown how in the dance the individual feels the society acting upon him, constraining him to join in the common activity and regulate his actions to conform with those of others, and, when he so acts in harmony with them, giving him the experience of a great increase of his own personal force or energy. All ceremonies in which the whole community takes part give the individual the experience of the moral force of the society acting upon him in somewhat the same way as the dance.

Thus in these and other ways the individual does experience the action of the society upon himself as a sort of force, not however as a physical force, but as a moral force, acting directly in his own mind and yet clearly felt as something outside his own self, and with which that self may be in conflict.

How is it, then, that this force comes to be projected into the world of nature? The answer to that question, which can only be very briefly indicated here, is to be found in the conclusions at which we have arrived with regard to social values. The moral force of the society is experienced by the individual not only directly but also as acting upon him indirectly through every object that has social value. The best example of this process is found in the things used for food. Thus, in the Andamans, food is very closely connected with the feeling of moral obligation, as we have seen. Further, food is one of the principal sources of those alternations of social euphoria and dysphoria in which, through the action of the collective emotion, the individual experiences the action of the society upon his own well-being. When food is plentiful happiness spreads through the community and the time is spent in dancing and feasting so that the individual feels a great increase in his own personal force coming to him from the society or from the food. On the other hand, when food is scarce and hunting unsuccessful the community feels itself thwarted and restrained and experiences a sense of weakness, which collective feeling has for its immediate object the food the lack of which is its origin.

Similarly with the phenomena of the weather and all other objects that have social value, they are all associated in the mind of the individual with his experience of the action of the society upon himself, so that the moral force of the society is actually felt as acting through them. . . .

[W]hat I have denoted as ceremonial consists of (1) collective actions, (2) required by customs, (3) performed on occasions of changes in the course of social life, and (4) expressing the collective sentiments relating to such social change . . .

. . . [L]egends are the expression of social values of objects of different kinds. By the social value of an object is meant the way in which it affects the life of the society, and therefore, since every one is interested in the welfare of the society to which he belongs, the way in which it affects the social sentiments of the individual. The system of social values of a society obviously depends upon the manner in which the society is constituted, and therefore the legends can only be understood by constant reference to the mode of life of the Andamanese.

The legends give us in the first place a simple crude valuation of human actions. Anger, quarrelsomeness, carelessness in observing ritual requirements are exhibited as resulting in harm. This is the moral element of the stories strictly so called, and is to be observed in many of them. The young men who failed to observe the rules laid down for those who have recently been through one of the initiation ceremonies were turned to stone. The quarrelsomeness of the lizard led to ancestors being turned into animals. The bad temper of one of the ancestors resulted in darkness covering the earth, or in a great cyclone in which many were destroyed.

Secondly, the legends as a whole give expression to the social value of the past, of all that is derived from tradition, whether it be the knowledge by which men win their sustenance, or the customs that they observe. In the wonderful times of the ancestors all things were ordered, all necessary knowledge was acquired, and the rules that must guide conduct were discovered. It remains for the individual of the present only to observe the customs with which his elders are familiar.

The legends of a man's own tribe serve also to give a social value to the places with which he is familiar. The creeks and hills that he knows, the camping sites at which he lives, the reefs and rocks that act as landmarks by reason of any striking feature they may present, are all for him possessed of a historic interest that makes them dear to him. The very names, in many cases, recall events of the far-off legendary epoch.

Again, many of the legends express the social value of natural phenomena. By reference to *Biliku* and *Tarai,* for instance, the native can express what he feels with respect to the weather and the seasonal changes that so profoundly affect the common life. Finally, in the legends he is able to express what he feels about the bright plumaged birds and the other creatures with which he is constantly meeting in the jungles, which are a source of perennial interest, and are yet so clearly a part of the world cut off from himself and his life, having no immediately discernible influence upon his welfare.

This system of social values, or rather this system of sentiments, that we find expressed in the legends is an essential part of the life of the Andamanese; without it they could not have organised their social life in the way they have. Moreover the sentiments in question need to be regularly expressed in some way or another if they are to be kept alive and passed from one generation to another. The legends, which are related by the elders to the young folk, are one of the means (the various ceremonial customs analysed in the last chapter being another) by which they are so expressed, and by which their existence is maintained.

> Although the term "social value" has been used as a convenient expression, yet the meaning of the legends might be expressed in other ways. We may say, for instance, that they give a representation of the world as regulated by law. The conception of law which they reveal is not, however, that to which we are accustomed when we think of natural law. We may perhaps adequately state the Andaman notion by saying that moral law and natural law are not distinguished from one another. The welfare of the society depends upon right actions; wrong actions inevitably lead to evil results. Giving way to anger is a wrong action, as being a cause of social disturbance. In the legends the catastrophes that overwhelmed the ancestors are in many instances represented as being caused by some one giving way to anger. There is a right way and a wrong way to set about making things such as a bow. We should explain this by saying that the right way will give a good serviceable weapon, whereas the wrong way will give an inferior or useless one. The Andaman Islander tends to look at the matter from a different angle; the right way is right because it is the one that has been followed from time immemorial, and any other way is wrong, is contrary to custom, to law. Law for the Andaman Islander, means that there is an order of the universe, characterised by absolute uniformity; this order was established once for all in the time of the ancestors, and is not to be interfered with, the results of any such interference being evil, ranging from merely minor ills such as disappointment or discomfort to great calamities. The law of compensation is absolute. Any deviation from law or custom will inevitably bring its results, and inversely any evil that befalls must be the result of some lack of observance. The legends reveal to our analysis a conception of the universe as a moral order.
>
> Here I must conclude my attempt to interpret the custom and beliefs of the Andaman Islanders, but in doing so I wish to point out, though indeed it must already be fairly obvious, that if my interpretation be correct, then the meaning of the customs of other primitive peoples is to be discovered by similar methods and in accordance with the same psychological principles.

Physiology of the Economic System

Radcliffe-Brown believed that individuals are united within a certain structure in pursuit of certain common social values and that social morphology identifies such structures (*e.g.*, a society's economic machinery or legal system). Other structures within which individuals unite to pursue common goals are the professions, which are demarcated by the division of labor, as well as religious organizations, ideological associations, and forms of government. The physiology of these structures shows how they exist and persist and reveals the direct and indirect relations of persons and groups within particular structures.[246] These relations include power, subordination, prestige, dependencies, reciprocal services, and so on.

246. Radcliffe-Brown, Structure and Function, *supra* note 7, at 195–96.

Radcliffe-Brown illustrated this structure by the physiology of the economic system, which is found in simple or complex form in every human society. At the heart of the economic system of every society he described a division of labor through which certain tasks for the sustenance of society ("gratification") are apportioned between various members who make up the group.[247] The activity in one provides some gratification for the other, but a complex web of mutual gratifications within a social system sustains society as a whole.

Radcliffe-Brown observed that economists generally specialize in the study of the kinds and quantities of goods produced and how they are distributed and disposed of; therefore, they use abstract techniques that have little connection with the social system. He also noted that when economic institutions are viewed as social structures, particularly in primitive societies, economic activities involving the exchange of goods and services reveal a dynamic set of human relations that maintain certain structures such as clans, lineages, and moieties, together with their corresponding distributions of rank, privilege, and prestige.[248]

He concluded that when the economic machinery of a society is studied in relation to its social structure, the seemingly isolated activities of the exchange of goods and services in fact show how they contribute to maintaining a certain structure through a network of human relations between persons and groups of persons. What to the economist may appear to be a completely wasteful activity may to the anthropologist represent a vital method maintaining the structures that carry various distributions of social standing in terms of rank and privilege.[249]

Physiology of Law

Similarly, according to Radcliffe-Brown, law and morality are not merely a set of abstract rules with objective meanings, all operating within an autonomous and independent legal system, even though the legal profession treats law in just this manner. He believed that like the economist, the lawyer will look at and study law in complete abstraction from the social system within which it operates and of which it is a part. A structural functional approach to law, which he advocated, would show that the law plays a vital and dynamic role in ensuring that social relations between individuals, between individuals and groups, between the groups themselves, and between individuals or groups and the government are maintained at a certain equilibrium. Moreover, if this equilibrium is disturbed the legal institutions will restore, adjust, or modify the relations as necessary. Acknowledging that the legal system is a complex mechanism that defines rights, duties, privileges, exemptions, and liberties in the service of a variety of social structures, he concluded that the law thus has a pervasive presence if not a "brooding omnipresence" (to borrow Oliver Wendell Holmes's phrase) in all aspects of society.

---

247. *Id.* at 197.

248. *Id.* at 198. *See also* Radcliffe-Brown, A Natural Science, *supra* note 212, at 126–27 (on the economic institution of the Potlatch of the Tlingit).

249. Radcliffe-Brown, Structure and Function, *supra* note 7, at 198.

In the next excerpt, Radcliffe-Brown explains the structural-functional approach to the physiology of economic and legal institutions.

A.R. Radcliffe-Brown, Structure and Function in Primitive Society 197–199 (1952).

Let us consider very briefly certain other branches of social anthropology and their relation to the study of social structure. If we take the social life of a local community over a period, let us say a year, we can observe a certain sum total of activities carried out by the persons who compose it. We can also observe a certain apportionment of these activities, one person doing certain things, another doing others. This apportionment of activities, equivalent to what is sometimes called the social division of labour, is an important feature of the social structure. Now activities are carried out because they provide some sort of 'gratification', as I propose to call it, and the characteristic feature of social life is that activities of certain persons provide gratifications for other persons. In a simple instance, when an Australian blackfellow goes hunting, he provides meat, not only for himself, but for his wife and children and also for other relatives to whom it is his duty to give meat when he has it. Thus in any society there is not only an apportionment of activities, but also an apportionment of gratification resulting therefrom, and some sort of social machinery, relatively simple or, sometimes, highly complex, by which the system works.

It is in this machinery, or certain aspects of it, that constitutes the special subject-matter studied by the economists. They concern themselves with what kinds and quantities of goods are produced, how they are distributed (i.e. their flow from person to person, or region to region), and the way in which they are disposed of. Thus what are called economic institutions are extensively studied in more or less complete abstraction from the rest of the social system. This method does undoubtedly provide useful results, particularly in the study of complex modern societies. Its weaknesses become apparent as soon as we attempt to apply it to the exchange of goods in what are called primitive societies.

The economic machinery of a society appears in quite a new light if it is studied in relation to the social structure. The exchange of goods and services is dependent upon, is the result of, and at the same time is a means of maintaining a certain structure, a network of relations between persons and collections of persons. For the economists and politicians of Canada the potlatch of the Indians of the north-west of America was simply wasteful foolishness and it was therefore forbidden. For the anthropologist it was the machinery for maintaining a social structure of lineages, clans and moieties, with which was combined as arrangement of rank defined by privileges.

Any full understanding of the economic institutions of human societies requires that they should be studied from two angles. From one of these the economic system is viewed as the mechanism by which goods of various kinds and in various quantities are produced, transported and transferred, and utilized. From the other the economic system is a set of relations between persons and groups which maintains, and is maintained by, this exchange or circulation of goods and services. From the latter point of view, the study of the economic life of societies takes its place as part of the general study of social structure.

Social relations are only observed, and can only be described, by the reference to the reciprocal behaviour of the persons related. The form of social structure has therefore to be described by the patterns of behavior to which individuals and groups conform in their dealings with one another. These patterns are partially formulated in rules which, in our own society, we distinguish as rules of etiquette, of morals and of law. Rules, of course, only exist in their recognition by the members of the society; either in their verbal recognition, when they are stated as rules, or in their observance in behavior. These two modes of recognition, as every field-worker knows, are not the same thing and both have to be taken into account.

If I say that in any society the rules of etiquette, morals and law are part of the mechanism by which a certain set of social relations is maintained in existence, this statement will, I suppose, be greeted as a truism. But it is one of those truisms which many writers on human society verbally accept and yet ignore in theoretical discussions, or in their descriptive analyses. The point is not that rules exist in every society, but that what we need to know for a scientific understanding is just how these things work in general and in particular instances.

Let us consider, for example, the study of law. If you examine the literature on jurisprudence you will find that legal institutions are studied for the most part in more or less complete abstraction from the rest of the social system of which they are a part. This is doubtless the most convenient method for lawyers in their professional studies. But for any scientific investigation of the nature of law it is insufficient. The data with which a scientist must deal are events which occur and can be observed. In the field of law, the events which the social scientist can observe and thus take as his data are the proceedings that take place in courts of justice. These are the reality, and for the social anthropologist they are the mechanism or process by which certain definable social relations between persons and groups are restored, maintained or modified. Law is a part of the machinery by which a certain social structure is maintained. The system of laws of a particular society can only be fully understood if it is studied in relation to the social structure, and inversely the understanding of the social structure requires, amongst other things, a systematic study of the legal institutions.

I have talked about social relations, but I have not so far offered you a precise definition. A social relation exists between two or more individual organisms when there is some adjustment of their respective interests, by

> convergence of interest, or by limitation of conflicts that might arise from divergence of interest. I use the term 'interest' here in the widest possible sense, to refer to all behaviour that we regard as purposive. To speak of an interest implies a subject and an object and a relation between them. Whenever we say that a subject has a certain interest in an object we can state the same thing by saying that the object has a certain value for the subject. Interest and value are correlative terms, which refer to the two sides of an asymmetrical relation.
>
> Thus the study of social structure leads immediately to the study of interests or values as the determinants of social relations. A social relation does not result from similarity of interests, but rests either on the mutual interest of persons in one another, or on one or more common interests, or on a combination of both of these. The simplest form of social solidarity is where two persons are both interested in bringing about a certain result and co-operate to that end. When two or more persons have a *common interest* in an object, that object can be said to have a *social value* for the persons thus associated. If, then, practically all the members of a society have an interest in the observance of the laws, we can say that the law has a social value. The study of social values in this sense is therefore a part of the study of social structure.

Among the social values mentioned at the end of the excerpt are rules of behavior, "usages" that are backed by sanctions.[250] The sanctions are positive or negative, diffused or organized. Diffused sanctions, which are spontaneous expressions of approval or disapproval at the community level, include rules of morality, etiquette, and religion. Organized sanctions, which are "social actions carried out according to some traditional and recognized procedure,"[251] are more clearly defined when they are negative, as opposed to positive. They are embodied as binding rules of behavior, the violation of which results in the organized application of a negative sanction in the name of society. Here, Radcliffe-Brown clearly has in mind the sanctions codified in legal rules and particularly in penal law.[252] Nonetheless, he also observed that a variety of nonlegal rules may not be compulsory but are complied with by the individual to obtain social recognition or approval. In somewhat Durkheimian fashion, he believed that such rules eventually became embedded in individual consciences.[253] Another Durkheimian trait in Radcliffe-Brown's treatment of sanctions is the notion of retaliation as a way of obtaining individual redress and group satisfaction,[254] such that the application of a sanction in any given case shows a condition of social dysphoria. The

---

250. *Id.* at 205.

251. *Id.*

252. *Id.* at 208.

253. *Id.* at 205.

254. Radcliffe-Brown, Structure and Function, *supra* note 7, at 209.

function of the sanction is to restore social euphoria by giving collective expression to the sentiments that have been offended by the deed in question.[255]

Radcliffe-Brown's physiology of sanction in legal institutions is designed to not only unveil the rich variety of sanctions in society but also demonstrate how they are linked to form a systematic whole and how they together bring about normative control and social integration. The following excerpt explains Radcliffe-Brown's physiology of sanction, particularly the legal sanction.

A.R. Radcliffe-Brown, Structure and Function in Primitive Society 208–211 (1952).

Organised negative sanctions, important among which are the penal sanctions of criminal law, are definite recognised procedures directed against persons whose behaviour is subject to social disapproval. There are many varieties of such procedures, the most important and widespread being the following: subjection to open expression of reprobation or derision, as, for example, through forcible public exposure by confinement in stocks; partial exclusion, permanent or temporary, from full participation in social life and its privileges, including permanent or temporary loss of civil or religious rights; specific loss of social rank, or degradation, the exact contrary of the positive sanction of promotion; infliction of loss of property by imposition of a fine or by forcible seizure or destruction; infliction of bodily pain; mutilation or branding in which pain is incidental to permanent exposure to reprobation; permanent exclusion from the community, as by exile; imprisonment; and punishment by death. These sanctions are legal sanctions when they are imposed by a constituted authority, political, military or ecclesiastic.

In any given society the various primary sanctions form a more or less systematic whole which constitutes the machinery of social control. There is an intimate relation between the religious sanctions and the moral sanctions, which varies, however, in different societies, and cannot be stated in any brief formula. The primary legal sanctions of criminal law, in all societies except the highly secularized modern states, show a close connection with religious beliefs.

Besides these primary social sanctions and resting upon them there are certain sanctions which may be termed secondary; these are concerned with the actions of persons or groups in their effects upon other persons or groups. In modern civil law, for example, when an individual is ordered by a court to pay damages, the primary sanction behind the order is the power of the court to make forcible seizure of his property or to imprison or otherwise punish him for contempt of court if he fails to obey. Thus secondary sanctions consist of procedures carried out by a community, generally through its representatives, or by individuals with the approval of the community,

255. *Id.* at 211.

when recognised rights have been infringed. They are based upon the general principle that any person who has suffered injury is entitled to satisfaction and that such satisfaction should be in some way proportioned to the extent of the injury.

One class of such procedures consists of acts of retaliation, by which is meant socially approved, controlled and limited acts of revenge. Thus in an Australian tribe when one man has committed an offense against another, the latter is permitted by public opinion, often definitely expressed by the older men, to throw a certain number of spears or boomerangs at the former or in some instances to spear him in the thigh. After he has been given such satisfaction he may no longer harbour ill feelings against the offender. In many preliterate societies the killing of an individual entitles the group to which he belongs to obtain satisfaction by killing the offender or some member of his group. In regulated vengeance the offending group must submit to this as an act of justice and must not attempt further retaliation. Those who have received such satisfaction are felt to have no further grounds for ill feeling . . .

In many preliterate societies procedures of indemnification are carried out under the diffuse sanction of public opinion, which compels an individual to indemnify one whose rights he has infringed. In some societies there is a recognised right of an injured person to indemnify himself by forcible seizure of the property of the offender. When society becomes politically organised, procedures of retaliation and indemnification, backed by diffuse sanctions, give place to legal sanctions backed by the power of judicial authorities to inflict punishment. Thus arises civil law, by which a person who has suffered an infringement of rights may obtain reparation or restitution from the person responsible.

In a consideration of the functions of social sanctions it is not the effects of the sanction upon the person to whom they are applied that are most important but rather the general effects within the community applying the sanctions. For the application of any sanction is a direct affirmation of social sentiments by the community and thereby constitutes an important, possibly essential, mechanism for maintaining these sentiments. Organised negative sanctions in particular, and to a great extent the secondary sanctions, are expressions of a condition of social dysphoria brought about by some deed. The function of the sanction is to restore the social euphoria by giving definite collective expression to the sentiments which have been affected by the deed, as in the primary sanctions and to some extent in the secondary sanctions, or by removing a conflict within the community itself. The sanctions are thus of primary significance to sociology in that they are reactions on the part of a community to events affecting its integration.

Physiology of Primitive Law

Surprisingly, Radcliffe-Brown's structural approach to primitive law adopts Roscoe Pound's modern Western definition that law is "social control through the systematic application of the force of politically organised society."[256] This narrow definition has two consequences. First, it emphasizes sanctions and defines the field of law as "coterminous with that of organized legal sanctions."[257] Second, simple societies can thus have no law per se, only customs that are enforced by nonlegal sanctions.

The distinction between law and custom and between legal and nonlegal sanctions are explained through Radcliffe-Brown's dichotomy of "the law of public delicts" and the "law of private delicts."[258] The occurrence of a public delict results in social dysphoria and triggers an "organized and regular procedure by the whole community" or its authorized representatives whereby responsibility is assigned and "some hurt or punishment" is inflicted, often through some form of ritual.[259] Capital punishment is also used. This sanction is penal in nature and its function is to restore social euphoria; thus its ceremonial or ritual aspects are particularly suited to such restoration.[260] Examples of public delicts in primitive societies are incest, sorcery, evil magic, repeated breaches of tribal custom, and certain forms of sacrilege.[261]

A private delict is analogous to a civil wrong in modern society. Here, personal injury has been caused by the infringement of a right. Typically, a duly constituted judicial authority would assign responsibility and order the defendant to indemnify the plaintiff. This sanction is restitutive rather than punitive in nature, although under modern law certain deeds (*e.g.*, homicides) may be subject to civil and criminal sanctions. Examples of private delicts in primitive law are killing, wounding, theft, adultery, and failure to pay debts. The sanction, however, is repressive and restitutive in that it functions to relieve social dysphoria as well as indemnify the injured party.[262] To satisfy the former, the sanction can be warfare, vengeance in the form of retaliation, or the inflection of equivalent damage to the offender or a member of his clan (*lex talionis*).[263] The restitutive element would be generally satisfied by the offender or his clan being required to hand over certain valuables to indemnify the loss.

Radcliffe-Brown believed that this dichotomy of public and private delicts, although focused on sanctions, shows that sanctions have no single origin. The same public delict may be subject to three different types of sanctions, as when it offends the moral sentiments of the group. In such a case the offender may be subjected simultaneously to diffuse moral reprobation, a ritual sanction for self-purification, and a penal sanction that expresses collective moral indignation and relieves social dysphoria.[264]

---

256. *Id.* at 212.

257. *Id.*

258. *Id.*

259. Radcliffe-Brown, Structure and Function, *supra* note 7, at 212.

260. Radcliffe-Brown, Method, *supra* note 206, at 41. Radcliffe-Brown, Andaman Islanders, *supra* note 233, at 324 *et seq.*

261. Radcliffe-Brown, Structure and Function, *supra* note 7, at 213.

262. *Id.* at 214.

263. *Id.* at 215.

264. *Id.* at 214–15. *See also* Radcliffe-Brown, Method, *supra* note 206, at 41.

Radcliffe-Brown's physiology of primitive law is excerpted here.

A.R. Radcliffe-Brown, Structure and Function in Primitive Society, 212–219 (1952).

Many historical jurists in contrast with the analytical school have used the term law to include most if not all processes of social control. The term is, however, usually confined to 'social control through the systematic application of the force of politically organised society' (Pound). The limited application, more convenient for purposes of sociological analysis and classification, will be adopted in this article; the field of law will therefore be regarded as coterminous with that of organised legal sanctions. The obligations imposed on individuals in societies where there are no legal sanctions will be regarded as matters of custom and convention but not of law; in this sense some simple societies have no law, although all have customs which are supported by sanctions.

The confusion which has resulted in the attempt to apply to preliterate societies the modern distinction between criminal law and civil law can be avoided by making instead the distinction between the law of public delicts and the law of private delicts. In any society a deed is a public delict if its occurrence normally leads to an organised and regular procedure by the whole community or by the constituted representatives of social authority, which results in the fixing of responsibility upon some person within the community and the infliction by the community or by its representatives of some hurt or punishment upon the responsible person. This procedure, which may be called the penal sanction, is in its basic form a reaction by the community against an action of one of its own members which offends some strong and definite moral sentiment and thus produces a condition of social dysphoria. The immediate function of the reaction is to give expression to a collective feeling of moral indignation and so to restore the social euphoria. Its ultimate function is to maintain the moral sentiment in question at the requisite degree of strength in the individuals who constitute the community.

Comparatively little precise information is available concerning penal sanctions in preliterate societies. Among the actions which are known to be treated as public delicts in the simpler societies are incest, i.e. marriage or sexual congress with persons with whom such relations are forbidden; sorcery, or evil magic, by one person against another within the community; repeated breaches of tribal custom; and various forms of sacrilege. In many preliterate societies the penal sanction is applied principally if not solely to actions which infringe upon customs regarded by the community as sacred, so that the sanction itself may almost be regarded as a special form of ritual sanction . . .

In the procedure of a law of private delicts a person or a body of persons that has suffered some injury, loss or damage by infringement of recognised rights appeals to a constituted judicial authority, who declares some other person or body of persons within the community to be responsible and rules that the defendant shall give satisfaction to the plaintiff, such satisfaction frequently taking the form of the payment of an indemnity or damages. A private delict is thus an action which is subject to what may be called a restitutive sanction. The law of private delicts in preliterate societies corresponds to the civil law of modern times . . .

In preliterate societies private delicts are for the most part killing, wounding, theft, adultery and failure to pay debts; and while they are primarily regarded as constituting an injury to some member of the community they are subject also to moral reprobation as anti-social actions. The sanction is frequently both restitutive and repressive, giving satisfaction to the injured person and inflicting punishment upon the person responsible for the injury . . . In its basic form the law of private delicts is a procedure for avoiding or relieving the social dysphoria which results from conflicts within a community. . . .

The distinction between public delicts and private delicts illustrates the fact that the law has no single origin. A deed committed by a member of the community which offends the moral sense of the community may be subject to three sanctions, the general or diffuse moral sanction, which makes the guilty person subject to the reprobation of his fellows; the ritual sanction, which produces in the guilty person a condition of ritual uncleanness that constitutes a danger to himself and to those with whom he is in contact—in such cases custom may require him to undergo ritual purification or expiation or it may be believed that as a result of his sin he will fall ill and die; the penal sanction, whereby the community through certain persons acting as its constituted judicial authorities inflicts punishment on the guilty person, which may be regarded either as a collective expression of the moral indignation aroused by the deed or as a means of removing the ritual pollution resulting from the deed by imposing an expiation upon the guilty person, or as both.

On the other hand, an action which constitutes an infringement of the rights of a person or group of persons may lead to retaliation on the part of the injured against the person or group responsible for the injury. When such acts of retaliation are recognised by custom as justifiable and are subject to a customary regulation of procedure, various forms of retaliatory sanctions may be said to prevail. In preliterate society generally warfare has such a sanction; the waging of war is in some communities, as among the Australian hordes, normally an act of retaliation carried out by one group against another that is held responsible for an injury suffered, and the procedure is regulated by a recognised body of customs which is equivalent to the international law of modern nations. The institution of organised and regulated vengeance is another of a retaliatory sanction. The killing of a man, whether intentional or accidental, constitutes an injury to his clan, local community

> or kindred, for which satisfaction is required. The injured group is regarded as justified in seeking vengeance and there is frequently an obligation on the members of the group to avenge the death. The retaliatory action is regulated by custom; the *lex talionis* requires that the damage inflicted shall be equivalent to the damage suffered and the principle of collective solidarity permits the avengers to kill a person other than the actual murderer, for example his brother, or in some instances any member of his clan . . . Retaliatory sanctions may also appear in relation to injuries of one person by another; for example, the recognised right in certain circumstances of one person to challenge another to fight a duel. Among Australian tribes an individual who has suffered injury from another may by agreement of the elders be given the right to obtain satisfaction by throwing spears or boomerangs at him or by spearing him in a non-vital part of the body, such as the thigh . . . In many societies retaliation is replaced more or less by a system of indemnities; persons or groups having injured other persons or groups provide satisfaction to the latter by handing over certain valuables. . . .
>
> An important step is taken towards the formation of a legal system where there are recognised arbitrators or judges who hear evidence, decide upon responsibility and assess damages; only the existence of some authority with power to enforce the judgments delivered by the judges is then lacking. It has been argued plausibly that in some societies a legal system for dealing with private delicts has grown up in this manner; disputes are brought before arbitrators who declare the custom and apply it to the case before them; such courts of arbitration become established as regular tribunals; and finally there is developed in the society some procedure for enforcing judgments. . . .
>
> In its most elementary developments law is intimately bound up with magic and religion; legal sanctions are closely related to ritual sanctions. A full understanding of the beginnings of law in simpler societies can therefore be reached only by a comparative study of the whole systems of social sanctions.

Physiology of Justice as a Universal Principle

Although Radcliffe-Brown's approach to physiology demands that all structures be studied in functional rather than abstract contexts, his methodology claims that certain abstract structural principles are found universally in all social systems. The principle of justice is one example.[265] He also takes pains to point out that the sociologist is not concerned with the content of justice (*i.e.*, what it ought to be); rather, he is only concerned with the forms it takes in various societies, regardless of how he might consider them just or unjust.

One of the universal forms through which justice manifests itself is the principle of just retribution, as embodied in the maxim "a person who does evil should suffer

265. Radcliffe-Brown, A Natural Science, *supra* note 212, at 131 *et seq.*

evil."[266] This principle can be displaced or have exceptions as when rank trumps the rule. Thus "the king can do no wrong" is an example of an exception; religious doctrine that identifies love rather than justice as governing human relations, and for judging or forgiving bad behavior, is an example of displacement. Notwithstanding these marginal situations, justice as an abstract type exists universally.

Another form of justice identified by Radcliffe-Brown is the principle of equivalent return, which is used principally to grant satisfaction for an injury (exemplified by the *lex talionis*).[267] It also finds expression in the principles of mutual aid and reciprocity, in which equivalent benefits are exchanged. Finally, this principle is found in regimes of indemnification and compensation for injuries, particularly under modern civil law systems. In the penal context, society as a whole reacts to offenses, on the theory that the wrongful deed has caused injury to the community at large. This reaction manifests in both primitive and modern systems, as seen in the previous section.

Yet another form of abstract justice identified by Radcliffe-Brown is the universal structural principle of expiation.[268] As seen in the previous section, expiation for wrongful conduct in primitive contexts frequently involves some form of ritual sanction of self-purification that is felt to have a cleansing effect.[269] Criminal justice is another example of the expiation of crime; but in the primitive context, such expiation is combined with the principle of just retribution, which relieves social dysphoria and restores social euphoria.[270]

A final example of abstract structural forms of justice are theories of economic justice. Radcliffe-Brown emphasized the use of these to determine the price and value of goods and services, based on the fundamental principle of equivalence and fair exchange. In primitive society this occurs through the exchange of equivalent gifts, in others through barter and/or purchase.[271] All economic relations involve the adjustment of interests between individuals on the basis of what is accepted by them to be their basic principles of economic justice. The functional approach shows how these relations are aligned, how they work, and most important, how they demonstrate that the individuals participating therein derive satisfaction. The basic premise of the principle of equivalence is that one will only be satisfied if one feels that what one gets is equivalent to what one has given. No mention is made by Radcliffe-Brown of the principle of charity as an abstract form of economic justice. Under this principle, of course, one would feel quite satisfied when one has given without expectation or thought of return:

> I hold there is in human societies the principle of just retribution. . . . We can, as a matter of fact, derive from this principle a second principle of equiv-

266. *Id.* at 132.

267. *See* text at note 263 *supra.*

268. Radcliffe-Brown, A Natural Science, *supra* note 212, at 135.

269. *See* text at note 260 *supra.*

270. *See* text at note 255 *supra.*

271. Radcliffe-Brown, A Natural Science, *supra* note 212, at 138.

alent return. . . . The third form of the principle occurs in indemnification for an injury. . . . I would say that principles of this sort, if rationally arrived at and empirically tested, will tie up systematically with other structural principles. The question is, do we get several sciences or one fairly completely unified science out of these processes? It seems to me that on the whole they make a unified system. If we can show, for instance, that the principle of justice gives us systematic propositions about law, it could then be combined with the principle of expiation to give us an adequate account of a great mass of religious phenomena. Without adding greatly to it, the principle of justice may also give us the basis of a theory of economics, namely that of value and price. If this can be demonstrated by rational analysis and application to empirical data, we shall have started with one single abstract principle, that of simple justice, and have tied up with it law, religion, and economics.[272]

272. *Id.* at 132–35.

Chapter 4

Cultural Marxism and Normativity

The focus of this chapter is the philosophy of social and normative determinism, as proposed in the theories of Karl Marx and Friedrich Engels, which challenged classical evolutionary determinism. In the next chapter, we examine the work of other cultural anthropologists influenced by Marx and Engels, including Marvin Harris, Leslie White, and Julian Steward. Harris's theory is known as cultural materialism, White's approach may be called "culturology" with a material base, and Steward's is known as cultural ecology.

We begin with a sketch of the basic tenets of Marxism. Marx's radical anthropology is better understood in the context of his basic philosophical and political tenets.

Basic Tenets of Marxist Political Philosophy

Marx saw societies as inherently unstable systems and attributed this instability to numerous contradictions that inevitably lead to social upheaval, change, and progress. He set out to study and explain how these contradictions arise and how they are resolved, in other words to theorize how social development and progress occur. He rejected the utilitarian belief that ideas are mere reflections of natural conditions in favor of Georg Hegel's emphasis on the human being as a thinking animal.[1] Like Hegel, Marx believed that human history differs from natural history because of the human ability to form mental concepts and ideas.[2] However, unlike Hegel, Marx believed that the ideas of man are grounded in his material reality,[3] and he criticized Hegelians for their belief that "the relationships of men, all their doings, their chains and their limitations are products of their consciousness."[4]

Marx adopted a part of Hegel's dialectic as the key to social development with two critical modifications. Hegel conceived of history as a process in which the Absolute unfolds itself progressively and believed this unfolding to be something understood in terms of the dialectic or union of opposites. Marx used the dialectic to explain both social conflict and its resolution, but he did not adopt Hegel's idealism. He replaced this idealism with a thoroughgoing materialist approach and theory of knowledge. This method was based on a form of dialectical materialism, which he called "historical materialism" when applied to human relations and social relations in a historical context.

1. Maurice Bloch, Marxism and Anthropology: The History of a Relationship 6 (1983).

2. *Id.*

3. *Id.*

4. Karl Marx & Friedrich Engels, The German Ideology 41 (C.J. Arthur ed., 1970).

Inverting Hegel's dialectic was Marx's second major modification. He proclaimed his method to be

> not only different from the Hegelian, but its direct opposite. To Hegel the life-process of the human brain, *i.e.*, the process of thinking, which, under the name of "the Idea," he even transforms into an independent subject, is the demiurgos of the real world, and the real world is only the external, phenomenal form of "the Idea." With me, on the contrary, the ideal is nothing else than the material world reflected by the human mind, and translated into forms of thought. . . . With [Hegel the dialectic] is standing on its head. It must be turned right side up again, if you would discover the rational kernel within the mystical shell.[5]

These two elements are the key to understanding not only Marx's general philosophy but also the place of legal and nonlegal norms within its overall scheme. By materialism, the first element, he meant human material conditions, primarily modes and relations of production. These constitute the base on which is founded the entire social and normative order (the "superstructure"), which includes ideology, religion, philosophy, and law. By reversing Hegel's dialectic, Marx asserted that forms of thought are determined by the material conditions of life and not vice versa.[6] He believed that relations of production together with their associated norms are similarly dictated by the material means of subsistence and thus are independent of individual will. For Marx, subsistence was the first sine qua non of social life.

Given the need in any society to produce its own material means of subsistence, the process of social production (which provides the means for subsistence) is only possible if people enter into normatively defined relations of production (*e.g.*, property in the means of production, the methods and modes of distribution of products).

> In the social production which men carry on they enter into definite relations that are indispensible and independent of their will; these relations of production correspond to a definite stage of development of their material powers of production. The sum total of these relations of production constitutes the economic structure of society—the real foundation, on which rise legal and political superstructures and to which correspond definite forms of social consciousness. The mode of production in material life determines the general character of the social, political and spiritual processes of life. It is not the consciousness of men that determines their existence, but, on the contrary, their social existence determines their consciousness.[7]

According to Marx, the relations of production are given expression through law. These relations are not stable in the sense of being permanent or universal. Instead,

---

5. 1 Karl Marx, Capital (Friedrich Engels, ed., Samuel Moore & Edward Aveling, trans., 1915).

6. "Life is not determined by consciousness, but consciousness by life." Marx & Engels, The German Ideology, *supra* note 4, at 47.

7. Karl Marx, A Contribution to the Critique of Political Economy 11 (N.I. Stone trans., 1911).

they are historically contingent, depending on the extant technologies of production and other forces and modes of production. As the latter change, as they must over time, they come into conflict with the existing relations of production (*i.e.*, with positive law). Marx saw this conflict as inevitable because he believed that the material conditions of life must trigger in men definite ideas about their lives, interests, and goals. Because these interests represent different competing economic classes, however, the competition eventually explodes into social revolution, resulting in the overthrow of the existing relations of production and the substitution of a new set of more progressive relations.

> In the social production which men carry on they enter into definite relations that are indispensible and independent of their will; these relations of production correspond to a definite stage of development of their material powers of production. The sum total of these relations of production constitutes the economic structure of society—the real foundation, on which rise legal and political superstructures and to which correspond definite forms of social consciousness. The mode of production of material life determines the general character of the social, political and spiritual processes of life. It is not the consciousness of men that determines their existence, but, on the contrary, their social existence determines their consciousness. At a certain stage of their development, the material forces of production in society come in conflict with the existing relations of production, or—what is but a legal expression for the same thing—with the property relations within which they had been at work before. From forms of development of the forces these relations turn into their fetters. Then comes the period of social revolution. With the change of the economic foundation the entire immense superstructure is more or less rapidly transformed.[8]

For Marx, the law, as well as the cultural elements constituting the superstructure, changes only after the fact. This "cultural lag" is neutralized only when superstructural changes catch up with the new material modes of production. For its part, the superstructure is not a mere passive reflection of the base—there is a certain measure of interaction between the two. Perhaps this interaction is best illustrated by Marx's conviction that the law develops concurrently with the establishment of private property. Thus, once civil law is developed, existing property relationships are considered to be the result of a general will. In turn, the number of property relationships grows and new areas of industry and commerce develop. The law then adjusts to the new means of acquiring property that result.

In the Marxist view, social development is a historically contingent phenomenon; therefore, there are no universal principles of law or eternal principles of natural law. Nor are there "neutral" laws. Instead, laws exist to protect and enforce particular relations. In addition, they favor the economically dominant classes, which own the

8. Karl Marx, A Contribution to the Critique of Political Economy 11–12 (N.I. Stone trans., 1911).

means of production and control political power. Therefore, these unequal economic power relationships sow the seeds of social conflict and eventual revolution, and the state is conceived to mediate hostility between the classes.

Marx emphasized that the political power of the ruling class, exercised through the state, strives to prevent or at least minimize the risk of social conflict. Moreover, once it has consolidated its power, the ruling class continually finds new ways to exploit the oppressed class. Compromises can be struck, but only when doing so does not threaten the prevailing order; in cases of threat, state coercion is applied.

Marx postulated that under capitalism, the state and its law exist as barriers to any meaningful social reform. Thus, the more the working class (proletariat) wishes to effect change in the modes of production and relations of production, the more it is frustrated by superstructural "lag." As class divisions deepen, the exploited class organizes itself for change through an explicitly class-based struggle; eventually, it finds that meaningful change can occur only with the complete overthrow of the state and the existing relations of production. The resulting violent revolution is followed by the establishment of the dictatorship of the proletariat, wherein the law is used as an instrument to promote the advent of a new communist society in which there is no private ownership of the means of production or private appropriation of surplus labor value, and class is not constructed along economic lines. Legal excesses during this stage are justified on the grounds that they do not benefit any single group or class to the detriment of another.

In the Marxist utopia, after the disappearance of class and the establishment of public ownership of the means of production, all surplus value goes to the state—which represents the people as a whole. As society moves toward true egalitarianism in the sharing of wealth, law as an instrument of social control fades away, accompanied by the withering of the state itself. With the establishment of communist society, there is little need for law, because people learn the rules of social behavior without compulsion.

The state, therefore, is only a historically contingent institution—not a universal one. In the famous words of Engels:

> The state, therefore, has not existed from all eternity. There have been societies which have managed without it, which had no notion of the state or state power. At a definite stage of economic development, which necessarily involved the cleavage of society into classes, the state became a necessity because of this cleavage. We are now rapidly approaching a stage in the development of production at which the existence of these classes has not only ceased to be a necessity, but becomes a positive hindrance to production. They will fall as inevitably as they once arose. The state inevitably falls with them. The society which organizes production anew on the basis of free and equal association of the producers will put the whole state machinery where it will then belong—into the museum of antiquities, next to the spinning wheel and the bronze ax.[9]

9. Friedrich Engels, The Origin of the Family, Private Property and the State 160 (Resistance Books, 2004).

In the following excerpt, Marx presents his materialist approach to human evolution.

Preface to A Contribution of the Critique of Political Economy, reprinted in KARL MARX, SELECTED WRITINGS IN SOCIOLOGY AND SOCIAL PHILOSOPHY 51–53 (T.B. Bottomore trans., 1956).

I. THE MATERIALIST CONCEPTION OF HISTORY

I was led by my studies to the conclusion that legal relations as well as forms of State could neither be understood by themselves, nor explained by the so-called general progress of the human mind, but that they are rooted in the material conditions of life.... In the social production which men carry on they enter into definite relations that are indispensable and independent of their will; these relations of production correspond to a definite stage of development of their material powers of production. The totality of these relations of production constitutes the economic structure of society—the real foundation, on which legal and political superstructures arise and to which definite forms of social consciousness correspond. The mode of production of material life determines the general character of the social, political and spiritual processes of life. It is not the consciousness of men that determines their being, but, on the contrary, their social being determines their consciousness. At a certain stage of their development, the material forces of production in society come in conflict with the existing relations of production, or—what is but a legal expression for the same thing—with the property relations within which they had been at work before. From forms of development of the forces of production these relations turn into their fetters. Then occurs a period of social revolution. With the change of the economic foundation the entire immense superstructure is more or less rapidly transformed. In considering such transformations the distinction should always be made between the material transformation of the economic conditions of production which can be determined with the precision of natural science, and the legal, political, religious, esthetic or philosophical—in short ideological, forms in which men become conscious of this conflict and fight it out. Just as our opinion of an individual is not based on what he thinks of himself, so can we not judge of such a period of transformation by its own consciousness; on the contrary, this consciousness must rather be explained from the contradictions of material life, from the existing conflict between the social forces of production and the relations of production. No social order ever disappears before all the productive forces for which there is room in it have been developed; and new, higher relations of production never appear before the material conditions of their existence have matured in the womb of the old society. Therefore, mankind always sets itself only such problems as it can solve; since, on closer examination, it will always be found that the problem itself arises only when the material conditions necessary for its solution already exist or are at least in the process of formation. In broad outline we can

> designate the Asiatic, the ancient, the feudal, and the modern bourgeois modes of production as progressive epochs in the economic formation of society. The bourgeois relations of production are the last antagonistic form of the social process of production; not in the sense of individual antagonisms, but of conflict arising from conditions surrounding the life of individuals in society. At the same time the productive forces developing in the womb of bourgeois society create the material conditions for the solution of that antagonism. With this social formation, therefore, the prehistory of human society comes to an end.

The quotation shows that society as a complex normatively structured whole (including state, law, culture) goes through successive historical changes that each mark additional progress. This unidirectional evolutionary scheme begins with the "primitive" phase, which has been described as an amalgam of the first six phases of cultural evolution devised by Lewis Henry Morgan.[10]

Marx's Radical Anthropology

Marx's analysis of social and economic evolution is based on conditions that he claimed are not mere abstractions or dogmas but are instead empirically verifiable.[11] For this empirical verification he turned to anthropological studies, particularly of primitive Asiatic, Roman, and post-Roman/feudal societies. He concluded that the "first premise of all human history" is the "existence of living human individuals," by which he meant their physical organization and their relation to nature. He found much support in the anthropological and ethnographic research of Morgan, whose book *Ancient Society* traces the conditions of subsistence of primitive societies as they evolved through what are called the three grand phases of human social evolution (savagery, barbarism, and civilization).

Marx argued that the natural facts of humanity's physical and material environment dictate that people must interact with nature to subsist and we do so by expending labor to produce life-sustaining goods. He asserted that this combination of labor and production is what distinguishes humans from other animals.[12] Marx also understood that by producing the means of subsistence, humans actively create the material conditions of life. Thus it is a fundamental premise of his materialist philosophy that as humans engage in the social process of production, they develop not only certain normative relations of production but also forms of consciousness that, although conditioned by their material existence, are independent of their will.

> The fact is, therefore, that definite individuals who are productively active in a definite way enter into these definite social and political relations. Empirical observation must in each separate instance bring out empirically, and without any mystification and speculation, the connection of the so-

10. Leopold Pospíšil, Anthropology of Law: A Comparative Theory 158 (1974).

11. Karl Marx, *The German Ideology*, *in* The Marx-Engels Reader, 110, 113 (Robert C. Tucker ed., 1972).

12. *Id.* at 114.

> cial and political structure with production. The social structure and the State are continually evolving out of the life process of definite individuals, but of individuals, not as they may appear in their own or other people's imagination, but as they *really* are; i.e., as they operate, produce materially, and hence as they work under definite material limits, presuppositions and conditions independent of their will.[13]

According to Marx, the material environment is man's natural environment. Therefore, man not only operates in nature but also takes from nature and at the same time manipulates and modifies it to suit his needs.[14] Interactions between man and nature also produce social evolution because man acts not only individually but also in society with other men. What man takes from nature by expending labor is an appropriation, expressed as the basic concept of property (not to be confused with private property, as we shall see).

For Marx, the most significant element of social evolution was its corresponding forms of property. These are symbolized by the division of labor, which in turn is linked to the relations of production.

> The various stages of development in the division of labor are just so many different forms of ownership, i.e., the existing stage in the division of labour determines also the relations of individuals to one another with reference to the material, instrument, and product of labour.[15]

A Materialist Anthropology of Evolution: Marx and Morgan

Marx and Engels drew on nineteenth-century anthropological approaches to human evolution in works such as *The German Ideology*, *Pre-Capitalist Economic Formations*, and *The Origin of the Family, Private Property and the State*. Both were particularly enthusiastic about the studies of Lewis Henry Morgan and viewed his classic work *Ancient Society* as confirming their materialist view of the evolution of human society.[16] It must be noted, however, that Morgan was not a Marxist in that he did not explicitly propose or endorse the dynamic of base and superstructure. Nor did he advance a structural theory that accounted for modes or relations of production and the conflicts and contradictions that drive social revolutions.[17]

---

13. *Id.* at 126.

14. Eric J. Hobsbawm, *Introduction*, *in* KARL MARX, PRE-CAPITALIST ECONOMIC FORMATIONS 9, 12 (Eric J. Hobsbawm ed., 1964).

15. Marx, *The German Ideology*, *supra* note 11, at 11.

16. William H. Shaw, *Morgan and Marx*, 23 HIST. THEORY 215, 222 (1984) (stating that "for Marx and Engels what really mattered was not Morgan's political judgments, but rather his theoretical approach to primitive times and the assistance *Ancient Society* gave to their theory in treating pre-history").

17. Elman R. Service, *The Mind of Lewis H. Morgan*, 22 CURR. ANTHROPOL. 25, 25 (1981) (discussing Morgan's materialism and suggesting that Morgan may be as much of an idealist as a materialist).

Nonetheless, Morgan made numerous and sufficient references in *Ancient Society*, as well as in *Systems of Consanguinity and Affinity*, to material factors that influence human evolution.

> The most advanced portion of the human race were halted . . . at certain stages of progress, until some great invention or discovery, such as the domestication of animals, or the smelting of iron ore, gave a new and powerful impulse forward.[18]

Morgan also emphasized what he called the "arts of subsistence," whose development distinguished the various stages of human evolution. This concept found ready incorporation in Marx's concept of productive forces. In other words, for Morgan as well as Marx, material production played a critical role in social evolution and was intimately connected with changes in a society's kinship relations as well as its system of property relations.

These and many other similar references by Morgan were seen by Marx and Engels as lending support to their theories. Indeed, Marx made extensive notes on Morgan's book, presumably to integrate his findings with his own theories. Thus, although Morgan was not a Marxist, one may conclude that Marx was (with some reservations) a Morganist. Although Marx's notes were not published until after his death, Engels made good use of them in *The Origin of Family, Private Property and the State.*[19]

It has been suggested that Morgan's alleged materialism was largely popularized by the prominence given to him by Marx and Engels as they developed their theories of historical materialism.[20] For example, Service has argued that Morgan's faith in the human spirit and in "the Almighty" as the force responsible for uplifting humanity from savagery strongly suggests that he was as much an idealist or "mentalist" as a materialist.[21] This position is controversial, however, and has been criticized by other scholars.[22]

Morgan's thesis of the arts of subsistence driving human evolution was arrived at retrospectively (*i.e.*, by his reconstruction of past society). Marx, who independently derived the same theory, used it prospectively (*i.e.*, for what he saw as the society of

---

18. Lewis Henry Morgan, Ancient Society 44 (1877); *see also id.* at 535, 539, 553. *See also* Lewis Henry Morgan, Systems of Consanguinity and Affinity 14, 492 (1871) for references to the importance of property in society.

19. For Marx's notes on Morgan's *Ancient Society see* The Ethnological Notebooks of Karl Marx (Lawrence Krader ed., 1972).

20. Service, *supra* note 17, at 29. *See also* Patrick Fleuret, Comment asserting that "our present-day fascination with Morgan is based less on Morgan himself than on the achievements of the powerful personalities (White and Marx) who drew attention to Morgan while developing their own statements about evolution and history." *Id.* at 32; *see also* Lawrence Krader, Comment arguing that Marx did *not* consider Morgan to be a materialist and that only Engels did. *Id.* at 34.

21. *Id.* at 25–27, 41. *See also* Alan Barnard, Comment asserting that "Service rightly criticizes Engels and White for reading into Morgan's mind concepts of "materialism" and "evolutionism" that probably were not there." *Id.* at 31.

22. *See* Adam Kuper, Comment, *id.* at 35, and John H. Moore, Comment, *id.* at 36 (accusing Service of an "anticommunist" bias), and Raoul Makarius, Comment, *id.* at 36 (challenging the view that Morgan was religious and asserting that Morgan became an agnostic in his later life).

the future). The following is the attempt of one commentator (Chattopadhyaya) to integrate the ideas of Morgan and Marx.

> This socio-historical process of the negation of the negation is propelled in fact by the same force, namely, that of the development of the technique or mode of production. Morgan saw this in his own way while looking back at past society, while Marx foresaw it while looking forward to the future society. Morgan's researches led to the assertion that the development of the technique of obtaining the means of subsistence, beginning from the early stage of savagery, reached, at what he called the upper stage of barbarism, a situation in which conditions were created for a qualitative transformation of the social organisation—the emergence of class society on the ruins of the pre-class society. According to the researches of Marx and Engels, the further development of the technique of production through the successive stages of class society reached again under modern capitalism a situation that called for a qualitative transformation in social organisation—the emergence of classless society on the ruins of the class society. There is thus a real connecting thread between the researches of Morgan and Marx, to which Engels drew our attention when he said, "Morgan rediscovered in America, in his own way, the materialist conception of history that had been discovered by Marx forty years ago."
>
> In short, the researches of Morgan and Marx are in need of integration. When integrated, we have a fuller understanding of the dialectics of social evolution as determined by the technique of production. We may briefly recapitulate the main points of this.
>
> In the primitive pre-class society, the technique of production was so rudimentary that the labour of the entire community was required to maintain it at the minimum level of subsistence. Human labour power was not yet capable of producing any surplus, hence there was no question of one section of the community living on the labour of another. With the development of the productive technique, human labour power became able to produce surplus—*i.e.*, more than was necessary for the bare maintenance of the labourer himself. Objective conditions were thus created for one section of the society to live on the labour of another. In other words, conditions were created for the possible division of society into two broad classes, namely, that of the direct producers and of those that expropriated their surplus product. Morgan, and following him Engels, showed how this possibility was actualised in human history. This was the negation of the primitive pre-class society by early class society, *i.e.*, as determined by the quantitative increase of human productive power reaching a qualitatively new level. The development of the technique of production continued through the successive stages of class society, culminating in capitalism. Under capitalism, however, the development of the productive technique reached again a qualitatively new character as a result of which it became increasingly incompatible with the

> division of society into classes. In other words, conditions were created again for the negation of class society by the classless society of the future or for communism, though this at an incomparably higher level.[23]

Chattopadhyaya also quotes a letter that Marx wrote to Engels in 1868, almost a decade before Morgan's book was published. The excerpted letter is followed by Chattopadhyaya's comment.

> It is the same with human history as with palaeontology. Even the best minds fail to see—on principle, owing to a certain judicial blindness—-things which lie in front of their noses. Later, when the moment has arrived, one is surprised to find traces everywhere of what one has failed to see. The first reaction against the French Revolution and the Enlightenment which is connected with it was naturally to regard everything mediaeval as romantic; even people like Grimm are not free from this. The second reaction *is to look beyond the Middle Ages into the primitive age of every nation, and that corresponds to the socialist trend,* although those learned men have no idea that they have any connection with it. Then they are surprised *to find what is newest in what is oldest*—even equalitarians, to a degree which would have made Proudhon shudder.

> As is characteristic of Marx's hurried notes, a considerable number of ideas and comments appears to be crowding the letter just quoted. But the main drift of his thought—the central theme connecting his ideas and comments—is not difficult to see. He comes across a few and fragmentary evidences of primitive communism or its survival in German and Roman history and, on the basis of these, gives us a glimpse of the dialectics of social development in the following remarkable expressions: "*to look . . . into the primitive age of every nation, and that corresponds to the socialist trend. . . . They are surprised to find what is newest in what is oldest—even equalitarians, to a degree which would have made Proudhon shudder.*" Without violently distorting Marx we have to admit that "what is newest" is of course communism and "what is oldest" is primitive communism; hence to see what is newest in what is oldest "corresponds to the socialist trend." It was precisely the same point that Morgan also wanted to emphasize in his own way, when he said: "It will be a revival, in a higher form, of the liberty, equality and fraternity of the ancient gentes." However, in 1860, when Marx was making this momentous formulation containing the crux of the dialectics of social development, Morgan's *Ancient Society* was yet to appear. We can well understand Marx's enthusiasm for it, for it contained a detailed and sustained study of "what is oldest" or the primitive pre-class society.[24]

---

23. Debiprasad Chattopadhyaya, *Dialectics of Social Evolution: Morgan, Marx and Engels*, 9 Soc. Sci. 3, 15–16 (1982).

24. *Id.* at 18.

Morgan's critical-historical perspective on the role of private property was highly appealing to both Marx and Engels.[25] Morgan argued that the dominance of private property was only temporary, that it was the source of many social ills, that it contained its own "elements of self-destruction," and that there would come a time when mankind would live in a "higher form of liberty, equality and fraternity."

> Since the advent of civilization, the outgrowth of property has been so immense, its forms so diversified, its uses so expanding and its management so intelligent in the interests of its owners, that it has become, on the part of the people, an unmanageable power. The human mind stands bewildered in the presence of its own creation. The time will come, nevertheless, when human intelligence will rise to the mastery over property, and define the relations of the state to the property it protects, as well as the obligations and the limits of the rights of its owners. The interests of society are paramount to individual interests, and the two must be brought into just and harmonious relations. A mere property career is not the final destiny of mankind, if progress is to be the law of the future as it has been of the past. The time which has passed away since civilization began is but a fragment of the past duration of man's existence; and but a fragment of the ages yet to come. The dissolution of society bids fair to become the termination of a career of which property is the end and aim; because such a career contains the elements of self-destruction. Democracy in government, brotherhood in society, equality in rights and privileges, and universal education, foreshadow the next higher plane of society to which experience, intelligence and knowledge are steadily tending. It will be a revival, in a higher form, of the liberty, equality and fraternity of the ancient gentes.[26]

Not only does this passage support Marx's own views on the exploitative nature of private property, Engels quoted it in full at the end of his own book.[27] The support for Marx's view in the passage lies in the anticipation of a dialectic of social development based on the idea of "the negation of the negation." Here, the primitive classless society of the gentes has been negated by the class society, which in turn will be negated by a yet higher form of classless society that revives the ancient equality and liberty enjoyed during primitive communism.[28]

Marx on Evolution

Marx's writings describe six epochs of human evolution: primitive communism, the Asiatic system, ancient slavery, feudalism, capitalism, and communism. These

25. Elisabeth Tooker, *L.H. Morgan and His Contemporaries*, 94 AM. ANTHROPOL. 357 (1922) (suggesting that Morgan was regarded as "a founder of 'Marxist Anthropology' ").

26. MORGAN, ANCIENT SOCIETY, *supra* note 18, at 552.

27. ENGELS, THE ORIGIN OF THE FAMILY, *supra* note 9, at 164. Service, *supra* note 17, at 26.

28. Chattopadhyaya, *supra* note 23, at 4.

phases are not given systematic treatment, nor is a strict unilinear scheme postulated for all humans in all geographical areas. Indeed, Marx and Engels make clear that they do not subscribe to a rigid unilinear view.

> The archaic or primary formations of our earth consist themselves of a series of layers of different age, superimposed upon one another. Similarly, the archaic structures of society reveal a series of different social types corresponding to progressive epochs.[29]

In another work Marx declares:

> Primitive communities are not all cut to a single pattern. On the contrary, taken together they form a series of social groupings, differing both in type and age, and marking successive phases of development.[30]

Yet both Marx and Engels maintained that there is a distinct progression of human society more or less in the order above, particularly in the sense that each phase is further removed from its previous (*i.e.*, less-developed) phase and historically closer to achieving communism. The latter phase, the epoch of classless society, heralds the end of private property and its attendant class antagonisms—the primary characteristics of all previous phases of human evolution.[31]

Apart from these very distinct views about the evolutionary progressions of human society, Marx and Engels's focus was not on cultural evolution *per se* but rather the various forms of property relations associated with each epoch. For this reason, they gave short shrift to epochs that they did not consider to be marked by stages of the division of labor (which for Marx were "just so many different forms of ownership").[32] For example, the first phase of primitive communism is described by Engels as a type of promiscuous society based on group marriage and matrilineal communistic households. His view of the evolution of the family into more complex forms of social union is described below; here, we need only note that this evolution was marked by little in the way of division of labor and notions of property.

The Asiatic model, which seems to have been for Marx less an evolutionary phase than a geographic or regional model, is also marked by the absence of property. It is founded on a centrally controlled irrigation system and other public works and has a rigid normative system run by a despotic government. Its land is tilled in common, and there is no ruling class. Its society is largely static.

> The Asiatic form necessarily survives longest and most stubbornly. This is due to the fundamental principle on which it is based, that is, that the individual does not become independent of the community; that the circle of

29. Karl Marx & Friedrich Engels, The Russian Menace to Europe 223 (Paul W. Blackstock & Bert F. Hoselitz eds., 1952).

30. Marx, Pre-Capitalist Economic Formations, *supra* note 14, at 144.

31. Karl Marx and Friedrich Engels, *Manifesto of the Communist Party*, *in* The Marx-Engels Reader, *supra* note 11, at 335.

32. *See* quotation in text at note 15, *supra*.

> production is self-sustaining, unity of agriculture and craft manufacture, etc. If the individual changes his relation to the community, he modifies and undermines both the community and its economic premises; . . .
>
> In all these forms the basis of evolution is the *reproduction* of relations between individual and community *assumed as given*—they may be more or less primitive, more or less the result of history, but fixed into tradition—and a *definite, predetermined objective* existence, both as regards the relation to the conditions of labour and the relation between one man and his co-workers, fellow-tribesmen, etc. Such evolution is therefore from the outset *limited*, but once the limits are transcended, decay and disintegration ensue.[33]

The communistic and Asiatic models were of interest to Marx and Engels only for their status as epochs that have evolved into normative systems that are more complex because of their increased divisions of labor and forms of ownership.

Marx identifies the first form of ownership as tribal (*stammeigentum*).[34] The division of labor here is still rather minimal because this is a community of hunter-gatherers whose chief means of subsistence are hunting, fishing, and rearing livestock. Division of labor is limited to the "natural" division of labor within the family. The social structure is limited to the extended family in the following hierarchy: patriarchal family chieftains, tribal members, and slaves. Slavery, which is "latent in the family,"[35] becomes more widespread with population growth, external trade, and conquests. The first advance in the division of labor is the separation of agricultural labor from industrial and commercial labor, a separation that manifests in the distinction and rivalry between town and country.

This diversification leads to the second form of ownership identified by Marx: the "ancient communal" model that manifests when tribes unified by agreement or conquest form a city. Slavery in this phase remains prevalent and, as explained in the excerpt below, the division of labor with its corresponding forms of property is more complex. For the first time class relations emerge, begin to compete, and become antagonistic. Examples include antagonism between the slave-owning class and the slaves themselves and between townspeople and country folk.[36]

Marx's third form of ownership is feudal or estate property,[37] which emerged during the Middle Ages after the decline of the Roman Empire.[38] Marx assigns the emergence of feudalism to the countryside (rather than the town, where the previous epoch had originated), in part because of the defeat of the Roman Empire by the Germanic tribal conquerors, which included the destruction of the empire's productive forces (*i.e.*, its agricultural and industrial bases). He also cited "the sparseness of the population at that time, which was scattered over a large area and which received no

---

33. Marx, Pre-Capitalist Economic Formations, *supra* note 14, at 83.

34. Karl Marx, *The German Ideology*, *supra* note 11, at 115.

35. *Id.*

36. *Id.*

37. *Id.* at 116.

38. *Id.* at 116–17.

large increase from the conquerors."[39] As in the ancient communal period, organizations in the feudal era thrived on the labor of a subjugated producing class (the serfs) but with a new set of relations of production.

The principal form of property in the feudal era was land ownership by feudal lords, "with serf labour chained to it."[40] According to Marx, this ownership was backed by the tribal conquerors and their Germanic institutions. By contrast, a parallel division in the towns valued the principal forms of property (*i.e.*, goods) more than the private labor of individuals who produced the goods. Some of these workers organized into guilds, which consisted of master craftsmen and merchants who employed apprentices and journeymen.[41] Thus new divisions of labor and corresponding property forms emerged: princes, nobles, clergy, and peasants in the country and master craftsmen, apprentices, and journeymen in the towns.

Although the feudal era is presented by Marx as chronologically following the second (ancient communal) epoch, he does not suggest a logical or causal nexus between them. Instead, feudalism appears at this time as an alternative evolutionary epoch,[42] when cities are few and population density is low.[43] However, once the new division of labor and the two-tier property system emerge,

> [t]he grouping of larger territories into feudal kingdoms was a necessity for the landed nobility as for the towns. The organization of the ruling class, the nobility, had, therefore, everywhere a monarch at its head.[44]

Marx maintains that, even if feudalism is not necessarily triggered by the ancient communal epoch, the transition from feudalism to capitalism is the product of feudal evolution.[45]

Karl Marx, *The German Ideology*, *in* The Marx-Engels Reader 113–119 (Robert C. Tucker ed., 1972).

> The premises from which we begin are not arbitrary ones, not dogmas, but real premises from which abstraction can only be made in the imagination. They are the real individuals, their activity and the material conditions under which they live, both those which they find already existing and those produced by their activity. These premises can thus be verified in a purely empirical way.
>
> The first premise of all human history is, of course, the existence of living human individuals. Thus the first fact to be established is the phys-

39. *Id.* at 116.

40. *Id.* at 117.

41. *Id.*

42. Shaw, *supra* note 16, at 218.

43. Hobsbawm, *supra* note 14, at 28.

44. Marx, *German Ideology*, *supra* note 11, at 118.

45. Marx & Engels, *The Communist Manifesto*, *supra* note 31, at 336–340.

ical organisation of these individuals and their consequent relation to the rest of nature. . . .

Men can be distinguished from animals by consciousness, by religion or anything else you like. They themselves begin to distinguish themselves from animals as soon as they being to *produce* their means of subsistence, a step which is conditioned by their physical organisation. By producing their means of subsistence men are indirectly producing their actual material life.

The way in which men produce their means of subsistence depends first of all on the nature of the actual means of subsistence they find in existence and have to reproduce. . . . As individuals express their life, so they are. What they are, therefore, coincides with their production, both with *what* they produce and with *how* they produce. . . .

The various stages of development in the division of labour are just so many different forms of ownership, i.e., the existing stage in the division of labour determines also the relations of individuals to one another with reference to the material, instrument, and product of labour.

The first form of ownership is tribal [*Stammeigentum*] ownership. It corresponds to the undeveloped stage of production, at which a people lives by hunting and fishing, by the rearing of beasts or, in the highest stage, agriculture. In the latter case it presupposes a great mass of uncultivated stretches of land. The division of labour is at this stage still very elementary . . .

The second form is the ancient communal and State ownership which proceeds especially from the union of several tribes into a *city* by agreement or by conquest, and which is still accompanied by slavery. Beside communal ownership we already find movable, and later also immovable, private property developing . . . The division of labour is already more developed. We already find the antagonism of town and country; later the antagonism between those states which represent town interests and those which represent country interests, and inside the towns themselves the antagonism between industry and maritime commerce. The class relation between citizens and slaves is now completely developed. . . .

The third form of ownership is feudal or estate property. If antiquity started out from the town and its little territory, the Middle Ages started out from the *country*. . . . The last centuries of the declining Roman Empire and its conquest by the barbarians destroyed a number of productive forces; agriculture had declined, industry had decayed for want of a market, trade had died out or been violently suspended, the rural and urban population had decreased. From these conditions and the mode of organisation of the conquest determined by them, feudal property developed under the influence of the Germanic military constitution. . . . As soon as feudalism is fully developed, there also arises antagonism to the towns. The hierarchical structure of landownership, and the armed bodies of retainers associated with it, gave the nobility power over the serfs. . . .

> This feudal system of landownership had its counterpart in the *towns* in the shape of corporative property, the feudal organisation of trades. Here property consisted chiefly in the labour of each individual person. The necessity for association against the organised robber nobility, the need for communal covered markets in an age when the industrialist was at the same time a merchant, the growing competition of the escaped serfs swarming into the rising towns, the feudal structure of the whole country: these combined to bring about the *guilds*. . . .
>
> Thus the chief form of property during the feudal epoch consisted on the one hand of landed property with serf labour chained to it, and on the other of the labour of the individual with small capital commanding the labour of journeymen. . . .
>
> The grouping of larger territories into feudal kingdoms was a necessity for the landed nobility as for the towns. The organisation of the ruling class, the nobility, had, therefore, everywhere a monarch at its head. . . .

The Transition from Feudalism to Capitalism in Evolutionary Context

Marx asserts that the capitalist era evolved directly out of the feudal system. Again, his explanation is thoroughly materialistic, grounded on his analysis of the economic conditions that presaged the downfall of feudalism. He identified the locus within feudal society from which capitalism was derived as the city, more particularly the city craftsmen and merchants ("burghers").[46] As seen in the previous section, members of this urban class were able to become private owners of their means of production. This achievement was important to Marx because it is precisely the emancipation granted by ownership of the means of production, in a way separate from the earlier communal basis for production, that enables society to separate labor from "the objective conditions of production."[47] Even so, as we saw in the previous section, Marx understood that the guilds existed separately from the landed nobility and were subsumed under it *via* the feudal monarch.

As Marx examined national and international markets, he concluded that evolving conditions had inevitably rendered the above system inadequate. The feudal system of industry, together with the closed guilds that eventually monopolized manufacturing and industry, could not meet the new needs of trade made possible by the opening of sea routes to America; travels around and beyond the Cape of Good Hope; the opening up of new trade routes to East India, China, and the British colonies in Asia; and the resultant increases in worldwide commerce and navigation. He concluded that feudal property relations as well as the guild system acted as "fetters" on the new demands.[48] They were eventually forced to make way for steam-driven machines

46. *Id.* at 336.

47. Hobsbawn, *supra* note 14, at 41. Karl Marx, Grundrisse 508–09 (Penguin Harmondsworth 1969).

48. Marx & Engels, *The Communist Manifesto*, *supra* note 31, at 340.

and railways that revolutionized industrial production and trade. In the process, the city burghers had to admit a new industrial middle class: the modern bourgeoisie.[49]

Karl Marx & Friedrich Engels, *The Manifesto of The Communist Party*, *in* THE MARX-ENGELS READER 336–340 (Robert C. Tucker ed., 1972).

Our epoch, the epoch of the bourgeoisie, possesses, however, this distinctive feature: it has simplified the class antagonisms: Society as a whole is more and more splitting up into two great hostile camps, into two great classes directly facing each other: Bourgeoisie and Proletariat.

From the serfs of the Middle Ages sprang the chartered burghers of the earliest towns. From those burgesses the first elements of the bourgeoisie were developed.

The discovery of America, the rounding of the Cape, opened up fresh ground for the rising bourgeoisie. The East-Indian and Chinese markets, the colonisation of America, trade with the colonies, the increase in the means of exchange and in commodities generally, gave to commerce, to navigation, to industry, an impulse never before known, and thereby, to the revolutionary element in the tottering feudal society, a rapid development. . . .

Each step in the development of the bourgeoisie was accompanied by a corresponding political advance of that class. An oppressed class under the sway of the feudal nobility, . . . the bourgeoisie has at last, since the establishment of Modern Industry and of the world-market, conquered for itself, in the modern representative State, exclusive political sway. The executive of the modern State is but a committee for managing the common affairs of the whole bourgeoisie. . . .

The bourgeoisie, wherever it has got the upper hand, has put an end to all feudal, patriarchal, idyllic relations. It has pitilessly torn asunder the motley feudal ties that bound man to his "natural superiors," and has left remaining no other nexus between man and man than naked self-interest, than callous "cash payment." . . .

The bourgeoisie keeps more and more doing away with the scattered state of the population, of the means of production, and of property. It has agglomerated population, centralised means of production, and has concentrated property in a few hands. The necessary consequence of this was political centralisation. Independent, or but loosely connected provinces, with separate interests, laws, governments and systems of taxation, became lumped together into one nation, with one government, one code of laws, one national class-interest, one frontier and one customs-tariff. . . .

We see then: the means of production and of exchange, on whose foundation the bourgeoisie built itself up, were generated in feudal society. At a certain stage in the development of these means of production and of ex-

---

49. *Id.* at 336.

change, the condition under which feudal society produced and exchanged, the feudal organisation of agriculture and manufacturing industry, in one word, the feudal relations of property became no longer compatible with the already developed productive forces; they became so many fetters. They had to be burst asunder; they were burst asunder.

Into their place stepped free competition, accompanied by a social and political constitution adapted to it, and by the economical and political sway of the bourgeois class.

The Transition from Capitalism to Communism in Evolutionary Context

According to Marx's evolutionist materialism, just as the feudal system of production had become a fetter on the newer and more developed needs of capitalism, so the capitalist system itself eventually would become a fetter on the greater aspirations and demands of communism. The difference, of course, is that instead of the bourgeoisie acting as a progressive force, such as the one that overthrew feudalism, the working class (the proletariat) forms the revolutionary force that will overthrow capitalism.

Thus, for Marx and Engels, the capitalist system of production was only one of six human evolutionary epochs, each characterized by its own division of labor, forms of property, and relations of production. According to Marx, because the study of a given epoch in retrospect would show that it was not always so, neither are the capitalist relations of production permanent, eternal, and natural. He did, however, appear to see labor as something that is naturally sold in the market, according to the laws of supply and demand, and wage levels therefore as similarly natural and inevitable. The goal of Marx's political activism was to prove that there was nothing inevitable about the helplessness and exploitation of workers and that this phenomenon was rather the result of the prevailing notions of property and the ownership of the means of production (*e.g.*, land, tools, machines).

Marx and Engels turned to anthropology to demonstrate that forms of property were not natural, God-given, and permanent, and found the evidence they sought in the evolutionary theories of Johann Bachofen and Morgan. For example, Engels had high praise for Morgan's theory of kinship among the Iroquois and for his studies of its prevalence and evolution in other parts of the world. In particular he cites Morgan's conclusion that the Native American system of kinship also prevailed among numerous tribes in Asia, Africa, and Australia; that it was preceded by a form of group marriage, the remnants of which were still evident in some Hawaiian and Australian islands; and that this form of marriage had left behind a kinship system that could only be explained by even earlier forms of group marriage and common property that were now extinct.[50]

---

50. Engels, The Origin of the Family, *supra* note 9, at 33. For further details on Morgan's classification of kinship systems *see* Chapter 1, text at notes 71–83.

Engels concluded that endogamous marriage (*i.e.*, marriage within the group) has existed everywhere in the world at one time or another when a tribe has consisted of members related by blood on the mother's side (gentes), because—as he postulated—paternity is always uncertain under such conditions. Engels further credited Morgan with the discovery that the *gens*, organized according to mother right, was the original form that led to the gens according to father right, found among the "civilized peoples" of ancient Greece and Rome. Indeed, for Engels the discovery that the mother-right gens was the antecedent of the father-right gens has the same significance for primitive society as Darwin's theory of evolution has for biology and Marx's theory of surplus value has for political economy.[51] Hence his indebtedness to Morgan.[52]

Marx and Engels's interest in anthropology was motivated by their desire to show that each epoch of human evolution is a specific product of its own history and that none are preordained. Marx (like Engels) often referred to systems other than the capitalist system, for example the feudal system of the Middle Ages, to show that the relations of production in the latter were different from capitalism. Feudalism was characterized by the personal relationship of the feudal lord and his serf, and the relation of subordination came from the lord's ownership and control of the land, with little, if any, division of labor. By contrast, the division of labor under the capitalist order is highly specialized and impersonal. Indeed, Marx argues that labor becomes a commodity under capitalism, and like any other commodity, it is bought and sold contractually. This process dehumanizes the worker and alienates him from the product of his own labor.

However, capitalism is afflicted with other ills that contain the seeds of its own destruction, as explained in the excerpt that follows. Note the similarity with Morgan's interpretation of how developments in the arts of subsistence affect kinship and property relations over the different "ethnical" periods of human evolution.

---

51. Engels, The Origin of Family, *supra* note 9, at 34–35.

52. "This is the point at which Morgan's chief work enters: *Ancient Society* (1877), the book upon which the present work is based. What Morgan only dimly surmised in 1871 is here developed with full comprehension. Endogamy and exogamy constitute no antithesis; up to the present no exogamous 'tribes' have been brought to light anywhere. But at the time when group marriage still prevailed—and in all probability it existed everywhere at one time or other—the tribe consisted of a number of groups related by blood on the mother's side, gentes, within which marriage was strictly prohibited, so that although the men of a gens could, and as a rule did, take their wives from within their tribe, they had, however, to take them from outside their gens. Thus, while the gens itself was strictly exogamous, the tribe, embracing all the gentes, was strictly endogamous. . . .

Morgan, however, did not rest content with this. The gens of the American Indians served him further as a means of making the second decisive advance in the field of investigation he had entered upon. He discovered that the gens, organised according to mother right, was the original form out of which developed the later gens, organised according to father right, the gens as we find it among the civilised peoples of antiquity. The Greek and Roman gens, an enigma to all previous historians, was now explained by the Indian gens, and thus a new basis was found for the whole history of primitive society." *Id.*

Karl Marx & Friedrich Engels, *The Manifesto of the Communist Party*, *in* The Marx-Engels Reader 340–345 (Robert C. Tucker ed., 1972).

Modern bourgeois society with its relations of production, of exchange and of property, a society that has conjured up such gigantic means of production and of exchange, is like the sorcerer, who is no longer able to control the powers of the nether world whom he has called up by his spells. . . . The productive forces at the disposal of society no longer tend to further the development of the conditions of bourgeois property; on the contrary, they have become too powerful for these conditions, by which they are fettered, and so soon as they overcome these fetters, they bring disorder into the whole of bourgeois society, endanger the existence of bourgeois property. The conditions of bourgeois society are too narrow to comprise the wealth created by them. . . .

But not only has the bourgeoisie forged the weapons that bring death to itself; it has also called into existence the men who are to wield those weapons—the modern working class—the proletarians.

In proportion as the bourgeoisie, *i.e.*, capital, is developed, in the same proportion is the proletariat, the modern working class, developed—a class of labourers, who live only so long as they find work, and who find work only so long as their labour increases capital. These labourers, who must sell themselves piece-meal, are a commodity, like every other article of commerce, and are consequently exposed to all the vicissitudes of competition, to all the fluctuations of the market. . . .

Modern industry has converted the little workshop of the patriarchal master into the great factory of the industrial capitalist. Masses of labourers, crowded into the factory, are organised like soldiers. As privates of the industrial army they are placed under the command of a perfect hierarchy of officers and sergeants. Not only are they slaves of the bourgeois class, and of the bourgeois State; they are daily and hourly enslaved by the machine, by the over-looker, and, above all, by the individual bourgeois manufacturer himself. The more openly this despotism proclaims gain to be its end and aim, the more petty, the more hateful and the more embittering it is. . . .

No sooner is the exploitation of the labourer by the manufacturer, so far, at an end, that he receives his wages in cash, than he is set upon by the other portions of the bourgeoisie, the landlord, the shopkeeper, the pawnbroker, etc.

. . . At this stage the labourers still form an incoherent mass scattered over the whole country, and broken up by their mutual competition. . . .

But with the development of industry the proletariat not only increases in number; it becomes concentrated in greater masses, its strength grows, and it feels that strength more. . . . Thereupon the workers begin to form combinations (Trades Unions) against the bourgeois; they club together in order to keep up the rate of wages; they found permanent associations in order to make provision beforehand for those occasional revolts. Here and there the contest breaks out into riots. . . .

The essential condition for the existence, and for the sway of the bourgeois class, is the formation and augmentation of capital; the condition for capital is wage-labour. Wage-labour rests exclusively on competition between the labourers. The advance of industry, whose involuntary promoter is the bourgeoisie, replaces the isolation of the labourers, due to competition, by their revolutionary combination, due to association. The development of Modern Industry, therefore, cuts from under its feet the very foundation on which the bourgeoisie produces and appropriates products. What the bourgeoisie, therefore, produces, above all, is its own grave-diggers. Its fall and the victory of the proletariat are equally inevitable.

The Radical Anthropology of Friedrich Engels

Introduction to Engels's Historicism

If Marx found that the research of Lewis Henry Morgan supported his own materialist view of evolution, Engels explicitly adopted Morgan's evolutionary phases in *The Origin of the Family, Private Property and the State* and even subtitled this work *In the Light of the Researches of Lewis H. Morgan.*[53] In writing this book, Engels had access to the extensive notes made by Marx after reading Morgan's book, presumably in order to integrate Morgan's theories into his own analysis of the material bases of human evolution. Thus Engels presents *The Origin of the Family, Private Property and the State* as "the fulfillment of a bequest" by Marx, who—according to Engels—had planned to present the results of Morgan's studies in connection with his own "materialist investigation of history."[54] Engels contends that Morgan "rediscovered" in America the materialist conception of history that had been discovered by Marx some forty years before Morgan.[55]

For Engels the materialist conception holds that the determining factor in history is the "production and reproduction of immediate life."[56] The development of social institutions is conditioned by two kinds of production: the production of the means of subsistence (*e.g.*, food, clothing, shelter, tools), as well as the production of human beings themselves (*i.e.*, the propagation of the species).[57] The former reflects the conditions of labor (specializations within, and the division of, labor); the latter denotes the family. Both of these social institutions evolve over time. The less developed the conditions of labor, the more limited is the volume of production; therefore, the

53. *Id.* at 39.

54. *Id.* at 25.

55. *Id.*

56. *Id.*

57. *Id.*

wealth of society is limited as well and the social order is dependent on gender-based ties within the family. But because society is never static, labor productivity and, with it, overall social wealth improve over time. As labor also becomes more and more specialized, private property and differences in wealth emerge. These developments occur because it is now possible for certain persons to buy the labor power of others, which creates class distinctions as well as antagonisms between labor and capital. These antagonisms eventually "burst asunder" the old family-centered system, which is then replaced by territorial groupings dominated by the property system.

> However, within this structure of society based on ties of sex, the productivity of labour develops more and more; with it, private property and exchange, differences in wealth, the possibility of utilising the labour power of others, and thereby the basis of class antagonisms: new social elements, which strive in the course of generations to adapt the old structure of society to the new conditions, until, finally, the incompatibility of the two leads to a complete revolution. The old society, built on groups based on ties of sex, bursts asunder in the collision of the newly developed social classes; in its place a new society appears, constituted in a state, the lower units of which are no longer groups based on ties of sex but territorial groups, a society in which the family system is entirely dominated by the property system, and in which the class antagonisms and class struggles, which make up the content of all hitherto *written* history, now freely develop.[58]

Engels on the Origin of the Family

Introduction

By Engels's logical inference, if the emergence of class antagonism and struggle mark the beginning of written history, the prior period must be *pre*-history. Thus Engels credits Morgan for having "discovered" and "reconstructed" the prehistoric foundation of human evolution. The foundational social unit of prehistory was the family, whose identity was based on ties of gender. Engels's authoritative point of departure was Bachofen's *Mother Right* (1861), which asserts that (1) the period of prehistory (for humans at least) was one of complete sexual promiscuity; (2) such promiscuity meant that lineage (as well as inheritance) could only be traced through the female line, since paternity could never be certain; and (3) women therefore had a high social status; being the only ascertainable parents of younger generations, women ruled the household and the family.[59]

According to Engels, Bachofen's hypothesis is confirmed empirically by Morgan's studies on the nature of kinship systems worldwide. He credited Morgan as having "discovered" that the prehistoric family consisted of gentes related by blood on the mother's side and that the gens organized according to mother right later evolved

58. *Id.* at 26.

59. *Id.* at 28.

into the gens according to father right as found in the civilized peoples of antiquity (*i.e.*, the Greek and Roman gens).[60] For Engels, this was a revolutionary development:

> The rediscovery of the original mother-right gens as the stage preliminary to the father-right gens of the civilised peoples has the same significance for the history of primitive society as Darwin's theory of evolution has for biology, and Marx's theory of surplus value for political economy.[61]

In other words, the Bachofen-Morgan thesis confirmed the materialist view (here with regard to the status of women) that social relations, particularly the relations of production, are not static and evolve as modes of production change. Under this thesis, women, originally the dominant force of society, lost this status and become an oppressed and exploited class along with other exploited classes. This loss of status seems to happen as society moves from being matrilineal to patrilineal; as men operate and have power over the means of production, women are confined to household duties regarded as less important.[62]

Evolution of the Family and the Changing Status of Women

Engels adopted Morgan's three great epochs of human evolution (savagery, barbarism, and civilization), together with the subdivision of the first two into lower, middle, and upper stages.[63] He tied these subdivisions to progress in the methods and means of subsistence. According to Engels, the evolution of the family "proceeds concurrently" with these epochs although it does not itself mark off or delimit these periods.[64]

Engels also followed Morgan's assertion that the first stage of the family, the consanguine family, developed out of the original condition of promiscuous intercourse among humans.[65] Thus he also maintained that the latter condition, characterized by the group family in which lineage is traced through the mother and inheritance is governed by mother right, arose during the period of savagery and the lower stage of barbarism.[66] By this logic, in the consanguine family, marriage groups ranged according to generations; only ancestors and descendants (parents and children) were excluded from marriage with one another.[67] The next advance in the form of the matrilineal group was the emergence of the punaluan family, which added the exclusion of siblings as well as first, second, and third cousins from marriage.[68] Next

60. *Id.* at 34.

61. *Id.* at 34–35.

62. *Id.* at 151.

63. For more discussion of these stages *see* Chapter 1 text at notes 84–100.

64. Engels, The Origin of the Family, *supra* note 9, at 39.

65. *Id.* at 51.

66. *Id.* at 55.

67. *Id.* at 51.

68. *Id.* at 52–53.

was the emergence of the pairing family in which, at first, one man had a principal wife (among others); however, this arrangement evolved to a condition in which one man lived with one woman (the classical pairing family) although polygamy and/or occasional infidelity remained a man's privilege (but not his wife's).[69] The pairing family emerges at "the border line between savagery and barbarism, mainly at the upper stage of savagery."[70] Lineage is still traced through the mother, however, which ensured her high social standing.

The progression from the consanguine to the punaluan to the pairing family, which shows the ever-widening exclusion of blood relatives from marriage, led Morgan to speculate that marriage between nonconsanguinous gentes created a "more vigorous stock physically and mentally."[71] Although, as he posited, the successive exclusion of closer and even remote relatives eventually led to the extinction of group marriage, the communistic household was maintained throughout these stages of family; even the pairing family was too weak and unstable to require an independent household.[72] As noted above, the communistic household ensured the supremacy of women in the house because of the impossibility of determining the natural father.

> The communistic household, in which most of the women or even all the women belong to one and the same gens, while the men come from various other gentes, is the material foundation of that predominancy of women which generally obtained in primitive times.... [T]he reports of travellers and missionaries about women among savages and barbarians being burdened with excessive toil in no way conflict with what has been said above. The division of labour between the two sexes is determined by causes entirely different from those that determine the status of women in society. Peoples whose women have to work much harder than we would consider proper often have far more real respect for women than our Europeans have for theirs. The social status of the lady of civilisation, surrounded by sham homage and estranged from all real work, is infinitely lower than that of the hard-working woman of barbarism, who was regarded among her people as a real lady... and was such by the nature of her position.[73]

Flux in marital forms does not, of course, occur in a vacuum. Socioeconomic forces foment these transitions; traditional sexual mores lose their "naive, jungle character" as a result of economic developments; and growing population density results in increased production and social wealth.[74] Group sexual relations appear degrading if not oppressive to women, who seek either chastity or monogamous

---

69. *Id.* at 59.

70. *Id.* at 64.

71. Morgan, *supra* note 18, at 468.

72. *Id.* at 60. Engels, The Origin of the Family, *supra* note 9, at 60.

73. *Id.* at 61.

74. *Id.* at 63.

relationships.[75] Thus it must be women who are the driving force of monogamy. As Engels wryly observes:

> This advance could not have originated from the men, if only for the reason that they have never—not even to the present day—dreamed of renouncing the pleasures of actual group marriage.[76]

He does add, however, that this victory is lopsided in that despite the successful introduction of strict monogamy, it was for women only.

Engels recognized that monogamy was also unfavorable to women in the economic sense. As natural selection completed its work in reducing the circle of community marriage to two, new social and economic forces emerged in the form of the domestication of animals and the breeding of flocks and herds; these animal groups created unprecedented wealth which, in turn, required entirely new social relationships among people.[77] For example, the previous necessity of hunting became a luxury.

This new wealth would have originally belonged to the gens, but private property developed in the name of the (male-dominated) family community or (male) family chief. Along with the introduction of the pairing family, the "natural mother" had to take into account the "natural father," on whom fell the task of procuring food and operating the heavy implements, which he also came to own together with a new instrument of labor: slaves. The following excerpt presents Engels's view of these transitions and the reversal of prior gender roles and statuses.

Friedrich Engels, The Origin of the Family, Private Property and the State 64–67 (Resistance Books, 2004).

> The pairing family arose on the border line between savagery and barbarism, mainly at the upper stage of savagery, and here and there only at the lower stage of barbarism.... For its further development to stable monogamy, causes different from those we have hitherto found operating were required.... If no new, *social* driving forces had come into operation, there would have been no reason why a new form of the family should arise out of the pairing family. But these driving forces did commence to operate.
>
> We now leave America, the classical soil of the pairing family. There is no evidence to enable us to conclude that a higher form of the family developed there, or that strict monogamy existed in any part of it at any time before its discovery and conquest. It was otherwise in the Old World.
>
> Here the domestication of animals and the breeding of herds had developed a hitherto unsuspected source of wealth and created entirely new

---

75. *Id.*

76. *Id.* at 63–64.

77. *Id.* at 64.

social relationships.... All previous means of procuring food now sank into the background. Hunting, once a necessity, now became a luxury.

But to whom did this new wealth belong? Originally, undoubtedly, to the gens. But private property in herds must have developed at a very early stage.... Equally certain is it that on the threshold of authenticated history we find that everywhere the herds are already the separate property of the family chiefs, in exactly the same way as were the artistic products of barbarism, metal utensils, articles of luxury and, finally, human cattle—the slaves....

Such riches, once they had passed into the private possession of families and there rapidly multiplied, struck a powerful blow at a society founded on pairing marriage and mother-right gens. Pairing marriage had introduced a new element into the family. By the side of the natural mother it had placed the authenticated natural father—who was probably better authenticated than many a "father" of the present day. According to the division of labour then prevailing in the family, the procuring of food and the implements necessary thereto, and therefore, also, the ownership of the latter, fell to the man; he took them with him in case of separation, just as the woman retained the household goods. Thus, according to the custom of society at that time, the man was also the owner of the new sources of foodstuffs—the cattle—and, later, of the new instrument of labour—the slaves. According to the custom of the same society, however, his children could not inherit from him....

[T]his was impossible as long as descent according to mother right prevailed. This had, therefore, to be overthrown, and it was overthrown.... The reckoning of descent through the female line and the right of inheritance through the mother were hereby overthrown and male lineage and right of inheritance from the father instituted....

The overthrow of mother right was the *world-historic defeat of the female sex*. The man seized the reins in the household also, the woman was degraded, enthralled, the slave of the man's lust, a mere instrument for breeding children....

To which Marx adds:

> The modern family contains in embryo not only slavery (*servitus*) but serfdom also, since from the very beginning it is connected with agricultural services. It contains within itself in *miniature* all the antagonisms which later develop on a wide scale within society and its state.

Such a form of the family shows the transition of the pairing family to monogamy.

Women and the Law

Marx and Engels theorized that the monogamian family arises in the period of transition from the middle to the upper stage of barbarism, at the dawn of civilization.[78] In this type of family, the marriage tie is far more rigid than in the pair-

78. *Id.* at 70.

ing family. As the foregoing excerpt mentions, monogamy arises out of economic conditions—namely, the victory of private property over common ownership. Here, Engels quotes Marx: "The first division of labour is that between man and woman for child breeding." Although Engels considered monogamy to be a great historical advance, he also considered it, along with slavery and private wealth, to be an institution riven with antagonism and exploitation.[79] Indeed, Engels declares the monogamian family to be the site of origin of the "first class antagonism in history."[80] By extension, every advance of each segment of society (prior to the communist epoch) is a relative detriment to another; for example, the uplifting, well-being, and development of males is attained at the expense, misery, and repression of females.

Engels asserts that marriage is falsely portrayed as a voluntary union by two subjects who are "equal" before the law, but he insists that such equality exists only on paper and that the union is highly unequal because of the class positions of the two parties. The wife, for example, is reduced to the status of domestic servant.[81] Nor does the law help this economically weaker party, as the following excerpt shows.

Given this oppression of women through monogamy (which Engels believed to acquire its most entrenched form under capitalism), little hope is given for their liberation. However, as seen previously, both Marx and Engels portrayed the capitalist system as containing the seeds of its own demise, which would be accompanied by the cessation of exploitation of all classes, including women. The social revolution they predicted would eliminate the economic foundations of monogamy, supplemented by adultery and prostitution (which would of course favor men).[82] Because monogamy arose due to the concentration of wealth in the man and his desire to pass on his wealth only to his own children, it was to be observed strictly by the woman. The man was to engage in overt or covert polygamy (including adultery and prostitution). Only the impending social revolution would transform most of the inheritable wealth (*i.e.*, the means of production) into social property, and only then could there be true equality of women and men before the law.[83]

Friedrich Engels, The Origin of the Family, Private Property and the State 78–81 (Resistance Books, 2004).

> Our jurists, to be sure, hold that the progress of legislation to an increasing degree removes all cause for complaint on the part of the woman. Modern civilised systems of law are recognising more and more, first, that, in order to be effective, marriage must be an agreement voluntarily entered into by both parties; and secondly, that during marriage, too, both parties must be on an equal footing in respect to rights and obligations. If, however, these

79. *Id.* at 73.

80. *Id.*

81. *Id.* at 79–80.

82. *Id.* at 80.

83. *Id.* at 80–81.

two demands were consistently carried into effect, women would have all that they could ask for.

This typical lawyer's reasoning is exactly the same as that with which the radical republican bourgeois dismisses the proletarian. The labour contract is supposed to be voluntarily entered into by both parties. But it is taken to be voluntarily entered into as soon as the law has put both parties on an equal footing *on paper*. The power given to one party by its different class position, the pressure it exercises on the other—the real economic position of both—all this is no concern of the law. And both parties, again, are supposed to have equal rights for the duration of the labour contract, unless one or the other of the parties expressly waived them. That the concrete economic situation compels the worker to forego even the slightest semblance of equal rights—this again is something the law cannot help.

As far as marriage is concerned, even the most progressive law is fully satisfied as soon as the parties formally register their voluntary desire to get married. What happens behind the legal curtains, where real life is enacted, how this voluntary agreement is arrived at—is no concern of the law and the jurist. And yet the simplest comparison of laws should serve to show the jurist what this voluntary agreement really amounts to. . . .

The position is no better with regard to the juridical equality of man and woman in marriage. The inequality of the two before the law, which is a legacy of previous social conditions, is not the cause but the effect of the economic oppression of women. In the old communistic household, which embraced numerous couples and their children, the administration of the household, entrusted to the women, was just as much a public, a socially necessary industry as the providing of food by the men. This situation changed with the patriarchal family, and even more with the monogamian individual family. The administration of the household lost its public character. It was no longer the concern of society. It became a *private service*. The wife became the first domestic servant, pushed out of participation in social production. Only modern large-scale industry again threw open to her—and only to the proletarian woman at that—the avenue to social production; but in such a way that, when she fulfills her duties in the private service of her family, she remains excluded from public production and cannot earn anything; and when she wishes to take part in public industry and earn her living independently, she is not in a position to fulfill her family duties. What applies to the woman in the factory applies to her in all the professions, right up to medicine and law. The modern individual family is based on the open or disguised domestic enslavement of the woman; and modern society is a mass composed solely of individual families as its molecules. Today, in the great majority of cases, the man has to be the earner, the breadwinner of the family, at least among the propertied classes, and this gives him a dominating position which requires no special legal privileges. In the family, he is the bourgeois; the wife represents the proletariat. In the industrial world, however, the specific character of the economic oppression that weighs down the proletariat stands out in all its sharpness only after all the special legal privileges of the capitalist class have been set aside and the complete juridical equality of both classes is established. The democratic republic does not abolish the antagonism between the two classes; on the contrary, it provides the field on which it is fought out. And, similarly, the peculiar character of man's domination over woman in the modern family, and the necessity, as well as the manner, of establishing real social equality between the two, will be brought out into full relief only when both are completely equal before the law. It will then become evident that the first premise for the emancipation of women is the reintroduction of the entire female into public industry; and that this again demands that the quality possessed by the individual family of being the economic unit of society be abolished. . . .

We are now approaching a social revolution in which the hitherto existing economic foundations of monogamy will disappear just as certainly as will those of its supplement—prostitution. Monogamy arose out of the concentration of considerable wealth in the hands of one person—and that a man—and out of the desire to bequeath this wealth to this man's children and to no one else's. For this purpose monogamy was essential on the woman's part, but not on the man's; so that this monogamy of the woman in no way hindered the overt or covert polygamy of the man. The impending social revolution, however, by transforming at least the far greater part of permanent inheritable wealth—the means of production—into social property, will reduce all this anxiety about inheritance to a minimum.

Conclusion

According to Engels, the status of women evolved with the various phases of human evolution. During the period of savagery the predominant social unit was the family as established by group marriage. Because paternity could never be certain under these conditions, lineage was necessarily traced by mother right—a system that ensured the social supremacy of the mother. The period of barbarism ushered in pairing marriage, which triggered the slow evolution of marital relations that eventually overthrew mother right; Engels regarded this development as the "world-historic defeat of the female sex"[84] and marked its consummation by the dawn of monogamy at the beginning of the period of civilization.

Marx and Engels believed that all societal changes are to be viewed in terms of their corresponding material and economic foundations, the economic foundation of monogamy being wealth inheritance through males. Thus, according to Engels, the monogamous family unit of civilized society was the first socially antagonistic unit.

---

84. *See* excerpt under heading "Evolution of the Family and the Changing Status of Women," *supra*.

In turn, it merged with larger antagonisms based on class in the capitalist system of production and private ownership of the means of production.

Engels on the Origin of the State and Law

Given Engels's embrace of Morgan's evolutionary epochs, it is not surprising to see that he saw the origin of the modern state machinery in the transition from barbarism to civilization. Here too, the material/economic conditions were key. Furthermore, these had to be viewed in evolutionary context, the highlights of which are sketched below.

Engels's starting point is the gentile order, which started in the middle stage of savagery, developed further during its upper stage.[85] It reached its prime in the lower stage of barbarism and declined during the upper stage of barbarism. Its demise was with the advent of civilization. The gentile order was based on mother right, a simple or "natural" division of labor between the sexes, and a communistic household. Whatever was produced was common property, as were the means of production.

Engels saw the creation of social wealth as originating with the domestication of animals and the invention of technologies having to do with food and fabrics. With the emergence of pastoral tribes emerged the first great social division of labor, which made regular exchange of goods (*e.g.*, meat, fabrics, milk, and meat products) possible for the first time. As the pastoral tribes converted their herds into separate property, the scope of exchange widened[86] with cattle becoming a commodity of exchange.

Engels credited the middle stage of barbarism with two crucial industrial innovations: the weaving loom and the smelting of metal ores from which tools, weapons, and utensils could be made. Increased cattle breeding, agriculture, and domestic handicrafts led to the production of food beyond what was necessary for society. Thus arises the "second great division of labor" between handicrafts and agriculture,[87] which fueled the desire for more labor power, a desire that was satisfied by slave labor (by captives of war, according to Engels). This resulted in the first great division of classes in society: masters and slaves.[88]

These developments in turn sparked a revolution in the structure of the family, symbolized by the decline of mother right and female supremacy. The economic dynamics now allowed certain individuals to become the owners of both the means and results of production; moreover, the matrilineal hierarchy was replaced by a patrilineal hierarchy.[89]

Engels noted that the upper stage of barbarism coincided with the Iron Age. Apart from its obvious economic benefits, the diversity of activities stemming from the

85. *Id.* at 148.

86. *Id.* at 150.

87. *Id.* at 152.

88. *Id.*

89. *See* previous section.

use of iron greatly enhanced the potential of human labor.[90] Not only did slaves become even more essential, the distinctions between rich and poor, freeman and slave, became firmly established.[91] Existing communistic household communities broke up, and the transition to private ownership was gradually accomplished with the transition from the pairing family to monogamy.[92] As a result, the individual family unit was now the economic unit of society.[93] As population density increased, the position of military commander also became essential, which aided in the creation of "military democracy" as war and the organization of war became more common.[94] Engels attributed man's increasing tendency to wage war to the greed and wealth that now consumed society; war was waged for the purpose of plunder.[95]

The second great division of labor between agriculture and goods, of course, increased the scope of exchange and commerce; as noted above, the contrast between town and country grew.[96] At this point a third division of labor occurs with its accompanying class, namely the merchant class. This class, however, does not engage in actual production but rather captures the *management* of production.[97] Although merchants make the exchange of commodities more efficient, they also amass wealth and influence as they "skim the cream off production";[98] Engels goes so far as to call them "a class of parasites."[99] With the merchant class came commercial expansion and the development of money, usury, landed property, and the mortgage.[100] These developments in turn resulted in the concentration of wealth in the hands of an aristocratic class, at the expense of the impoverished masses.[101]

Like Marx, Engels emphasized that this newer society, with its class antagonisms between freeman and slaves and between the rich and the exploited poor, could not exist in a state of open and continuous struggle. The rich and the powerful classes would need a new institution, the state, to manage and contain these conflicts and contradictions.

> Such a society could only exist either in a state of continuous, open struggle of these classes against one another or under the rule of a third power which, while ostensibly standing above the classes struggling with each other,

90. Engels, The Origin of the Family, Private Property and the State, *supra* note 9, at 152.

91. *Id.*

92. *Id.*

93. *Id.*

94. *Id.* at 152–53.

95. *Id.* at 153.

96. *Id.* at 154. *See also* excerpt from *The German Ideology* in the section (above) titled "Marx on Evolution."

97. Engels, The Origin of the Family, Private Property, and the State, *supra* note 9, at 154.

98. *Id.*

99. *Id.*

100. *Id.* at 155.

101. *Id.*

> suppressed their open conflict and permitted a class struggle at most in the economic field, in a so-called legal form. The gentile constitution had outlived its usefulness. It was burst asunder by the division of labour and by its result, the division of society into classes. Its place was taken by the *state*.[102]

The state, according to Engels, is a product of society at a certain stage of development; specifically, a society that has developed to a point of "insoluable contradictions" due to class struggle.[103] It has several distinguishing features: (1) it divides subjects according to territory;[104] (2) it establishes public power that no longer coincides with armed force;[105] (3) it taxes the citizens and creates public debts, in order to maintain public power; and thus (4) it is dominated by public officials.[106] The entire machinery of the state and its rules for order, power, and taxes are enforced by law—law which, like the officials who administer it, stands "above" society and which, as seen in the excerpt that follows, is portrayed by the state as neutral, sacred, and inviolable.

Engels saw the state as the institution of the most powerful, economically dominant class, and thus as a tool for exploiting the oppressed classes.[107] Therefore, when society develops to a point where classes no longer exist, the state will go the way "of the spinning wheel and the bronze axe."

> The state, then, has not existed from all eternity. There have been societies that did without it, that had no idea of the state and state power. At a certain stage of economic development which was necessarily bound up with the split of society into classes, the state became a necessity owing to this split. We are now rapidly approaching a stage in the development of production at which the existence of these classes not only will have ceased to be a necessity, but will become a positive hindrance to production. They will fall as inevitably as they arose at an earlier stage. Along with them the state will inevitably fall. Society, which will reorganise production on the basis of a free and equal association of the producers, will put the whole machinery of state where it will then belong: into the museum of antiquities, by the side of the spinning wheel and the bronze axe.[108]

The following excerpt outlines the origin of the state in evolutionary context, beginning with the waning of the gentile communistic order in the face of new economic challenges, the establishment of private property of the means of production, and the emergence of the merchant class.

---

102. *Id.* at 156–57.

103. *Id.* at 157.

104. *Id.* at 158.

105. *Id.*

106. *Id.*

107. *Id.*

108. *Id.* at 160.

Friedrich Engels, The Origin of the Family, Private Property and the State 153–160 (Resistance Books, 2004).

In this manner the organs of the gentile constitution were gradually torn from their roots in the people.... This could not have happened had not the greed for wealth divided the members of the gentes into rich and poor; had not "property differences in a gens changed the community of interest into antagonism between members of a gens" (Marx); and had not the growth of slavery already begun to brand working for a living as slavish and more ignominious than engaging in plunder.

This brings us to the threshold of civilisation. This stage is inaugurated by further progress in division of labour.... Civilisation strengthened and increased all the established divisions of labour, particularly by intensifying the contrast between town and country (either the town exercising economic supremacy over the country, as in antiquity, or the country over the town, as in the Middle Ages) and added a third division of labour, peculiar to itself and of decisive importance: it created a class that took no part in production, but engaged exclusively in exchanging products—the *merchants*.... Here a class appears for the first time which, without taking any part in production, captures the management of production as a whole and economically subjugates the producers to its rule; ... a class of parasites arises, genuine social sycophants, who, as a reward for very insignificant real services, skim the cream off production at home and abroad, rapidly amass enormous wealth ...

The thing they had been striving for most just before that time was liberation from the claim of the gentile community to their parcels of land, a claim which had become a fetter for them. They were freed from this fetter—but soon after also from their new landed property. The full, free ownership of land implied not only possibility of unrestricted and uncurtailed possession, but also possibility of alienating it.... Just as hetaerism and prostitution clung to the heels of monogamy, so from now on mortgage clung to the ownership of land....

Commercial expansion, money, usury, landed property and mortgage were thus accompanied by the rapid concentration and centralisation of wealth in the hands of a small class, on the one hand, and by the increasing impoverishment of the masses and a growing mass of paupers, on the other.... Such a society could only exist either in a state of continuous, open struggle of these classes against one another or under the rule of a third power which, while ostensibly standing above the classes struggling with each other, suppressed their open conflict and permitted a class struggle at most in the economic field, in a so-called legal form. The gentile constitution had outlived its usefulness. It was burst asunder by the division of labour

> and by its result, the division of society into classes. Its place was taken by the *state*. . . .
>
> As distinct from the old gentile order, the state, first, divides its subjects *according to territory*. . . .
>
> The second distinguishing feature is the establishment of a *public power* which no longer directly coincides with the population organising itself as an armed force. This special public power is necessary because a self-acting armed organisation of the population has become impossible since the split into classes. . . . This public power exists in every state; it consists not merely of armed men but also of material adjuncts, prisons and institutions of coercion of all kinds, of which gentile [clan] society knew nothing. . . .
>
> In order to maintain this public power, contributions from the citizens become necessary—*taxes*. These were absolutely unknown in gentile society; but we know enough about them today. As civilisation advances, these taxes become inadequate; the state makes drafts on the future, contracts loans, public *debts*. Old Europe can tell a tale about these, too.
>
> Having public power and the right to levy taxes, the officials now stand, as organs of society, *above* society. The free, voluntary respect that was accorded to the organs of the gentile [clan] constitution does not satisfy them, even if they could gain it; being the vehicles of a power that is becoming alien to society, respect for them must be enforced by means of exceptional laws by virtue of which they enjoy special sanctity and inviolability. . . .
>
> Because the state arose from the need to hold class antagonisms in check, but because it arose, at the same time, in the midst of the conflict of these classes, it is, as a rule, the state of the most powerful, economically dominant class, which, through the medium of the state, becomes also the politically dominant class, and thus acquires new means of holding down and exploiting the oppressed class. Thus, the state of antiquity was above all the state of the slave owners for the purpose of holding down the slaves, as the feudal state was the organ of the nobility for holding down the peasant serfs and bondsmen, and the modern representative state is an instrument of exploitation of wage labour by capital. . . .
>
> The state, then, has not existed from all eternity. There have been societies that did without it. . . .

The progressive evolutionary scheme of Marx and Engels has been criticized, as has their first putative phase of a lawless, communally centered primitive society, which has been called speculative and not empirically verifiable.[109] The notion of the withering of the state has been dismissed as utopian. In fact, in societies where Marxist regimes have existed, neither state nor law has disappeared; on the contrary, they show strong and repressive tendencies.[110]

---

109. Pospíšil, *supra* note 10, at 165.

110. *Id.*

Pospíšil has even challenged Marx's use of the dialectical method as ethnocentric because it is based on knowledge of Western culture only. He asserts that Hegel's dialectic (used by Marx) is based on Western philosophy with its dyadic conceptualization of the universe.[111] He points to his fieldwork of the Kapauku Papúans, whom he characterizes as "stone age people" of the Highlands of New Guinea where the inhabitants "think in terms of continua rather than dichotomies,"[112] and challenges the notion of economic determinism with examples of their economic interactions. He also challenges the notion of primitive communism by asserting that the means of production in the Papúan economy were privately owned and that there were no commonly owned economic goods.[113] He cites a variety of other examples from the life of the Papúans that oppose Marxist claims about primitive societies, such as the complexity of their economy, their strong individualism, and their use of law.

Historical Materialism and Law

Introduction

Historical materialism is the general theory of Marxism that explains how social systems work and how societies are transformed. At their most basic level, the material conditions of life are the elementary factors that make human survival possible (through the satisfaction of minimum biological and physiological needs). These needs are satisfied as man subjugates nature by whatever technologies are available during a particular historical period. As the technologies are used for various processes of production of material goods, men enter into *relations of production*; which type depends on the available natural resources and the extant technologies for their exploitation. Together, these elements constitute the *forces of production*.

Marx saw an intimate connection between the relations of production and their material base. In the preface to *A Contribution to the Critique of Political Economy*, Marx asserted that all social institutions as well as the structures of political authority of a community, including law, arise from and adapt themselves to the prevailing relations of production.[114] This "base/superstructure" thesis asserts that the material economic base of every society exerts primary influence on the legal, political, and ideological superstructure.

The Importance of Property and Law

Historical materialism asserts that as productive forces become more sophisticated, they come into conflict with the existing relations of production "or—what is but a

111. Leopold Pospíšil, *Empirical Critique of Marxist Theories of Law and Social Control*, 5 Windsor Yearbook of Access to Justice 3, 16 (1985).

112. *Id.* at 17.

113. *Id.* at 23.

114. *See* excerpt *supra* from the *Preface*. The economic base is the "real foundation on which rises a legal and political superstructure."

legal expression for the same thing—with the property relations."[115] Property relations are therefore expressed through law, and "it is in the interest of the ruling section of society to sanction the existing order as law."[116] Law protects property rights and ensures stability because order, stability, predictability, and the elimination of arbitrariness are indispensable for any mode of production.

> [H]ere as always it is in the interest of the ruling section of society to sanction the existing order as law and to legally establish its limits given through usage and tradition. Apart from all else, this, by the way, comes about of itself as soon as the constant reproduction of the basis of the existing order and its fundamental relations assumes a regulated and orderly form in the course of time. And such regulation and order are themselves indispensable elements of any mode of production, if it is to assume social stability and independence from mere chance and arbitrariness. These are precisely the form of its social stability and therefore its relative freedom from mere arbitrariness and mere chance. Under backward conditions of the production process as well as the corresponding social relations, it achieves this form by mere repetition of their very reproduction. If this has continued on for some time, it entrenches itself as custom and tradition and is finally sanctioned as an explicit law.[117]

The totality of laws do no "more than proclaim, express in words, the will of economic relations."[118] In other words, "Law is only the official recognition of [material] fact."[119]

Marx and Engels dismiss as "illusion" the claim that the development of law is based on free will.[120] Contemporary Marxists likewise dismiss as "legal fetishism" the belief that law and legal systems are an essential component of social order and civilization.[121] On law as the product of free will, both Marx and Engels deny that law has any particular role as an agent for deliberative change in historical processes; in the words of Marx, "revolutions are not made by laws."[122] Indeed, the opposite is the case in the Marxist view of social dynamics: revolutions are the cause of new legal formations.

With regard to the "fetishism" that views law as the *sine qua non* of society, Marx and Engels assert the essentially instrumental origins of law. Both viewed early prim-

---

115. *Id. See* section above titled "Marx on Evolution," showing how Marx's entire evolutionary scheme was based on the function of property in each evolutionary period, note 32 *et seq. supra*.

116. 3 Karl Marx, Capital 793 (Lawrence & Wishart, London, 1972).

117. *Id.*

118. Karl Marx, *The Poverty of Philosophy*, *in* Karl Marx & Friedrich Engels, Collected Works 147 (1976).

119. *Id.* at 150.

120. Karl Marx & Friedrich Engels, *The German Ideology*, *in* 5 Karl Marx & Friedrich Engels, Collected Works 90–92 (1976).

121. Hugh Collins, Marxism and Law 10, *et seq.* (1982).

122. Marx, Capital, *supra* note 5, at 823.

itive societies as classless communities in which property was commonly shared.[123] The inference that such societies had no "law" in the sense that civilized societies know it is strong.[124] Thus, "[c]ivil law develops simultaneously with private property out of the disintegration of the natural community."[125] In other words, the "natural community" did not have property laws.

Similarly, they noted, the Roman system had its own set of property laws, which remained stable and unchanged because modes of production during the Roman era remained unchanged. Subsequent feudal and capitalist societies did experience change, however, particularly when feudalism was overthrown by the bourgeoisie's unrequited demands for greater industry and trade. New forms of private property were thus able to emerge under civil law.[126] These evolutionary and revolutionary trends, which have already been discussed,[127] are noted here only to emphasize that Marxism views the law as fulfilling particular historical and social needs and not as the driver of change, much less an idealized institution to be glorified in the Hegelian (or Aristotelian) sense.

In the following passage from *The German Ideology*, Marx and Engels argue that property relations are falsely portrayed as voluntary and consensual and thus as the product of the general will. They also refuse to reify the *jus utendi et abutendi* (the right to use and dispose of property) as something that exists independently of society and reject the notion that rights associated with private property are the incidents of private will. They argue instead that property relations are not consensual because they are dictated by the material conditions of life and therefore arise independently of individual will. By this logic, the right to use and/or dispose of property is not only limited but also dictated by economic conditions. This situation then results in the "juridical illusion" that law (*i.e.*, property law) is the expression of individual will, which leads to the paradox that an individual may have legal title to a thing without actually having it.[128] An example would be when an income-producing property becomes totally unproductive due to capitalist rules that allow free competition (the owner retains title to the property but is unable to do anything with it). Yet the "illusion of the jurists" persists, namely that everyone is free to contract (or not to contract, in the case of the hapless and impoverished owner of the unproductive land) and that all economic relations are the product of the individual free will of the contracting parties.

---

123. *See* sections on "The Radical Anthropology of Karl Marx," and "The Radical Anthropology of Friedrich Engels," *supra*.

124. Paul Phillips, Marx and Engels on Law and Laws 30 (1980) (arguing that Marx and Engels's conclusions about the "natural community" are problematic in that cattle existed as private property in such communities).

125. Marx & Engels, *The German Ideology*, *supra* note 120, at 90.

126. *Id.* at 90–92.

127. *See* text at notes 45 *et seq.*

128. Marx & Engels, *The German Ideology*, *supra* note 120, at 91–92. *See also* Phillips, *supra* note 124, at 33.

> In civil law the existing property relations are declared to be the result of the general will. The *jus utendi et abutendi* itself asserts on the one hand the fact that private property has become entirely independent of the community, and on the other the illusion that private property itself is based solely on the private will, the arbitrary disposal of the thing. In practice, the *abuti* has very definite economic limitations for the owner of private property, if he does not wish to see his property and hence his *jus abutendi* pass into other hands, since actually the thing, considered merely with reference to his will, is not a thing at all, but only becomes a thing, true property, in intercourse, and independently of the law (*a relationship*, which the philosophers call an idea). This juridical illusion, which reduces law to the mere will, necessarily leads, in the further development of property relations, to the position that a man may have a legal title to a thing without really having the thing. If, for instance, the income from a piece of land disappears owing to competition, then the proprietor has certainly his legal title to it along with the *jus utendi et abutendi*. But he can do nothing with it: he owns nothing as a landed proprietor if he has not enough capital elsewhere to cultivate his land. This illusion of the jurists also explains the fact that for them, as for every code, it is altogether fortuitous that individuals enter into relations among themselves (e.g., contracts); it explains why they consider that these relations [can] be entered into or not at will, and that their content [rests] purely on the individual free will of the contracting parties.
>
> Whenever, through the development of industry and commerce, new forms of intercourse have been evolved (e.g., insurance companies, etc.), the law has always been compelled to admit them among the modes of acquiring property.[129]

A New Division of Labor: Emergence of the Professional Jurist

Engels asserts that at a certain point of social evolution, the need for a common rule to unify "the daily recurring acts of production, distribution and exchange of products" will arise.[130] These acts are regulated by law, whose chief organ of public authority is the state. As production, distribution, and exchange relationships become more complex, so does the law. The legal system thus becomes highly specialized and autonomous, as well as seemingly independent of other social, political, and economic processes. Its operative principles of right/duty/free will/justice create the illusion of autonomy such that people forget they are really triggered by the economic conditions of life.

---

129. Marx & Engels, *The German Ideology*, *supra* note 120, at 91–92.

130. Friedrich Engels, *The Housing Question*, *in* 3 Karl Marx & Friedrich Engels, Selected Works 365 (1970).

At this point a new division of labor emerges in the form of the professional jurist who believes that he is operating with *a priori* propositions. But in reality, these propositions are mere reflections of the economy. This illusion creates a false "inversion" of the relationship between law and economics along with a certain ideological outlook. The latter is a human or cultural phenomenon that can lead to demands that are at odds with or contradict existing power relationships. It therefore falls to the law to harmonize these demands with the dominant precepts of the economic base and to modify the latter within certain limits. Nonetheless, to maintain its façade of autonomy and neutrality, the law can never appear as "the blunt, unmitigated, unadulterated expression of the domination of a class."[131]

The following passage by Engels is from *The Housing Question*:

> At a certain, very primitive stage of the development of society, the need arises to bring under a common rule the daily recurring acts of production, distribution and exchange of products, to see to it that the individual subordinates himself to the common conditions of production and exchange. This rule, which at first is custom, soon becomes *law*. With law organs necessarily arise which are entrusted with its maintenance—public authority, the state. With further social development, law develops into a more or less comprehensive legal system. The more intricate this legal system becomes, the more is its mode of expression removed from that in which the usual economic conditions of the life of society are expressed. It appears as an independent element which derives the justification for its existence and the substantiation of its further development not from the economic relations but from its own inner foundations or, if you like, from "the concept of the will." People forget that their right derived from their economic conditions of life, just as they have forgotten that they themselves derive from the animal world. With the development of the legal system into an intricate, comprehensive whole a new social division of labour becomes necessary; an order of professional jurists develops and with these legal science comes into being. In its further development this science compares the legal systems of various peoples and various times not as a reflection of the given economic relationships, but as systems which find their substantiations in themselves. The comparison presupposes points in common, and these are found by the jurists compiling what is more or less common to all these legal systems and calling it *natural right*. And the stick used to measure what is natural right and what is not is the most abstract expression of right itself, namely, *justice*. Henceforth, therefore, the development of right for the jurists, and for those who take their word for everything, is nothing more than a striving to bring human conditions, so far as they are expressed in legal terms, ever closer to the ideal of justice, *eternal* justice. And always this justice is but the ideologised, glorified expression of the existing economic relations, now

---

131. Friedrich Engels, *Letter to Conrad Schmidt 27 October 1890, in* Karl Marx & Friedrich Engels, Selected Correspondence 481 (1942).

from their conservative, and now from their revolutionary angle. The justice of the Greeks and Romans held slavery to be just; the justice of the bourgeois of 1789 demanded the abolition of feudalism on the ground that it was unjust. . . . The conception of eternal justice, therefore, varies not only with time and place, but also with the persons concerned . . . While in everyday life, in view of the simplicity of the relations discussed, expressions like right, wrong, justice, and sense of right are accepted without misunderstanding even with reference to social matters, they create, as we have seen, the same hopeless confusion in any scientific investigation of economic relations as would be created, for instance, in modern chemistry if the terminology of the phlogiston theory were to be retained. The confusion becomes still worse if one, like Proudhon, believes in this social phlogiston, "justice," or if one, like Mülberger, avers that the phlogiston theory is as correct as the oxygen theory.[132]

The following passage by Engels is from a letter to Conrad Schmidt:

As soon as the new division of labour which creates professional lawyers becomes necessary, another new and independent sphere is opened up which, for all its general dependence on production and trade, has also a specific capacity for reacting upon these spheres. In a modern state, law must not only correspond to the general economic condition and be its expression, but must also be an *internally coherent* expression which does not, owing to internal conflicts, contradict itself. And in order to achieve this, the faithful reflection of economic conditions suffers increasingly. All the more so the more rarely it happens that a code of law is the blunt, unmitigated, unadulterated expression of the domination of a class—this in itself would offend the "conception of right". Even in the *Code Napoléon* the pure, consistent conception of a right held by the revolutionary bourgeoisie of 1792–96 is already adulterated in many ways, and, in so far as it is embodied in the Code, has daily to undergo all sorts of attenuations owing to the rising power of the proletariat. This does not prevent the *Code Napoléon* from being the statute book which serves as the basis of every new code of law in every part of the world. Thus to a great extent the course of the "development of law" simply consists in first attempting to eliminate contradictions which arise from the direct translation of economic relations into legal principles, and to establish a harmonious system of law, and then in the repeated breaches made in this system by the influence and compulsion of further economic development, which involves it in further contradictions. (I am speaking here for the moment only of civil law.)

The reflection of economic relations in the form of legal principles is likewise bound to be inverted: it goes on without the person who is acting being conscious of it; the jurist imagines he is operating with *a priori* propositions, whereas they are really only economic reflections; everything is therefore

132. Engels, *The Housing Question*, *supra* note 130, at 365–66.

upside down. And it seems to me obvious that this inversion, which, so long as it remains unrecognised, forms what we call *ideological outlook*, influences in its turn the economic basis and may, within certain limits, modify it.[133]

In sum, Engels asserts that law merely reflects relationships of production, distribution, and exchange. As these become more complex, so does the law—which also becomes more specialized. As it acquires a life of its own, law must also eliminate contradictions that arise from the translation of economic relations into legal rules so that a harmonious legal system may be established. Thus the development of law includes the elimination of contradictions that arise from the repeated breaches caused by the influence of progressive economic development. The jurist may imagine he is operating with *a priori* propositions, but in fact he is operating according to economic conditions.

Revolutions Are Not Made by Law

It was Marx who declared that revolutions are not made by law.[134] This assertion was made as a rejection of the idealist tradition that conceived law as an autonomous principle that potentially plays a creative role in historical processes.[135] Under the Marxist approach, the relationship between revolution and law is inverse. Law does not cause revolution; rather, revolution causes new legal formations. A good illustration is provided by Hugh Collins, who invokes a very early primitive group of nomadic hunters with extremely crude hunting weapons such as sticks and stones. This limited technology would require cooperative hunting to maximize success. If, however, in this group of hunters "some rule was announced forbidding hunting in groups, then in order to avoid starvation either an entirely new mode of production would have to be discovered, or more likely there would be a revolution against the authority which was attempting to impose the rule."[136]

Another important principle of Marxism posits that social evolution develops from conflicts between the forces of production and the relations of production.[137] Therefore, challenges to laws that govern the existing relations of production can signal pressures for change. If laws inhibit the development of new production arrangements, social groups that seek to use new technology will engage in political struggle to change the laws. As seen above, land tenure laws of the feudal era governing rights and duties over land were seen as having been appropriate to the agricultural modes of production of precapitalist societies and the then-prevailing technologies. The serf rendered certain services to his lord who, in return, allowed the serf to use his land to sustain himself. This arrangement, as well as the existence of closed guilds, impeded the use of land as a capital asset that could be freely bought and sold and/

133. Engels, *Letter to Conrad Schmidt*, *supra* note 131, at 479–82.

134. *See* text at note 122, *supra*.

135. Maureen Cain & Alan Hunt, Marx and Engels on Law 51 (1979).

136. Collins, *supra* note 121, at 19.

137. *See* section above titled "Basic Tenets of Marxist Political Philosophy."

or exploited by wage laborers as the new bourgeoisie demanded. The feudal system of property also impeded the use of land for the numerous manufacturing processes that became available due to new technologies.[138] For these reasons, according to Marxist theory, the old land tenure laws became the focus of political struggle that eventually toppled them in favor of a system of private property that was conducive to the emergence of the new commercial society.

In addition to explaining the content of the laws of any historical epoch, historical materialism aims to explicate the various forms in which law emerges. It links certain modes of production with a customary informal style of law, whereas modern relations of production are described as requiring legal systems equipped with courts, legislatures, and lawyers. For example, the abolishment of land tenure law of England in 1660 took the form of statute to be enforced by a complicated court system, rather than a general transition of meaning in a set of customary rules.[139]

The conclusion of course is that in the long run, just as "revolutions are not made by law," men do not have the freedom to develop legal doctrinal thought and legal reasoning. Instead, the institutional framework and substance of legal rules, as well as their forms, are ultimately determined by the material mode and relations of production and exchange. Law is thus merely an epiphenomenon of its material base.

The Base-Superstructure Relationship: A Crude Instrumentalism?

The extent to which law and other social institutions are the mere epiphenomena of the material base has been long debated. In particular, such crude instrumentalism is said to obscure the role of social institutions as well as the relationship between government and law, the family and law, and law and morality. Many family matters, including marital relationships, are outside the scope of production relations. There are also many technical laws apportioning legal competence and limiting the discretion of governmental and administrative agencies in ways that are of no consequence to the relations of production and exchange. Similarly, prohibitions against rape, murder, assault, etc. cannot be said to reflect the material base in any meaningful sense.[140]

These difficulties were partly addressed by the second generation of Marxist thinkers after Marx died in 1883, particularly by Lenin, but also by Engels (who outlived Marx by twelve years).[141] Engels admitted that he and Marx were "partly to blame" for their theoretical emphasis on economic factors but claimed that it had been made in reaction to those who denied the importance of these factors.[142] In 1890, Engels asserted a far more robust role for legal, political, and other factors:

---

138. *See* excerpt from the Communist Manifesto *supra*.

139. Collins, *supra* note 121, at 21–22.

140. *Id.* at 24 *et seq.*

141. Phillips, *supra* note 124, at 211.

142. Friedrich Engels, *Letter to J. Bloch 21 September 1890*, *in* Karl Marx & Friedrich Engels, Selected Correspondence, *supra* note 131, at 396.

> According to the materialist conception of history, the *ultimately* determining factor in history is the production and reproduction of real life. Neither Marx nor I have ever asserted more than this. Hence if somebody twists this into saying that the economic factor is the *only* determining one, he transforms that proposition into a meaningless, abstract, absurd phrase. The economic situation is the basis, but the various elements of the superstructure—political forms of the class struggle and its results, such as constitutions established by the victorious class after a successful battle, etc., juridical forms, and especially the reflections of all these real struggles in the brains of the participants, political, legal, philosophical theories, religious views and their further development into systems of dogmas—also exercise their influence upon the course of the historical struggles and in many cases determine their *form* in particular.[143]

Such statements as well as one that follows show that Engels accepted the notion of the relative autonomy of the superstructure,[144] which had in fact stemmed from his view that the material relations of production, distribution, and exchange must all be given "juristic form" in order to be sanctionable. Once given legal expression, he felt, these forms take on a life of their own in which they become specialized and autonomous.

> But once the state has become an independent power *vis-a-vis* society, it produces forthwith a further ideology. It is indeed among professional politicians, theorists of public law and jurists of private law that the connection with economic facts gets lost for fair. Since in each case the economic facts must assume the form of juristic motives in order to receive legal sanction; and since, in so doing, consideration of course has to be given to the whole legal system already in operation, the juristic form is, in consequence, made everything and the economic content nothing. Public law and private law are treated as independent spheres, each having its own independent historical development, each being capable of and needing a systematic presentation by the consistent elimination of all inner contradictions.[145]

Lenin, who asserted a different kind of instrumentalism, argued that the modern state is an instrument of the ruling class, that law is an integral part of the state apparatus, and that both are deliberately used to repress the subordinate classes.[146] He asserted that law protecting private property and private ownership of the means of production, as well as laws against theft, are the direct emanations of the will of the ruling class.

---

143. *Id.* at 394–95.

144. Phillips, *supra* note 124, at 214.

145. Friedrich Engels, *Ludwig Feuerbach and the End of Classical German Philosophy*, *in* Marx & Engels Selected Works in One Volume 627–28 (1968).

146. Vladimir Lenin, The State and Revolution 10–12 (Kessiger Publishing, 2004).

This conception of law strongly critiqued traditional liberal political theories, for example the idea advanced by Hobbes and Locke that the law provides the necessary "rules of the game" to make sure that no one can secure an "unfair advantage." The Marxist argument was, of course, that the law is anything but fair because it preserves and protects a particular set of production relations and its corresponding class structure, thereby ensuring that social wealth and power remain with a small fraction of the population.[147]

A less grim post-Leninist refinement of the above "conspiratorial" or "imperativist" view is that the ruling class does not necessarily conspire to be a deliberate or conscious agent of oppression. Although social and cultural attitudes do arise from the relations of production, over time these permeate all aspects of social life in the form of ideology; for their part, laws are enacted pursuant to this ideology. Under this view, the ruling elites are not even aware of their dominant class position and have no diabolic plan to subjugate or oppress the subordinate classes. The dominant ideology simply appears as part of the natural social order, and law is simply an instrument for maintaining this order rather than an instrument of oppression.

> [T]he central argument is that ideologies arise from and are conditioned by social practices in the relations of production. Since the class of owners of the means of production share similar experiences and perform approximately the same role in the relations of production, there emerges a dominant ideology which permeates their perceptions of interest. Laws are enacted pursuant to this ideology. Thus the Marxist theory of ideology has subtly transformed the claim about class oppression. Initially that claim indicated the presence of a conspiracy amongst an élite group who knew exactly where their best interests lay. There is no need, however, on the theory of ideology presented here to suggest that the ruling class is aware of its class position and deliberately sets out to crush opposition. Instead, its perceptions of interest will appear to be the natural order of things since they are confirmed by everyday experience. A corollary of this is that laws enacted according to the dictates of a dominant ideology will appear to the members of that society as rules designed to preserve the natural social and economic order. The ruling class will not have the oppression of other classes in mind, but simply the maintenance of social order.[148]

Hugh Collins, in rejecting what he calls the "imperativist" doctrine of law in the above passage, assigns a fairly benign character to law. However, he also gives it a *creative* or *deliberative* role within the base/superstructure dynamic, with the perceptive observation that additional ideologies may emerge from legal rules and have a "snowball effect" on the evolution of the entire social formation.[149] According to Collins, the law's dual mission of regulating conduct and resolving disputes can have a huge

147. Collins, *supra* note 121, at 28.

148. *Id.* at 43.

149. *Id.* at 89.

impact on the organization of the mode of production, the definition of relations of production, and the accompanying definitions of rights and obligations. Sophisticated real estate law, complex doctrines of contract law, the law of corporations, banking law, etc., which are just a few modern examples, can influence the development of further superstructural phenomena. As legal institutions develop and specialize, they become important purveyors of the dominant ideology. Lawyers and judges engage in discourses that articulate the values of the material economic base, for example private ownership, use and disposal of private property, the method and mechanisms of such use and disposal, etc. Eventually, these values become inculcated in the belief system of every citizen through constant exposure to legal rhetoric.

Hugh Collins, Marxism and Law 89–91 (1982).

Furthermore, the legal rules serve as a material basis from which additional ideologies may arise, and in a snowball effect the whole social formation will slowly emerge. For example, during bartering and exchanges of commodities, customary conceptions about the appropriate standards to observe will develop. This ideology will then provide the substance for legal regulation of disputes and the organization of the mode of production. In turn, the more exact definitions of obligations within a set of relations of production provided by the law will create the opportunity for the development of further superstructural phenomena, such as complex legal doctrines to govern sophisticated contracts.

Thus the connection between base and superstructure is one of ideological derivation and incremental growth. The superstructure is derived from the relations of production because it is created according to the dictates of the dominant ideology which is produced in practices associated with the relations of production. Laws which are superstructural in origin then serve as rules to govern the material base, and because they render the customs irrelevant to social behaviour, the legal rules actually constitute, define, and express the relations of production. This close regulation then permits, perhaps encourages, further complicated social structures to arise. The pattern of interaction between base and superstructure is cumulative rather than circular. The process of accumulating a sophisticated political and cultural life will continue with the aid of law until a revolution transforms the relations of production abruptly, and then a new dominant ideology will arise to determine gradually the content of another social formation.

An incidental advantage of this formulation of the base and superstructure model is that it becomes unnecessary to distinguish clearly between social rules and legal rules once it is conceded that the base and superstructure do not always differ in form or function. Legal rules may be superstructural in origin and then serve as part of the material base, and no importance need be attached to the term law. Thus whether or not the rules governing the capture of prey in the hunter-gatherer society are custom or law is a matter of indifference. The rules will be superstructural in origin even though they now constitute and govern the productive activities. . . .

. . . Thus the rule against pollution was certainly superstructural in origin, but rapidly it began to function as a rule constituting the relations of production. Of course, this analysis destroys the simplicity of traditional interpretations of the base and superstructure metaphor, but it has the merits of preserving the key element of material determination and providing a persuasive interpretation of the origins and contents of laws. . . .

[T]he traditional Marxist claim (is) that law is an instrument of class oppression. This traditional analysis of law led to the adoption by Marxists of an imperativist image of law. For writers like Lenin, the legal system was a coercive organization which issued orders backed by threats in the form of criminal codes. Together with the remainder of the State apparatus the law ensured that the wishes of the dominant class were carried out. Legal rules were in the basic form of commands addressed to the masses to do or to abstain from doing something, and the significance of law in a society depended entirely upon its potential to affect behaviour by threats of sanctions. Yet this traditional imperativist concept of law must now be rejected in the light of the broader functions of law. . . .

From our investigation of social formations according to the principles of historical materialism two overlapping functions of law have been emphasized. In the first place law resolves conflicts within a community by approving and enforcing standards of behaviour which are consistent with the dominant ideology. A second function of law is ideological. Legal institutions are some of the most important purveyors of the dominant ideology. Not only do the judges operate as articulate mouthpieces for the dominant ideology, but also the whole of legal discourse expresses concepts such as private ownership which become inculcated in the values of every citizen through their constant exposure to legal rhetoric.

Conclusion

Marx's evolutionary scheme was based almost entirely on the function of property in distinct epochs of human social development. He viewed property relations as but the legal expression of the relations of production. By this logic, law serves a purely instrumental purpose and is not an institution that should be idealized or glorified in the Hegelian sense. The instrumentalism of the law and its outward appearance of specialization and autonomy create the "juristic illusion" that it is a product of free will. But in fact its actual mission is to translate economic relations into a harmonious set of legal rules. In addition, just as "revolutions are not made by law," men do not have the freedom to give doctrinal content to law. The content and form of law is instead ultimately determined by its material base, so that law is merely an epiphenomenon of the base.

The era after Marx's death yielded a more supple view of the base/superstructure dynamic among subsequent generations of Marxists, who treated it as a mere metaphor and included within it a more benign if not creative role for the law. They began to view law as the prime vehicle for the articulation of ideology, discourse over which is internalized by the citizenry at large without stark references to oppression, class cleavage, or class antagonisms.

Back to the Future: Marxism Today

Today, 130 years after the death of Marx, interest in Marxist philosophy remains strong, as evidenced by the emergence of Marxist and neo-Marxist trends in social critique in the twentieth and twenty-first centuries. Some of these contemporary trends in "classical" Marxism are sketched below; the ones that are more appropriately called "neo-Marxist" are examined in Chapter 5.

The first major twentieth-century trend, structural Marxism, appeared briefly in the second half of the twentieth century. This is discussed next, followed by a discussion of newer trends in contemporary cultural Marxism that emerged at the end of the twentieth century and continue to thrive.

Structural Marxism

Introduction

Radical social movements emerged in the late 1960s and early 1970s in the United States and in Europe, particularly France and Germany. Classical European colonialism, mostly in Africa, came to an end in the 1960s as well. During these years, the most powerful critiques of the existing order in the West and its influence abroad were inspired by Marxism, which not only provided a philosophy that was antithetical to capitalism at home and colonialism and imperialism abroad but also offered theoretical alternatives. Structural Marxism sought to respond to particular challenges of the times, including but not limited to the explanation of precapitalist social formations, Marx's reversal of the Hegelian dialectic as applied to such social formations, the emergence of the Eastern bloc, and colonialism and the Third World.

In confronting these challenges, the new school of structural Marxism introduced a number of doctrinal and methodological innovations that reconfigured classical Marxism. As a result, this school viewed cultural normativities as determined not so much by the natural environment or technology but within certain structures of social relations, particularly relations of production. Structural Marxists viewed technology, ecology, and the environment not as discrete subjects but rather as symbols, reflections, or explanations of social relations and modes of production. Normative relations established by the institutions of marriage, family, clan, or lineage, together with their systems of beliefs and values, were identified as making up the ideology of culture and explaining the processes of social production. This approach gave structural Marxism a decidedly functional character.

We have already seen that "structuralism" and "functionalism" are complementary terms in social science, and we have also seen the emergence of theories labeled "structural-functional." Modern functionalism, as reviewed in previous chapters, can be traced to the works of Darwin, Durkheim, and Marx. In the twentieth century, it became the theoretical foundation of British social anthropology, as seen in the writings of Radcliffe-Brown and Malinowski.

More recently, structuralism and functionalism have enjoyed a rebirth in the thought of structural Marxism. In its most basic sense, functionalism is a type of holistic explanation whose premise is that the whole can best be understood with reference to its parts. In order to grasp the fullness of the whole, structural functionalists study the interconnectedness of the parts or structures. Thus, functional theory "is an attempt to account for regularities in behavior that do not appear to result from the conscious desires of individuals. Explanation is framed in terms of the properties of a social whole, whose purposes are served by the actions of individuals."[150] Structural Marxism endorses this view and further examines socioeconomic formations within the framework of a "totalizing movement" in which the various components or structures of society interact and evolve together in accordance with the law of the whole.[151]

Hegelian philosophy advanced the doctrine of *Geist* (variously translated as *Idea* or *World Spirit*) according to which the world as a "whole" is supposed to evolve dialectically toward certain preordained goals. Under this view all worldly phenomena are only the reflection of the *Idea*, translated into forms of thought (consciousness). In other words, consciousness determines being. Marx not only disagreed but insisted that it is being that determines consciousness.[152] Structural Marxism accepted the basic premise of this reversal but contended that it did not go far enough and proceeded to reconfigure Marx's reversal. Remaining faithful to the functional method, it embraced the assumption that human actions and historical processes, which are independent of human will, are either structurally or systemically determined by objective conditions. One set of such conditions would be the structure of ideology; another would be the capitalist world system.

Basic Tenets of Structural Marxism

Structural Marxism began with the pioneering thought of Louis Althusser, whose disciples included Étienne Balibar, Claude Meillassoux, and Emmanuel Terray, among others. For our purposes, the doctrinal innovations of this new subschool within Marxism coalesce around Althusser's reconfiguration of (a) Marx's reversal of the Hegelian dialectic, (b) Marx's base/superstructure dynamic, and (c) Marx's law of historical inevitability. Collateral methodological innovations included the development

150. James Duncan & David Ley, *Structural Marxism and Human Geography: A Critical Assessment*, 72 ANN. ASSOC. AM. GEOGR. 30, 41–42 (1982).

151. *Id.* at 42.

152. *See* text at notes 1–8 *supra*.

of the notion of "overdetermination" and the rejection of reductionism, subjectivism, and teleology.

Reconfiguring Marx's Inversion of the Hegelian Dialectic

Regarding the Hegelian dialectic, which Marx had sought to put "right side up,"[153] the new school considered that Marx had not quite fully liberated himself from Hegel's idealism and that Marx's inversion of the dialectic was materialist in name only. A second objection of structural Marxism was that Marx had also remained trapped within Hegel's historical teleology (*i.e.*, the notion that history has a goal or end toward which it always moves).[154] Marx's inversion of Hegel's dialectic was thus viewed as an incomplete break with Hegel's historicist problematic,[155] and this failure served as the primary justification for the structural Marxist rejection of historical teleology. The new school also rejected all notions of idealism on the ground that Hegelian idealism tended to reduce complex social institutions and historical processes to their simple essences.[156] For Hegel, as we have seen, the essence of civil society is to be found in the state; by contrast, Marx's anatomy of civil society and of political economy shows that the state is the instrument of the dominant class.

Althusser's contention is that Marx's inversion shows that more than just the terms of the essence-appearance relationship have changed; it shows that the relationship itself has changed. Similarly, as Hegelian notions of simplicity and essence can be expressed as easy binary or symmetrical relations such as "essence-appearance," the essence of civil society is manifested in the state. But a materialist inversion of Hegel's dialectic as applied to the state shows a variety of asymmetrical relations that are so different and complex that not only the terms of the dialectical relationship but also the relationship itself are changed. Thus, under the structural Marxist approach, the state is no simple reflection of the dominant class but rather the result of a complex set of heterogeneous and autonomous, yet interrelated, structures constituting the state as a whole.

In contrast to Hegel's philosophical method, which reduces complexity to an essential simplicity, structural (Marxist) materialism is committed to recognizing the irreducible complexity of social totalities. The state, other political institutions, legal institutions, and ideologies do not simply reflect any inner essence through which the whole can be understood. Instead, each must be studied on its own and only after such study may each structure be contextualized within the general structure.[157]

When such studies are completed, according to structural Marxism, it becomes clear that social formations and their evolution are best understood by first distin-

---

153. *See* text at note 5 *supra*.

154. Ted Benton, The Rise and Fall of Structural Marxism: Althusser and his Influence 60 (1984).

155. *Id.*

156. *Id.* at 62.

157. *Id.* at 62. Robert Paul Resch, Althusser and the Renewal of Marxist Social Theory 23 (1992).

guishing between economic foundations and ideological-political superstructures. One must also recognize that superstructural structures are not only complex but also relatively autonomous, and that they are determined by the economic foundation "in the last instance." The caveat of "last instance" both moves away from any notion of direct monocausality and accommodates the idea of the relative autonomy of superstructural elements. These ideas are discussed further in the next section.

Along with his "new and improved" reconfiguration of Marx's inversion of the Hegelian dialectic, Althusser advanced a more dynamic view of "contradiction" by asserting that the Marxist view of contradiction must be accompanied by the commitment to accept the irreducible complexity of social totalities. No single contradiction, such as between labor and capital, can explain the diverse sets of social contradictions; rather, a multiplicity of simultaneously occurring contradictions "overdetermine" one another. (Of course, like Marx, Althusser concluded that when these contradictions are condensed, they lead to revolutionary rupture.)[158] Althusser's reconfiguration of the Hegelian dialectic, as well as the ideas of "last instance," the "irreducible complexity of social totalities," "contradiction," "overdetermination," and other key notions are explained in the excerpt that follows.

Ted Benton, The Rise and Fall of Structural Marxism: Althusser and his Influence 60, 62–63 (1984).

Historical teleology (the idea that history has a goal or end state) is, then, central to historicism, as is the idea of a linear series of stages through which the process must pass. In this sense, Hegel, certainly as Althusser reads him, is a historicist. In so far as the Hegelian pattern of dialectical motion in history is taken over by Feuerbach and the early Marx, notwithstanding their inversion of the *elements* in that pattern, then so far is their work governed by a historicist problematic. To merely *invert* Hegel is to remain trapped within Hegel's problematic, which is a historicist problematic.

... But, argues Althusser, if Marxism goes beyond the mere 'inversion' of Hegel's idealism, discovering, independently, new structures and mechanisms in the real historical process, how can a method which served the purposes of Hegel's idealist philosophy possibly be appropriate to this new object of study? For example, the essence of civil society is located in the state for Hegel, whereas in Marx, the 'anatomy of civil society' is sought in political economy, whilst the Hegelian conception of the state as embodying the general interest is replaced by the idea of the state as a mechanism of the dominant class. But not only the *terms* of the relationship have changed, so has the relationship itself: there is no simple inversion of the essence-appearance relationship, but rather, the idea of an asymmetrical relationship

158. Benton, *supra* note 154, at 63. Bridget O'Laughlin, *Marxist Approaches in Anthropology*, 4 Annu. Rev. Anthropol. 341, 344 (1975).

of mutual determination is introduced (relative autonomy of the superstructures, determination in the last instance by the economic).

Althusser draws from these considerations two conclusions about the distinctive character of the Marxist dialectic. First, the conception of the nature of the *totality* upon which the dialectic is supposed to operate is quite different in Hegel and Marx. The Hegelian notion of totality is what Althusser calls 'expressive', in the sense that each specific element or 'moment' of a *seemingly* complex whole is interpreted as 'expressing' in its own particular way some general or essential character of the whole: the appearance of complexity is reduced by the Hegelian philosophical method to an *essential* simplicity. By contrast, the respect for the independent and specific reality of the concrete objects of study imposed by Marxist materialism commits historical materialism to a recognition of the irreducible complexity of social totalities: ideological forms, particular forms of the state, and so on, do not 'reflect' or 'express' any inner principle through which the whole can be grasped, but rather must be first analysed in their specificity, and only then explained in general terms.

Althusser uses historical texts by Marx, Lenin and Mao . . . The distinction between economic foundation and ideological-political superstructures, and the notions of the determination in the last instance by the economic, and the relative autonomy of the superstructures are, for Althusser, the most important . . .

Althusser's second conclusion is intimately linked with this first one. It is that, to analyse complex 'structures in dominance' and their forms of motion and change, a new conception of 'contradiction' is required. Here, again, the main difference between Marxist and Hegelian concepts of contradiction centres on the *complexity* of the former. Lenin's notebooks reveal his analysis of the revolutionary situation in Russia as a synthesis of numerous distinct contradictions: the presence of both feudal and the most advanced capitalist relations, an imperialist country subject itself to imperialist domination, a simultaneous peasant revolt against landlords, and a workers' revolution. Borrowing terms from Lacanian psychoanalysis, Althusser comments that the Marxist conception of contradiction is not a simple one, in which apparently diverse contradictions are manifestations of a single underlying one (capital versus labour), but one in which a multiplicity of co-existing contradictions *overdetermine* one another, the *condensation* of these determinations producing a revolutionary rupture. Mao's distinctions, too, between principal and secondary contradictions, and principal and secondary aspects of a contradiction, are used to show that the classic writers of Marxism have always explicitly or implicitly recognised the complexity of the Marxian concept of contradiction, a complexity indicated in Althusser's term 'overdetermined contradiction'.

Structural Marxism and Anthropology

The affinity between structural Marxism and the field of social anthropology resulted in the generic descriptive term "anthropological structural Marxism" (ASM).[159] One reason for this is, as seen above, classical Marxist anthropology was not particularly rich in ethnographic data but was largely prospective in outlook; Marx and Engels drew on anthropological speculations about past (particularly precapitalist) social formations and applied these to capitalist and postcapitalist social systems. At the very least, ASM was the original force within social anthropology for legitimizing Marxism in the discourse of the field as a whole.

As a collective movement, ASM rejected reductionism, humanism, subjectivism, and teleology. In fact, two of the defining characteristics of Althusser's thought, and of ASM in general, were the elaboration of a "nonreductive" view of economic determinism and the assertion of a variety of uneven, heterogeneous, noneconomic yet interrelated structures that influence the economic, political, legal, and ideological institutions of society. The economy is determinant, but only "in the last instance."[160] What may be called "superstructure" in classical Marxism is thus viewed as far more complex and creative in social formations. In order to study the latter, which would mean to reach the "deep structure" of society, the various heterogeneous and relatively autonomous superstructural and infrastructural levels must be penetrated.[161] At this deep level lies the mode of production, within which can be found a subnormative order comprising the relations of ownership as well as the relations of production between laborers and nonlaborers. These relations operate in structures that are seemingly not only autonomous but also noneconomic. It is therefore necessary to distinguish between the deep structure of the mode of production and the dominant role that a particular political or legal institution may have at the surface level of society.[162]

Althusser's collaborator Étienne Balibar asserted that modes of production are specific combinations of three elements: the laborer/producer, the means of production, and the nonlaborer/owner who appropriates the surplus.[163] These elements are combined to form Marx's original modes of production (Asiatic, ancient, feudal, capitalist, communist). In a nonreductive Balibarian view:

> Economic relations, centrally those between owners and direct producers, are always determinant (in the last instance) with respect to the other levels or 'instances' in a society, and with respect to the configuration of society as a whole, but that this determination by the economic structure takes the rather indirect form of assigning to the other, non-economic levels, their

159. Stephen Nugent, *Some Reflections on Anthropological Structural Marxism*, 13 J. Roy. Anthropol. Inst. 419, 420 (2007).

160. Louis Althusser, For Marx 200 *et seq.* (1970). Resch, *supra* note 157, at 23. O'Laughlin, *supra* note 158, at 367.

161. Duncan & Ley, *supra* note 150, at 46.

162. Resch, *supra* note 157, at 23.

163. Benton, *supra* note 154, at 68–69.

place in a hierarchy of *dominance* with respect to one another, and the *kind* of articulation between them.[164]

In short, the complexity of the social formation, as illustrated by its variety of heterogeneous but interrelated structures, makes possible the articulation of a plurality of modes of production within a single social formation.[165]

The basic tenets of structural Marxism and their applicability to precapitalist social formations are well summarized in the following excerpt.

Robert Paul Resch, Althusser and the Renewal of Marxist Social Theory 23–24, 26–27 (1992).

The object of Structural Marxist analysis is a social formation structured on the basis of a mode of production. Structural Marxists insist that the economy is determinant "in the last instance," but they conceptualize economic determination not directly, in reflectionist terms, but indirectly, in terms of a hierarchy of heterogeneous, unequal, yet interrelated structures, exercising various economic, political, and ideological functions. The mode of production, comprised of relations of ownership and production obtaining between laborers and non-laborers with respect to the means of production, defines the economic function. The economic function is held to be determinant; that is, the mode of production is understood by Structural Marxists as constituting the deep structure of a social formation.

The economic functions of ownership and production united in the mode of production may be separated at the surface level of the social formation. The function of economic ownership may be exercised within institutional apparatuses distinct from economic production and thus, at least superficially, non-economic in nature. Given this state of affairs, it is necessary to distinguish the determinant role of the economic function, the deep structure of the mode of production, from the dominant role that a particular institutional apparatus, be it political, ideological, or economic, may exercise at the surface level of the social formation. It is typically the case that the institutional apparatus exercising the function of economic ownership will be dominant at the level of the social formation. However, it is always the deep structure of the mode of production that accounts for dominance at the level of the social formation.

Structural Marxism conceives of economic determination within a modernist framework of structural causality. The social formation is a parallelogram of economic, political, and ideological forces manifested in determinate social structures and relations. While the economic function is primary, political and ideological functions have their own distinct character and effec-

164. *Id.* at 72.

165. *Id.* at 118.

tivity, and all determinate structures and relations—political, ideological, and economic—are simultaneously, if unequally, at work as a structured whole, the social formation. In addition, Structural Marxism lacks any teleology or goal toward which economic determination is propelling the social formation. Economic determination refers to the historical effectivity of the social formation as a complex whole on individual structures and relations. The social formation, in other words, constitutes the historical matrix or intransitive conditions of existence of individual structures, yet it exists only as the "complex unity" of their present or transitive effectivities. Because the economic function is always primary within the historical matrix (if not always dominant as a distinct institutional form), all social structures and practices are "always already" assigned a place and a function indirectly—that is, in the last instance—determined by the economy.

Structural Marxism also recognizes contradictory tendencies within and between social structures, contradictions stemming from the uneven development of the social whole and the relative autonomy of individual structures. The primacy of the economy sets boundaries or limits on political and ideological structures, but it does not specify each and every political institution, nor does it directly determine ideological apparatuses such as the family, the university, or the church. Political and ideological structures have a relative autonomy and an internal dynamic that is not coordinated in advance with the development of the economy. At the same time, economic determination is itself contradictory since the production of objective changes within the economic structures and relations themselves may not readily facilitate their reproduction. Thus economic determination "in the last instance" respects the variety of causal determinations at work within the social whole, neither ignoring their particularity nor presuming their reproduction over time. . . .

Since technology only exists in the context of class struggle, and since class powers and interests only exist in the unity of the forces and relations of production, Structural Marxists reformulate the question of historical development in terms of distinct modes of production and their interrelationship (articulation). In the case of any mode of production, the relations of production are dominant because it is the function of ownership to appropriate the social product and to allocate a portion for reproducing the existing forces of production. In the case of any articulation of two different modes of production, it is always a matter of the dominance of the more productive over the less productive mode and the subordination of the reproduction of the latter to that of the former. Individuals exercising the ownership function within a mode of production, of course, constitute its ruling class, and the ruling class of the dominant mode within a given articulation will dominate the dominant class of the subordinate mode. In sum, within any given mode of production we may speak of the dominance of the relations over the forces, yet the question of technological determinism versus class

> struggle cannot be meaningfully posed. However, within any articulation of two modes of production, we may speak of technological determinism but only in the sense of the one mode (one unity of forces and relations and one class struggle) dominating a second.
>
> The concept of a mode of production also permits Structural Marxists to demonstrate the relevance of economic determination to non-capitalist social formations. First, by conceptualizing the forces and relations of production as two social relations among three elements—laborers, technology, and non-laborers—Structural Marxists are able to isolate the economic functions of ownership and production within any given social formation. Second, by distinguishing both economic and non-economic functions from particular institutions that are the bearers of those functions (the lineage, the manor, and so on), Structural Marxist analysis is able to specify relations of determination invisible to methodologies that are content simply to describe institutions and behavior patterns. Third, by specifying relations and their structured interrelationship, Structural Marxists are able to balance general theory and concrete research in a productive and interactive fashion, developing general concepts of a variety of distinct modes of production while respecting the historical individuality of social formations in a given time and place. In short, the concept of a mode of production posits, in classic modernist fashion, abstract structural determinations as objectively real as gravity, yet like the force of gravity, visible only in their effects.

ASM also rejected humanism, even Marxist humanism of, for example, the Sartrean variety. Well before Althusser, Jean-Paul Sartre advanced a nonreductive critique in social theory by arguing that existentialism was a form of humanism based on volition, subjectivism, and rational choice.[166] ASM, by contrast, asserted that while objectivism was needed, subjectivism was not, and that only the "objective" account of ASM could provide an epistemologically accurate account of all precapitalist and capitalist social formations. ASM also rejected all teleological explanations of social causality. In other words, they rejected the classical Marxist "law" of historical inevitability, which postulates first that capitalism contains the seeds of its own destruction, and second that such self-destruction will necessarily, inevitably, and spontaneously result in a communist social formation.[167]

ASM did remain faithful to the basic and fundamental Marxist doctrines of historical materialism, modes of production, and class struggle.[168] The uniquely structuralist doctrines regarding modes of production, social formation (in the sense of a dynamic and reinvigorated superstructure), and the notion of economic determination "in the last instance" were advanced by ASM as transhistorical and cross-culturally applica-

---

166. *See* Isaak Dore, The Epistemological Foundations of Law 778–787 (2007); Jean-Paul Sartre, Existentialism & Humanism (Bernard Frechtman, trans., 1947).

167. Benton, *supra* note 154, at 113.

168. *Id.* at 115. *See also* Sherry B. Ortner, *Theory in Anthropology Since the Sixties*, *in* Law and Anthropology 126, 172 (Peter Sack & Jonathan Aleck eds., 1992); Resch *supra* note 157, at 23.

ble.[169] Their epistemological claim, which was quite strong, posited that these concepts are universally applicable and have explanatory power regardless of divergent social formations and what period of human history or prehistory is under study. Indeed, ASM purported to remedy and reinforce the Marxist project in the face of a number of challenges, as exemplified by Ted Benton:

1. A range of problems connected with the analysis of "pre-capitalist" societies. Marx's own indications were peripheral to his main concerns, and very schematic. Can a rigorous typology of pre-capitalist economic forms (modes of production) be produced which is both consistent with the main propositions of Marxist theory and capable of providing illuminating analysis of the rich empirical data field of anthropology and cognate disciplines? Can the Marxist thesis of determination by the economic be sustained against the apparently overwhelming importance of such institutions as kinship, religion and the state in pre-capitalist formations?
2. A nexus of questions concerned with the Marxist conception of the social totality: how should the supposed determination by the economic of the other 'levels' of society be conceived, and how can this determination be reconciled with an autonomy on the part of the non-economic levels? Can the distinctions between the levels even be sustained, and are they unequivocally the same distinctions when they are applied to radically different forms of society?
3. A range of questions having to do with the explanation of historical change. Short of a schematic philosophy of history, can anything be said in abstract theoretical terms about the possibility of, and the forms of transition from one socio-economic formation to another? Can such a theory avoid teleological or 'historicist' modes of explanation? Can, in particular, the transition from Feudalism to Capitalism in the West be explained in terms consistent with the basic concepts and propositions of historical materialism? And what of the transformation of Capitalism itself? Does Marxism have a coherent theory of socialism as a socio-economic form, and its historical conditions of possibility? How can the [then] prevailing socio-economic forms of Eastern Europe be conceptualised using historical materialist categories?
4. Given that Marxist theory conceptualises a number of distinct actual or possible socio-economic forms, how does it theorise their relationships of co-existence? Colonialism, imperialism and war are all examples of phenomena of the inter-relation of different socio-economic formations for which classical Marxism offered explanations. What do the Althusserian reconstructions of classical Marxist concepts have to offer in response to the difficulties encountered by these attempts at explanation?[170]

169. Benton, *supra* note 154, at 115.

170. *Id.* at 116–17.

Structural Marxism and Precapitalist Societies: Case Studies

The first challenge ASM wished to take on was how Marxism could give a better account of precapitalist or "primitive" societies, since Marx had very little actual data on such societies and since such societies were in any case "peripheral" to his main concerns.[171] ASM met this challenge, in part, through its use of a nonreductionist conceptualization of the modes of production and their relation to social formations, now broadly conceived as explained above.[172] This conceptualization included the notion of the complexity of the social formation, in terms of several levels of autonomous institutions superimposed on the deep structure of the economic base. The latter was considered complex enough for a plurality of modes of production to be articulated within a single social formation.[173]

These ideas were harnessed by ASM to explain not only precapitalist social formations but also the transition from feudalism to capitalism, developments in the Eastern bloc, colonial occupation and postcolonial transformations of Third World countries, and so on. What is immediately relevant for our purposes is ASM's approach to precapitalist formations, which is illustrated by Meillassoux's study of the tribal society of the Gouro in the Ivory Coast,[174] the study of social formations within Indonesian peasant society by Joel Kahn, and the study of eating taboos among women of the Mbum tribe in West Africa by Bridget O'Laughlin.

In brief, the latter attempted to show that Mbum Kpau women were prohibited from eating chicken or goat primarily for economic reasons, but also for noneconomic reasons such as pregnancy; there were also food taboos that supposedly protected women from sterility or even death during childbirth. The taboo also reflected the superiority of the male (who had a preferred right of access to meat) as well as the economic dependence of women.[175] O'Laughlin's structural/functionalist analysis shows how control over an important economic resource (meat) permitted the maintenance of culturally legitimated power.[176] Similarly, Kahn studied how subsistence and petty commodity production affected social structures within a Sumatran peasant culture.[177] Jack Goody and P. M. Worsley sought to show that kinship relations are determined by the way in which production is organized; thus,

171. *See* passage above.

172. *See* text at notes 159–165, *supra.*

173. Louis Althusser & Étienne Balibar, Reading Capital 225 (Ben Brewster trans., 1970); Emmanuel Terray, Marxism and "Primitive" Societies 98 (Mary Klopper trans., 1972).

174. Claude Meillassoux, L'Anthropologie économique des Gouro de Côte d'Ivoire (1981).

175. Bridget O'Laughlin, *Mediation of Contradiction: Why Mbum Women Do not Eat Chicken, in* Women, Culture and Society, 301–339 (M. Rosaldo, L. Lamphere & J. Bamberger eds., 1974).

176. Nugent, *supra* note 159, at 424.

177. Joel Kahn, *Economic Scale and the Cycle of Petty Commodity Production, in W. Sumatra, in* Marxist Analysis and Social Anthropology 137–58 (Maurice Bloch ed., 1975).

Worsley argued that the particular forms of Tale kinship were determined by the fixed farms and their dependence on cooperative agricultural labor.[178]

These studies, as well as the one by Meillassoux discussed below, show that ASM conceives social formations as relational systems composed of superstructural normative arrangements that are ultimately connected to the economic base, which may itself articulate plural modes of production. This conception of a social formation entails the methodological principle that every social institution (*e.g.*, kinship, family, or state) must be viewed normatively in terms of the human/social relations that define it, and that these must be linked to the base. Only then can the social formation be understood as a whole.[179]

Meillassoux's study of the Gouro is a particularly good example. His goal was to study plural modes of production within a lineage-based agricultural society with a particular kinship structure. He found that all culturally significant activity was organized through relationships of kinship and descent. Thus, among the Gouro, it was kinship relations that governed

> the allocation of individuals and instruments of production to production units, the redistribution of the product, and the circulation of women in exchange for a 'bride price' paid in 'élite goods' . . . the 'locus' of these distributions and allocations resting with the elders of the lineage . . .
>
> Life and death act as disturbances and tend to break down the natural family. Economic imperatives, among others, contribute to the creation of new units whose members are tied by relations of production and consumption. The biological family cannot stay within its narrow geneaological framework and is replaced by functional families whose members are associated with consanguinity. Under such a dynamic, the bonds of kinship have to be sufficiently elastic to adapt to such modification.[180]

These observations confirm the structural Marxist thesis that the economic factor is critical to the culturally significant activities of social formations, and (in this case) that kinship ties are best understood when linked to their economic base. Among the Gouro, the allocation of productive and redistributive activities were determined by kinship relations; even brides were acquired through the exchange of culturally significant economic goods. But the economic factor was determinative only in the last instance, due to the presence of other factors such as life and death cycles and considerations of consanguinity. The latter, which are part of what in Althusserian terms would be called "the irreducible complexity of the social totality," are also illustrative of how kinship norms and kinship relations are "overdetermined" through a synthesis of multiple cultural vectors.

> Kinship as a system of social relationships does not correspond to geneaology: it is geneaology modified by the requirements of production and repro-

178. P. M. Worsley, *The Kinship System of the Tallensi: A Reevaluation*, 86 J. Roy. Anthropol. Inst. 37 (1956). Jack Goody, Technology, Tradition and the State in Africa (1971).

179. O'Laughlin, *supra* note 158, at 350.

180. Benton, *supra* note 154, at 119–20 (quoting Meillassoux, *supra* note 174, at 168–69).

> duction, so that, in Terray's terms 'relations of production can be "realised" within it.' For Terray, the Althusserian concept of overdetermination provides the key to an analysis of the place of kinship relations in the 'primitive' social formation: comparably with class relations in more advanced formations, kinship relations cannot be identified with one or other 'level' of the mode of production, but are the effect of a *synthesis of determinations* by the economic base, and its ideological and juridico-political superstructures. It is in this sense that kinship relations 'realise' economic, political and ideological relations: they are the form of appearance taken by these relations in lineage-based societies.[181]

Emmanuel Terray's interpretation of Meillassoux's ethnography of the Gouro seems to be at variance with the views of Claude Lévi-Strauss. As we see in Chapter 6, Lévi-Strauss's structuralism asserted that kinship and marriage in "primitive" societies were the dominant structures and were the key to understanding such societies. Terray's came to the opposite conclusion (*i.e.*, that kinship relations were not dominant in all primitive societies, and even when dominant, did not govern all culturally significant activities).

For Terray, identification of the modes of production (*i.e.*, agriculture, hunting, and gathering) among the Gouro was of primary importance. By accomplishing this, he concluded that he could prove the Marxist thesis of the correspondence between the forces and relations of production and social relations. Thus, he portrayed the Gouro as having two modes of production with corresponding social structures: (1) hunting and gathering, which required complex cooperation necessitating social organization at the tribal-village level; and (2) agricultural and domestic production that required simple cooperation at the lineage level.[182]

Maurice Godelier's studies also illustrate the twin notions of overdetermination and synthesis of determinations. He asserts that one of the primary concerns of precapitalist society is the control of access to women and the regulation of their "circulation" (by which he meant sexual availability as well as physical freedom of mobility) and assigned the primacy of this concern to the fact that precapitalist kinship structures operate at the level of both infrastructure and superstructure. Thus the economist may be able to identify the productive role of kinship structures in such societies but may not be able to discern their autonomous relations of production. Indeed,

> the multifunctionality of kinship structures acts as a limit to the development of the productive forces and explains the generally slow rhythm of their development . . . [K]inship relations constrain the independently determined technological system.[183]

---

181. Benton, *supra* note 154, at 120 (quoting Terray, *supra* note 173, at 141); *See also* O'Laughlin, *supra* note 158 at 344.

182. Terray, *supra* note 173, at 115.

183. O'Laughlin, *supra* note 158, at 357 (quoting Maurice Godelier, Rationality and Irrationality in Economics 290 (1972)).

The "irreducible complexity of the social totality" is illustrated by Godelier's example of precapitalist societies in which there are a multiplicity of kinship levels, so that kinship structures operate at the level of base/infrastructure and superstructure. It is thus possible that kinship relations at the superstructural level (which enjoy a relative autonomy) may act as a break (or "fetter" to use Marx's term) on the productive structure at the base level. In this nonreductive explanation of social totality, not only is the base not the sole determinant of kinship relations, the base itself is not self-reproducing. This explanation also illustrates the "synthesis of determinations" by the economic base and juridico-political superstructures. In other words, a more complete picture of both economic and social life is revealed when kinship is studied in its multifunctional roles. Because social and economic relations thus represent a synthesis of these various cultural vectors, this example also illustrates the overdetermination of social and economic relations through a multiplicity of interactive influences. In short, every mode of production will show not only its base but also its corresponding forms of superstructure.

Conclusion

Structural Marxism clearly offers a holistic rather than an individualistic explanation of culture. In this sense, it shares common ground with classical Marxism, under which large-scale social and cultural evolution is unaffected by individual thought and action. This deterministic approach is endorsed by ASM with some qualifications, principally that economic determination occurs only "in the last instance." Interstitially, however, robust interaction occurs between base and superstructure and is captured by the doctrines of overdetermination, syntheses of determinations, and irreducible complexity of the social totality.

This softer form of determinism is the result of the Althusserian reconfiguration of Marx's reversal of the Hegelian dialectic. If Hegel saw world history in idealistic terms (*i.e.*, in terms of history having a preordained *telos* or end), ASM rejected teleology and substituted a greater degree of flux and complexity in human evolution and in social processes. However, the structural aspects of ASM's holism may have unwittingly embraced Hegelian holism.[184] Hegel's doctrine of the "World Spirit" or *Geist* described it as a transcendental force that manifests itself in all things and guides their evolution;[185] however, man is the chief agent through which *Geist* manifests itself in history. Here, Hegel used Aristotle's distinction between formal cause and efficient cause in that *Geist* is the formal cause and man the efficient cause through which *Geist* manifests itself. Hegel thus viewed the world (and human evolution) holistically, implying that the individual is a mere passive agent of *Geist* and is therefore incapable of shaping the course of human (and world) history.

Marx, in reversing the Hegelian dialectic, claimed the opposite (that man is capable of taking control of his own destiny) and proposed a theory of human evolution called historical materialism. However, claiming that Marx had not made a

184. Duncan & Ley, *supra* note 150, at 34, 55.

185. *Id.* at 33.

successful break with Hegelian idealism, historicism, and teleology, Althusser and his followers rejected teleology and proposed the "last instance" doctrine, which they complemented with the doctrines of overdetermination, plurality in the modes of production, syntheses of determinations, and the irreducible complexity of social totalities. Nevertheless, ASM remained largely committed to Hegelian holism by substituting "social formation" for Hegel's "*Geist*" and Marx's "capital." This commitment raises the question of whether the whole social formation can be viewed as the "formal cause" with man as the "efficient cause" through which the goals of the social form are implemented. After all, Althusser himself affirmed the priority of the whole over its structures and contradictions, as well as his belief that individuals are only the bearers or agents of the structures.[186] Still, it can be argued that this criticism is flawed, given that ASM deliberately eschewed teleology and that its doctrines of irreducible complexity, overdetermination, plural modes of production, and so on, posited a more active and dynamic role for the individual. Put differently, ASM did not conceive the social formation as a reified supra-individual entity, as did Hegel with *Geist* and Marx with capital.

> One of the virtues of structural Marxism, then, was that there was a place for everything in its scheme. Refusing to see inquiries into material relations and into "ideology" as opposed enterprises, its practitioners established a model in which the two "levels" were related to one another via a core of social/political/economic processes. In this sense, they offered an explicit mediation between the "materialist" and "idealist" camps of sixties anthropology. The mediation was rather mechanical . . . but it was there. More important . . . the structural Marxists put a relatively powerful sociology back into the picture. They cross-fertilized British social anthropological categories with Marxist ones, and produced an expanded model of social organization ("mode of production") which they then proceeded to apply systematically to particular cases. Whereas other Marxisms emphasized relations of political/economic organization ("production") almost exclusively, the structural Marxists were, after all, anthropologists, trained to pay attention to kinship, descent, marriage, exchange, domestic organization, and the like. They thus included these elements within their considerations of political and economic relations (often giving them a more Marxist ring by calling them "relations of reproduction") and the total effect was to produce rich and complex pictures of the social process in specific cases. Given the relative paucity . . . of detailed sociological analysis in the various sixties schools, this was an important contribution.[187]

186. Louis Althusser, Politics and History: Montesquieu, Rousseau, Hegel and Marx 183 (1972). *See also* Althusser & Balibar, *supra* note 173, at 180.

187. Ortner, *supra* note 168, at 173–74.

Contemporary Cultural Marxism

Introduction

Contemporary Marxist methodology as an analytical tool for sociocultural developments is based on the following interrelated claims: that consciousness is sensuous rather than abstract (in the Hegelian sense); that sensuous consciousness is determined by man's material existence which, in turn, is reflective of the extent to which man modifies nature to suit his material and sociocultural needs; that the possibilities for universal human freedom can be unveiled only if social ills are diagnosed in terms of class conflict; and that the law of historical inevitability (predicting the demise of capitalism) must be replaced by the law of historical necessity under which universal freedom can be controlled by individuals only when it is controlled by all.

These claims are elaborated below, although their underlying reasons have already been discussed. For example, the anti-Hegelian conception of the sensuous nature of consciousness (the first claim) and its material foundation (the second claim) both flow from Marx's famous maxim[188] that it is not consciousness that determines being, but rather being that determines consciousness. The third claim also naturally flows from the belief of Marx and Engels (expressed in the *Communist Manifesto*)[189] that the whole of human history can be understood as a history of class struggle.

The final claim involving the law of historical inevitability presents the greatest challenges to Marxism. Although the demise of capitalism remains a theoretical possibility, its inevitability has been questioned, if not abandoned. Yet, here too accommodation has been made consistently with the fundamental Marxist tenet that true freedom (*i.e.*, freedom from exploitation and alienation) can be achieved *only* if the productive forces of society are controlled by all. Thus even if public ownership of the means of production is not inevitable, it is *necessary*. The law of historical inevitability is thus supplanted by the law of historical necessity, yet the goal for both is identical. In other words, the end remains the same; only the means to the end has been tweaked.

The Material Foundation of Sensuous Consciousness

> The chief defect of all hitherto existing materialism . . . is that the thing, reality, sensuousness, is conceived only in the form of the *object* or of *contemplation*, but not as *human sensuous activity*, *practice*, not subjectively.[190]

The subjectivity referred to by Marx in the above quotation is the result of the totality of activities by which man transforms nature to meet his material needs.[191] This transformation consists of three analytical categories: (1) the manipulation of

---

188. *See* text at notes 1–8, *supra*.

189. *See* text at notes 11–52, *supra*.

190. Karl Marx, *Theses on Feuerbach*, *in* THE MARX-ENGELS READER, *supra* note 11, at 107.

191. John Brenkman, *Theses on Cultural Marxism*, 7 SOCIAL TEXT 19, 21 (1983).

nature for the production of material goods necessary for human subsistence; (2) the production and reproduction of social relations; and (3) the establishment of symbolic and other forms of social interaction (*i.e.*, culture).[192]

> Culture comprises the entire continuum of symbolic interactions and expressive forms through which a collectivity establishes solidarity from its relation to nature and from the antagonisms it experiences in the social relations. Cultural practices elaborate the multilayered dialectic of identity and difference, of solidarity and struggle, of possible community and actual social conflict.[193]

The keywords here are "solidarity," "struggle," "nature," and "antagonisms." In essence, as he tames nature, man is what he makes of himself. This Sartrean existentialist approach contrasts with the Hegelian conception of automatic progress toward perfection over which man has no control. It also conceives man as both a product of and manipulator of nature. Nature is ontologically prior to man, but man is capable of intelligible conceptions of nature, which leads him to modify it to suit his needs. Thus while ASM rejected Sartre's humanism, contemporary cultural Marxism appears to reembrace it.

> Especially in his early writings, as well as in his Hegel-critique, the anthropological component in Marx's thinking becomes visible, because according to him Hegel overlooked human reality and interpreted the world as a spiritual category. "For Hegel," as Marx puts it, "human nature, man, is equivalent to self-consciousness" . . . which leads him to make the claim that man cannot see the real suffering and alienation of mankind that was historically produced through private property, labor division and the development of social classes. Hegel's misconception of human reality as a reflection of the absolute subject is the central point for Marx, as it misses the fact that we are tied to nature, and that human beings and their social reproduction are both part and product of nature. Because Hegel did not realize man's reality he overlooks human reality as a whole, and therefore his philosophy must be conceived as ideology, Marx writes:
>
>> sensuous consciousness is not abstractly sensuous consciousness, but humanly sensuous consciousness, religion, wealth, etc., are only the estranged reality of human objectification, of human essential powers born into work, and therefore only the way to true human reality. . . .
>
> Marx invokes human reality as the main issue of philosophy and, as a successor of Feuerbach, re-establishes anthropological thinking within the development of 19th century thought. Marx destroys every reference to the epistemological distinction between empirical and transcendental knowledge as well as between existence and the underlying essential structure of actuality, which was central for Hegelian philosophy and its absolute metaphysics.

192. *Id.*

193. *Id.* at 31.

> In its place he elaborates only on the ontological distinction between man and nature. Human reality can no longer be understood by references to spirit or to God; neither does it relate itself to an eternal nor to a substantial truth. "For man," as Marx points out in his *Critique of Hegel's Philosophy of Right*, "the root is man himself . . . for man the supreme being is man." . . . Consequently, philosophy comes to an end as soon as it is realized in practice, because it no longer expresses and possesses a higher and more substantial form of truth which is separated from reality. In other words, the nature of human kind in its development comes to an end through the development of culture. Through culture, which is the process of history, man returns to himself and realizes what he is.[194]

Contemporary Marxism argues that traditional theory treats culture as standing apart from material necessity and as having an almost spiritual or transcendental quality that is insulated from and unaffected by the divisions and conflicts within society.[195] The Marxist view takes the opposing stance that sociocultural relations are directly affected by the material conditions of life, including its attendant divisions of labor and class conflicts. This influence, according to the Marxists, is what gives consciousness its sensuous quality.

For Marxism, freedom is a critical aspect of sociocultural relations, particularly freedom from domination and exploitation. Under the capitalist system such freedom is not possible; there is instead "unfreedom," and true freedom remains an unfulfilled promise or (at best) a latent possibility.[196] The promise is fulfilled only when productive forces are appropriated for the benefit of all, followed by the establishment of a classless society.

John Brenkman, *Theses on Cultural Marxism*, 7 Social Text 19, 21–22, 30 (1983).

> . . . Subjectivity is not spirit as opposed to matter, nor is it identical with consciousness, for it is grounded in human sensuous activity or praxis. Humanity produces and reproduces itself through the totality of activities by which it transforms nature into human reality.
>
> There are thus three moments in praxis. The transformation of nature includes: (1) the production of material goods for the satisfaction of human needs; (2) the production and reproduction of social relations; and (3) the production of symbolic interactions and expressive forms. Culture is this third moment or aspect of praxis. How to construe the relative autonomy of culture with respect to the other two moments of praxis—this is the core of

194. Christian Lotz, *From Nature to Culture? Diogenes and Philosophical Anthropology*, 28 Human Studies 41, 44–45 (2005) (quoting Karl Marx, Early Writings 385 (R. Livingston & G. Benton trans., 2005)).

195. Brenkman, *supra* note 191, at 21.

196. *Id.*

critical theory's dispute with traditional theory. Traditional theory considers culture to be a realm apart from society, a spiritual realm standing above material necessity, a transcendent sphere of meanings and values unaffected by the divisions and conflicts of society. For critical theory, humanity does not achieve self-realization in a separated realm of culture, spiritually and without overcoming the social division of labor. A free and universal humanity can only emerge when self-activity extends to all members of society in the whole of their endeavors and interactions. Marx and Engels: "A complete and no longer restricted self-activity . . . consists in the appropriation of a totality of productive forces and in the thus postulated development of a totality of capacities. Modern universal intercourse can be controlled by individuals, therefore, only when controlled by all."

Cultural Marxism is the theoretical and interpretive project that approaches culture in its dialectic relation to the social totality. This totality, however, is not an achieved unity, but rather an unfulfilled promise or possibility latent within human history. Totality remains obstructed so long as the cultural realm of freedom, as well as the material realm of necessity, is founded upon unfreedom in the relations among human beings. . . .

That individuals or classes, however, are made to serve as wealth, as the source of satisfaction, for others without controlling the products of their own labor and without enjoying the recognition of their own desires—this is the inessential, massively real condition of all class societies. Domination is the result of the social division of labor—among classes, among races and peoples, between men and women. . . .

Hence the philosophical and political stakes in cultural Marxism's insistence on the dialectical connection of the social relations and the symbolic. Culture is not independent of material production for the reason that material production itself—the satisfaction of human needs through the interchange with nature—is at the same time a set of interhuman relations. . . . Culture is the lived symbolization of interhuman relations and of the relation to nature. These symbolizations veil and unveil the forms of domination that organize the uses one human being or class makes of another for the satisfaction of its own needs. . . .

Marx contested, politically and philosophically, the state as a unity transcending the social relations deriving from the capitalist division of labor. The contradictions of class could not be resolved or abolished in the armed logos of the state, but only in the revolutionary processes that would found a classless society. Marx ultimately located this historic conflict in the developing antagonism between society's productive capacity (forces of production) and the social relations (relations of production). For Marx, the revolutionary transformation of capitalism would be driven by this tendency for society's productive capacity to break the social relations which constrain it.

Diagnosing Social Ills through the Prism of Class Struggle

Marx rejected Hegel's glorification of the state as a higher form of social organization and asserted that class contradictions cannot be mediated within the logos of the state. Such discourse, when mediated by the state, tends to obfuscate the class character of social injustice, hinders movements for change, and thwarts critical thought about the moral implications of the existing relations of production. For these reasons, Anthony Marcus's ethnographic field work on the homeless of New York City during the Reagan/Bush era of the 1980s and 1990s led him to conclude that many social ills could not be remedied because they were misdiagnosed. He asserted that the failure to diagnose the problems of poverty, homelessness, housing, employment, and health care in America as class phenomena (*i.e.*, in the Marxist tradition) led to inept and unsuccessful attempts to tackle these social ills. He explains how discourses on poverty fell under vague and impressionistic categories such as "underclass," "the Other America," "homeless," "the poor," etc. These discourses excluded a Marxist analysis and confused attempts to understand the true nature of poverty,[197] largely because they treated the poor as separate and distinct from the rest of society and favored "social shame" as the means for tackling such social ills.[198]

A Marxist diagnosis of these ills would be based on the following two tenets:

> [T]he capitalist class who own the means of production and derive benefit from channelling a higher percentage of the social product into profit and the employed working class who share with "the poor" an interest in channelling a higher percentage of the social product into use values and a lower percentage into profit.[199]

The failure to heed these two fundamental tenets of social analysis has two consequences. First, the dominant cultural symbol of the Other essentially guarantees that the poor are not seen as a distinct class. In other words, the cultural model replaces the class model and by doing so denies the commonality of interest between the well-paid doctor working for a major insurance company and a minimum wage clerk in a store. The cultural model naturalizes the capitalist labor market and also ensures that working-class demands to increase the social wage and reduce profits are excluded from discourses on poverty and inequality.

Here, social shame is substituted for the proletariat as the means to fight poverty. Under Marxist theory, it is the proletariat that fights for reductions in profit and increases in use value of the social product and is, therefore, the agent seeking changes in the division and distribution of social wealth. This quest, which lies at the heart of class struggle, is best achieved by the deliberate and conscious recognition and articulation of class contradictions along class lines.

According to Marcus and Brenkman, the above discourses based on the cultural model and the model of shame are buttressed by two theoretical models that further

---

197. Anthony Marcus, *The Culture of Poverty Revisited: Bringing Back the Working Class*, 47 ANTHROPOLOGICA 35, 36 (2005).

198. *Id.*

199. *Id.* at 36–37.

naturalize the capitalist mode of production and distribution. The first was put forward by Max Weber, whose characterization of the system of capitalism of Western Europe as based on "logically formal rationality" portrays the capitalist society as rational, formal, impartial, and equal.[200] Under this model, economic and political history have little to do with the perpetuation of poverty. The second model, the somewhat more liberal Durkheimian one, embraces limited social welfare programs such as food stamps and housing assistance to mitigate the effects of poverty.[201] Both models reject the Marxist tenets mentioned above and also fail to recognize the existence of systemic political and economic contradictions in society. A superficial compromise ("the Fordist compromise") is struck between capital and labor, aimed at increasing the standard of living, increasing consumer choice, and decreasing class consciousness.[202]

> However, in war and in peace and in economic sickness and health, the U.S. poverty studies industry, often composed of academics like myself, who think of themselves as Marxists and advocates for their social class, have actively participated in maintaining and nurturing a set of influential intellectual discourses and categories of difference that disappear the U.S. working class and any potential working-class resolutions. These discourses and categories are often shot through with corrosive caste/colour prejudices, illusory notions of social harmony under capitalism, and faith in the moral and ethical behaviour of enlightened elites and their capitalist employers.
>
> However, such discourses are actually quite fragile, due to their deep contradictions, procrustean unwieldiness and declining support from government funding agencies. It is difficult to know exactly what conscious Marxist anthropologies of poverty would look like. There is no roadmap or blueprint that can substitute for conscious and cumulative discussion, debate and practice. However, as a start it is worth reiterating that providing fine tuning for even the broadest program directed at an "other America" represents a "retreat from class" and a barrier to providing a clear Marxist analysis. Following this, the use of Weberian consumption categories such as "poor" and "middle class" or "practical" categories based on emergency considerations such as housing, food, healthcare, or employment as the unit of analysis may be useful or important in a variety of scholarly, professional and policy contexts, but it tends to obscure larger conflicts involving the entire working class and the social product that it produces. These conflicts must be highlighted and examined in order to develop a thoroughly dialectical materialist history of who is doing what to whom.[203]

---

200. Max Weber, Max Weber on Law in Economy and Society 1 (Max Rheinstein ed., Max Rheinstein & Edward Shils trans., Free Press 1954) (1925).

201. Marcus *supra* note 197, at 38.

202. *Id.* at 42.

203. *Id.* at 48.

The Law of Historical Inevitability Displaced by the Law of Historical Necessity

According to Marxism, only when dialectical materialism unveils "who is doing what to whom" can class solidarity be mobilized for the revolutionary overthrow of exploitative relations of production. As already noted, it also holds that true freedom of the individual can exist only when it exists for all; in other words, when the social product is shared by all. Traditional Marxism also holds that capitalism contains the seeds of its own destruction. Thus, just as feudalism was overthrown by a new set of productive forces and relations of production under capitalism, so capitalism will inevitably be overthrown by communism.

This prognostication stands as the biggest challenge for contemporary Marxism. Indeed, not only has capitalism shown its staying power, but the breakup of the Soviet empire has shown the opposite trend. In attempting to explain this paradox, John Brenkman frankly admits that the law of historical inevitability is "no longer compatible" with Marxism. Instead, he seeks reconciliation by reference to another traditional precept of Marx:

> (M)odern universal intercourse can be controlled by individuals, . . . only when controlled by all.[204]

The above is posited as the law of historical necessity. If social ills are diagnosed along Marxist lines, class categories will replace cultural categories and the proletariat will be at the forefront of change. Even if change is not historically inevitable, it is a historical necessity. Thus the proletariat must take the necessary action.

> The most difficult lesson that Marxism has had to learn in the 20th century is that social transformation and liberation can no longer follow the quantitative increase of the productive forces. Marx derived the dialectic of quantity and quality from the process of industrialization which made the economic development of capitalism in the 19th century appear to be the driving force for the overthrow of the very social relations of capitalism. But the moment has been missed in which the quantitative growth of the economy and the progressive destitution of the worker could dialectically turn into a qualitative transformation of society as a whole. The law of historical inevitability is no longer compatible with the critical power of Marxism. Utopian thought, not scientific dictum, has become the vital support of the critical theory of society. Another sense of historical necessity alone has relevance for contemporary Marxism, a sense which is persistent though latent in Marx's writings, as in the statement from *The German Ideology*: "Modern universal intercourse can be controlled by individuals, therefore, only when controlled by all." Here Marx and Engels evoke historical necessity in the sense of a condition or requirement: *if* humanity is to achieve the autonomy and freedom, the self-activity, that bourgeois society abstractly attributes to indi-

204. Brenkman, *supra* note 191, at 26 (citing MARX, THE GERMAN IDEOLOGY).

viduals, there *must be* a revolutionary reorganization of society which frees all individuals to control the whole of their interrelations and interactions. Indeed, this expresses the utopian moment in communist consciousness, the recognition that every human being will become an existence *for itself* only when he or she can freely develop as an existence *for others*.

Culture—the continuum of knowledges and representations, interactions and symbolizations—contains this consciousness as its obstructed horizon and its historically denied possibility. The conflict of interpretations, that is, the struggle over the self-understanding of cultural practices, is therefore a political struggle to redeem what is possible from what is real, our reality being but the systematic obstruction of the possible.[205]

205. *Id.* at 26–27.

Chapter 5

Neo-Marxist Cultural Materialism and Normativity

The theories of Marx and Engels, though formulated in the mid-nineteenth century, continue to influence cultural anthropology. The present chapter discusses this influence upon three major thinkers of the twentieth century: Leslie White (1900–1975), Julian Steward (1902–1972), and Marvin Harris (1927–2001). Harris, who is the acknowledged and most influential standard-bearer of contemporary cultural Marxism, coined the descriptive label of "cultural materialism"—a term that also serves as a general description of the theories of White and Steward. We begin with the neo-Marxist theories of White, continue with those of Steward, and conclude with Harris's concept and methodology of cultural materialism.

Leslie White: Cultural Evolution and Technology

A new subschool of thought that espoused an essentially neo-Marxist evolutionist approach emerged in the middle of the twentieth century, largely as a reaction to the relativism of the Boasian tradition and of structural functionalism. This school earned the label "neo-evolutionist" although White, one of its main protagonists, rejected the label out of concern that his theories belonged to the classical evolutionist school in the same way the theories of Tylor and Spencer had.[1] In his essay "Energy and the Evolution of Culture," White labels his theories evolutionist.

> The theory set forth in the preceding pages was, as we have made clear, held by the foremost thinkers of the Evolutionist school of the nineteenth century, both in England and in America. Today they seem to us as sound as they did to Tylor and Morgan, and, if anything, more obvious. It seems almost incredible that anthropologists of the twentieth century could have turned their backs upon and repudiated such a simple, sound, and illuminating generalization, one that makes the vast range of tens of thousands of years of culture history intelligible. But they have done this. The anti-evolutionists, led in America by Franz Boas, have rejected the theory of evolution in cultural anthropology—and have given us instead a philosophy of "planless hodge-podge-ism."[2]

1. Leslie White, The Evolution of Culture ix (1959).
2. Leslie White, *Energy and the Evolution of Culture*, 45 Am. Anthropol. 335, 355 (1943).

Technoenvironmental Basis for White's Basic Law of Cultural Evolution

Like Marx, White believed human survival depends on the ability to master one's environment and secure the material conditions of life. White also thought that humankind's evolutionary track is determined by the extent to which people are able to harness energy to modify their natural environment through advances in technology. The greater the advances in technology, the greater the level of normative integration in society. Thus energy and technology (*i.e.*, the "instrumental means of putting the energy to work") are key factors of cultural and normative development. Based on this claim, White boldly proposes a basic law of cultural evolution:

> Other factors remaining constant, culture *evolves as the amount of energy harnessed per capita per year is increased, or as the efficiency of the instrumental means of putting the energy to work is increased. . . .* [3]

White offers the survival of the human species over the ages as proof of his theory of the technological basis for cultural systems:

> The technological basis of cultural systems is rather easily demonstrated. All living organisms can maintain themselves as individuals and perpetuate themselves as species only if a certain minimum adjustment to the external world is achieved and maintained. There must be food, protection from the elements, and defense from enemies. These life-sustaining, life-perpetuating processes are technological in a broad, but valid, sense; i.e., they are carried on by material, mechanical, biophysical, and biochemical means.[4]

White identifies three factors to be analyzed when studying culture: energy, tools, and product. He explains the interaction among the three as follows:

> As we have seen, culture is a mechanism for serving the needs of man. And to do this it must harness energy and put it to work. The use of energy requires technological apparatus, and we may extend the use of the term *tools* to cover all the material means with which energy is harnessed, transformed, and expended. We shall designate all goods and services capable of serving the needs of man that have been produced or formed by the cultural use of energy, the *product*. . . . [5]

In addition to explaining how culture evolves, White explained why culture evolves. "In the case of man . . . the power to invent and to discover, the ability to select and use the better of two tools or ways of doing something—these are the factors of cultural evolution."[6]

---

3. Leslie White, The Science of Culture 368–69 (1949) (emphasis in original).
4. White, The Evolution of Culture, *supra* note 1, at 19.
5. *Id.*
6. White, *Energy and the Evolution of Culture*, *supra* note 2, at 339.

White finds that technological advances are made possible through the efficient harnessing and conversion of energy. Thus, culture itself evolves as the amount of energy per capita per year is increased.[7] After defining energy as "the ability to do work" and going on to say that "[e]nergy and work are interchangeable terms,"[8] White summarizes his discussion of energy and tools in a law of cultural development: "[C]ulture advances as the amount of energy harnessed per capita per year increases, or as the efficiency or economy of the means of controlling energy is increased, or both."[9]

White divided culture into three components: technological, sociological, and ideological. The technological sector consists of the material, mechanical, physical, and chemical means by which humans define their existence in their natural habitat. The sociological sector, which is the network of normative relations, includes kinship, economic, ethical, legal, political, religious, and military systems. The ideological sector includes belief systems, philosophies, knowledge, science, and literature.[10] White gives primacy to the technological sector because he saw a direct causal connection between it and the other two.

According to White, culture is primarily a mechanism for harnessing energy to service human needs. Only secondarily is it a mechanism for regulating behavior that is not directly connected to subsistence. Thus the social system is "determined" by the technological system of material subsistence, whereas art and philosophy express experience as defined by technology and "refracted" by the social system.[11] Under this view it would be reasonable to locate law or the legal system in the sociological sector, but White does not give it this placement in any explicit manner. It could also easily be placed in the ideological/philosophical sector, although the precise location of law for White would be academic, given the primacy he assigned to the technological sector.

Although White did not acknowledge Marx or Engels as inspirations behind his notion of social advancement through mastery of the environment and technological change, the influence of Marxism is clear in his work.[12] White even espoused the Marxist theory that technical advances in production come into conflict with existing social relations, which eventually must change to accommodate these advances.[13] He also observes that a social system may able to constrain the emergence of a new technological system. When this happens, cultural advance is "arrested" and can be revived only by harnessing a new source of energy of sufficient magnitude to "burst asunder the social system," so that "the new technology will form a new social system,

---

7. Marvin Harris, The Rise of Anthropological Theory 636 (updated ed. 2001).

8. White, The Evolution of Culture, *supra* note 1, at 40.

9. *Id.* at 56; *see also*, White, *Energy and the Evolution of Culture*, *supra* note 2, at 345.

10. White, The Science of Culture, *supra* note 3, at 365–66. *See* excerpt below.

11. *Id.* at 366.

12. Harris, *supra* note 7, at 637.

13. Elvin Hatch, Theories of Man and Culture 132–33 (1973).

one congenial to its growth, and culture will again advance until, perhaps, the social system once more checks it."[14]

This analysis clearly resembles Marx and Engels's account of the way the relations of production act as "fetters" on the emergence of new productive forces, such as in the incompatability of the system of property during the feudal era with the use of land as a freely alienable asset that could be exploited through wage labor under the capitalist system.[15] Furthermore, as in the Marxist analysis, White seems to view the push/pull between culture and technology as a recurring phenomenon, declaring that "This fact has become commonplace today."[16]

Invoking the theories of Morgan and Tylor, White emphasizes the technological basis of the evolutionary shift of mankind from savagery to agricultural society.

> Culture develops as man's control over his environment, especially over the food supply, increases. Mankind advanced from savagery to barbarism when they took to agriculture.... Social evolution comes as a consequence of technological development: To this "change of habit [i.e., from a wild food economy to agriculture] may be plainly in great part traced the expansion of industrial arts and the creation of higher social and political institutions.... [17]

Echoing Marx's diagnosis that capitalism contains the seeds of its own destruction, White first observes that the needs of European capitalism led to the search for new markets, new empires, colonialism, and imperialism. Next, he notes that the collapse of this colonial-imperialist order in the mid-twentieth century (when he was writing) showed that the social system of Western Europe was also decaying and needed to be changed. The rejection of evolutionary thought by the Boasian school represented to White nothing more than a reactionary movement against change.[18]

White's thesis of the technological basis of cultural systems is explained in the following excerpt.

Leslie A. White, The Science of Culture 364–391 (1949).

> Culture is an organized, integrated system. But we may distinguish subdivisions within, or aspects of, this system. For our purpose, we shall distinguish three subsystems of culture, namely, technological, sociological, and ideological systems. The technological system is composed of the material, mechanical, physical, and chemical instruments, together with the techniques of their use, by means of which man, as an animal species, is articulated with his natural habitat. Here we find the tools of production, the means of subsistence, the materials of shelter, the instruments of offense and defense. The so-

---

14. White, *Energy and the Evolution of Culture*, *supra* note 2, at 348.

15. *See* Chapter 4, text at notes 46–49.

16. White, *Energy and the Evolution of Culture*, *supra* note 2, at 348.

17. *Id.* at 353.

18. Hatch, *supra* note 13, at 133.

ciological system is made up of interpersonal relations expressed in patterns of behavior, collective as well as individual. In this category we find social, kinship, economic, ethical, political, military, ecclesiastical, occupational and professional, recreational, etc., systems. The ideological system is composed of ideas, beliefs, knowledge, expressed in articulate speech or other symbolic form. Mythologies and theologies, legend, literature, philosophy, science, folk wisdom and common sense knowledge, make up this category . . .

. . . The primary role is played by the technological system. This is, of course, as we would expect it to be; it could not be otherwise. Man as an animal species, and consequently culture as a whole, is dependent upon the material, mechanical means of adjustment to the natural environment. Man must have food. He must be protected from the elements. And he must defend himself from his enemies. These three things he must do if he is to continue to live, and these objectives are attained only by technological means. The technological system is therefore both primary and basic in importance; all human life and culture rest and depend upon it.

Social systems are in a very real sense secondary and subsidiary to technological systems. In fact a social system may be defined realistically as the organized effort of human beings in the use of the instruments of subsistence, offense and defense, and protection. A social system is a function of a technological system. . . .

Ideological, or philosophical, systems are organizations of beliefs, in which human experience finds its interpretation. But experience and interpretations thereof are powerfully conditioned by technologies. . . . A pastoral, agricultural, metallurgical, industrial, or military technology will each find its corresponding expression in philosophy. One type of technology will find expression in the philosophy of totemism, another in astrology or quantum mechanics. . . .

We may view a cultural system as a series of three horizontal strata: the technological layer on the bottom, the philosophical on the top, the sociological stratum in between. These positions express their respective roles in the culture process. The technological system is basic and primary. Social systems are functions of technologies; and philosophies express technological forces and reflect social systems. The technological factor is therefore *the* determinant of a cultural system as a whole. It determines the form of social systems, and technology and society together determine the content and orientation of philosophy. This is not to say, of course, that social systems do not condition the operation of technologies, or that social and technological systems are not affected by philosophies. They do and are. But to condition is one thing; to determine, quite another. . . .

We can now formulate the basic law of cultural evolution: Other factors remaining constant, *culture evolves as the amount of energy harnessed per capita per year is increased, or as the efficiency of the instrumental means of putting the energy to work is increased.* Both factors may increase simultaneously of course. We may now sketch the history of cultural development from this standpoint. . . .

. . . Since the degree of cultural development—the amount of human need-serving goods and services produced per capita—is proportional to the amount of energy harnessed and put to work per capita per year, other factors remaining constant, these earliest cultures of mankind, dependent as they were upon the meager energy resources of the human body, were simple, meager, and crude, as indeed they had to be. No cultural system, activated by human energy alone, can develop very far. . . .

Thus we trace the development of culture from anthropoid levels to the present time as a consequence of periodic increases in the amount of energy harnessed per capita per year effected by tapping new sources of power. There is, however, another technological factor involved which we have merely mentioned incidentally so far; we must now consider it more fully, namely, the role of tools in the culture process. Energy is of course neither created nor annihilated, at least not within cultural systems; it is merely transformed. It is harnessed and it is put to work or expended. But this requires tools and machines. The amount of energy harnessed may, and the amount of human need-serving goods produced per unit of energy does, depend upon the efficiency of the tools employed. So far, we have been holding the tool factor constant and varying the energy factor. We now hold the energy factor constant and vary that of tools. We get, then, the following generalization: *the degree of cultural development varies directly as the efficiency of the tools employed, other factors remaining constant*. . . .

Technology is the hero of our piece. This is a world of rocks and rivers, sticks and steel, of sun, air and starlight, of galaxies, atoms and molecules. Man is but a particular kind of material body who must do certain things to maintain his status in a cosmic material system. The means of adjustment and control, of security and survival, are of course technological. Culture thus becomes primarily a mechanism for harnessing energy and of putting it to work in the service of man, and, secondarily, of channelling and regulating his behavior not directly concerned with subsistence and offense and defense. Social systems are therefore determined by technological systems, and philosophies and the arts express experience as it is defined by technology and refracted by social systems. . . . Technology builds but it may also destroy. The belief and faith that civilization, won at such great cost in pain and labor, simply cannot go down in destruction because such an end would be too monstrous and senseless, is but a naive and anthropocentric whimper. The cosmos does little know nor will it long remember what man has done here on this tiny planet. The eventual extinction of the human race—for come it will sometime—will not be the first time that a species has died out. Nor will it be an event of very great terrestrial significance.

Ambiguities and Contradictions in White's Thought

There are certain aspects of White's thought that appear to move away from, if not abandon, the base/superstructure dynamic fundamental to Marxism. These aspects seem to indirectly embrace a type of functional evolutionism reminiscent of the thought of Boas, Durkheim, Radcliffe-Brown, and Benedict.

White's theory of evolution views culture as always progressive and, indeed, as having a life of its own that is preserved and transmitted through symbols. In addition, White theorizes that culture molds the individual and the individual's ideas and beliefs, and not vice versa.

> Everyone—every individual, every generation, every group—has since the very earliest period of human history, been born into a culture, a civilization, of some sort.... No people makes its own culture; it inherits it ready-made from its ancestors or borrows it from its neighbors. It is easy enough for man to believe that he has made his culture, each generation contributing its share, and that it is he who controls and directs its course through the ages. Does he not chip the arrowheads and stone-axes, build carts and dynamos, coin money and spend it, elect presidents and depose kings, compose symphonies and carve statues, worship gods and wage war? But one cannot always rely upon the obvious. It was once obvious that the earth remained stationary while the sun moved; anyone could see that for himself. We are now approaching a point in modern thought where we are beginning to suspect that it is not man who controls culture but the other way around.[19]

This, the culturological aspect of evolutionary theory, is explained by White as follows: because culture is "the distinctive feature of man... the scientific study of this feature should be called *culturology* rather than *sociology*."[20] This particular aspect of White's culture study is treated in some scholarly circles as different from, if not incompatible with, his utilitarian view on culture, which in turn is tied to the primacy of technology as the driving force of all cultural formations. Ironically, the culturological aspects of White's theory have been interpreted as largely consistent with Boasian anthropology because the culturological approach appears to reject an understanding of culture in terms of the environment. Instead, culture is to be treated as *sui generis*.

Of course, Boas and his followers (*e.g.*, Kroeber) rejected any approach that reduced culture to the level of the individual. As discussed in Chapter 3, the Boasian argument was that it is not the individual who creates culture but culture that creates the individual. White seemingly embraced this antireductionist and deterministic view of culture, as seen in the following quotations from *The Science of Culture.*

---

19. White, The Science of Culture, *supra* note 3, at 337.

20. *Id.* at 116.

> If, then, we cannot explain cultures in terms of race or physical type, or in terms of psychological processes, and if appeal to environment is equally futile, how *are* they to be accounted for and made intelligible to us?
>
> There seems to be only one answer left and that is fairly plain—after one becomes used to it, at least. Cultures must be explained in terms of culture. As we have already noted, culture is a continuum. Each trait or organization of traits, each stage of development, grows out of an earlier cultural situation.... What a man thinks, feels, and does is determined by his culture. And culture behaves in accordance with its own laws.[21]

Indeed, Richard Barrett argues that—as between the culturological versus the materialist/utilitarian approach—White gave preference to his culturological approach by insisting that "[c]ultures must be explained in terms of culture."[22]

> In the foregoing, a significant trend can be discerned in White's scholarship: the tendency to modify positions adopted in his evolutionism to make them more compatible with his cultural determinism. It was noted earlier that when White developed his evolutionary and materialist perspective, he did not then revise positions that he had adopted earlier even though they appeared to contradict his materialism.... We can now understand why this was so: the trend in his thought was just the opposite. On the rare occasions when White perceived a conflict between his materialist-evolutionary theory and his culturology, it was the culturology that prevailed.[23]

Barrett (with the apparent agreement of Elvin Hatch)[24] further argues that by 1975, White realized the incompatibility between his culturological and utilitarian/materialistic approaches and renounced the latter. In 1975, White wrote:

> At this point I must reverse a position that I have held for years. In *The Evolution of Culture* (1959) I wrote: "The purpose and function of culture are to make life secure and enduring for the human species."
>
> [I] no longer think of culture as designed to serve the needs of man; culture goes its own way in accordance with laws of its own. Man lives within the embrace of cultural systems, and enjoys or suffers whatever they mete out to him.[25]

There has been speculation that with such declarations, White (together with his contemporaries Julian Steward and Betty Meggars) deliberately concealed their Marx-

21. White, The Science of Culture, *supra* note 3, at 339, 344.

22. *Id.* at 339.

23. Richard Barrett, *The Paradoxical Anthropology of Leslie White*, 91 Am. Anthropol. 986, 993 (1989).

24. Elvin Hatch, *Leslie White's Materialism: A Comment on Barrett*, 92 Am. Anthropol. 1018 (1990).

25. Leslie White, The Concept of Cultural Systems 9, 159 (1975); *but see* Patrick J. Crowe, *The Unity of White's Anthropological Theory: A Response to Barrett*, 92 Am. Anthropol. 1018 (1990) (arguing that there is no conflict between White's materialism and his culturology).

ist leanings due to the political tensions of McCarthyism (1950–1956) and the Second Red Scare (1947–1950s) when they were writing.[26]

Given the rather strong evidence that White renounced materialism,[27] the culturological aspects of his determinism invite comparisons with Durkheim, Kroeber, Radcliffe-Brown, and Benedict, all decidedly non-Marxist scholars.[28]

White's determinism insists that it is at this level of society at large that, according to him, such cultural molding is manifested. Individual behavior, by contrast, may depend on one's biological makeup; one individual may respond to cultural stimuli in a different way from another individual. Nonetheless, culture as the more powerful force generally overrides the biological factor. White, like Benedict, emphasizes the importance of culture in behavior, but unlike her does not ignore humanity's biological nature.

Durkheim's desire to avoid reductionism compelled him to reject any examination of the utility of social institutions, whereas Radcliffe-Brown's functionalism compelled him to treat as valuable only those institutions that had a functional value in the maintenance of social cohesion. He treated as irrelevant Durkheim's notion of the autonomy of the collective consciousness. White, however, is firmly in the Durkheimian camp in terms of his notion of the autonomy of culture and its pervasive influence on behavior, beliefs, and sentiments.[29] He is also in agreement with Durkheim on the significance of symbol and ritual. To White, culture is transmitted through symbols, and symbolic rituals reinforce common sentiments and normative order. However, the social function of symbol and symbolic ritual is outside the conscious awareness of the individual himself.[30]

Radcliffe-Brown's functionalism signals, paradoxically, a parallel to White's early utilitarianism, because a utilitarian view of culture must take into account the interrelatedness of social institutions. It has been said that White's thought also incorporates an "integrational form of functionalism."[31] As seen above, Benedict was the chief proponent of the theory of normative integration or configurationalism[32] (if culture is seen as a mosaic of configurations making up the whole, then these configurations must be seen as functionally interdependent). White's theory of increasing cultural integration coupled with technological advances similarly shows

---

26. David H. Price & William J. Peace, *Un-American Anthropological Thought: The Opler-Meggers Exchange*, 59 J. ANTHROPOL. RES. 183, 183–85 (2003).

27. See text at notes 19–25, *supra*.

28. *See generally* Chapters 2 and 3.

29. John W. Copeland, *Culture and Man: Leslie A. White's Thesis Re-Examined*, 19. S.J. ANTHROPOL. 109, 110 (1963) (suggesting the parallel with Durkheim but also arguing that White is being unduly dogmatic in clinging to the view that culture controls the individual and not the other way round).

30. WHITE, THE EVOLUTION OF CULTURE, *supra* note 1, at 157.

31. HATCH, *supra* note 13, at 145.

32. *See* Chapter 2 text at notes 149–208.

that human institutions must have some interrelated functions if they are to result, eventually, in progress.

Insofar as progress is natural, indeed inevitable, there are parallels in White's thought with that of the early classical evolutionists. White found it "incredible" that anthropologists of the twentieth century had ignored the "simple, sound and illuminating" theories of Tylor, Morgan, and Spencer.[33]

Unlike Julian Steward,[34] White does not consider the environment to have a notable impact on cultural evolution.

> We may ... dispose of the environmental factor now, once and for all, so far as evolutionist theory is concerned ... every culture is of course affected by environmental factors. But the relationship between culture and environment is not a one-to-one correlation by any means. Environment does not "determine" culture in the sense that "given the environment, we can predict the culture." Environments vary, and their influence and effect upon cultures vary likewise ... if one is concerned with culture as a distinct class of phenomena, if one wishes to discover how cultural systems are structured and how they function as cultural systems, then one does not need to consider the natural habitat at all.[35]

More specifically, in *The Science of Culture*, White supports his assertion that the environment does not affect culture.

> We may say that culture as a whole serves the need of man as a species. But this does not and cannot help us at all when we try to account for the variations of specific cultures.... The functioning of any particular culture will of course be conditioned by local environmental conditions. But in a consideration of culture as a whole, we may average all environments together to form a constant factor which may be excluded from our formulation of cultural development.[36]

Julian Steward: Cultural Ecology and Multilinear Evolution

Introduction and Critique of Unilinear Evolutionism

If White tried to reclaim the high ground of classical evolutionism, his contemporary Steward explicitly rejected a major tenet of nineteenth-century evolutionism: the principle of unilinear evolution. But Steward also rejected the particularism of the antievolutionists, including that of the Boasian school, although as a student of

33. *See* text at notes 1–2, *supra*.

34. See next section, "Julian Steward: Cultural Ecology and Multilinear Evolution."

35. White, The Evolution of Culture, *supra* note 1, at 50–51.

36. White, The Science of Culture, *supra* note 3, at 338–39.

Kroeber he embraced a form of normative integrationalism similar to that of Kroeber and Benedict. This similarity is discussed below, including Steward's appropriation of Kroeber's term "super-organic." Indeed, Hatch has argued that the materialist aspects of the thought of White and Steward is "the natural offspring" of Boasian thought.[37]

Steward's theory can be seen as an attempt to bridge the gap between the classical evolutionists (including White's unique brand of evolutionism) and the cultural relativism of the Boasian tradition. While acknowledging that White had moved beyond nineteenth-century evolutionism, Steward criticized White's model as so general that it robbed evolutionism of all its force and appeal. By this logic, if the sequences of normative patterns (referred to by Steward as "regularities") are compared to identify only their common denominators, then all differences and variations in evolutionary cycles are sidelined at best or ignored at worst.

> The present need is not to achieve a world scheme of culture development or a set of universally valid laws, though no doubt many such laws can even now be postulated, but to establish a genuine interest in the scientific objective and a clear conceptualization of what is meant by regularities. It does not matter whether the formulations are sequential (diachronic) or functional (synchronic), on a large scale or a small scale. It is more important that comparative cultural studies should interest themselves in recurrent phenomena as well as in unique phenomena, and that anthropology explicitly recognize that a legitimate and ultimate objective is to see through the differences of cultures to the similarities, to ascertain processes that are duplicated independently in cultural sequences, and to recognize cause and effect in both temporal and functional relationships. Such scientific endeavor need not be ridden by the requirement that cultural laws or regularities be formulated in terms comparable to those of the biological or physical sciences, that they be absolutes and universals, or that they provide ultimate explanations. Any formulations of cultural data are valid provided the procedure is empirical, hypotheses arising from interpretations of fact and being revised as new facts become available.[38]

This sidelining, according to Steward, was the main defect of the universalist and unilinear approach of the classical evolutionists: "Their principal undoing was, of course, the notion that progress (*i.e.*, toward the goal of European civilization) was the guiding principle in human development."[39] According to Steward, Tylor's unilinear theories failed because "[t]he inadequacy of unilinear evolution lies largely in the postulated priority of patriarchal matters over the other kinship patterns and in the indiscriminate effort to force the data of all precivilized groups of mankind,

---

37. Elvin Hatch, *The Growth of Economic, Subsistence and Ecological Studies in American Anthropology*, 29 J. Anthropol. Research 221, 231–32 (1973).

38. Julian Steward, Theory of Culture Change: The Methodology of Multilinear Evolution 180 (1953).

39. Julian Steward, Evolution and Ecology 59 (1977).

which included most of the primitive world, into the categories of 'savagery' and 'barbarism.'"[40] Steward found that White's theory of universal evolution was very similar to "the heritage of nineteenth-century unilinear evolution . . . in the scope of its generalizations but not in its treatment of particulars."[41] Steward asserted that twentieth-century ethnographic research had amassed overwhelming evidence to support the conclusion that particular cultures diverge significantly from each other and do not pass through unilinear phases.

Multilinear Evolution

Steward proposed a multilinear approach that would take into account not only the similarities and variations but also the importance of cultural individuality.

> Multilinear evolution is essentially a methodology based on the assumption that significant regularities in cultural change occur, and it is concerned with the determination of cultural laws. Its method is empirical rather than deductive. It is inevitably concerned also with historical reconstruction, but it does not expect that historical data can be classified in universal stages. It is interested in particular cultures, but instead of finding local variations and diversity troublesome facts which force the frame of reference from the particular to the general, it deals only with those limited parallels of form, function, and sequence which have empirical validity. What is lost in universality will be gained in concreteness and specificity. . . . It recognizes that the cultural traditions of different areas may be wholly or partly distinctive, and it simply poses the question of whether any genuine or meaningful similarities between certain cultures exist and whether these lend themselves to formulation.[42]

Steward thus set out to investigate the interrelationships of particular social phenomena that recur cross-culturally but are not necessarily universal.[43] In doing so, he encouraged the study of even remote cultural and normative connections in similar environments, no matter how tentative the resulting conclusions.

> Unless anthropology is to interest itself mainly in the unique, exotic, and non-recurrrent particulars, it is necessary that formulations be attempted no matter how tentative they may be. It is formulations that will enable us to state new kinds of problems and to direct attention to new kinds of data

40. Steward, Theory of Culture Change, *supra* note 38, at 15. *See also* Samuel Gerald Collins, *Scientifically Valid and Artistically True: Chad Oliver, Anthropology, and Anthropological SF*, 31 Sci. Fict. Stud. 243, 245–46 (2004) (tying Steward's rejection of "unilinear" evolution to the notion that unilinear evolution wrongly posited Western culture as the "apogee of cultural advancement" vis-a-vis a "savage lot" of non-Western cultures).

41. Steward, Theory of Culture Change, *supra* note 38, at 16.

42. *Id.* at 18–19.

43. *Id.* at 29.

> which have been slighted in the past. Fact-collecting of itself is insufficient scientific procedure; facts exist only as they are related to theories, and theories are not destroyed by facts—they are replaced by new theories which better explain the facts.[44]

The methodology of cultural ecology (discussed in the following passage) provided Steward with both the analytical framework and the empirical basis for his theory of multilinear evolution.

> The methodology of evolution contains two vitally important assumptions. First, it postulates that genuine parallels of form and function develop in historically independent sequences or cultural traditions. Second, it explains these parallels by the independent operation of identical causality in each case. The methodology is therefore avowedly scientific. . . . It endeavors to determine recurrent patterns and processes and to formulate the interrelationships between phenomena in terms of "laws."[45]

In simple terms, Steward claims in the foregoing passage that similar causal factors give rise to correspondingly similar social formations cross-culturally and that these can be formulated as laws.[46] His approach, which was extremely empirical, included the independent variables of economy and environment, with ideology (*inter alia*) as a dependent variable. Steward tested his hypothesis by examining cultures so widely separated that cultural parallels between them could only be explained in terms of his hypothesis.

He compared five disparate centers of ancient civilization: Mesopotamia, Egypt, China, Mesoamerica, and the Andes.[47] Because these were largely arid regions, he reasoned that their economies were only sustainable through irrigation and floodwater agriculture. As this technology increased food production and surpluses, it led to population growth and allowed lifestyles to exceed mere subsistence. Then, as agricultural productivity reached its limits, competition over natural resources grew, often leading to warfare. Militarism as well as empires thus grew, and corresponding political institutions emerged. This growth was accompanied by parallel integrating social and normative formations, including occupational specializations, religious institutions, and other political and legal institutions.[48]

Steward concluded that these largely dispersed regions of the world developed similar social and political formations entirely due to their common technoenvironmental factors (*i.e.*, the irrigation and floodwater agriculture that made them habitable). He declared that these evolutionary sequences were due neither to some supposed universal scheme of evolution nor to diffusion.

---

44. *Id.* at 209.

45. *Id.* at 14.

46. *Id.* at 181.

47. *Id.* at 178–209.

48. *Id.* at 208.

> How shall dense, stable populations organize their sociopolitical relations? Obviously, they will not remain inchoate mobs until diffused patterns have taught them how to live together. (And even diffused patterns had to originate somewhere for good and sufficient reasons.) In densely settled areas, internal needs will produce an orderly interrelationship of environment, subsistence patterns, social groupings, occupational specialization, and over-all political, religious, and perhaps military integrating factors. These interrelated institutions do not have unlimited variability, for they must be adapted to the requirements of subsistence patterns established in particular environments; they involve a cultural ecology. Traits whose uniqueness is proof of their diffusion are acceptable if they are congruent with the basic socio-economic institutions. They give uniqueness and local color, and they may help crystallize local patterns in distinctive ways, but they cannot per se produce the underlying conditions of, or the need for, greater social and political organization. It is therefore possible to concede wide diffusion of particulars within the hemispheres and even between the hemispheres without having to rely upon diffusion as the principal explanation of cultural development.[49]

Methodology of Cultural Ecology

> Steward proposed a methodology he called cultural ecology, which he defined as the study of processes by which a society adapts to its environment. Its principal problem is to determine whether these adaptations initiate internal social transformations of evolutionary change. It analyzes these adaptations, however, in conjunction with other processes of change. Its method requires examination of the interaction of societies and social institutions with one another and with the natural environment.[50]

It is distinct from biological, human, and social ecology: "The principal meaning of ecology is 'adaptation to environment. . . .'";[51] "Man enters the ecological scene . . . not merely as another organism which is related to other organisms in terms of his physical characteristics. He introduces the super-organic factor of culture."[52] (Kroeber had been the first to use the term "super-organic," which was controversial at the time, to describe culture.[53]) Steward's proposed method was designed to supplement the traditional historical approach of anthropology to allow discovery of the creative processes at work in the adaptation of a culture to its environment. This adaptation, of course, took place through technological advances. Yet, Steward also

49. *Id.* at 208–09.

50. Steward, Evolution and Ecology, *supra* note 39, at 43.

51. Steward, Theory of Culture Change, *supra* note 38, at 30.

52. *Id.* at 31.

53. *See* Chapter 2 text at notes 67–85.

realized that not all technologies are used in the same manner in every society; nor do all societies that have the same technology exhibit the same sociocultural forms. Therefore, to the extent that their environments differ, cultural adaptations and social arrangements will vary in different social groupings.[54]

> All men, it is true, have the biological basis for making rational solutions, and specific features of culture may develop from the application of reason. But since circumstances differ (e.g., in the conditions for hunting), solutions take many forms. Moreover, much culture develops gradually and imperceptibly without deliberate thought.[55]

Steward declared that "the environment is not only permissive or prohibitive with respect to these technologies, but special local features may require social adaptations which have far-reaching consequences."[56] In other words, the forms of technology that do emerge enable humans to exert control over their environment. The more technologically advanced the society, the greater its freedom from environmental limitations and the wider the range of latitude in its sociocultural forms. He also thought the ecological approach to be "less applicable to complex societies than to primitive ones, because a society with a sophisticated technology enjoys greater freedom from environmental limitations and hence a wider range of latitude,"[57] which for him meant that such societies are able to achieve a higher level of normative integration.

Steward believed that similar environmental conditions are likely to spawn similar patterns of normative organization. For example, if animal hunting is the means of subsistence, the presence of large game herds in particular areas will result in the emergence of cooperative hunting by larger population groups because that method would be advantageous within the prevailing hunting conditions.[58] But if the game in one area is nonmigratory and found only in small or scattered clusters, the best form of hunting there would be conducted by small and dispersed family groups of expert hunters.[59] Even if the same technology for hunting is used by groups in dissimilar areas, different material conditions of subsistence (*e.g.*, hunting) would require different forms of social organization.[60] Steward thus assigned a creative power to the environment by crediting it with selecting the most appropriate social forms from the

54. Steward, Theory of Culture Change, *supra* note 38, at 38–39.

55. Steward, Evolution and Ecology, *supra* note 39, at 62.

56. Steward, Theory of Culture Change, *supra* note 38, at 38.

57. Hatch, *supra* note 13, at 120; *see also* Steward, Theory of Culture Change, *supra* note 38, at 40.

58. Steward gave as examples of societies organized for cooperative hunting the Athabaskans and Algonkians of Canada. These groups were organized as multifamily or multilineage groups. Steward, Theory of Culture Change, *supra* note 38, at 38.

59. The small group hunters were the Bushmen and the Fuegians, made up of small localized patrilineal lineages or bands. *Id.*

60. Steward gives as examples the Eskimo and the Nevada Shoshoni. These two groups used similar technology in dissimilar environments. Yet neither of the two environments were conducive to cooperative hunting, leading to dispersed family groups in both cases. *Id.*

possible options. He also thought that the environment has a limiting force insofar as it excludes or modifies certain social forms.

Thus in two hunting communities, one with large herds of bison or caribou and the second with a smaller-species, nonmigratory game population, Steward thought that despite similarities between their cultural repertories of hunting devices, the large-scale cooperative hunting of the former would lead to multifamily or multilineage social formations, whereas the small group of expert hunters in the latter would result in localized patrilineal lineages. He refers to the multilineage social formations of the Athabaskans and Algonkians of Canada as examples of the cooperative hunting community in the first scenario and the small localized bands among the Bushmen, Australians, Congo Negritoes, Tasmanians, and Fuegians as examples of the community of expert hunters in the second scenario. Steward is keen to point out that the localized bands of the second scenario are similar not because their total environments are the same—indeed, the Bushmen and Australians live in deserts whereas the Congolese Negritoes live in rainforests—but "because the nature of the game and therefore of their subsistence problem is the same in each case."[61]

Steward found another demonstration of the environment's creative power over sociocultural formations in the differing environments of subsistence among the Eskimo and the Shoshoni of Nevada. According to his analysis, the Eskimo were dispersed into small family groups due to the effect of the scarcity of fish and sea mammals upon their quest for subsistence, which had resulted in a sparse population unconducive to cooperative hunting. He noted that the Alacaluf Indians of the Chilean archipelago, who were in a similar predicament due to the erratic occurrence of shellfish (their principal food) had also dispersed into nomadic food-collecting families.[62] But he thought that the Shoshoni Indians of Nevada were dispersed into independent family groups for different reasons: the scarcity of game and the predominance of seeds as their basis of subsistence. As discussed in the case study below, subsistence in this particular environment was also unconducive to cooperative economic activity.[63]

Noting that the ecological conditions of subsistence (including natural resources) among the ten communities he studied varied from migratory to nonmigratory, abundant to scarce, and aquatic-based to agrarian-based, Steward reasoned that even if their technology of subsistence was roughly the same, these societies exhibited different normative patterns that were commensurate with their own particular ecological environments. Thus he concluded that cultural ecology demands not the study of "the web of life for its own sake" but also the isolation of the relevant environmental factors that condition cultural and normative adaptations and considered the material means of subsistence to be the key environmental factor. It is the first of his three fundamental procedures of cultural ecology and clearly drives the other two.

---

61. *Id.* at 38.

62. Steward, Evolution and Ecology, *supra* note 39, at 54.

63. Steward, Theory of Culture Change, *supra* note 38, at 38–39.

> First, the interrelationship of exploitative or productive technology and environment must be analyzed. This technology includes a considerable part of what is often called "material culture." . . . Second, the behavior patterns involved in the exploitation of a particular area by means of a particular technology must be analyzed. . . . The third procedure is to ascertain the extent to which the behavior patterns entailed in exploiting the environment affect other aspects of culture.[64]

Steward's concept and method of cultural ecology are more fully set forth below.

Julian H. Steward, Theory of Culture Change 30, 36–42 (1963).

The principal meaning of ecology is "adaptation to environment." . . .

It differs from the relativistic and neo-evolutionist conceptions of culture history in that it introduces the local environment as the extracultural factor in the fruitless assumption that culture comes from culture. Thus cultural ecology presents both a problem and a method. The problem is to ascertain whether the adjustment of human societies to their environments require particular modes of behavior or whether they permit latitude for a certain range of possible behavior patterns. . . .

The problem of cultural ecology must be further qualified, however, through use of a supplementary conception of culture. According to the holistic view, all aspects of culture are functionally interdependent upon one another. The degree and kind of interdependency, however, are not the same with all features. Elsewhere, I have offered the concept of *cultural core*—the constellation of features which are most closely related to subsistence activities and economic arrangements. The core includes such social, political, and religious patterns as are empirically determined to be closely connected with these arrangements. Innumerable other features may have great potential variability because they are less strongly tied to the core. These latter, or secondary features, are determined to a greater extent by purely cultural-historical factors—by random innovations or by diffusion—and they give the appearance of outward distinctiveness to cultures with similar cores. Cultural ecology pays primary attention to those features which empirical analysis shows to be most closely involved in the utilization of environment in culturally prescribed ways. . . .

Whether or not new technologies are valuable is, however, a function of the society's cultural level as well as of environmental potentials. All pre-agricultural societies found hunting and gathering techniques useful. Within the geographical limits of herding and farming, these techniques were adopted. More advanced techniques, such as metallurgy, were acceptable

---

64. *Id.* at 40–41.

only if certain pre-conditions, such as stable population, leisure time, and internal specialization were present. These conditions could develop only from the cultural ecological adaptations of an agricultural society.

The concept of cultural ecology, however, is less concerned with the origin and diffusion of technologies than with the fact that they may be used differently and entail different social arrangements in each environment. The environment is not only permissive or prohibitive with respect to these technologies, but special local features may require social adaptations which have far-reaching consequences. Thus, societies equipped with bows, spears, surrounds, chutes, brushburning, deadfalls, pitfalls, and other hunting devices may differ among themselves because of the nature of the terrain and fauna. If the principal game exists in large herds, such as herds of bison or caribou, there is advantage in co-operative hunting, and considerable numbers of peoples may remain together throughout the year . . .

The adaptative processes we have described are properly designated ecological. But attention is directed not simply to the human community as part of the total web of life but to such cultural features as are affected by the adaptations. This in turn requires that primary attention be paid only to relevant environmental features rather than to the web of life for its own sake. Only those features to which the local culture ascribes importance need be considered. . . .

The Method of Cultural Ecology

. . . Three fundamental procedures of cultural ecology are as follows:

First, the interrelationship of exploitative or productive technology and environment must be analyzed. This technology includes a considerable part of what is often called "material culture," but all features may not be of equal importance. In primitive societies, subsistence devices are basic: weapons and instruments for hunting and fishing; containers for gathering and storing food; transportational devices used on land and water; sources of water and fuel; and, in some environments, means of counteracting excessive cold (clothing and housing) or heat. In more developed societies, agriculture and herding techniques and manufacturing of crucial implements must be considered. In an industrial world, capital and credit arrangements, trade systems and the like are crucial. . . .

Second, the behavior patterns involved in the exploitation of a particular area by means of a particular technology must be analyzed. Some subsistence patterns impose very narrow limits on the general mode of life of the people, while others allow considerable latitude. . . .

The use of these more complex and frequently co-operative techniques, however, depends not only upon cultural history—i.e., invention and diffusion—which makes the methods available but upon the environment and its flora and fauna. . . .

The exploitative patterns not only depend upon the habits concerned in the direct production of food and of goods but upon facilities for transporting the people to the source of supply or the goods to the people. Watercraft have been a major factor in permitting the growth of settlements beyond what would have been possible for a foot people. Among all nomads, the horse has had an almost revolutionary effect in promoting the growth of large bands.

The third procedure is to ascertain the extent to which the behavior patterns entailed in exploiting the environment affect other aspects of culture. Although technology and environment prescribe that certain things must be done in certain ways if they are to be done at all, the extent to which these activities are functionally tied to other aspects of culture is a purely empirical problem....

The third procedure requires a genuinely holistic approach, for if such factors as demography, settlement pattern, kinship structures, land tenure, land use, and other key cultural features are considered separately, their interrelationships to one another and to the environment cannot be grasped. Land use by means of a given technology permits a certain population density. The clustering of this population will depend partly upon where resources occur and upon transportational devices. The composition of these clusters will be a function of their size, of the nature of subsistence activities, and of cultural-historical factors. The ownership of land or resources will reflect subsistence activities on the one hand and the composition of the group on the other....

The Methodological Place of Cultural Ecology

Cultural ecology has been described as a methodological tool for ascertaining how the adaptation of a culture to its environment may entail certain changes. In a larger sense, the problem is to determine whether similar adjustments occur in similar environments. Since in any given environment, culture may develop through a succession of very unlike periods, it is sometimes pointed out that environment, the constant, obviously has no relationship to cultural type. This difficulty disappears, however, if the level of sociocultural integration represented by each period is taken into account. Cultural types therefore, must be conceived as constellations of core features which arise out of environmental adaptations and which represent similar levels of integration.

Cultural diffusion, of course, always operates, but in view of the seeming importance of ecological adaptations its role in explaining culture has been greatly overestimated. The extent to which the large variety of world cultures can be systematized in categories of types and explained through cross-cultural regularities of developmental process is purely an empirical matter. Hunches arising out of comparative studies suggest that there are many regularities which can be formulated in terms of similar levels and similar adaptations.

Primacy of Ecological Base

Steward rejects relativistic and neo-evolutionist conceptions of culture, particularly the opinion (most recently associated with Leslie White) that "cultures must be explained in terms of culture."[65] Instead he identified an extracultural factor, the local ecological environment, as the driving force of cultural formations.

The main points of the foregoing excerpt are summarized as follows. First, cultural ecology is the study of the processes through which a society adapts itself to its environment. Second, cultural ecology thus presents the problem to be investigated as well as the method of investigation. The problem is to examine whether social and normative adaptations to local environments require particular modes of behavior or whether they allow leeway for a certain range of possible patterns of behavior. In other words, the problem is to investigate how such adaptations cause internal social transformations and evolutionary change.

As to the third, the method of investigation, Steward proposes a three-pronged methodology. The first step is analysis of the relationship between the local ecological environment and an exploitive or productive technology. The second step is analysis of the behavior patterns for the exploration of a particular resource by a particular technology. The final step is the ascertainment of the extent to which the behavior patterns for exploiting the environment affect other aspects of culture.

In Marxist terminology, this methodology gives primacy to the material base, with the second and third levels of inquiry being concerned largely with superstructure, which Steward refers to as the "web of life."[66] However, like White, Steward did not specifically embrace Marx's methodology of historical materialism. Given that both were writing during the politically charged McCarthy era, there is scholarly speculation that White and Steward concealed their Marxist leanings and were careful not to be associated with the Left.[67] Indeed, Steward expressly acknowledged this danger in a letter to Marvin Harris.[68]

David Price and William Peace, who classify the writings of White and Steward as examples of "crypto-Marxist anthropology," state that "Steward claimed a much stronger influence by Marx than was apparent in any of his writings."[69] Lending credence to these claims, Steward himself emphasizes that in studying adaptative

---

65. *See* text at note 22, *supra*.

66. Steward, Theory of Culture Change, *supra* note 38, at 39.

67. Ian McKay, *Historians, Anthropology, and the Concept of Culture*, 8/9 Labour/Le Travail 185, 191 (1981–1982) (stating that the historical tensions of the period created an "uncongenial climate" for materialist studies).

68. Price & Peace, *supra* note 26, at 183–85 (quoting Letter from Julian Steward to Marvin Harris, March 8, 1969).

69. *Id.* at 185.

processes, primary attention must be paid "only" to the environmental factors rather than the web-of-life factors:

> The adaptative processes we have described are properly designated ecological. But attention is directed not simply to the human community as part of the total web of life but to such cultural features as are affected by the adaptations. This in turn requires that primary attention be paid only to relevant environmental features rather than to the web of life for its own sake.[70]

The primacy of the environmental base is well illustrated by Steward's study of the Shoshoni. As described in the foregoing excerpt, their sparse natural resources were thought by Steward to be unconducive to the emergence of large social groupings, and their society was dispersed into small nomadic families as a result. But he also observed polygyny and polyandry, two other cultural features that he considered to be directly tied to the material/ecological environment of Shoshonean society. Steward asserts that the dire conditions of subsistence and the perpetual quest for food made husband and wife of equal importance; thus spouses had equal status. Steward noted the difference between the Shoshoni and other societies where plural marriage was practiced, in which only males were allowed to have more than one spouse. His conclusion was that the gender equality encouraged by Shoshonean economic exigencies made it possible for them to practice both polygyny and polyandry.[71]

Steward interpreted the complex system of property rights associated with the modes of subsistence of Shoshonean culture, which is described in detail below,[72] as another indicator of ecological primacy. When evaluating this perspective, it must be kept in mind that certain forms of land ownership were impossible among the Shoshoni due to the Basin-plateau ecology.[73] Overall, Steward gives clear primacy to the ecoenvironmental base in culture formations but also distinguishes "secondary," "variable" features that are not strongly tied to the core. He considered that these "are determined to a greater extent by purely cultural-historical factors—by random innovations or by diffusion. . . ."[74]

Cultural Core, Cultural Type, and Integrationalism

Steward accepts the holistic conception of culture under which all aspects of culture are functionally interdependent. This conception, which is very much in the tradition of cultural integrationalism as championed by Kroeber, Benedict, and other adherents of Boasian particularism, is opposed to the "shreds and patches" image of culture.[75] However, Steward points out that the degree and kind of interdepen-

---

70. STEWARD, THEORY OF CULTURE CHANGE, *supra* note 38, at 39.

71. Julian Steward, *Shoshoni Polyandry*, 38 AM. ANTHROPOL. 561 (1936).

72. *See infra* section labeled "Cultural Ecology and Law: A Case Study."

73. HATCH, *supra* note 13, at 120.

74. STEWARD, THEORY OF CULTURE CHANGE, *supra* note 38, at 37.

75. HATCH, *supra* note 13, at 121.

dency is not the same for all cultural components. In this sense, Steward's holism deliberately accommodates the idea of cultural variability. Only those components that lie at the cultural core are the focus of his methodological approach. As to the question of what is found at the core of a culture, Steward proposed only those social and normative formations that are directly connected to subsistence activities.[76] This reply would seem to flow logically from the primacy of the material base, but for Steward the core also includes such superstructural features as social, political, legal, and religious patterns that are "empirically determined to be closely connected with these subsistence arrangements."[77] Under this approach, law and the legal system of a culture falls within the cultural core as demonstrated by Steward's study of the Shoshonean Indians, discussed below.[78]

According to Steward, just as the kind and degree of normative integration and interdependency are not the same for all cultural components, so they are not similarly affected by ecological adaptations. For example, the political and legal systems may evolve, but the prevailing language will remain the same. Humanistic and stylistic cultural manifestations may retain their traditional forms but may acquire new functions; thereby societies change through a series of nonuniform structural and functional transformations.[79] These transformations are, in turn, driven by the material conditions of subsistence, more particularly by "cooperative productive activity."[80] These relations of production give rise to parallel social forms or cultural types, which can be at the level of a family, a clan of families, an entire kinship, or community-wide (later in his career, Steward added band, tribe, chiefdom, and state to this list).[81]

The emergence and evolution of cultural types, according to Steward, begins with the most rudimentary forms of subsistence, which lead to normative organization in the form of interpersonal or interfamilial arrangements. But where food sources are scarce, there is social segmentation (if not fragmentation) in the form of competitive nuclear family units—another cultural type. A third cultural type occurs when there is an abundance of game, which tends to foster cooperative hunting, socially cohesive patterns of behavior, and closely knit social groupings. A farming community, yet another cultural type, is likely to have a permanent community organization. Steward concluded that similar cultural types will show similar levels of integration. He also concluded that the greater the potential for increased productive capacity due to improved technology, the greater the likelihood of specialization and social stratification.[82] Steward's cultural ecology thus focuses on those societal features that

76. Steward, Theory of Culture Change, *supra* note 38, at 37.

77. *Id.*

78. *See* text at notes 90–95 *infra*.

79. Steward, Evolution and Ecology, *supra* note 39, at 50.

80. *Id.*

81. Merwyn S. Garbarino, Sociocultural Theory in Anthropology: A Short History 90 (1977).

82. Steward, Evolution and Ecology, *supra* note 39, at 51.

empirical analysis shows to be most closely connected to the use of the material environment in culturally prescribed ways.[83]

Steward reasoned that if cultural types are conceived as constellations of core features arising out of environmental adaptations and representing similar levels of integration, it follows that cultures with similar core features will be of the same cultural type. In other words:

> they show the same general responses to similar environments and are assumed to have the same structural functional interrelationships.[84]

He therefore suggests that sociocultural systems be compared in terms of levels of normative integration.[85] Steward proposed three levels of integration: family, multifamily, and state.[86] He placed the biological or nuclear family, the most basic level of integration, as historically antecedent to higher forms. Citing the simple society of the Western Shoshoni, Steward observes that almost all culturally significant features are integrated into and function at the family level. Children are reared in relative isolation, food is procured to satisfy family needs only, and all other activities and cultural routines take place within the basic family unit. But as productive processes become more complex (*e.g.*, through collective hunting, fishing, herding, or farming) the need for a suprafamily (or multifamily) organization arises with a set of normatively integrated economic, kinship, and property rules, and the nuclear family becomes integrated into the larger kinship structure. Integration at the state level, which unites the multifamily structure under a single overarching economic and political union, is accompanied by large-scale infrastructural projects such as roads, irrigation projects, and rules for business and laws to protect property. Eventually, complex new state institutions emerge to regulate all aspects of life.

Steward, however, wished to go beyond describing the family, the multifamily, and the state, which he referred to as mere "taxonomic concepts."[87] He wanted to emphasize that transformations occur at all three levels at different stages and through different processes, that they are functionally specialized and dependent upon the whole structure, and that they play a vital role in integrating various aspects of culture. Then, as a culture becomes more complex, new forms of integration emerge so that an advanced culture shows different forms of integration than a simple culture does.

This idea is not new; in fact, Steward laments its association with now-discredited schemes of evolution.[88] Thus it is not entirely surprising that, in a biological analogy, he states that higher forms of life have different organizing principles than lower ones and that this difference has nothing to do with the evolution of particular species.

---

83. Steward, Theory of Culture Change, *supra* note 38, at 37.

84. Garbarino, *supra* note 81, at 90.

85. Steward, Theory of Culture Change, *supra* note 38, at 47.

86. *Id.* at 54–55.

87. *Id.* at 55.

88. *See* Collin's reference to the perception created by unilineal evolutionists that non-Western societies are all lumped together as a "savage lot." Text of note 40, *supra*.

Similarly, the concept of cultural integration has nothing to do with evolution and does not purport to explain the developmental sequences of cultural types.

> The cultural evolution of Morgan, Tylor, and others is a developmental taxonomy based on concrete characteristics of cultures. The concept of levels of sociocultural integration, on the other hand, is simply a methodological tool for dealing with cultures of different degrees of complexity. It is not a conclusion about evolution.[89]

Steward designed his concept of integrationalism as a tool for cross-cultural comparison. As he mentions in the foregoing excerpt, comparative study of culture is rendered difficult because various cultures develop through a succession of very unlike periods. Furthermore, because the environment remains a constant through these changes, it is tempting to conclude that it has no relationship to culture type. But Steward points out that these difficulties disappear if one keeps in mind two key methodological approaches: first, conceiving culture types as constellations of core features of environmental adaptations; and second, considering the level of normative integration represented by each developmental period when comparing one culture type to another.

Steward used his concept of levels of integration as a typology for culture types, as shown by his survey of South American cultures in his book *Native Peoples of South America*, in which he presented a single continuum with irrigation societies at the top and hunter/gatherer societies at the bottom. Without claiming that his illustration is an evolutionary scheme, Steward uses it as a typological scheme to present a wide variety of cultures under a common framework.[90]

Cultural Ecology and Law: A Case Study

As seen above, the concept and method of cultural ecology seek to discover how the ecological environment of a society influences its culture forms. Its methodology was applied by Steward to study the Great Basin Shoshoni Indians. Some of their cultural processes as described by Steward, particularly their system of property rights, shed light on how an ecological approach may be applied to law. Steward's study of Shoshoni culture provides a textbook example of how sparse food resources are unconducive to cooperative relations of production and how the legal system of a society falls within its "cultural core."

The natural resources available to the Shoshoni for exploitation were extremely limited;[91] vast areas of terrain were virtually waterless. The tribes could thus only forage for vegetable foods, seeds, nuts, and small creatures such as rats, mice, go-

89. Steward, Theory of Culture Change, *supra* note 38, at 52.

90. Julian Steward & Louis Faron, Native Peoples of South America (1959); Hatch, *supra* note 13, at 118.

91. Steward, Theory of Culture Change, *supra* note 38, at 103.

phers, locusts, ants, and so on. Moreover, their food chain was highly unstable due to unpredictable rainfall.

But the absence of large cooperative groupings in Shoshonean society was not just due to the scarcity of their food resources. At the time they were observed by Steward, they also had not mastered the techniques of smoking and drying meat and fish for long-term storage. Thus such game as they were able to hunt (*e.g.*, rabbits, antelope, and fish) spoiled quickly. Had the Shoshoneans been able to preserve their meats, large-scale permanent populations might have emerged—particularly around lakes and streams abundant with fish. Under such circumstances, the primary goal of subsistence was to ward off starvation by constantly moving from one area to another. This could only be done in small groups comprising one or two related families.

One mode of sustenance was gathering and consuming pine nuts. Because the gathering process is necessarily prior to consumption, suitable areas had to be identified and assigned. Thus arose a customary rule whereby each family restricted itself by mutual agreement to a limited area. It was also commonly understood that each family stood to harvest more if it worked alone and without interference from another family. Whatever was harvested by each family was stored in earth caches and belonged to it alone.

> The concept of property rights among the Shoshoneans was directly related to this way of life. These Indians assumed that rights to exclusive use of anything resulted from work expended by particular individuals or groups and from habitual use. This is a rather obvious, simple, and practical concept, and it seems to have entailed a minimum of conflict.[92]

Because other natural resources were considered common property, any family could fish in rivers, lakes, and streams. In cases of potential conflict between families over access to and exploitation of natural resources, the applicable rule was based on the principle of "first come first served."[93] Thus when a family started to harvest seeds in a particular area, before any other family came along, they had priority in the right to gather seed. The same rule applied to hunting game.

> This principle of property rights was essential to survival in the Shoshonean area. Owing to the erratic annual and local occurrence of foods, the arbitrary exclusion of territorially delimited groups of families from utilization of other territories would have caused starvation and death. With few exceptions, the habitat of most families always provided such uncertain subsistence that the territorial interpenetration of families living in different localities was necessary to the survival of all. The absence of property claims of local groups to delimitable areas of natural resources upon which work had not been expended was the corollary of the fragmented nature of Shoshonean society.[94]

92. *Id.* at 107.

93. *Id.*

94. *Id.* at 108.

In the few areas where resources were comparatively abundant, families set up permanent villages from which they made daily trips to exploit the resources. Eventually, habitual use of these resources led to the rule that each local village or group of villages had exclusive rights to resources within bounded areas. According to Steward, "This economic stability and permanent residence of a particular group of families provided a basis for association, leadership, and organization in band groups."[95]

From Steward's ethnographic study of the Shoshoni we may conclude first that the normative relations of production and consumption are dictated by the material/ecological environment; second, that these productive relations determine the nature and complexity of social interactions as well as the nature and complexity of social groups and organization; and finally, that the legal system of rights and duties is triggered by the modes and means of production and therefore falls within the cultural core of society.

Conclusion

Steward's thought, like that of White, shows traces of determinism. The Boasian school also espoused determinism, but its particular form was cultural whereas Steward's is largely economic. Similarly, whereas Boas, Kroeber, and Benedict viewed the phenomenal world as the reflection of individual subjectivism, for Steward it was the other way around. One is reminded of Marx's reversal of the Hegelian dialectic, whereby the material world conditions individual thinking. As Marx described this relationship:

> In the social production which men carry on they enter into definite relations that are indispensable and independent of their will; these relations of production correspond to a definite stage of development of their material powers of production. The sum total of these relations of production constitutes the economic structure of society—the real foundation, on which rise legal and political superstructures and to which correspond definite forms of social consciousness. The mode of production in material life determines the general character of the social, political and spiritual processes of life. It is not the consciousness of men that determines their existence, but, on the contrary, their social existence determines their consciousness.[96]

Steward took the position that the objective world of productive relations and the material conditions of subsistence were responsible for individual thought. In this sense he would agree also with Durkheim that sociocultural phenomena occur outside of individual control. His studies of the Athabaskans, the Bushmen, the Eskimo, and the Shoshoni showed the importance of the objective conditions of subsistence. Nevertheless, like the Boasians, Steward did see culture as a normatively integrated whole and can be said to have adopted an integrational form of analysis, albeit within environmental limitations.

---

95. *Id.*

96. Karl Marx, Preface to The Critique of Political Economy 11–12 (I.N. Stone, trans. 1904).

Marvin Harris: Cultural Materialism

In the preface of his book *Cultural Materialism*, Marvin Harris declares this concept to be a "strategy" that is based on "the simple premise that human social life is a response to the practical problems of earthly existence."[97] He also makes the relatively modest claim that cultural materialism leads to a "better scientific" understanding of sociocultural phenomena, albeit not the whole truth about them. This approach contrasts with the broad claims of the Durkheimian school: Durkheim himself argued that his sociological method could establish scientific truths on par with those of natural science; Radcliffe-Brown claimed to have discovered universal "sociological laws" about human society; and White claimed to have discovered a law of cultural evolution based on a culture's ability to harness energy. By contrast, Harris expressly states that he is making no such claims; indeed, he refers to cultural materialism as a "strategy" rather than a "methodology" and is content to say that it is a "good bet," in the sense that it offers a better explanation than its rival theories, without calling for the abandonment of the latter.[98]

Influence of Marxism

The goal of cultural materialism is to understand the "causes of differences and similarities" among societies and cultures.[99] In this regard, this goal is similar to that of the evolutionists and the structuralists; the main difference is that whereas its rival theories acknowledge (in varying degrees) the importance of man's material conditions, Harris adopts materialism as his exclusive point of departure. In doing so he acknowledges that cultural materialism is founded on the teachings of Marx, with certain modifications.[100] These constitute, in the main, the rejection of the philosophical underpinnings of Marxism, particularly the Hegelian notion that history unfolds through a dialectical process of contradictory negations, similar to the Heraclitean notion of flux.[101]

Hegel maintained that the world in flux is perceived by the human mind. In other words, the mind "creates" the phenomenal world through its perceptions. As we have seen numerous times, Marx reversed the Hegelian premise and argued that it is the material reality of the phenomenal world that creates forms of consciousness. The question is one of matter over mind, not of mind over matter, hence the term "dialectical materialism."

97. Marvin Harris, Cultural Materialism: The Struggle for a Science of Culture ix (1979).

98. *Id.* at 57.

99. *Id.* at ix.

100. Marvin Harris, Theories of Culture in Postmodern Times 142 (1999).

101. *See* Isaak Dore, The Epistemological Foundations of Law 47, 65 (2007) (on the Heraclitean notion of flux).

Harris professes to reject dialectical materialism and proposes to "improve" Marx's methodology "by dropping the Hegelian notion that all systems evolve through a dialectic of contradictory negations" and adding "reproductive pressure and ecological variables" as the two primary material conditions that determine sociocultural phenomena.[102]

Harris expressly chose Marx's materialist approach because he was convinced of its explanatory power and because he believed Marx, whom he called the "Darwin of the social sciences," had made it possible to have a "science" of human society.[103] Harris quotes with approval Marx's proposition that the material means of subsistence determine state institutions (*e.g.*, law, art, and religion) and not vice versa.

> The "materialism" in "cultural materialism" is therefore intended as an acknowledgment of the debt owed to Marx's formulation of the determining influence of production and other material processes.[104]

In the end, Harris seems to reject only the Hegelian dialectic of progress through the negation of opposites. In place of Hegel, Harris substitutes the utilitarianism of the British empiricists, particularly David Hume, to the point of adopting Hume's opinion that knowledge of the material world ("matters of fact") can only be based on inferences drawn from observation of recurrent or conjoined events. Harris also explains that dropping the word "dialectical" does not mean that cultural materialism does not take into account such things as "continuities and harmonies," "function and dysfunction," and "adaptation and maladaptation"—concepts that would be at the very core of any dialectical approach. He further explains that cultural materialism rejects biological and racial explanations of cultural similarities and differences. In addition, he states that it transcends national boundaries and is therefore truly cross-cultural, creating a "pan-human" science of society based on empirically verifiable data.[105]

The Methodology of Cultural Materialism

Even if the goal of cultural materialism is to develop an empirical science of sociocultural phenomena, it faces a unique methodological challenge: the fact that the human "object" of study is also a "subject." One may contrast this with any endeavor in natural science, such as astronomy, in which the objects of study are stars and other celestial bodies, or atomic physics, in which the objects of study are atoms and subatomic particles. In neither of these fields are the objects of study thought to have developed thoughts and attitudes or the capacity to make judgments. In this lack of conscious thought lies the fundamental difference between the science of nature and the science of society.

---

102. Harris, Cultural Materialism, *supra* note 97, at ix.

103. *Id.* at x.

104. *Id.* at xi.

105. *Id.* at xii.

Cultural materialism's methodology must therefore distinguish between what people say, think, and do as objects of study and what they say and think as subjects.[106] The latter is a matter of the mind, the former of matter. Where Marx asserted the primacy of matter over mind, cultural materialism maintains that both mind and matter have reality, as well as that matter and ideas exist independently of each other. In other words, "thoughts about things and events are separable from things and events."[107] The epistemological project of cultural materialism, which is to gain scientific knowledge of both realms, proposes two distinctions for this purpose. The first is that between mental and behavioral events, and the second is the distinction between emic and etic events. These two distinctions are examined next.

A. The Mental and Behavioral Fields

According to Harris behavioral events are the totality of human bodily motions and their environmental effects, whereas the mental field is that of thought and feelings of humans. Each of these fields requires a distinct methodological approach. In order to understand bodily motions and their effects, one does not have to enter the mind of the individual. Similarly, to describe mental experiences one does not enter the behavioral field. Nonetheless, mental and behavioral events can both be studied from two different perspectives: the perspective(s) of the participant(s) and the perspective(s) of the observer(s).[108] Both perspectives can yield true or scientific accounts of mental and behavioral phenomena, although the methodological approach does vary with the participant–observer distinction. In anthropology, the participant is usually a native informant who is deferred to as the final judge of the accuracy of the information he or she relays. The native view is the emic view, or the view from within. As such it requires the ethnologist-observer to acquire intimate knowledge of native folkways (*i.e.*, of the various means, rules, and etiquettes of thinking and acting as a native).

The emic method is contrasted with the etic approach, in which the ethnographer-observer is the ultimate judge of the data gathered, including the various folkways and etiquettes of the culture under study. Here, the objective is again to generate scientifically testable theories about sociocultural and normative similarities and differences on a panhuman scale. However, in the interests of "science" and "objectivity," the observer may use measurements or examine juxtaposed activities in a way that may seem meaningless to the native informer. In other words, under the etic approach, the observer uses his own framework of discourse, which could include his own categories of time, numbers, place, weight measures, body motion, environmental effects, etc. When a native description is responsive to the observer's framework of discourse, that description is etic.[109]

---

106. *Id.* at 29.

107. *Id.* at 30.

108. *Id.* at 31.

109. *Id.* at 36.

In either case, for anthropologists, mental experience must be kept separate from behavioral events, and the yields of emic and etic methods must not be combined. Harris gives an example of a situation in which the emic and etic approaches to a single case led to contradictory results. The case involved the killing of domesticated bovines in the southern Indian state of Kerala. Every native farmer professed that he would never kill a cow because the species is regarded as sacred by Hindus. However, due to a scarcity of feed for cows and little need for traction animals in the state, farmers ended up simply starving male calves to death. Here an emic account was clearly incompatible with the etic conclusion that the economic conditions required the cattle sex ratios to be adjusted systematically to meet local economic needs.[110]

For our purposes, the important conclusion is that if ethnographers fail to distinguish between the mental and the behavioral and between the etic and the emic, they will fail to develop scientific theories explaining the causes of sociocultural and normative differences and similarities. At the same time, Harris cautions against embracing the etic to the total exclusion of the emic. Rather, the ethnographer must embrace both points of view and use each one judiciously, as called for.

According to Harris, there are four operational domains of sociocultural inquiry:

(1) Emic/behavioral
(2) Etic/behavioral
(3) Emic/mental
(4) Etic/mental

The relationship between emic and etic approaches is explained in the following excerpt.

Marvin Harris, Cultural Materialism: The Struggle for a Science of Culture 36, 38–39, 45 (1979).

Etics, Emics, and Informants

A common source of misunderstanding about the emic/etic distinction is the assumption that etic operations preclude collaboration with native informants. But as a matter of practical necessity, observers must frequently rely on native informants to obtain their basic information about who has done what. Recourse to informants for such purposes does not automatically settle the epistemological status of the resultant descriptions.

Depending on whose categories establish the framework of discourse, informants may provide either etic or emic descriptions of the events they have observed or participated in. When the description is responsive to the observer's categories of time, place, weights and measure, actor types, numbers of people present, body motion, and environmental effects, it is etic. Census taking provides the most familiar example. If one merely asks an in-

110. *Id.* at 32–33.

formant, "Who are the people who live in this house?" the answer will have emic status, since the informant will use the native concept of "lives here" to include and exclude persons present in or absent from the household....

Mental Etics and Behavioral Emics

IF THE TERMS "emic" and "etic" are not redundant with respect to the terms "mental" and "behavioral," there should be four objective operationally definable domains in the sociocultural field of inquiry:

	Emic	*Etic*
Behavioral	I	II
Mental	III	IV

To illustrate with the example of the sacred cow:

I *Emic/Behavioral*: "No calves are starved to death."
II *Etic/Behavioral*: "Male calves are starved to death."
III *Emic/Mental*: "All calves have the right to life."
IV *Etic/Mental*: "Let the male calves starve to death when feed is scarce."

The epistemological status of domains I and IV creates the thorniest problems. What is the locus of the reality of the emic behavioral statement, "No calves are starved to death"? Does this statement refer to something that is actually in the behavior stream, or is it merely a belief about the behavior stream that exists only inside of the heads of the Indian farmers? Similarly, what is the locus of the reality of the etic mental rule: "Let the male calves starve to death when feed is scarce"? Does this rule exist inside the heads of the farmers, or is it merely something that exists inside of the head of the observer?

Let me turn first to the problem of the status of emic behavioral descriptions. Descriptions of the behavior stream from the actor's point of view can seldom be dismissed as mere figments of the imagination and relegated to a purely mental domain. First of all, there are many instances where there is a very close correspondence between the actor's and observer's views of what is going on in the world. When Indian farmers discuss the steps they take to transplant rice or to get a reluctant cow to let down its milk, their emic descriptions of behavior stream events are as accurate as any ethnographer's etic description would be. Moreover, even when there are sharp divergences between them, the emic and etic viewpoints are not likely to cancel each other out entirely. Even in the present rather extreme example, note that the farmers do not see the culling of unwanted animals as "bovicide" and that the mode of achieving the death of unwanted animals is sufficiently ambiguous to warrant that interpretation. Clearly the amount of discrepancy between the emic and etic versions of events in the behavior stream is an important measure of the degree to which people are mystified about events taking place around them.

> Only if people were totally mystified could one claim that their behavioral descriptions referred exclusively to mental phenomena.
>
> The other thorny category, the etics of mental life (IV), has similar implications. People can be mystified about their own thoughts as well as about their behavior. Such mystifications may come about as the result of repressing certain thoughts to an unconscious or at least a nonsalient level of attention. In the example under consideration, the existence of the rule "when feed is scarce, let the male calves starve to death" can be inferred from the recurrently lopsided sex ratios. As I mentioned earlier, something very close to this rule can be elicited from some Kerala farmers when they are confronted with the question of why male calves eat less than female calves. Etic descriptions of mental life, in other words, can serve the function of helping to probe the minds of informants concerning less salient or unconscious beliefs and rules.
>
> The road to etic knowledge of mental life is full of pitfalls and impasses. Extreme caution is called for in making inferences about what is going on inside people's heads even when the thoughts are those of our closest friends and relatives....
>
> THE EMICS OF THE OBSERVER
>
> PARTISANS of idealist strategies seek to subvert the materialist efforts by claiming that "all knowledge is ultimately 'emic.'" ... The allegation is that in the name of demystifying the nature of social life, the observers merely substitute one brand of illusion for another. After all, who are the "observers"? Why should their categories and beliefs be more credible than those of the actors? The answer to these questions is entirely dependent on whether one accepts the scientific way of knowing as having some special advantages over other ways of knowing. To deny the validity of etic descriptions is in effect to deny the possibility of a social science capable of explaining sociocultural similarities and differences. To urge that the etics of scientific observers is merely one among an infinity of other emics—the emics of Americans and Chinese, of women and men, of blacks and Puerto Ricans, of Jews and Hindus, of rich and poor, and of young and old—is to urge the surrender of our intellects to the supreme mystification of total relativism.
>
> True, the practitioners of science do not constitute a community apart from the rest of humanity, and we are filled with prejudices, preconceptions, and hidden agendas. But the way to correct errors resulting from the value-laden nature of our activity is to demand that we struggle against our strategic competitors and critics of all sorts to improve our accounts of social life, to produce better theories, and to achieve higher, not lower, levels of objectivity with respect to both the emics and etics of mental and behavioral phenomena. Once again we must ask: "What is the alternative?"

The rhetorical question "What is the alternative?" at the end of the foregoing excerpt confirms the tentative and provisional nature of Harris's epistemology. Cultural materialism "struggles" to produce only "better" theories and "higher" levels of objectivity. That these goals are clearly limited shows the modesty of Harris's epistemological project. Although he claims that his approach is scientific, he does not press his claim to the point of infallibility. In contrast to Durkheim and Radcliffe-Brown, for example, he openly admits that rival methodologies may contribute to scientific accounts of sociocultural phenomena and rejects any *a priori* position that excludes divergent (if not rival) methodologies for the scientific study of culture.[111]

Nevertheless, Harris declares that the etic approach will ultimately save the day. In his example of "bovicide" in southern India, it is the etic approach that correctly exposes the unconscious beliefs of the native farmers. To deny the validity of the etic approach would result in the debacle of the "supreme mystification of total relativism."[112] The preponderance of the etic approach is also very much in evidence in the methodology of cultural materialism.

B. Basic Methodological Principles

Almost all of the major ethnologists we have seen discussed in previous chapters started with certain basic postulates about the human condition. Wissler, for example, identified basic normative characteristics of social organization without which society could not endure. He called this the "universal pattern" that subsumes components such as speech, material traits, social regulation, etc.[113] Malinowski's theory of needs identified certain essential biological and physiological needs of the individual around which "cultural imperatives" evolved.[114] Radcliffe-Brown identified certain "necessary conditions" that had to be satisfied for a society to endure.[115] Marx postulated man's material needs for subsistence as the *sine qua non* triggering relations of production, consumption, and social organization.[116]

Harris likewise proposes a "universal pattern" for sociocultural systems worldwide. As with Marx, he begins with the etic need of subsistence as the first *sine qua non* for society;[117] this need in turn triggers an etic behavioral mode of production. The second requirement is an etic behavioral mode of reproduction, which consists of methods and mechanisms for maintaining population size. These two requirements are collectively known as the infrastructure. The third requirement is the necessity of maintaining normative order, particularly in the economic sector, which consists of etic behavioral domestic and political economies. These maintain family structures, allocate the division of labor, and govern social discipline and political organization. The domestic and political economies together constitute the structure. Fourth and finally is the etic behavioral superstructure, which consists of recurrent and recreational, sportive, and aesthetic products and services.

---

111. *Id.* at x.

112. *See* second last paragraph of foregoing excerpt.

113. *See* Chapter 2, text at note 40–42.

114. *See* Chapter 3, text at notes 130–44.

115. *See* Chapter 3, text at notes 221–32.

116. *See* Chapter 4, text at notes 1–9, *supra*.

117. HARRIS, CULTURAL MATERIALISM, *supra* note 97, at 51.

In summary, the universal pattern shows that every society will have infrastructure, structure, and superstructure. In terms of economic activity, modes of subsistence (*i.e.*, the predominant practices of production such as factory production, industry, agriculture, etc.) are classified as infrastructure.[118] By contrast, what Marx calls the social relations of production (*i.e.*, relations governed by institutions of private property, communal property, wages, other forms of compensation, exchanges, etc.), belong to structure which is normative in nature. By this logic, industrial factories are an infrastructural feature, but the actual organization of the factory (*e.g.*, whether it is privately owned or publicly owned, run by elite managers or by workers' committees) is a structural feature.[119]

According to Harris, these etic behavioral components have corresponding emic mental components as well. They are:

Etic infrastructure: ethnobotany, magic, religion, and taboos
Etic structure: kinship, political ideology, magic, religion, and taboos
Etic superstructure: symbols, myths, philosophies, aesthetic standards, magic, religion, and taboos

The emic mental components are collectively placed under the rubric of mental and emic superstructure. Harris thus postulates four major universal characteristics of sociocultural systems, established through native accounts or etic observer accounts. These are:

(1) The etic behavioral infrastructure
(2) The structure
(3) The superstructure
(4) The mental and emic superstructure

Of these, (1) is key because it triggers all other social and normative formations. This primacy is declared expressly by Harris in accordance with Marx's thesis that the mode of production and the material conditions of life determine in general the nature of the social, political, spiritual and other normative processes of life.[120] Harris, however, proposes two refinements to Marx's notion of "the modes of production." The first is to include under this rubric the technology of subsistence (*i.e.*, food and other forms of energy), technoenvironmental relations, ecosystems, and work patterns. The second is the addition of a new category, modes of reproduction, under which is included the technology for expanding, limiting, and maintaining population size. This category also has normative implications in that it includes matters of demography, mating patterns, fertility, natality, mortality, nurture of children, medical control of demographic patterns, contraception, abortion, and infanticide.[121]

118. Harris, Theories of Culture in Postmodern Times, *supra* note 100, at 142.

119. *Id.*

120. Karl Marx, Selected Writings in Sociology and Social Philosophy 51 (T.B. Bottomore trans., T.B. Bottomore & Maximilien Rubel eds. 1956).

121. Harris, Cultural Materialism, *supra* note 97, at 52.

The inclusion of these matters is, however, more than a mere refinement to Marx's treatment of the modes of production: it represents a major philosophical departure from classical Marxism, which conceives of modes of production as evolving through the development of contradictions between the means of production and the relations of production.[122] This process, according to Harris, leaves Marxism wedded to the old Hegelian dialectic, which he rejects.

> In Marx's dialectic of history no less than in Hegel's, each epoch or social formation is urged onward toward its inevitable negation by an uncanny teleological thrust. For Hegel, it was the growth of the idea of freedom; for Marx, the development of the forces of production. In order for Marx's contradiction between forces and relations to provide the motive force of a sociocultural evolution faithful to Hegel's vision of a spiritualized cosmos dialectically negating itself into a heavenly utopia, the mode of production must tend toward maximum realization of its power over nature. As Marx put it: "No social order ever disappears before all the productive forces for which there is room in it have been developed." Why should one expect this to be true?[123]

Harris explains the development of better or higher productive forces through "modes of reproduction," of children in particular and the expansion of demographic forces in general.[124] Thus, this development includes controlling and managing technologies to increase or limit population, as necessary.

This is Harris's more detailed version of Marx's notion of "base," which Harris calls "infrastructure."[125] For Marx, the base determined other social formations; for Harris, the infrastructure "probabilistically determine[s] the etic behavioral domestic and political economy."[126] This relationship is the foundation of Harris's principle of infrastructural determinism,[127] in which the domestic and political economy (*i.e.*, the structure) reflect the etic and emic superstructures, although in some cases the latter may acquire a measure of autonomy from the etic infrastructure.[128]

In addition to such autonomy within structure and superstructure, structure and superstructure play an important role in maintaining society as a functioning whole, very much in the traditional functionalist sense. They are no mere "mechan-

---

122. *See* Chapter 4, text at note 8, *supra*.

123. Harris, Cultural Materialism, *supra* note 97, at 66.

124. *Id.*

125. A modification by Harris to Marx's notion of base, as seen above, is the reallocation of Marx's concept of the "relations of production" and "ownership of the means of production" to "structure" and "superstructure." Harris, Theories of Culture in Post-modern Times, *supra* note 100, at 142. Harris, Cultural Materialism, *supra* note 97, at 64–65.

126. Harris, Cultural Materialism, *supra* note 97, at 55.

127. *Id.* at 56.

128. *Id.* at 65. For example, price values, capital, wages, and commodity markets are parts of structure and superstructure, and they may achieve a degree of autonomy.

ical epiphenomena" playing a passive role in history.[129] Instead, they provide negative "system-maintaining" feedback that is of vital importance to the conservation of the system as a whole. Beyond this, it is possible that fermentation within structure and superstructure may foment (but not directly cause) change in infrastructure.

> Nothing in this formulation of the probabilistic outcome of infrastructural changes warrants the inference that structure or superstructure are insignificant, epiphenomenal reflexes of infrastructural factors. On the contrary, structure and superstructure clearly play vital system-maintaining roles in the negative feedback processes responsible for the conservation of the system. Productive and reproductive processes are functionally dependent on etic domestic and political organization, and the entire etic conjunction is functionally dependent on ideological commitments to values and goals that enhance cooperation and/or minimize the costs of maintaining order and an efficient level of productive and reproductive inputs. It follows from this that ideologies and political movements which lessen the resistance to an infrastructural change increase the likelihood that a new infrastructure will be propagated and amplified instead of dampened and extinguished. Furthermore, the more direct and emphatic the structural and superstructural support of the infrastructural changes, the swifter and more pervasive the transformation of the whole system.
>
> In other words, although I maintain that the probability is high that certain kinds of changes in the modes of production and reproduction will change the system, I also maintain that functionally related changes initiated simultaneously in all three sectors will increase the probability of systemic change. Indeed, it would be irrational to assert that ideological or political struggle could not enhance or diminish the probability of systemic changes involving all three sectors. But the crucial question that separates cultural materialism from its rivals is this: to what extent can fundamental changes be propagated and amplified by ideologies and political movements when the modes of production and reproduction stand opposed to them? Cultural materialism holds that innovations are unlikely to be propagated and amplified if they are functionally incompatible with the existing modes of production and reproduction—more unlikely than in the reverse situation (that is, when there is an initial political and ideological resistance but none in the modes of production and reproduction). This is what cultural materialists mean when they say that in the long run and in the largest number of cases, etic behavioral infrastructure determines the nature of structure and superstructure.[130]

---

129. *Id.* at 70. *See also* Harris, Theories of Culture in Postmodern Times, *supra* note 100, at 147.

130. Harris, Cultural Materialism, *supra* note 97, at 72–73.

Cultural materialism stresses the priority of etic conditions and processes over emic/mental conditions and processes. As for the reason for this priority of the etic behavioral infrastructure:

> The principle of the primacy of infrastructure holds that innovations that arise in the infrastructural sector are likely to be preserved and propagated if they enhance the efficiency of the productive processes that sustain health and well-being and that satisfy basic human biopsychological needs and drives.[131]

Below are examples of infrastructural primacy.

Of Unclean Pigs and Sacred Cows: Applied Infrastructuralism

In the example of bovicide in Kerala, India, infrastructural economic conditions (the scarcity of animal feed) led to the systematic killing of male calves.[132] Other examples of infrastructural primacy given by Harris explain how vegetarianism takes root and forbids the consumption of meat. He believed that as farming communities possessing domestic animals increased rapidly in early societies, they faced a choice between growing more crops or raising more animals. These ancient states and empires always gave priority to raising crops because the net calorie return on each calorie of human effort put into crop growing is approximately ten times greater than the net calorie return from animal production. Thus it is more efficient for humans themselves to consume their crops than to lengthen the food chain by placing animals between humans and their crops.[133] Furthermore, some animals were worth more alive than dead because they could be used for agricultural husbandry and for milk and milk products. Thus, according to Harris, meat consumption became a luxury in the Old World; then consumption of the flesh of the more prized species became forbidden altogether and, in some regions, meat itself became ritually unclean.[134]

Harris speculated that this was particularly the case with the raising of pigs, who were considered unclean and thus unfit for consumption by the Jews of the Ancient Middle East (around 1200 BCE). When the pig was domesticated, the region was full of forests and swamps, but by 700 BCE intensive farming had drastically reduced the forests to grasslands. The pigs, deprived of their natural diet, had to be fed grains, which put them in direct competition with humans. They also needed artificial sheds and moisture since human economic activity had largely depleted the region of the natural environment in which pigs thrive. In short, Harris thought that pigs became an ecological as well as an economic burden, which led them to be eventually declared unclean and unfit for human consumption.[135]

Harris provides a similar economic infrastructural explanation for the origin of the "sacred cow" phenomenon in India. Prior to about 600 BCE the Brahmins, the Hindu

---

131. Harris, Theories of Culture in Postmodern Times, *supra* note 100, at 142.

132. Harris, Cultural Materialism, *supra* note 97, at 32–33. *See* text at note 110 *supra*.

133. Marvin Harris, Cannibals and Kings 129 (1977).

134. *Id.* at 130.

135. *Id.* at 132–33.

priestly caste, engaged in eating animal flesh as well as animal sacrifice. However, with the development of agriculture, cows became necessary for agricultural labor (particularly plowing) and the provision of fertilizer, in the form of manure. As a result, meat became available only to some privileged Brahmins and other higher castes. By contrast, the common farmer felt compelled to preserve his stock for traction, milk, milk products, and dung.

By the middle of the sixth century BCE, according to Harris, resentments had developed over the great gulf between the privileged meat-eating aristocracy and the "impoverished meatless peasantry."[136] The subsequent emergence of Buddhism and Jainism fomented the belief in the sacredness of all life, and eventually the cow came to be regarded as a sacred animal.

Harris offers these examples in the context of cultural materialism as explanations of economic infrastructural determinism that affect lifestyles and permeate ideational beliefs and attitudes in the structure and superstructure. He also considered, however, that emic/mental processes may function as last resorts for the researcher when no other testable etic behavioral theory has explanatory power. He further justified infrastructural priority by the fact that it is the primary interface between nature and culture. In other words, in order to survive, human beings (like all bioforms) must engage in life-sustaining activities that are dependent on the particular technologies available at any given historical moment and that mark the boundaries within which humanity's technology interacts with its physical, ecological, and chemical environment. Sociocultural and normative practices thus necessarily emerge as people attempt to modify and/or overcome the restraints imposed on them by nature. According to Harris, it follows that similar infrastructural complexes in different societies will trigger the formation of similar structural and superstructural formations.[137]

> Innovations that are adaptive (i.e., that increase the efficiency of production and reproduction), are likely to be selected for, even if there is a marked incompatibility (contradiction) between them and preexisting aspects of the structural and symbolic-ideational sectors. Moreover, the resolution of any deep incompatibility between an adaptive infrastructural innovation and the preexisting features of the other sectors will predictably consist of substantial changes in those other sectors. In contrast, innovations of a structural or symbolic-ideational nature are likely to be selected against if there is any deep incompatibility between them and the infrastructure—that is to say, if they reduce the efficiency of the productive and reproductive processes that sustain health and well-being and that satisfy basic human biopsychological needs and drives.
>
> A logical entailment of the principle of the primacy of infrastructure is that, given similar evolved infrastructural complexes in different societies, one can expect convergence toward similar structural relationships and

136. *Id.* at 143.

137. Harris, Theories of Cultures in Postmodern Times, *supra* note 100, at 143.

symbolic-ideational features. The reverse also holds: different infrastructures lead to different structures and different symbols and ideas.[138]

The excerpt below explains Harris's basic methodological principles based on a reformulation of Marx's base-superstructure relationship.

Marvin Harris, Cultural Materialism: The Struggle for a Science of Culture 51–57 (1979).

Universal Pattern in Cultural Materialist Strategy

The universal structure of sociocultural systems posited by cultural materialism rests on the biological and psychological constants of human nature, and on the distinction between thought and behavior and emics and etics. To begin with, each society must cope with the problems of production—behaviorally satisfying minimal requirements for subsistence; hence there must be an *etic behavioral mode of production*. Second, each society must behaviorally cope with the problem of reproduction—avoiding destructive increases or decreases in population size; hence there must be an *etic behavioral mode of reproduction*. Third, each society must cope with the necessity of maintaining secure and orderly behavioral relationships among its constituent groups and with other societies. In conformity with mundane and practical considerations, cultural materialists see the threat of disorder arising primarily from the economic processes which allocate labor and the material products of labor to individuals and groups. Hence, depending on whether the focus of organization is on domestic groups or the internal and external relationships of the whole society, one may infer the universal existence of *etic behavioral domestic economies* and *etic behavioral political economies*. Finally, given the prominence of human speech acts and the importance of symbolic processes for the human psyche, one can infer the universal recurrence of productive behavior that leads to etic, recreational, sportive, and aesthetic products and services. *Behavioral superstructure* is a convenient label for this universally recurrent etic sector.

In sum, the major etic behavioral categories together with some examples of sociocultural phenomena that fall within each domain are:

Mode of Production: The technology and the practices employed for expanding or limiting basic subsistence production, especially the production of food and other forms of energy, given the restrictions and opportunities provided by a specific technology interacting with a specific habitat.

Technology of subsistence
Techno-environmental relationships
Ecosystems
Work patterns

---

138. *Id.*

Mode of Reproduction: The technology and the practices employed for expanding, limiting, and maintaining population size.

Demography
Mating patterns
Fertility, natality, mortality
Nurturance of infants
Medical control of demographic patterns
Contraception, abortion, infanticide

Domestic Economy: The organization of reproduction and basic production, exchange, and consumption within camps, houses, apartments, or other domestic settings.

Family structure
Domestic division of labor
Domestic socialization, enculturation, education
Age and sex roles
Domestic discipline, hierarchies, sanctions

Political Economy: The organization of reproduction, production, exchange, and consumption within and between bands, villages, chiefdoms, states, and empires.

Political organizations, factions, clubs, associations, corporations
Division of labor, taxation, tribute
Political socialization, enculturation, education
Class, caste, urban, rural hierarchies
Discipline, police/military control
War

Behavioral Superstructure:

Art, music, dance, literature, advertising
Rituals
Sports, games, hobbies
Science

I can simplify the above by lumping the modes of production and reproduction together under the rubric *infrastructure*; and by lumping domestic and political economy under the rubric *structure.* This yields a tripartite scheme:

Infrastructure
Structure
Superstructure

However, these rubrics embrace only the etic behavioral components of sociocultural systems. What about the mental components? Running roughly parallel to the etic behavioral components are a set of mental components whose conventional designations are as follows:

Etic Behavioral Components	*Mental and Emic Components*
Infrastructure	Ethnobotany, ethnozoology, subsistence, lore, magic, religion, taboos
Etic Behavioral Components	*Mental and Emic Components*
Structure	Kinship, political ideology, ethnic and national ideologies, magic, religion, taboos
Etic superstructure	Symbols, myths, aesthetic standards and philosophies, epistemologies, ideologies, magic, religion, taboos

Rather than distinguish the mental and emic components according to the strength of their relationship to specific etic behavioral components, I shall lump them together and designate them in their entirety as the *mental and emic superstructure*, meaning the conscious and unconscious cognitive goals, categories, rules, plans, values, philosophies, and beliefs about behavior elicited from the participants or inferred by the observer. Four major universal components of sociocultural systems are now before us; the etic behavioral infrastructure, structure, and superstructure, and the mental and emic superstructure. . . .

The Major Principles of Cultural Materialism

The kernel of the principles that guide the development of interrelated sets of theories in the strategy of cultural materialism was anticipated by Marx . . . in the following words: "The mode of production in material life determines the general character of the social, political, and spiritual processes of life. It is not the consciousness of men that determines their existence, but on the contrary, their social existence determines their consciousness." As stated, this principle was a great advance in human knowledge, surely equivalent in its time to the formulation of the principle of natural selection by Alfred Wallace and Charles Darwin. However, in the context of modern anthropological research, the epistemological ambiguities inherent in the phrase "the mode of production," the neglect of "the mode of reproduction," and the failure to distinguish emics from etics and behavioral from mental impose the need for reformulation.

The cultural materialist version of Marx's great principle is as follows: The etic behavioral modes of production and reproduction probabilistically determine the etic behavioral domestics and political economy, which in turn probabilistically determine the behavioral and mental emic superstructures. For brevity's sake, this principle can be referred to as the principle of infrastructural determinism.

The strategic significance of the principle of infrastructural determinism is that it provides a set of priorities for the formulation and testing of theories and hypotheses about the causes of sociocultural phenomena. Cultural materialists give highest priority to the effort to formulate and test theories in which infrastructural variables are the primary causal factors. Failure to identify such factors in the infrastructure warrants the formulation of theories in which structural variables are tested for causal primacy. Cultural materialists give still less priority to exploring the possibility that the solution to sociocultural puzzles lies primarily within the behavioral superstructure; and finally, theories that bestow causal primacy upon the mental and emic superstructure are to be formulated and tested only as an ultimate recourse when no testable etic behavioral theories can be formulated or when all that have been formulated have been decisively discredited. In other words, cultural materialism asserts the strategic priority of etic and behavioral conditions and processes over emic and mental conditions and processes, and of infrastructural over structural and superstructural conditions and processes; but it does not deny the possibility that emic, mental, superstructural, and structural components may achieve a degree of autonomy from the etic behavioral infrastructure. Rather, it merely postpones and delays that possibility in order to guarantee the fullest exploration of the determining influences exerted by the etic behavioral infrastructure.

Why Infrastructure?

The strategic priority given to etic and behavioral production and reproduction by cultural materialism represents an attempt to build theories about culture that incorporate lawful regularities occurring in nature. Like all bioforms, human beings must expend energy to obtain energy (and other life-sustaining products). And like all bioforms, our ability to produce children is greater than our ability to obtain energy for them. That strategic priority of the infrastructure rests upon the fact that human beings can never change these laws. . . .

Infrastructure, in other words, is the principal interface between culture and nature, the boundary across which the ecological, chemical, and physical restraints to which human action is subject interact with the principal sociocultural practices aimed at overcoming or modifying those restraints. . . . To endow the mental superstructure with strategic priority, as the cultural idealists advocate, is a bad bet. Nature is indifferent to whether God is a loving father or a bloodthirsty cannibal. But nature is not indifferent to whether the fallow period in a swidden field is one year or ten. We know that powerful restraints exist on the infrastructural level; hence it is a good bet that these restraints are passed on to the structural and superstructural components.

C. Thought Over Behavior: A Case of Mistaken Priority

Two recurring themes of cultural materialism, which are also related, are its probabilistic epistemology and the priority of etic infrastructural behavioralism over its emic counterparts. According to the first theme, cultural materialism does not claim that its methodology necessarily excludes its rivals. Instead, it is against all forms of dogmatism and remains open to any test that will verify or falsify its theories.[139] As seen in the foregoing excerpt, the causal chain asserting infrastructural determinism is based only on a probabilistic theory. Infrastructural priority is only advanced as a good bet, and giving priority to the emic superstructure is said to be a bad bet.

With this qualification, cultural materialism goes on to explain why infrastructural priority is a better bet. The explanation is essentially that mental and emic elements of life are transient; they come and go and are mere acts of will. By contrast, production and reproduction are grounded in nature; they cannot be made to appear and disappear by mere acts of will.[140]

> Thought changes nothing outside of the head unless it is accompanied by the movements of the body or its parts. It seems reasonable, therefore, to search for the beginnings of the causal chains affecting sociocultural evolution in the complex of energy-expending body activities that affect the balance between the size of each human population, the amount of energy devoted to production, and the supply of life-sustaining resources. Cultural materialists contend that this balance is so vital to the survival and well-being of the individuals and groups who are its beneficiaries that all other culturally patterned thoughts and activities in which these individuals and groups engage are probably directly or indirectly determined by its specific character. But we do not contend this out of any final conviction that we know what the world is really like; we contend it merely to make the best possible theories about what the world is probably like.[141]

The second theme of the priority of etic behavior over emic thought is in some ways counterintuitive. In other words, cultural materialism maintains the opposite of what most people intuitively believe to be true, namely, that thought governs behavior. Thus, for example, for a culture to develop hunting tools such as bow and arrow or rifle, someone must first think about the need for these tools, design them, and decide to build them.

As cultural materialism reaches for a deeper explanation of such processes, it stresses that it is not concerned with how technological inventions originate in the individual mind but rather with how they come to have a material social existence and how they affect production and reproduction. No innovation will have a material social existence unless the material conditions for their social acceptance are ripe.

---

139. Harris, Cultural Materialism, *supra* note 97, at 76.

140. *Id.* at 58.

141. *Id.*

Even in cultures in which freedom of thought is highly valued, simple acts like going out to dinner or an evening at the theater do not materialize out of thin air; instead, they are chosen from a preexisting range of typical acts characteristic of the culture in question.[142]

> The issue of behavioral versus mental determinism is not a matter of whether the mind guides action, but whether the mind determines the selection of the inventory of culturally actionable thoughts. As Schopenhauer said, "We want what we will, but we don't will what we want." Thus the human intuition concerning the priority of thought over behavior is worth just about as much as our human intuition that the earth is flat.[143]

Some thinkers of the Boasian tradition (*e.g.*, Kroeber, Sapir, Benedict, and Mead) also asserted the primacy of cultural forces over individual behavior. Kroeber's "superorganic" postulated a force in culture that is all-pervasive. Similarly, Sapir, Benedict, and Mead subscribed to the notion that cultural forces are so strong that the individual conforms to them unconsciously. These parallels are only superficial, however; cultural materialism's disciplined focus on the economic and material imperatives of life awards to these conditions an almost coercive rather than unconscious effect on behavior, to the point of creating paradoxical situations in which the poor and the exploited seem trapped into deliberately perpetuating their own misery (thus showing the powerlessness of thought).

> Obviously there are many innovations which are bio-psychologically more satisfying to some members of a society than to others. Purdah, the veiling of women in Moslem societies, facilitates domestic and political control by men over women. Presumably the bio-psychological rewards of purdah are greater for men than for women—indeed, one might say that for the women there are severe penalties. But the men have the power to make their own well-being weigh more heavily in the balance of advantages and disadvantages than the well-being of women. The more hierarchical the society with respect to sex, age, class, caste, and ethnic criteria, the greater the degree of exploitation of one group by another and the less likely it is that the trajectory of sociocultural evolution can be calculated from the average bio-psychological utility of traits. This leads to many puzzling situations in which it appears that large sectors of a society are acting in ways that diminish their practical well-being instead of enhancing it. In India, for example, members of impoverished menial castes avidly uphold the rule of caste endogamy and insist that marriages be legitimized by expensive dowries. Abstractly, it would appear that the members of such impoverished castes would be materially better off if they practiced exogamy and stopped insisting on big marriage payments. But the victims of the caste system cannot base their behavior on

142. *Id.* at 59–60.

143. *Id.* at 60.

long-term abstract calculations. Access to such menial jobs as construction worker, toddy-wine maker, coir maker, and so forth depends on caste identity validated by obedience to caste rules. In the lower castes if one fails to maintain membership in good standing one loses the opportunity to obtain work even of the most menial kind, and plunges still further into misery. To throw off the weight of the accumulated privileges of the upper castes lies entirely beyond the practical capacity of those who are at the bottom of the heap; hence, perverse as it may seem, those who benefit least from the system ardently support it in daily life.[144]

Conclusion

Cultural materialism is the contemporary bearer of the Marxist mantle in anthropology. It adopts the basic thesis of Marx that the material conditions of life influence forms of thought as well as social institutions. However, cultural materialism departs from orthodox Marxism in that it rejects the Hegelian dialectic and substitutes reproductive forces. Cultural materialism is not therefore concerned with such ontological questions as the essence of being or whether it manifests itself through matter, idea, or spirit.

More specifically, cultural materialism argues that sociocultural transformation is primarily driven by the etic behavioral infrastructure, which is composed of the modes of production and reproduction. The latter, in turn, are made up of practices of production for subsistence and forces of reproduction. Together, the forces of production and reproduction represent the economic, technological, environmental, and demographic variables of social life, which are collectively called the "infrastructure." The latter is then complemented by two other universal institutions that render the system into a functioning whole: the "structure," which is made up of the largely normative sectors of the domestic and political economy, and the "superstructure," which is made up of the symbolic and ideational sector of society.

Cultural materialism acknowledges its debt to Marx (whom Harris describes as the "Darwin of the social sciences") but disclaims any particular political program. Unlike Marxism, which advocates revolution through political action, cultural materialism declines to propose a program of action. It thus purports to be a descriptive rather than a prescriptive methodology.

Finally, while this methodology is claimed to be "scientific," it expressly admits that there is more than one way of knowing and therefore claims no privileged access to the truth. Indeed, its epistemology is probabilistic and open to falsification. For example, Harris expressly invokes Hume's critique of induction as a founding block for the epistemology of cultural materialism. Briefly, Hume's philosophy drew a distinction between knowledge of relationships between logical propositions and knowledge about relationships between matters of fact. Reason gives certain knowledge in the former realm, for example, in mathematics. One cannot doubt that $2+2=4$. In the

144. *Id.* at 61–62.

empirical world of facts, however, reason cannot establish conclusions about factual relationships because it is always logically possible to assert the contrary of any factual situation without ending in a contradiction.[145] Thus Hume's conclusion, adopted by Harris, is that the only way to make sense of causation in the phenomenal world is through inferences drawn by careful and repeated observation. These inferences do not constitute knowledge, but they are the best that one can do to cope with the material and physical world as one finds it. For these reasons, Harris does not exclude rival theories and simply asserts that cultural materialism is a better bet than any other theory for gaining scientific knowledge of the sociocultural world.

145. For further discussion, *see* Harris, Cultural Materialism, *supra* note 97, at 9–10. *See also* Isaak Dore, The Epistemological Foundations of Law 355–63 (2007).

Chapter 6

Cultural Cognitivism and Normativity: Cognitive Functionalism, Ethnoscience, and Neostructuralism

The 1950s ushered in a new era of retrospection and reassessment in anthropological thought. The direction of future cultural studies was so central to the debate that one prominent anthropologist lamented that the field "appears to be a thing of shreds and patches, of individuals and small coteries pursuing disjunctive investigations and talking mainly to themselves."[1] Unable to agree on a common approach, anthropologists split into two main groups, each with its own subgroups. Debate between the groups centered on whether ethnographers should take an emic or etic approach to the study of cultural normativity. Briefly, the emic approach studies thought and behavior from the point of view of the in-culture participant, whereas the etic approach studies the same using thoughts and concepts of the outside observer.

> The test of the adequacy of emic analyses is their ability to generate statements the native accepts as real, meaningful, or appropriate. In carrying out research in the emic mode, the observer attempts to acquire a knowledge of the categories and rules one must know in order to think and act as a native. One attempts to learn, for example, what rule lies behind the use of the same kin term for mother and mother's sister among the Bathonga; or one attempts to learn when it is appropriate to shame one's guests among the Kwakiutl....
>
> The test of the adequacy of etic accounts is simply their ability to generate scientifically productive theories about the causes of sociocultural differences and similarities. Rather than employ concepts that are necessarily real, meaningful, and appropriate from the native point of view, the observer is free to use alien categories and rules derived from the data language of science. Frequently, etic operations involve the measurement and juxtaposition of activities and events that native informants may find inappropriate or meaningless.[2]

---

1. Sherry B. Ortner, *Theory in Anthropology Since the Sixties*, 26 Comp. Stud. Soc'y & Hist. 126, 126 (1984).

2. Marvin Harris, Cultural Materialism: The Struggle for a Science of Culture 32 (1979).

The split in anthropological thought was reflected by the emergence of two disparate schools in the 1960s: the tangible anthropologists, or cultural materialists (who favored an etic approach), and the intangible cognitive anthropologists, or cultural idealists (who favored an emic approach).[3] For our purposes, the idealist conception of culture simply means the individual is considered to be the main agent of culture change and is seen to creatively shape its normative order. By extension, there is a move away from reifying culture as something separable from the individual and which the latter cannot control, either in the sense of Kroeber's super-organic or under the determinist approach of Marxism.[4]

The cultural materialists used economic and ecological models to explain normativity in culture, as seen in Chapters 4 and 5. Marx, White, and Steward were the pioneers of the materialist approach. Marvin Harris is the contemporary standard bearer of cultural materialism.

The idealistic or ideational approach was initially spurred by what was seen as the reconciliation by Max Weber of the two hitherto irreconcilable theories of materialism and idealism. Although it is beyond the scope of this work to examine Weber's theories about religion and capitalism, it is worth noting that his theoretical model was understood by anthropologists as giving creative power to the individual while remaining grounded in the essentially Marxian categories of the relations of production and reproduction.[5] However, other anthropologists explicitly reject materialist explanations (particularly by Harris) and embrace the idealist approach as defined above.[6]

For analytical purposes, the emic cognitive anthropologists (or idealists) can be subdivided into five interrelated subschools: emic cognitive functionalism, cognitive ethnoscience, cognitive neostructuralism, symbolic anthropology, and interpretivism. These subschools concentrate on the mental and psychological variables that constitute culture and thus emphasize how the individual understands life at the group level (*i.e.*, how one gives meaning to that life and how that meaning, in turn, serves as a normative guide to behavior and interaction between individuals). The first three subschools are examined in this chapter. The last two are examined in the next chapter.

---

3. *Id.* at 569.

4. Paul A. Erickson & Liam D. Murphy, A History of Anthropological Theory 132 (2d ed., 2003).

5. *See* Max Weber, The Protestant Ethic and the Spirit of Capitalism (1930); Max Weber, Sociology of Religion (1920). On the "rediscovery" of Max Weber by anthropologists, *see* Erickson & Murphy, *supra* note 4, at 131–35.

6. Janet L. Dolgin, David S. Kemnitzer, & David M. Schneider, *Introduction*, *in* Symbolic Anthropology: A Reader in the Study of Symbols and Meanings 3, 6 (Janet L. Dolgin, David S. Kemnitzer, & David M. Schneider eds., 1977).

Emic Cognitive Functionalism: Definitional Issues

In 1957, Ward Goodenough proposed that culture be defined as "whatever it is one has to know or believe in order to operate in a manner acceptable to its members."[7] The three key elements of this formulation are what one has to "know" in order to "operate" in a way that is acceptable in society. These essentially functional elements formed the basis for a new subfield in anthropology for investigating the unity that underlies diverse sociocultural phenomena. Some twenty years after Goodenough's formulation, a newer and more refined definition, also functional in nature, was put forward and became the basis for a new methodological approach. This new (and current) definition, its accompanying methodological approach, and its epistemological implications are discussed next.

The current classic definition of culture by the emic functionalists is that "Culture is the learned and shared knowledge that people use to generate behavior and interpret experience."[8]

Under this definition, culture is treated as a type of knowledge; it is not behavior. Furthermore, this knowledge consists of codes and rules that are socially acquired. Like all knowledge, it is "in people's heads" and exists in the form of mental categories that each individual learns from others during maturation.[9] The other two elements of the above definition of culture are related. First, knowledge is the causal factor of behavior; it "generates" behavior. Second, knowledge helps people to understand (or give meaning to) their social experiences by helping them to interpret their experience in the form of symbols. The above definition thus connotes that human experience and behavior are products of symbolic meaning systems.[10] A symbol is, quite simply, any object or event that has a socially assigned meaning.[11] The meanings of symbols, as well as their interpretation, combination, and adaptation, are arrived at through rules that in their totality constitute the cultural code of society.[12]

By this logic, the mind of the individual is a blank slate at birth (*i.e.*, it lacks culture). Therefore, all individuals undergo a form of "universal schooling" whereby as they grow up they learn their society's system of beliefs and acquire knowledge of customary patterns of behavior. And although certain human acts, gestures, and bodily movements are genetically programmed actions and reactions, the questions of when and how they are to occur or to be suppressed are regulated by cultural rules.

---

7. Ward H. Goodenough, *Cultural Anthropology and Linguistics*, *in* Report of the Seventh Annual Round Table Meeting on Linguistics and Language Study 167 (Monograph Series on Language and Linguistics no. 9, Paul L. Garvin ed., 1957).

8. James P. Spradley & David W. McCurdy, Conformity and Conflict: Readings in Cultural Anthropology 2 (11th ed., 2003).

9. *Id.*

10. James P. Spradley & David W. McCurdy, Anthropology: The Cultural Perspective 5 (1975).

11. *Id.* at 20, 27.

12. *Id.* at 27.

In this way, knowledge is thought to be the causal factor of individual behavior; it also helps individuals give meaning to their social experiences. Here "meaning" takes on a plainly relativist significance because the same experiences in different cultural contexts can have different meanings.[13] For example, dogs are treated as part of the household in North American culture, whereas they are treated as pests and nuisances in Indian culture.[14] The experience of having a dog (as a pet or otherwise) therefore has different meanings in the two cultures, and these meanings are learned as part of growing up in each culture.

Where culture as knowledge can be expressed in words, it is referred to as "explicit culture." Where words are lacking, as in a set of sound categories (such as d/e/f) referred to by anthropological linguists as phonemes, the individual learns these unconsciously by hearing and replicating them in speech.[15] This realm of knowledge of culture is called "tacit culture." Another example of wordless tacit culture is the notion of speaking distances. Thus when the Latin American speaks at a close distance to the North American the latter may interpret this as a gesture of intimacy when the speaker may not have intended it to be so. It is also well known that when one person considers a gesture of intimacy improper (in his or her cultural context) all sorts of negative consequences may follow.

The emic functionalists do not study the people of a culture as subjects; rather, they study the culture through an informant who is a member and therefore has the necessary knowledge. The informant's task is to teach the ethnographer to understand a culture from within. The ethnographer must be wary about not making suppositions that all cultures are similar or that certain issues are viewed in the same way in all cultures. The latter approach, called "naive realism," will result in cultural meanings being overlooked.[16]

The same dangers lurk if ethnographers fail to shed their own ethnocentrism when studying a foreign culture. They may be surprised or even shocked by what they see. Not only will they then not know how to act appropriately in the new context, but they may suffer anxiety and culture shock.

Methodological Approach

The emic approach maintains that the above dangers can be minimized if the correct methodology is used for ethnographic research. That methodology, known as "participant observation," requires the professional anthropologist to engage in

---

13. Stephen A. Tyler, *Introduction*, *in* Cognitive Anthropology 1, 3, 13 (Stephen A. Tyler, ed., 1969).

14. Spradley & McCurdy, Conformity and Conflict, *supra* note 8, at 2.

15. *Id.* at 3.

16. *Id.* at 4. *See also* Mary Black & Duane Metzger, *Ethnographic Description and the Study of Law*, 67 Am. Anthropol. 141, 143 (1965).

ethnographic fieldwork with the goal "to understand another way of life from the native point of view."[17] This method was pioneered by Bronislaw Malinowski.[18]

The ethnographer's activity is a learning experience. Rather than studying people and possibly imposing their own frameworks on these people's lives and experiences, such anthropologists learn from them about how they see their world and how they speak, think, and act in ways that are different from the ethnographer's frame of reference. This willingness to learn from their subjects underlies the designation of such ethnographers as emic functionalists.[19]

Because the search is for internal meaning within cultures, emic functionalists regard cultures as "cognitive organizations."[20] In contrast to the evolutionists, as well as the structural functionalists and Marxists who seek to identify uniformities or what is typical or normal in all cultures, the emic functionalists propose a new theoretical orientation. They propose to learn how different cultures organize and understand the principles underlying their normative relations. As explained in the following excerpt, they reject the attempt of their predecessors to construct universal organizational types linked either by the way they evolved or by similarities of their internal structure. In addition, whereas their predecessors sought to explain foreign cultures in the native language of the ethnographers, the cognitivists understand and explain cultures in the native tongues of these cultures themselves. Their assumption is that the language of the natives best explains their mental codes.

Stephen A. Tyler, *Introduction*, *in* Cognitive Anthropology 1, 3–6 (Stephen A. Tyler ed., 1969).

> [C]ognitive anthropology constitutes a new theoretical orientation. It focuses on *discovering* how different peoples organize and use their cultures. This is not so much a search for some generalized unit of behavioral analysis as it is an attempt to understand the *organizing principles underlying* behavior. It is assumed that each people has a unique system for perceiving and organizing material phenomena—things, events, behavior, and emotions . . . The object of study is not these material phenomena themselves, but the way they are organized in the minds of men. Cultures then are not material phenomena; they are cognitive organizations of material phenomena. Consequently, cultures are neither described by mere arbitrary lists of anatomical traits and institutions such as house type, family type, kinship type, economic type, and personality type, nor are they necessarily equated with some over-all integrative pattern of these phenomena. Such descriptions may tell us something about the way an anthropologist thinks about a culture, but there is little, if

17. James P. Spradley, Participant Observation 3 (1980).

18. *See* Chapter 3. Malinowski is also regarded as the father of functionalism, the approach that studies society from the point of view of the individual.

19. Spradley, Participant Observation, *supra* note 17, at 3.

20. Tyler, *supra* note 13, at 3.

any, reason to believe that they tell us anything of how the people of some culture think about their culture.

In essence, cognitive anthropology seeks to answer two questions. What material phenomena are significant for the people of some culture; and how do they organize these phenomena? Not only do cultures differ among one another in their organization of material phenomena, they differ as well in the kinds of material phenomena they organize. The people of different cultures may not recognize the same kinds of material phenomena as relevant, even though from an outsider's point of view the same material phenomena may be present in every case. For example, we distinguish between dew, fog, ice, and snow, but the Koyas of South India do not. They call all of these *mancu*. Even though they can perceive the differences among these if asked to do so, these differences are not significant to them. On the other hand, they recognize and name at least seven different kinds of bamboo, six more than I am accustomed to distinguish. . . .

Not only may the same phenomena be organized differently from culture to culture, they may also be organized in more than one way in the same culture. There is, then, *intracultural* variation as well as *intercultural* variation. . . .

A consequence of this interest in variation is the idea that cultures are not unitary phenomena, that is, they cannot be described by only one set of organizing principles. For each class of relevant phenomena there may be several alternative organizations. The realization or choice of one alternative to the exclusion of some other is dependent upon a variety of factors. For example, some people have more or less knowledge of some phenomena, or certain alternatives may be acceptable only in particular contexts. . . . If these variants are used only in certain identified situations, or if there is a hierarchy of choice so that variants are ordered on the basis of their relative desirability, we can say that they are complementary distribution and do not conflict with one another. In such a situation it is possible for a large number of variants to coexist. But, if these variants conflict in their organization and the situations in which they occur, there must be some means of harmonizing the contrast. This can be achieved by some change in the principles of organization or in the situations in which they occur. For example, among the Koyas, the pig is classed as an edible animal, but among neighboring Muslims the pig is classed as inedible and defiling. Suppose a Koya woman were married to a Muslim man. While in her husband's home she could not act on her classification of the pig as an edible by eating pork; while visiting her parents in the absence of her husband she could. So long as the two systems of classification can be realized in these isolated contexts there is no necessary conflict between them, and both may persist. If these contexts were not in complementary distribution, some rearrangement of the two contrasting systems of classification would have to take place if the marriage were to persist.

> In fact, this is an argument for a different kind of unitary description which sees unity as emerging from the ordered relations between variants and contexts. Variants are not mere deviations from some assumed basic organization; with their rules of occurrence *they are the organization*.... It must be emphasized, however, that such a unitary description can be achieved only by the anthropologist. It is highly unlikely that the members of a culture ever see their culture as *this kind of* unitary phenomenon. Each individual member may have a unique unitary model of his culture, but is not necessarily cognizant of all the unique, unitary models held by other members of his culture. He will be aware of and use some, but it is only the anthropologist who completely transcends these particular models and constructs a single, unitary model. This cognitive organization exists solely in the mind of the anthropologist....
>
> The "theory" here is not so much a THEORY OF CULTURE as it is *theories of cultures*, or a theory of descriptions. The aim of such a theory is to provide answers to the questions: How would the people of some other culture expect me to behave if I were a member of their culture; and what are the rules of appropriate behavior in their culture? Answers to these questions are provided by an adequate description of the rules used by the people in that culture. Consequently, this description itself constitutes the "theory" for that culture, for it represents the conceptual model of organization used by its members. Such a theory is validated by our ability to predict how these people would expect us to behave if we were members of their culture....
>
> In a sense, cognitive anthropology is not a new departure. Many anthropologists have expressed interest in how the natives see their world. Yet, there is a difference of focus between the old and the new. Where earlier anthropologists sought categories of description in their native language, cognitive anthropologists seek categories of description in the language of their natives. Ultimately, this is the old problem of what do we describe and how do we describe it? Obviously, we are interested in the mental codes of other peoples, but how do we infer these mental processes? Thus far, it has been assumed that the easiest entry to such processes is through language, and most of the recent studies have sought to discover codes that are mapped in language. Nearly all of this work has been concerned with how other peoples "name" the "things" in their environment and how these names are organized into larger groupings. These names are thus both an index to what is significant in the environment of some other people, and a means of discovering how these people organize their perceptions of the environment. Naming is seen as one of the chief methods for imposing order on perception.

Terms such as "cousin," "marriage," "friendship," "family," "kinship obligationism," and so on, have different meanings in different cultures. Thus the insider view, expressed in the language of natives, is a different species of knowledge than that of an outsider. The latter must strive to adopt the belief, which may at times feel counterintuitive, that reality is viewed differently in different cultures. One is predisposed to believe that the world has certain objective facts (*e.g.*, dew, fog, ice, life, death, food, trees, animals, snow, love, worship, etc.) and that these things, along with others, have the same meanings across all cultures.[21] Even if the enlightened ethnographer rejects ethnocentric approaches and, with them, naive realism, such predispositions may unconsciously affect his understanding.

The concept of culture as a cognitive organization views human experience as the sum total of three fundamental elements: cultural behavior, cultural artifacts, and cultural knowledge. The first two are easy enough to see because they consist respectively of what people do and the things they use. Books, for example, are artifacts, and the act of reading them is the behavioral aspect. Beyond this, however, lies a vast realm of cultural knowledge that remains largely hidden: how to read, which in turn implies knowledge of a language and its rules of grammar; knowledge about how written words in a language are arranged (*e.g.*, left to right, or right to left, from the top of the page to the bottom, from one page to the next); and knowledge about how to read specific texts (*e.g.*, a newspaper, a magazine, a billboard, a bus ticket, etc.). This knowledge is used with different artifacts to engage in the behavior called "reading." This analogy underlies the above definition of culture as the acquired knowledge that people use to interpret experience and generate behavior.[22] Calling culture a "cognitive organization" says the same thing.

The above definition shifts the emphasis from behavior and artifacts to their meaning. The ethnographer's task is to go beyond mere observation of behavior and artifacts to give meaning to them; that is, the meaning as given or revealed by the insider/informant. Frequently, this knowledge is given by express language (*i.e.*, explicit culture); however, a large portion of cultural knowledge remains tacit. Examples of the latter are rules of etiquette about breathing, coughing, or touching in the company of others.

The concept of culture as acquired knowledge is related to the theory of symbolic interactionism. This theory of meaning in sociocultural contexts is based on three premises. The first is that human beings are moved toward things on the basis of the meaning those things have for them. The second is that this meaning arises from social interaction. Because the latter is a dynamic phenomenon, meaning is defined, revised, or changed in accordance with particular interactional contexts. The third and final premise of symbolic interactionism is that meaning is arrived at through an interpretive process. Again, interpretations can differ in particular sociocultural contexts.[23]

The interpretive process is shown more clearly if culture is viewed as a cognitive map that serves as a guide to individual action and for interpreting experience. The map is only a contextual guide, however; it does not compel particular courses of action because human actions and interactions are as varied as they are unpredictable.

---

21. *Id.* at 11.

22. *See* text at note 8 *supra*.

23. Spradley, Participant Observation, *supra* note 17, at 8–9.

People within a culture are thus not just map readers but also map makers because through particular interactional contexts, they both apply old meanings and create new ones.[24] Cognitive anthropologists therefore regard cultural norms as the embodiment of "public, socially established symbolic systems rooted in the individual."[25]

Epistemological Implications

Meanings are not "things" that exist (contrary to Durkheim). Instead they are inferences, rather in the style of David Hume as interpreted by Marvin Harris in his cultural materialist methodology. Unlike Harris's, however, the emic functional approach does not press any particular epistemological argument. Its point is only that every culture exhibits the "universal pattern" of meaningful but different inferences drawn from behavior, artifacts, and explicit and tacit cultural knowledge.[26] The ethnographer's task is to learn the totality of the inferences made by the people by entering their semantic domain (*i.e.*, to give expression to them in their native tongue).[27] The inferences drawn by the ethnographer will be deduced from what is said in response to "controlled eliciting," which uses sentence frames derived from the local semantic domain.[28] Inferences are also drawn from behavior observed and artifacts used. Every inference must be treated initially only as a hypothesis to be tested repeatedly until the ethnographer is "relatively certain that people share a particular system of cultural meanings."[29]

Given the views of Durkheim, Radcliffe-Brown, Harris, and Marx, who claimed to advance a science of man on par with natural science, cognitive anthropology asserts that cultural anthropology is a formal science, not a natural one.[30] Its data is characterized as mental in nature, rather than material, and the assumption is that mental data is capable of formal analysis in the same way as the formal systems of mathematics and logic. Thus, an epistemological argument lurks just beneath the surface of the formalist argument: if the data of cognitive anthropology has the same cognitive status as mathematics, then its inferences and deductions presumably have the same certainty as mathematical deductions.

Many philosophers, including Locke and Hume, have argued that true knowledge exists only in the realm of mathematics and that human reason is incapable of producing knowledge of the phenomenal world. If so, the cognitivists are making an epistemological claim that is even stronger than those of Harris, Radcliffe-Brown, Durkheim, Marx, *et al.* This conclusion, however, results from a chain of interpo-

---

24. *Id.* at 9.

25. Janet W. D. Dougherty, *Introduction*, *in* Directions in Cognitive Anthropology 3, 9 (Janet W. D. Dougherty ed., 1985).

26. The term "universal pattern" is not used by the cognitivists. It is used here for obvious comparative reasons. *See further* Goodenough, *supra* note 7.

27. Tyler, *supra* note 13, at 11.

28. *Id.* at 12. *See also* Dougherty, *supra* note 25, at 4.

29. Spradley, Participant Observation, *supra* note 17, at 10.

30. *Id.*; Tyler, *supra* note 13, at 14.

lations, beginning with the assumption that the mental data of cognitive studies has the same rank as mathematical data. This conclusion, which remains debatable, is implicit in the argument of cognitive anthropology.

Another approach to the epistemological question is *via* the claim that cultures are cognitive organizations. One clear association of the term "cognitive" here is with "meaning," which is generally associated with knowledge. The absence of knowledge about any social or natural phenomenon would show that no meaningful explanation can be given about it. Therefore, a variety of cognitive devices are used to derive meaning in cognitive methodology; the three primary ones are symbols, cultural concepts, and cultural categories.

As defined above, culture as knowledge that people use to generate behavior and interpret experience implies that human experience and behavior are products of symbolic meaning systems. Thus a symbol is any object or event that has a socially assigned meaning.[31] Symbols are formed, interpreted, and combined in accordance with a socially transmitted cultural code.[32] The meanings assigned to symbols are called concepts. These, in turn, are subsumed by a set of commonly shared cultural categories, which are classificatory schemes under which similar things, objects, and events are treated as equivalents. The categories facilitate understanding by the human mind of the phenomenal world.

One study of human thought identifies six major cultural categories:

1. *Cultural categories reduce the complexity of the environment.* Take color as one example. While normal color vision enables a person to discriminate among more than 1 million different colors, the color categories of a culture reduce this complexity to a relatively small number.
2. *Cultural categories enable us to identify the objects of the world about us.* Identification of people, things, and events involves placing them in some category. This reduces the anxiety of constantly encountering unknown things.
3. *Cultural categories reduce the necessity of constant learning.* Once a tramp learns the defining attributes of each kind of "bull," he can categorize new individuals without having to learn their identity. We do not have to be taught at each encounter with an automobile or a book that the object is, indeed, an automobile or a book. Children in every society learn more than what things are; they learn the principles for categorizing and thereby reduce the necessity for constant learning.
4. *Cultural categories provide direction for instrumental activity.* When we can categorize some object as "hot," we then know how to act. Once a source of water is categorized as "contaminated," we probably avoid drinking it. Knowing what to do in most situations requires the use of cultural categories.
5. *Cultural categories permit us to order and relate classes of events.* Cultural meaning systems involve sets of related categories. A simple idea such as "children

31. *See* text at note 11 *supra*.

32. Spradley & McCurdy, Anthropology, *supra* note 10, at 27.

should obey their parents" relates at least two categories of relatives. Most human endeavors, from making a spear to complex scientific experiments are based on ordering and relating categories.

6. *Cultural categories permit the anticipation of future events and preparation for coping with them.* "It is not simply that organisms code the events of their environment into equivalence classes, but that they utilize cues for doing so that allow an opportunity for prior adjustment to the event identified." . . . An orderly social life is based on this ability to correctly anticipate events and prepare to act appropriately. Categories ensure a measure of predictability for the human experience in every society.[33]

Cognitive anthropology acknowledges, of course, that there are many varieties and combinations of categories through which human understanding operates. As noted above, symbols facilitate this understanding within the categories. Just as genetic information is coded chemically in DNA, cultural information is coded symbolically. The symbols are arranged, combined, and adapted in accordance with cultural rules or codes that allow for the infinite number of ways in which human behavior varies and adapts itself.[34] These cultural codes are, furthermore, far from ephemeral. They survive generation after generation as part of the acquired culture of society. Variation occurs not just between generations but within generations. Human relationships are dynamic, crisscrossing biological, environmental, physical, psychological, and social needs. These needs, in turn, boil down to a single imperative: survival. Humans as a species have had to adapt over millions of years in order to survive and flourish. Alongside genetic evolution, cultural knowledge has played an important role in such adaptation. The task of the cognitive anthropologist is to give specific cultural descriptions of particular societies during adaptation.[35]

Applied Cognitive Anthropology: Case Studies in Law

While it is no surprise that cognitivism views law as a cultural institution, it may be somewhat surprising that it embraces functionalism in its study of law. The particular function of law with which cognitivism is concerned is the maintenance of social order. Because the settlement of disputes is one of the main methods of maintaining social order, cognitivism views dispute settlement as the chief function of law and examines the normative values that underlie legal principles used for settling disputes.

The origin of this method, generally known as the case method, can be traced to the seminal book by Karl Llewellyn and E. Adamson Hoebel, *The Cheyenne Way*. In this book, the authors identify three approaches to study the "law-stuff" of a culture: rules (norms), practice (behavior), and disputes arising from behavior ("trouble

---

33. *Id.* at 24–25 (citing JEROME S. BRUNER, JACQUELINE J. GOODNOW, & GEORGE A. AUSTIN, A STUDY OF THINKING 11-15 (1956)).

34. SPRADLEY & MCCURDY, ANTHROPOLOGY, *supra* note 10, at 27–29.

35. *Id.* at 33–35.

cases"). Of these, they pick the latter as the most promising approach for describing the law-stuff of a culture.[36]

A typical illustration of the case method is Laura Nader's month-long study in 1957 of sixty cases recorded in the Zapotec town court of Ralu'a (Mexico). As seen next, Nader extracted a number of generalizations about various aspects of Zapotec culture and social organization from these cases. She also used the ethnographic data gleaned from them to predict future disposition of cases in the community.[37]

Discussed in the following are six case studies of applied cognitive anthropology. The first explains the functional focus. Discussed thereafter is how law is viewed as a cultural code by the cognitivists, followed by a section on how cultural values underlie every legal system. Next are three sections that describe cognitivism in the courtroom.

A. Cognitivism, Functionalism, and Law

The two leading cognitivists, James Spradley and David McCurdy, describe law as a "universal feature of culture."[38] Consistently with the classical definition of culture as knowledge used to generate behavior,[39] they claim that law is defined as "part of the cultural knowledge that people use to organize and interpret behavior."[40] Their focus on behavior shows a preference for a functional rather than a formal approach to law. The latter is the predominant approach in Western legal systems, in which law is defined with reference to formal institutions for making and enforcing it as well as for settling disputes. Some early Western scholars maintained that primitive cultures had no law because they did not have such formal institutions as courts, police, judges, and so on.[41]

The cognitivists' preference for a functional approach to law comprises formal as well as informal legal institutions, with a focus on how they maintain social order.[42] An orderly social life is taken as a basic or universal human desire, and cultural rules (both formal and informal) reinforce order through social conformity. Social pressure, rewards, recognition, reprobation, ostracism, and ridicule are examples of informal means that induce conformity. Religious rituals and secular ceremonies are examples of the more formal methods of reinforcing common values and individual commitments to follow them. Nonconforming behavior may be dealt with informally as long as it yields socially satisfactory results. However, when this is not possible, a dispute will arise and need resolution.

---

36. Karl N. Llewellyn & Edward A. Hoebel, The Cheyenne Way: Conflict and Case Law in Primitive Jurisprudence 20–21, 29 (1941).

37. Laura Nader, *An Analysis of Zapotec Law Cases*, 3 Ethnology 404, 407 (1964).

38. Spradley & McCurdy, Anthropology, *supra* note 10, at 386.

39. *See* text at note 8 *supra.*

40. Spradley & McCurdy, Anthropology, *supra* note 10, at 388.

41. *Id.* at 387.

42. *Id.* at 388; Nader, *Zapotec Law Cases*, *supra* note 37, at 406.

The law shows one of its chief functions here, as each culture contains agreed-upon methods to settle disputes.[43] But the law has other functions as well, and the ethnographer's task is to trace its relations with other social institutions.[44] However, as noted above, dispute settlement is the law's principal function. Law is therefore defined (or redefined) as "cultural knowledge that people use to settle disputes by means of agents who have recognized authority."[45]

According to the case method, once an appropriate authority has been recognized as having the legal competence to settle disputes, a variety of disputes will inevitably come before it. These disputes and the process of their settlement constitute the raw material that ethnographers must study and from which they can draw generalized conclusions about the range of grievances to be resolved, the likely parties in particular grievances, the dyads that appear in opposition, how particular rules applied to settle disputes demonstrate the dominant cultural values, and how law is related to social structure.

In the following excerpt, Nader explains the task of the ethnographer using the case method.

Laura Nader, *The Anthropological Study of Law*, 67 Am. Anthropol. 3, 23–25 (1965).

If field studies of law are to result in comparable data what essential materials should be covered by the ethnographer? First, several assumptions should be made clear: 1) there is a limited range of dispute for any particular society; that is, all societies do not fight about all the possible things human beings could fight about; 2) a limited number of formal procedures are used by human societies in the prevention of and/or settlement of grievances (e.g. courts, contests, ordeals, go-betweens, etc.); 3) there will be a choice in the number and modes of settlement (e.g. arbitration, mediation, compromise, adjudication, and so on). How people resolve conflicting interests and how they remedy strife situations is a problem with which all societies have to deal; and usually they find not one but many ways to handle grievances. In any society also there are various remedy agents which may be referred to when a grievance reaches a boiling point, and an understanding of all such agencies is necessary for a comprehensive analysis of social control and for a sophisticated contextual analysis of the court system, should one exist.

Having in mind the range of remedy agents (or agencies) in a society certain empirical questions come to mind: 1) What do people fight and argue about publicly, and how, when, and where do conflicts come about? 2) How do societies handle disputes and what is the outcome for the individual(s) involved as well as for the society? 3) Within what groups are disputes con-

---

43. Spradley & McCurdy, Anthropology, *supra* note 10, at 389.

44. *Id.*

45. *Id.* at 390.

centrated? 4) How do disputes at one group level (family, kindred, lineage, etc.) affect that at another (village, region, nation, etc.)?

Information on these four areas should enable us to provide answers to such developmental questions as: At what ages (speaking of biological and sociological age) in the life cycle, in what roles, at what rank, and under what conditions do citizens fit into the picture as parties to specific disputes? What is the relation between the composition of the family, the frequency of crime, and the use of the courts? The Gluecks (1950) and B. Whiting in this volume suggest a relation between the composition of the family and delinquent acts. A relation between family structure and the use of the courts is illustrated by the Zapotec situation where the absence of a father and/or brother often forced women to take recourse to formal law agencies as plaintiffs. Why should this be? What are the social and cultural correlates of sex and age-linked offenses? Among the Zapotec for example, women are rarely defendants in dispute cases involving assault and battery, while men on the other hand are rarely defendants in slander cases. These informations should also enable us to answer the question: 5) What are the manifest and latent jobs of the law and how are they related to the social structure?

A quantitative and qualitative sampling of dispute cases from each society could provide key material around which comparison would be made—provided that sampling problems are resolved or indeed that one could guarantee witnessing more than a handful of cases in some populations. The dispute case, unlike any particular form of adjudication or class of disputes or functions, is present in every society. Universally such cases share most of the following components depending on what stage the dispute is in: the dispute or grievance (property, custody, theft, homicide, marital obligations, or however the society may class such disputes); the parties to a grievance (sex, age, rank, status, relation between parties); presentation of the grievance (before a remedy agent such as a judge, go-between, lineage head); procedure or manner of handling a grievance; the outcome; the termination of the grievance; and the enforcement of a decision. Mapping the component parts of a case so that the sociological aspects of conflict can be systematically discerned has been attempted for the Zapotec material. . . . The results are mainly descriptive generalizations which have proved useful as a springboard for comparative work. . . .

In examining monographs that included case materials, certain neglected areas were noted: frequency estimates, sociological data on the parties such as age and status, detailed descriptions of the legal and extralegal factors determining the outcome. The decision-making process is often ignored or barely mentioned. Typically, for example, there might be a statement of a case, then a sentence declaring that "after much wrangling" the case was settled in such and such a manner. We need to know more about the "wrangling." If we are dealing with a society with courts we need to investigate the

> dispute case in the context of the range of social institutions which adults use in the resolution or prevention of trouble situations, that is, we should sample out-of-court cases as well as court cases. In this way we may reveal the intricate balance between the use patterns of various authority systems....
>
> But how do we arrive at an understanding of our last question: 6) What jurisprudential ideas are expressed in legal reasoning? If prior to field work we attempt to make a category listing of substantive areas of the law such as family law, tort law, property law, we run into difficulties. Who could say, at this stage of knowledge, what the major categories of family law would be when viewed cross-culturally? The range of possibilities in terms of substantive law are too great to be handled in the same way as procedure, given our present knowledge. Is inheritance, for example, a universal category of law?... Llewellyn and Hoebel might suggest that we "find" substantive law by noting cases of breach, and this one can do in the field only. But there is another possibility, one which admittedly has its drawbacks. Field workers, both implicitly and explicitly, have described the law ways of preliterate and nonliterate groups usually against a backdrop of Western European law. Hence the familiar chapters of family, property, contract, torts, etc. This has been the subject of much criticism. While I do not believe that we can adopt wholesale Western jurisprudential categories of law for use in non-Western cultures, it is possible that we could explicitly state that we are using an outline of Anglo-American common law, for example, against which or from which we view exotic legal systems. At least we would be clear about what our biases were....

The ethnographer's main task is to describe the process of dispute settlement of a given culture. This process may settle disputes even if no agents with authority are clearly identifiable; among the Zapotec people, for example, some disputes may be settled through extralegal methods or may fester without resolution. Nader and Harry Todd identify seven procedures used worldwide to settle disputes: adjudication, arbitration, mediation, negotiation, coercion/conquest, avoidance (or withdrawal of a claim), and "lumping it." The latter term refers to the failure on the part of the complainant to pursue and obtain a final resolution.[46] Whereas avoidance implies a complete rupture in the social relationship between the antagonists, lumping it implies a lack of final resolution without necessary rupture. This phenomenon has been observed among the Hopi, as well as Scandinavians and Koreans.[47]

Max Gluckman suggests that the ethnographer who studies the process of disputing in any given culture must be mindful of the nature of the relationships between the disputants. After studying the Lozi in what is now Zambia, he argued that this relationship may determine the procedural form of settlement—which, in turn, may

---

46. Laura Nader & Harry F. Todd, Jr., *Introduction*, *in* THE DISPUTING PROCESS—LAW IN TEN SOCIETIES 1, 9 (Laura Nader & Harry F. Todd, Jr. eds., 1978).

47. *Id.* at 9–10.

determine the nature of the outcome.[48] For example, the more complex the relationship and the greater the desire to continue that relationship, the more likely the parties will be to choose a negotiated solution that is mutually satisfactory. Likewise, the more simple the relationship, the greater the likelihood of an imposed or coerced settlement.[49]

Other variables that affect disputing are political power and control over resources. Some disputing mechanisms maintain and legitimize the existing distribution of political and economic power; in short, those in power control the mechanisms of dispute settlement and thus their outcomes.[50] Such arguments would certainly find favor among Marxist and cultural materialist ethnographers. The ethnographer must also be alert to motive, for example a monetary payoff, an out-of-court settlement, an apology, or to soothe pride.[51] Yet another important variable, the notion of the multiplicity of legal levels within a single society, was chiefly promoted by Durkheim and Malinowski.[52] According to this view, society does not have just a single, monolithic legal system, and every functioning subgroup within society has its own legal system. Thus, the settlement of disputes depends on how authority to settle disputes is distributed at the various levels, and failure to settle a dispute at one level may not necessarily exclude it from settlement at another level.[53]

Under the functional approach, a dispute becomes "legal" only when it is resolved by an authority that has the socially recognized competence to settle disputes. This is the first of three types of disputes. It is possible for a dispute to arise outside the legal process and fester until such time as a recognized authority takes cognizance of the dispute and settles it.[54] If no official cognizance is taken, it is usually because the dispute is not socially significant and may thus exist at the infralegal level. Different cultures have different ways of dealing with infralegal disputes, including avoidance, fighting, verbal insults, prayer, and settlement by mutual agreement. Infralegal disputes are the second of the three types of dispute. The third type are extralegal disputes. These remain outside the legal process but degenerate into violence and war between political groups or feuds between subgroups and gangs. Among the Zapotec, unsettled feuds are not unknown; in one case, a Zapotec farmer's crops were stolen but no action was taken against the suspected thief because of the absence of proof.[55]

48. Max Gluckman, The Judicial Process Among the Barotse of Northern Rhodesia 18–20 (1955).

49. Nader & Todd, *supra* note 46, at 13.

50. *Id.* at 20–21. *See also* Laura Nader & Elisabetta Grande, *Current Illusions and Delusions about Conflict Management—In Africa and Elsewhere*, 27 Law & Soc. Inquiry 573, 590 (2002).

51. Nader & Todd, *supra* note 46, at 22.

52. Leopold Pospíšil, Kapauku Papuans and Their Law 272 (1958).

53. For a case study of this phenomenon, *see* Laura Nader & Duane Metzger, *Conflict Resolution in Two Mexican Communities*, 65 Am. Anthropol. 584 (1963).

54. Spradley & McCurdy, Anthropology, *supra* note 10, at 392. *See also* Nader, *Zapotec Law Cases*, *supra* note 37, at 407. Nader reports the case of a physically abusive Zapotec husband who ignored infralegal remonstrations at the family and church levels, and who had to be finally dealt with by the town court.

55. Spradley & McCurdy, Anthropology, *supra* note 10, at 394.

The distinctions among legal, infralegal, and extralegal disputes are only an analytical device that shows the variety of disputes likely to arise in a culture. They are not mutually exclusive categories. Indeed, many disputes arise that defy easy categorization. For example:

(1) Among the Comanche, the willful killing of a man's horse permits the owner to kill the transgressor himself through the socially approved act of self-redress.
(2) A dispute may be settled by a go-between who negotiates a settlement, as often happens in disputes between different kinship groups among the Ifugao of the Philippines.
(3) Among the Eskimo, disputes are often settled by a game of skill in which the disputants engage in mental or physical combat in accordance with certain rules.
(4) Disputes may also be settled by ordeal whereby the accused is subjected to a painful or dangerous test, the outcome of which is supposed to be controlled by supernatural forces.[56]

Most of these methods are alien to Western notions of maintaining social discipline, yet they show that non-Western societies have a variety of formal and informal cultural mechanisms for maintaining normative order. As to whether these examples are legal, infralegal, or extralegal, number four would hardly qualify as legal in the Western sense. Nevertheless, it undeniably has a disciplinary function in the same way as Western law. Indeed, one study shows how legal and supernatural systems work in complementary fashion to uphold the social system.[57]

B. Law as a Cultural Code

The definition that cultural knowledge is, in its totality, a code or grammar for interpreting experience and generating behavior has special implications for law.[58] The legal system is an integral part of culture; therefore, it too is "a code for interpreting and settling disputes."[59] This code contains answers to such questions as what types of issues typically arise in a dispute, who seeks legal recourse, who is in the wrong, what rules have been violated, and who can authoritatively settle the dispute. The authority will draw from code, rules, and principles to answer the questions raised in a dispute in a manner that the rest of society recognizes as appropriate. These settlements and decisions may serve as guides for resolving future disputes.

The ethnographer's task of learning law as a code of culture is confronted by a potential difficulty; namely, of confusing ideal law with actual law, or law as it ought to be and law as it is. When the participant observer learns through an informant, the latter may feel the natural urge to state rules in terms of how people ought to

56. *Id.* at 396–98.

57. David M. Schneider, *Political Organization, Supernatural Sanctions on the Punishment for Incest on Yap*, 59 AM. ANTHROPOL. 791 (1957).

58. *See* Nader & Todd, *supra* note 46, at 28 on the "emic" dimension of the disputing process.

59. SPRADLEY & MCCURDY, ANTHROPOLOGY, *supra* note 10, at 394.

behave rather than make a statement of actual behavior. To guard against this danger, the ethnographer must develop a multipronged strategy that draws on several sources, such as:

1. Informal discussion with informants.
2. Clear statements from informants as to the ideal rule.
3. Clear statements from informants as to what actual behavior is.
4. The ethnographer's own observations,
5. Other professional reports as to behavior.[60]

What follows is a statement about how Nader was able to marshal the above sources to gain cultural knowledge of Zapotec law and to anticipate the contours of future disputes and their resolution.

> On the basis of these and other sources of information, one constructs a cultural grammar and then tests it with further observations and questions. The goal, as in all ethnography, is to anticipate appropriate behavior and to identify inappropriate actions in the same way informants do.
>
> The idealized reports that the anthropologist received from some Zapotec informants she recorded as part of her data. In addition, she remained alert for actual trouble cases that occurred in the course of daily life. She also gained the trust of informants who gave firsthand reports of other cases. From these sources she was able to make important inferences about the cultural knowledge of law that the Zapotec used to settle disputes. Eventually, like the Zapotec themselves, she was able to anticipate such things as the trouble spots where conflicts were most likely to occur, the kinds of persons involved in disputes, the kinds of disputes that would arise, the various ways they would be settled, and even the expected fines or other outcomes for individual cases. For instance, after examining many cases handled by the *presidente*, she discovered that he operated with an implicit cultural rule for penalizing men and women. "For the same crimes men should be punished by fines, required public work, or jail sentence, whereas women should be punished by fines, on rare occasions by jail sentences, and never by required public work." Having discovered this cultural rule, the anthropologist could anticipate the outcome of cases involving women. Like the Zapotec themselves, she would have been very surprised if the *presidente* had sentenced a woman to perform public work. Indeed, the *presidente* himself would probably never do such a thing because the outcry from members of the pueblo would be too great. For the lifelong resident of Ralu'a or the visiting anthropologist, this ability to anticipate such behavior comes from an understanding of Zapotec legal knowledge.[61]

60. *Id.* at 401.

61. *Id.*

Law reflects the fundamental values of the culture within which it operates. These values are contained in legal principles that express societal conceptions of what is considered to be a desirable state of affairs for that society. These principles give rise to substantive and procedural law.[62] Zapotec culture is characterized by two fundamental principles for promoting social order.[63]

C. Cultural Values and Legal Principles: The Harmony Model

This section illustrates the above with Nader's examination of dispute settlement in two Zapotec communities in Mexico. One study was of the mountain Zapotec village of Talea de Castro; the other was of the town of Ralu'a. Nader contends that together, these studies show that Zapotec culture is characterized by two fundamental principles in the promotion of normative order, namely maintaining harmony and balance (*erj.goonz*).[64] Talea best illustrates the harmony model, whereas Ralu'a best illustrates the model of balance, although both are closely related.

Harmony as ideology. Nader describes how the promotion of harmony in Talea de Castro emerged and has operated as a political strategy during the colonial and postcolonial periods. Her ethnohistorical example is based on fieldwork and historical records. In studying Talea, Nader adopts an approach that she describes as "internalist" in that it shows "how the 'natives' use the harmony model."[65]

The sixteenth-century colonial policy of Spain left a permanent mark on Talea and its courts.[66] A hallmark of this policy was the creation of semi-autonomous village communities in Mexico. Talea has jealously guarded its autonomy as a way of avoiding interference from the national government. Village feuds and dissension provoke national attention, if not intervention; thus, noninterference and nonintervention by the national authorities has depended on how well the village manages its internal affairs. In such matters, the Zapotec espouse an ethos of moderation and symmetry.

> It is unappealing to be too rich or too poor, too fat or too thin, too pretty or too ugly. Asymmetry is often the underlying cause of envy, witchcraft accusations, or disputes in courts.[67]

This almost self-effacing ethos is a way of avoiding attention and thereby preventing impingement of a superordinate power. Aside from this strategy of prevention and

---

62. *Id.* at 414.

63. Nader, *Zapotec Law Cases*, *supra* note 37, at 405.

64. Laura Nader, *The Crown, The Colonists, and the Course of Zapotec Village Law*, *in* HISTORY AND POWER IN THE STUDY OF LAW : NEW DIRECTIONS IN LEGAL ANTHROPOLOGY 320 (June Starr & Jane F. Collier eds., 1989) (study of Talea de Castro); Nader, *Zapotec Law Cases*, *supra* note 37 (study of Ralu'a).

65. Nader, *The Crown, The Colonists, and the Course of Zapotec Village Law*, *supra* note 64, at 333, 341.

66. *Id.* at 321.

67. *Id.* at 328.

resistance, the Zapotec adopt two additional strategies: "appeal to tradition and rigorous attention to legality."[68]

Since the sixteenth century, the central village court of Talea has had broad jurisdiction to hear cases. It is a place where tradition is recognized and given expression and where village autonomy is symbolized. Additionally, Nader asserts that "the main feature of style in the Talean court [is] one that values the achievement of balance between principals in a case."[69] This balance is achieved as "compromise arrived at by adjudication" or even "adjudication based on compromise."[70] In either instance, the process is always to establish harmony.

The desire for harmony is internalized by the Zapotec; it is their emic self-image of what differentiates them from other strife-riven communities of Mexico. Nader reports the popular belief of the Taleans that if they do not live peaceful, harmonious lives, the national government will intervene and take over local affairs.[71] The ideology of harmony is then the political basis for their claim to autonomy in their *relaciones exteriores*.[72] In addition, the concept of autonomy serves as a powerful judicial tool with which the village court demands private parties to be accountable to the community and to promote other community values. In both areas, the goal is to minimize the sense of injustice and outrage.

Nader explains these basic normative values of Zapotec culture, how they are reflected through law, and how the harmony model is a cardinal symbol of Zapotec society.

Laura Nader, *The Crown, the Colonists, and the Course of Zapotec Law*, *in* History and Power in the Study of Law: New Directions in Legal Anthropology 320, 332–342 (June Starr & Jane F. Collier eds., 1989).

> ... At the core, the harmony style and its associated ideology, as I described them for the Zapotec, are internal accommodations to conquest and domination....
>
> ... If we look at style as a component of a political ideology, however, we come closer to understanding that the Talean harmony model is a tool for restricting the encroachment of external, superordinate power.
>
> Why have I stressed harmony or balance in my work on the Taleans? In spite of my observations and interviews, which revealed considerable discord in Talean social life, I emphasize the importance of harmony and balance not only because I read Durkheim and the structural-functionalists, but also

68. *Id.* at 329 (quoting Elizabeth Colson, Tradition and Contract: The Problem of Order 76 (1974)).

69. Nader, *The Crown, The Colonists, and the Course of Zapotec Village Law*, *supra* note 64, at 332.

70. *Id.*

71. *Id.* at 335.

72. *Id.*

because I learned from the Taleans that they themselves prefer that disputes be settled on the basis of these principles. Even when one becomes more of an insider and hears of many instances of conflict and division, Taleans still present themselves as peaceful and harmonious. Harmony, they argue, is what differentiates them from others—the people of the sierra or the Valley of Oaxaca or the Cajones, where people are not peaceful. We are thus more in the domain of ideology than of observational reality. Taleans strongly believe that if they were not living peaceful, harmonious lives the state would interfere in their business. It is also their theory about how their society related first to the Crown and later to the Mexican state. The image of harmony thus dominates how they present themselves to outsiders in what they like to describe as *relaciones exteriores.* As they state: "We are peaceful in this village, and by being peaceful and minding our own business we keep control of our village. We keep it in local hands, and by so doing we can maintain a relative autonomy." And as we shall see, this attempt to present a united front in response to external contact is not an uncommon reaction to colonization and what Wolf . . . called "the tug of war between conquerors and conquered."

The political effectiveness of the Talean court depends on democratic participation, whereby it disperses power and reinforces community solidarity. In the name of harmony the court can hold private power accountable for the general good of the village. In the name of autonomy the court encourages decision-making that is accountable. In the name of solidarity it makes decisions reflecting concerns about long-term consequences. Through its legal processes the court expresses and ranks social values that are important to the village and to its relationship with the outside world. The village court can compete effectively with the district court, for villagers generally opt for local dispute-handling processes. . . . The courts are the expression of political interest pursued through democratic legal procedures that are governed by the concepts of harmony and balance. These concepts enable conflicting interests to be accommodated in dispute settlement. In terms of actual case-handling, the harmony model reflects less attention to the facts of specific cases than to the language of disputing in the village court as opposed to that used in state courts. Through their ideology of harmony, villagers create an image of their society as cohesive and independent and thus fend off the outside world. . . .

It is worth reiterating that the features of Talean court style have something in common with models presented by anthropologists and sociologists for people in other parts of the world, despite great organizational and cultural differences. . . .

Ethnographies on Africa, as Colson . . . has pointed out, report cases of societies managing to maintain local autonomy in face of colonial incursion by using local law. . . .

In the United States during the 1960s, adversarial law was highly valued as the means for attaining civil rights. At that time this legal model was

> broadened to include attainment not only of rights but also of remedies in such domains as civil rights, consumer rights, environmental rights, and the rights of women, Native Americans, and the elderly. Opponents of the adversarial model moved with surprising speed to supplant it within ten years by a harmony model that has been translated into action and institution-building.... Again, I believe the rapidity with which the change in styles of dispute-resolution was accepted can be attributed to the growing movement in Christian fundamentalism in the United States. This example of the shift from adversary to harmony models in the United States, as fundamentalism has gained new strength, inspires me to consider the spread of Christianity around the globe as a possible source of the harmony model in reality and in anthropological theory....
>
> ... The ideology of harmony thus becomes transformed into the image of themselves that Taleans present to outsiders, and it may reflect to some extent what missionaries have preached to them over 400 years—that harmony is the Christian way. This ideology and image of Talean social life has not only been approved by outsiders, but also helped maintain village solidarity.
>
> Anthropological theory is shaped by the ideologies presented to them by informants, as well as by the Western world and such social philosophers as Emile Durkheim. That this ideology may have had Western origins makes it even more interesting as we attempt to trace the origins of anthropological ideas and to determine why Taleans employ the principles of harmony and balance in dispute settlement and in dealings with outsiders. Although I have focused here on how the "natives" use the harmony model, this issue has brought me closer to understanding how anthropologists use the natives' harmony model and how anthropological theory has been shaped both by colonial policies and by Christianity as preached to indigenous peoples. It thus appears likely that structural-functionalists have influenced colonial policy and been influenced by colonial policies through the resulting indigenous harmony ideologies. In the history of anthropological theory, structural-functionalism becomes more understandable when we realize how our informants have used colonial policies and how these people and their ideology have been reflected in our analyses. Fact, indigenous ideology, and anthropological theory thus become part of a common temporal perspective on law. If the early functionalists were internalist in their analyses focused on structure, continuity, or equilibrium, while contemporary anthropologists are more interested in transformations and in the role of external forces of change, both periods contribute to the understanding of continuity and transformation in law.

D. Cultural Values and Legal Principles: The Principle of Balance

Nader's description of the court system of the Zapotec town of Ralu'a explains that its three judges (the *presidente*, the *alcalde*, and the *sindicio*) are selected by town citizens because of their reputations as persons who would be able to maintain balance.[73] Under the principle of maintaining balance, finding fault is not as important as finding a compromise solution that accommodates the demands of all parties and restores peace. Nor does the court hesitate to advise parties about their future conduct. These traditions do not mean that substantive rules are ignored and fault is never assigned. Rather, a solution is found, without blame and with minimum loss of face, that reinforces the substantive rule in question.

Nader examines a number of cases in Zapotec culture that illustrate this principle. In one case, a truck driver damaged a basket of chilies belonging to the plaintiff. Both parties appeared before the court; the chilies were examined; the defendant was asked to pay a nominal three pesos for only the portion of the contents of the basket that was damaged; and the court advised the plaintiff to avoid placing his chilies in areas of traffic.[74] In another case, the alleged wrongdoer was encouraged (without being ordered) to make a modest financial settlement to help the plaintiff seek remedial help.[75] In both of these cases, the balance was considered to have been restored by terminating all grievances. Thus, the Zapotec ideal is not to exact revenge but to restore equilibrium between the parties.[76] The idea of striking a balance between two extremes such as winning and losing, working too hard and not enough, being sociable and antisocial, is central to Zapotec culture.[77] Thus law as part of the culture is just as strongly affected by the principle of social equilibrium as all other aspects of social interaction.

The maintenance of personal reputation and integrity is another cultural value demonstrated by Nader's study, in which slander was more severely punished than citizen insubordination and even assault and battery. Another conclusion was that women in Zapotec culture enjoyed high status, as demonstrated by the fact that Zapotec women regularly took their husbands to court and that decisions of the male head of household were frequently overruled in court.[78]

The general point, of course, is that "[u]nderlying every legal system are those shared values that give meaning to a particular way of life."[79]

E. The Tramp in Court

This section and the next two inject some realism into the function of the legal system in a specifically judicial context. The first two sections consider an urban nomad charged with drunkenness in public. The functional inquiry shows that in its actual operation, the legal system may well fall short of the values it aspires to protect. Furthermore, *as per* the cognitivist mission of faithfully reporting the insider's

---

73. Laura Nader, *Styles of Court Procedure: To Make the Balance*, *in* LAW AND CULTURE IN SOCIETY 69, 73 (Laura Nader ed., 1997).

74. *Id.* at 74–75.

75. *Id.* at 75–76.

76. *Id.* at 73.

77. *Id.*

78. Nader, *Zapotec Law Cases*, *supra* note 37, at 418.

79. SPRADLEY & MCCURDY, ANTHROPOLOGY, *supra* note 10, at 417.

point of view, this section includes the perspective of the urban nomad in his various brushes with the judicial system in the city of Seattle.

In one particular study, poignantly titled "They Make You Feel Like a Bum," Spradley describes in detail the squalid conditions of detention prior to the defendant's appearance in court, followed by descriptions of the procedures of arraignment, trial, and sentencing. The urban nomad had various options for responding to the charge (*e.g.*, guilty, not guilty, bail out, bond out, plead extenuating circumstances, request a treatment center, etc.).[80] However, Spradley reported a judicial system so stacked against the nomad that most feel it would be futile to plead not guilty. Thus, some 94% of a sample pleaded guilty and almost 97% of drunkenness cases resulted in convictions.

The emic/cognitive perspective is clearly shown in the following excerpt. Not only did most nomads believe that "You can't win the case" and "You are guilty anyway," they also felt that pleading guilty was the best way to receive a lighter sentence. The alternative was further delay and re-detention under the depressing conditions of the drunk tank, even if the nomad believed in his own innocence. Hence the exasperated cry of: "[Y]ou look and feel like a bum whether you are or not."[81]

Thus, all the legal network of protections are effectively denied to the nomad. He is coerced into violating his own integrity by surrendering to the system through a guilty plea. There is a bitter sense of alienation when the nomad sees that the affluent segment of society, with resources and lawyers, gets different (and more favorable) treatment.

James P. Spradley, You Owe Yourself a Drunk: An Ethnology of Urban Nomads 180–184, 190–192 (1970).

> The most widely used way to beat a drunk charge is a passive one—*plead guilty* and hope for the best. Ninety-four per cent of the sample reported they usually pleaded guilty to a drunk charge even when they felt sure they were not really drunk at the time of arrest. Almost 97 per cent of the drunk cases heard in this court result in convictions. Tramps firmly believe that "you can't beat the charge," "you can't win the case," and it doesn't make any difference what you plead, "you are guilty anyway." Most men felt they actually had "no other choice," and it is this feeling that leads them to see this, and other courts, which hear drunk cases, purely as kangaroo courts. Most men also believe they will be rewarded by the judge if they take this passive role and plead guilty. One man stated, "In my opinion you get a lighter sentence"; another said, "It's the best out."
>
> Another important reason given for pleading guilty is that there might be additional punishment if you do not. This could manifest itself in any number of ways. Often it means that one returns to the drunk tank to await

80. James P. Spradley, You Owe Yourself a Drunk: An Ethnography of Urban Nomads 173 (1970).

81. *Id.* at 192.

trial; more than 30 per cent of those who reported pleading not guilty had waited in the drunk tank for their trial, some for more than ten days. Twenty-seven per cent of the sample had, at one time or another, entered a plea of not guilty, although only four men reported they had been acquitted. One man stated:

The judge told me if I didn't think I was guilty to plead not guilty, which I did. He moved my case ahead 30 days and I spent 30 days in jail, was found guilty and sentenced to 30 days! . . .

One man recalled:

I pled not guilty lots of times and they had to appear against me and so they lost a little time and they got mad. Every time the wagon went around and they seen me, to jail I went.

Another said: "If you plead not guilty you have the arresting cops against you so you can't win anyway!"

Finally, men plead guilty most of the time because they believe the courts are in collusion with the police against them. "All a cop has to do is say you were drunk—the judge never goes against a cop!" . . . Tramps not only know the assumptions and rules of our legal system, they also know that the law enforcement agencies violate these rules as far as they are concerned: they are assumed to be guilty rather than innocent; they are rewarded for pleading guilty even when they are innocent; they have no way to provide themselves with a defense attorney; and they are punished if they go against the system by pleading not guilty. The network of protections for the innocent are stripped away from the process of criminal justice for these men and in their place is an overwhelming tide of pressure coercing them into violating their own integrity by agreeing with the verdict of the system. He is asked to speak against himself on those occasions when he feels sure he is not guilty, and he knows he must comply because the immediate consequences will be worse than if he defends himself. . . . Yet the long-range consequences may be devastating: the act of publicly and repeatedly repudiating himself increasingly alienates the man from himself, creating an inner vacuum obliterating his true identity. . . .

Equal justice for all under the law is the maxim of this court, yet when we consider to whom the judge gives sentences to and who escapes them, we must conclude that some men are more equal than others. The legal system of America and the criminal justice practice are based on norms and values which are in contrast to those of the urban nomad. Judges are socialized into the dominant society and learn to dispense justice on the basis of those values. This practice means essentially that the man with the *most resources* is rewarded. Unto whom much is given, little shall be required. As a man moves into the world of tramps he loses many of the things which middle-class Americans consider important: steady employment, wife and family, interest in working, and a sedentary existence. The man who has retained any of these resources has a better chance of escaping incarceration than others. . . .

Consider how these men feel. They are arrested for the public nature of their life style; those who live in better parts of town and behave in similar ways are not. They are robbed and roughed up because they are tramps; other citizens are not treated this way. They are kept in jail for days after each arrest awaiting court because they are too poor to bail out; those with money are released in a few hours. They are brought into court and arraigned with no opportunity for a defense counsel; those with wealth may hire an attorney. They are induced by the system to plead guilty to escape the consequences of using other means which require self-assertion; those with money never even face this dilemma because they have bailed out. With these contrasts in mind it is with ironic disbelief that the tramp views the sign hanging over the judge's bench: EQUAL JUSTICE FOR ALL UNDER THE LAW, and it is no surprise that 64 per cent of the men in the sample reported they did not feel that the Seattle Criminal Court provided them with such justice. But there is a deeper and perhaps more significant aspect of the court experience which concerned most men.

Those in our society who define these men as alcoholics, bums, or common drunks often believe that they have "reached bottom" and lost all respect for themselves. They appear in public in a condition which offends other people and many would find it hard to believe that they are concerned about the image of themselves they portray to others. My first observations in the court aroused feelings of shock and pity for the men who appeared on public drunkenness charges; they were unshaven, unkempt, poorly groomed individuals who appeared to be the dregs of humanity. It was a long time before I was to discover that they may have spent five days and nights in a crowded cement drunk tank with no possible opportunity to prepare themselves personally for their appearance in court. The men in the sample were asked, "What do you feel is the worst thing about appearing in court on a drunk charge?", and though their answers were varied, they consistently fell into the following major categories:

The public humiliation	53%
The waiting, loss of time	24%
Facing the judge without a defense	17%
Loss of food, liquor, and physical comfort	6%

Those who felt the worst aspect of their experience in court was the public humiliation were especially worried about their physical appearance, which is always important for maintaining a viable self-image:

Your appearance, it is degrading to lay in the drunk tank over weekend and appear in court—no shave, no comb to even comb your hair, clothes all wrinkled.

It is as if the drunk tank were especially designed to desecrate a man before he is placed on exhibit in court:

A person is usually sick and dirty from laying on the concrete floor and to have to appear in front of a lot of people in that condition is very humiliating. . . .

. . . The worst thing about court is being "herded around like a bunch of cattle—dumb animals." From the moment a man is taken to the court docket until he receives his sentence in court, he feels more like the victim of our legal institutions than their beneficiary. He may attempt one or more strategies for beating the charge, but these almost always end in failure and he quickly learns it is best to comply with the system. Yet, in so doing, the sense of alienation from oneself and others increases; he has moved even further away from those respected identities he had when arrested for the first time, and as he finally goes to the court docket and the courtroom he finds, as Mr. Tanner put it, that "you look and feel like a bum whether you are or not."

F. Procedural Law

The ethnographer's task of gaining knowledge of legal norms extends to procedural law as well as substantive law at various legal levels of society (*e.g.*, the family, the church, village officials, witches and sorcerers, etc.). The procedural law to be studied by the ethnographer is the procedural law *de facto* (*i.e.*, the actual procedural law, whether written or not). Procedural law reflects the agreed-upon ways to settle disputes. Such law can have different consequences when applied to the same rules of substantive law, as shown in the extract that follows regarding the experiences in court of the urban nomads of Seattle.

James P. Spradley & David W. McCurdy, Anthropology: The Cultural Perspective 409 (1975).

Procedural Rules in U.S. Society

Procedural rules in our own legal system are not always clearly specified. The ethnographer seeks to make these rules explicit, thereby shedding light on substantive rules and the entire process of law. The ethnographic research among the tramps in Seattle, Washington, mentioned earlier, revealed an implicit procedural rule that held enormous significance for this population. It involves a procedural rule for sentencing that can be stated as follows.

If a man is poor and has been arrested many times for being drunk in public, he shall be sentenced with greater severity than those with money or with no record of previous arrests for drunkenness.

On the basis of this rule, two men could be arrested at 10:00 p.m. on Monday on the same block in Seattle and plead guilty in court to public drunkenness. One would be given a 2-day suspended sentence and would walk out of the courtroom a free man. The other would be given 90 days in jail. Why this difference? The first man had not been arrested for this crime during the preceding 6 months, whereas the other had been arrested seven times.

But the most significant part of this procedural rule involves differences in wealth. Take two men, for example, who were arrested 10 to 15 times each year for public drunkenness. Each time they were picked up by the Seattle police they had to spend several hours in the jail "drying out." Then both men were allowed to post a $20 bail, *if they had the money*. Only one of the men has this amount, and he alone was immediately released from jail. He might be arrested again within a few days or weeks and repeat the process. Over the course of 15 or 20 years such a man might spend several thousand dollars for bail, each time walking away from jail after a few hours of sleep. Although a man who posted bail was expected to appear in court for his arraignment, no one did, choosing instead to forfeit this money than face a judge and possible jail sentence. The man who could not post bail, on the other hand, waited several days in the drunk tank, appeared in court, pleaded guilty, received his sentence, and then returned to jail to serve his time. Thus, violation of the same *substantive rule* can lead to enormously different consequences, depending on the nature of related *procedural rules*.

G. The Rom in Court

Examined next is the case involving a Rom (Gypsy), presented from the emic perspective of the Rom himself. This perspective is presented by anthropologist Anne Sutherland, who testified in court on his behalf.[82]

The case involved a Rom, SN, who was convicted of the crime of using his nephew's Social Security number in his application for a car loan. When the purchase was questioned by the car dealership, SN returned the car and was arrested on a felony charge of using a false Social Security number. There was no allegation that SN intended to deprive anyone of property, and the statute did not require proof of an intention to defraud or wrongful purpose.

At this point it is important to note the testimony of Sutherland that Romany culture is unique in several ways. For example, the Roma do not have a single or "real" name but have several "American" names; their social identity is defined by what cognatic descent group or *vitsa* they belong to. The Roma are a traditionally nomadic people who frequently borrow each other's names and, in the U.S., Social Security cards; the latter are viewed as the corporate property of the kin group or *vitsa*. In fact, their sense of self and identity are so different from the traditional North American sense that they do not formally register births or obtain birth certificates.

During Sutherland's first meeting with SN, in federal prison, she discovered he had lost fifteen pounds and was visibly distressed. This was partly because he was isolated from his kinfolk, but most importantly he feared he would become defiled (*marime*) by eating food prepared by people who did not follow the rules of cleanliness required by his culture. Once declared *marime*, he would be shunned and ostracized by other Roma. SN had gone to great lengths to avoid being so branded and stigmatized.

82. Spradley & McCurdy, Conformity and Conflict, *supra* note 8, at 318.

In court, SN's defense argued that the statute under which he was charged was objectionable for two reasons. First it had a disproportionate and discriminatory impact on Roma, contrary to the equal protection clause guaranteed by the Fifth Amendment of the U.S. Constitution. Second, because in cases of deprivation of property felonious intent had to be proven, the statute's failure to require this was a serious flaw, and in SN's case there was no felonious intent. Finally, he argued that SN was merely following a time-honored cultural tradition of remaining anonymous and that his own Social Security card had been used by other Roma.[83]

These arguments were rejected, and SN was sentenced to a six-month term in prison. In the following excerpt, Sutherland explains the case and her role of anthropologist hired as an expert witness for the defense.

James Spradley & David W. McCurdy, Conformity and Conflict: Readings in Cultural Anthropology 321–325 (11th ed., 2003).

The Anthropologist as Cultural Broker

S.N.'s defense attorney contacted me after finding that he was less confused about S.N. after reading my book about Gypsies. He sought my help in determining whether S.N. was a Gypsy, what his name was, and any other cultural information (such as the use of social security numbers by Gypsies) that would help him with his case. . . .

For S.N., the most immediately effective action I could take was to see that he got the food he needed to stay "clean" in jail. When I met him he had lost fifteen pounds and was suffering demonstrable distress and nervousness. He was upset at being cut off from his culture and people for the first time in his life. In addition, he was distressed at being incarcerated and fearful for his safety. More importantly, he was worried he would become defiled or *marime*. A major concern of his was that if he ate food prepared by non-Gypsies who did not follow rules of cleanliness considered essential in the Gypsy culture, he would become *marime*, a condition of ritual impurity that would result in his being shunned by his relatives and other Gypsies. To protect himself, he avoided eating prison food in the hopes that when he was released from prison he would be able to return to his family without a period of physical exile, also called *marime* (or "rejected" as the Gypsies translate it into English). I arranged for his lawyer to provide him with money to buy food from the concession because it is packaged and untouched by non-Gypsies and therefore considered clean by Gypsy standards. He bought milk in cartons, candy bars and soft drinks and other packaged foods that, though they may lack in nutrition, at least were not defiling and kept him from starvation.

83. *Id.* at 320.

A further complicating factor for S.N. was that he spoke English as a second language. He had only a rudimentary ability to read, thus straining his grasp of his defense. And his only contact with relatives was by telephone since neither he nor they could write with any ease. Even though his limited English made it difficult for him to follow his own trial, the court did not provide a translator. . . .

The purpose of my testimony was to establish that S.N. *was* a Gypsy and that Gypsies often use false identification without intent to defraud. They do so because as members of a *vitsa*, or cognatic descent group, identification is corporate in nature. Members of the group have corporate access to property owned by other members of the group. That property includes forms of identification. . . .

I was also asked to testify on my own personal experience with discrimination against Gypsies by the Minneapolis Police Department. One instance of discrimination I related to the court occurred during a talk I gave to some twenty police officers to help them understand Gypsy culture. When I had spoken about the strong sense of family and community among the Gypsies and how much they value their children, a police officer suggested that since the main problem law enforcement officers have is how to detain the Gypsies long enough to prosecute them, removing Gypsy children from their homes on any pretext would be an effective way to keep the parents in town.

Prejudice against Gypsies often goes unrecognized even by culturally and racially sensitive people. The assistant district attorney prosecuting S.N. offered me an article that he used to understand the Gypsies, entitled "Gypsies, the People and their Criminal Propensity," . . .

Conclusions: Anthropology and Cultural Differences in The Courtroom

. . . First is the question of the cultural conflict between a historically nomadic group and the state bureaucracy of settled people. Identification—a serious legal issue in a bureaucratic society composed of people with fixed abodes and a written language—has virtually no meaning for the nomadic Gypsies who consider descent and extended family ties the defining factor for identification.

Second is the conflict between Gypsy religious rules regarding ritual pollution and prison regulations. The Gypsies avoid situations, such as a job or jail, that require them to be in prolonged contact with non-Gypsies. Jail presents special problems because the Gypsies can become *marime*, that is, defiled by unclean food and living conditions. The psychological trauma that results from isolation from their community is compounded if they then emerge from jail and have to undergo a further isolation from relatives because of becoming *marime* in jail.

Finally, this case illustrates a cultural clash between the Rom Gypsy value on corporate kinship and the American value on individual rights. The rights

> and status of an individual Rom Gypsy is directly linked to his or her membership in the *vitsa*. Furthermore, the status of all members of the *vitsa* is affected by the behavior of each individual *vitsa* member. Since they are so intricately linked, reciprocity between *vitsi* members is expected. Members of a *vitsa* and family share economic resources, stay in each other's homes, help each other in work and preparation of rituals, loan each other cars, information, identification, and money. They also share the shame of immoral or incorrect behavior by one member and the stigma (*marime*) attached to going to jail. For the Gypsies, the American ideal of each individual having only one name, one social security number, or a reputation based entirely on their own behavior is contrary to their experience and culture.
>
> The analysis of an event such as a trial, especially an event that brings to the fore cultural difference, can be instructive for both cultures. In this article I have tried to present fundamental differences in the practices of American culture and U.S. law and the practices of Roma law and Gypsy culture. Understanding differences does not necessarily resolve conflict, but it can lead to a more humanitarian application of the law to different cultures. The United States, a country based on immigration and diversity, is in no position to ignore the cultural foundations of different ethnic groups, nor are different cultures in the United States exempt from a law because it is contrary to custom. However, the more aware the legal system is of cultural histories and custom, the greater its capacity for justice.

Conclusion

The cognitive approach requires participant observers to learn the cultural codes that underlie their normative orders. Additionally, they must learn the entire culture as a particular cognitive enterprise that enables its individuals to understand and give meaning to experience itself, in addition to generating meaningful rules of behavior. The epistemological claim is implicit not only in the search for meaning but also in the claim that all cultures exhibit universal patterns of meaningful inferences drawn from behavior, artifacts, and other aspects of humanity's biosocial environment. Thus, the quest for knowledge of the cultural codes and symbols subsumed under mental categories of cognition allow a group to survive, adapt, and flourish.

We may assume in Kantian tradition that certain universal features of cognition in the human mind enable it to process experience and learn behavior.

> In order to account for the enormous diversity in human behavior from one society to another, anthropologists employ the concept of culture. Culture is the acquired knowledge people use to interpret experience and generate social behavior. Culture is like a recipe for organizing the necessary ingredients for a viable social life.
>
> Cultural knowledge consists of symbols and concepts. Anything can become a symbol by attaching some meaning to it. The meanings assigned to symbols are called concepts. Cultural concepts involve categories, sets

> of different objects that are treated as if they were equivalent. The set of rules for forming symbols, combining symbols, and interpreting symbols is called a cultural code.
>
> Cultural knowledge is learned and shared. The knowledge that people talk about is explicit; knowledge that cannot be articulated is tacit. The boundary between explicit and tacit cultural knowledge is a permeable one, and anthropologists work to assist people in making their tacit knowledge explicit.
>
> Cultural knowledge systems provide the basic means of adaptation for the human animal. Underlying the process of adaptation are important physical, psychological, and social requirements for survival. The function of culture refers to what a specific cultural practice does in general and its consequences for human adaptation.[84]

Applying these theoretical and methodological principles to law and legal contexts shows that law is part of culture, and the legal principles of any culture reflect the culture's conception of what is socially desirable. These principles give rise to the substantive and procedural law of particular cultures. The anthropologist's task is to study the operation of law as a code for settling disputes and maintaining order. Doing so results in a methodology that may be called cognitive functionalism, the goal of which is to portray the actual rather than an idealized operation of the legal system. When applied to specific judicial, and in particular, courtroom contexts, the emic descriptions reveal that the legal system does not always live up to the values it aspires to protect. This conclusion is true from the emic *and* etic perspective.

Cognitive Ethnoscience and Law

In the late 1950s and 1960s the cognitive approach to law became enmeshed with other cognitive sciences.[85] Among these were psychology, linguistics, semantics, and knowledge structures of ethnoscience domains in different societies.[86] The areas of focus of cognitive anthropology continued to expand well into the 1990s.

> In the 1970s decision models and narrative grammars were added to the cognitive approach. In the 1980s methods were developed in discourse semantics, in the mapping of consensus in knowledge and belief among individuals of culture-sharing groups, and in applications of artificial intelligence to the study of knowledge structures and procedural representations in ethnography. In the 1990s were added cognitive theories of emotion, studies of the linkage of cognitive and emotional processes with health and well-being, studies of the cognitive aspects of religious symbolism, and development of

---

84. Spradley & McCurdy, Anthropology, *supra* note 10, at 40–41.

85. Roy G. D'Andrade, The Development of Cognitive Anthropology 1, 248 (1995).

86. Benjamin N. Colby, *Cognitive Anthropology*, *in* 1 Encyclopedia of Cultural Anthropology 209, 209 (David Levinson & Melvin Ember eds., 1996).

computer-aided forms of discourse analysis and content analysis through microfeatures.[87]

Most of these developments are beyond the scope of this book. What is relevant is how cognitive anthropology has drawn from the disciplines of linguistics, psychology, and componential analysis in ethnoscience to unveil the phenomenon of law.[88] This revelation is the focus of the materials that follow. But first, some background is provided to place cognitive ethnoscience in historical context.

Historical Roots of Ethnoscience

The historical origins of cognitive anthropology in general, and ethnoscience in particular, can be traced to Franz Boas and the effort to ethnographically preserve the cultural heritage of Native American groups.[89] But in more general terms, cognitive anthropology is an emic approach rooted in Boasian cultural relativism, with input from anthropological linguistics.[90] One can see the early influence of the linguistic work of Edward Sapir, who saw cultural behavior as symbolic and culture as abstractions of ideas and behavior patterns with different meanings for different individuals.[91] Paula Erickson and Liam Murphy see the Sapir-Whorf hypothesis—that the mental structures of languages and cultures are so correlated that each influences the other—as a precursor to cognitive anthropology.[92]

With the emergence of detailed ethnographies came frequent disagreements and inconsistencies; cognitive anthropology first attempted to address this validity problem through language.[93] Cognitive anthropologists were inspired by the concept of the phoneme—the elementary unit of psychologically meaningful sound,[94] which they used to study larger units of meaning. In the process they developed interview techniques and analytical procedures to bring out native categories of thought rather than impose the analyst's own cultural system.[95]

Cognitive anthropology emerged as a formative subdiscipline at Yale University in the 1950s under the names "ethnoscience," "ethnographic semantics," and "the new ethnography," and, finally, as cognitive anthropology,[96] although Garbarino notes that

---

87. *Id.*

88. Ward H. Goodenough, *Componential Analysis and the Study of Meaning*, 32 LANGUAGE 195, 195 (1956).

89. Colby, *supra* note 86, at 210.

90. ERICKSON & MURPHY, *supra* note 4, at 115.

91. Floyd G. Lounsbury, *A Semantic Analysis of the Pawnee Kinship Usage*, 32 LANGUAGE 158, 159 (1956); MERWYN S. GARBARIO, SOCIOCULTURAL THEORY IN ANTHROPOLOGY: A SHORT HISTORY 82 (1977). For discussion of Sapir *see* Chapter 2, text at notes 108–148.

92. ERICKSON & MURPHY, *supra* note 4, at 115–16.

93. Colby, *supra* note 86, at 210–11.

94. *Id.* at 211; Goodenough, *supra* note 88, at 195–96.

95. Colby, *supra* note 86, at 211.

96. *Id.*

the term can be used broadly to include the subcategories of ethnoscience, symbolic anthropology, and the mazeway formulation of Anthony Wallace.[97] Ethnoscientists initially turned to linguistic procedures to elicit information without placing it in the preconceived classifications of the ethnographer, thereby producing taxonomies or models through componential analyses.[98] The analyses were "componential" in the sense that they aimed at producing a taxonomy or model of all components germane to the universe of enquiry free from the biases and categories of the enquirer. The ethnoscience or New Ethnography movement of the 1950s was thus an effort to extend the mentalist approach (*i.e.*, to grasp the native view) as urged by Boas and Malinowski.[99] Merwyn Garbarino notes that "[b]ecause it is so totally individualistic and mentalistic, ethnoscience has unkindly been called the last gasp of cultural relativism."[100]

As noted above, the early advocates of ethnoscience were inspired by linguistics to improve their methodological rigor through componential analyses. Their goal was to describe native cognition as a semantic domain or a domain of meaning with a cognitive code.[101] The goal of componential analysis was to uncover the criteria underlying folk taxonomies that would classify cultural realms using hierarchies of categories defined by cultural criteria.[102] By analyzing whether contrasting sounds were meaningful to the native informant, anthropological linguists using componential analysis produced "cultural grammars," or maps of semantic domains.[103] This methodology is based on the belief that culture is a formal system of rules for guiding thought and behavior.[104] The next section presents a unique case study in ethnoscience, in the form of a series of componential analyses aimed at presenting the legal grammar of the law of land tenure of a remote tribal society, the Kapauku Papuans of New Guinea.

---

97. Garbarino, *supra* note 91. Wallace's concept of the mazeway is premised on the assumption (basic to most if not all cognitive approaches) that all individuals organize or classify experience in meaningful ways. Each individual thus has a "cognitive map" to navigate through society with culturally appropriate behavior. Society will thus have as many overlapping mazeways as its members. The extent to which they overlap marks the boundaries of shared expectations and mutually predictable behaviors. According to Wallace, no individual has total knowledge of socially appropriate behavior, and individuals therefore need their fellow members of society to complement their behavior. Thus "cognitive variability rather than cognitive consonance" characterizes social interaction. The principal thesis of the mazeway concept is that culture change prompts a reordering of mazeways. If such change is too rapid or drastic, a mazeway will break down and be replaced by a new one; if it is gradual the mazeway will be adjusted as necessary, thus providing the individual with a new (or newer) cognitive map for guiding behavior.

98. *Id.*

99. *Id.*

100. *Id.*

101. Erickson & Murphy, *supra* note 4, at 116–17.

102. *Id.* at 117. *See also* Black & Metzger, *supra* note 16, at 143.

103. Erickson & Murphy, *supra* note 4, at 117.

104. *Id.*

Pospíšil's Analysis of the Kapauku Law of Land Tenure

Leopold Pospíšil used the method of componential analysis to unveil a comprehensive subnormative system of land tenure of the Kapauku Papuans of New Guinea. In Pospíšil's own words, his componential analysis is done "through an application of various methods of formal analysis drawn from the fields of ethnoscience and linguistics."[105] In particular, Pospíšil uses the taxonomic approach of Harold Conklin for his folk classifications; he also adopts the componential analysis used in structural linguistics and kinship terminology by Ward Goodenough and Floyd Lounsbury.[106] What distinguishes Pospíšil from the authors he cites is that he is not necessarily reflecting native cognition.

> Even if we accept the assumption (certainly erroneous) that all peoples could provide us, through explicit utterances or drawings, with statements about their cognitive categories, it still does not mean that these statements necessarily reveal the cognitive processes. It has long been recognized that there is often a significant discrepancy between what people think they do and what they say they do, and between what they say they do and *actually* do.[107]

Even though Pospíšil used informants to gain native insight, his analysis does not claim to portray the native point of view. Indeed, he claims his informants engaged in "folk hocus-pocus" when they erroneously informed him that the legal rules pertaining to their natural terrains were derived from their physical characteristics. Pospíšil contradicts this by claiming that economic and legal significance rather than physical characteristics were the dominant factors in the division of the various terrain types of the Kapauku's natural habitat.[108] He thus argues that his informants were "in error" with regard to certain categorizations of their land and water terrains.[109]

His use of the phrase "in error" may have meant the informants were mistaken about what was actually the correct native perception—in which case he believed the ethnographer must guard against this danger if and when necessary and substitute his own conclusion, one that is faithful to the native view. In such a situation, perhaps he meant the ethnographer's own conclusion could be claimed as the "correct" representation of native cognition. If so, Pospíšil appears to belong to the emic side of the emic/etic divide although he does not explicitly say so. Moreover, as seen in the following, the taxonomy of his semantic domain is entirely emic.

---

105. Leopold Pospíšil, Anthropology of Law: A Comparative Theory 274 (1974).

106. Harold C. Conklin, *Comment, in* Anthropology and Human Behavior 86–93 (Thomas Gladwin & William C. Sturtevant eds., 1962); Goodenough, *supra* note 88, at 195; Lounsbury, *supra* note 91, at 158.

107. Pospíšil, Anthropology of Law, *supra* note 105, at 278.

108. *Id.* at 290.

109. *Id.* at 278. *See* text of note 115, *infra*.

Kapauku Folk Taxonomy of Land and Water Categories

Pospíšil's universe of investigation was the matrix of land and water categories that constituted the material and physical environment of Kapauku Papuan society. In all, he presented fourteen categories or "terrain types" into which the Kapauku had classified their natural environment in accordance with their physical, biotic, and economic features.[110]

1. *Bugi*: The garden; land under cultivation.
2. *Juwuuda*: The yard; uncultivated land used for multiple purposes including ceremonies, meetings, cooking, as a playground for children, etc.
3. *Geiga*: Fallow grassland, a consequence of crop rotation.
4. *Gapuuga*: Fallow bush, overgrown by fast growing bushes and willow-like trees. It is used by hunters and trappers to trap various mammals and birds.
5. *Gamouda*: Exploited virgin forest. This is an area that has been stripped of most of its resources, such as rattan vines and canoe and plank trees.
6. *Buguwa*: Virgin forest. It has the resources for the canoe builder and carpenter, and it is also a valuable preserve of wild game and birds and thus a good source of protein.
7. *Ita*: A path, usually leading through fallow land and is usually exempt from cultivation on a permanent basis. Paths belong to the owner of the plots through which they cross and are used by all members of the local sublineage, and are open to all travelers.
8. *Begadimi*: A mountain summit. It is agriculturally unproductive. It provides limited hunting opportunities.
9. *Bago*: A crag akin to a rocky mountain peak. It has very few resources and is practically speaking a wasteland.
10. *Takapaka*: A swampy area that, like *Begadimi*, is agriculturally unproductive, but unlike it, the area provides excellent fishing and hunting.
11. *Dego-uwo*: An unnavigable brook, generally considered to be the property of the sublineage and sometimes also shared with a neighboring sublineage. This area is economically not important, although there are limited opportunities to catch fish and frogs.
12. *Pekuu*: A small lake accessible (for fishing and hunting duck) to all members of the political confederacy to which the unilineal kinship group belongs.
13. *Uwo ibo*: A large lake owned by lineages and sublineages which belong to several different political confederacies. Open to all for fishing and hunting.
14. *Onee*: A river capable of navigation by canoe, and also good for fishing and hunting.

These terrain types are the folk categories of the Kapauku and are classified under four general levels of inclusiveness, as shown in the chart that follows (Chart 1). Thus *bugi* (garden), *juwuuda* (yard), *geiga* (fallow grassland), and *gapuuga* (fallow bush) are included under the general category of agricultural land, whereas *gamouda* and

110. Pospíšil, Anthropology of Law, *supra* note 105, at 279–84.

Chart 1*

<table>
<tr><td colspan="14">Uwoje-makije
(World)</td></tr>
<tr><td colspan="10">Maki
(Land)</td><td colspan="4" rowspan="2">Uwo
(Water)</td></tr>
<tr><td colspan="4">Mude
(Agricultural Land)</td><td colspan="2">Pijaida
(Wooded Area)</td><td rowspan="2">Ita
(Path)</td><td colspan="3">Peu-maki
(“Bad Land”)</td></tr>
<tr><td>Bugi
(Garden)</td><td>Juwuuda
(Yard)</td><td>Geiga
(Fallow Grassland)</td><td>Gapuuga
(Fallow Bush)</td><td>Gamouda
(Exploited Virgin Forest)</td><td>Buguwa
(Virgin Forest)</td><td>Begadimi
(Mt. Summit)</td><td>Bago
(Crag)</td><td>Takapaka
(Swamp)</td><td>Dego-uwo
(Brook)</td><td>Pekuu
(Small Lake)</td><td>Uwo ibo
(Large Lake)</td><td>Onee
(River)</td></tr>
</table>

Kapauku Taxonomy of the Economically Important Terrain Types

*Leopold Pospíšil, Anthropology of Law: A Comparative Theory 285 (1974)

buguwa (respectively, exploited and unexploited virgin forest) are included under the general category of wooded area, and so on.

The foregoing taxonomy arranges all the legally relevant categories of terrain in vertical order and shows the hierarchical relationship of the categories in terms of their lexical inclusion. In other words, categories of the same degree of inclusiveness are on the same level.

The next section presents a componential analysis of the fourteen categories in terms of their folk components (*i.e.*, their distinctive features as identified by informants). This analysis differs from the analysis of the taxonomy in several ways. Whereas the taxonomy presented the categories irrespective of their degree of inclusiveness, the componential analysis employs a matrix of terrain categories that are of the same degree of inclusiveness, are in contrastive distribution, and appear at the lowest level of the taxonomy. Thus the main focus of the next section is to compare and contrast the fourteen terrain types in terms of Kapauku folk components, an essentially emic enterprise.

Componential Analysis in Terms of Physical and Economic Attributes

Pospíšil's componential analysis of the terrain types reveals six contrasting dimensions "which the natives have recognized as significant"[111] and thus constitute their "folk components."[112] The emic nature of Pospíšil's approach is quite apparent, in that the meaning or significance for the natives is in terms of the physical and economic attributes of each of the fourteen types of terrain. Thus the first contrasting dimension is "land versus water," given that each of the terrains is either land or water. As seen above, each has its physical and economic uses.

The second dimension contrasts land that is agricultural, or potentially cultivable, exempt from cultivation, or unfit for cultivation. As seen in Chart 1, the second dimension can apply only to the first ten land types (the other four are water types). Thus *bugi* (garden), *juwuuda* (yard), *geiga* (fallow grassland), and *gapuuga* (fallow bush) are agricultural land. These four terrains contrast with *gamouda* (exploited virgin forest) and *buguwa* (virgin forest), which are both potentially cultivable. The latter two contrast with *ita* (path), which is exempt from cultivation. *Ita* then contrasts with *begadimi* (mountain summit), *bago* (crag/rocky mountain peak), and *takapaka* (swamp), all of which are unfit for cultivation.

The third dimension contrasts degrees of permissible vegetation disturbance (*i.e.*, complete, substantial, or slight). Chart 1 shows that this dimension can apply only to the first six land terrains. Thus *bugi* (garden) allows complete removal of vegetation, which contrasts with *juwuuda* (yard) and *gamouda* (exploited virgin forest), where vegetation may be substantially disturbed. In contrast to these, vegetation may be only slightly disturbed in fallow land (*geiga* and *gapuuga*) and virgin forest (*buguwa*).

The fourth dimension contrasts the type of vegetation on the terrains (*e.g.*, grass versus trees, versus swamp grass, versus slight vegetation). Chart 1 shows that this

111. *Id.* at 287.

112. *Id.* at 286.

dimension only applies to the five land terrains. Thus fallow grassland (*geiga*) is well known for its grass and reed cover, whereas fallow bush (*gapuuga*) has shrubbery. The short grass of the mountain summit (*begadimi*) contrasts with the crag/rocky mountain peak (*bago*), which has very little vegetation. The swamp (*tapakaka*) of course has swampy grass.

The fifth dimension contrasts the small with the large. The brooks (*dego-uwo*) and small lakes (*pekuu*) belong to the small category, whereas large lakes (*uwo ibi*) and large rivers (*onee*) fall in the category of large.[113] The final contrast, with reference to "kinetic quality" (stream versus static), applies only to water types. Brook (*dego-uwo*) is thus contrasted with small lake (*pekuu*), and large lake (*uwo ibo*) is contrasted with river (*onee*).[114]

Chart 2 presents a componential analysis of the fourteen Kapauku terrain types in terms of their contrasting physical and economic usefulness.

Componential Analysis of the Legal Attributes of Terrain Types

Having presented the analysis of Kapauku terrain types in terms of their economic and physical attributes, Pospíšil proceeds to analyze the fourteen terrain types in terms of their legal attributes.[115] Because legal rights were associated with the fourteen terrain types, Pospíšil felt justified in using them as contrasting categories, even though their contrastive features were not inherent in the terrain concepts.[116] Pospíšil hoped his new analysis would reveal something more culturally significant than would a mere taxonomy based on folk components.[117] The legal principles, together with their functions and values, served as "contrastive correlates" and, like the above components, had a contrastive function.[118] The contrastive legal correlates for the fourteen terrain types revealed seven mainly binary contrasting dimensions:

1. Kind of ownership (individual versus nonindividual). The first six land classes are individually owned; land water and rights of the remaining eight terrain types are group-owned (*i.e.*, at the level of the sublineage, the lineage, or the Kapauku people as a whole). Thus the garden (*bugi*), yard (*juwuuda*), fallow grassland (*geiga*), fallow bush (*gapuuga*), exploited virgin forest (*gamouda*), and virgin forest (*buguwa*) are individually owned, in contrast with the remaining terrain types, which are nonindividually owned (*see* Chart 3).
2. Degree of legal exemption from control of sublineage members (less exempt versus more exempt). This dimension applies only to the last eight nonin-

113. *Id.* at 287–88.

114. *Id.*

115. It is here that Pospíšil distances himself somewhat from the emic approach. He is prompted to do so by the discovery of his informants' "error," which consisted of misdescribing the importance of physical features of land terrains. Pospíšil was of the opinion that economic and legal considerations were the dominant factors, not the physical characteristics of the terrains. *See* text at note 109 *supra*.

116. Pospíšil, Anthropology of Law, *supra* note 105, at 291.

117. *Id.*

118. *Id.*

Chart 2*

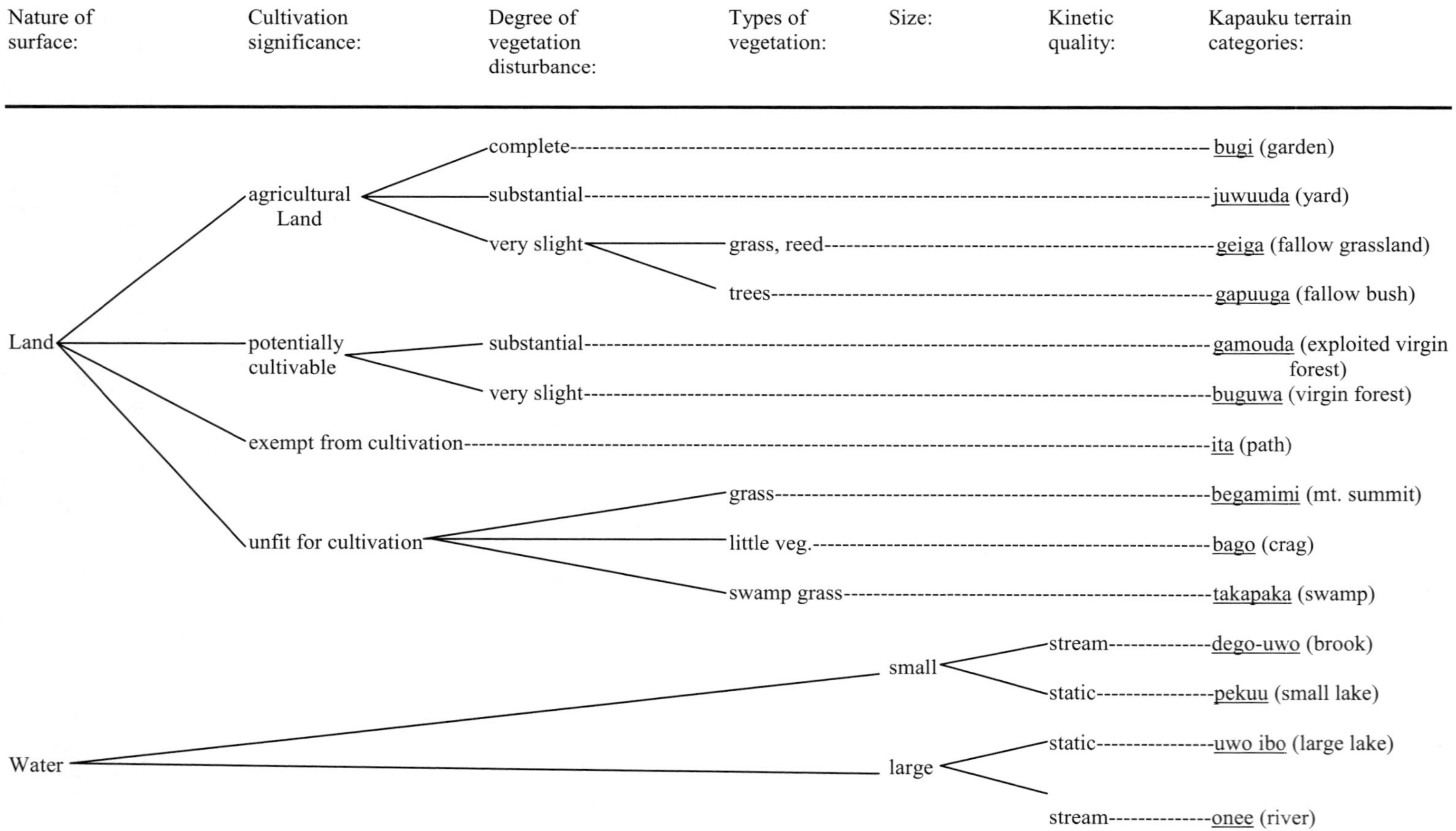

Componential Analysis of Kapauku Terrain Types in Terms of their Physical and Economic Attributes

*Leopold Pospíšil, Anthropology of Law: A Comparative Theory 289 (1974)

dividually owned terrain types. These eight categories are divided into two subcategories, the first of which (*ita*, *begadimi*, *bago*, *takapaka*, and *dego-uwo*) contain terrains owned and controlled exclusively by members of the local sublineage. These are to be contrasted with the terrains of the second subcategory (*pekuu*, *uwo ibo*, and *onee*), which the local sublineage must share with a larger group (*e.g.*, the lineage or general public).

3. Degree of limitation of the right to trespass, fish, and gather (limited to special individuals versus no limitation). Here *bugi*, *juwuuda*, *geiga*, *gapuuga*—where rights are limited to members of the local group (sublineage or lineage)—contrast with *gamouda*, *buguuwa*, *ita*, *begadimi*, *bago*, and *takapaka*, where there are no limitations and where anyone may fish or gather. These in turn may be contrasted with *dego-uwo*, where such rights are limited; *pekuu*, where rights are limited, is contrasted with *uwo ibo* and *onee*, where there are no limitations.
4. Scope of people entitled to fell secondary trees (owner versus sublineage). This dimension applies only to the first six terrain types and contrasts second-growth trees with virgin forest trees. The latter are exclusively owned by the owner of the plot. The former are owned by the local sublineage, whose members may fell trees regardless of the wishes of the plot owner. The contrasts are *bugi*, *juwuuda*, and *geiga* in *gapuuga*; and *gamouda* in *buguwa*.
5. Relative importance of laws regulating gathering of frogs (important versus not important). Importance is to be understood in terms of whether the right to catch frogs is restricted to a specific group or is open to all. The contrasts under this dimension are *ita*, *begadimi*, and *bago* with *takapaka*, and *uwo ibo* with *onee*.
6. Relative scope of people entitled to fell old trees. This dimension is not binary; it has two correlates (inapplicable versus smaller, versus larger). It applies to six land terrains that distinguish those on which there are no old first-growth trees from those in which old trees may be felled by a smaller category of persons and from those terrains in which old trees may be felled by members of a more inclusive group (*i.e.*, local sublineage).

In the contrast between garden on one hand and yard and fallow grassland on the other, smaller means the individual owner and larger refers to the local sublineage. In the contrast between path and mountain summit, smaller means the local sublineage and larger refers to any Papuan. Here *bugi* contrasts with *juwuuda* and *geiga*, and *ita* with *begadimi* and *bago*.

The rationale for the restriction on old trees is that felling an old tree is a complex operation that is likely to cause collateral damage to crops. It is therefore restricted to the discretion of the *bugi* owner.

7. Relative size of the group entitled to hunt "nonrats" (smaller versus larger). This dimension contrasts the yard (*juwuuda*) with fallow grassland (*geiga*) in that only members of the local sublineage may shoot marsupials and birds, whereas any member of the whole local lineage may do so in fallow grassland.

The above legal analysis is delineated in Chart 3.

The preceding analysis focused on the terrain types and presented the distinguishing legal principles giving them their *raison d'être*. In contrast, the analysis that follows focuses on the legal principles and their relationship to the fourteen classes of terrain.

Cognitive Map of Kapauku Land Tenure Law

As Pospíšil observes, analysis such as the one above is not helpful from a substantive legal point of view.[119] Like all componential analyses, it focuses only on those elements of land tenure that have contrastive significance. Thus, substantive legal rules of land tenure such as the rule that the individual owner has the exclusive right to hunt in his own garden are not revealed by the tabulation of contrastive correlates. In order to focus on the legal rules themselves, rather than their function as contrastive criteria, Pospíšil embarks on another analysis in which he includes correlates of a contrasting as well as noncontrastive nature.

Eight dimensions (or "legal correlates") are presented to reveal the specific rights of various parties to the fourteen terrain types. They are the right of ownership; to shoot rats; to plank and canoe trees; to fell secondary trees; to fish, navigate, and gather; to fell old trees; to hunt "nonrats" (*i.e.*, birds, marsupials, wild boar); and to collect frogs. Here, Pospíšil's goal is to present a comprehensive cognitive map or "legal grammar" of Kapauku law of land tenure. Through his eight dimensions, he reveals the entire range and type of possible rights one may have in every terrain, the subjects of those rights—that is, who has the right(s) in question—and where they exist—that is, the object(s) of those rights, namely the terrains.

The first dimension, right of ownership, delineates who owns each terrain type in terms of individual, sublineage, lineage, or common ownership. Garden, yard, fallow grassland, fallow bush, exploited virgin forest, and virgin forest are individually owned. Path, mountain summit, crag, swamp, and brook are owned by the sublineage; the small lake is owned by the lineage. Large lake and river are commonly owned. The right to shoot rats, the second dimension, is distributed at the individual, sublineage, and common levels. This pattern of rights is evident in the remaining six dimensions *mutatis mutandis*, as explained and tabulated in the following excerpt.

Leopold Pospíšil, Anthropology of Law: A Comparative Theory 296–302 (1974).

> Analysis of the Kapauku land and water categories in terms of legal correlates employs eight dimensions, whose correlates define the fourteen categories in terms of specific rights and types of entitled parties and present all the Kapauku rules of land and water tenure in a concise, encyclopedic outline at the same time. Because of its different nature and purpose, this method presents eight instead of six dimensions, in the form of specific

119. *Id.* at 296.

Chart 3*

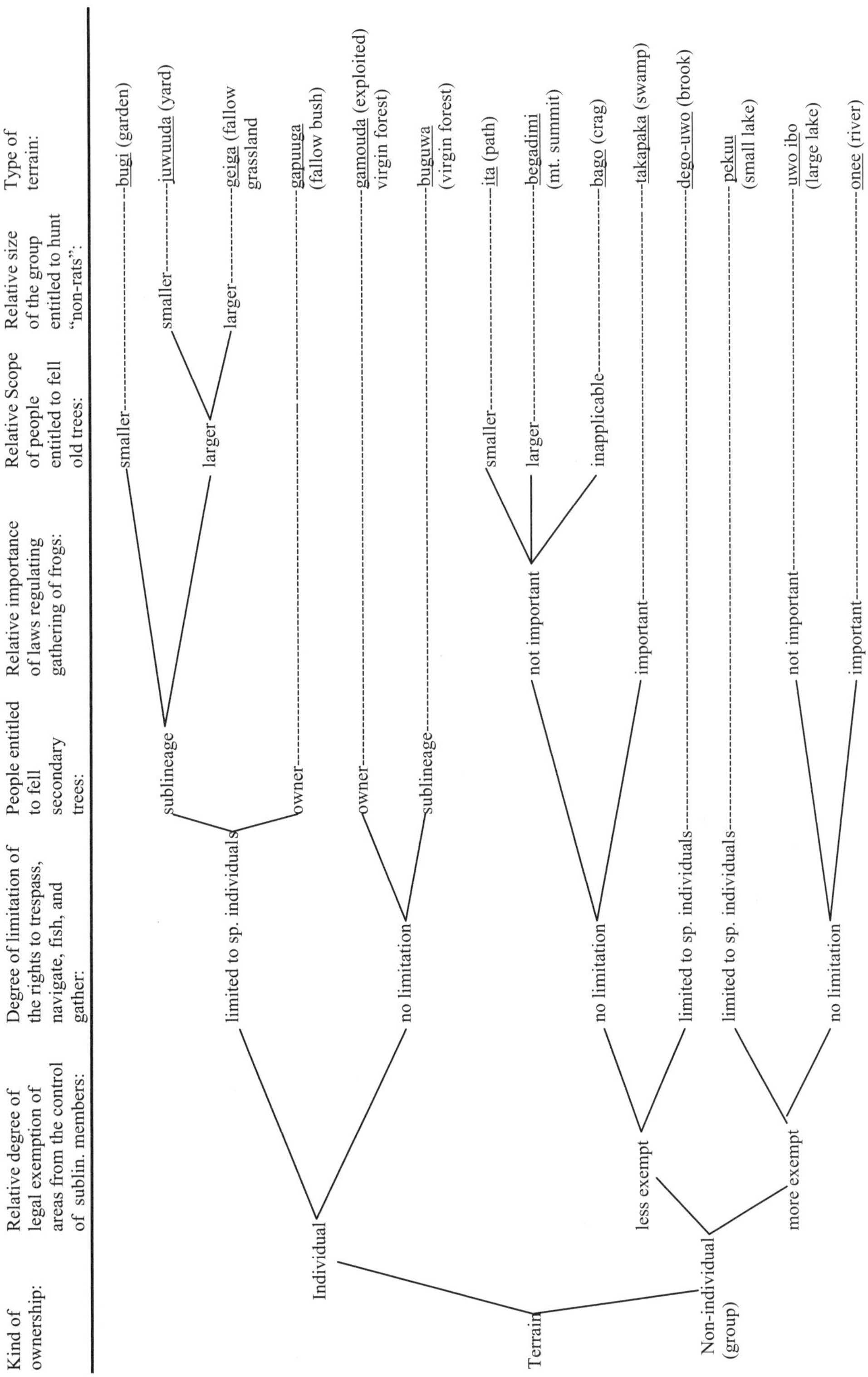

Analysis of Kapauku Terrain Types in Terms of their Contrastive Correlates

*Leopold Pospíšil, Anthropology of Law: A Comparative Theory 298 (1974)

rather than generalized rights, with correlates that precisely specify the types of the entitled parties.

1. *Right of ownership* (individual versus sublineage, versus lineage, versus everyone).... However, there is a bundle of specific rights that any owner (individual, sublineage, lineage, or the general public—"everyone") possesses with respect to his (their) property that may pertain to any of the fourteen terrain classes. If any of these rights is exercised by someone other than the owner (*ipuwe*), this happens only on the basis of a contractual agreement between the two (contrariwise, the other rights, not listed in this "ownership" dimension, may limit the owner without such an agreement). These specific rights, or the concept of "general land and water ownership," constitute our first dimension. This type of Kapauku ownership consists of the following rights: exclusive right with regard to a piece of land or water to negotiate a contractual agreement (sale, lease, barter, *servitus*, etc.), right to cultivate, right to trap, right to cut *moane* trees (best material for canoe construction), right to hunt by means of fire (burning dry grasslands), and right to collect indemnity for damage done to the terrain by others. The dimension of "right of ownership" applies to all fourteen terrain types and distinguishes among them on the basis of "individual" ownership (garden, yard, fallow grassland, fallow bush, exploited virgin forest, virgin forest), sublineage ownership (path, mountain summit, crag, swamp, brook), lineage ownership (small lake), and everyone's ownership (large lake, river). Consequently, this dimension contrasts *bugi, juwuuda, geiga, gapuuga, gamouda, buguwa,* with *ita, begadimi, bago, takapaka, dego-uwo,* with *pekuu,* and with *uwo ibo, onee.*
2. *Right to shoot rats* (inapplicable versus owner, versus sublineage, versus everyone). Unlike the preceding dimension, this one does not apply a legal regulation to all the Kapauku terrain categories for the reason that there are no rats in the water categories. In [Chart 4] the word "inapplicable" signifies no legal disposition because of scarcity or absence of the object of the particular right in the given environment. However, because an absence of legal regulation does carry a contrastive value, it must be included as a value in this analysis. The present dimension distinguishes types of water without any legal disposition (*dego-uwo,* brook; *pekuu,* small lake; *uwo ibo,* large lake, *onee,* river) from types of land on which the right to hunt rats is restricted exclusively to the individual owner (*bugi,* garden; *juwuuda,* yard; *geiga,* fallow grassland; *gapuuga,* fallow bush), from those land categories where the right is held in common by all members of the local sublineage (*gamouda,* exploited virgin forest; *ita,* path), and from land where hunting rats is permitted to everyone (*buguwa,* virgin forest; *begadimi,* mountain summit; *bago,* crag; *takapaka,* swamp).

3. *Right to plank and canoe trees* (inapplicable versus owner, versus sublineage). This dimension includes rules pertaining to the allocation of the right to plank and canoe trees (except *moane*) growing on the various types of land. It contains three different types of values. "Inapplicable" indicates an absence of any legal regulation and pertains to: *ita*, path; *begadimi*, mountain summit; *bago*, crag; *takapaka*, swamp; *dego-uwo*, brook; *pekuu*, small lake; *uwo ibo*, large lake; *onee*, river. The second reserves to the individual owner of the plot the exclusive right to the plank and canoe trees growing in his *bugi*, garden; *juwuuda*, yard; *geiga*, fallow grassland; *gapuuga*, fallow bush; and *gamouda*, exploited virgin forest. The last asserts common ownership for all local sublineage members of the valuable trees that grow in their virgin forest (*buguwa*).
4. *Right to fell secondary trees* (inapplicable versus owner, versus sublineage). Among the Kapauku the right to "second-growth trees," for all practical purposes, is reserved to the individual owner of the grove. Sublineage members may share in felling only those secondary trees that grow on those types of land where they are very scarce. . . . The dimension, then, distinguishes classes of land and water with no related legal disposition pertaining to the felling of secondary trees (*ita*, path; *begadimi*, mountain summit; *bago*, crag; *takapaka*, swamp; *dego-uwo*, brook; *pekuu*, small lake; *uwo ibo*, large lake; *onee*, river) from those in which felling of secondary trees is reserved to the individual owner of the plat (*gapuuga*, fallow bush; *gamouda*, exploited virgin forest), from those in which this prerogative belongs to all the members of the local sublineage (*bugi*, garden; *juwuuda*, yard; *geiga*, fallow grassland; *buguwa*, virgin forest).
5. *Right to fish and navigate, trespass and gather* (sublineage versus lineage, versus everyone). . . . Accordingly, this dimension distinguishes classes of land and water where the rights to fish, navigate, gather, and trespass belong collectively to all members of the local sublineage (*bugi*, garden; *dego-uwo*, brook) from classes where these rights are shared by all members of the local lineage (*juwuuda*, yard; *geiga*, fallow grassland; *gapuuga*, fallow bush; *pekuu*, small lake), and from classes where these rights are extended to everyone (*gamouda*, exploited virgin forest; *buguwa*, virgin forest; *ita*, path; *begadimi*, mountain summit; *bago*, crag; *takapaka*, swamp; *uwo ibo*, large lake; *onee*, river).
6. *Right to fell old trees* (inapplicable versus owner, versus sublineage, versus everyone). In the exploited virgin forest and virgin forest those old hardwoods unsuitable for canoes or planks belong in the category of "old trees." . . . This dimension distinguishes classes of land and water without legal provision for the felling of old trees (*bago*, crag; *dego-uwo* [,] brook; *pekuu*, small lake; *uwo ibo*, large lake; *onee*, river) from classes whose old trees may be cut only by the owner of the plot (*bugi*, garden), from classes on which this right is reserved to the members of the local sublineage (*juwuuda*, yard; *geiga*, fallow grassland; *gapuuga*, fallow bush; *ita*, path;

takapaka, swamp), from classes where the right to harvest old trees is explicitly free for all without any restriction (*gamouda*, exploited virgin forest; *buguwa*, virgin forest; *begadimi*, mountain summit).

7. *Right to hunt "non-rats"* (inapplicable versus owner, versus sublineage, versus lineage, versus everyone). The objects of this right are all types of animals hunted with bow and arrow or club except the common rat (*Rattus*, sp.). Accordingly, in this category belong all types of birds, marsupials, and rodents except the rat, wild boar, bats, and two species of python. Other small animals, such as lizards, frogs, and invertebrates, are gathered or fished for rather than hunted, and their acquisition is subject to other legal regulations. The dimension distinguishes classes of environment in which the native law makes no provisions for this hunting right (*dego-uwo*, brook) from classes of land and water where the right is reserved for the individual land-owner (*bugi*, garden), from classes where the right is extended to all members of the local sublineage (*juwuuda*, yard), from classes where the right is allocated to all members of the local lineage (*geiga*, fallow grassland; *gapuuga*, fallow bush; *pekuu*, small lake), from classes where the native law specifically gives permission to everyone to hunt (*gamouda*, exploited virgin forest; *buguwa*, virgin forest; *ita*, path; *begadimi*, mountain summit; *bago*, crag; *takapaka*, swamp; *uwo ibo*, large lake; *onee*, river).
8. *Right to collect frogs* (inapplicable versus sublineage, versus lineage, versus everyone).... The dimension distinguishes classes of environment for which the law makes no provision because of absence of a substantial number of frogs (*bugi*, garden; *juwuuda*, yard; *geiga*, fallow grassland; *gapuuga*, fallow bush; *gamouda*, exploited virgin forest; *buguwa*, virgin forest; *ita*, path; *begadimi*, mountain summit; *bago*, crag) from a class where the right to collect frogs is restricted to the members of a local sublineage (*dego-uwo*, brook), from classes of land and water where the right is extended to the membership of the local lineage (*takapaka*, swamp; *pekuu*, small lake; *onee*, river), from the class of large lakes in which everyone is permitted to collect these amphibians (*uwo*, *ibo*, large lake).

The total picture and the structure of the analysis of the Kapauku rules of land tenure is presented in [Chart 4] in which the vertical columns represent the eight dimensions (identified by headings) and their specific values (expressed in terms of the identification of the entitled parties); the horizontal levels summarize the legal dispositions with regard to the fourteen Kapauku terrain categories that are identified at the end of each horizontal line and that form the last vertical column. In other words, the vertical columns list all the various kinds of allocation of a particular right with respect to the fourteen different land and water classes; the horizontal lines present all the legal provisions pertaining to a given category of terrain with respect to the eight clusters of rights which I have used as dimensions for the analysis. This

Chart 4*

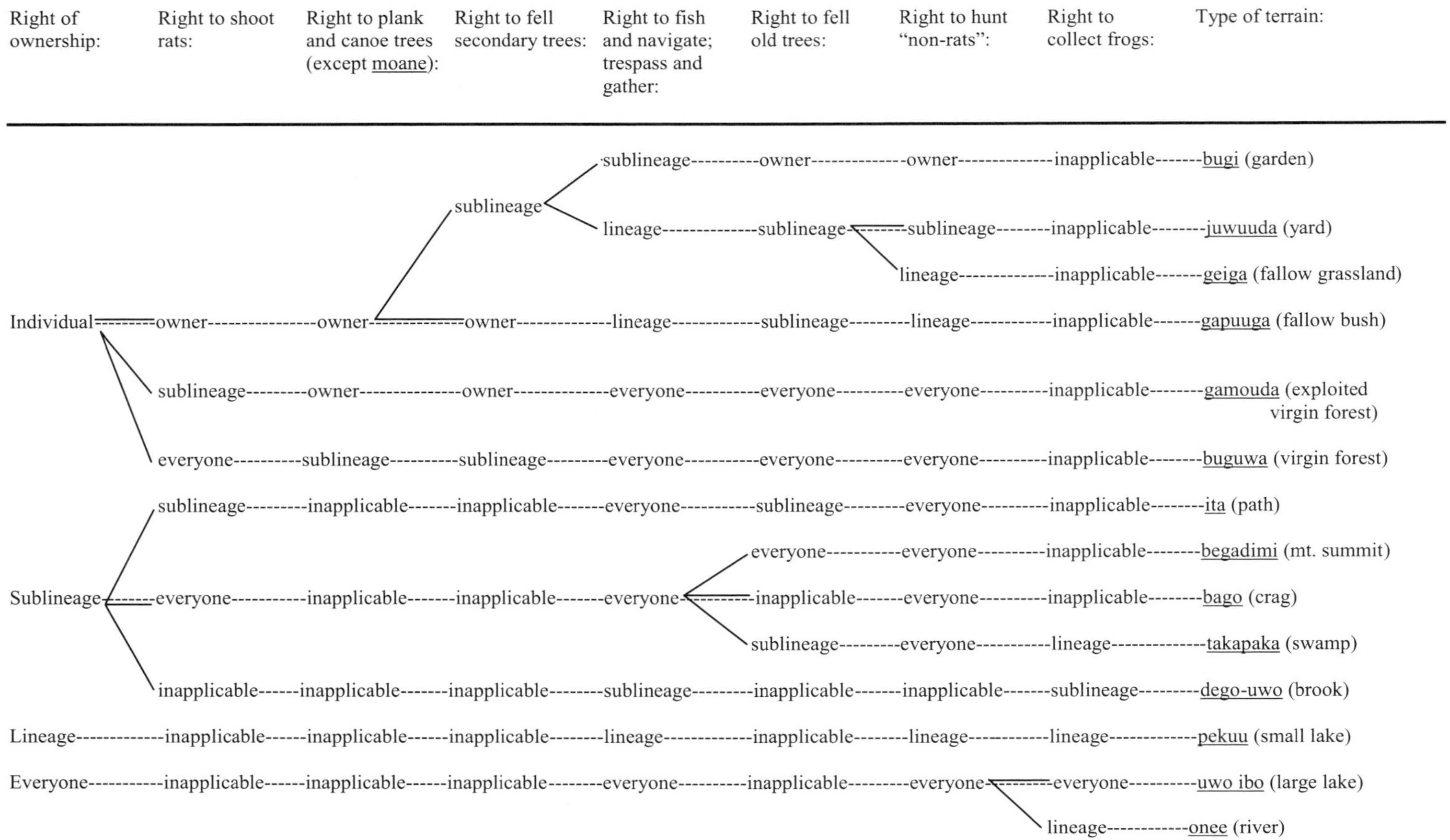

Analysis of Kapauku Terrain Types in Terms of their Legal Correlates

*Leopold Pospíšil, Anthropology of Law: A Comparative Theory 297 (1974)

> tabulation of legal correlates of the fourteen terrain classes . . . gives a concise and full account of the Kapauku laws of land tenure.

Conclusion

The goal of componential analysis in general is to uncover the criteria that underlie folk taxonomies that classify hierarchies of cultural domains as defined by cultural criteria. With help from linguistics, the ethnographer can analyze contrasting sounds that represent the cognitive categories of a native culture. By doing so, the anthropological linguist uses componential analysis to produce the cultural grammar of a native culture as a whole or (as in the case of Pospíšil) a subnormative system within it.

In analyzing the Kapauku system of land ownership, Pospíšil claims to have presented a complete legal grammar and encyclopedic outline of the Kapauku law of land tenure.[120] He started his project by employing the taxonomic approach to folk classifications and componential analysis (the latter being popular in structural linguistics and kinship terminology). He thus abstracted distinctive semantic components that he grouped into several folk categories. These were the classes of terrain into which the Kapauku had classified their natural environment in accordance with physical and economic features.

After describing the fourteen terrain types of the Kapauku natural habitat, he presented them as part of a folk taxonomy. He further presented an essentially emic description of how the Kapauku distinguished one terrain type from another by collecting native criteria of contrast, and used these as components in a formal analysis. These were more or less fairly standard applications of ethnoscience that resulted in a complex componential analysis of Kapauku terrain types in terms of their physical and economic attributes.

He discovered the "error" of his informants when he concluded that the Kapauku classes of terrain were not based on their physical features but on their economic-legal significance. Pospíšil then decided to analyze and compare the fourteen terrains in terms of these criteria. In embarking on this task, Pospíšil hoped to show something more culturally significant than what a taxonomy based on folk components would show. He thus abstracted legal principles from Kapauku rules as his dimensions and used their specific values as correlates. He then analyzed the matrix of fourteen terrain types in terms of their contrastive features, in order to show how the legal features contributed to the Kapauku classification of their natural terrains.

However, such analysis does not reveal the content of substantive rules because it focuses only on the contrastive legal correlates and therefore can show only the legally relevant contrasts among the land and water terrains. Hence his final goal: to present a comprehensive legal grammar of Kapauku land tenure law that simultaneously tabulated, in relation to the fourteen terrains, the entire range and type of rights possible (listed in eight dimensions), the subjects of the rights (who owned what right), and the object of the rights (the fourteen terrains).

120. *Id.* at 296, 337.

Neostructuralism and Law

Lévi-Strauss and Structural Anthropology

Claude Lévi-Strauss's structural anthropology lends itself to ready classification as a subschool of cognitive anthropology. If culture is defined as a form of knowledge that individuals must have in order to structure and organize their social behavior and social relations, Lévi-Strauss's methodological model, which is based on structural linguistics, can also be viewed as an emic quest for cultural knowledge.

Lévi-Strauss was one of the most original thinkers of anthropology in the twentieth century. He embraced linguistics as his methodological model for anthropological research. By the time he was writing, linguistics had already made the transition from functionalism to structuralism. The functional aspect was the idea each item of language (*e.g.*, a sentence, morpheme, or phoneme) serves a communicative function. The structural notion was that no element of language can be communicated unless it is first understandable (*i.e.*, has meaning), which is possible only if each linguistic element is considered in relation with other elements. Thus the idea of relation is the foundation of the theory: language is a system of relations. The totality of these relations constitutes the grammar of which the speaker is unconscious.

By choosing linguistics as his methodological model, Lévi-Strauss did not intend to transfer linguistic analysis into anthropology, but to translate it into anthropological terms. Following is an outline of Lévi-Strauss's approach to the nature of human understanding (*i.e.*, how the mind operates to give meaning to cultural data).

Lévi-Strauss on the Nature of Human Understanding

According to Lévi-Strauss, all humans have a deep-seated mental desire for normative order.[121] Mankind has a universal need to understand its social and moral world through mentally constructed categories and classifications, what Lévi-Strauss calls "the systematic cataloging of relations."[122] This is akin to a form of "Kantianism without a transcendental subject."[123] Indeed, if there is a transcendental subject in Lévi-Strauss's Kantianism, it is society itself (somewhat in the tradition of Radcliffe-Brown).

Regardless of subject, the urge to classify and understand reveals deep mental structures (again similar to the Kantian cognitive categories) that are common to mankind. These structures are not apparent in the outward behavior of humans; they are, rather, innate to the very psychobiological nature of all humans.[124] As such they should be flushed out and studied by the structural anthropologists. A good

---

121. Claude Lévi-Strauss, The Savage Mind 10 (George Weidenfeld & Nicolson Ltd. trans., 1966).

122. *Id.*

123. Paul Ricoeur, *Symbole et temporalité*, *in* Archivio di Filosofia 24 (1963).

124. Garbarino, *supra* note 91, at 84–85.

restatement of the Kantianism of the structuralist argument is the following by Edmund Leach:

> The general argument runs something like this: what we know about the external world we apprehend through our senses. The phenomena which we perceive have the characteristics which we attribute to them because of the way our senses operate and the way the human brain is designed to order and interpret the stimuli which are fed into it. One very important feature of this ordering process is that we cut up the continua of space and time with which we are surrounded into segments so that we are predisposed to think of the environment as consisting of vast numbers of separate things belonging to named classes, and to think of the passage of time as consisting of sequences of separate events. Correspondingly, when, as men, we construct artificial things (artifacts of all kinds), or devise ceremonials, or write histories of the past, we imitate our apprehension of Nature; the products of our Culture are segmented and ordered in the same way as we suppose the products of Nature to be segmented and ordered.[125]

Just as the Kantian categories make objects of perception conform to the mind, thereby making sense of what would otherwise remain a jumble of senseless data, structuralism argues that processes of the brain impose form on otherwise formless phenomena, and these forms are then organized through classifications to enable better understanding and more efficient communication.

Lévi-Strauss set out to prove that the phenomenon of myth, which to many may seem bizarre and irrational, reveals that the human mind constructs empirical categories that are used by it as conceptual tools to elaborate abstract ideas, which are then combined to form propositions.[126] These categories, which are binary (*e.g.*, raw/cooked, fresh/decayed, moist/burned, etc.), can be identified by ethnographic observation that takes into account "the standpoint of a particular culture."[127]

As Lévi-Strauss notes, mythology has no obvious practical function as do the laws of marriage, the prohibition of incest, or the rules of kinship. The latter show the reality of normative relations as well as their function and purpose. Myth, by contrast, has no obvious social function and does not show an objective reality of the type underlying the laws mentioned above. It is merely a form of "intellectual *bricolage*"[128]—the noun is a French term for work done by a *bricoleur*, a type of handyman trying his best to repair things with limited skills and tools. Myths for Lévi-Strauss are *bricolage* in the sense that man creates them and believes in them to cope with difficult-to-understand worldly phenomena. By this logic, myths are similarly built—without proper science, without logic, without continuity, and with

---

125. The Structural Study of Myth and Totemism 21 (Edmund Leach ed., 1970).

126. 1 Claude Lévi-Strauss, The Raw and the Cooked: Introduction to the Science of Mythology: 1 (John Weightman & Doreen Weightman trans., 1970).

127. *Id.*

128. Lévi-Strauss, The Savage Mind, *supra* note 121, at 17.

limited conceptual tools—thus, they have limited explanatory power. Albeit weak in explanatory power, myths do reveal a subnormative system of coping with the world; of imposing order in the face of disorder and/or bewilderment.

Lévi-Strauss therefore quotes Franz Boas with approval: "It would seem that mythological worlds have been built up only to be shattered again, and that new worlds were built from the fragments."[129] However, although he believed myths to be thus contingent, Lévi-Strauss also believed that the apparent arbitrariness of myths is "belied by the outstanding similarity between myths collected in widely different regions."[130] Lévi-Strauss's "Kantian" project had an additional, and more limited, goal for studying myths, as the following excerpt explains.

Lévi-Strauss's basic argument is that the laws of marriage, incest, and kinship may appear contingent, superficial, and incoherent at first, but (like myths) their study reveals deep mental structures of which the individual is unaware but that also reveal a "complex mass of customs and practices."[131] This mass of customs, practices, and meanings are examined in the materials that follow, with a focus on the laws of marriage, incest, and kinship. Through his "experiment" in mythology, Lévi-Strauss wanted to show that myths operate by way of mental categories of which the individual is unconscious. Hence his claim that "[I]f the human mind appears determined even in the realm of mythology, *a fortiori* it must also be determined in all its spheres of activity."[132]

1 Claude Lévi-Strauss, The Raw and the Cooked: Introduction to a Science of Mythology 10–12 (John Weightman & Doreen Weightman trans., 1970).

> The experiment I am now embarking on with mythology will consequently be more decisive. Mythology has no obvious practical function: unlike the phenomena previously studied, it is not directly linked with a different kind of reality, which is endowed with a higher degree of objectivity than its own and whose injunctions it might therefore transmit to minds that seem perfectly free to indulge their creative spontaneity. And so, if it were possible to prove in this instance, too, that the apparent arbitrariness of the mind, its supposedly spontaneous flow of inspiration, and its seemingly uncontrolled inventiveness imply the existence of laws operating at a deeper level, we would inevitably be forced to conclude that when the mind is left to commune with itself and no longer has to come to terms with objects, it is in a sense reduced to imitating itself as object; and that since the laws governing its operations are not fundamentally different from those it exhibits in its

129. Claude Lévi-Strauss, *The Structural Study of Myth*, 68 J. Am. Folklore 428, 428 (1955) (quoting Franz Boas, *Introduction*, *in* James Teit, Traditions of the Thompson River Indians of British Columbia 18 (1898)).

130. *Id.* at 429.

131. Lévi-Strauss, The Raw and the Cooked, *supra* note 126, at 10.

132. *Id.*

other functions, it shows itself to be of the nature of a thing among things. The argument need not be carried to this point, since it is enough to establish the conviction that if the human mind appears determined even in the realm of mythology, *a fortiori* it must also be determined in all its spheres of activity.

In allowing myself to be guided by the search for the constraining structures of the mind, I am proceeding in the manner of Kantian philosophy, although along different lines leading to different conclusions. The ethnologist, unlike the philosopher, does not feel obliged to take the conditions in which his own thought operates, or the science peculiar to his society and his period, as a fundamental subject of reflection in order to extend these local findings into a form of understanding, the universality of which can never be more than hypothetical and potential. Although concerned with the same problems, he adopts an opposite approach in two respects. Instead of assuming a universal form of human understanding, he prefers to study empirically collective forms of understanding, whose properties have been solidified, as it were, and are revealed to him in countless concrete representational systems. And since for him, belonging as he does to a given social milieu, culture, region, and period of history, these systems represent the whole range of possible variations within a particular type, he chooses those that seem to him to be the most markedly divergent, in the hope that the methodological rules he will have to evolve in order to translate these systems in terms of his own system and vice versa, will reveal a pattern of basic and universal laws: . . .

I am perfectly aware that it is this aspect of my work that Ricoeur is referring to when he rightly describes it as "Kantism without a transcendental subject." But far from considering this reservation as indicating some deficiency, I see it as the inevitable consequence, on the philosophical level, of the ethnographic approach I have chosen; since, my ambition being to discover the conditions in which systems of truths become mutually convertible and therefore simultaneously acceptable to several different subjects, the pattern of those conditions takes on the character of an autonomous object, independent of any subject.

I believe that mythology, more than anything else, makes it possible to illustrate such objectified thought and to provide empirical proof of its reality. . . . It is the same with myths as with language: the individual who conscientiously applied phonological and grammatical laws in his speech, supposing he possessed the necessary knowledge and virtuosity to do so, would nevertheless lose the thread of his ideas almost immediately. In the same way the practice and the use of mythological thought demand that its properties remain hidden: otherwise the subject would find himself in the position of the mythologist, who cannot believe in myths because it is his task to take them to pieces. Mythological analysis has not, and cannot have, as its aim to show how men think. In the particular example we are dealing with here, it is doubtful, to say the least, whether the natives of central Brazil, over and above the fact that they are fascinated by mythological stories, have any understanding of the systems of interrelations to which we reduce them. And when by appealing to such myths we justify the existence of certain archaic or colorful expressions in our own popular speech, the same comment can be made, since our awareness is retrospective and is engineered from without and under the pressure of a foreign mythology. I therefore claim to show, not how men think in myths, but how myths operate in men's minds without their being aware of the fact.

The Linguistic Model and Methodological Approach of Lévi-Strauss

According to Lévi-Strauss, naming is one way of organizing or classifying perceptions and experience, as well as communicating them through a common language shared by participants of the same culture. Those who are members of a different culture will still be able to communicate cross-culturally through universally shared infrastructures.[133] What is common to language and certain cultural representations such as kinship, exchange, and myths is that they are all forms of communication:

> In any society, communication operates on three different levels: communication of women, communication of goods and services, communication of messages. Therefore, kinship studies, economics, and linguistics approach the same kinds of problems on different strategic [that is, methodological] levels and really pertain to the same field.[134]

Therefore, according to Lévi-Strauss, society as well as its normative subsystems (such as marital and kinship relations) should be studied as if they were languages. Just as language has deep-seated rules of grammar that are not immediately apparent to or even known by the speaker, social behavior and social relations have underlying structures of which the actor is unconscious. The structures are largely based on thought that strives to give meaning by drawing contrasts such as night/day, life/death, white/black, and so on. These dualisms or binary oppositions are responsible for overall structures of a variety of social "representations" (to use Durkheim's term)[135] such as kinship systems and myths. These may appear to be arbitrary at first, but when subjected to structural study they reveal systematized cognitive maps of their own.

This is of course not to say that Lévi-Strauss believed all societies have identical structures. He recognized that societies do differ from each other just as their surface grammars differ. The same may be said of languages. But he maintained that all

---

133. Garbarino, *supra* note 91, at 85.

134. Claude Lévi-Strauss, Structural Anthropology 296 (Claire Jacobson & Brooke Grundfest Schoepf trans., 1963).

135. *See* Ch. 3 text at note 64. Lévi-Strauss also uses this term. Lévi-Strauss, Structural Anthropology, *supra* note 134, at 3.

societies have innate mental structures explaining particular social representations, be they myths or a moiety organization.

Lévi-Strauss maintains that structural linguistics offered revolutionary insights to the social sciences in the same way that nuclear physics revolutionized the physical sciences.[136] First, structural linguistics shifted the focus of study of conscious linguistic phenomena to the unconscious infrastructure. Second, it shifted attention from the study of terms themselves to the study of the relations between terms. Third, "Modern phonemics does not merely proclaim that phonemes are always part of a system; it *shows* concrete phonemic systems and elucidates their structure."[137]

In other words, structural linguistics demonstrated the importance of showing the concrete existence of systems of relationships of meaning. Finally, structural linguistics made it possible to discover general laws through induction or logical deduction.[138] The latter made it possible for social science to formulate necessary relationships.[139]

Thus, like phonemes, kinship terms and the rules of marriage represent meaningful social structures. Also like phonemes, they acquire meaning only if they are integrated into systems. Furthermore, marital and kinship systems, such as phonemic systems, exist in the mind as unconscious thought. Finally, the recurrence of similar kinship patterns in different cultures suggests that kinship patterns, like their linguistic counterparts, follow the same general laws.

In the following excerpt, Lévi-Strauss explains the importance of linguistics to ethnography, how it helps to reveal unconscious thought patterns that otherwise escape notice, and how kinship systems are analogous to phonemic systems.

Claude Lévi-Strauss, Structural Anthropology 18–21, 33–34 (Claire Jacobson & Brooke Grundfest Schoepf trans., 1963).

> The principle that anthropology draws its originality from the unconscious nature of collective phenomena stems (though in a still obscure and ambiguous manner) from a statement made by Tylor. Having defined anthropology as the study of "Culture or Civilization," he described culture as "that complex whole which includes knowledge, belief, art, morals, law, custom, and any other capabilities and habits acquired by man as a member of society." We know that among most primitive peoples it is very difficult to obtain a moral justification or a rational explanation for any custom or institution. When he is questioned, the native merely answers that things have always been this way, that such was the command of the gods or the teaching of the

136. Lévi-Strauss, Structural Anthropology, *supra* note 134, at 33.

137. *Id.* (quoting Nikolai Troubetzkoy, *La Phonologie actuelle*, *in* Psychologie Du Language 243 (1933)).

138. Lévi-Strauss, Structural Anthropology, *supra* note 134, at 33.

139. *Id.*

ancestors. Even when interpretations are offered, they always have the character of rationalizations or secondary elaborations. There is rarely any doubt that the unconscious reasons for practicing a custom or sharing a belief are remote from the reasons given to justify them. Even in our own society, table manners, social etiquette, fashions of dress, and many of our moral, political, and religious attitudes are scrupulously observed by everyone, although their real origin and function are not often critically examined. We act and think according to habit, and the extraordinary resistance offered to even minimal departures from custom is due more to inertia than to any conscious desire to maintain usages which have a clear function. There is no question that the development of modern thought has favored the critical examination of custom. But this phenomenon is not something extraneous to anthropological study. It is, rather, its direct result, inasmuch as its main origin lies in the tremendous ethnographic self-consciousness which the discovery of the New World aroused in Western thought. And even today, secondary elaborations tend to acquire the same unconscious quality as soon as they are formulated. With surprising rapidity—which shows that one is dealing with an intrinsic property of certain modes of thinking and action—collective thought assimilates what would seem the most daring concepts, such as the priority of mother-right, animism, or, more, recently, psychoanalysis, in order to resolve automatically problems which by their nature seem forever to elude action as well as thought.

Boas must be given credit for defining the unconscious nature of cultural phenomena with admirable lucidity. By comparing cultural phenomena to language from this point of view, he anticipated both the subsequent development of linguistic theory and a future for anthropology whose rich promise we are just beginning to perceive. He showed that the structure of a language remains unknown to the speaker until the introduction of a scientific grammar. Even then the language continues to mold discourse beyond the consciousness of the individual, imposing on his thought conceptual schemes which are taken as objective categories. Boas added that "the essential difference between linguistic phenomena and other ethnological phenomena is, that the linguistic classifications never rise to consciousness, while in other ethnological phenomena, although the same unconscious origin prevails, these often rise into consciousness, and thus give rise to secondary reasoning and to reinterpretations." But this difference, which is one of degree, does not lessen their basic identity or the high value of linguistic method when it is used in ethnological research. . . .

Actually Boasian ethnographic analysis, which is incomparably more honest, solid, and methodical than that of Malinowski, remains, like Malinowski's, on the level of individual conscious thought. Boas of course refused to consider the secondary rationalizations and reinterpretations, which retained so much hold over Malinowski that he managed to discard those offered by the natives only by substituting his own. But Boas continued to utilize the categories of individual thought. His scientific scruples only deprived it of its human overtones. He restricted the scope of the categories that he compared, but he did not re-create them on a new level. When the work of fragmentation seemed to him impossible, he refrained from making comparisons. And yet linguistic comparison must be supported by something more than a mere fragmentation—namely, a real analysis. From words the linguist extracts the phonetic reality of the phoneme; and from the phoneme he extracts the logical reality of distinctive features. And when he has found in several languages the same phonemes or the use of the same pairs of oppositions, he does not compare individually distinct entities. It is the same phoneme, the same element, which will show at this new level the basic identity of empirically different entities. We are not dealing with two similar phenomena, but with one and the same. The transition from conscious to unconscious is associated with progression from the specific toward the general.

In anthropology as in linguistics, therefore, it is not comparison that supports generalization, but the other way around. If, as we believe to be the case, the unconscious activity of the mind consists in imposing forms upon content, and if these forms are fundamentally the same for all minds—ancient and modern, primitive and civilized (as the study of the symbolic function, expressed in language, so strikingly indicates)—it is necessary and sufficient to grasp the unconscious structure underlying each institution and each custom, in order to obtain a principle of interpretation valid for other institutions and other customs, provided of course that the analysis is carried far enough. . . .

The advent of structural linguistics completely changed this situation. Not only did it renew linguistic perspectives; a transformation of this magnitude is not limited to a single discipline. Structural linguistics will certainly play the same renovating role with respect to the social sciences that nuclear physics, for example, has played for the physical sciences. In what does this revolution consist, as we try to assess its broadest implications? N. Troubetzkoy, the illustrious founder of structural linguistics, himself furnished the answer to this question. In one programmatic statement, he reduced the structural method to four basic operations. First, structural linguistics shifts from the study of *conscious* linguistic phenomena to study of their *unconscious* infrastructure; second, it does not treat *terms* as independent entities, taking instead as its basis of analysis the *relations* between terms; third, it introduces the concept of *system*—"Modern phonemics does not merely proclaim that phonemes are always part of a system; it *shows* concrete phonemic systems and elucidates their structure"—; finally, structural linguistics aims at discovering *general laws*, either by induction "or . . . by logical deduction, which would give them an absolute character."

Thus, for the first time, a social science is able to formulate necessary relationships. This is the meaning of Troubetzkoy's last point, while the preceding rules show how linguistics must proceed in order to attain this end. It is not for us to show that Troubetzkoy's claims are justified. The vast majority of modern linguistics seem sufficiently agreed on this point. But when an event of this importance takes place in one of the sciences of man, it is not only permissible for, but required of, representatives of related disciplines immediately to examine its consequences and its possible application to phenomena of another order.

New perspectives then open up. We are no longer dealing with an occasional collaboration where the linguist and the anthropologist, each working by himself, occasionally communicate those findings which each thinks may interest the other. In the study of kinship problems (and, no doubt, the study of other problems as well), the anthropologist finds himself in a situation which formally resembles that of the structural linguist. Like phonemes, kinship terms are elements of meaning; like phonemes, they acquire meaning only if they are integrated into systems. "Kinship systems," like "phonemic systems," are built by the mind on the level of unconscious thought. Finally, the recurrence of kinship patterns, marriage rules, similar prescribed attitudes between certain types of relatives, and so forth, in scattered regions of the globe and in fundamentally different societies, leads us to believe that, in the case of kinship as well as linguistics, the observable phenomena result from the action of laws which are general but implicit. The problem can therefore be formulated as follows: Although they belong to *another order of reality*, kinship phenomena are *of the same type* as linguistic phenomena.

Structural Analysis of Matrimonial Law

One may examine marriage and kinship rules in structural terms by beginning with the prohibition against incest. It is a universal rule, enforced in all cultures; yet before Lévi-Strauss wrote on the subject, the rule was not accorded rational explanation but tended to be justified in religious or mythical terms. According to Lévi-Strauss, a structural explanation for the incest taboo would run along the following lines: The universality of the taboo is analogous to the universality of language. The taboo is not found in lower animals; thus it is a uniquely human institution. Since it is not found in the animal kingdom it cannot have a biological or instinctual origin. Being a human institution, the taboo also does not have any effective philosophical teleological or biological explanation, nor an explanation based on eugenics. Finally, neither can the taboo be explained in Freudian terms such as a son's desire for his mother and murder of his father. Lévi-Strauss dismisses the Freudian hypothesis as only a "symbolic dream" that, rather than being the origin of the taboo, is its consequence.[140]

Having explained what the incest taboo is not, structuralism proceeds to explain what it is in terms of its normative value. First, the taboo—like language—is a complex institution with an unconscious thought structure. Second, the taboo does not have purely negative implications. Rather than suppressing unions it differentiates

140. Octavio Paz, Claude Lévi-Strauss: An Introduction 17 (J.S. Bernstein & Maxine Bernstein trans., 1970).

them. By showing what unions are prohibited, it paves the way for a whole range of unions that are permitted, thus revealing a yes/no binary opposition analogous to elementary linguistic structures.

According to Lévi-Strauss, the prohibition of incest is not so much a rule forbidding marriage with sister, daughter, or mother as the rule that allows sister, daughter, or mother to be given to others in marriage.[141] These exchanges, which he believes have the nature of "gifts," take place on the basis of reciprocity. Lévi-Strauss also believed that if these elements are not understood, two serious misunderstandings arise. First, the very nature of the institution of marriage is mistakenly viewed as a discontinuous process having limits that are internal to each particular marriage, when in fact, according to Lévi-Strauss, marriage is an institution with a continuous process that draws its life from the serial exchange of women. The second misunderstanding, again according to Lévi-Strauss, is that the incest prohibition is thought to be founded in some quality intrinsic to women, the mother, daughter, and sister being seen to possess these qualities. However, there are no inherent biological facts pointing to such qualities; rather, mother/daughter/sister are terms that represent a set of social relations (*i.e.*, relationships between themselves and the rest of the world).

> One is therefore drawn infallibly towards biological considerations, since it is only from a biological, certainly not a social, point of view that motherhood, sisterhood or daughterhood are properties of the individuals considered. However, from a social viewpoint, these terms cannot be regarded as defining isolated individuals, but relationships between these individuals and everyone else. Motherhood is not only a mother's relationship to her children, but her relationship to other members of the group, not as a mother, but as a sister, wife, cousin or simply a stranger as far as kinship is concerned. It is the same for all family relationships, which are defined not only by the individuals they involve, but also by all those they exclude. This is true to the extent that observers have often been struck by the impossibility for natives of conceiving a neutral relationship, or more exactly, no relationship. We have the feeling—which, moreover, is illusory—that the absence of definite kinship gives rise to such a state in our consciousness. But the supposition that this might be the case in primitive thought does not stand up to examination. Every family relationship defines a certain group of rights and duties, while the lack of family relationship does not define anything; it defines enmity:
>
> 'If you wish to live among the Nuer you must do so on their terms, which means that you must treat them as a kind of kinsman and they will then treat you as a kind of kinsman. Rights, privileges and obligations are determined by kinship. Either a man is a kinsman, actually or by fiction, or he is

141. Claude Lévi-Strauss, The Elementary Structures of Kinship 481 (Revised ed., James Harle Bell & John Richard von Sturmer trans., 1969). We must, of course, differentiate Lévi-Strauss's use of the term "incest" to mean a marital union of near relations from the term as it is commonly used today (sexual relations between close relatives).

> a person to whom you have no reciprocal obligations and whom you treat as a potential enemy.'[142]

A related point is that, according to Lévi-Strauss, incestuous relationships appear to threaten the integrity of the family unit only because culture has defined the one to irreducibly exclude the other. People could have chosen otherwise, in which case the conception of marriage would today be quite different; for this reason, Lévi-Strauss believed, the origin of the incest prohibition cannot be explained in terms of ideas derived from within it.[143] The explanation must thus necessarily be found in reasons external to the prohibition, *i.e.*, its normative function. For Lévi-Strauss, those reasons are to be found in the social benefits derived from the principles of exchange, gift, and reciprocity (even if today, half a century after Lévi-Strauss, the idea of reducing human beings to items of gift and exchange is morally repulsive).

Furthermore, he thought the complexity and social significance of the institution of marriage lies in the fact that on it depends the entire flow of future generations. Its positive aspects are in distinguishing, mediating, differentiating, selecting, and combining sexual unions so that they become meaningful systems. It is a rule "by which and in which the transition from nature to culture is fulfilled."[144] Thus, "raw animal sexuality" is transformed into a complex human matrimonial system with laws and regulations that uphold its basic way of life.

Lévi-Strauss recognized that the laws of matrimony go well beyond mediating the "exchange" of women.[145] As seen next, he thought they led to the creation of the basic family unit and, eventually, the social state itself. If reappearing natural sounds in articulate speech acquire meaning, so the law against incest leads to other laws that mediate the evolution of the biological family. The minimal kinship elements are not the natural (or biological) ones of father, mother, and son but are made up of four terms: brother and sister, father and daughter. According to Lévi-Strauss, the law against incest means ultimately that "in human society a man cannot get a woman except from another man, who entrusts him with his daughter or sister."[146]

Apart from the basic purpose of incest law being to facilitate the circulation of women, Lévi-Strauss noted that the exchange is reciprocal in nature.

> Because marriage is exchange, because marriage is the archetype of exchange, the analysis of exchange can help in the understanding of the solidarity which unites gift and counter-gift, and one marriage with other marriages.[147]

---

142. *Id.* at 482 (quoting E. E. Evans-Pritchard, The Nuer: A Description of the Modes of Livelihood and Political Institutions of a Nilotic People 183 (1940)).

143. Lévi-Strauss, The Elementary Structures of Kinship, *supra* note 141, at 486–87.

144. Paz, *supra* note 140, at 18.

145. Lévi-Strauss, The Elementary Structures of Kinship, *supra* note 141, at 478.

146. Paz, *supra* note 140, at18.

147. Lévi-Strauss, The Elementary Structures of Kinship, *supra* note 141, at 483.

The prohibition is the counterpart of the obligation to give; as such it is shared and communicated between men as a kind of language involving a group of operations having messages and meanings. At the broader level, the law of matrimony (together with the incest taboo) orders the positions and statuses of all individuals and links them as individuals and as groups:[148] "Marriage is thus a dramatic encounter between nature and culture, between alliance and kinship . . . marriage is an arbitration between two lovers, parental and conjugal."[149]

The foregoing quotation contains several important ideas. First is that marriage is a fundamental social institution; it marks the transition from "nature" to "culture." The implication here is that with the institution of marriage man progresses from his rude natural condition to a higher social and cultural form; otherwise, "society might not have been."[150] Marriage also shows the link between it and kinship. Second is that the institution of marriage is ontologically prior to any intelligible conception of kinship (*i.e.*, there can be no kinship relations without marriage). Finally, marriage is the font of conjugal love (the "alliance") as well as parental love; these two types of love also mark two different types of normative relations (*i.e.*, between husband and wife and between parents and offspring).

The triumph of culture over nature is seen as a positive development. The rules of exchange and of marriage, and the incest prohibition, have social value. They provide

> the means of binding men together, and of superimposing upon the natural links of kinship the henceforth artificial links—artificial in the sense that they are removed from chance encounters or the promiscuity of family life—of alliance governed by a rule.[151]

Lévi-Strauss goes so far as to proclaim that "the rules of kinship and marriage are not made necessary by the social state. They are the social state itself."[152]

The following section presents an analysis of how kinship can be analyzed from the structural point of view.

A Structural Analysis of Kinship

In his major tome, *The Elementary Structures of Kinship*, Lévi-Strauss examines kinship from a structural viewpoint. Given the necessary connection between marriage as an institution and kinship, Lévi-Strauss considers marriage itself to be a set of kin relations between husband/wife, parents/children, mother/daughter, mother/son, father/son, father/daughter. What is important for Lévi-Strauss is that these terms represent "attitudes."[153]

---

148. Marcel Henaf, Claude Lévi-Strauss and the Making of Structural Anthropology 9 (Mary Baker trans., 1998).

149. Lévi-Strauss, The Elementary Structures of Kinship, *supra* note 141, at 489.

150. *Id.* at 490.

151. *Id.* at 480.

152. *Id.* at 490.

153. Lévi-Strauss, Structural Anthropology, *supra* note 134, at 37.

Thus he theorized that any kinship system comprises two orders of reality. At the first order are the terms through which the various family relations are expressed (*i.e.*, the nomenclature of kinship). This system of terminology expresses the various rights and duties that exist between members of the family. At the second level exists a system of attitudes of a psychological and social nature.[154] They ensure group cohesion and equilibrium, and thus their function is clear. However, Lévi-Strauss urges an inquiry beyond function, so that one may understand the nature of the interconnections between the various attitudes as well as their necessity.[155] As in the case of language, one may know the function of a phoneme, but its system remains unknown.

Lévi-Strauss claimed that some of these attitudes may not be institutionalized and are therefore not helpful in explaining the system. They are diffuse and uncrystallized and mere reflections or transpositions of terminology on the psychological level. For him, the more important attitudes are those that are the stylized, prescribed, and enforced privileges and/or taboos. They are institutionalized and expressed through fixed rituals.[156] They clarify and resolve contradictions in the first order level of terminology.

Lévi-Strauss uses the relation of the nephew and maternal uncle (the avunculate) as a point of departure for his theory of attitudes, given that the avunculate is a recurring feature in most cultures. Just as there is a vast range of linguistic sounds that can be uttered through the human vocal apparatus, so there can be a wide range of the types of human interpersonal relationships. However, despite the variety of sounds, each language in the end retains only a small number of the possible sounds. In linguistics this raises two questions: Why are only certain sounds selected? and What is the relationship between one or several of the chosen sounds and all the others? The avunculate can be studied by asking analogous questions. When this is done the two orders of reality become apparent. At the first order is the terminological system of the avunculate; at the second is the attitudinal system revealing a rich tapestry of psychophysiological material.[157]

In adopting the example of the avunculate in South Africa, as presented by Radcliffe-Brown,[158] Lévi-Strauss asserts that the relationship reveals "two antithetical systems of attitudes."[159] In one, the maternal uncle represents family authority and is not only feared and obeyed but also possesses certain rights over his nephew. In the other, the relationship between uncle and nephew is easy and familiar. Furthermore, the attitudes between uncle and nephew and between nephew and father are inversely linked. Thus when the relationship of uncle and nephew is easy and familiar, the relationship between the latter and his father is formal, and *vice versa*.

---

154. *Id.*

155. *Id.* at 37–38.

156. *Id.* at 38.

157. *Id.* at 40.

158. Lévi-Strauss, Structural Anthropology, *supra* note 134, at 40 *et seq.*

159. *Id.* at 40.

> We find the two systems of attitudes in both cases, but they are inversely correlated. In groups where familiarity characterizes the relationship between father and son, the relationship between maternal uncle and nephew is one of respect; and where the father stands as the austere representative of family authority, it is the uncle who is treated with familiarity. Thus the two sets of attitudes constitute (as the structural linguist would say) two pairs of oppositions.[160]

Lévi-Strauss adopts Radcliffe-Brown's explanation that descent determines the choice of oppositions, with one important reservation. He accepts Radcliffe-Brown's explanation that in patrilineal societies where the father represents authority and the mother is an indulgent figure, the maternal uncle's relationship with his nephew is easy and familiar. The opposite occurs in matrilineal societies, where authority is vested in the maternal uncle and feelings of love and tenderness evolve between father and son.[161] However, Lévi-Strauss finds that Radcliffe-Brown's scheme "arbitrarily" excludes other relations that, together with the mother's brother/sister's son and father/son relation, constitute the "irreducible" unit of kin. In addition to the ones identified by Radcliffe-Brown, Lévi-Strauss would add the relations of brother/sister and husband/wife. These additions are discussed after the following excerpt, which explains the two "different orders of reality" in kinship systems (*i.e.*, the terminological and attitudinal systems). It then examines these phenomena in the context of the avunculate to show the two pairs of inversely related oppositions among uncle, nephew, and father.

Claude Lévi-Strauss, Structural Anthropology 37–41 (Claire Jacobson & Brooke Grundfest Shoepf trans., 1963).

> What is generally called a "kinship system" comprises two quite different orders of reality. First, there are terms through which various kinds of family relationships are expressed. But kinship is not expressed solely through nomenclature. The individuals or classes of individuals who employ these terms feel (or do not feel, as the case may be) bound by prescribed behavior in their relations with one another, such as respect or familiarity, rights or obligations, and affection or hostility. Thus, along with what we propose to call the *system of terminology* (which, strictly speaking, constitutes the vocabulary system), there is another system, both psychological and social in nature, which we shall call the *system of attitudes*. Although it is true (as we have shown above) that the study of systems of terminology places us in a situation analogous, but opposite, to the situation in which we are dealing with phonemic systems, this difficulty is "inversed," as it were, when we examine systems of attitudes. We can guess at the role played by systems of attitudes,

160. *Id.* at 41.

161. *Id.*

that is, to insure group cohesion and equilibrium, but we do not understand the nature of the interconnections between the various attitudes, nor do we perceive their necessity. In other words, as in the case of language, we know their function, but the system is unknown.

Thus we find a profound difference between the *system of terminology* and the *system of attitudes,* and we have to disagree with A.R. Radcliffe-Brown if he really believed, as has been said of him, that attitudes are nothing but the expression or transposition of terms on the affective level. The last few years have provided numerous examples of groups whose chart of kinship terms does not accurately reflect family attitudes, and vice versa. It would be incorrect to assume that the kinship system constitutes the principal means of regulating interpersonal relationships in all societies. Even in societies where the kinship system does function as such, it does not fulfill that role everywhere to the same extent. Furthermore, it is always necessary to distinguish between two types of attitudes: first, the diffuse, uncrystallized, and non-institutionalized attitudes, which we may consider as the reflection or transposition of the terminology on the psychological level; and second, along with, or in addition to, the preceding ones, those attitudes which are stylized, prescribed, and sanctioned by taboos or privileges and expressed through a fixed ritual. These attitudes, far from automatically reflecting the nomenclature, often appear as secondary elaborations, which serve to resolve the contradictions and overcome the deficiencies inherent in the terminological system. . . . The system of attitudes constitutes, rather, a dynamic integration of the system of terminology.

Granted the hypothesis (to which we whole-heartedly subscribe) of a functional relationship between the two systems, we are nevertheless entitled, for methodological reasons, to treat independently the problems pertaining to each system. This is what we propose to do here for a problem which is rightly considered the point of departure for any theory of attitudes—that of the maternal uncle. We shall attempt to show how a formal transposition of the method of structural linguistics allows us to shed new light upon this problem. Because the relationship between nephew and maternal uncle appears to have been the focus of significant elaboration in a great many primitive societies, anthropologists have devoted special attention to it. It is not enough to note the frequency of this theme; we must also account for it. . . .

A few further remarks here may underline the striking analogy between the development of this problem and certain stages in the evolution of linguistic theory. The variety of possible attitudes in the area of interpersonal relationships is almost unlimited; the same holds true for the variety of sounds which can be articulated by the vocal apparatus—and which are actually produced during the first months of human life. Each language, however, retains only a very small number among all the possible sounds, and in this respect linguistics raises two questions: Why are certain sounds selected?

What relationships exist between one or several of the sounds chosen and all the others? Our sketch of the historical development of the avuncular problem is at precisely the same stage. Like language, the social group has a great wealth of psycho-physiological material at its disposal. Like language too, it retains only certain elements, at least some of which remain the same throughout the most varied cultures and are combined into structures which are always diversified. Thus we may wonder about the reason for this choice and the laws of combination.

For insight into the specific problem of the avunculate we should turn to Radcliffe-Brown. His well-known article on the maternal uncle in South Africa was the first attempt to grasp and analyze the modalities of what we might call the "general principle of attitude qualification." We shall briefly review the fundamental ideas of that now-classic study.

According to Radcliffe-Brown, the term *avunculate* covers two antithetical systems of attitudes. In one case, the maternal uncle represents family authority; he is feared and obeyed, and possesses certain rights over his nephew. In the other case, the nephew holds privileges of familiarity in relation to his uncle and can treat him more or less as his victim. Second, there is a correlation between the boy's attitude toward his maternal uncle and his attitude toward his father. We find the two systems of attitudes in both cases, but they are inversely correlated. In groups where familiarity characterizes the relationship between father and son, the relationship between maternal uncle and nephew is one of respect; and where the father stands as the austere representative of family authority, it is the uncle who is treated with familiarity. Thus the two sets of attitudes constitute (as the structural linguist would say) two pairs of oppositions. Radcliffe-Brown concluded his article by proposing the following interpretation: In the final analysis, it is descent that determines the choice of oppositions. In patrilineal societies, where the father and the father's descent group represent traditional authority, and maternal uncle is considered a "male mother." He is generally treated in the same fashion, and sometimes even called by the same name, as the mother. In matrilineal societies, the opposite occurs. Here, authority is vested in the maternal uncle, while relationships of tenderness and familiarity revolve about the father and his descent group.

It would indeed be difficult to exaggerate the importance of Radcliffe-Brown's contribution, which was the first attempt at synthesis on an empirical basis following Lowie's authoritative and merciless criticism of evolutionist metaphysics. To say that this effort did not entirely succeed does not in any way diminish the homage due this great British anthropologist; but we should certainly recognize that Radcliffe-Brown's article leaves unanswered some fundamental questions. First, the avunculate does not occur in all matrilineal or all patrilineal systems, and we find it present in some systems which are neither matrilineal nor patrilineal. Further, the avuncular relationship is not limited to two terms, but presupposes four, namely, brother, sister, brother-in-law,

> and nephew. An interpretation such as Radcliffe-Brown's arbitrarily isolates particular elements of a global structure which must be treated as a whole....

Structural Characteristics of the Basic Kin Unit

As Lévi-Strauss asserts at the end of the foregoing excerpt, Radcliffe-Brown's analysis "arbitrarily isolates particular elements of a global structure which must be treated as a whole."[162] To determine what is missing and to locate the missing elements, Lévi-Strauss examines data on kin relations in tribal cultures such as the Trobriand Islanders, the Pschav and the Cherkess of the Caucasus, the Tonga in Polynesia, and so on. He notes Malinowski's findings that among the Trobriands the husband and wife live in an atmosphere of "tender intimacy" and in a relationship characterized by reciprocity,[163] whereas the Trobrian relationship between brother and sister is "dominated by an extremely rigid taboo." Therefore, it is a major insult to tell a man that he resembles his sister. By contrast, the brother-sister relationship among the Pschav is loving and tender, whereas the husband-wife relationship among the Cherkess is so rigid that a Cherkess man will not appear in public with his wife, will only visit her in secret, and will not talk about her in public.

In light of these findings about the Cherkess, Trobriand, and other societies, Lévi-Strauss concludes that it is not enough to confine the correlation of attitudes between father/son and uncle/sister's son. This correlation is, according to Lévi-Strauss, only one aspect of a global system that (analogous to a language's complete system of phonological contrasts) contains four types of relationships: brother/sister, husband/wife, father/son, and mother's brother/sister's son. These two groups yield a "law" such that

> [i]n both groups, the relation between maternal uncle and nephew is to the relation between brother and sister as the relation between father and son is to that between husband and wife. Thus if we know one pair of relations, it is always possible to infer the other.[164]

This structure then rests on four terms (brother, sister, father, son).[165] They are linked by two pairs of correlative oppositions so that in each of the two generations there is a positive and a negative relationship.[166] Thus one has to know two of the relations in order to predict the other two. For example, one must know the father/son and husband/wife relation in order to predict the uncle/nephew and brother/sister relation.[167]

Consistently with his structuralist methodology, Lévi-Strauss's goal is to go beyond the terms and reveal their underlying normative relations. The totality of

---

162. *Id.*

163. Lévi-Strauss, Structural Anthropology, *supra* note 134, at 42.

164. *Id.*

165. *Id.* at 46.

166. *Id.*

167. Marvin Harris, The Rise of Anthropological Theory 496 (updated ed., 2001).

relations are captured by his basic kinship unit, a unit that is irreducible in the sense that it contains the minimum set of relations among kin that cannot be reduced further without breaking up the unit itself. Furthermore, as explained in the following excerpt, the fundamental unit of kinship results from the prohibition against incest and the ongoing exchange of women, both of which are interconnected with the law of marriage.

Claude Lévi-Strauss, Structural Anthropology 46 (Claire Jacobson & Brooke Grundfest Shoepf, trans., 1963).

Thus we see that in order to understand the avunculate we must treat it as one relationship within a system, while the system itself must be considered as a whole in order to grasp its structure. This structure rests upon four terms (brother, sister, father, and son), which are linked by two pairs of correlative oppositions in such a way that in each of the two generations there is always a positive relationship and a negative one. Now, what is the nature of this structure, and what is its function? The answer is as follows: This structure is the most elementary form of kinship that can exist. It is, properly speaking, *the unit of kinship*.

One may give a logical argument to support this statement. In order for a kinship structure to exist, three types of family relations must always be present: a relation of consanguinity, a relation of affinity, and a relation of descent—in other words, a relation between siblings, a relation between spouses, and a relation between parent and child. It is evident that the structure given here satisfies this threefold requirement, in accordance with the scientific principle of parsimony. But these considerations are abstract, and we can present a more direct proof for our thesis.

The primitive and irreducible character of the basic unit of kinship, as we have defined it, is actually a direct result of the universal presence of an incest taboo. This is really saying that in human society a man must obtain a woman from another man who gives him a daughter or a sister. Thus we do not need to explain how the maternal uncle emerged in the kinship structure: He does not emerge—he is present initially. Indeed, the presence of the maternal uncle is a necessary precondition for the structure to exist. The error of traditional anthropology, like that of traditional linguistics, was to consider the terms, and not the relations between the terms.

Conclusion

Lévi-Strauss's structural methodology is based on the assumption that the human mind is predisposed to impose order on the formless data of its perceptions of the world outside it, which essentially preserves the Cartesian dichotomy of *res cogitans* and *res extensa*.[168] But more important for Lévi-Strauss was to theorize about how the

168. *See* Isaak Dore, The Epistemological Foundations of Law 315, n. 47 (2007).

mind imposes order. He believed it does so through mental categories; thus man is disposed to understand and give meaning to his material and social world in terms of things and relations belonging to named classes or categories.

Focusing on the social world, Lévi-Strauss sought to understand basic normative relations (*e.g.*, marriage, kinship, and myths) in structural terms. This meant going beyond the terminological aspects and focusing on the relational aspects of social representations. Doing so meant adopting linguistics as the methodological model. Structural linguistics (which held that each linguistic element must be considered in relation to other elements) inspired the notion that marital and kinship laws must be studied in terms of the relations they entail. Lévi-Strauss borrowed the notion that, like language, these relations in their totality constitute the grammar of which the individual participant in culture is unconscious.

For these reasons, Lévi-Strauss studied myth as an experiment to bolster his claim that the human mind operates through binary categories to give order and meaning to life. If so contingent a phenomenon as myth was given meaning through mental categories, Lévi-Strauss believed there was an *a fortiori* argument that other social representations such as marriage and kinship arrangements can be studied as complex systems of binary opposite relations.

Thus, like the basic elements of language, Lévi-Strauss deemed these representations to be meaningful social structures that acquire meaning only when integrated into systems that show their interrelationships. Furthermore, he thought these relations, like linguistic elements, exist largely as unconscious thought. Finally, the recurrence of similar myths and similar kinship patterns in different cultures suggested to Lévi-Strauss that, like their linguistic counterparts, they follow the same general laws.

In subjecting marriage and kinship to structural analysis, Lévi-Strauss attempted to show them to be founded on the law against incest containing a yes/no binary opposition. He concluded that the prohibition of some types of relations shows the range of those that are permitted. Thus he viewed incest laws as having emerged from a rational if not utilitarian basis: they allowed the establishment of the basic nuclear family unit which was a vital component of the social state. It is here, Lévi-Strauss believed, that man makes the transition from nature to a higher normative order, *i.e.*, culture.

According to Lévi-Strauss, the existence of the matrimonial family leads to the creation of kinship relations. These relations must therefore be studied beyond their terminological aspects so that the underlying reality of attitudes and relations, as well as their interconnections, are exposed. The prime example is the avunculate showing two binary oppositions, in which the attitudes between uncle and nephew and nephew and father are inversely linked.

Lévi-Strauss, however, criticizes Radcliffe-Brown's analysis of the avunculate on the ground that it arbitrarily excludes certain relations that make up the total structure. Thus, analogously with a language's complete system of phonological contrasts, Lévi-Strauss proposed four types of relationships: brother/sister (*i.e.*, mother: mother's brother), husband/wife (*i.e.*, father: mother), father/son, and mother's brother/sister's son (*i.e.*, uncle: nephew).

By adding the husband/wife and brother/sister relation to Radcliffe-Brown's father/son and uncle/nephew relation, Lévi-Strauss claims to have identified the most elementary and irreducible kinship form. In other words, the kinship must be seen as only one relationship within an overall structure of attitudinal oppositions.

Chapter 7

Cultural Cognitivism and Normativity: Symbolism and Interpretivism

The preceding chapter focused on three schools of emic cognitivism: cultural functionalism, ethnoscience, and neostructuralism. The present chapter is devoted to the last two schools in this domain: symbolic anthropology and interpretivism.

Symbolic Anthropology: Basic Tenets

All five schools discussed in this and the previous chapter are interrelated; their separation here is for analytical purposes only. It will be readily seen that the study of symbols is closely related to cognitive functionalism, which defines culture as learned knowledge that helps members of a cultural grouping to understand or give meaning to social experience in the form of symbols.[1] Here, a symbol is simply an object or event that has a socially assigned meaning. These meanings are interpreted, adapted, and/or combined through rules that together make up the cultural code of society.

> The focus of symbolic anthropology is the study of meaning in human social life—how we make sense of and interpret each other and our environs, and how, on the basis of our understandings, we create shared communicative worlds, or cultural systems of meaning. As the term suggests, symbolic anthropology approaches these vast questions by concentrating on symbols and symbolization—things and ideas we imbue with meaning and the cognitive and communicative processes by which we do so. Its central concern with the role of representation, meaning and interpretation in shaping culturally distinctive forms of understanding gives symbolic anthropology ties to a number of other subdisciplines, most notably cognitive anthropology, folklore, psychological anthropology, and sociolinguistics.[2]

One premise of symbolic anthropology is that beliefs considered in isolation from each other may well seem irrational or unintelligible; however, they become highly meaningful when examined as part of cultural webs of understandings. These understandings in their totality express a *weltanchaung* or worldview that explains even the

1. *See* Chapter 6 text at notes 7–12 *supra*.

2. Mary Des Chene, *Symbolic Anthropology, in* 4 Encyclopedia of Cultural Anthropology 1274, 1274 (David Levinson & Melvin Ember eds., 1996).

most mundane of materially grounded activities.[3] For this reason, symbolic anthropology is considered to be idealist rather than materialist in orientation.[4]

The field of symbolic anthropology embraces all of the primary social and cultural representations (*e.g.*, political and kinship systems, religion, art, dance, myth, ritual, oratory, cosmology). These representations are taken to encode a culture's fundamental beliefs and are understood, interpreted, and communicated between individuals through a variety of material and verbal symbols.[5] When different symbolic representations are considered together, they foster overall coherence in social life.[6]

Symbolic anthropology is particularly influenced by structuralism, pioneered by Lévi-Strauss (discussed in Chapter 6), and by structural functionalism (discussed in Chapter 3). However, unlike Lévi-Strauss, whose binary classifications were designed to reduce diverse cultural representations such as kinship systems and myths to their common elements, symbolic anthropology seeks to portray the rich and complex tapestry of cultural life while adhering to the structuralist belief in the universality of certain forms of human cognition (*i.e.*, the belief in the universal human capacity to symbolize). This capacity exists at the individual level and extends to the group, and not *vice versa*.

From structural functionalism, symbolic anthropology borrows the presumption that societies are functionally integrated wholes in which all individual social institutions work together pragmatically to maintain overall normative order. Symbolic anthropology shares the structural functional belief in the pragmatic social consequences of belief systems and how symbols (as belief systems) foster solidarity and a sense of emotional attachment. For example, David Schneider studied American kinship as an integral system of symbols without connecting it to its biological or psychological characteristics. According to him, although kinship represents its obvious biological facts, these facts are something more than facts; they acquire qualitative meanings such as love, bonding, "enduring solidarity," and trust.[7] Similarly, Clifford Geertz considers religion to be a symbolic system that reinforces the emotions with which humans interpret the real world.[8] Mary Douglas likewise explains the social categories of cultural meanings through symbols. By taking a Durkheimian approach, she explains how cultural statements about symbolic purity and impurity (*e.g.*, food

---

3. Clifford Geertz, *Religion as a Cultural System*, *in* CLIFFORD GEERTZ, THE INTERPRETATION OF CULTURES: SELECTED ESSAYS 87, 99 (1973).

4. JERRY D. MOORE, VISIONS OF CULTURE: AN INTRODUCTION TO ANTHROPOLOGICAL THEORIES AND THEORISTS 227 (2d ed., 2004).

5. VICTOR TURNER, THE FOREST OF SYMBOLS: ASPECTS OF NDEMBU RITUAL 30 (1967).

6. Janet L. Dolgin, David S. Kemnitzer & David M. Schneider, *Introduction*, *in* SYMBOLIC ANTHROPOLOGY: A READER IN THE STUDY OF SYMBOLS AND MEANINGS 3, 4–5 (Janet L. Dolgin, David S. Kemnitzer & David M. Schneider eds., 1977).

7. David M. Schneider, *Kinship, Nationality, and Religion in American Culture: Toward a Definition of Kinship*, *in* SYMBOLIC ANTHROPOLOGY: A READER, *supra* note 6, at 63, 66–67.

8. Geertz, *Religion as a Cultural System*, *supra* note 3, at 90.

taboos) express a sense of uniqueness and, indeed, the very identity of a particular culture.[9]

The following excerpt is one perspective on the nature of symbolic anthropology that explains not only its structural-functional orientation but also (somewhat paradoxically) the importance of purposive individual (as opposed to group) action.

Janet L. Dolgin, David S. Kemnitzer & David M. Schneider, *Introduction, in* Symbolic Anthropology: A Reader in the Study of Symbols and Meanings 33–43 (Janet L. Dolgin, David S. Kemnitzer & David M. Schneider eds., 1977).

It is now time to return to the place where this excursion began, that being the notion that human beings form societies, that the members of society share a system of symbols and meanings, technically called "culture," and that this system of symbols and meanings represents the reality of the world in which they live their lives. Whether this system of symbols and meanings is tightly and closely integrated (or even loosely integrated) is a question around which there is much disagreement. But there is little debate about the fact that it is a system to some degree—that it is more or less integrated and does not constitute a merely *ad hoc* collection of disparate items. This becomes self-evident when it is remembered that the group of people—be they two or three hundred or a few hundred million—have to act with respect to each other. Hence their roles must articulate in some degree; their definitions of what it is all about must be shared in some measure, even if not everyone agrees with everyone else's definition. They must have at least *some* notion of what other people believe, they must be able to have a reasonable expectation of what their response to others, and others' response to them, will be, in order to interact with them and certainly to communicate with them. And communication is the *sine qua non* of any human society.

If the culture of a group of people constitutes, in some sense, an integrated whole, what is the *ground* for its integration? One mode of integration has to do with the roles people play to fulfill the functional prerequisites for the maintenance of any social system and, of course, the people within it. People must be fed. They must reproduce. And there must be some order to this; the integration of the cultural system provides common definitions of the state of affairs called life, some way to conceptualize all of those things which make physical and social life possible; and gives sense, too, to those that make it *worth* living; the style of life which is any people's uniqueness, and identity, has been proven by people time and time again to be as valuable as eating. Culture is thus indispensable to the integration of the social system in two senses: it provides the constitution, as it were, of the individual

9. *See* Mary Douglas, Purity and Danger: An Analysis of Concepts of Pollution and Taboo (1966).

roles and relations out of which the daily life is built; and it provides the unifying features—which might be seen as an aesthetic dimension—of these activities. Whatever the postulated relationship between culture and society, between thought and action—whether they can be seen as distinguishable in analysis (as argued by Kroeber and Parsons 1958), or as one embedded in the other, or as inseparable aspects of a single unity—life must have meaning, the things people do must be communicable—and this entails a system of signs or symbols in which this meaning is embedded and expressed.

Functionalist queries notwithstanding, we do not know enough about people's cultural life—in the narrow sense in which we use the term—to be able to spell out how, precisely, it is adaptive, and to what, and whether it can be accounted for on those grounds; or whether we need species specific grounds, which simply say "that's the nature of the human animal." Even here we know enough to know how little we know. We assume—we must assume—the capacity to learn language, to invent language, to use it as a form of communication; that it is no rude tool by any means. History may tell us that the people who live on the island of Yap speak Yapese now because they spoke it for some time, and that proto-Yapese is probably what they spoke before that. What, however, is the structure of Yapese, the rules which govern the way in which its signs and meanings are used? How does it vary from other languages? These, only comparative study can tell us. The same questions can be asked about human cultures. Even accepting that there are species-specific capacities for culture, the question as to what the parameters of these are, what the universals (if any) are, what the range of variants are and in what regard they occur, remain.

It is important, too, that we do not reify culture to the point that we no longer see it as an aspect of what people do. Every act that every person performs has its symbolic aspect, its meanings. That we abstract these meanings in order to understand a system of meanings is true, but we must remember that *we abstract them from the concrete actions of people* As an abstraction, culture cannot follow laws of its own; rather, what regularities it shows are those which inhere in the actions from which the symbolic and the meaningful are abstracted.

Fundamental to the study of symbolic anthropology is the concern with how people formulate their reality. We must, if we are to understand this and relate it to an understanding of their (and our own) action, examine *their culture,* not *our theories* (and if we study our theories, we must study them *as* "their culture"); study their systems of symbols, not our *ad hoc* presumptions about what it might or should be; what they actually do, not what we presume to be universal and therefore attribute to them—all too often only to discover that what we thought to be universal was not so universal after all. In other words, our task is not to study forms, but to study *praxis* (which makes use of, creates, and relates to forms)—self-consciousness and conscious action—and for that, we need a method, theory, which does not dissolve it before we begin. . . .

. . . A more symbolic approach understands ritual as a direct embodiment of social transitions and movements, this symbolic embodiment being credited as responsible for the dynamic effectiveness of ritual as a therapeutic agent. . . . Within the symbolic perspective it has been suggested that rituals develop in reaction, and encapsulate a cultural retort, to socially menacing objects and events. Both of these somewhat different explanations of ritual assume the (logical or temporal) priority of a nonsymbolic social system which induces stress which is met in turn by ritual responses. So, while economics is seen to deal with fundamental reality in an outside world and kinship with fundamental realities of human biology, ritual is taken to deal with problems which social life creates for itself, problems which follow, by and large, from the *a priori* "givens" of social life itself.

Such analyses assume ritual and its kindred "expressive" activities to be analogous to a bandage for the social body; religion and art (including graphics, music, dance) are examined as symbolic statements of the trouble with life and are thought to have the same function. So religion, in general, like ritual, is seen to provide comforts, is seen as a form of self-expression projecting in representational form the joy or the hell of living.

However, there is no reason to assume that this Band-Aid theory is correct, . . . There is nothing more "down to earth" or "basic" about kinship, economics, or status changes than there is about rituals. . . .

When ritual and kinship are compared, we find that each entails a system of statuses, roles, and rules for how the roles should be played out, how the statuses relate to each other, and how persons move through these statuses. Each has its uses; each has its symbolic and meaningful aspects. Indeed, the belief that kinship orders *the* facts of biological reproduction is itself an interesting cultural statement. It is no longer enough to distinguish semantic domains which contrast, interact, or remain independent, and to associate meanings, symbols, or functions to these. Symbols exist in the context of other symbols, in ordered structures; the symbolic forms must be followed out through the structures if we are to do more than consider the problems we pose externally, if, that is, we are to explore the structures of meaning in use.

Toward Praxis

. . . Our analysis of *some* formal problems in practical interpretation has led us to two basic points about symbolic activity: (1) formal symbolic structures are structures *in use* (they are entities which are used *by* one person or group to refer to a different entity, *for* an audience); (2) the functional relations between symbolic structures and other aspects of social life must be understood, not as a superorganic operation which serves an *a priori* role in the relations of other superorganic operations, but as a structure of actors' intentions. . . .

Symbolic action is part of a total mode of production and expression of creative human energy. The only *reference* of symbolic action is to the other aspects of the creative enterprise; symbolic action may determine, or be determined by, other aspects of social action, in any particular concrete empirical instance; but *in theory,* symbolic action always refers only to *itself:* to other symbolic action (because all action and all aspects of human action are symbolically constituted). Of course, for many Marxist writers, symbolic action is shaped by other forces, particularly economic structures; and indeed, on Marx's view, symbolic action *may* be secondary to other dimensions of action. This is not, however, a necessary condition of symbolization, according to Marx; the alternative to symbolic meaning is not as Durkheim and Weber insisted, chaos. Such chaos *does not exist,* since for people, everything is symbolic, created (in part at least) by the mind.

This creation by the mind, moreover, is an *active* process, part and parcel of the human tendency to act on the world; if symbolic action is created by anything, it is by the predilection for action in a certain mode—which is to say, by previous action, previous meanings. What this view requires is a concentration on symbolic *processes,* instead of requiring that the analysis of meaning show only how a particular form represents a more elementary one; and it demands also that the process whereby people give meaning to their world and their action in it, be seen as a part of their lives and actions, a part of the general pattern of social relationship, instead of being artificially separated from it. . . .

. . . As we have tried to make clear above, theories of meaning are shared by the self-consciousness of people and their response to their own situation. Our contemporaries who cling to the opposition between meaning and chaos do so largely out of a desire—perhaps not expressed or expressible, but nonetheless present and powerful—to escape the realities of freedom which the alternative view offers them and the responsibilities that reality carries with it. That responsibility is twofold: on the one hand, to combat the mystification to which we are subject as members of our own culture, and, on the other, to struggle for the implementation of a world which sets the human spirit—and its apparently infinite potential to create new dimensions of meaningful existence—truly free.

People act on the basis of belief. To study belief in action—whether in New Guinea or New York—is to examine the possibilities of freedom, and the roots of oppression and alienation. But these can be studied only in the context of a *practical* commitment to freedom and a determination to overcome that which stands in its way. People made it, is the principal lesson of modern anthropology; people can remake it, must become the principal lesson of our work in the future.

This excerpt ends on an optimistic if not idealistic note. It emphasizes the importance of freedom and creative human choice, in contrast to the determinism of Marx and the social solidarism of Durkheim.

The emic nature of the inquiry is also clearly intentionalist in nature. It is designed to explore the "structure of actors' intentions," "theories of meaning," and "self-consciousness of people."[10] According to Mary Des Chene, it is designed to "emphasize the actor's point of view," as to how symbols constitute the epistemology for comprehending the world and guiding social relations.[11] The cognitive or "mentalist" nature of the approach is also evident.[12]

This explanation does not entail any evaluation of the scientific truth of beliefs associated with a symbol. Thus, some may believe in ghosts, others may not; among those who do, ghosts are treated by the anthropologist as real. In other words, that which is thought to be real is treated as real.[13]

Human Creativity Versus Determinism and Solidarism

The intentionalist nature of symbolic anthropology shows that symbols are socially constructed and serve distinct human ends ("If people can make it, they can re-make it"). It is with regard to the questions of individual freedom and creativity that symbolic anthropology is at variance with structural functionalism, despite its other affinities with it.

As we have seen, a number of structural functionalist theories inspired by the writings of Kroeber, Sapir, Benedict, and Mead portray individuals as unconscious of the cultural forces that control them. This conclusion, if not the entire Durkheimian project itself, is viewed by the symbolic anthropologists as not giving proper credit to the individual; thus, it is viewed as too narrow. For example, contrary to Durkheim's "mechanical solidarity" argument (*i.e.*, that primitive societies are somehow bound together by a primordial need), Victor Turner advances the quasi-Freudian argument that primitive humans used symbols as tools to cope with the challenges of the forces of nature that threatened their very existence.[14] In Durkheimian terms, symbols are the means to achieve social solidarity. The belief that the latter do not arise "mechanically" but are consciously constructed results in the conclusion that symbols are the means to achieve particular social ends.[15] The particularism of the Boasian approach has been viewed as equally unacceptable because it is devoid of theory and eclipses the individual.[16]

10. *See* above excerpt.

11. Des Chene, *supra* note 2, at 1275; *see also* Moore, *supra* note 4, at 228.

12. Merwyn S. Garbarino, Sociocultural Theory in Anthropology: A Shorty History 83 (1977).

13. Dolgin, Kemnitzer & Schneider, *supra* note 6, at 5.

14. For a concise explanation of the influence of Freud on symbolic anthropology, *see id.* at 5–6.

15. Victor Turner, Revelation and Divination in Ndembu Ritual 52–53, 171–74 (1975).

16. Paul A. Erickson & Liam D. Murphy, A History of Anthropological Theory 135–36 (2d ed., 2003).

Other philosophical currents have centered on the individual. Kant's emphasis on the moral worth of the individual (who is assumed to be endowed with the capacity to reason) and Edmund Husserl's phenomenology (which argues that culture cannot be studied as if it is a natural science and that cultural life must be understood subjectively, as "lived experience") also position the individual as the focal point of social science.[17] (As we have seen, Durkheim and Radcliffe-Brown argued that social facts are "things" and can therefore be studied scientifically in the same way as material facts.) Thus, just as Kant claimed to have effected a "Copernican revolution" by arguing that in the phenomenal world, the object conforms to the mind and not the other way around, so emic cognitivism, culminating in symbolic anthropology, may be credited with an intellectual paradigm shift by claiming that the individual controls culture and not vice versa.

The study of the individual had, and still has, the added appeal of being amenable to sound empirical investigation. Thus it falls easily within the Cartesian dualism of mind and body, which could otherwise be restated as the distinction between the observer and the observed.

Symbolism in Law: Case Studies

A. The Law of Forfeiture

One example of symbolism in law is the law of civil forfeiture, or the law of the deodand, derived from the Latin *deo dandum* ("given to God").[18] This type of law dates back to ancient Greece (and possibly before) but was also popular under the old common law of England, where the king as the earthly representative of God received forfeited objects and property deemed harmful to the social and moral order of the community.[19] Under this law, inanimate objects such as trees, statues, and javelins, as well as animals such as horses, donkeys, pigs, and so on, could be confiscated and "exiled" to a place outside the community if they were the cause of injury to humans.[20]

As seen earlier, symbolic anthropology seeks to unearth the narratives that underlie symbols, in order to understand their meanings. Symbolism in law is analogous to symbolism in other areas of social life, such as religion. According to Geertz, religious narratives and their accompanying rituals are ways of giving meaning to bewildering and frightening phenomena that people encounter in the real world, such as death and catastrophic events.[21] By this logic, such narratives affirm social solidarity and faith and serve as frameworks for understanding crises that disrupt order. Explained

---

17. *See* Isaak Dore, The Epistemological Foundations of Law 414–18 (2007) (on Kant). Edmund Husserl, The Basic Problems of Phenomenology: From the Lectures, Winter Semester, 1910–1911, 4–5 (Ingo Farin & James G. Hart trans., 2006).

18. Paul Schiff Berman, *An Anthropological Approach to Modern Forfeiture Law: The Symbolic Function of Legal Action Against Objects*, 11 Yale J. L. & Human. 1, 25 (1999).

19. *Id.* at 25–26.

20. *Id.* at 26.

21. Geertz, *supra* note 3, at 108.

next is how the symbolism underlying forfeiture law embodies a narrative of social meaning as to how social harm is cleansed and solidarity restored.

Two of the primary functions of law are to maintain order and, when that order is disturbed, to restore it. The law of civil forfeiture of animate and inanimate objects (*deo dandum*) fulfils the same normative goals. It is a symbolic way of restoring the social equilibrium that has been disturbed by the object in question. As such it is pursued on behalf of the community and is independent of any criminal or civil penalties that might be levied against the owner.[22]

Paul Schiff Berman, *An Anthropological Approach to Modern Forfeiture Law: The Symbolic Function of Legal Actions Against Objects*, 11 Yale J. L. & Human. 1, 23–26 (1999).

After the collapse of the Roman Empire, many societies in Europe developed traditions whereby inanimate objects and animals that caused the death of human beings were cast out of the human community. Evidence of these proceedings stretches as far back as the ninth century and continues even into the twentieth century. As with the examples from ancient Greece, there is no indication that these legal proceedings against inanimate objects and animals served as proxies for actions against negligent or culpable owners. Instead, we again see communities constructing narratives of guilt after the breach of a social norm and then creating a symbolic way of cleansing the community to preserve the societal order.

The proceedings against animals and inanimate objects, both in England and on the Continent, appear to derive from the Bible where, in the Book of Exodus, an ox that killed a human being was sentenced to death by stoning, and its flesh could not be eaten. The punishment of stoning is a distinctive sentence in the Bible, reserved for only a few types of crimes.

In those cases, there is no designated "executioner," for the community assembled is the common executioner of the sentence. Offenses that entail this mode of execution must therefore be of a character that, either in theory or in fact, "offend" the corporate community or are believed to compromise its most cherished values to the degree that the commission of the offense places the community itself in jeopardy.

The Biblical treatment of the ox indicates that, as in ancient Greece, actions against non-human transgressors were treated as crimes against the community as a whole. Moreover, it was irrelevant whether or not the ox was "morally" guilty. Rather, the guilt was treated as an objective contagion that "must be eradicated in the most public way, and the public must participate in the act of eradication as a demonstration that it is consciously and effectively restoring the order that had been disturbed."

22. Berman, *supra* note 18, at 20.

In addition to this Biblical command, the English law of the deodand also derived from reaction to the ancient tradition of the blood feud, wherein the kin of the deceased would seek vengeance against whomever was the cause of the death. To stop the cycle of violence caused by these feuds, communities adopted codes intended to persuade the relatives of the deceased to accept pecuniary compensation rather than exacting their revenge in blood. This tradition was known as "noxal surrender." Eventually an offering was also given both to the lord over the place where the wrong was done and to the lord whose subject had been slain. These monetary payments implicitly acknowledged that it was not only the victim's kin that needed redress, but the broader society as well:

> In the [payment], we can see the germ of the idea that wrong is not simply the affair of the injured individual—an idea which is the condition precedent to the growth of a criminal law. A wrong is regarded as a breach of the [peace] of the king, of a community.

The various offerings appeased both the kin and the community and therefore restored harmony.

The ninth-century Anglo-Saxon laws of Alfred the Great blended the Biblical tradition with these offerings and created a proceeding resembling forfeiture that later became known as deodand in the English common law. Under this code, rather than condemning an animal transgressor to death by stoning, the animal was surrendered to the authorities for retribution. In addition, if a tree fell on someone, the victim's kin were permitted to take the tree in order to expiate the death. Significantly, the guilty object was given to the kin not as compensation for the loss suffered, but rather as an object upon which their vengeance must be wrought before the dead person could lie in peace.

Ultimately, the Crown replaced the kin as the prosecuting entity. The word "deodand" derives from the Latin phrase "deo dandum" which literally means "given to God." Thus, the offending object "was forfeited to God, that is, to the King, God's Lieutenant on earth, to be distributed in works of charity for the appeasing of God's wrath." Indeed, the King originally used money collected as a result of the deodand to fund a mass for the dead person's soul, emphasizing the connection between forfeiture and religious expiation.

Many instances of deodand forfeitures exist in the historical literature. An early treatise refers to mischances involving falls from trees, ships, boats, carts, horses, and mills, and decrees that the objects causing the death in these cases shall be adjudged deodands. Another history refers to horses, oxen, carts, boats, mill-wheels, and cauldrons as the most common deodand. Thus, for example, a boat that capsized, causing a fisherman to die, was beached, cursed, and allowed to rot, and a horse that carried a man over a cliff or into water, drowning him, was forfeited.

Berman gives modern examples of several cases of civil forfeiture decided by the U.S. Supreme Court, which he criticized for not properly articulating the normative rationale in upholding forfeitures of "inanimate transgressors." The two cases that are his focus of discussion are *Bennis v. Michigan*[23] and *United States v. Ursery*.[24] In *Bennis*, one John Bennis was arrested while he was engaged in an illicit act with a prostitute in a 1977 Pontiac he owned jointly with his wife. He was charged, convicted, and fined for gross indecency. The state authorities then went further and confiscated the vehicle under a public nuisance statute that allowed seizure of property used in criminal activity. The Supreme Court ultimately upheld the constitutionality of the forfeiture under the Due Process Clause of the Fifth Amendment, giving as its main reason that forfeiture may serve a deterrent function; Justice Clarence Thomas's concurring opinion maintained that a law that could be traced to such ancient usage under the common law as received and applied in the U.S. should be presumed to comport with due process requirements.[25]

In *Ursery*, police found marijuana growing adjacent to the defendant's house as well as marijuana seeds, stems, and stalks inside the house. The U.S. commenced civil forfeiture proceedings against the house on the ground that it was being used to facilitate the production of a controlled substance. The defendant was also given a six-year jail term for manufacturing marijuana. The Supreme Court upheld the forfeiture on the ground that it did not constitute a punishment for purposes of the Double Jeopardy Clause, and therefore the clause did not apply. Again, the court affirmed the long line of cases in which Congress had authorized *in rem* civil forfeiture and which, in the court's opinion, were not punishment because they constituted "remedial civil action."[26]

> [This] forfeiture proceeding . . . is *in rem*. It is the property which is proceeded against, and, by resort to a legal fiction, held guilty and condemned as though it were conscious instead of inanimate and insentient. In a criminal prosecution it is the wrongdoer in person who is proceeded against, convicted, and punished. The forfeiture is no part of the punishment for the criminal offense. The provision of the Fifth Amendment to the Constitution in respect of double jeopardy does not apply.[27]

Berman notes the storm of criticism from commentators to the effect that the court was resorting to empty fictions and perpetrating injustice,[28] but his critique focuses on the court's failure to fully articulate the social and cultural symbolism of civil forfeiture. Although he makes no normative claim as to the desirability of forfeiture law, Berman does explain its normative rationale in sociocultural terms:

---

23. 516 U.S. 442 (1996).
24. 518 U.S. 267 (1996).
25. *Bennis*, 516 U.S. at 454–455.
26. *Ursery*, 518 U.S. at 274, 278.
27. Various Items of Personal Property v. United States, 282 U.S. 577, 581 (1931).
28. Berman, *supra* note 18, at 16.

Paul Schiff Berman, *An Anthropological Approach to Modern Forfeiture Law: The Symbolic Function of Legal Actions Against Objects*, 11 YALE J. L. & HUMAN. 1, 18–19, 37–38, 44–45 (1999).

When a transgressor breaches a societal norm, the act, by definition, causes a rift in the social fabric. In response, the community must construct a narrative, or provide "social meaning" for understanding and healing that breach. Anthropologists have long recognized that narratives are the vehicle by which we construct the meaning we take from the world around us. These narratives provide a framework to interpret what we experience and a language for describing reality. "Every telling is an arbitrary imposition of meaning on the flow of memory . . . every telling is interpretive."

Narratives are particularly relied upon in times of change, disorientation, and trauma. Thus, a disaster will stimulate "pronouncements, prayers, eulogies, addresses, white papers, and other formal offerings that later dissolve back into the welter of conversation characterizing the ordinary business of living together." A society's primary social institutions must function as storytellers at such crisis moments. Religious narratives and their accompanying rituals are the clearest example of an institution constructing meaning out of death and other irrational and frightening events. The rites link us to our past and future by enacting enduring and underlying patterns. And the narratives provide explanations, or affirmations of faith, or parables, all of which create a framework for understanding the crisis event and healing psychological wounds. Thus, it has been said that cultural narratives provide a "shield against terror."

Courts too are social institutions that tell stories about chaotic events. Legal processes provide cultural narratives for imposing order and asserting the primacy of the community. . . .

B. Narratives of Degradation

Most modern writers who have discussed the social function of trials have emphasized the courts' chief role as dispute resolvers. However, it is important to see that trials also function as cultural storytellers and that legal processes provide narratives that permit the community to respond to the breach of a social norm. Thus, trials not only redress the harm to a community by punishing a guilty individual; they also "perform the laws" so that the community can reenact a sense of its own order and redraw its boundaries. The tainted transgressor is therefore reduced in status, reclassified as an "other," and symbolically removed from the polity.

Social scientist Harold Garfinkel has called this type of ritual a "status degradation ceremony," defined as "[a]ny communicative work between persons, whereby the public identity of an actor is transformed into something looked on as lower in the local scheme of social types." According to Garfinkel, the act of expressing moral indignation towards a transgressor of the established order reinforces group solidarity. Indeed, he describes a degradation ceremony as "a secular form of communion."

A degradation ceremony can be particularly useful in cases where the transgressor is not a human being. When statues fall from the sky or pigs kill a small child or the branch of a tree crushes someone, there is a sense of disorder and irrationality that the society's institutions must address: "Such random acts of violence caused by insensate agents bring a deep feeling of lawlessness: not so much the fear of laws being broken, but the far worse fear that the world might not be a lawful place at all." By permitting the community to reaffirm its boundaries and reestablish its solidarity, a status degradation ceremony helps to impose order on a world of random violence. And while it is unclear whether communities considered the guilty animals or inanimate objects actually to have lost status as a result of legal proceedings against them, it is significant that these proceedings mirrored the trials of human perpetrators and relied on the same ritualized forms of justice. Therefore, the form of the status degradation ceremony, with its focus on community purification, was retained.

The legal proceedings against inanimate objects and animals . . thus can be understood as status degradation ceremonies that helped to heal the community in at least two ways. First, the trials asserted the moral order of the community by defining the offending animal or object as guilty of a crime. Then, the proceedings performed an act of purification by removing the transgressor from the community, either through banishment, forfeiture, excommunication, or execution. And although action might also be taken against a human agent involved in the killing, such action was seen as entirely distinct from the proceedings against the non-human agent. . . .

Moreover, once we take seriously the idea that forfeiture actions exist as much to heal the community as to punish the owner, we are able to identify various ramifications and avenues for further study. For example, psychological and sociological research might reveal whether the removal of a symbol of neighborhood blight (for example, a car that is recognized in a community as a drug courier vehicle) actually brings therapeutic benefits over and above the arrest of the human perpetrators. If so, then discussion of forfeiture policy could be informed by current scholarship regarding the use of "social norms" to enforce societal order through such practices as shaming rituals. Under this view, we might be concerned that modern forfeiture practice does not always seem calculated to achieve a symbolic cleansing or a community catharsis. As we can see from the large number of people who turned out to watch as the content of O.J. Simpson's home were carted away, there may be a perceived need for the community actually to participate more actively in the forfeiture event. Therefore, rather than permitting the State to sell the Bennis's car at auction (where, theoretically, a new person could purchase it and begin cruising the same neighborhood for prostitutes), perhaps the car should have been given to neighborhood residents for a ritual destruction, as with the burning of the abandoned crack house. Along the same lines, forfeiture law might be changed to apply only in those instances when the seizure of the object truly has symbolic or therapeutic value. Or, in contrast, we may reject the basic premise that the perceived needs of the community should be allowed to trump individual civil liberties. But these questions cannot be resolved without first taking seriously the notion that, at least in some situations, forfeiture can have an independent community value and is not simply an irrational and unjust practice built on a devious "fiction." Finally, this study fits within a broader project whereby anthropologists and legal scholars have come to realize that law is in part concerned with the construction of narratives and social meanings that influence the way a community perceives reality. Thus, for every legal question, we must study the language being used to analyze the question, the symbolic content of the proceedings at issue, and the meaning being created. Such inquiry permits us to understand the social role that law fulfills for a community beyond its traditional role in dispute resolution. In the end we must realize that it is not only so-called "primitive" societies that create rituals to make sense of the world. We have legal rituals as well, and the forfeiture of an automobile or a house is not simply a deterrent legal action; it is a symbolic event. Only by recognizing the symbolic content of our own rituals of justice can we begin to decide which legal rules and procedures are truly best.

Conclusion

The Supreme Court fails to explain the social meaning underlying the concept of forfeiture. Instead it relies on the deterrent effect of forfeiture. Second, it mentions the "legal fiction" through which a nonhuman aggressor is found to be "guilty and condemned as though it were conscious."[29] Finally, it cites the long line of precedent in English and U.S. law in support of forfeiture. Critics, however, also miss the point when they attack the court for relying on a custom that they allege to be unjust as well as archaic and nonsensical.

Berman, rejecting the arguments of the court and its critics alike, offers a different rationale for forfeiture of nonhuman aggressors. Historically the deodand permitted a community to heal and restore balance after the breach of a social norm; hence the banishment of a (symbolic) aggressor through a legal but symbolic ritual perceived as cleansing the community of the wrong done to it. In this view, law is thus very much concerned with the construction, through symbols, of narratives and social meanings that indicate how a society perceives reality.

29. *Various Items of Personal Property*, 282 U.S. at 581.

B. Narratives in Law as Community Discourse

Two anthropologists and a lawyer teamed up to study attitudes toward law in three ordinary communities (one each in Massachusetts, Illinois, and Georgia).[30] The researchers anticipated that the residents of such widely dispersed areas would have very different meanings about community, conflict, law, and law avoidance but were surprised at the incidence of similar views.

1. Narratives of Avoidance: General Characteristics

One area of similarity concerned "the assiduous avoidance of law."[31] Indeed, this research belied the myth of the supposed litigiousness of U.S. society and found instead that narratives of law avoidance were normatively valuable because not only did they foster community solidarity but also promoted the ethic of self-discipline and tradition, as alternative mechanisms for ensuring social order.[32] The narratives of avoidance were not necessarily descriptive of everyday behavior, but they did constitute the ideal for the community as a whole. Like the symbol of banishing a nonhuman transgressor, the narrative of avoidance served several normative goals. It constituted a symbolic affirmation of solidarity and order in society, a symbolic reaffirmation of the *status quo*, a strategy to cope with change, and finally, a symbol of equality and individualism.[33]

In some respects one could say that the cultural norm of law avoidance was itself a myth because the law and legal institutions did have important roles in all three communities. Not only did the courthouse have prominence in each town, but residents vigorously supported the enforcement of criminal law. Nevertheless, even if law avoidance was a myth it was, from an emic perspective, a native construct (*i.e.*, its symbolism had its "own place in the mythology of the happy community constructed by residents").[34] Again, as with the law of forfeiture that served a popular penal purpose (namely, banishment), the residents' vigorous embrace of criminal law enforcement can be seen to serve the popular goals of restoring order, cleansing society of wrongs, and promoting solidarity.

The "happy myth" of law avoidance was further belied by the general acceptance and approval of actions landlords brought for rent collection and evictions, actions to recover debt, the enforcement of contractual obligations, enforcement of the obligation to pay child support, and actions for dissolution of marriage. Perhaps one could view these actions as symbolizing the core minimum values of the communities for which resort to law was deemed appropriate, but outside of which law avoidance was the norm.

---

30. Carol J. Greenhouse, Barbara Yngvesson & David M. Engel, Law and Community in Three American Towns (1994).

31. *Id.* at 118.

32. *Id.* at 118–19.

33. *Id.* at 119.

34. *Id.*

What became apparent to the researchers was the selectivity of popular understandings about when to invoke law and when to avoid it. They saw this choice as depending on the social relations that were implicated. Through their narratives of law use and conflict management, the residents of the three communities showed what relations were valued, thereby creating normative hierarchies of relations and values that were dear to them. These hierarchies then became part of the cultural fabric of each community. For example, community discourse on litigiousness marked social boundaries expressing "place," or what it meant to belong to the community.[35] Avoidance discourse and social discourse on litigiousness were "linked to the processes by which people sought order and 'place' in social relationships and to the processes by which the identity and direction of those relationships were determined and defined as 'community.'"[36]

If a particular conflict had a "place" in court, it represented a relationship that was valued inside the community; one that was not, such as litigation for personal injury (viewed as selfish or greedy), was frowned on and viewed as an outsider claim.[37] Thus the researchers concluded that notion of place denoted not only the social and moral boundaries of the community but also specific values and relationships. For example, a claim by a minister who sued for compensation in a slip-and-fall case was viewed as out of place, whereas a landlord's claim for eviction and back rent was met with approval.[38] Such seemingly random cases of approval and disapproval were thus revealed to be not at all patternless, because they could be reconciled in terms of the overarching values and customs of the community.

The researchers also observed that, just as *in rem* forfeiture results in status degradation of the object forfeited and banished, so labeling someone "out of place" results in a degradation of personal status. This is constructive banishment, in that the person degraded is no longer viewed to have a legitimate role in the community. Such persons may be stigmatized as uncultured, poor, ethnically undesirable, unchristian, and so on.[39] Through the narrative of avoidance whereby outsiders are banished, insiders are able to reaffirm their own status, identity, and solidarity. Again, the normative parallel with forfeiture proceedings is obvious.

> Viewed in this way, in the three settings discourse concerning litigiousness and the virtues of avoidance becomes part of a more general process of establishing and maintaining social boundaries. Condemnation of certain types of litigation almost immediately transforms itself into degradation of the plaintiffs themselves as poor, uncultured, ethnically undesirable, or unchristian. By contrast, praise of avoidance becomes the chorus in a hymn to the virtues of community insiders: rooted, established, selfless, "good neighbors," religiously and ethnically acceptable, and respectful of traditional ways. Of course, those who are

35. Greenhouse, Yngvesson & Engel, *supra* note 30, at 121.

36. *Id.* at 127.

37. *Id.* at 121.

38. *Id.* at 121, 127.

39. *Id.* at 121.

> condemned as "litigious" may hold different ideas about good neighbors and the boundaries of the community. For ethnic outsiders or blue-collar workers, avoidance may be a less salient value than acceptance, and "litigiousness" may be a lesser evil than discrimination or economic exploitation. For them, the attempt to negotiate a niche in the community involves asserting claims to fair treatment and, in some instances, compensation, in the face of the broadly stated denunciation of litigiousness.[40]

However, the researchers found neither the ethic of exclusion nor the narrative of avoidance to be monolithic, unidirectional processes. Those who were legally excluded did not passively accept seclusion; they fought back for inclusion, fair treatment, and even compensation. They pressed for alternative visions of community to the point that the community as a whole was often forced to negotiate and redefine its values.[41] The researchers cautioned that these outcomes should not detract from the fact that the more outsider claims seemed to challenge settled practices or threatened existing institutions, the greater the potential for the proverbial circling of the wagons of the insiders—motivated by a concern for the future of their community.[42]

Carol J. Greenhouse, Barbara Yngvesson & David M. Engel, Law and Community in Three American Towns 118–121, 124–127, 188 (1994).

> The locale (Massachusetts, Georgia, Illinois) is indeed a source of variation; yet, . . .
>
> Our three studies were conducted during an era in which it was widely perceived that American society had become excessively "legalized" and its people litigious. However, the narratives of law avoidance and of law involvement were still told by some members of these three communities in ways that did not differ significantly. . . . A pervasive norm of nonlitigiousness was apparent in many of these narratives, contrary to popular perceptions that American society had become completely enamored of litigation. Although law and order were highly valued in all three towns, so was the ethic of rejecting law and of embracing forms of social order based on self-discipline and tradition rather than legal enforcement. . . .
>
> . . . The "narratives of avoidance" that were recounted in all three settings were not necessarily descriptions of typical, everyday behavior but were ideological statements whose purpose and function within the community were both important and complex. They were a means by which some attempted to create or impose order within the community, to define or deflect change, and to articulate a philosophy of individualism and equality that could also be reconciled with their tenacious defense of the status quo.

---

40. Greenhouse, Yngvesson & Engel, *supra* note 30, at 121.

41. *Id.* at 125.

42. *Id.* at 128.

It must be emphasized that, despite the importance of law avoidance as a cultural norm, law and legal institutions were central to the culture of the three towns and, therefore, had their own place in the mythology of the happy community constructed by residents. In each setting, the courthouse itself occupied a symbolically prominent position in the town square. The courthouse buildings and their occupants figured importantly in local histories of the communities. There were, in fact, some valued forms of litigation that partook of the symbolic centrality of the courthouse in the community. Energetic enforcement of the criminal law was strongly supported by those who decried litigiousness in general terms and was not viewed as evidence of excessive legalization of the society. On the contrary, the criminal justice system was thought to embody many of the community's most fundamental values and beliefs.... There was little sympathy for those who violated the criminal law, and there was no sense that a proliferation of arrests or criminal prosecutions indicated a legal system that had gone out of control.

Other forms of law invocation were also deemed appropriate by those who were otherwise suspicious of court use: actions by landlords to collect rent or to evict tenants who were in default, debt collections and other forms of contract enforcement, the enforcement of child-support obligations, and even divorce actions were all considered consistent with the culturally central role of the court in the community. Although the underlying social causes of such litigation might be regretted, the invocation of law was not condemned in itself.

Avoidance of and involvement with the law thus carried complex and variable cultural meanings. "Litigiousness" was indeed of great importance in all three settings, but its importance lay chiefly in its role as a signifier. Attempts to study litigiousness in particular communities or societies have always been problematic precisely because there are so many questions of meaning embedded in the processes of disputing and litigation themselves. We chose to approach this issue not by converting questions of meaning or signification into questions of frequency but by exploring how interpretations of the meanings of litigiousness are negotiated and deployed by different groups in the community.

What was consistent in all three communities was the selectivity of popular understandings as to the occasions on which law was to be invoked or avoided. Among different groups in these communities, certain kinds of litigation were highly valued; other kinds were devalued. Much depended on the nature of the social relationships underlying the different types of cases. In their narratives of law and conflict management in the community, residents created and reinforced distinctive categories of appropriate and inappropriate court use. These categories became a part of the cultural fabric of the community itself....

... But this sense of the appropriate "place" for particular forms of conflict also expresses understandings of other kinds of social boundaries and other notions of where things and people should be. In all three settings there were people who were perceived as "out of place" in the community. To condemn their legal claims was to reaffirm their status as outsiders and to mark the social boundaries that excluded them from a legitimate role in the community. On the whole, perceptions of excessive litigation appear to be associated with perceptions of certain people as "outsiders"; affirmations of the ethic of avoidance appear to be part of a process by which insiders reaffirm their own status and identity.

Viewed in this way, in the three settings discourse concerning litigiousness and the virtues of avoidance becomes part of a more general process of establishing and maintaining social boundaries. Condemnation of certain types of litigation almost immediately transforms itself into degradation of the plaintiffs themselves as poor, uncultured, ethnically undesirable, or unchristian. By contrast, praise of avoidance becomes the chorus in a hymn to the virtues of community insiders: rooted, established, selfless, "good neighbors," religiously and ethnically acceptable, and respectful of traditional ways. Of course, those who are condemned as "litigious" may hold different ideas about good neighbors and the boundaries of the community. For ethnic outsiders or blue-collar workers, avoidance may be a less salient value than acceptance, and "litigiousness" may be a lesser evil than discrimination or economic exploitation. For them, the attempt to negotiate a niche in the community involves asserting claims to fair treatment and, in some instances, compensation, in the face of the broadly stated denunciation of litigiousness. . . .

. . . In all three communities, the good citizen was defined by negative reference to the bad citizen, whose failures were most obviously apparent in the public conflicts and lawsuits he or she brought. Such lawsuits were of critical importance, for they were often interpreted and represented as occasions when "outsiders" engaged in characteristic efforts to press alternative visions of the community and its norms and thus to manipulate their own social status in self-serving ways. Such talk about litigation provided one of the most important occasions in all three communities for articulating, negotiating, and redefining the personal qualities and behavior that were most highly valued and disvalued. . . .

. . . But what about comparable claims by people who are locally viewed as insiders? Did "insiders" never suffer injuries? Did they never fight among themselves? Did their children never get in trouble in the schools? Although (by definition, if for no other reason) accidents and conflicts may have been somewhat more prevalent among those who were considered outsiders, it would be absurd to maintain that "insiders" did not encounter similar situations at times. By virtue of their public identity as insiders, however, they were able to handle such matters without recourse to law in many cases. A discreet phone call, a conversation at the club, a discussion over the back

> fence could provide a smooth and private resolution. "Citizenship" has its privileges. . . .
>
> In conversation, avoidance and litigiousness were, therefore, linked to the processes by which people sought order and "place" in social relationships and to the processes by which the identity and direction of those relationships were determined and defined as "community." Praise for the farmer who demonstrated forbearance when his neighbors needed extra time to make payments; praise for the landlord who sued to evict his undesirable tenants and collect back rent; blame for the minister who sought compensation in a slip-and-fall case. These seemingly inconsistent judgments on local citizens and on litigation all can be reconciled in terms of overarching concerns about community order in the face of changes that threatened traditional ways and values.

C. Narratives of Avoidance: Ethical Dimensions

It is worth noting that the narrative of avoidance in the three communities had an ethical as well as a religious dimension. The ethical dimension, which sought to mediate the tension between individualism and communitarianism on one hand and conflict between egalitarianism and hierarchy on the other, is discussed next.

Individualism v. communitarianism. Successful reconciliation depended on whether individualism as practiced implicated rights and entitlements or emphasized self-reliance and independence. The first was assumed to be concerned with the protection of personal interests, the second with the notion of self-sufficiency. The narrative of avoidance applied to the latter notion. Those who avoided judicial recourse were viewed as stoic and unselfish, as people who did not enrich themselves at the expense of others but instead advanced their material and social standing through free and fair competition in the marketplace. This approach blends with the U.S. *laissez-faire* capitalist ethic whereby self-interested competition in the economic marketplace is perceived to ultimately advance rather than undermine the collective good. Such self-reliance is viewed as lacking when judicial recourse is sought.

> By extolling avoidance as an *ethical* position, one can pursue self-interest and yet remain selfless, struggle for success and yet exhibit self-restraint and control, seek individual rewards and yet sustain the values of community solidarity. . . .
>
> Avoidance narratives allow a speaker simultaneously to invoke culturally preferred solidarities (of family and town, for example) *and* to distinguish individual interests within those social fields. In this way, avoidance emerges as a culturally appropriate means of resolving some of the contradictions between self-interest and the collective good. Its counterpart, confrontation, which is derived from conceptions of individualism based on rights and entitlements and is associated with a stereotype of the outsider, utterly fails this test. Confrontation, viewed from this perspective, appears to pit the individual irreconcilably against the collectivity. From the same perspective,

> whatever gains an individual may obtain by invoking law are at the expense of the community.[43]

Egalitarianism v. hierarchy. Thus far we have seen that narratives of avoidance established two related public symbols: community boundaries and the distinction between insiders and outsiders. Additionally, the narratives of avoidance reinforce the ethics of self-reliance, self-restraint, and autonomy by mediating the tension between individual and collective good.

Avoidance understood as an ethic of self-reliance, self-restraint, and autonomy also mediates the tension between egalitarian and hierarchical conceptions of community. Here, however, the mediation in fact results in perpetuating hierarchy. This is so because once the narrative of avoidance becomes internalized as a social value, then all attempts by outsiders (*e.g.*, minorities seeking equal protection) to invoke the law are condemned as undermining the social fabric. This rhetoric has the effect of transforming what is really a defense of hierarchy in the face of a democratic challenge into a defense of the so-called community.[44] The narrative of avoidance can thus play a highly antiegalitarian and antidemocratic role in society.

> Through its openness, its sense that "all can play," the avoidance ethic superficially appears to conform to egalitarian values consistent with the American tradition. Anyone, at least hypothetically, could convert individual instances of self-restraint into the general currency of social ascension; however, the narratives of avoidance and involvement have important underlying antiegalitarian implications. Hierarchy is preserved when those who are most disadvantaged and most susceptible to the deprivation of rights are told that any attempt to assert their interests will be interpreted as evidence that they are neither saved nor civilized and that their "litigiousness" is reprehensible. They are given a Hobson's choice. For those who occupy the lowest position in the social hierarchy, the decision to resist will be condemned, but realistically the decision to avoid conflict and accept the status quo is more likely to perpetuate their problems than to solve them.
>
> Avoidance both creates hierarchy and is its outcome. It is an index of civility and cultural astuteness, separating those who are saved from those who are not, but it also involves an ethic that tends to preserve the existing status system and suppress challenges and conflict from below. Avoidance thus reproduces existing patterns of class and ethnic division, which in turn become a framework of potential conflict that explains and justifies avoidance. Even as the happy community ... defines itself, it constitutes a worldview in which challenges to the established order are most likely to fail and those defined as outsiders are least likely to usurp the position held by the local elite.[45]

---

43. *Id.* at 129.

44. *Id.* at 130.

45. Greenhouse, Yngvesson & Engel, *supra* note 30, at 132.

Discussed next is the religious dimension of the narrative of avoidance. Of special interest is how this local narrative has influenced discourse at the national level.

D. Religious Foundation of the Narrative of Avoidance: Local and National Implications

Carol Greenhouse, one of the three researchers, compiled a separate study of the narrative of avoidance that focused only on the town in Georgia (called "Hopewell" in the study). Her ethnography showed that the Baptist community of Hopewell couched its narrative of avoidance in religious terms by creating a symbolic equation between harmony and Christianity and thereby viewing recourse to law as disruptive of harmony.[46] By their logic, recourse to law invoked human authority in the person of the judge and other officers of the state, which was believed to be contrary to the Christian designation of Jesus as the ultimate and only legal authority who could be invoked only by faith.[47] This rejection of disputing was directly based on scriptural advice to "turn the other cheek," to submit to whatever was demanded, and to leave all judgments to Jesus. As with the more secular communities of Massachusetts and Illinois, the religious narrative of Hopewell translated into self-restraint and self-reliance as independent human virtues. The other, the outsider, was the non-Baptist who was assumed to be contentious and litigious as well as damned or unsaved.[48]

The Baptists of Hopewell viewed prayer as the chief method to achieve order and personal well-being and considered that law was for those who were unsaved (*i.e.*, those who could only achieve their vision of order by law use). This law was manmade, or positive law; it was not the law of God, or natural law as they viewed it. The latter operated *in foro interno*, whereas the former was thought to be external law and an imposition via human agency.

Carol J. Greenhouse, *Interpreting American Litigiousness*, *in* History and Power in the Study of Law: New Directions in Legal Anthropology 252, 256–57 (June Starr and Jane F. Collier eds., 1989).

In Hopewell, many Baptists explained to me that disputing is a profoundly unchristian act because the Bible states clearly that Jesus is the judge of all people. The implication seems to be that to enter into a dispute is to stand as judge over another person, and to do so not only reveals lack of faith in Jesus, but preempts Jesus' power ("All vengeance is mine . . . saith the Lord"). . . .

On another dimension, Baptists acknowledge that disputing and "making a case for oneself" is a strong temptation in everyday life, and they present

46. Carol J. Greenhouse, *Interpreting American Litigiousness*, *in* History and Power in the Study of Law: New Directions in Legal Anthropology 252, 254 *et seq.* (June Starr & Jane F. Collier eds., 1989).

47. *Id.* at 255.

48. *Id.*

their own assiduousness in avoiding disputes as the product of concerted effort buttressed by prayer.... Prayer is a form of narrative that accompanies the performance of everyday activities or, more accurately from the Baptist perspective, inserts some textuality into the looming chaos of "the world" ("the world" refers specifically to a society dominated by the unsaved, until the Day of Judgment). Prayer is verbal and is addressed directly to Jesus ("So I said to the Lord, 'Lord ...'" was the beginning of many prayer narratives I heard in conversation). The most frequent themes of prayer narrated to me were pleas for Jesus' support in refraining from disputing and from having feelings of conflict within a family or friendship group, and prayers for the salvation of some particular individual. Prayers for interpersonal harmony consist of potentially lengthy explanations, spoken aloud or verbalized silently, of the history of the conflict.

While prayer is held to be adequate for the faithful as a means of achieving order in their personal lives, Baptists acknowledge the difficulties of accomplishing harmony for people with stunted, misdirected, or absent "prayer lives." The law, they say, helps these people live in peace. It is only in this sense—of making the world of the unsaved safe—that the Baptists in Hopewell concede any valid place to the law. Man made law (they stress "man-made") is by definition a conceit, because it is not the law of God. It is important to note that Hopewell's Baptists do not conceive of God's law as a set of rules ...; they do, however, understand man-made law as rules. God's law—the central tenets of the Christian life—are individually *felt*. This is part of the significance of the Baptists' insistence that the Scriptures are accessible to all Baptists by virtue of their faith, but that the "Christian life" is reason itself. The contrast to the world of rules, lawyers, judges, and (in Baptist eyes) the exaltation of contention could not be clearer: where God's law is felt, man's law is imposed; where God's law is reason itself, man's law is artificial; where God's law promises eternal life, man's law thrives on enmity and conflict; where God's law is expressed in prayer, man's law is expressed in rules. Under God's law, all people are equal—all people *become* equal, shedding the inequalities (particularly the ultimate vanity of basing status on material possessions) that Baptists see in the non-Baptist world.

Thus, like other Americans, Baptists in Hopewell see their own way of life as by definition legal, although they carefully locate its legality in reason, the source of which is God, and in nature, which is understood as God's dominion. The Baptists' vision of social order, which comes about by extending God's word to the unsaved, is a vision of a society at peace because each individual "does right" and "knows right in his heart." Authoritative intervention is not necessary to the achievement of this order, although Hopewell Baptists do concede a role for the law in the interim period before Judgment Day.

The origins of the Baptist view on conflict avoidance date back to the pre- and post-Civil War periods. In those eras it was a political strategy that insulated the church from the most urgent contemporary issues: states' rights, removal of the Cherokee from "white" lands, and the abolition of slavery.

> The church in Hopewell was apparently deeply divided over these questions, and at one point its membership may have fallen to as low as seven. At this period in Hopewell's history, survival of the order demanded that the church somehow transcend, or at least contain, politics. It finally did so by stressing its theological objections to the human authority that would be inescapably constituted in any overt dispute. By reiterating the contradictions between God's law and human authority over a period of twenty or more years, the local Baptist church association was finally successful in symbolically linking conflict with the unsaved. The Civil War marked an end to any mention of disputing in the church record, and the life of good witness became doubly that of the aspiring Baptist and the defeated Southerner.[49]

Recourse to law, because it is usually adversarial, provided further ammunition in favor of the supposedly pacifist religious posture of the church. In such cases, the plaintiff would suffer immediate status degradation in much the same way as the banished object under the law of forfeiture.[50] The human authority whose intervention was called for was denounced as inappropriate, given the belief that only God should render judgment. Earthly legal recourse was therefore claimed to be an unnatural interference with the natural order of relations between equals. The latter argument filtered into political discourse at the national level, with the emergence of the political doctrine of nonintervention by the state in social affairs which, by definition, were based on the principle of egalitarianism.

Thus, at the national level, Americans were urged to reject any type of legal (or other) discourse that revealed hierarchy and inequality in relationships that were otherwise presumed to be equal.[51] What originated as a religious doctrine at this point acquired a secular foundation in the popular American belief that ordinary life is ordered and thus naturally "legal." The community studied in Illinois (Sander County) openly viewed litigious groups as troublemakers.

> People in Sander County see troublemakers and litigious groups as people for whom the ordinary bonds of the natural legal order are not effective or not sufficient. Specifically, it is personal-injury disputes that generate anxieties over litigiousness in Sander County, not contract disputes. . . . : "Duties generated by socially imposed obligations to guard against injuring other people were seen as intrusions upon existing relationships, as pretexts for forced exchanges, as inappropriate attempts to redistribute wealth, and as limitations upon individual freedom." Engel's study suggests that, in the eyes of Sander County residents, concerns about litigiousness channel diffuse anxieties about the community's increasing pluralism. Hopewell Baptists show

49. *Id.* at 258–59.

50. *See* text at note 20 *supra*.

51. Greenhouse, *supra* note 46, at 264.

a similar response in somewhat different terms; they see disputing and litigation as defining characteristics of the unsaved.[52]

If the perceptions are that there is already order in society and that order must predate the law, any effort to effect change through "official" law is seen as injecting unwanted, unnatural, adversarial, and competitive elements into social relations. The formalistic discourse of official law ("May it please the court," "Your Honor") also separates the ordinary person from official law. Americans tend to espouse a natural law philosophy in the structural functional sense of society but an essentially positivist philosophy in the practice of law.[53] The following excerpt explains these attitudes and the linkage between discourse at local and national levels.

Carol J. Greenhouse, *Interpreting American Litigiousness*, *in* History and Power in the Study of Law: New Direction in Legal Anthropology 252, 269–71 (June Starr and Jane F. Collier eds., 1989).

In effect, Americans seem to hold two views of the law. The ethnographic and historical literature suggests that Americans hold a natural-law philosophy ... when the question is the functioning structure of society itself, but when the question turns to the nature of official law, Americans are positivists. To put this another way, Americans may see society as intrinsically ordered by collective contractual arrangements (hence its legal quality), but they simultaneously see official law as rules imposed externally by elite institutions ... The natural-rights theorizing of Americans suggests that Americans identify with the law and view its use in a positive light. On the other hand, their positivist theorizing suggests that confrontations with the law are likely to be risky encounters on almost literally unfamiliar territory—in a strange language, around strange principles devised by strangers. Indeed, statistical and ethnographic studies of Americans' use of the courts reflects this ambivalence, as disputants either litigate or avoid confrontations altogether.... The important point ... is that Americans hold these two views simultaneously and apply them to two different populations: the regular folk who "get along" and "litigious Americans."

This ambivalence is expressed in the discourse of authority and its place in social relations. As we have seen, to the extent that Americans resist the law in personal affairs, one aspect of the resistance is linguistic. Specifically, this resistance is aimed at the intertextuality of the official law and everyday life; it is a resistance that would cancel the discourse of official law altogether (indeed, in 1810 the Georgia legislature entertained a bill to

52. *Id.* at 266. The language quoted in the passage is of Engel, *See* David M. Engel, *The Oven Bird's Song: Insiders, Outsiders, and Personal Injuries in an American Community*, 18 Law & Society Rev. 551, 575 (1984).

53. Greenhouse, *supra* note 46, at 269.

prohibit the practice of law). The embedded imagery of the law as a genre of discourse is helpful to our discussion, because it sheds light on how litigiousness acquires some of its negative value in the cultural complex at issue here. To continue the notion of legal discourse in a metaphor, litigation is a form of apostrophe, a diversion of ordinary dyadic exchanges to some third party, an interruption of context.... The plaintiff sets the outsider—the lawyer, the policeman, the judge—above his neighbor. The embarrassment of apostrophe in social relations deemed to be already legal is the sudden overturning of a supposed relation of equality by a relation of hierarchy and authority. From this perspective, it is the possibility of equality's transformation into hierarchy that makes litigiousness seem to be the very unmaking of the Revolution.

What are the connections between the case of Hopewell's Baptists and other Americans? Drawing on an interdisciplinary literature concerning American patterns of disputing, the politics of identity, and culture, we can point to some parallels: their shared sense (expressed by Schneider) of the definition of society as a set of legal contracts. These contracts, or this legality, is not intrinsic to relationships, but is brought to them—perhaps by virtue of citizenship, or by salvation, or by some other attribute. On this particular point, we might expect considerable diversity. There is also a second obvious parallel in the extent to which Hopewell's Baptists and those Americans who decry litigation by others condemn litigiousness as both a cause and a sign of social disintegration. Third, the negative valuation of disputing and litigation that both Hopewell Baptists and other (though certainly not all other) Americans express resides in the formal aspects of their discourse—in the creation and reproductions of generic categories of others, sometimes named, sometimes not, whose social predations are served by their allegedly inappropriate use of courts. The Baptists of Hopewell have used generic classifications to convey the meaning of litigiousness across the generations since the mid-nineteenth century; they remain in form but have changed in content. Today's concerns in Hopewell focus not on the anti- Cherokee, hard-line Democrats but on godless businessmen or self-absorbed city people, and so on. These categories reiterate the generic forms of the outsider and the power elite, as well as the futility and sacrilege of confronting them.

The Baptist church is thriving in Hopewell, where the new temptations of affluence in the Sunbelt fuel a continuing felt need for salvation. This observation leads to a concluding point: to the extent that Americans worry about litigiousness, they share with Hopewell's Baptists a cultural vision that reveals at once a cultural model of society and a portrait of its enemies. The cultural model of society is, as we have seen, a harmoniously functioning web of contractual relationships among equals. The portrait of the enemy lacks a face—he might be one's neighbor, one's customer, one's client, or one's patient—but (and on this the portrait is clear) he has stolen the mantle of the king.

Conclusion

The narratives of avoidance, though derived from only three widely separated communities in three different regions of the United States, are nevertheless of general significance to the nation as a whole. Indeed, the discourse of avoidance has filtered into the national political dialogue. It represents a worldview (à la Geertz) that is the prism through which society and its politicians engage in political discourse that encourages free enterprise and market-based economics, the deregulation of commerce, and the ending of rules regarding worker health and safety, as well as gutting environmental protections and cutting back social services with a corresponding emphasis on voluntarism and self-reliance. Thus, law use and law avoidance are clearly intertwined with the construction of narratives and social meanings as to how a local or national community perceives social reality.

In addition, the narratives of avoidance create a number of symbolic oppositions between the two semantic categories of insiders and outsiders. Each of these semantic categories has rich and nuanced local meanings. The former are the culturally, politically, and economically privileged segments of society, usually the indigenous white middle and upper classes, while the latter are often racial, ethnic, or immigrant minorities. The former are usually religious Christians; the latter are not. The former have roots in "the community"; the latter do not. The former define their identity and values in terms of their original foundational beliefs and traditions, to which the latter are viewed as a mortal threat. The latter seek redress through law but are seen by the former as lacking in self-restraint. The former perceive their community to embody the values of self-reliance, independence, autonomy, and self-restraint; the latter are perceived by them as greedy, self-serving, and an overall threat to the established order.

The discourse of avoidance not only creates these symbolic oppositions but also serves as an antiegalitarian bulwark that resists change in favor of reinforcing hierarchies and the status quo. The hierarchies show segments of the population as belonging to the upper or lower echelons, as restrained or unrestrained, as self-reliant or greedy, and as included or excluded.

E. Symbolism of Punishment in Criminal Law: Public Executions

We begin with mid-eighteenth-century European criminal law, whose graphic symbolism of punishment was a regular feature of most parts of early modern Europe. Vandals, robbers, and murderers were subjected to gruesome forms of punishment in public in ways that were intended to mirror the nature of their crimes.[54] Punishments included hanging, breaking on the wheel, garroting, decapitation, burning, and whipping, as well as banishment and incarceration.[55] Each of these methods was supposed to reveal something about the nature of the crime for which they were applied. The condemned were executed in a prominent place and were escorted thence with much

54. Anton Blok, *The Symbolic Vocabulary of Public Executions*, *in* History and Power in the Study of Law, *supra* note 46, at 31, 46.

55. *Id.* at 36.

ceremony, as much to reinforce their humiliation as to instill fear in the public.[56] A constable carrying a "red-painted rod of justice" (indicating that a sentence had been passed) would lead such processions, followed by a bailiff, an alderman, local militiamen with ceremonial feathers on their hats, a drummer, and an executioner. The bailiff would read the sentence, after which the condemned would walk (if possible) to the actual site of hanging, burning, or other means of punishment.[57]

The mirroring of punishment and crime embodied a symbolic narrative. For example, robbers had their faces blackened and fingers cut off prior to being killed because prior to committing their crime they had disguised themselves by blackening their faces.

> The symbolic vocabulary included the case of one man who, before he was hanged, had his face blackened and two fingers of his right hand cut off....
>
> Because many robbers had also broken into churches and committed various profanities, their execution included several combinations of capital punishments as well as various forms of burning at the stake. No less than twenty Bokkerijders were garroted and then burned. At least one robber was executed the same way, after having his right hand first smeared with sulfur, then burned, and finally chopped off. Several others, who had held leading positions in the bands, were broken on the wheel and decapitated, after having the right hand burned and chopped off; their bodies, together with severed limbs, were displayed on the wheel, and their heads were put on iron pins.
>
> Some of these executions assumed the character of true *spiegelstraffen* (literally, mirror punishments)—that is, the executions, or certain stages of them, were meant to reflect exactly the nature of the crimes the condemned had committed. This was the case, for example, with the robbers who had blackened their faces while breaking into houses and farms. Similar literal reenactments of the delicts were included in the execution of two skinners. One of them had, among other things, murdered a traveler with his stick and killed an innkeeper with his knife. Before he was broken on the wheel and burned, he received a stab with a knife in his side and four blows with the stick on his head. His brother, who had misled the judges, had his tongue sliced off before he was burned at the stake.[58]

The theatrical and symbolic elements in the administration of punishment were also evident on those convicted of lesser crimes, for which they were flogged and banished. Such people were put on the scaffold with the hangman's rope around their necks, giving the message that their next offense would be punishable by death.[59]

As Michel Foucault noted, the body of the condemned person was the central element in the ceremonial of public executions in eighteenth-century Europe.

---

56. *Id.* at 47–50.

57. *Id.* at 47.

58. *Id.* at 48.

59. *Id.* at 49–50.

> It was the task of the guilty man to bear openly his condemnation and the truth of the crime that he had committed. His body, displayed, exhibited in procession, tortured, served as the public support of a procedure that had hitherto remained in the shade; in him, on him, the sentence had to be legible for all.[60]

Foucault's penetrating studies on power, domination, and state control of the (human) body are beyond the scope of this work; however, his analysis of the prison system and the various modern techniques or "disciplines" of individual control by the state are relevant to the inquiry of how draconian punishments have evolved into more subtle forms of control.

Foucault argues that the old technology of punishment was simply a crude and unrefined contest between the violence of the accused and the violence of the state, which he depicts by discussing a graphic torture scene in 1757 France. It concerned a man condemned for attempting to assassinate the King of France. His punishment consisted of drawing and quartering by four horses, after which a combination of molten lead, boiling oil, burning resin, wax, and sulphur would be poured over his torn body.

> On 2 March 1757 Damiens the regicide was condemned 'to make the *amende honorable* before the main door of the Church of Paris', where he was to be 'taken and conveyed in a cart, wearing nothing but a shirt, holding a torch of burning wax weighing two pounds'; then, 'in the said cart, to the Place de Grève, where, on a scaffold that will be erected there, the flesh will be torn from his breasts, arms, thighs and calves with red-hot pincers, his right hand, holding the knife with which he committed the said parricide, burnt with sulphur, and, on those places where the flesh will be torn away, poured molten lead, boiling oil, burning resin, wax and sulphur melted together and then his body drawn and quartered by four horses and his limbs and body consumed by fire, reduced to ashes and his ashes thrown to the winds' . . .
>
> 'Finally, he was quartered,' recounts the *Gazette d'Amsterdam* of 1 April 1757. 'This last operation was very long, because the horses used were not accustomed to drawing; consequently, instead of four, six were needed; and when that did not suffice, they were forced, in order to cut off the wretch's thighs, to sever the sinews and hack at the joints . . .
>
> 'It is said that, though he was always a great swearer, no blasphemy escaped his lips; but the excessive pain made him utter horrible cries, and he often repeated: "My God, have pity on me! Jesus, help me!" The spectators were all edified by the solicitude of the parish priest of St. Paul's who despite his great age did not spare himself in offering consolation to the patient.'
>
> Bouton, an officer of the watch, left us his account: 'The sulphur was lit, but the flame was so poor that only the top skin of the hand was burnt, and

60. Michel Foucault, Discipline and Punish: The Birth of the Prison 43 (Alan Sheridan trans., 1977).

that only slightly. Then the executioner, his sleeves rolled up, took the steel pincers, which had been especially made for the occasion, and which were about a foot and a half long, and pulled first at the calf of the right leg, then at the thigh, and from there at the two fleshy parts of the right arm; then at the breasts. Though a strong, sturdy fellow, this executioner found it so difficult to tear away the pieces of flesh that he set about the same spot two or three times, twisting the pincers as he did so, and what he took away formed at each part a wound about the size of a six-pound crown piece.

'After these tearings with the pincers, Damiens, who cried out profusely, though without swearing, raised his head and looked at himself; the same executioner dipped an iron spoon in the pot containing the boiling potion, which he poured liberally over each wound. Then the ropes that were to be harnessed to the horses were attached with cords to the patient's body; the horses were then harnessed and placed alongside the arms and legs, one at each limb . . .

'The horses tugged hard, each pulling straight on a limb, each horse held by an executioner. After a quarter of an hour, the same ceremony was repeated and finally, after several attempts, the direction of the horses had to be changed, thus: Those at the arms were made to pull towards the head, those at the thighs towards the arms, which broke the arms at the joints. This was repeated several times without success. He raised his head and looked at himself. Two more horses had to be added to those harnessed to the thighs, which made six horses in all. Without success . . .

'After two or three attempts, the executioner Samson and he who had used the pincers each drew out a knife from his pocket and cut the body at the thighs instead of severing the legs at the joints; the four horses gave a tug and carried off the two thighs after them, namely, that of the right side first, the other following; then the same was done to the arms, the shoulders, the arm-pits and the four limbs; the flesh had to be cut almost to the bone, the horses pulling hard carried off the right arm first and the other afterwards.

'When the four limbs had been pulled away, the confessors came to speak to him; but his executioner told them that he was dead, though the truth was that I saw the man move, his lower jaw moving from side to side as if he were talking. One of the executioners even said shortly afterwards that when they had lifted the trunk to throw it on the stake, he was still alive. The four limbs were untied from the ropes and thrown on the stake set up in the enclosure in line with the scaffold, then the trunk and the rest were covered with logs and faggots, and fire was put to the straw mixed with this wood.

'. . . In accordance with the decree, the whole was reduced to ashes.'[61]

This gruesome scene graphically illustrates the power of the state. The punishment is designed to frighten and deter, but its stark brutality is also designed to communicate that the power of the state is superior to that of the individual. Foucault's

61. *Id.* at 3–5.

studies show that the naked nature of state power became less obvious over the four historical periods in Europe over which law and political power evolved: the feudal era, large-scale administrative monarchies, late sixteenth- and seventeenth-century religious wars, and the post-eighteenth-century period of parliamentary democracy.[62]

According to Foucault, the contemporary subtlety of state power is proportional to its ability to hide itself.[63] This hiddenness functions to obscure the fact of domination by those who have power, even as it perpetuates and reinforces their domination. Just as the narrative of avoidance served as cover for perpetuating power, privilege, hierarchy, and the status quo in the three American communities already discussed,[64] what may be called (in Foucaultian terms), the narrative of "right" as expressed in law serves as a facade for the numerous or "polymorphous techniques of subjugation."[65] The numerous methods and techniques of subjugation that Foucault wishes to unearth are supposed to show that the individual is controlled not merely by the formal law of the state (*i.e.*, statutes, administrative law, criminal law, and case law) but by a vast regulatory process made up of a variety of institutions such as prisons, schools, banks, hospitals, corporations, and so forth. Each has its own method or "technology" for controlling the individual.[66]

For these reasons, argues Foucault, the Hobbesian model of the unitary sovereign is obsolete: the law of the sovereign is only one of many technologies of power. The birth of the modern prison in Foucault's famous case study, *Discipline and Punish*, represents the diffusion of power from the sovereign to other institutions. Whereas the criminal law of seventeenth- and eighteenth-century France focused on the public infliction of physical pain through the use of torturers and executioners, who performed their duties in public, modern criminal law exercises a different technology over the body of the criminal. To drive the point home, Foucault begins his 1975 book with the account in the foregoing excerpt.[67]

Between 1769 and 1810, a new age of penal justice was ushered in all over Europe and the United States during which legally sanctioned torture as a public spectacle disappeared.[68] The new approach, which emphasized imprisonment and surveillance, was enforced by "a whole army of technicians" (*e.g.*, judges, lawyers, doctors, psychologists, psychiatrists, prison wardens).[69] It was characterized by techniques that avoided the infliction of pain for its own sake and substituted less direct penalties

---

62. Michel Foucault, Power/Knowledge: Selected Interviews and Other Writings, 1972–1977 171 (Colin Gordon, ed., Colin Gordon et al. trans., 1980).

63. Michel Foucault, The History of Sexuality Volume I: An Introduction 86 (Robert Hurley trans., 1980).

64. *See* text at notes 30–45 *supra*.

65. Foucault, Power/Knowledge, *supra* note 62, at 96.

66. Ian Ward, An Introduction to Critical Legal Theory 151 (1998). *See also* Michel Foucault, *Governmentality*, *in* The Foucault Effect: Studies in Governmentality 93–95 (Graham Burchell et al. eds., 1991).

67. Michel Foucault, Discipline and Punish, *supra* note 60, at 3–6.

68. *Id.* at 7.

69. *Id.* at 11.

such as imprisonment, confinement, forced labor, surveillance, deportation, and so on. However, Foucault asserts that these are merely new means for the exercise of control over the bodies of others, and they are dictated by the political interests of those who have the power to punish.[70]

Conclusion

Anton Blok and Foucault give persuasive accounts of how European criminal law and social thought made the transition from gruesome public punishment to other forms of control of the body. These accounts show the symbolism of the old and the new. The old symbolism was crude and unrefined, but the new symbols are so refined as to be almost hidden. The function of the old and new symbols, however, remains the same: control over the body, dictated by the political interests of those who have the power to punish.

Turner: The Cognitive Role of Symbols

Victor Turner focused on the cognitive and emotional role of ritual symbols in maintaining normative order and ensuring its continuity when normative relations within that order are transformed due to various social forces.[71] The latter issue was a critical aspect of his thought. Turner had been schooled in the tradition of classical British structural functionalism as pioneered by Durkheim and developed by Malinowski and Radcliffe-Brown. However, he went beyond the study of what strengthens normative order to examine conditions under which order is threatened and how society confronts and neutralizes threats through ritual.[72] Related to these matters is how society goes through transformative changes without losing its sense of cohesion, for example, as when a new king or chief is installed, or after an initiation ceremony.

For Turner, ritual is directly connected to social change.

> I found that I could not analyze ritual symbols without studying them in a time series in relation to other "events," for symbols are essentially involved in social process. I came to see performances of ritual as distinct phases in the social processes whereby groups became adjusted to internal changes and adapted to their external environment. From this standpoint the ritual symbol becomes a factor in social action, a positive force in an activity field. The symbol becomes associated with human interests, purposes, ends, and means, whether these are explicitly formulated or have to be inferred from the observed behavior. The structure and properties of a symbol become those of a dynamic entity, at least within its appropriate context of action.[73]

---

70. *Id.* at 24–28. Anton Blok, "The Symbolic Vocabulary of Public Executions," in History and Power in the Study of Law: New Directions in Legal Anthropology, June Starr and Jane F. Collier eds. at 31 (1989).

71. Erickson & Murphy, *supra* note 16, at 137.

72. Turner, The Forest of Symbols, *supra* note 5, at 93–111.

73. *Id.* at 20.

The centrality of ritual as "a positive force" in the maintenance and continuity of normative order is Turner's key focus. Unlike Lévi-Strauss and Durkheim, who considered symbolic contrasts and correspondences to be universal mental phenomena that connect people, Turner considered social unity to be basically problematic and asserted that order and unity cannot be taken for granted.[74] In this way, Turner almost reversed the Durkheimian premise that social solidarity emerges due to humankind's deep primordial psychological need to bond.

Turner viewed societies as inherently unstable, meaning that they are forced to confront the forces of instability to produce and reproduce order.[75] Ritual symbols, particularly those Turner refers to as "dominant" symbols, are the tools for the processes whereby society renews itself, because they can "embrace" the contradictory forces and forge renewal.[76] In their aggregate, dominant symbols stand for the unity and continuity of society at its widest and most inclusive level. They are ends in themselves, in other words, to be contrasted with "instrumental symbols" that serve only as means to achieve the ends of particular rituals.[77] Given that rituals (both dominant and instrumental) are the processes for social continuity and transformation, Turner refers to his study as a "processual view of society."[78]

Turner wished to study stability as well as change, and continuity as well as transformation. Traditional structuralism stood only for continuity and stability; hence, "positive structuralism can only become processualism by accepting the concept of social anti-structure as a theoretical operator."[79] Antistructure, another key concept for Turner, stands for the second aspect of his study: change and transformation of structure. In this way Turner departs from the Durkheimian notion of change as immanent in the structure of society.[80]

> The functionalists of my period in Africa tended to think of change as "cyclical" and "repetitive" and of time as structural time, not free time. With my conviction as to the dynamic character of social relations I saw movement as much as structure, persistence as much as change, indeed, persistence as a striking aspect of change. I saw people interacting, and, as day succeeded day, the consequences of their interactions. I then began to perceive a form in the process of social time. This form was essentially *dramatic*. My metaphor and model here was a human esthetic form, a product of *culture* not of nature.[81]

---

74. Erickson and Murphy, *supra* note 16, at 137.

75. *Id.*

76. Turner, The Forest of Symbols, *supra* note 5, at 46. This book is reviewed by James Peacock in *The Forest of Symbols: Aspects of Ndembu Ritual by Victor Turner*, 70 Am. Anthropol. 984 (1968).

77. Turner, The Forest of Symbols, *supra* note 5, at 45.

78. Victor Turner, Dramas, Fields, and Metaphors: Symbolic Action in Human Society 231, 37 (1974).

79. *Id.* at 45.

80. *Id.* at 31.

81. *Id.* at 32.

As Turner points out in the foregoing passage, the form of social change is essentially dramatic. These key concepts of Turnerian thought (*i.e.*, structure, antistructure, symbolism in ritual, and its dramatic form) are discussed in greater detail in the following.

Social Change, Ritual, and Drama

Turner viewed the social world not as "a world in being" but as "a world in becoming."[82] Indeed, study of the former is "irrelevant" because society is always in flux, never static. He proposed to study ritual in order to show the dynamic nature of social order through the symbolic form of social drama because, as noted previously, he perceived social change as taking an essentially dramatic form. Adopting the neo-Kantian distinction between the natural and cultural ("phenomena" and "noumena" in Kantian terms), Turner emphasized that natural systems exist independently of experience. Cultural systems, by contrast, depend on conscious volitional human relations that are stable as well as changing. These relations not only give meaning to cultural systems (the cognitive aspect) but also are responsible for their existence.

> I felt I had to bring the "humanistic coefficient" into my model if I was to make sense of human social processes.[83]

When social relations stand in opposition, the result is social drama. Turner recognized that not every drama finds resolution but nonetheless claims that when he studied the social life of the Ndembu of Zambia, enough dramas got resolved to give "processional form" to drama.[84] Upon embarking on a cross-societal comparison, he became convinced that social dramas with "the same temporal or processual structure as . . . detected in the Ndembu case, can be isolated for study in societies at all levels of scale and complexity."[85] He claims that social drama in so remote a setting as the African village of the Ndembu resembles Greek drama.[86]

Social drama has two general dimensions: structure and *communitas*.[87] The former has a processual content but is not dramatic in nature, for example, as when nonconflictual or "harmonic" decisions based on considerations of rationality, utility, and convenience are taken freely and cooperatively to pursue mundane economic tasks. The latter, however, is dramatic; thus, all social dramas are units of "aharmonic" or "disharmonic" processes that reveal conflicting relations. The next section examines these ideas in more detail.

---

82. *Id.* at 24.

83. Turner, Dramas, Fields, and Metaphors, *supra* note 78, at 33.

84. *Id.*

85. *Id.*

86. Victor Turner, Schism and Continuity in African Society: A Study of Ndembu Village Life 94 (1957).

87. Turner, Dramas, Fields, and Metaphors, *supra* note 78, at 33.

Communitas, Antistructure, and Processualism

The second dimension of social drama, *communitas*, emerges as part of a fourfold analysis of conflictual drama. First there is a breach of a regular social norm of crucial importance to ongoing social interaction. The breach may not necessarily be a crime; it may instead be an "obvious symbol of dissidence" or a "symbolic trigger of confrontation" taken consciously or unconsciously on behalf of others and not merely for oneself. It could also take the form of a symbolic "separation" of an individual from his or her community.[88]

Second, following the breach or separation, a gradual sense of a supervening *crisis* or uncertainty develops. If not immediately contained or resolved, this sense can spread and engulf the entire society by dividing it into antagonistic camps.

> This second stage, *crisis*, is always one of those turning points or moments of danger and suspense, when a true state of affairs is revealed, when it is least easy to don masks or pretend that there is nothing rotten in the village. Each public crisis has what I now call liminal characteristics, since it is a threshold between more or less stable phases of the social process, but it is not a sacred limen, hedged around by taboos and thrust away from the centers of public life. On the contrary, it takes up its menacing stance in the forum itself and, as it were, dares the representatives of order to grapple with it. It cannot be ignored or wished away.[89]

The third phase involves redressive action taken formally or informally, institutionally or on an *ad hoc* basis, to resolve the crisis. The methods, means, and types of action vary with the social significance of the separation or breach, the level of inclusiveness of the affected group, and the way the latter influences societal relations in the wider context. The redressive action can take the form of personal advice, resolution through mediation, arbitration, judicial settlement, or the performance of public ritual.

> Study carefully what happens in phase three, the would-be redressive phase of social dramas, and ask whether the redressive machinery is capable of handling crises so as to restore, more or less, the status quo ante, or at least to restore peace among the contending groups. Then ask, if so, how precisely? And if not, why not? It is in the redressive phase that both pragmatic techniques and symbolic action reach their fullest expression. For the society, group, community, association, or whatever may be the social unit, is here at its most "self-conscious" and may attain the clarity of someone fighting in a corner for his life. Redress, too, has its liminal features, its being "betwixt and between," and, as such, furnishes a distanced replication and critique of the events leading up to and composing the "crisis." This replication may be in the rational idiom of a judicial process, or in the metaphorical and symbolic

88. *Id.* at 38.

89. *Id.* at 39.

> idiom of a ritual process, depending on the nature and severity of the crisis. When redress fails there is usually regression to crisis. At this point direct force may be used, in the varied forms of war, revolution, intermittent acts of violence, repression, or rebellion. Where the disturbed community is small and relatively weak vis-à-vis the central authority, however, regression to crisis tends to become a matter of endemic, pervasive, smoldering factionalism, without sharp, overt confrontations between consistently distinct parties.[90]

The final phase, *reintegration* of the disaffected group or person or a recognition that an unbridgeable schism exists between the opposing groups, may result in one legitimately seceding from the other. However, reconciliation and reintegration can occur years later, after a major public ritual in which all parties are involved.[91]

The second phase of the crisis represents the threshold of transition—which Turner refers to as the "liminal" phase. He borrowed the concept of liminality from Belgian anthropologist Arnold van Gennep, who contended that the ritual process involves the transition of individuals from one social condition or state to another. Furthermore, van Gennep asserted that this transition occurs through a threefold process of "separation" from the group, "transition" to a new state, and "incorporation" or "re-incorporation" into the social order.[92] In van Gennep's view, the second (threshold) period is one in which individuals are neither what they were before separation nor what they will become upon incorporation. In Turner's words, the individual is "betwixt and between."[93]

Turner elaborated on van Gennep's notion of liminality to argue that during this phase, all notions of normativity and structure are undone through a symbolic as well as a physical separation of an individual (or individuals) from society. He called this temporary negation of social structure "anti-structure."

> Anti-structure is possible, Turner argued, because the liminal state is one in which all the limitations of everyday structure are dispensed with and new creative possibilities opened up. A central aspect of this theory is that, throughout all inversion and liminal transformation of norms and identities, members of a society ultimately come to recognize and reaffirm the basic structural cohesion that they had known all along in their routine existence outside of ritual. It is by way of this new-found solidarity, or reintegration, that society avoids the truly revolutionary implications of liminality, and is instead fused by what Turner called **communitas**—an increased awareness of the social order, reminiscent of Durkheim's idea that rituals are emotionally effervescent events.[94]

---

90. *Id.* at 40–41.

91. Turner, Schism and Continuity in African Society, *supra* note 86, at 288–317.

92. Turner, The Forest of Symbols, *supra* note 5, at 94. Erickson & Murphy, *supra* note 16, at 138.

93. Victor Turner, The Ritual Process: Structure and Anti-Structure 95 (1969).

94. Erickson & Murphy, *supra* note 16, at 139.

The following excerpt is representative of Turner's concepts of antistructure, liminality, *communitas*, and processual symbolism. The latter is further discussed after the excerpt.

Victor Turner, Dramas, Fields and Metaphors: Symbolic Action in Human Society 273–274 (1974).

I have used the term "anti-structure," but I would like to make clear that the "anti" is here used only strategically and does not imply a radical negativity. . . . When I speak of anti-structure, therefore, I really mean something positive, a generative center. I do not seek the eradication of matter. . . .

Roughly, the concepts of liminality and communitas define what I mean by anti-structure. Liminality—a term borrowed from van Gennep's formulation of the processual structure of ritual in *Les Rites de passage*—occurs in the middle phase of the rites of passage which mark changes in an individual's or a group's social status and/or cultural or psychological state in many societies past and present. Such rites characteristically begin with ritual metaphors of killing or death marking the separation of the subject from ordinary secular relationships (in which status-role behavior tends to prevail even in informal situations) and conclude with a symbolic rebirth or reincorporation into society as shaped by the law and moral code. The biological order of birth and death is reversed in rites of passage—there one dies to "become a little child." The intervening liminal phase is thus betwixt and between the categories of ordinary social life. Symbols and metaphors found in abundance in liminality represent various dangerous ambiguities of this ritual stage, since the classifications on which order normally depends are annulled or obscured—other symbols designate temporary antinomic liberation from behavioral norms and cognitive rules. This aspect of danger requiring control is reflected in the paradox that in liminality extreme authority of elders over juniors often coexists with scenes and episodes indicative of the utmost behavioral freedom and speculative license. Liminality is usually a sacred condition protected against secularity by taboos and in turn prevented by them from disrupting secular order, since liminality is a movement between fixed points and is essentially ambiguous, unsettled, and unsettling.

In liminality, communitas tends to characterize relationships between those jointly undergoing ritual transition. The bonds of communitas are anti-structural in the sense that they are undifferentiated, equalitarian, direct, extant, nonrational, existential, I-Thou (in Feuerbach's and Buber's sense) relationships. Communitas is spontaneous, immediate, concrete—it is not shaped by norms, it is not institutionalized, it is not abstract. Communitas differs from the camaraderie found often in everyday life, which, though informal and egalitarian, still falls within the general domain of structure, which may include interaction rituals. . . . It tends to ignore, reverse, cut across, or occur outside of structural relationships. In human history, I see

> a continuous tension between structure and communitas, at all levels of scale and complexity. Structure, or all that which holds people apart, defines their differences, and constrains their actions, is one pole in a charged field, for which the opposite pole is communitas, or anti-structure, the egalitarian "sentiment for humanity" of which David Hume speaks, representing the desire for a total, unmediated relationship between person and person, a relationship which nevertheless does not submerge one in the other but safeguards their uniqueness in the very act of realizing their commonness. Communitas does not merge identities; it liberates them from conformity to general norms, though this is necessarily a transient condition if society is to continue to operate in an orderly fashion.
>
> I have discussed elsewhere . . . how, among the Ndembu people of Zambia, in the liminal phase of their rites of passage, communitas is both metaphorically represented and actually engendered by ritual leveling and humiliation.

Before presenting the Ndembu ritual to illustrate Turnerian liminality, it is worth noting that Turner associated the properties of *communitas* with a variety of binary oppositions that stood for the basic dichotomy or opposition of *communitas* to structure. Examples include transition/state, anonymity/systems of nomenclature, silence/speech, totality/partiality, status/absence of status, sexual continence/sexuality, absence of rank/distinctions based on rank, unselfishness/selfishness, equality/inequality, and so forth.[95] Most of these oppositions, but particularly the last six, are illustrated in the Ndembu ritual next.

Turner also regarded such oppositions to be present in religious pilgrimages and as underscoring the transitional phase of liminality. Pilgrimages exhibit *communitas* in the processual sense in that they initially shed all outward symbols of social rank and mimic equality. Turner gives the examples of Tolstoy and Gandhi, who renounced worldly goods and tried "to approximate in dress and behavior the condition of the poor."[96] These examples, which show both a merger and an inversion of normal social rankings, are echoed in the Ndembu ritual discussed next.[97]

Liminality and *Communitas* in Ndembu Ritual

The prototypical processual ritual is a rite of passage or initiation ceremony. The rite marks some form of change, usually one of place, state, social position, or age.[98] The attributes of liminality are necessarily ambiguous because the person detached is in a condition that eludes classification under the normal rules that "place" people in cultural space.[99] The ambiguity is expressed by a rich variety of symbols and metaphors of death, darkness, solar or lunar eclipse, bisexuality, nakedness, and so on, the

95. Turner, The Ritual Process, *supra* note 93, at 106–07.

96. Turner, Dramas, Fields, and Metaphors, *supra* note 78, at 243.

97. Moore, *supra* note 4, at 255–56.

98. Turner, The Ritual Process, *supra* note 93, at 94.

99. *Id.* at 95.

latter being a particularly appropriate way to show lack of status or lack of ownership of material goods. The person is thus "being reduced or ground down" so as to be refashioned anew, endowed with new status and new powers.

The following abstract describes an initiation ceremony in the form of an installation rite for the senior chief (*Kanongesha*) of the Ndembu tribe of Zambia.

Victor Turner, The Ritual Process: Structure and Anti-Structure 100–104 (1969).

To return to the installation rites of the Kanongesha of the Ndembu; the liminal component of such rites begins with the construction of a small shelter of leaves about a mile away from the capital village. This hut is known as *kafu* or *kafwi*, a term Ndembu derive from *ku-fwa*, "to die," for it is here that the chief-elect dies from his commoner state. Imagery of death abounds in Ndembu liminality. . . . The chief-elect, clad in nothing but a ragged waist-cloth, and a ritual wife, . . . are called by Kafwana to enter the *kafu* shelter just after sundown. The chief himself, incidentally, is also known as *mwadyi* or *lukanu* in these rites. The couple are led there as though they were infirm. There they sit crouched in a posture of shame (*nsonyi*) or modesty, while they are washed with medicines mixed with water. . . .

Next begins the rite of *Kumukindyila*, which means literally "to speak evil or insulting words against him"; we might call this rite "The Reviling of the Chief-Elect." It begins when Kafwana makes a cut on the underside of the chief's left arm—on which the *lukanu* bracelet will be drawn on the morrow—presses medicine into the incision, and presses a mat on the upper side of the arm. The chief and his wife are then forced rather roughly to sit on the mat. The wife must not be pregnant, for the rites that follow are held to destroy fertility. Moreover, the chiefly couple must have refrained from sexual congress for several days before the rites. . . .

After this harangue, any person who considers that he has been wronged by the chief-elect in the past is entitled to revile him and most fully express his resentment, going into as much detail as he desires. The chief-elect, during all this, has to sit silently with downcast head, "the pattern of all patience" and humility. . . . The chief may not resent any of this or hold it against the perpetrators in times to come.

Attributes of Liminal Entities

The phase of reaggregation in this case comprises the public installation of the Kanongesha with all pomp and ceremony. . . . Our present focus is upon liminality and the ritual powers of the weak. These are shown under two aspects. First, Kafwana and the other Ndembu commoners are revealed as privileged to exert authority over the supreme authority figure of the tribe. In liminality, the underling comes uppermost. Second, the supreme political authority is portrayed "as a slave," recalling that aspect of the coronation of a pope in western Christendom when he is called upon to be the "*servus servorum Dei*." . . . The chief has to exert self-control in the rites that he may be able to have self-mastery thereafter in face of the temptations of power. But the role of the humbled chief is only an extreme example of a recurrent theme of liminal situations. This theme is the stripping off of preliminal and postliminal attributes.

Let us look at the main ingredients of the *Kumukindyila* rites. The chief and his wife are dressed identically in a ragged waist-cloth and share the same name—*mwadyi*. This term is also applied to boys undergoing initiation and to a man's first wife in chronological order of marriage. It is an index of the anonymous state of "initiand." These attributes of sexlessness and anonymity are highly characteristic of liminality. In many kinds of initiation where the neophytes are of both sexes, males and females are dressed alike and referred to by the same term. . . . Symbolically, all attributes that distinguish categories and groups in the structured social order are here in abeyance; the neophytes are merely entities in transition, as yet without place or position.

Other characteristics are submissiveness and silence. Not only the chief in the rites under discussion, but also neophytes in many *rites de passage* have to submit to an authority that is nothing less than that of the total community.

The neophyte in liminality must be a *tabula rasa*, a blank slate, on which is inscribed the knowledge and wisdom of the group, in those respects that pertain to the new status. The ordeals and humiliations, often of a grossly physiological character, to which neophytes are submitted represent partly a destruction of the previous status and partly a tempering of their essence in order to prepare them to cope with their new responsibilities and restrain them in advance from abusing their new privileges. They have to be shown that in themselves they are clay or dust, mere matter, whose form is impressed upon them by society.

Another liminal theme exemplified in the Ndembu installation rites is sexual continence. This is a pervasive theme of Ndembu ritual. Indeed, the resumption of sexual relations is usually a ceremonial mark of the return to society as a structure of statuses. . . . The undifferentiated character of liminality is reflected by the discontinuance of sexual relations and the absence of marked sexual polarity.

It is instructive to analyze the homiletic of Kafwana, in seeking to grasp the meaning of liminality. The reader will remember that he chided the chief-elect for his selfishness, meanness, theft, anger, witchcraft, and greed. All these vices represent the desire to possess for oneself what ought to be shared for the common good. An incumbent of high status is peculiarly tempted to use the authority vested in him by society to satisfy these private and privative wishes. But he should regard his privileges as gifts of the whole community, which in the final issue has an overright over all his actions.

Structure and the high offices provided by structure are thus seen as instrumentalities of the commonweal, not as means of personal aggrandizement.

Conclusion

Turner subscribed to the Durkheimian notion of social solidarity but added cognitive and emotional content. He moved beyond the structural functionalist thesis that normative change is simply repetitive and cyclical by advancing the concepts of antistructure and *communitas*, which together offer a far more dynamic view of normative change and of the persistence of social structures through time. His studies of ritual demonstrated how societies manage change, for example, during the installation rites for a new chief or the initiation of boys and girls as they come of age. He developed the idea of social drama, with its four phases, to analyze social transformation and normative continuity.

According to Turner, social drama brings out the cognitive, emotional, and "humanistic" aspects of ritual in social life. Ritual creates the "liminal" conditions through which normative transformations can be symbolically enacted and understood. Thus, for Turner, ritual has a direct connection with normative structure, which led him to claim that "I came to see performances of ritual as distinct phases in social processes whereby groups adapted to their external environment."[100]

Geertz: Interpretivism and Thick Description

Introduction to Geertz's Semiotic Phenomenology

> The concept of culture I espouse . . . is essentially a semiotic one. Believing, with Max Weber, that man is an animal suspended in webs of significance he himself has spun, I take culture to be those webs, and the analysis of it to be therefore not an experimental science in search of law but an interpretive one in search of meaning.[101]

Clifford Geertz's semiotic theory holds that cultural acts are signifiers of meaning that ethnographers must carefully interpret and isolate from an entire range or "web" of possible meanings. In an approach reminiscent of the phenomenological methodology of Husserl, who argued that cultural life has meaning only as "lived experience,"[102] Geertz's interpretive theory argues that the task of ethnography is to show how "lived experience is integrated in a coherent, public system of symbols that both renders the world intelligible and seems uniquely suited to do so."[103]

---

100. Turner, The Forest of Symbols, *supra* note 5, at 20.

101. Clifford Geertz, *Thick Description: Toward an Interpretive Theory of Culture, in* Geertz, The Interpretation of Cultures, *supra* note 3, at 5.

102. Edmund Husserl, The Crisis of the European Sciences and Transcendental Phenomenology 240 (1970).

103. Erickson & Murphy, *supra* note 16, at 140.

However, Geertz cautions that finding the correct meaning is no easy task because human behaviors, including symbolic acts, have multiple layers of meaning. This captures the idea of normativity; *i.e.*, that meaningful norms exist in layers, and that their meanings vary situationally. The task of ethnography is to decipher such normativity through "thick description," a term Geertz borrowed from Gilbert Ryle.[104]

> Doing ethnography is like trying to read (in the sense of "construct a reading of") a manuscript—foreign, faded, full of ellipses, incoherencies, suspicious emendations, and tendentious commentaries, but written not in conventionalized graphs of sound, but in transient examples of shaped behavior.[105]

In going about the task of thick description the ethnographer does not, of course, arrive intellectually empty-handed. He brings theoretical ideas from past interpretive studies, which are adapted and applied to new interpretive contexts. Just as natural scientists "describe" and then "explain" natural phenomena, the ethnographer gives "thick description" and "specification" of cultural phenomena. Thick description gives the meaning that particular social actions have for their actors; by contrast, specification is the ethnographer's statement of what the knowledge so obtained tells us about the society in question. The ethnographer has the double task of unveiling the conceptual structure (meaning) of the subjects' acts from the subjects' point of view and deducing therefrom what is unique about the actions of the subjects.

> Although one starts any effort at thick description, beyond the obvious and superficial, from a state of general bewilderment as to what the devil is going on—trying to find one's feet—one does not start (or ought not) intellectually empty-handed. Theoretical ideas are not created wholly anew in each study; as I have said, they are adopted from other, related studies, and, refined in the process, applied to new interpretive problems. If they cease being useful with respect to such problems, they tend to stop being used and are more or less abandoned. If they continue being useful, throwing up new understandings, they are further elaborated and go on being used.
>
> Such a view of how theory functions in an interpretive science suggests that the distinction, relative in any case, that appears in the experimental or observational sciences between "description" and "explanation" appears here as one, even more relative, between "inscription" ("thick description") and "specification" ("diagnosis")—between setting down the meaning particular social actions have for the actors whose actions they are, and stating, as explicitly as we can manage, what the knowledge thus attained demonstrates about the society in which it is found and, beyond that, about social life as such. Our double task is to uncover the conceptual structures that inform our subjects' acts, the "said" of social discourse, and to construct a system of analysis in whose terms what is generic to those structures, what belongs to them because they are what they are, will stand out against the other deter-

104. Geertz, *Thick Description*, *supra* note 101, at 10.

105. *Id.*

> minants of human behavior. In ethnography, the office of theory is to provide a vocabulary in which what symbolic action has to say about itself—that is, about the role of culture in human life—can be expressed.[106]

This particular form of description aims to account for culture from the point of view of the native without the ethnographer actually "going native" (*i.e.*, becoming a member of and assimilating totally into the group being studied).[107] Certain forms of behavior or gestures can have more than one meaning depending on whether they are done deliberately, accidentally, or instinctively and on whether they are directed to someone in particular, done publicly or secretly, and so on. Geertz illustrates this point in the next excerpt by distinguishing between an involuntary eyelid twitch and a deliberate wink to show how these two simple gestures can acquire complex and different meanings depending on social context. An actor who is a member of the group may only be aware of the one meaning he or she is desiring to communicate; the astute ethnographer, however, would be able to unearth all layers of meaning through careful interpretation. Borrowing a term from psychoanalysis, Geertz describes the former as "experience-near" (the level at which the actor member, whom we may think of in this context as the informant, acts naturally and effortlessly) and the latter as "experience-distant" (the level at which the ethnographer-analyst studies and interprets meaning).[108]

The Normative Critique

Geertz attacks the "myth" created by Malinowski of the ethnographer as "the chameleon field worker, perfectly self-tuned to his exotic surroundings, a walking miracle of empathy, tact, patience, and cosmopolitanism."[109] For Geertz, ethnography does not demand such superhuman qualities.[110] He thus signals the approach embraced by the deconstructionist anthropologists, namely that there is no longer an unbridgeable gap between observing and participating, scientist and native, and "Self and Other."[111]

There is a corresponding rejection by Geertz of the attempt to describe ethnography as "subjective," "objective," "materialist," "idealist," or "mentalist." He maintains that these labels become irrelevant once it is accepted that human behavior consists of symbolic acts that signify public meanings. In other words, it is nonsensical to examine whether culture is patterned conduct (as Benedict and Mead claimed) or a frame of mind (as cultural idealists such as Turner or Goodenough argued) or a

106. *Id.* at 27.

107. *Id.* at 13. The term "going native" is used by Barbara Tedlock, *From Participant Observation to the Observation of Participation: The Emergence of Narrative Ethnography*, 47 J. ANTHROPOL. RES. 69, 71 (1991). *See also*, Clifford Geertz, *"From the Native's Point of View": On the Nature of Anthropological Understanding, in* CLIFFORD GEERTZ, LOCAL KNOWLEDGE: FURTHER ESSAYS IN INTERPRETIVE ANTHROPOLOGY 55, 57–58 (1983).

108. Geertz, *"From the Native's Point of View," supra* note 107, at 57.

109. *Id.* at 56.

110. *Id.* at 70.

111. Tedlock, *supra* note 107, at 71.

combination of both. It is neither, according to Geertz, who rejects the notion of culture as an autonomous "super organic" force as claimed by Kroeber. Geertz also rejected the various approaches associated with ethnoscience, componential analysis, and cognitive anthropology.[112] As explained in the following excerpt, in his view the aforementioned approaches obscure the basic truth that ethnography is concerned not with the ontological status of cultural behavior but what it means. As Geertz wryly observes, playing the violin requires skills, habits, knowledge, and mood—but the act of playing the violin is not these things in and of themselves. Nor does the act of playing the violin confer any ontological status on the instrument (*i.e.*, the act of playing the violin does not reify it).

The notion of culture as "super organic" does reify it, however, as does the claim that culture is knowledge one must have to guide one's behavior. This claim conceives culture as being made up of psychological or mental structures that guide individual or group behavior. Linguistic codes, grammatical codes, and legal codes are then promulgated through various tabulations and charts to represent "the native point of view." But these efforts, according to Geertz, only create further confusion and internal debates among ethnographers as to what the natives "really" think.[113]

Clifford Geertz, *Thick Description: Toward an Interpretive Theory of Culture*, *in* Clifford Geertz, The Interpretation of Cultures: Selected Essays 5–12 (1973).

The concept of culture I espouse . . . is essentially a semiotic one. Believing, with Max Weber, that man is an animal suspended in webs of significance he himself has spun, I take culture to be those webs, and the analysis of it to be therefore not an experimental science in search of law but an interpretive one in search of meaning. . . .

In anthropology, or anyway social anthropology, what the practitioners do is ethnography. . . . What defines it is the kind of intellectual effort it is: an elaborate venture in, to borrow a notion from Gilbert Ryle, "thick description." . . .

Consider, he says, two boys rapidly contracting the eyelids of their right eyes. In one, this is an involuntary twitch; in the other, a conspiratorial signal to a friend. The two movements are, as movements, identical; from an I-am-a-camera, "phenomenalistic" observation of them alone, one could not tell which was twitch and which was wink, or indeed whether both or either was twitch or wink. Yet the difference, however unphotographable, between a twitch and wink is vast; as anyone unfortunate enough to have had the first taken for the second knows. The winker is communicating, and indeed communicating in a quiet precise and special way: (1) deliberately, (2) to someone in particular, (3) to impart a particular message, (4) according to a

112. Geertz, *Thick Description*, *supra* note 101, at 10–11.

113. *Id.* at 11.

socially established code, and (5) without cognizance of the rest of the company. As Ryle points out, the winker has not done two things, contracted his eyelids and winked, while the twitcher has done only one, contracted his eyelids. Contracting your eyelids on purpose when there exists a public code in which so doing counts as a conspiratorial signal *is* winking. That's all there is to it: a speck of behavior, a fleck of culture, and—*voilà!*—a gesture.

That, however, is just the beginning. Suppose, he continues, there is a third boy, who "to give malicious amusement to his cronies," parodies the first boy's wink, as amateurish, clumsy, obvious, and so on. He, of course, does this in the same way the second boy winked and the first twitched: by contracting his right eyelids. Only this boy is neither winking nor twitching, he is parodying someone else's, as he takes it, laughable, attempt at winking. Here, too, a socially established code exists (he will "wink" laboriously, overobviously, perhaps adding a grimace—the usual artifices of the clown); and so also does a message. Only now it is not conspiracy but ridicule that is in the air. If the others think he is actually winking, his whole project misfires . . . completely. . . . But the point is that between what Ryle calls the "thin description" of what the rehearser (parodist, winker, twitcher . . .) is doing ("rapidly contracting his right eyelids") and the "thick description" of what he is doing ("practicing a burlesque of a friend faking a wink to deceive an innocent into thinking a conspiracy is in motion") lies the object of ethnography: a stratified hierarchy of meaningful structures in terms of which twitches, winks, fake-winks, parodies, rehearsals of parodies are produced, perceived, and interpreted . . .

Right down at the factual base, the hard rock, insofar as there is any, of the whole enterprise, we are already explicating: and worse, explicating explications. Winks upon winks upon winks . . .

Doing ethnography is like trying to read (in the sense of "construct a reading of") a manuscript—foreign, faded, full of ellipses, incoherencies, suspicious emendations, and tendentious commentaries, but written not in conventionalized graphs of sound but in transient examples of shaped behavior.

Culture, this acted document, thus is public, like a burlesqued wink or a mock sheep raid. Though ideational, it does not exist in someone's head; though unphysical, it is not an occult entity. The interminable, because unterminable, debate within anthropology as to whether culture is "subjective" or "objective," together with the mutual exchange of intellectual insults ("idealist!"—"materialist!"; "mentalist!"—"behaviorist!"; "impressionist!"—"positivist!") which accompanies it, is wholly misconceived. Once human behavior is seen as (most of the time; there *are* true twitches) symbolic action—action which, like phonation in speech, pigment in painting, line in writing, or sonance in music, signifies—the question as to whether culture is patterned conduct or a frame of mind, or even the two somehow mixed together, loses sense. The thing to ask about a burlesqued wink or a mock

> sheep raid is not what their ontological status is. It is the same as that of rocks on the one hand and dreams on the other—they are things of this world. The thing to ask is what their import is: what it is, ridicule or challenge, irony or anger, snobbery or pride, that, in their occurrence and through their agency, is getting said.
>
> This may seem like an obvious truth, but there are a number of ways to obscure it. One is to image that culture is a self-contained "superorganic" reality with forces and purposes of its own; that is, to reify it. Another is to claim that it consists in the brute pattern of behavioral events we observe in fact to occur in some identifiable community or other; that is, to reduce it. But though both these confusions still exist, and doubtless will be always with us, the main source of theoretical muddlement in contemporary anthropology is a view which developed in reaction to them and is right now very widely held—namely, that, to quote Ward Goodenough, perhaps its leading proponent, "culture [is located] in the minds and hearts of man."
>
> Variously called ethnoscience, componential analysis, or cognitive anthropology (a terminological wavering which reflects a deeper uncertainty), this school of thought holds that culture is composed of psychological structures by means of which individuals or groups of individuals guide their behavior. "A society's culture," to quote Goodenough again, this time in a passage which has become the *locus classicus* of the whole movement, "consists of whatever it is one has to know or believe in order to operate in a manner acceptable to its members." And from this view of what culture is follows a view, equally assured, of what describing it is—the writing out of systematic rules, an ethnographic algorithm, which, if followed, would make it possible so to operate, to pass (physical appearances aside) for a native. In such a way, extreme subjectivism is married to extreme formalism, with the expected result: an explosion of debate as to whether particular analyses (which come in the form of taxonomies, paradigms, tables, trees, and other ingenuities) reflect what the natives "really" think or are merely clever simulations, logically equivalent but substantively different, of what they think. . . .
>
> To play the violin it is necessary to possess certain habits, skills, knowledge, and talents, to be in the mood to play, and (as the old joke goes) to have a violin. But violin playing is neither the habits, skills, knowledge, and so on, nor the mood, nor (the notion believers in "material culture" apparently embrace) the violin.

In the foregoing excerpt, Geertz analogizes what he calls "cognitive fallacy" with the confusion between knowing how to wink and the act of winking itself, which involves forgetting or ignoring the fact that a wink can have many different meanings, depending on context. In the realm of culture, the cognitivist fallacy claims that mental phenomena constitute culture itself; by contrast, Geertz would argue that what is needed is an understanding of the meanings that underlie these phenomena and that these can only be interpretations by way of thick description. Such descriptions are necessarily "second- or third-order" interpretations, the "first-order" interpretation being that of the natives themselves.[114]

Geertz asserts that most ethnographers do give second and third interpretations but are unaware that they are doing so. In fact, ethnographers always give their "own constructions of other people's constructions" so that there are layers of meanings to given cultural acts. Thus, we have "winks upon winks upon winks."[115] However, when the ethnographer tries to comprehend a particular act, ritual, or custom, the latter is insinuated as background information, and an explanation is given as if after the fact. This procedure gives the impression that ethnographic research is "more of an observational and rather less of an interpretive activity than it really is."[116]

Epistemological Implications of the Interpretivist Critique

Geertz asserts that understanding ethnography as interpretive means that "the line between mode of representation and substantive content is as undrawable in cultural analysis as it is in painting."[117] This statement threatens the objective status of anthropological knowledge; however, according to Geertz, the threat is "hollow"[118] because thick description will distinguish between public meanings and will contextually "verify" or "appraise" its interpretative conclusions.

> It is not against a body of uninterpreted data, radically thinned descriptions, that we must measure the cogency of our explications, but against the power of the scientific imagination to bring us into touch with the lives of strangers.[119]

The epistemological claim is fairly modest. Geertz's interpretivism is not supposed to lead to the discovery of "autogenous principles of order, universal proprieties of the human mind, or vast, *a priori weltanschauugen*."[120] Careful appraisal of alternative interpretations enables the ethnographer to distinguish "a better account from a worse one" so that in the end,

> cultural analysis is (or should be) guessing at meanings, assessing the guesses, and drawing explanatory conclusions from the better guesses, not discovering the Continent of Meaning and mapping out its bodiless landscape.[121]

For these reasons, Geertz concludes that ethnographic findings and conclusions are not privileged, just particular.[122] Nor do they lead to grand narratives (*e.g.*, "Jonesville

---

114. *Id.* at 15.

115. *Id.* at 9.

116. *Id.*

117. Geertz, *Thick Description*, *supra* note 101, at 16.

118. *Id.*

119. *Id.*

120. *Id.* at 20.

121. *Id.* at 20.

122. Geertz, *Thick Description*, *supra* note 101, at 23.

is America writ large").[123] He makes no bold or express claim that particular interpretations (appraised and verified) are inherently privileged but rather believes that "better" interpretations can be sorted from "worse" ones. This stand is reminiscent of Marvin Harris, who claims (as seen in Chapter 4) that cultural materialism gives a "better" account than other approaches to sociocultural phenomena.[124]

> Cultural analysis is intrinsically incomplete. And, worse than that, the more deeply it goes the less complete it is. It is a strange science whose most telling assertions are its most tremulously based, in which to get somewhere with the matter at hand is to intensify the suspicion, both your own and that of others, that you are not quite getting it right. But that, along with plaguing subtle people with obtuse questions, is what being an ethnographer is like.
>
> There are a number of ways to escape this—turning culture into folklore and collecting it, turning it into traits and counting it, turning it into institutions and classifying it, turning it into structures and toying with it. But they *are* escapes. The fact is that to commit oneself to a semiotic concept of culture and an interpretive approach to the study of it is to commit oneself to a view of ethnographic assertion as, to borrow W.B. Gallie's by now famous phrase, "essentially contestable." Anthropology, or at least interpretive anthropology, is a science whose progress is marked less by a perfection of consensus than by a refinement of debate. What gets better is the precision with which we vex each other.[125]

Case Studies in Interpretivism

A. The Balinese Cockfight

One graphic illustration of experience-distant thick description is Geertz's interpretation of the Balinese cockfight, which he interprets as symbolic affirmation from the native point of view not only of male sexual prowess but also of male honor and status, extending to the kin group. Because kin solidarity is affirmed through bets on the fight, one never bets against a cock owned by a kinsman. This norm extends to allied kingroups and beyond to the village as a whole, especially when the rival cock is not a "home bird."[126] Finally, the gory ritual is also a form of blood sacrifice to appease evil spirits.

---

123. *Id.* at 21–22.

124. *See* Chapter 5 *supra*, text at notes 97–98.

125. Geertz, *Thick Description*, *supra* note 101, at 29.

126. Clifford Geertz, *Deep Play: Notes on the Balinese Cockfight*, *in* GEERTZ, THE INTERPRETATION OF CULTURES, *supra* note 3, at 412, 437–38.

Clifford Geertz, *Deep Play: Notes on the Balinese Cockfight, in* Clifford Geertz, The Interpretation of Cultures: Selected Essays 412, 417–422, 433 (1973).

Of Cocks and Men

To anyone who has been in Bali any length of time, the deep psychological identification of Balinese men with their cocks is unmistakable. The double entendre here is deliberate. It works in exactly the same way in Balinese as it does in English, even to producing the same tired jokes, strained puns, and uninventive obscenities. Bateson and Mead have even suggested that, in line with the Balinese conception of the body as a set of separately animated parts, cocks are viewed as detachable, self-operating penises, ambulant genitals with a life of their own....

But the intimacy of men with their cocks is more than metaphorical. Balinese men, or anyway a large majority of Balinese men, spend an enormous amount of time with their favorites, grooming them, feeding them, discussing them, trying them out against one another, or just gazing at them with a mixture of rapt admiration and dreamy self-absorption ... Red pepper is stuffed down their beaks and up their anuses to give them spirit. They are bathed in the same ceremonial preparation of tepid water, medicinal herbs, flowers, and onions....

... In identifying with his cock, the Balinese man is identifying not just with his ideal self, or even his penis, but also, and at the same time, with what he most fears, hates, and ambivalence being what it is, is fascinated by—"The Powers of Darkness."

The connection of cocks and cockfighting with such Powers, with the animalistic demons that threaten constantly to invade the small, cleared-off space in which the Balinese have so carefully built their lives and devour its inhabitants, is quite explicit. A cockfight, any cockfight, is in the first instance a blood sacrifice offered, with the appropriate chants and oblations, to the demons in order to pacify their ravenous, cannibal hunger....

In the cockfight, man and beast, good and evil, ego and id, the creative power of aroused masculinity and the destructive power of loosened animality fuse in a bloody drama of hatred, cruelty, violence, and death....

The Fight

Cockfights (*tetadjen; sabungan*) are held in a ring about fifty feet square. Usually they begin toward late afternoon and run three or four hours until sunset....

Most of the time, in any case, the cocks fly almost immediately at one another in wing-beating, head-thrusting, leg-kicking explosion of animal fury so pure, so absolute, and in its own way so beautiful, as to be almost abstract, a Platonic concept of hate. Within moments one or the other drives home a solid blow with his spur....

> It is, in fact, in shallow games, ones in which smaller amounts of money are involved, that increments and decrements of cash are more nearly synonymous for utility and disutility, in the ordinary, unexpanded sense—for pleasure and pain, happiness and unhappiness. In deep ones, where the amounts of money are great, much more is at stake than material gain: namely, esteem, honor, dignity, respect—in a word, though in Bali a profoundly freighted word, status. It is at stake symbolically, for (a few cases of ruined addict gamblers aside) no one's status is actually altered by the outcome of a cockfight; it is only, and that momentarily, affirmed or insulted. But for the Balinese, for whom nothing is more pleasurable than an affront obliquely delivered or more painful than one obliquely received—particularly when mutual acquaintances, undeceived by surfaces, are watching—such appraisive drama is deep indeed.

Here, the cock and the cockfight are presented as two related symbols. Each has its own set of meanings that together reveal additional ones: (1) male pride; (2) male sexual prowess; (3) male honor; (4) male status; (5) pride, status, and solidarity of the cock owner's kin group; (6) pride, status, and solidarity of allied kin groups; (7) pride, status, and solidarity of the village as a whole; (8) method of making money through bets; (9) method of appeasing evil supernatural spirits.

B. A Javanese Funeral

As previously stated, thick description bequeaths a twofold mission to the ethnographer: to uncover the cognitive structures that inform behavior, the "said" of social discourse, and to deduce therefrom what is unique about the actions of the subjects under study.[127] The former task ascertains the principles of "logico-meaningful integration," which one might find "in a Bach fugue, in Catholic dogma, or in the general theory of relativity."[128] In other words, the first task requires mastering what gives a system its unity, style, and value. Geertz calls the second task "causal-functional integration,"[129] which refers to how all parts of a system are united in a single causal web, with each part working to "keep the system going."[130] Because these two types of normative integration are not identical, meaning the form of one does not dictate the form of the other, conflict between them is possible.

---

127. *See* text at note 106 *supra*.

128. Clifford Geertz, *Ritual and Social Change: A Javanese Example*, *in* Clifford Geertz, The Interpretation of Cultures, *supra* note 3, at 142, 145.

129. *Id.* These terms are borrowed by Geertz from Pitirim Sorokin, Social and Cultural Dynamics (1937).

130. Geertz, *Ritual and Social Change*, *supra* note 128, at 145.

Clifford Geertz, *Ritual and Social Change: A Javanese Culture*, *in* Clifford Geertz, The Interpretation of Cultures: Selected Essays 142, 144–145 (1973).

> One of the more useful ways—but far from the only one—of distinguishing between culture and social system is to see the former as an ordered system of meaning and of symbols, in terms of which social interaction takes place; and to see the latter as the pattern of social interaction itself. On the one level there is the framework of beliefs, expressive symbols, and values in terms of which individuals define their world, express their feelings, and make their judgments; on the other level there is the ongoing process of interactive behavior, whose persistent form we call social structure. Culture is the fabric of meaning in terms of which human beings interpret their experience and guide their action; social structure is the form that action takes, the actually existing network of social relations. Culture and social structure are then but different abstractions from the same phenomena. The one considers social action in respect to its meaning for those who carry it out, the other considers it in terms of its contribution to the functioning of some social system.
>
> The nature of the distinction between culture and social system is brought out more clearly when one considers the contrasting sorts of integration characteristic of each of them. This contrast is between what Sorokin has called "logico-meaningful integration" and what he has called "casual-functional integration." By logico-meaningful integration, characteristic of culture, is meant the sort of integration one finds in a Bach fugue, in Catholic dogma, or in the general theory of relativity; it is a unity of style, of logical implication, of meaning and value. By casual-functional integration, characteristic of the social system, is meant the kind of integration one finds in an organism, where all the parts are united in a single causal web; each part is an element in a reverberating causal ring which "keeps the system going." And because these two types of integration are not identical, because the particular form one of them takes does not directly imply the form the other will take, there is an inherent incongruity and tension between the two and between both of them.

This background allows us to examine why a Javanese ritual failed to function properly. The ritual involved funeral rites following the death of a ten-year-old boy. According to Geertz, no approach that fails to distinguish the "logico-meaningful" aspects of the ritual from the "causal-functional" (or social cultural aspects) could properly account for the failure of the ritual.

The typical Javanese traditional funeral ceremony is relatively short and subdued, after which the deceased is quickly buried. A communal feast (*slametan*) is held, incense is burned, and a Moslem prayer is recited by the Modin; all mourners depart quickly. The spirits are deemed to have been appeased by the proceedings, and communal solidarity is reaffirmed.[131] But at this particular funeral the ceremony was stalled and considerable social tension resulted. The problem was that the funeral was to occur at a non-Moslem home, and the Modin refused to perform the funeral rites or recite any prayers there unless the homeowner first converted to Islam.

The homeowner belonged to the Permai, a vigorously anti-Moslem politico-religious cult that had evolved over the fifty-year post-independence period in Indonesia. He refused to convert to Islam. The vivid details of the setting, of life in the *kampongs* (off-street neighborhoods), and of political and religious factionalism of Suharto's Indonesia are not immediately relevant and are not reproduced here. It is sufficient to note the family was able to muddle through the funeral over a protracted period, with much crying and wailing (unusual at Javanese funerals). Thus, the self-control and calm (*iklas*) that normally prevails at Javanese funerals unraveled.

What concerns us is Geertz's analysis of the crisis. He contends that the traditional functional structural analysis along the lines of Malinowski's *Magic, Science and Religion* would have been as follows:

> And here into this play of emotional forces, into this supreme dilemma of life and final death, religion steps in, selecting the positive creed, the comforting view, the culturally valuable belief in immortality, in the spirit independent of the body, and in the continuance of life after death. In the various ceremonies at death, in commemoration and communion with the departed, and worship of ancestral ghosts, religion gives body and form to the saving beliefs. . . . Exactly the same function it fulfills also with regard to the whole group. The ceremonial of death, which ties the survivors to the body and rivets them to the place of death, the beliefs in the existence of the spirit, in its beneficent influences or malevolent intentions, in the duties of a series of commemorative or sacrificial ceremonies—in all this religion counteracts the centrifugal forces of fear, dismay, demoralization, and provides the most powerful means of reintegration of the group's shaken solidarity and of the re-establishment of its morale. In short, religion here assures the victory of tradition over the mere negative response of thwarted instinct.[132]

According to Geertz, as he interpreted the facts of the event, religion—far from affirming or reaffirming solidarity—caused a serious rift. Geertz also rejects the functionalist counterargument.

> To this the functionalist has a ready answer, which takes one of two forms depending upon whether he follows the Durkheim or the Malinowski tradition: social disintegration or cultural demoralization. Rapid social change has disrupted Javanese society and this is reflected in a disintegrated culture; as the unified state of traditional village society was mirrored in the unified slametan, so the broken society of the kampong is mirrored in the broken slametan of the funeral ritual we have just witnessed. Or, in the alternate

131. *Id.* at 147.

132. *Id.* at 164 (quoting Bronislaw Malinowski, Magic Science and Religion 33–35 (1948)).

> phraseology, cultural decay has led to social fragmentation; loss of a vigorous folk tradition has weakened the moral ties between individuals.
>
> It seems to me that there are two things wrong with this argument, no matter in which of the two vocabularies it is stated: it identifies social (or cultural) conflict with social (or cultural) disintegration; it denies independent roles to both culture and social structure, regarding one of the two as a mere epiphenomenon of the other.[133]

Geertz's explanation is that not all Kampong residents shared the same set of highly integrated values for funerals and that this difference resulted in a discontinuity at the funeral between the dimension and form at the cultural logico-meaningful level, as well as the dimension and form of integration at the social structural or causal-functional level.[134] By this logic, the residents of the home at which the funeral was to take place were caught up in the processes of social and political modernization. They were "in between" the urbanized elite and the traditionally organized peasantry.[135] When there is this kind of lack of congruity between cultural and social structural dimensions, the result is not social disintegration but social conflict.

Geertz's thick description of funeral rites was able to distinguish between the dual missions of the ethnographer as well as between cultural structure and social structure. Traditional functionalism treats these two phenomena as mere reflections of one another and not as independent and interdependent variables.

> In sum, the disruption of Paidjan's funeral may be traced to a single source: an incongruity between the cultural framework of meaning and the patterning of social interaction, an incongruity due to the persistence in an urban environment of a religious symbol system adjusted to peasant social structure. Static functionalism, of either the sociological or social psychological sort, is unable to isolate this kind of incongruity because it fails to discriminate between logico-meaningful integration and causal-functional integration; because it fails to realize that cultural structure and social structure are not mere reflexes of one another but independent, yet interdependent, variables. The driving forces in social change can be clearly formulated only by a more dynamic form of functionalist theory, one which takes into account the fact that man's need to live in a world to which he can attribute some significance, whose essential import he feels he can grasp, often diverges from his concurrent need to maintain a functioning social organism. A diffuse concept of culture as "learned behavior," a static view of social structure as an equilibrated pattern of interaction, and a stated or unstated assumption that the two must somehow (save in "disorganized" situations) be simple mirror images of one another, is rather too primitive a conceptual

133. Geertz, *Ritual and Social Change*, *supra* note 128, at 163.

134. *Id.* at 164.

135. *Id.*

apparatus with which to attack such problems as those raised by Paidjan's unfortunate but instructive funeral.[136]

C. Interpretivism and Law

When one thinks of the internal harmony of a Bach fugue or the scientific principles that underlie the general theory of relativity, one might also think of their systemic unity, in other words, what gives these things coherence and meaning. In the context of culture, what may come to mind is an ordered system of meaning and of symbols at the widest and most inclusive level, the terms by which people interact. Turner described these symbols as "dominant" and "instrumental."[137] Dominant symbols, as we have seen, in their aggregate stand for the unity and continuity of society in its widest and most inclusive sense. They are viewed as desirable in themselves or as ends in themselves. Instrumental symbols are the means to particular ends.

Geertz's conception of unity at the widest, most inclusive level is captured by the dimension of logico-meaningful integration, which he described as containing "a framework of beliefs, expressive symbols and values in terms of which individuals define their world, express their feelings and make their judgments."[138] He described causal-functional integration as the process and patterns of social interaction itself. For a system to work, he believed, both must be in harmony.

According to Geertz, law or the legal system of a society clearly supports logico-meaningful integration. Nader's studies of the Mexican communities of Talea de Castro and Ralu'a have met the first part of this definition by showing that law reflects the basic cultural beliefs at the most inclusive community level. In the second part of Geertz's definition, law is a system of "expressive symbols and values." As we know, people certainly use the law to make judgments (officially and unofficially) about what to do or not to do, and judgments about what others do or do not do. Many of the values codified in law are ends in themselves and thus constitute the "dominant" symbols of society in the Turnerian sense. But law also serves an "instrumental" function since people use it to interact on a daily basis; hence its "causal-functional" role in society.

One may also use the conception of a legal system proposed by H. L. A. Hart, who stated that a legal system may be viewed as a union of primary and secondary rules.[139] Primary rules comprise the basic or dominant values; secondary rules, including Hart's "rule of recognition," are the instrumental means whereby people make the kind of judgments listed previously.

In the context of the Javanese funeral, specific legal principles of logico-meaningful integration were in dispute. This is not the point of greatest interest, however. Instead, we must note that a sufficiently strong degree of integration in the logico-meaningful sense did not take place. It could not have taken place because the body had not been

136. *Id.* at 169.

137. *See* text at note 77 *supra*.

138. Geertz, *Ritual and Social Change*, *supra* note 128, at 144–45.

139. H. L. A. Hart, The Concept of Law 94 (2d ed., 1994).

prepared for burial, buried, prayed over, and mourned at graveside with the required rituals. Had these activities gone on unhindered, communal solidarity would have been reaffirmed. In Turnerian terms, the dominant ritual was a proper Moslem burial for the deceased, and the actual procedures were the instrumental means by which to achieve it.

The difficulty, as previously mentioned, arose from the fact that not all Kampong residents shared the same set of funeral beliefs and that the Moslem Modin refused to perform the funeral rites in the home of a nonbeliever (one whom, in addition, was ideologically committed to an anti-Moslem political party). Thus a necessary discontinuity between culture and integration at the inclusive level occurred and social interaction in the causal-functional sense was disrupted. This lack of congruity led to social conflict but not to social disintegration.

Laura Nader's Harmony Model may also be analyzed in interprevist terms.[140] As seen in her studies of the two Mexican communities, the village courts of both communities were able to successfully mediate disputes in the spirit of harmony and social balance. The dominant motivation for harmony (in the case of Talea) was to avoid the attention of and interference from the national government. In this case, a strong and inclusive sense of logico-meaningful integration in these communities resulted, in the "causal-functional" sense, in social interaction as well as dispute settlement in ways that satisfactorily preserved harmony and balance.

One may also understand the narratives of avoidance in interpretivist terms, as in the study discussed earlier of three widely dispersed American communities that demonstrated a highly integrated ethos of avoiding recourse to law, which in turn fitted into a web of ideological commitments at the local and at the most inclusive national level.[141] It was this integrative solidarity that facilitated smooth social interaction or causal-functional integration. In addition, Berman's critique of Supreme Court decisions in *Bennis v. Michigan* and *United States v. Ursery* cases involving forfeiture law can be examined in interpretivist terms. The critique was that by showing slavish adherence to precedent, the court failed to articulate the proper rationale for forfeiture law in logico-meaningful terms. Berman felt that the court should have acknowledged that forfeiture was historically viewed as restoring social solidarity through the symbolic banishment of nonhuman agents that offended community morality.[142]

From these examples, we may draw three conclusions:

(1) That law embodies the basic values of a culture (in the logico-meaningful sense) and also provides the bases for social structural interaction (in the causal-functional sense).
(2) That law plays both a dominant and an instrumental role in society.
(3) That if the dominant premises of law are not shared in the aggregate by the members of the group, there will be social conflict.

140. *See* Chapter 6, text at notes 64–72 *supra.*

141. *See* text at notes 30–45 *supra.*

142. *See* text at notes 18–29 *supra.*

D. Legal Interpretivism as Hermeneutics

Geertz's interpretivism often seems to take the form of legal hermeneutics, as influenced by the thought of Ludwig Wittgenstein, Husserl, and Hans-Georg Gadamer. According to Wittgenstein, a particular concept need not have perfect clarity of meaning in order to serve as an effective means of communication. His famous example of the phrase "stand roughly here" demonstrates that although it is inexact, depending on context it is meaningful enough for everyday conversation.[143] For Wittgenstein, different contexts lead to different meanings, so that no single meaning can account for every potential contextual contingency.[144]

Similarities may be detected in the thought of Heidegger and Gadamer. According to Gadamer, interpretation is not an attitude of the subject projected onto nature but is something that "precedes and informs subjectivity."[145] In other words, the act of interpretation is not an activity but a mode of being. Thus, interpretation is just one way of being in the world.[146] Other ways of being, which are abundant, become clear when all the varieties of life experiences are brought to bear on attempts to understand the world. These statements are typical of hermeneutics, the study of the ways existence gives meaning to the world.[147]

However, according to Geertz and other proponents of hermeneutics, whatever meanings are given cannot be proclaimed as final. Instead, meaning is arranged along a continuum that begins with finality and objectivity, otherwise referred to as dogmatic or metaphysical realism; at the other end are indeterminacy and subjectivity. The hermeneutic approach goes beyond the subjective/objective dichotomy for meaning in law without a total surrender to subjectivism. Gadamer's goal was to clarify the conditions in which meanings are given. For our purposes, these are the conditions that make interpretation in law possible.[148]

First among these conditions are the prejudices and foremeanings that the interpreter brings to any communicative encounter. Second is the "effective history" of the text; Gadamer urges interpreters to transcend their predispositions and prejudices and take historical conditions into account. Third, he urges the interpreter to try to understand "the otherness of the other," because meaning is derived from a fusion of the horizons of the interpreter and the other (*i.e.*, the speaker).[149] Thus humans as hermeneutical beings are always interpreting. The primordial act of the first in-

---

143. Ludwig Wittgenstein, Philosophical Investigations ¶ 79 (G.E.M. Anscombe trans., 3d ed., 2001).

144. Lon Fuller, The Morality of Law 137–41 (2d ed. 1969) (citing Wittgenstein for the proposition that language carries with it certain tacit understandings that need not be spelled out in every case).

145. Francis J. Mootz III, *Is the Rule of Law Possible in a Postmodern World?*, 68 Wash. L. Rev. 249, 295 (1993).

146. *Id.*

147. Hans-Georg Gadamer, Truth and Method 263 (Garrett Barden & John Cumming trans., 2d ed., 1975).

148. *Id.* at 263.

149. *Id.* at 267–74.

terpretation is itself an interpretive event, and all subsequent acts are second-order acts of interpretation. If one tries to consciously reflect on the first-order perception, eventually we realize this attempt was, in itself, an interpretation.[150]

Geertz, who asserts that what the ethnographer reports is a construction of other peoples' construction, understood that one can never give a first-order interpretation.[151] Geertz also invokes Husserl and Wittgenstein in his essay *Thick Description* to argue that culture is not a mental phenomenon that can be captured and described through formal methods such as mathematics and logic.[152] For him, meanings are public and not always easy to establish (particularly when dealing with strange people who have unfamiliar traditions).

Geertz argues that studying law in comparative perspective well illustrates the point that "cultural contextualization of incident is a critical aspect of legal analysis."[153] Thus he cautioned that interpretive approaches to foreign cultures and their laws should not be ethnocentric or nihilistic; instead, the goal of the researcher should be to craft an approach that welds the processes of self-knowledge to those of "other-knowledge, other-perception, other-understudying . . . sorting out who we are and sorting out whom we are among."[154] This exhortation is, in essence, what Geertz refers to as the "hermeneutics of legal pluralism."[155]

By this logic, sorting out "whom we are among" involves the quest for public structures of meanings that are complex, layered, and contextualized. Legal structures can be studied comparatively in the same way. As Geertz explains in the following excerpt, contextualizing law and its varying structures of meaning shows that legal pluralism is to be celebrated, not suppressed.

Clifford Geertz, *Local Knowledge: Fact and Law in Comparative Perspective*, *in* Clifford Geertz, Local Knowledge: Further Essays in Interpretive Anthropology 167, 182, 215–216 (1983).

The turn of anthropology, in some quarters at least, towards a heightened concern with structures of meaning in terms of which individuals and groups of individuals live out their lives, and more particularly with the symbols and systems of symbols through whose agency such structures are formed, communicated, imposed, shared, altered, reproduced, offers as much promise for the comparative analysis of law as it does for myth, ritual, ideology, art, or classification systems, the more tested fields of its application. "Man,"

150. *Id.* at 446.

151. *See* text at notes 114–115 *supra*.

152. Geertz, *Thick Description*, *supra* note 101, at 12–13.

153. Clifford Geertz, *Local Knowledge: Fact and Law in Comparative Perspective*, in Geertz, Local Knowledge, *supra* note 107, at 167, 181.

154. *Id.* at 181–82.

155. *Id.* at 225. *See also* Geertz, *From the Native's Point of View*, *supra* note 107, at 69.

as A.M. Hocart remarked, "was not created governed," and the realization that he has become so, severally and collectively, by enclosing himself in a set of meaningful forms, "webs of signification he himself has spun," to recycle a phrase of my own, leads us into an approach to adjudication that assimilates it not to a sort of social mechanics, a physics of judgment, but to a sort of cultural hermeneutics, a semantics of action. What Frank O'Hara said of poetry, that it makes life's nebulous events tangible and restores their detail, may be true as well, and no less variously accomplished, of law. . . .

Law, I have been saying, somewhat against the pretensions encoded in woolsack rhetoric, is local knowledge; local not just as to place, time, class, and variety of issue, but as to accent—vernacular characterizations of what happens connected to vernacular imaginings of what can. It is this complex of characterizations and imaginings, stories about events cast in imagery about principles, that I have been calling a legal sensibility. This is doubtless more than a little vague, but as Wittgenstein, the patron saint of what is going on here, remarked, a veridical picture of an indistinct object is not after all a clear one but an indistinct one. . . .

Elusive or not, such a view has a number of much less shadowy implications. One is that the comparative study of law cannot be a matter of reducing concrete differences to abstract commonalities. Another is that it cannot be a matter of locating identical phenomena masquerading under different names. And a third is that whatever conclusions it comes to must relate to the management of difference not to the abolition of it. Whatever the ultimate future holds—the universal reign of *gulag* justice or the final triumph of the market-mind—the proximate will be one not of a rising curve of legal uniformity, either across traditions or (something I have, so far, had rather to neglect here) within them, but their further particularization. The legal universe is not collapsing to a ball but expanding to a manifold; and we are headed rather more toward the convulsions of alpha than the resolutions of omega.

This view that things look more like flying apart than they do like coming together (one I would apply to the direction of social change generally these days, not just to law), opposes, of course, some of the leading doctrines in contemporary social science: that the world is growing more drearily modern—McDonald's on the Champs Elysées, punk rock in China; that there is an intrinsic evolution from *Gemeinschaft* to *Gesellschaft*, traditionalism to rationalism, mechanical solidarity to organic solidarity, status to contract; that post capitalist infrastructure in the form of multinational corporations and computer technology will soon shape the minds of Tongans and Yemenis to a common pattern. But it opposes as well, or at least raises doubts about, a leading view concerning the social potency of law: namely that it depends upon normative consensus.

At the end of the foregoing excerpt, Geertz takes what appears to be a controversial position when he opposes the "consensus" theory of law and seems to reject the claim that law reflects community values. However, a closer reading shows that Geertz finds "more than a grain of truth" in this claim.[156] His point is that the consensus theory neglects the creative role of law, along with other symbols and beliefs. Law is "constructive," "constitutive," and "formational."[157] It is not a mere instrumental means to an end but can hold grander visions for society.[158] Furthermore, when the creative role of law is thus understood and the effort is other-oriented, an expansion of the established means of discourse in the comparative study of law should result, as well as tolerance for cultural heterogeneity and normative dissensus.[159]

Conclusion

What Geertz terms the "hermeneutics of legal pluralism" calls for a form of Gadamerian intercultural dialogue, even within cultures that contain incommensurably opposing views. The hope here is that their respective horizons can be fused and understanding may be forged, given that law is a species of social imagination and given its imaginative force. A certain measure of uncertainty will be generated during this dialogue, but, in the fashion of Wittgenstein, not only is this no bar to continuing the dialogue; in fact we have no other choice.

> An hermeneutics of legal pluralism—an attempt to represent Ethiopic situations, whether in the Third World, the Second, or . . the First, in a reasonably intelligible fashion—does not imply [that] everything counter, original, spare, strange, can be blankly and neutrally said. . . .
>
> But a serious effort to define ourselves by locating ourselves among different others—others neither distanced as Martians, discredited as Primitives, nor disarmed as universal Everypersons, bent like us on sex and survival—involves quite genuine perils, not the least of which are intellectual entropy and moral paralysis. The double perception that ours is but one voice among many and that, as it is the only one we have, we must needs speak with it, is very difficult to maintain. What has been well called the long conversation of mankind may be growing so cacophonous that ordered thought of any sort, much less the turning of local forms of legal sensibility into reciprocal commentaries, mutually deepening, may become impossible. But however that may be, there is, so it seems to me, no choice. The primary question, for any cultural institution anywhere, now that nobody is leaving anybody else alone and isn't ever again going to, is not whether everything is going to come seamlessly together or whether, contrarywise, we are all going to persist

156. Geertz, *Local Knowledge*, *supra* note 153, at 218.

157. *Id.*

158. *Id.* at 231.

159. *Id.* at 225.

sequestered in our separate prejudices. It is whether human beings are going to continue to be able, in Java or Connecticut, through law, anthropology, or anything else, to imagine principled lives they can practicably lead.[160]

160. *Id.* at 225, 234.

Chapter 8

Postmodern Ethnographies in Normativity

The term "postmodernism" was first used in architecture in the late 1940s[1] to represent a movement that rejected modernist industrial designs.[2] It later spread to the social sciences, particularly to studies of literature and society.[3] As a social and intellectual movement, postmodernism rejects the modern era's faith in human reason and challenges its espousal of the inevitability of human progress.[4] Postmodernism has thus rejected claims to linear progress of knowledge by challenging notions of objectivity, predictability and permanence, "not simply as a gesture of political opposition but more particularly as an acknowledgement of the indeterminate structuration of the lifeworld."[5] These critiques of objectivity and indeterminacy have challenged many of our basic beliefs about norms and normativity as seen below.

Postmodernism today is a political critique as well as a social and intellectual movement. Because postmodernists emphasize the social construction of knowledge, they argue that all knowledge is "constructed out of unequal, or hegemonic, relations of power among people."[6] Generally, Lawrence Kuznar describes the primary tenets of postmodernism as

(1) an elevation of text and language as the fundamental phenomena of existence,
(2) the application of literary analysis to all phenomena,
(3) a questioning of reality and representation,
(4) a critique of metanarratives,
(5) an argument against method and evaluation,
(6) an advocacy of polyvocality,
(7) a focus upon power relations and hegemony, and
(8) a general critique of Western institutions and knowledge.[7]

---

1. Marvin Harris, Theories of Culture in Postmodern Times 153 (1999).

2. Lawrence A. Kuznar, Reclaiming a Scientific Anthropology 69 (1977).

3. *Id.*

4. Roy Boyne & Ali Rattansi, *The Theory and Politics of Postmodernism: By Way of an Introduction*, *in* Postmodernism and Society 1 (Roy Boyne & Ali Rattansi eds., 1990).

5. Bruce A. Arrigo, *The Peripheral Core of Law and Criminology: On Postmodern Social Theory and Conceptual Integration*, 12 Just. Q. 447, 452 (1995).

6. Kuznar, *supra* note 2, at 82.

7. *Id.* at 125.

Postmodernism and Anthropology

These ideas gained a foothold in anthropology in the 1960s and 1970s. Anthropology is fertile disciplinary ground for postmodern thinking because it is "unavoidably a political and ethical discipline."[8] Thus, legal ethnography and normative ethnography in general are especially amenable to postmodernism's tenets because of the cultural forces and power relations deeply intertwined in the "icons of modernist justice."[9] Bruce Arrigo contends that "embedded in the language of expressions such as 'burdens of *proof*,' 'a demand for *factual evidence*,' '*actual* legal intent,' '*expert* testimony,' '*causes* of crime,' and 'the *reasonable* wo/man standard' are notions of power, conveying only certain truths and representing the ideology of the male-centered master *discourse*."[10] This leads Marvin Harris to conclude that for postmodernists, " 'reasonable' ways are always brutally unfair to somebody" because the "reason" and "truth" that guide modernists are always embedded in power relations.[11] The political critique of postmodern ethnography, particularly its portrayal of law as a symbol of cultural hegemony, is discussed later in this chapter. Here it will suffice to emphasize the postmodernist juxtaposition of knowledge and power, which will be discussed later.

Whereas modernism embraced the idea that Western science and technology are the keys to human improvement,[12] postmodernism considers knowledge or science as an "ideological product embedded in a particular cultural context."[13] Thus, scientific truth viewed through a postmodern lens is at best "persuasive fiction."[14] Rather than seeking scientific knowledge, postmodernism seeks "narrative knowledge."[15] As Arrigo argues, "Truth, justice, reason, progress, and other similar abstractions are based on myths, symbols, and metaphors representing the historicity of a given culture as an incomplete and unfolding life story."[16] That is, postmodernism seeks to include the narratives and voices that have been excluded from the histories of a particular culture's stories of truth, justice, reason, and progress. Postmodern knowledge is narrative because it is relational, not discrete; "meaning is contingent, not certain"; and "understanding is fragmented, not complete."[17] The narratives of the excluded that postmodern ethnography seeks to unveil (as seen below) are those of the poor, the unrepresented working classes, ethnic minorities, and peoples of developing countries, and so on.

---

8. *Id.* at 89 (quoting Dell Hymes, Reinventing Anthropology 48 (1974)).

9. Arrigo, *supra* note 5, at 461.

10. *Id.*

11. Harris, *supra* note 1, at 155.

12. Marshall Berman, All That Is Solid Melts into Air 16 (1982).

13. Harris, *supra* note 1, at 154.

14. *Id.*

15. Arrigo, *supra* note 5, at 461.

16. *Id.*

17. *Id.*

The claim that reality is uncertain, contingent, and/or fragmented is directly related to postmodernism's rejection of the conception of the all-knowing "subject" of the modernist era and its attendant subject/object distinction. By this logic, the subject is represented by an "I"—a consciousness embodied in the person of an observer. Hence:

> The Western conception of the person as a bounded, unique, more or less integrated motivational and cognitive universe, a dynamic center of awareness, emotion, judgment, and action organized into a distinctive whole and set contrastively both against other such wholes and against its social and natural background.[18]

This notion of subject as person, endowed with cognitive abilities and the capacity to reason and make judgments, is contrasted with "other such wholes," namely "objects" found in society and in nature, which exist independently of persons and can be apprehended by the senses.

The philosophical origin of this conception is the Cartesian dualism of mind and body, *res cogitans* and *res extensa*.[19] This fundamental dualism, which has dogged Western philosophy since the 1600s, conceives subject and object to exist independently of each other. This distinction is rejected by postmodern thinking, which in some circles has given rise to the notion of the "death" of the subject.[20]

The Death—and Resurrection—of the Subject in Postmodern Anthropology

The subject/object distinction is foundational to modernist thinking. As originally conceived, it was not only applicable to one's observation of material reality (*e.g.*, things, trees, people) but also, equally, to one's observation of immaterial reality (*e.g.*, ideas, goodness, justice, culture). Anthropological postmodernism (APM) rejects such clear-cut distinctions, especially between subject and object, in favor of the view that individual subjects are neither autonomous nor self-constituting.[21] First, subjects are not autonomous because they never exist independently from their environment; more to the point, subjects never exist independently of objects. As soon as a subject begins to observe something, it becomes part of the reality of the thing being observed; it no longer exists independently from the object, and vice versa. Second, subjects are not self-constituting; that is, they are what they are only in terms of their environment and are constituted by their environment. Even the conscious "I" of self-expression—the personality—has become that only in reaction to, and

18. Clifford Geertz, Local Knowledge: Further Essays in Interpretative Anthropology 59 (1983).

19. *See* Isaak Dore, The Epistemological Foundations of Law 315 n. 47, 324 (2007).

20. *Id.* at 845, 847.

21. *See* Arrigo, *supra* note 5, at 454–55.

is dependent on, outside stimuli and factors that are truly formative. Indeed, one cannot identify the "I" until one encounters another person—a "Thou"—to whom the former addresses itself.

The very definition of subject thus necessarily includes what has previously been thought of as separate from its object. From the perspective of APM, ethnographers inevitably become part of the culture they are observing, and the culture becomes part of them. It is impossible for ethnographers to separate themselves from the reality they are observing, nor can they take on the mantle of a third-party "objective" observer. Instead, a constitutive interplay is at work among all components of reality, and although the individual components may be separable and distinguishable for certain purposes, the modernist subject/object distinction proves itself to be too neat at best and false at worst.

Laura Nader captures the interplay between subject and environment through what she calls "the mutuality of the gaze" between the ethnographer and the observed culture. Ethnographers should not reach their conclusions exclusively though their own value systems; rather, their conclusions should be considered in the comparative context of, and be informed by, the value system(s) of the cultures they are observing.

> Even though one may not see oneself as a comparativist, thinking comparatively is probably universal. When we look at others objectively, we cannot help but at least implicitly be comparing what we see with what we already know. In the 1980s, I wrote about comparative consciousness arguing that without making explicit our implicit comparisons the validity of our work was diminished. I used as illustrations what the West notices about the conditions (legal and otherwise) of Islamic women and what Islam may observe about women in the West. I recognized "the mutuality" of the gaze—each seeing the other as repressive—legally and otherwise. For example, Western legal observers see plural marriage as impinging on women's status, while Islamic legal scholars might argue that such arrangements come with legal responsibilities while having mistresses in Europe does not.[22]

The untidiness (if not the falsity) of the subject/object distinction is exposed by APM's approach to describing culture "from the native's point of view." Geertz, who can be classified as one of APM's pioneers, asserts that "The ethnographer does not, and ... largely cannot, perceive what his informants perceive."[23] He reaches this conclusion because he believes that natives have an "experience-near" perspective of their culture, whereas the ethnographer has only an "experience-distant" conception. Experience-near knowledge is produced by internal categories of cognition of the natives that are not shared by the outsider. If the latter tries to be "the chameleon fieldworker, perfectly self-tuned to his exotic surroundings, a walking miracle of

---

22. Laura Nader, *What the Rest Think of the West—Legal Dimensions*, 32 Hasting Int'l. & Comp. L. Rev. at 765, 766 (2009).

23. Geertz, *supra* note 18, at 58.

empathy, tact, patience, and cosmopolitanism,"[24] he is only acting out a myth and creating the illusion that he is representing the native point of view.[25] Referring to natives, Geertz remarks:

> In one sense, of course, no one knows this better than they do themselves; hence the passion to swim in the stream of their experience, and the illusion afterward that one somehow has. But in another sense, that simple truism is simply not true. People use experience-near concepts spontaneously, unselfconsciously, as it were colloquially; they do not, except fleetingly and on occasion, recognize that there are any "concepts" involved at all. That is what experience-near means—that ideas and the realities they inform are naturally and indissolubly bound up together. What else could you call a hippopotamus? Of course the gods are powerful, why else would we fear them? The ethnographer does not, and, in my opinion, largely cannot, perceive what his informants perceive. What he perceives, and that uncertainly enough, is what they perceive "with"—or "by means of," or "through" . . . or whatever the word should be.[26]

For these reasons, APM seeks to clarify who is the knowing subject in situations in which the ethnographer tries to "swim in the stream" of the experience of the natives (*i.e.*, the native him- or herself or the ethnographer), and who is the object of observation. If the natives are the object of observation, the ethnographer must face the challenge of giving a true picture of native life without, as experience-distant observer, possessing the "spontaneous" and "unselfconscious" cognitive categories of the natives.

The mission of the ethnographer, however, is not without hope. At the end of the foregoing passage, Geertz suggests that the fieldworker must strive to unearth how the natives understand their lives, that is, by searching out the means through or with which they perceive themselves. This involves "searching out and analyzing the symbolic forms—words, images, institutions, behaviors—in terms of which, in each place, people actually represented themselves to themselves and to one another."[27]

The Concept of Person as Subject: Case Studies in APM

The concept of person as subject is the vehicle by which Geertz proposes to describe three native cultural viewpoints; it is the symbolic form of analysis for each culture, Javanese, Balinese, and Moroccan. Geertz justifies his choice of symbol on the ground that the concept of person (*i.e.*, what a human individual is) is universal and therefore cross-culturally applicable.[28]

---

24. *Id.* at 56.
25. *Id.* at 58.
26. *Id.*
27. *Id.* at 59.
28. *Id.* at 60.

True to this thesis, Geertz demonstrates the importance of personhood and identity in all three cultures. He demonstrates that (in contrast to the West) the subject is normatively constituted by culture in these societies in the sense that she acquires not only her identity and place through culture, but also internalizes certain behavioral norms. At the same time, he promotes the thesis that the Western conception of the person or subject as a "dynamic centre of awareness," endowed with certain cognitive abilities and the capacity to reason and make judgments, is unique to Western culture. Therefore, he concludes that attempts to understand personhood in other cultures within the framework of the Western conception of person are inappropriate. Because every culture has its own categories of selfhood, ideas of selfhood in Java, Bali, and Morocco would naturally be not only radically different from those in the West but also different from each other.

A. Personhood in Java

In Java, a person is defined in two realms: inside and outside. "Inside" refers to "the felt realm of human experience" and "outside" to "the observed realm of human behavior."[29] Geertz is quick to point out that these contrasts neither correspond to the Western subject/object distinction nor parallel the Western soul/body distinction. The inside refers not to an individual's own detached experience, but rather to "the emotional life of human beings taken generally."[30] Individuality is "effaced," meaning that experience is identical for all persons. By the same token, outside refers not to the body (of one's self or others) as "object" but rather to outward behavior in the forms of "external actions, movements, postures, speech."[31]

In short, the two realms denote a bifurcated conception of the self: inward feelings and outward actions. The two need to be properly balanced so that the total person (in thought/emotion and behavior/action) reflects desirable moral values and avoids undesirable ones. Desirable values fall under the general category of *alus*, whose subset includes values such as "smooth," "pure," "refined," or "subtle." Undesirable values fall under the general category of *kasar*, the subset of which includes values such as "vulgar," "coarse," or "insensitive."

Geertz believes that smoothness on the inside is achieved through religious discipline, and smoothness on the outside is achieved by following rules of etiquette. He cites as an example a young man who had just lost his beloved wife, yet did not express his sorrow but instead greeted everyone with a smile and apologized for his wife's absence. Geertz contrasts this behavior with the kind of grief-related behavior Western culture might expect, which would be based on the sincere expression of deeply negative feelings. In Java, by contrast, a person's external expression must correspond to social norms rather than individual feelings and thoughts. These social norms have

29. GEERTZ, *supra* note 18, at 60.

30. *Id.*

31. *Id.* at 60–61.

a "force of law"[32] so powerful that they efface individuality *via* voluntary suppression of individual thoughts and feelings. The grieving widower, for example, could not only not show his grief but also had to hide his pain to the point of denying it.

Clifford Geertz, *"From the Native's Point of View": On the Nature of Anthropological Understanding*, *in* Clifford Geertz, Local Knowledge: Further Essays in Interpretative Anthropology 55, 59–62 (1983).

In Java . . . life was altogether far from promising . . . . Yet in the midst of this depressing scene there was an absolutely astonishing intellectual vitality, a philosophical passion really, and a popular one besides, to track the riddles of existence right down to the ground. Destitute peasants would discuss questions of freedom of the will, illiterate tradesmen discoursed on the properties of God, common laborers had theories about the relations between reason and passion, the nature of time, or the reliability of the senses. And, perhaps most importantly, the problem of the self—its nature, function, and mode of operation—was pursued with the sort of reflective intensity one could find among ourselves in only the most recherché settings indeed.

The central ideas in terms of which this reflection proceeded, and which thus defined its boundaries and the Javanese sense of what a person is, were arranged into two sets of contrasts, at base religious, one between "inside" and "outside," and one between "refined" and "vulgar." These glosses are, of course, crude and imprecise; determining exactly what the terms involved signified, sorting out their shades of meaning, was what all the discussion was about. But together they formed a distinctive conception of the self which, far from being merely theoretical, was the one in terms of which Javanese in fact perceived one another and, of course, themselves.

The "inside"/"outside" words, *batin* and *lair* . . . refer on the one hand to the felt realm of human experience and on the other to the observed realm of human behavior. . . . *Batin*, the "inside" word, does not refer to a separate seat of encapsulated spirituality detached or detachable from the body, or indeed to a bounded unit at all, but to the emotional life of human beings taken generally. It consists of the fuzzy, shifting flow of subjective feeling perceived directly in all its phenomenological immediacy but considered to be, at its roots at least, identical across all individuals, whose individuality it thus effaces. And similarly, *lair*, the "outside" word, has nothing to do with the body as an object, even an experienced object. Rather, it refers to that part of human life which, in our culture, strict behaviorists limit themselves to studying—external actions, movements, postures, speech—again conceived as in its essence invariant from one individual to the next. These two sets of phenomena—inward feelings and outward actions—are then regarded not

32. *Id.* at 61.

as functions of one another but as independent realms of being to be put in proper order independently.

It is in connection with this "proper ordering" that the contrast between *alus*, the word meaning "pure," "refined," "polished," "exquisite," "ethereal," "subtle," "civilized," "smooth," and *kasar*, the word meaning "impolite," "rough," "uncivilized," "coarse," "insensitive," "vulgar," comes into play. The goal is to be *alus* in both the separated realms of the self. In the inner realm this is to be achieved through religious discipline, much but not all of it mystical. In the outer realm, it is to be achieved through etiquette, the rules of which here are not only extraordinarily elaborate but have something of the force of law. Through meditation the civilized man thins out his emotional life to a kind of constant hum; through etiquette, he both shields that life from external disruptions and regularizes his outer behavior in such a way that it appears to others as a predictable, undisturbing, elegant, and rather vacant set of choreographed motions and settled forms of speech.

There is much more to all of this, because it connects up to both an ontology and an aesthetic. But so far as our problem is concerned, the result is a bifurcate conception of the self, half ungestured feeling and half unfelt gesture. An inner world of stilled emotion and an outer world of shaped behavior confront one another as sharply distinguished realms unto themselves, any particular person being but the momentary locus, so to speak, of that confrontation, a passing expression of their permanent existence, their permanent separation, and their permanent need to be kept in their own order. Only when you have seen, as I have, a young man whose wife—a woman he had in fact raised from childhood and who had been the center of his life—has suddenly and inexplicably died, greeting everyone with a set smile and formal apologies for his wife's absence and trying, by mystical techniques, to flatten out, as he himself put it, the hills and valleys of his emotion into an even, level plain ("That is what you have to do," he said to me, "be smooth inside and out") can you come, in the face of our own notions of the intrinsic honesty of deep feeling and the moral importance of personal sincerity, to take the possibility of such a conception of selfhood seriously and appreciate, however inaccessible it is to you, its own sort of force.

Conclusion

This study of personhood in Java shows, first, that the (unique) Javanese concept of person is the symbol through which Geertz, the Western subject, peers at his object, Javanese culture. Second, it shows that the Javanese person is not the knowing subject as understood in Western culture. Third, what confers personhood on an individual in Java is not so much his cognitive universe or his ability to reason and make judgments (as in Western culture) but his ability to harmonize his bifurcated self (*i.e.*, his "inner world of stilled emotion" and his "outer world of shaped behavior") in conformity with the Javanese values of smoothness and good etiquette. In short, the person is normatively constituted by Javanese culture.

B. Selfhood in Bali

Geertz's second non-Western notion of selfhood comes from Bali, where there is a similar normative relationship between personhood and culture. A person is important not for any individual characteristics or skills they possess but because of their place in the social order and the roles they play within it. The human person is viewed as "an appropriate representative of a generic type, not a unique creature with a private fate."[33] Each generic type has a socially assigned role to act out in life. Such acting out is done through a set of observable symbolic forms. These forms constitute a repertoire of designations and titles derived from birth order, kinship terms, gender terms, and so on. These in turn disclose a complex set of acceptable cultural practices and terminology. Each person is but the temporary occupant of an otherwise permanent social position with its own socially expected role. Each such role is permanent and thus standardized. The standardization of roles tends to efface biological, historical, psychological, and emotional individuality.

Geertz uses the way children are named in Bali as an example. Every child is given a birth-order name that implies whether he or she is first-born, second-born, and so on. After the fourth-born, the cycle begins again, so a fifth child would also be a first-born. Because dead children and stillborn children are also named in this way, the name of any child may reveal nothing about the place that he or she holds in the actual birth order (*e.g.*, a "second-born" child may actually be older than the "first-born" in the same family). Geertz concludes that these names, like all the other titles and designations, serve to emphasize "the most time-saturated aspects of the human condition."[34]

The worst fate for an individual in Balinese society is to experience *lek* (often translated as "shame"). Geertz prefers "stage fright"—the fear that the illusion of one's given place in the ordered world will not be maintained—"that the actor will show through his part."[35] A person's cultural location commits him or her to a role; therefore, nothing could be worse than to fail in that role.

Clifford Geertz, *"From the Native's Point of View": On the Nature of Anthropological Understanding, in* Clifford Geertz, Local Knowledge: Further Essays in Interpretative Anthropology 55, 62–64 (1983).

What is philosophy in Java is theater in Bali.

As a result, there is in Bali a persistent and systematic attempt to stylize all aspects of personal expression to the point where anything idiosyncratic, anything characteristic of the individual merely because he is who he is physically, psychologically, or biographically, is muted in favor of his assigned place in the continuing and, so it is thought, never-changing

33. *Id.* at 63.

34. *Id.* at 64.

35. *Id.*

pageant that is Balinese life. . . . There is no make-believe; of course players perish, but the play does not, and it is the latter, the performed rather than the performer, that really matters.

Again, all this is realized not in terms of some general mood the anthropologist in his spiritual versatility somehow captures, but through a set of readily observable symbolic forms: an elaborate repertoire of designations and titles. The Balinese have at least a half-dozen major sorts of labels, ascriptive, fixed, and absolute, which one person can apply to another (or, of course, to himself) to place him among his fellows. There are birth-order markers, kinship terms, caste titles, sex indicators, teknonyms, and so on and so forth, each of which consists not of a mere collection of useful tags but a distinct and bounded, internally very complex, terminological system. When one applies one of these designations or titles (or, as is more common, several at once) to someone, one therefore defines him as a determinate point in a fixed pattern, as the temporary occupant of a particular, quite untemporary, cultural locus. To identify someone, yourself or somebody else, in Bali is thus to locate him within the familiar cast of characters—"king," "grandmother," "third-born," "Brahman"—of which the social drama is, like some stock company roadshow piece—*Charley's Aunt* or *Springtime for Henry*—inevitably composed.

The drama is of course not farce, and especially not transvestite farce, though there are such elements in it. It is an enactment of hierarchy, a theater of status. But that, though critical, is unpursuable here. The immediate point is that, in both their structure and their mode of operation, the terminological systems conduce to a view of the human person as an appropriate representative of a generic type, not a unique creature with a private fate. To see how they do this, how they tend to obscure the mere materialities—biological, psychological, historical—of individual existence in favor of standardized status qualities would involve an extended analysis. But perhaps a single example, the simplest further simplified, will suffice to suggest the pattern.

All Balinese receive what might be called birth-order names. There are four of these, "first-born," "second-born," "third-born," "fourth-born," after which they recycle, so that the fifth-born child is called again "first-born," the sixth "second-born," and so on. Further, these names are bestowed independently of the fates of the children. . . . The birth-order naming system does not identify individuals as individuals, nor is it intended to; what it does is to suggest that, for all procreating couples, births form a circular succession of "firsts," "seconds," "thirds," and "fourths," an endless four-stage replication of an imperishable form. . . . All the designation and title systems, so I would argue, function in the same way: they represent the most time-saturated aspects of the human condition . . .

Nor is this sense the Balinese have of always being on stage a vague and ineffable one either. It is, in fact, exactly summed up in what is surely one of their experience-nearest concepts: *lek*. *Lek* has been variously translated

> or mistranslated ("shame" is the most common attempt); but what it really means is close to what we call stage fright. Stage fright consists, of course, in the fear that, for want of skill or self-control, or perhaps by mere accident, an aesthetic illusion will not be maintained, that the actor will show through his part. . . . In Bali, the case is the same: what is feared is that the public performance to which one's cultural location commits one will be botched and that the personality—as we would call it but the Balinese, of course, not believing in such a thing, would not—of the individual will break through to dissolve his standardized public identity. When this occurs, . . . men become suddenly . . . locked in mutual embarrassment, as though they had happened upon each other's nakedness. It is the fear of faux pas, rendered only that much more probable by the extraordinary ritualization of daily life, that keeps social intercourse on its deliberately narrowed rails and protects the dramatistical sense of self against the disruptive threat implicit in the immediacy and spontaneity even the most passionate ceremoniousness cannot fully eradicate from face-to-face encounters.

Conclusion

As in the case of Java, one can easily distinguish the Balinese concept of selfhood from its Western counterpart. The self in Bali is culturally constituted in terms of role-playing. In both Java and Bali, individuality and emotion are suppressed in favor of wider social goals. In Java, those goals are essentially moral as shown by the injunction against vulgar conduct and the promotion of smooth, pure, civilized conduct. In Bali, the roles have moral significance in that they collectively hold together the social fabric in desirable ways (although Geertz does not identify specific Balinese values as he does with Java). The difference is that personhood in Java is defined in terms of morality and etiquette, which have the force of law, whereas in Bali it is defined in terms of role-playing, which has an equal force of law.

C. Selfhood in Morocco

Geertz's third study of a culture through the symbol of selfhood is set in Morocco, which he describes as "a Wild West sort of place without the barrooms or the cattle drives."[36] Geertz focuses on the Moroccan practice of attaching some sort of relational concept, a *nisba*, to a person's name. The *nisba* often indicates place or tribe of origin (*e.g.*, Mujhammed Al-Sussi literally means "Mujhammed of the Sussi region"). Geertz observes that no matter how little one may know of someone in Morocco (*e.g.*, personal characteristics, wealth, location of residence), one will certainly know this relational part of his name. Therefore, he concludes that the people "gain their definition from associative relations they are imputed to have with the society that surrounds them. They are contextualized persons."[37] Of course, because everyone from the same place would share the same *nisba*, other *nisbas* are used within the

36. Geertz, *supra* note 18, at 64.

37. *Id.* at 66.

local community to differentiate persons. Thus, depending on context, within a single community the same person may be known by many different names or *nisbas*, such as with reference to occupation or religious orientation. Moroccans, Geertz writes, "do not float as bounded psychic entities, detached from their backgrounds and singularly named. As individualistic, even willful, as the Moroccans in fact are, their identity is an attribute they borrow from their setting."[38]

The *nisba* pattern of naming is no isolated custom; it is a highly complex linguistic nomenclature with morphological, grammatical, and semantic dimensions that engulf the total pattern of social interaction. This nomenclature has systemic normative consequences because it governs the domains within which people are distinguished from one another (*e.g.*, law, education, marriage, worship) and those in which they are connected (*e.g.*, work, politics, trade). The *nisba* nomenclature regulates the foregoing and at the same time balances its requirements by guaranteeing to the individual a relative freedom to pursue personal life and subjective experiences in privacy.

Clifford Geertz, *"From the Native's Point of View": On the Nature of Anthropological Understanding*, in Clifford Geertz, Local Knowledge—Further Essays in Interpretative Anthropology 65–68 (1983).

Yet no society consists of anonymous eccentrics bouncing off one another like billiard balls, and Moroccans, too, have symbolic means by which to sort people out from one another and form an idea of what it is to be a person....

Nisba itself, then, refers to a combination morphological, grammatical, and semantic process that consists in transforming a noun into what we would call a relative adjective but what for Arabs is just another sort of noun by adding *ī* (f., *īya*): *Sefrū*/Sefrou—*Sefrūwī*/native son of Sefrou; *Sūs*/region of southwestern Morocco—*Sūsī*/man coming from that region; ...

Thus, at one level, everyone in Sefrou has the same nisba, or at least the potential of it—namely, Sefroui. However, within Sefrou such a nisba, precisely because it does not discriminate, will never be heard as part of an individual designation. It is only outside of Sefrou that the relationship to that particular context becomes identifying. Inside it, he is an Adluni, Alawi, Meghrawi, Ngadi, or whatever. And similarly within these categories: there are, for example, twelve different nisbas (Shakibis, Zuinis, and so forth) by means of which, among themselves, Sefrou Alawis distinguish one another....

Now as with the Javanese inside/outside, smooth/rough phenomenological sort of reality dividing, and the absolutizing Balinese title system, the nisba way of looking at persons—as though they were outlines waiting to be filled in—is not an isolated custom, but part of a total pattern of social life.... It copes with it by distinguishing, with elaborate precision, the

38. *Id.* at 67.

contexts—marriage, worship, and to an extent diet, law, and education—within which men are separated by their dissimiltudes, and those—work, friendship, politics, trade—where, however warily and however conditionally, they are connected by them.

To such a social pattern, a concept of selfhood which marks public identity contextually and relativistically, but yet does so in terms—tribal, territorial, linguistic, religious, familial—that grow out of the more private and settled arenas of life and have a deep and permanent resonance there, would seem particularly appropriate. Indeed, the social pattern would seem virtually to create this concept of selfhood, for it produces a situation where people interact with one another in terms of categories whose meaning is almost purely positional, location in the general mosaic, leaving the substantive content of the categories, what they mean subjectively as experienced forms of life, aside as something properly concealed in apartments, temples, and tents. Nisba discriminations can be more specific or less, indicate location within the mosaic roughly or finely, and they can be adapted to almost any changes in circumstance. But they cannot carry with them more than the most sketchy, outline implications concerning what men so named as a rule are like. Calling a man a Sefroui is like calling him a San Franciscan: it classifies him, but it does not type him; it places him without portraying him.

It is the nisba system's capacity to do this—to create a framework within which persons can be identified in terms of supposedly immanent characteristics (speech, blood, faith, provenance, and the rest)—and yet to minimize the impact of those characteristics in determining the practical relations among such persons in markets, shops, bureaus, fields, cafés, baths, and roadways that makes it so central to the Moroccan idea of the self. Nisba-type categorization leads, paradoxically, to a hyperindividualism in public relationships, because by providing only a vacant sketch, and that shifting, of who the actors are—Yazghis, Adlunis, Buhadiwis, or whatever—it leaves the rest, that is, almost everything, to be filled in by the process of interaction itself. What makes the mosaic work is the confidence that one can be as totally pragmatic, adaptive, opportunistic, and generally ad hoc in one's relations with others—a fox among foxes, a crocodile among crocodiles—as one wants without any risk of losing one's sense of who one is. Selfhood is never in danger because, outside the immediacies of procreation and prayer, only its coordinates are asserted.

Conclusion

Viewed from the perspective of APM, like its Balinese (and possibly even Javanese) counterpart, Moroccan culture demonstrates a strong interaction between subject and object if "subject" is defined as the individual person and "object" is defined as social context (*i.e.*, culture). All Moroccan individuals are contextualized in terms of categories that are purely positional, so that they do not "float as bounded psychic entities" in the Western sense.[39] Thereby we may see that the notions of personhood or selfhood in all three cultures are radically different from their Western counterparts. Nonetheless, even if (as APM contends) the environment is what constitutes the subject, the three cultures (particularly those of Bali and Morocco) show that there can be no complete merger of subject and object. The subject, which is constituted only at birth in a particular social place or setting, remains so; its interface with culture does not result in complete effacement of individual personality. The Balinese recognize the constitutive nature of the environmental objects but retain a notion of the independence of the subject once it has been constituted by its environment. Moroccan culture similarly makes a deliberate effort to preserve privacy, in life and subjective experience (*e.g.*, in the domains of procreation and prayer), within the complex nomenclature of *nisba*.

The APM perspective may draw validation in two ways. First, the self is normatively constituted by culture in all three societies. Second, both Balinese and Javanese cultures (particularly the latter) show a distinct tendency to suppress individuality and emotion in favor of wider sociocultural imperatives. These conclusions bring up two additional issues. The first involves assessing the validity of the insight, taught by APM, that culture molds the subject and suppresses individuality. As we have seen, Sapir, Kroeber, Benedict, Mead, Steward, and others demonstrated the superior force of culture over the individual many decades before the emergence of postmodernist thought. The second issue, which is epistemological, concerns whether APM proposes a better methodology to represent accurately the native point of view or whether it claims that such representation is impossible. This issue involves the paradox, already noted, that arises from the status of ethnographer *qua* subject in the Western sense. Geertz himself believed that the ethnographer "cannot perceive what his informants perceive,"[40] yet proceeded to study Javanese, Balinese, and Moroccan cultures. He did so because, for him, "going native" does not mean "putting oneself into someone else's skin" (*i.e.*, acting like a native)[41] and "seeing" what such a native would see. Rather, he carried out his ethnographic mission by "searching out and analyzing the symbolic forms—words, images, institutions, behaviors—in terms of which, in each place, people actually represented themselves to themselves and to one another."[42]

For Geertz, peering at a culture through its symbolic forms compensates for the ethnographer's inability to "be" a native, which would mean thinking like the native and seeing what the native sees. He therefore claims that even if he cannot directly present an experience-near native point of view, he can present that same point of view inferentially through the study of a culture's symbolic forms. Geertz's belief in himself as the knowing subject in the classic Western sense thus remains intact, as does his belief in the "object" of his studies of Javanese, Balinese, and Moroccan cultures. At the same time, he engagingly presented three concepts of personhood

---

39. *See* text at note 38, *supra.*

40. *See* text at note 23, *supra.*

41. Geertz, *supra* note 18, at 58.

42. *Id.*

or subject that are different from their Western counterparts and from each other. This work should reassure the modernist who fears the death of his subject as a result of postmodernist revisionism; APM has resurrected the subject and preserves the subject/object distinction.

The foregoing sections focused on some postmodern themes of subject and object in terms of capturing the native point of view of a culture that is foreign or exotic to the ethnographer. The next section shifts focus from the foreign to the local (*i.e.*, ethnographic studies within the ethnographer's own culture), also known as the "reflexive" turn.[43] The focus on capturing a point of view is retained, but the vehicle for such capture is different. Just as Geertz used the symbol of self and personhood to peer at different cultures, a lawyer and cultural anthropologist team up to capture the layperson's perception of the American system of justice in the informal setting of small claims courts. Their vehicle for this endeavor is discourse: the actual language used by average laypersons, and the associative mental dispositions revealed thereby, as they seek justice in a court of law.

From "Going Native" to "Going Local": APM's Reflexive Turn

Part I

A good example of APM's move from studying the exotic-far to the familiar-near is the study of legal normativities in terms of power relations. In postmodernist spirit, John Conley and William O'Barr debunk the myths of the neutrality of the law, the impartiality of judges, and objective meaning in legal rules.[44] They do this not by using the case as the traditional unit of legal analysis but by presenting an ethnography of legal discourse among laypersons (hence the subtitle of their book). These authors rejected the case method because it gives a limited perspective of the law that is shaped only by the professional establishment, which is composed largely of lawyers and judges. The perspective of the layperson is thus entirely excluded. They contend that the narrowness of the case method is shown by its emphasis on winning and losing and the role of precedent (*i.e.*, rules and the "facts" at issue).[45]

Conley and O'Barr's ethnography of legal discourse, which involves more than 150 cases, presents a model of the encounter between the lay public and the legal system in informal small claims courts in the United States. Like traditional ethnography, their methodology focuses on inductive analysis through detailed and careful observation; the difference is that the approach treats discourse (or language) as its

---

43. John M. Conley & William M. O'Barr, *Legal Anthropology Comes Home: A Brief History of the Ethnographic Study of Law*, 27 Loy. L.A. L. Rev. 41, 48 (1993).

44. John M. Conley & William M. O'Barr, Rules versus Relationships: The Ethnography of Legal Discourse (1990).

45. *Id.* at 4.

object of study rather than merely its instrument of analysis.[46] The fact that Conley and O'Barr remain the knowing subjects in the classic Western sense confirms that the subject/object distinction is not problematic for APM.

Case Studies in the Ethnography of Legal Discourse

The case studies of Conley and O'Barr first reveal a dramatic dissonance in approach to law between laypersons and the professional legal establishment. Second is their division of lay discourse in law into two ideal types: rule-oriented discourse and relational discourse.[47] The former is couched in neutral terms that transcend individual need or social status to reveal a conception of law as a seamless web of objective rules that are routinely applied by impartial judges to specific facts. As one might imagine, this conception tends to resonate well with the professional legal establishment. All legal training, of lawyer and judge alike, is done around clusters of facts categorized and classified as cases, to which specific legal rules are applied to reach outcomes that can be trusted to be legally correct. Case law is constituted by judicial opinions that are presented as unproblematic applications of law through the process of legal reasoning; the goal of every student of the law is to master this process. This conception has come under increasing criticism in postmodern times but remains the dominant paradigm in the teaching and practice of law.

The relational orientation, by contrast, shows a predisposition on the part of the individual lay litigant to approach law and justice in a personalized manner. This approach is predicated on the idea of social interdependence from which rights, entitlements, and responsibilities flow. When this conception collides with that of the judge (particularly one who is rule-oriented), the latter's decision is incompatible with the litigant's relational orientation, and great frustration and alienation result.[48] In such situations, litigant and judge are playing two different "language games." What the litigant advances as a matter of truth, justice, and social responsibility is dismissed by the judge as irrelevant and inappropriate, and the litigant is treated as unprepared, imprecise, or even as "rambling, and straying from the central issues."[49] Given these parameters, lay litigants before a small claims court are likely to be untrained in the law and are therefore likely to be disappointed with their experience in court. In addition, such feelings and sentiments are more likely to appear in courts in which strict evidentiary rules do not impose constraints on what can be said or produced.

A. Relational Legal Discourse

The following excerpt is the partial testimony of a lay plaintiff with a relational disposition. The plaintiff (Rawls) had sued a neighbor (Bennett) for removing a hedge

---

46. *Id.* at xi.

47. *Id.* at ix, 58 *et seq.*

48. *Id.* at 58.

49. *Id.*

on her side of their common property line. Rawls's responses to the judge's questions reveal that she approached the matter in terms of social relations rather than legal doctrine. Her testimony is not on point and meanders into several anecdotal accounts of a personal nature that have nothing to do with the "legal issues" before the court.

JUDGE: You're alleging that these trees and, and the shrubs and apparently the hedge included were removed. When did this happen?

RAWLS: Oh, well now that happened this year. At uh—

JUDGE: And how did it happen?

RAWLS: Well I can, well, well I have to jump back because, uh, for three years when Mr. Bennett moved back—because he was there once before and then he moved and then he come back into that house—and all the time before—I have to say this though judge—because all the time before everybody took care of that hedge and they wouldn't let me take care of it. They trimmed it and I even went to Mr. Bennett when he was there before—

JUDGE: Wait a moment. Now the question that I asked you—and I would like to have you answer it—and that is how did the hedge get removed?

RAWLS: Well, um, Mr. Bennett said he told me when he moved back in, uh, because I was taking care of my trees coming up through the hedge, I was cutting them off and he told me not to do that. He said, "Don't do it," he said, "I'm going to have, the church is going to pay to take them out of there, because my wife wants to put a fence and plant roses on the other side." He said, "Is that alright with you?" I said, "I don't care what you do with it," you know, and I said, "If you need, uh, money for tools, maybe I can rent a tool and help in that respect because I can't dig," you know. And I said, "If you need uh, a tool to help you remove the hedge," I said, "uh, I will," well it wasn't the hedge then it was all the stumps underneath because he wanted that removed because he, his wife wanted the fence and she wanted roses on it. And so then three years went by and they let these trees grow up like you see the picture there. I think you've got it. And they're so big and then when he told me to stop taking them out because he was gonna take out that hedge, uh, the stumps, why uh, in the meantime I called a man and I had them, because I'm getting crippled up and I can't bend down sir, and here I was still taking out those trees and he wasn't coming to help me like he said he was. So then I had a man come—here Jim give him this—and I paid $45. There's the bill there and he cut it right off down level with the ground. Well, I knew that wouldn't take it but at least it would keep me for a little bit trying to get them tree things out of that shrubbery there. Well, um, Mr. Bennett, when he finally come out he said, "You know, that isn't going to do it," and that's when he told me, "My wife wants to put a fence," and he said, "You know that isn't going to do it. Those stumps are going to have to be taken out." And that's when I told him, and he said he would do it, "I and the church would

> take them out," and I, that's when I told him, "If you need, uh, money for a tool or something to help you. I'll pay for the tool or whatever." And he told, didn't do it, and so then I just had a, the Milehigh, uh, Tree Service come uh, uh, and um, a, and Mr., I had his name here—Mr., uh, Cook come and he come in the house and sat down with me and he looked at that and he said well he surely should help in the shrubbery in the back because there's shrubbery in the back that was over on my line that I've got to take out and I've got pictures of that too, sir. And he said he didn't know what the man or what the man was because the tree was dead why didn't he take it out? Well all he wants to do is harass me so he leaves it there so I have to keep taking the stuff out and bending over and using my trashcan, you know. This is something else. I only got one can. Why don't he pick up his own trash? And so I went ahead and paid it. He told me he would come if I need. He says, "I'll cut it when you need me." Yet I could never get this man. I tried to have him subpoenaed, yet I could never get him because I think Bennett got to him first. But, anyway I got the Milehigh Tree Service here for 275, and I got his mess in the backyard—if you want the pictures here—that's what I took them for. Did you give him the ones with the trees?[50]

A relational argument, as in Rawls' case, will probably be viewed as poorly pleaded from a legal perspective. Not only did Rawls not advance any specific legal rule or argument, she seemed more interested in complaining about Bennett's behavior as a neighbor. She was also unhelpful in establishing even the basic facts of her case, which led to the following comment from the authors of the study:

> Rawls's testimony typifies the tendency of relational account-givers to analyze and describe legal problems in terms of social relations rather than the kinds of rules that constitute legal doctrine. She rarely responds specifically to the issues raised in the judge's questions. Instead, his questions evoke lengthy digressions about the history of her relationship with Bennett. These digressions meander through time and place, drawing her audience ever deeper into her social world, but providing little information about the specific issues that are of interest to the court. Her account contains frequent references to personal status (e.g., . . . "I'm getting crippled up;" . . . "I only got one [trash] can"), items which are significant to her social situation but are irrelevant to the court's more limited and rule-centered agenda. Additionally, the account assumes that the listener shares her knowledge of background events and places. Although the assumption of shared knowledge is common and appropriate in familiar conversation, it creates difficulties for a stranger who is trying to extract a set of facts to apply strict legal rules to them. . . . One might wonder whether Rawls is less concerned about the dispute over

50. *Id.* at 61–63.

the hedge than finding a means of getting back at Bennett for the many injustices she feels he has done to her over the years.[51]

B. Rule-Oriented Legal Discourse

Next we contrast the foregoing illustration of relational discourse with testimony about a landlord-tenant dispute. The landlord (Broom) evicted a tenant (Grumman) and sued for back rent, late fees, and cleaning charges, as well as expenses for replacing a heating system the tenant had installed contrary to his wishes. Grumman, who denied that any back rent was due, claimed that an implicit agreement had been struck under which Broom would give Grumman credit for the value of the heating system. Broom's testimony, which is precise, is limited to the questions posed by the judge on calculating the rent and damages and on the reasons for replacing Grumman's furnace.

JUDGE: Alright. Now several other questions can be answered this way, what are the arithmetic parts of your 487? How did you get there and why?
BROOM: May I submit this as a—
JUDGE: Come right ahead. Mark this likewise for the plaintiff. This being a letter of June 29, '87 addressed to the defendant and uh, citing certain statutes and uh, rental for May '87 at the 375 plus the 50 late charge. Is, does the lease contain a provision for a late charge in that amount?
BROOM: Yes sir, your, your attention is directed to a—
JUDGE: A written-in portion about a third of the way down?
BROOM: Yes, sir. I said, "Postmarked after the fifth, add $50."
JUDGE: Then you're looking for recouping those first four days of June—
BROOM: Yes sir.
JUDGE:—at the rate of 12.50 and, without going through the arithmetic process, is that based on a 30-day month into 375?
BROOM: Yes it is.
JUDGE: The next is to clean up, and that turns into a $185 amount, including a dumpster for 125, broken glass, debris, and uh, the labor.
BROOM: 35 for dog feces on the floor, sir.
JUDGE: Alright sir. So that added in brings you to 310.
BROOM: Yes.
JUDGE: Then we're just going over the arithmetic. We're gonna back up to the 185 item just a moment. And labor to remove unauthorized gas service you had installed, labor, materials that he installed comes to 182. And then deducting the deposit brings you to a 487 figure. Then let's backup to, where's the furnace at this date?
BROOM: It's, it's discarded, was put in the dumpster, sir. . . .
JUDGE: Alright.

51. Conley and O'Barr, *supra* note 44, at 61.

BROOM: And if, he had called me and said, you know "Uh, Mr. Broom, can I take out your furnace and, your heating unit and put this in, that I obviously got left over from a job?", I would have said, "No, because I don't want that kind of a heating unit in my building because if you have gasoline or volatile fumes or anything of that nature in these areas, those fumes can lie on the floor and be sucked into this furnace." Now it might be one chance in a thousand, but I would rather have that furnace up in the air and it's my building and I certainly could decide what kind of heating I wanted. But instead without my permission, he took my heater out and installed this, this house-type of furnace. Now I understand, I know that he's gonna say, "You know, I incurred a lot of expense and time and labor and such as that to put this in." But my rebuttal is, "I didn't want that furnace and I don't think that uh. . . ." It cost me money then to, I had to go buy another heater. I hired some people to install the furnace. I had to first take his furnace out, all the ducting and all the grills and everything, I got rid of that and then I had to install this overhead furnace at my expense.[52]

Broom is clearly prepared to present the legal rules he believes to be at issue, including the rule that written contracts (*i.e.*, the lease) are binding. Broom's testimony also minimizes personal references with no bearing on the dispute and does not include reference to personal or social factors that could conceivably mitigate the terms of the lease. At the outset of the excerpt, he directs the court's attention to the specific provisions of the lease that justify a late charge of $50. He also responds directly to the judge's questions about damages.

Grumman's testimony, by contrast, clearly demonstrates a relational posture. He recites personal problems to explain why he did not pay the rent and offers a litany of complaints as to the poor condition of the leased building. He also fails to produce two critical documents, the first of which allegedly gave him extra time to stay in the building and the second of which allegedly contained the promise from Broom to give credit for the furnace.[53] Thus, from the legal perspective, the relational orientation makes for yet another poorly pleaded case.

GRUMMAN: Well, what it conc-, that the windows were broken when I went into the building and the window was cracked, the stool was leaking and I also fixed the stool on the other side and ran a copper line to the other side, which I never charged nobody for. I fixed the roof on the building, I fixed the roof on the shed back behind and I hauled all the trash off that was back behind the building.

JUDGE: Anything further sir?

GRUMMAN: Also my, at the time, he, when he served the three day notice, I went to my attorney because I couldn't be out of there in three days and my attorney contacted his attorney and asked his attorney for me to stay the additional four days right there.

---

52. *Id.* at 68–70.

53. *Id.* at 70–74.

JUDGE: What was that deal?
GRUMMAN: That everything would be fine and use the deposit because he was doing nothing, he wasn't standing by and had men standing by. Brown's right next door was empty and he wasn't doing anything with that building either.
JUDGE: Was this deal uh, reduced to writing?
GRUMMAN: Beg your pardon?
JUDGE: Was this reduced to writing, the deal to stay until the fourth of June? Did the lawyers put anything down on paper?
GRUMMAN: No, they, I don't think they did. They had an agreement between them. It cost me actually where I paid my attorney $200 for taking care of the matter, before this popped up.
JUDGE: Anything else you want me to know? Do you understand the nature of the claim, the plaintiff is seeking rent for uh, the month of May, and uh, for the removal, installation, removal of your furnace, the installation of the, a replacement and then the uh, clean up cost of 185 and the late charge.
GRUMMAN: I understand it. But I mean when he, when he offered to give me credit for that furnace and he took the other furnace that I took down, that I planned on reinstalling, at the time that I left.
JUDGE: What happened after this memo, which states, "I will give you credit for the heater that you've installed as a fixture"? What happened after that? Did anything get put down in writing, other than that lease?
GRUMMAN: I've got another, sir, I've got another letter that I cannot find where he was gonna sue me if I took the heater out of the building.[54]

Poor pleading puts Grumman at a clear disadvantage in court. He complains about the condition of the building, which he may have considered to be a mitigating factor. Instead, from the court's point of view, these facts are "extraneous." He testified that he had repaired a leaking toilet (by running a new copper line at his own expense) and the roof on a shed behind the building, had hauled off trash, and so on. These recitations were presumably done in the hope that the court (and the landlord) would find a reciprocal balance to offset the back rent. Indeed, the court could have independently used the principle of unjust enrichment to reduce Broom's figures, or it could have inferred an agreement of credit for work done from the conduct of the parties. However, Broom's rule-oriented discourse, together with the court's own natural bias toward it, ensured that Broom would prevail.

> The law would have permitted the judge to evaluate the case in terms other than those suggested by Broom. For example, he could have considered whether Broom was unjustly enriched by Grumman's uncompensated work on the building, or whether an agreement to credit Grumman for some of the value he added to the premises could be inferred from the parties' conduct. Once Broom provides a familiar framework, however, the judge works

54. Conley and O'Barr, *supra* note 44, at 73–74.

entirely within it. Grumman's plea to probe the underlying social relations evokes no response. Thus, Broom seems to benefit from approaching the court as a limited-purpose institution which deals most readily with issues that are presented in a rule-oriented format. Conversely, Grumman seems disadvantaged by his implicit assumption that the court has the willingness and ability to impose solutions on broader social problems.

What is particularly interesting is that the way that each party deals with the dispute in court appears to mirror the way that he dealt with it as it occurred. Grumman ignored such technicalities as leases, he did what he thought was socially appropriate, and he expected others to do the same. Broom, by contrast, ignored Grumman's social expectations, and instead took care to define all the terms of their relationship in writing. The radically different accounts given at trial epitomize these equally different approaches to life.[55]

Conclusion

According to APM, the two types of discourse and their normative consequences are functions of a person's socialization, depending on whether the sphere is public or private. According to Conley and O'Barr, gender roles are also a factor in that male socialization tends to focus on preparing men for public and business life, where attention to rules is the dominant concern.[56] The two authors also suggest that women, whose socialization may be different, may assume roles traditionally occupied by males (*e.g.*, in business and management) and therein adapt readily to rule-oriented postures.

In the end, the two paradigms are a function of social class rather than gender or race. APM, which usually defines social class in terms of political and economic power, argues that law is responsive primarily to the discourse of the dominant class, even as the official discourse of the law maintains a façade of neutrality. The dominant class has the skills and wherewithal to manipulate indeterminate legal doctrines to empower its political and economic interests. Thus the APM scholar would not be surprised that the landlord prevailed in the dispute just discussed and that the narrative of the layperson was excluded. The result would also confirm the overall thesis that the law is the instrument of the dominant classes.

Closely linked to the idea of law as power is the distinction between powerful and powerless speech. In the landlord/tenant dispute it was Broom, the landlord, who had the advantage of powerful speech; Grumman's speech style proved powerless. Powerless speech style is generally associated with the relational orientation, whereas its counterpart is associated with rule orientation. The burden of stylistic powerlessness tends to fall mostly on women, minorities, the poor, and the undereducated, who collectively compose the underprivileged class.

---

55. *Id.* at 78.

56. *Id.* at 79.

The social and political significance of the class factor can best be appreciated from the perspective of the critical legal studies movement. Critical legal scholars argue that law is the domain of a political and economic elite who manipulate indeterminate legal postulates in furtherance of their economic and ideological objectives. Under this view, rule-orientation could be characterized as an acquired skill which is the property of the literate and educated business and legal class. The mastery of rule-orientation is an instrument of class hegemony: the dominant class maintains its authority over those below it by seeing to it that legal and business affairs follow a system of logic that members of the subject classes have little opportunity to acquire. This system of control is both subtle and particularly effective because rule-oriented decision making has an appearance of strict neutrality. Thus, those whose relational orientation denies them access to legal and economic power derive false comfort from the illusion of a system that treats all people equally.

The factor of race may operate in a similar manner because it is still the case that disproportionate numbers of blacks in America are poor, undereducated, and relegated to occupations on the peripheries of economic and political power.

The distribution of the rule and relational orientations appears to parallel the distribution of powerful and powerless speech styles that we described in a previous program of research. . . . Our experimental research on speech style and its effects on legal decisionmakers demonstrated that powerless speakers are believed significantly less often than their powerful counterparts. We find a convergence of the tendencies toward the powerless speech style and the relational orientation, and a complementary convergence of rule-orientation and the absence of powerless stylistic features. Thus, it may be that the burden of stylistic powerlessness, which falls most heavily on women, minorities, the poor, and the uneducated, is compounded on the discourse level by the tendency among the same groups to organize their legal arguments around concerns that the courts are likely to treat as irrelevant.[57]

From "Going Native" to "Going Local": APM's Reflexive Turn

Part II

We now consider APM's conception of power, assuming that law is the instrument of the class(es) that have the greatest power. This section presents an anatomy of power in an anthropological context (*i.e.*, one that retains a "local" or nonexotic focus). The various visible and invisible methods and mechanisms of the deploy-

57. *Id.* at 80–81.

ment of power in U.S. culture, the interests it promotes, and its normative consequences are central to this focus.

The goal of APM's anatomy of power is analogous to the ethnography of legal discourse, which debunks the myths of the neutrality of law, impartiality of judges, and objective meaning of rules. By analyzing power as a hegemonic or controlling force, APM seeks, in keeping with the postmodernist spirit, to dispel a number of hegemonic myths both locally and globally. Among these myths are that the *status quo* is both normal and natural, that the beneficiaries of power are somehow its rightful custodians, and that the economy and its growth are as impersonal as they are natural and therefore uncontrollable. However, acceptance of the idea that economic and/or social relations are matters beyond individual control necessarily entails a corresponding acceptance of powerlessness. Just as powerlessness finds its natural ally in powerless speech/discourse, so does powerful speech find its domain in the economically powerful classes. One anthropologist illustrated the notion of economic powerlessness as follows:

> In 1994 . . . just ten individuals helped direct 37 American companies whose combined assets of $2 trillion represented nearly 10 percent of all corporate assets in U.S. for profit businesses. As long as everyone believes that the economy is beyond human control and can grow forever, the elite will be able to resist more equitable redistributive change.[58]

Another noted anthropologist has presented a sophisticated anatomy of power as a hegemonic force in U.S. culture through the notion of controlling processes, as described in the following section.

Power as Hegemonic Force in U.S. Culture: Case Studies

As the subtitle of her Mintz Lecture indicates, Nader's goal was to trace the dynamic components of power in U.S. culture. She does this by showing how certain cultural notions such as harmony, free choice, civilization, beauty, and science become mechanisms or controlling processes for exercising power in the United States. She demonstrates these normative consequences through three ethnographic case studies of U.S. culture. These studies were designed to show how power is constructed and exercised, how certain social and cultural dogmas are configured, and how entire segments of the American population are controlled and subtly persuaded to accept these dogmas as normal and natural.[59] When such dogmas become normalized, she concludes, the primary beneficiaries are the economically powerful classes.

Nader, who uses a neo-Foucaultian approach to conceiving power, does not view power as confined merely in persons and institutions, but rather as a force that permeates all aspects of social life "with no real center and no one employing power

---

58. John H. Bodley, Comment on Laura Nader, *Controlling Processes: Tracing the Dynamic Components of Power*, 38 Curr. Anthropol., 711, 725 (1997).

59. Alicia Barabas, Comment to Nader, *Controlling Processes*, *supra* note 58, at 723.

tactics."[60] Like Foucault, Nader asserts that when certain codes of behavior are internalized (or "normalized," in Foucault's terminology) they give meaning to and can even transform institutionalized social relations and patterns of consumption.

Nader proves this thesis through ethnographic accounts in law, medicine, and museology. In doing so, she is mindful that "anthropologists (just like other citizens) are conditioned by their own society."[61] This orientation might have certain implications for the subject/object distinction, particularly whether anthropologists studying their own citizens are conditioned by their own societies and whether this conditioning merges subjects with their objects. Nader is mindful of this pitfall but nevertheless perseveres with her domestic/local ethnographic agenda. Like Geertz, she is studying her own culture through the filter of certain cultural symbols (*e.g.*, the controlling processes of harmony ideology, beauty ideology, and civilization). Geertz too admitted that the ethnographer cannot know the native point of view (in his case, of foreign cultures); however, he felt that this did not invalidate the mission as long as the ethnographer did not try "to get into someone else's skin" (*i.e.*, try to be a native) but instead studied them through the filter of their cultural symbols.[62]

Geertz feared his inability to have an experience-near point of view due to his status as a nonnative. In terms of Nader's ethnography, we might assume that she, as a native citizen, would necessarily have an experience-near perspective. She raises the same concern, however.

A. Power as Hegemonic Force in Law

Nader gives an anatomy of power as a hegemonic force in U.S. law through her harmony model, which she developed in the 1950s and 1960s during her studies of Zapotec mountain culture in Mexico. She hypothesized that the harmony model functioned as a tool for pacification in the service of European (*i.e.*, Spanish) colonization as well as for achieving a coercive compromise and consensus that would maintain local autonomy and ward off intervention by the central government of Mexico.[63] Thus, the Zapotec converted a hegemonic tool of the Spanish Crown into a counterhegemonic mechanism of control in order to preserve local autonomy.

Nader's ethnographic research worldwide enabled her to trace the origins of what she calls "ideology of harmony" to the work of European Christian missionaries in tandem with European colonial conquests. Whereas the missionaries preached conciliation and compromise as the principal component of "Euro-Christian harmony ideology,"[64] Nader found analogous harmony ideologies in the legal workings of modern Western European democratic states as well. Such ideologies then became entrenched in schools, hospitals, workplaces, and other public and private places.

---

60. Nader, *Controlling Processes*, *supra* note 58, at 711.

61. *Id.* at 712.

62. *See* text at notes 40–42, *supra*.

63. *See* Chapter 6, text at notes 64–72.

64. Nader, *Controlling Processes*, *supra* note 58, at 713.

Nader sees the origin of this transformation in the decades of social activism that began in the 1960s over civil rights, women's rights, consumer rights, environmental rights, and so forth. But these great social issues, which raised fundamental questions of peace and justice, were rapidly eclipsed by a movement in favor of "alternative dispute resolution" (*i.e.*, methods and mechanisms for resolving claims for social justice in fora other than courts). In short, this movement emphasized mandatory mediation and/or arbitration with a discourse of peace rather than confrontation. Thus, it was psychological rather than legal and as such had wide political appeal to both the right and left wings of the American political establishment.

> Mandatory mediation-arbitration (in itself a contradiction in terms) replaces contention with "peace" and win-win solutions. The language of alternative dispute resolution is heavily psychological rather than legal, and it has attracted strange bedfellows—right-wing politicians concerned with the prospect of the success of the rights agendas, left-wing activists concerned with improving the judicial process, religious communities, psychotherapy groups, businesses tired of paying enormous sums in lawyers' fees, and administrators wishing to facilitate bureaucratic procedures. Dogmas of harmony and consensus appeal to a wide spectrum of political positions from right to left and, because they have deep cultural roots in American society, leave room for instrumental manipulations and more.[65]

Between 1969 and 1986, under Chief Justice Warren Burger, the U.S. Supreme Court played a pivotal role in promoting this trend. As harmony ideology permeated U.S. culture, its social consequences resulted in an invisible redistribution of power[66] that ironically disenfranchised the poor and progressive sectors of society because it is always the stronger of two parties that prefers negotiation, where the principle of equality does not apply. For example, in environmental issues, the emphasis was to avoid win-loss outcomes and balance competing interests. Unions were pressured into finding mutually satisfactory solutions with management. Religious sects such as the Southern Baptists preached a narrative of avoidance of law in favor of a narrative of consensus. Chief Justice Burger claimed that it was not "civilized" to resort to litigation and denigrated the adversarial model. As such attitudes took root in U.S. culture, harmony ideology took the character of "coercive harmony" and even spread abroad.[67] Thus, although the rhetoric of alternative dispute resolution proclaimed that it was intended to facilitate access to justice, it had the opposite effect of imposing a coercive consensus.[68]

On the international plane, the United States claims to prefer negotiation over compulsory judicial settlement. Nonetheless, having lost a case in the World Court against Nicaragua, it terminated its acceptance of the compulsory jurisdiction of the

65. *Id.*

66. *Id.* at 714.

67. *Id.*

68. Guita Grin Debert, Comment to Nader, *Controlling Processes*, *supra* note 58, at 726.

International Court of Justice.[69] It is of course no secret that the country's negotiating power is greater than that of almost any other; however, the United States has also declined to sign on to many important international treaty regimes, including the Rome Statute, which established the International Criminal Court and the United Nations Convention on the Law of the Sea (UNCLOS). This trend is also visible with other countries acting in the international arena. For example, in international water disputes the stronger parties usually prefer negotiation over judicial settlement.[70]

Laura Nader, *Controlling Processes: Tracing the Dynamic Components of Power*, 38 Curr. Anthropol. 711, 713–15 (1997).

Warren Burger, Chief Justice of the U.S. Supreme Court, played a pivotal role in the alternative dispute resolution movement from his appointment in 1969 until his retirement in 1986. Burger adumbrated a manner of thinking about social relations, structural problems of inequality, and cultural solutions to these problems that foreshadowed a cultural shift with ramifications far beyond the law. The movement was against the contentious and against concerns with root causes and toward control over the disenfranchised. For the most part the elements of such control were invisible, but they were pervasive....

The point of calling attention to the use of the harmony law model is not to valorize an adversarial model but to attempt to understand how and why legal ideologies shift from tolerance for controversy to the pursuit of harmony over time and with what consequences ... Certainly the history of global replacement of adversarial models by harmony models does not indicate that harmony ideology is benign. On the contrary, during the past three decades harmony ideology has resulted in an invisible redistribution of power....

Burger's legacy is evident everywhere today. A major purpose of environmental conferences, for example, is to see whether the emphasis can be shifted from a win-lose situation to a balance-of-interest approach. American Indians on reservations are being persuaded by negotiators from Washington to take nuclear waste as a win-win solution—climbing out of their misery while contributing to their country ... Timber activists are pressured with consensus meetings. Unions are deluged with quality-control plans whereby workers and management can cooperate in harmony ... Family problems are mediated, and, ironically, in many states such mediation is mandatory ... Ghetto school "troublemakers" and leaders are taught how to mediate disputes rather than search for justice. In Washington, D.C., there is now a Government Office of Consensus Conference Planning, and we have

69. Nicaragua v. United States of America, 1984 ICJ REP. 392 (June 27, 1986).

70. Nader, *Controlling Processes*, *supra* note 58, at 715.

elected presidents whose preference for consensus has been widely noted. Carol Greenhouse's (1986) work has called attention to the Southern roots of Presidents Carter and Clinton and the latter's position on consensus; her study of a Southern Baptist community in Georgia reveals the cultural roots of an alternative-dispute-resolution explosion in which the contemporary equation of Euro-American Christianity with harmony instills law avoidance, law aversion, and the value of consensus—"a strategy that transformed conflict." . . .

Thus, it appears that in the effort to quell the rights movements of the 1960s and to cool Vietnam-war protests, harmony became a virtue. Burger argued that to be more "civilized" Americans had to abandon their reliance on the adversarial model. It was by means of such rhetoric that the present-day "tort-reform" movement was born. Though the general public was largely unaware of it, the plan attracted enough attention to shift public emphasis and empathy away from courts and injured plaintiffs. A burgeoning dispute-resolution industry institutionalized the shift from "the acrimonious" to "the harmonious" through an empirically ungrounded discourse about the United States as "overlitigious" . . . The powerful tend to become advantaged by alternative dispute resolution, and coercive harmony can be repressive. . . .

Why this valorizing of negotiation? An international legal scholar . . . put his finger on the key—elasticity: "The less 'civilized' were doomed to work toward an equality which an elastic standard of civilization put forever beyond their reach." Edward Said (1978) had noticed this earlier when he observed that the valorizing of one cultural form over another is frequently linked to imbalances of power. Now that the "primitives" have courts, we move to alternative dispute resolution, a culturally encapsulated form of international negotiation that has emerged in the United States from the disciplines of law, economics, social psychology, political science, and psychotherapy.

What was different about the new international negotiators was not their practice of mediation or negotiation but their distaste for confrontation, the adversary process, justice acquired by win-lose methods, and equality before the law. They were also linked by an indifference to the international court, which since the emergence of new nations (many of them "Third World") was being used to represent new interests. For example, in 1984 Nicaragua filed suit against the United States, which withdrew from the case and shortly thereafter (along with the U.S.S.R.) withdrew from the agreement to comply with the decisions of the court. Controlling processes are double-edged.

Water resource disputes illustrate the shift of dispute resolution away from adjudication and arbitration toward negotiation. . . . Toxic poisoning is referred to as a "perception of toxic poisoning," and the question becomes how cultural behavior can be used or neutralized. The international "privatization" of justice through alternative dispute resolution centers in the United States is striking, as is the contempt for the judicial process.

> Many writers on international negotiation imply the existence of a "universal diplomatic culture" of negotiators. . . . However, what is claimed to be universal here is instead hegemonic, developed in the United States in the 1970s and exported worldwide by an expanding alternative dispute resolution industry; it is a coercive harmony whose primary function is producing order of a repressive sort. In the international river disputes it is the stronger parties that prefer negotiation.
>
> Harmony legal models or adversarial models may originate locally and spread or be imposed for purposes of control or resistance to control, resulting in the redistribution of power. Anthropologists know, of course, that dispute resolution ideologies have long been used as a mechanism for the transmission of hegemonic ideas, and indeed we no longer speak of culture as referring simply to shared traditions passed from one generation to another. The study of structures and activities that cross boundaries, including the boundaries of what has long been shared culture, illuminates places where power may be reconfigured and societies transformed. The question of choice is just such a place.

B. Power as Hegemonic Force in the Beauty and Medical Industries

The preceding passage ends by noting that power as a controlling force can transform society. The previous section bears out this claim by showing how certain cultural notions such as harmony, or what it is to be civilized, serve as vehicles for the exercise of transformative power. The passage also notes that choice is another cultural notion through which power operates. Nader, whose focus is the idea of free choice in a consumer society, unveils (again, in the postmodernist spirit) the coercive nature of culturally conditioned choices made by consumers. In doing so she dispels as myth the idea of the American consumer as an autonomous and self-regulating psychic entity who buys and consumes products in a free market on the basis of free choice.

Nader examines this question in the context of a market in which women are the primary consumers: breast enhancement surgery. She cites marketing strategies promoting the idea that breast implantation enhances feminine appearance.[71] Nader rejects the argument that breast implantation in the United States is a matter of free choice by adult women by countering that "the beauty-industrial complex" has adopted and successfully marketed a sophisticated strategy (which she calls beauty ideology) that has resulted in the commodification of the female body. She notes that the major corporations that are the beneficiaries of the female cosmetic industry have segmented the female body, targeting each segment with a corresponding beauty product. The female breast, as one such segment, has generated a multi-million dollar industry.

---

71. *Id.*

According to Nader, the marketing and sale of female beauty products has created a veritable beauty ideology, with its own discourse, that ensnares hundreds of thousands of women into seeking silicone gel and other types of breast implants. The ideological discourse treats small breasts as hypertrophy or deformity—a disease that can only be cured by implants.[72] Women in this condition are made to feel inadequate, less feminine, and not self-confident. Enlargement is marketed as a method that enhances their quality of life and as something necessary for their psychological health. Beauty ideology and its discourse become internalized or normalized by their target population, which then succumbs to its various demands.[73]

> The discourse became a sales pitch. Women "seek" breast implants to keep their husbands or their jobs, to attract men, or to become socially acceptable. [Linda] Coco calls this "patriarchal capitalism" and questions whether this is free choice or "mind colonization."
>
> Understanding "choice" led Coco to an examination of the power both in the doctor-patient relationship and in the control of information. By various means certain women—the insecure consumers—are led to trust and believe in modern medical technology. What is most important in being "caught" is their internalization of the social message. Coco's conclusion that American women are subtly indoctrinated to recognize and desire a certain kind of beauty presents an interesting possibility. Women "were told by the media, plastic surgeons, women's magazines, other women, and the business world that they could enhance their lives by enhancing their bust lines. . . . The social imperative for appearance was personalized, psychologized, and normalized." . . . Social surveys indicate that, to the extent that women internalize the social imperative, they feel they are making the decision on their own.
>
> Not surprisingly, women whose surgery resulted in medical complications often came to recognize the external processes of coercive persuasion that had led them to seek implants. In some ways, they resembled former cult members who had been deprogrammed: their disillusionment caused them to question the system that had encouraged them to make the decision in the first place . . . The result was a gradual building of protest against the industry, expressed in networks, newsletters, support groups, workshops, and seminars. As have some former cult members, women have brought suit, testified before lawmakers, and challenged in other ways some of the largest corporations and insurance companies in the land. The choice of implants, they learn, is part of a matrix of controlling processes in which women are subjects. Given the right circumstances it could happen to anyone. In the Sudan . . . , the young girl is told that circumcision and infibulation are done

72. *Id.* at 716.

73. *But see* Susan Drucker-Brown, Comment to Nader, *Controlling Processes*, *supra* note 58, at 727 (raising the possibility of women opting for breast enhancement for their own "empowerment"). Contrast this with Nader's response: "Indeed these women are empowered, as the saying goes, to roam in a four-cornered cage of someone else's design." Nader, *Controlling Processes*, *supra* note 58, at 734.

> *for* her and not *to* her. In the United States the mutilation of natural breasts is also done for the re-creation of femininity. Although power is exercised differently in these two cases, Coco notes the similarity: "The operation on the female breast in America holds much of the same social symbolism and expression of cultural mandates as does infibulation in Sudan. Thus, the question of why women choose breast augmentation becomes moot."[74]

Experience-Near Understanding When Ethnography "Goes Local"

> In the United States, culture may appear natural and inevitable because it is deliberately made to appear so by the manipulation of cultural images that articulate what people should be, should think, should buy (not that they always do). A strong belief in free will often impedes understanding of how lives are changed by cultural practices that are external to the individual and intended to modify individual behavior, for example, through political propaganda or economic marketing. Anthropologists witness and experience the construction of culture for financial gain. We are a marketing society. Yet for the most part our professional stance has been somewhat analogous to that of the anthropologists of the colonial period, who were criticized for writing about "pure native" culture before it disappeared while all around them native cultures were changing. When we close our eyes and minds to the possibilities of ethnographic research in taking a vertical slice of contemporary colonizers and colonized, we still practice anthropology in much the same way. In spite of recent gains we still ignore the ramifications of the commercial world and the multinationals—as if they were not changing every one of us, whether consciously resistant or not. More and more, modern technologies, population movements, and changing social organizations make us captives of our cultures.[75]

The foregoing passage addresses the question whether ethnographers can give an epistemologically reliable account of their own culture. Nader's answer is clearly in the affirmative, as Geertz's was.[76] But Nader warns that one faces the same pitfalls in observing one's own culture as when observing a foreign one. If ethnographers do not shed their cultural blinders, they will give an inaccurate account of their own culture. An ethnographer blinded by cultural notions of free will or free choice will not understand how "lives can be changed," as for example when women are coerced into seeking breast implants. Nader's point is that accuracy is more likely if the ethnographer can unmask and become self-aware of controlling processes. The latter

---

74. Nader, *Controlling Processes*, *supra* note 58, at 716–17.

75. *Id.* at 721–22.

76. *See* text at notes 21–26, *supra.*

are aimed at producing "conformity and selective blindness";[77] only by transcending these barriers (*i.e.*, by adopting "counterhegemonies") and understanding their modes of operation can the ethnographer render an epistemically reliable account of his or her own culture.

The ethnographer who adopts these counterhegemonies achieves the requisite measure of "cultural deprogramming" to give a true picture of his or her own culture.[78] Anthropology has hitherto concentrated on the study of far-away societies, but when the lens is turned toward home ground, the rendering of true ethnographic accounts raises difficulties that are not dissimilar. Anthropologists have tried to minimize or overcome these difficulties in both enterprises. Geertz, for example, proposed to peer at far-away cultures through their cultural symbols instead of going native. Nader proposes to study her own culture by adopting counterhegemonies aimed at self-cultural deprogramming. In the same vein, Conley and O'Barr used discourse as the symbolic vehicle for studying lay perceptions of law and justice in the United States.

Conclusion

According to Nader, beauty ideology in medicine (like harmony ideology in law) becomes "personalized, psychologized, and normalized."[79] These essentially Foucaultian notions show that the effectiveness of power as a controlling process is proportional to its ability to hide itself.[80] Its most overt form is when power is naked, ostensibly (*i.e.*, visibly) vested in individuals and institutions, and exercised to control individuals or groups and relationships. Such situations would typically be called instantiations of power for social control. At the other end of the power spectrum is hidden power, where there is no overt mode or manifestation. Here, power controls the mind. The former process controls social reflexes whereas the latter controls cultural reflexes, where growth of power is incremental rather than abrupt so that it "slides in" unnoticeably[81] and is thus more effective. The control of cultural reflexes through subtle exercises of power also creates the impression that such use of power is inherent in the natural evolution of all social processes, and particularly that the resulting normative order respects individual autonomy and choice; this impression, however, is illusory.

When cultural control of the mind is hegemonic, it appears to be impersonal, embedded, and invisible, akin to a Durkheimian form of "mechanical solidarity."[82] Because the ideology is internalized, beneficiaries and victims alike are often unaware

---

77. Nader, *Controlling Processes*, *supra* note 58, at 722.

78. *Id.* at 723.

79. *See* text at note 74, *supra*.

80. 1 Michel Foucault, The History of Sexuality: An Introduction 86 (Robert Hurley trans. 1980).

81. Nader, *Controlling Processes*, *supra* note 58, at 722.

82. Miguel Alberto Bartolomé, Comment to Nader, *Controlling Processes*, *supra* note 58, at 724.

of it or do not understand it and therefore cannot give an experience-near account of it. Even if the controlling processes are nonideological, they are defended if not legitimized in terms of other ideological or metaideological doctrines such as free market competition, self-realization, self-determination, and free choice.[83]

Anthropologists on home ground must therefore transcend these barriers and deprogram themselves culturally by adopting counterhegemonies that set them apart from the hegemonic nature of the operative controlling processes of their culture.

> Malinowski . . . recognized that controls operate most effectively through symbols that society places beyond the jurisdiction of its formal and social control system. Mintz illustrated how ideas linked to the disparities of power grow and are nurtured through interlocking institutions. Cultural control is often the result of incremental, not abrupt, change, and when it is achieved incrementally it is powerful indeed because it slides in rather unnoticed and comes to be considered natural. The controlling processes I have described here have gradually come to seem natural: in the first example, "harmony" became desirable as the natural order of things; the existence of "choice" was assumed in the second and strengthened by the belief in individualism; . . .
>
> Individuals may move in and out of various controlling processes, be caught by them, and remake them as did the women who had breast implants. The same controls may be effective across class lines, as in the events leading to the spread of harmony ideologies from the ghettos to the workplace to environmental activism. Implicit persuasion is easier to manage than overt coercion.
>
> A catholic view of culture, one that recognizes that the world is always only partly integrated or coherent or in effect only partly shared, changes the questions we ask and the perceptions we mold. If there is general value to be derived from this line of research, it is not only in the documentation of how controlling processes work to change behavior without force and violence or the unmasking of power but also in the recognition of how quickly they can do so. Considering counterhegemonies implies possibilities for general cultural deprogrammings, including a questioning of basic assumptions that may be impediments to anthropologists working on home ground. The relationship between colonizers and colonized studied by anthropologists in some ways parallels the interaction between industrialists and their target populations . . . Power is implicated in both settings, and so is resistance. The colonizing of minds and bodies does not differentiate between subjects, and yet—why is still unexplained—we know even less of industrial subjects than we do of colonized ones.[84]

83. Nader, *Controlling Processes*, *supra* note 58, at 720.

84. *Id.* at 722–23.

Cultural Domination through Discourse in Working-Class America

Sally Engle Merry's 1990 study of legal consciousness among average working-class white Americans in Massachusetts complements Nader's ethnography of controlling processes. Merry studied the attitudes of working people toward the American system of justice as they sought help with a variety of personal problems that involved neighbors, friends, lovers, and spouses.[85] She shows how recourse to the courts in 170 cases led to paradoxical consequences, namely, that although plaintiffs felt empowered to have judicial recourse, at the same time they became subjected to the control of the judicial apparatus, were denied the very remedies that the law promised, and thus experienced great disillusionment.

Cultural Domination of Legally Sanctioned Discourse

Disillusionment among plaintiffs was due to the fact that they became ensnared (both in court and in mediation) by one of three normative discourses, only one of which was that of law. And even when the discourse was that of law, the plaintiff did not necessarily obtain justice because the law is essentially "an ideology with hegemonic characteristics."[86] Hegemony is viewed by Merry as the imposition of a persuasive image of social order without violence or force.[87]

In all material senses, Merry adopts Foucault's notion of discourse as a mechanism for the exercise of power in subtle and disguised ways.[88] But the other two discourses, discourse of morality and discourse of the helping professions, are also hegemonic. Plaintiffs who come to court after having framed their disputes in one or more of these discourses find that court personnel reframe their dispute in another discourse, with adverse consequences for the plaintiff.

Discourses, which are part of the culturally constructed world, are part of the human consciousness, particularly regarding how to structure interpersonal relations. The apparent naturalness of cultural forms of discourse is one reason for their power.[89] Therefore, one natural way of conducting discourse is through naming.[90] For example, the cause of a family problem framed in terms of a "mean or vengeful father" results in a different outcome than if the father is portrayed as being "afflicted with the disease of alcoholism."[91] In the former situation, the outcome for the father is likely to be punitive; in the latter, it is likely to be remedial. Because the success of

---

85. Sally Engle Merry, Getting Justice and Getting Even: Legal Consciousness Among Working-Class Americans (1990).

86. *Id.* at 7.

87. *Id.*

88. *Id.* at 110.

89. *Id.* at 111.

90. *Id.* at 130 *et seq.*

91. Merry, *supra* note 85, at 111.

any party in court depends on his or her ability to harness the controlling discourse, naming is one way to exercise domination.

> Actors attempting to assert the discourses within which their problems are framed operate from structurally unequal positions. The supplicant, asking for help, is inevitably constrained to present his or her request in the language of the institution from which help is sought. In her study of marriage and inequality, Jane Collier argues cogently that when women seek to divorce their husbands they must present their demands in the discourse of marriage found in that society (1988). For example, if the discourse specifies that men are entitled to women by virtue of their prowess in war and raiding, women must contest their entitlement in those terms, not in others which might give them greater power. Thus, she argues, the choice of discourse itself is a product of the structure of the society, and the supplicant must adopt the discourse available to her.[92]

A party who finds a particular discourse to be ineffective may switch to another—as do court personnel such as clerks, judges, and mediators. The discourse of law usually invokes labels such as "breach of contract," "harassment," "assault," and so on. Discourse of morality involves moral duties between neighbors, parents, children, and others. Discourse of help invokes the need for therapy, stressing environmental factors such as stress or crowding, rather than individual fault.

For example, in one case a plaintiff (George) criticized his neighbor in decidedly legal discourse, claiming invasion of privacy and protection of property.[93] George complained about his many confrontations with the defendant's son, who in one instance allegedly threw eggs at George's house. The plaintiff's complaint form read in part:

> Repeated obscene telephone calls, damaging personal property, constant harassment from said family. Death threats to my 10-year-old son and flashing knives. Constantly threatening my son on the way to and from school and while playing on and around our own property. Has thrown eggs at my property on numerous occasions.[94]

The court clerk refused to issue the complaint and referred the case to mediation.[95] During mediation the defendant, Jane, used mostly moral and therapeutic discourse, which was also favored by the mediators:

> The complaint was harassing phone calls, but it is much, much more. George's family moved in two years ago. They have a little boy, and my son was friendly with him. The problem was their son's inability to communi-

---

92. *Id.*

93. *Id.* at 116.

94. *Id.* at 117.

95. *Id.*

> cate with his peers. They all picked on him, and the kids started to fight, especially Bobby and their son. George would intervene and start to fight with my children. This is the problem. There have been eggs thrown at both houses, and we have tried to get at a resolution for the bickering. My biggest complaint is that whatever my children did to his house, George did to mine; then he boyishly admits it. He has a low frustration tolerance and quite a temper. He is childish—he has knocked over a picnic table, hit Bobby with a baseball—and I had to call the police. I am at home all the time, and I see this. My son has been disrespectful to George, but he is disrespectful back. I intervene to protect their son sometimes. George once kicked in my door, and my kids were afraid. George also called my son, and I wrote down what he said. I told him: "When my children do wrong to you, I knock on the door and tell you and tell them to take the eggs off. I don't think you would do the same for me." I feel intimidated. I am recently divorced, and I don't need this aggravation. And the problem is not the wife or son; it is George. I am not the type of person to call all the time and say what your son does, but it is George who has chased us and hit us. He always blames us for things we do and don't do. The day that the children were playing with wood in our backyard I was nice about it.[96]

Language such as "their son's inability to connect with his peers," "they picked on him," "he has a low frustration level and quite a temper," and so forth, shows a combination of moral and therapeutic discourse on Jane's part.

The final agreement, which was drawn up after completion of the mediation process, showed a shift from the legal discourse in the original complaint to a moral discourse:

1. The parents, expressing full confidence in the ability of their sons to solve their own problems, agree to allow them to resolve their differences.
2. The three boys [including Bobby's older brother] will feel free to talk with one another over any problem that may arise.
3. All agree that there will be no further harassment.
4. Jane and Betsy will feel free to discuss any future problems on a one-to-one basis should the need arise. All three parents will encourage friendly terms.

Whenever the plaintiff used legal discourse during the mediation, the mediators interjected and steered him to think in moral terms such as friendship, neighborly duties, or parental responsibility. The mediators ignored "legal" evidence from the plaintiff in the form of documents and photos.

---

96. *Id.* at 117–18.

The Paradox of Legal Entitlement

The ability to seize the reigning discourse is one aspect of power; the other is the power of naming. In the foregoing case, as in others, when a legal claim is diffused and shifted to moral or therapeutic discourse, parties who framed their claims in legal terms are immediately disadvantaged, since they must now reframe their complaints and seek solutions that are not their first preference. The irony of course is that this shifting of discourse occurs under the authority of the court to whom the plaintiff turned for help in the first place. The plaintiff is coerced into accepting a different way to settle in the hope that this will strengthen his or her case in court "the next time," in case the mediated agreement does not work.

In this way, according to Merry, working-class Americans are discouraged from using the courts to settle their personal problems. Merry asserts the category under which a dispute falls (*e.g.*, neighborhood, family, marital, boyfriend-girlfriend) is irrelevant. Instead, the discourses in which disputes are embedded constitute the subtle processes of cultural domination in the lives of working-class white Americans.

Merry observed that when Americans resort to the courts to settle mundane personal problems, this is due neither to the allegedly litigious nature of American society nor to the theory that there has been some sort of "breakdown" in social cohesion and communal life. Rather, she concluded that it is due to the values of individualism, autonomy, privacy, and egalitarianism that permeate U.S. culture.[97] These values are also responsible for the historical trend that began with the founding of the nation of people migrating away from their communities to the suburbs and beyond: "What held Americans together . . . was their ability to live apart. Society depended on segmentation."[98]

The trend of living "apart" was itself an expression of personal autonomy; as such, it was further buttressed by the rapid expansion of social and judicial services from the state during most of the twentieth century. Recourse to the courts was viewed by underprivileged groups such as women and racial minorities as a form of empowerment and self-determination, consistent with basic American values. This view, of course, is confronted by the paradox that once litigants arrive in court, they find that their legal consciousness differs from that of the court system. Problems believed to be legal are diffused, downgraded, and recategorized as moral or therapeutic, and thus litigants are denied the very legal process they have been invited to invoke. Instead of having their rights vindicated, plaintiffs are coerced into accepting a different discourse, lectured by mediators about how to structure interpersonal relations, and convinced to settle in the hope that they may have better luck during their next courtroom encounter. This process is a demonstration of cultural domination through law, wherein the state uses its legal authority to reframe personal disputes and, in doing so, to deny the very protection it promises.

---

97. *Id.* at 176 *et seq.*

98. *Id.* at 174 (quoting Robert Wiebe, The Segmented Society: An Introduction to the Meaning of America 46 (1975)).

Sally Engle Merry, Getting Justice and Getting Even: Legal Consciousness Among Working-Class Americans 180–182 (1990).

This can be seen as a form of cultural domination in that the court uses its legal authority to frame the problems in other discourses, to offer nonlegal solutions, and to deny the forms of protection and help promised by the legal system itself....

There is a fundamental paradox to the consciousness of legal entitlement. The use of law by those at the bottom of the society hierarchy empowers the individual with relation to his or her neighbors and family members. On the other hand, it increases his dependence on the institutions of the state. The plaintiff draws on the symbolic power of the law to gain strength in fights with those he or she knows, but he or she loses control over this power when the problem moves into the courts. As the working-class citizen turns to the courts for protection against spouses, friends, and neighbors, he or she becomes vulnerable to the intervention of the rules and practices of the legal system and to the groups with the power to generate them. Thus, the use of the courts furthers the subordination of the working-class to those who manage and dispense court services. The more that working-class people become conscious of their legal rights and use the legal system to assert them, the more they can challenge traditional hierarchies which control their lives. But, at the same time, they become more dependent on the laws to mount that challenge and to define its terms.

This is the paradox of going to court: freedom from the control of the community comes at the price of domination by the state, in the form of the courts. To return to court again is to offer the court the opportunity to shape the problem in *its* discourses, to name it, and to point toward its solution. As the average person returns to court with new demands, he strengthens the power of the law over his life, both its direct coercive power and its ideological domination, its capacity to interpret and make sense of his problems. The use of the law challenges existing social hierarchies, but the discourses of the courthouse continue to constrain and restrict the way these problems are understood. Plaintiffs rebel against the social order, but their complaints are held within a framework established by the law, by traditions of social relationships, and by the language of therapy and help.

The consciousness of legal entitlement and the consequent turning to the law are profoundly democratic, radically egalitarian, and fundamentally American. This legal entitlement is an outgrowth of faith in the law, a faith observed early by Tocqueville and other commentators on the American scene. Cultural values of autonomy, self-reliance, individualism, and tolerance have led local courthouses to become the nearest moral authority for dealing with family and neighborhood problems....

> But, the irony of court use for these working-class plaintiffs is that as they seek to use the law to establish a more autonomous life, one regulated by law rather than by violence, they become more dependent on the law to order their lives. There is, in this sense, a new relationship forged between the individual and the state. The individual seeks to construct a social world of autonomy and individualism, a vision deeply entrenched in American culture, by establishing closer ties to the state as a way to order family and neighborhood life. The individual allows the institutions of the state, in this case the courts, to expand their supervision and governance of his intimate world of neighborhood and family. These plaintiffs free themselves from the control of their neighbors and spouses but tie themselves more closely to the state.
>
> Thus, the paradox of legal entitlement poses a fundamental dilemma for American society and for its legal order founded on liberalism. This is a society which celebrates individualism and equal access to the due process of the law. Yet there are some problems which seem less worthy of this equal access and less appropriate for legal intervention. This book concerns an arena of behavior which lies in the gray area between that traditionally regulated by the state and that which is private and beyond state control. The location of this boundary between public and private is now recognized as a profoundly political boundary and is being hotly contested, particularly by feminists ... To see family and neighborhood problems as being within the scope of the law is to expand that boundary and to increase government supervision over areas of life long defined as private; to deny access for these problems is to violate the expectations of relatively powerless citizens that the authority of the law is available to them as well as to the more privileged. This paradox is inherent in the legal order of contemporary America itself.

If the paradox of legal entitlement reveals a failure of justice for the average working-class American, the paradox of the revictimization of people who have been raped exposes an even darker side of the law. Such failure also involves discourse and power, both of which are closely intertwined with law.

Domination through Legal Discourse: Revictimizing Rape Victims

The following case study considers how language, discourse, and power are intertwined with the law. It shows how victims of rape who seek justice in court are, paradoxically, not only denied the justice they seek but also forced to publicly relive their ordeal to no avail. The discourses of the law, both on the macro and micro levels, perpetuate male-oriented hierarchies of domination over women, as revealed in the prosecution of an alleged rapist. Examination of courtroom discourse in a rape trial reveals how the proceedings actually serve the very person who is accused of domination, to the detriment (*i.e.*, the revictimization) of the victim.

A. Language, Discourse, and Power

A major theme of APM is the central role of language and discourse in the production, exercise, and subversion of legal power. As to the distinction between language and discourse, language is the *lingua franca* of the law in that law is expressed through language, whether this is done in a contract, a judicial opinion, a statute, or some other medium. Discourse, by contrast, has a linguistic as well as a social component; it overlaps with language but becomes specialized depending on its forum (*e.g.*, courtroom discourse, medical discourse) and has its own special vocabulary. Social discourse usually signifies a locus of power. As Michel Foucault wrote, discourse can be an instrument and an effect of power.[99]

Normativity in discourse is shown not only by how people talk about a social question but also how they think about it and, ultimately, act in accordance with it. In this sense, discourses on social issues such as punishment, discipline, sexuality, and human rights arise and compete for dominance. The discourse that eventually emerges as dominant is therefore a source of power; it becomes accepted or internalized by the population at large, whose behavior converges around it. The power structure thus enforced by the dominant discourse at the society-wide level is called the macrodiscourse; it must be distinguished from microdiscourse, which operates only in the linguistic sense but which is of no less normative significance.

In order to understand the concrete manifestation of the law's power at the social (*i.e.*, macro) level, Conley and O'Barr sifted through numerous microdiscourses of law. In their appropriately titled book, *Just Words*, in which they set out to explain how "the details of legal discourse matter,"[100] they contend that through language the power of law is "realized, exercised, reproduced, and occasionally challenged and subverted."[101] Simply put, law is

> the talk between disputants; the talk between lawyers and clients; the courtroom talk among lawyers, parties, judges, and witnesses; the legal talk that gets reduced to writing as statutes and judicial opinions; and the commentary on all of this other talk that people like us engage in.[102]

Accordingly, Conley and O'Barr argue that one must analyze law's microdiscourse in order to understand—and find concrete manifestations of—law's power.[103] By studying this microdiscourse, one can observe how power is exercised, identify points at which the law might be challenged, and surmise which challenges to existing law are likely to work.[104]

---

99. Foucault, *supra* note 80, at 101.

100. John M. Conley & William M. O'Barr, Just Words: Law, Language, and Power 129 (2d ed. 2005).

101. *Id.*

102. *Id.*

103. *Id.*

104. *Id.*

The following case study from Conley and O'Barr, which explores the revictimization of rape victims, offers a telling empirical perspective on exactly how "the details of legal discourse matter."

B. The Revictimization of Rape Victims

According to Conley and O'Barr, the political, social, and scholarly discourses surrounding the crime of rape all focus on rape as an exercise of power.[105] Though the definition of rape is not necessarily restricted to male/female encounters or even as occurring only between adults, the case study examined here involves a male/female incident. Besides the obvious physical exercise of power in which a man violates a woman's sexual autonomy, the abuse of power that occurs during rape has been interpreted as reflecting broader abuses of power at the macro level—abuses society condones and even promotes.[106] For example, that nonconsensual sex between master and slave or between man and wife have not historically been considered rape demonstrates a societal presumption that women have no choice but to be subjected to the power of men.[107]

But the "power politics" of rape, according to Conley and O'Barr, extend well beyond the commission of the crime. Not only are rapes grossly underreported, but when they are prosecuted, the elements of the crime are inherently patriarchal in that "a woman who did not actively, indeed aggressively, resist will be seen as having consented to sex."[108] Their harshest criticism of the system focuses on what happens in the courtroom. In what is commonly referred to as revictimization, not only is a woman forced by male-dominated legal discourse to relive her rape in her testimony, but this courtroom reenactment results in the victim actually being blamed for the crime that has been committed against her.[109]

> Defense lawyers exploit male-biased legal definitions of consent to badger the victim about ambiguous signals she might have sent to the perpetrator ... The vigor of her resistance will probably be questioned, again by male standards ... Trivial inconsistencies in her testimony will be blown out of proportion to suggest a faulty memory, if not mendacity. She will also be attacked if any aspects of her post-rape behavior fail to conform to male notions of logical response to a crime—for example, if she did not flee the scene and report the crime as soon as physically possible.[110]

Most controversially, prosecutors are allowed to question the rape victim about her sexual history in order to imply consent on the occasion in question, which means

105. *Id.* at 15.

106. Conley and O'Barr, *supra* note 100, at 16.

107. *Id.*

108. *Id.*

109. *Id.*at 16–17.

110. *Id.* at 17.

they are allowed to portray her as devoid of morals to increase the odds of a successful defense of consent.[111] Scholars argue that recent attempts at legal reform have had little impact on the occurrence of revictimization.[112]

C. Linguistic Features of Courtroom Proceedings

Conley and O'Barr employ Matoesian's method of microlinguistic analysis, also known as conversation analysis,[113] to "unlock the conundrum of power."[114] In other words, by understanding the microlinguistic details of courtroom conversation, Conley and O'Barr seek to understand exactly how the power dynamics of rape function. Because courtrooms, like all institutional environments, employ special conversational rules that govern interactions (*i.e.*, lawyers ask questions and witnesses answer them),[115] Conley and O'Barr examine five linguistic features of a rape trial that lawyers manipulate to control witnesses. These are: (1) silence, (2) question form, (3) topic management, (4) evaluative commentary, and (5) challenges to the witness's capacity for knowledge.[116]

Silence. There are several ways that lawyers use silence to accomplish strategic objectives that are otherwise not permitted by the rules of courtroom turn taking. Lawyers use silence to (1) manipulate the question-and-answer format and (2) comment critically on a witness's credibility.[117] For example, when a witness fails to respond immediately to a question, the lawyer may cut the witness off after two and a half seconds and loudly repeat the end of the question. This technique suggests that the witness knows the answer but refuses to give it.

> LAWYER: Then they're not in substantially the same condition, are they? [2.5] ARE THEY?[118]

Or, the lawyer can allow the silence to continue for more than six seconds and then disparage the witness's apparent failure of memory:

> LAWYER: Well WHAT were the items that you hadn't remembered when

111. *Id.*

112. *Id.* "Some states, for example, have done away with requirements that the victim prove active physical resistance in order to defeat the consent defense . . . Specifically trained rape units, often staffed by women, have become ubiquitous in police departments and district attorneys' offices. Some jurisdictions have experimented with closing courtrooms and protecting the identities of rape victims from the press. And in what is widely viewed as the most significant reform, many states have enacted 'rape shield' laws, which prevent defense lawyers from putting the victim's prior sexual history before the jury." *Id.*

113. *See generally*, GREGORY MATOESIAN, REPRODUCING RAPE (1993).

114. CONLEY & O'BARR, JUST WORDS, *supra* note 100, at 18.

115. *Id.* at 21.

116. *Id.* at 22 et seq.

117. *Id.* at 22–23.

118. *Id.* at 23.

you—remember as of Friday? [6.2] Or don't you remember that?[119]

Or, as shown next, the 45 seconds of silence following a witness's answer can create a pin-drop effect[120] that serves as a commentary on her credibility.

> LAWYER: Is it your sworn testimony [1.0] under sworn, SWORN oath [.08] that in four hours at the Grainary you had only two drinks?
> [1.2]
> WITNESS: Yes.
> [45.0]
> LAWYER: Linda . . . [121]

In each of the foregoing examples, lawyers use silence to manage and control courtroom discourse, and witnesses are powerless to resist their tactics.

Question Form. Through question form, lawyers can strategically limit the range of possible answers from a witness, or even place blame on the witness, regardless of the answer.[122] In the following, a defense attorney initially asks an open-ended question about the definition of "partying" before switching to "tag" questions (*i.e.*, questions that require a yes/no answer)[123] to imply an unhealthy interest in sex and drugs on the part of the witness.

> LAWYER: What's meant by partying? You, you're what? Nineteen? Were you nineteen at the time?
> WITNESS: Yes.
> LAWYER: What's meant among youthful people, people your age, Brian's age, by partying?
> WITNESS: Some take it just to go and, with some friends, people, and have a few drinks, and some do smoke, some do take pills.
> LAWYER: Partying.
> WITNESS: (Drugs.)
> LAWYER: Is it not true, partying among people your age, does not mean to go to a party?
> WITNESS: That's true.
> LAWYER: It implies to many people that, implies sexual activity, doesn't it?
> [*An objection by prosecuting attorney at this point is overruled by judge.*]
> LAWYER: To many people your age that means sexual activity, does it not?
> WITNESS: To some, yes, I guess.
> LAWYER: And at the very least it means the use of intoxicants?
> WITNESS: Yes.
> LAWYER: So, when they suggested, who suggested that you go partying?

---

119. *Id.*

120. CONLEY AND O'BARR, *supra* note 100, at 24.

121. *Id.*

122. *Id.*

123. *Id.*

WITNESS: I don't know who first brought it up. They [did mention]—
LAWYER: [Then did—]
WITNESS:—did mention that, uh, there would be friends who had the apartment who would be having a party.
LAWYER: So the word partying, let's go party, some like that, (inaudible) not just go to a party?
WITNESS: Mmhmm.
LAWYER: Correct?
WITNESS: Mmhmm.[124]

The witness's answers are rendered all but irrelevant because each tag question is preceded by a statement that is damaging to the witness. By controlling the form of the questions, the lawyer is able to present a self-serving monologue in lieu of actual cross-examination.[125]

Topic Management. A lawyer uses this approach by posing a particular question to regain control of an evasive witness by "repeating, rephrasing, or elaborating on questions that have failed to elicit the desired answers."[126] For example, the lawyer in the foregoing scenario employs a topic management strategy to define partying as an activity that includes drugs, alcohol, and sex. The lawyer then executes a topic shift to establish that this was the definition of partying the witness consented to on the night of the alleged rape. The witness thus subtly becomes an unwitting collaborator in the undermining of her own claim. By contrast, the witness in the following excerpt attempts to challenge the lawyer's question by deviating from the specific topic.

LAWYER: You were attracted to Brian, weren't you?
WITNESS: I thought he was a nice clean-looking man.
LAWYER: He was attractive-looking, correct?
WITNESS: Yeah.
LAWYER: And basically when you left that parking lot all you knew about him was that he was a good-lookin' man, isn't that true?
WITNESS: Yeah.[127]

Although the witness attempts to shift the topic to how the man looked, rather than whether or not she was attracted to him, the lawyer was still able to use her own word ("looking") in order to insinuate that she willingly went off with the defendant.

Commentary. Although the courtroom's prescribed question-and-answer format does not allow for a lawyer to comment directly on a witness's behavior, lawyers are able to embed this type of commentary in questions. For example, note that the purpose of each of the following questions is to implicitly comment on a discrepancy in the witness's story. The lawyer does this by offering an evaluative comment in his question and then demanding that the witness confirm this evaluation in her answer.

124. *Id.* at 25.
125. *Id.* at 26.
126. *Id.*
127. *Id.* at 27.

LAWYER: Isn't it true that on direct examination by Mrs. Roberts you never once answered a question with "I don't know" or "I don't remember"?

: . . .

LAWYER: Isn't it true that on cross-examination by Mr. Billings you, on numerous occasions, indicated you didn't know or didn't remember?[128]

Next, the lawyer implicitly attacks the witness's credibility by insinuating that her testimony is fabricated.

LAWYER: Did you ever say that three people got into your car?
WITNESS: Yes, I did.
LAWYER: How often did you say that?
WITNESS: A few times.
LAWYER: Before you talked to the prosecutor in this case?
WITNESS: Yes.
LAWYER: Was that because you thought that made your story sound better?[129]

The witness has no linguistic recourse available to counter the lawyer's commentary because any commentary by the witness is objected to as nonresponsive. However, a witness may attempt to downgrade the lawyer's question and diminish its significance:

LAWYER: Can you drink over at Saint Louis?
WITNESS: No.
LAWYER: So you come over here so you can get some alcohol, is that correct?
WITNESS: That's not the sole purpose, no.
LAWYER: That's one of the purposes, is it not?
WITNESS: Yea.[130]

Though the witness attempts to diminish the significance of the lawyer's assessment ("That's not the sole purpose"), the lawyer is able to counter by pointing out that consuming alcohol was one of the purposes for the witness's actions. This is yet another example of "the structure of courtroom interaction giv[ing] the lawyer an insurmountable advantage."[131]

The Witness's Capacity for Knowledge. Lawyers call into question the specific facts witnesses claim to know, sources of claimed knowledge, and, ultimately, whether the witness is capable of knowing anything at all. These techniques are known as "epistemological filters."[132] In the following passage, the lawyer continuously challenges the witness's seemingly reasonable identification of the place to which the defendant drove her the night of the alleged rape. Notice that the lawyer's control over the turn taking process allows him to press the issue and end with a damaging evaluative comment, despite the plausibility of the witness's initial answer:

---

128. CONLEY AND O'BARR, *supra* note 100, at 28.

129. *Id.*

130. *Id.* at 29.

131. *Id.*

132. *Id.*

LAWYER: You say that Brian's car led the way over to this Glen Carbon area?
WITNESS: Mmhmm.
LAWYER: How do you know that was Glen Carbon?
WITNESS: There's a water tank? Maybe? A big silver [bubble]—
LAWYER: [(What?)]
WITNESS:—thing that says Glen Carb–, Glen Carbon.
LAWYER: (Okay) but you don't actually know whether or not you were in Glen Carbon, or had you been told you were in Glen Carbon at that point in time?
WITNESS: I was told that was a part of Glen Carbon.
LAWYER: By the police officers?
WITNESS: Mmhmm.
LAWYER: (Okay), so you don't actually know it was Glen Carbon of your own personal knowledge.
WITNESS: No I assumed it when I'd seen [(that big)]—
LAWYER: [And when] the police officers told you.[133]

In this exchange, the lawyer accomplishes two important goals. First, he attacks the witness's theory of knowledge that she was in Glen Carbon. Second, he advances an alternative theory, namely that it was the police that planted the idea in the head of the witness.

Conley and O'Barr also underline the power dynamics of this exchange based on gender:

> Could a lawyer so readily challenge a *male* witness's ability to draw factual inferences from his observations? Or does the challenge depend on the cultural stereotype of women as being incapable of logical deduction and having diminished capacity for knowledge generally?[134]

D. Linguistic Domination, the "Sexual Double Bind," and Sexual History

The preceding linguistic features of a rape trial demonstrate how the question-and-answer conversational rules employed in the courtroom allow lawyers to manipulate and control witnesses. None of these techniques are unique to rape trials; rather, they are common cross-examination strategies used by lawyers in all trial settings. To find out what it is about a rape trial that leads to these techniques being used as tools for revictimization, Conley and O'Barr consider them against the background of the crime of rape itself.[135] The crime of rape is unique in that the jury must decide whether a common act—sexual intercourse—was in fact an act of involuntary

133. CONLEY AND O'BARR, *supra* note 100, at 30.

134. *Id.* at 31.

135. *Id.* at 31–32.

domination.[136] Of course, the foregoing linguistic strategies—silence, question form, topic management, evaluative commentary, and challenges to the witness's capacity for knowledge—are also strategies of domination.[137] When they are used in a rape trial, they paradoxically serve the interests of the very person who is accused of domination, to the detriment (or revictimization) of his accuser. Revictimization in a rape trial manifests linguistically when "a woman telling a story of physical domination by one man is subjected to linguistic domination by another."

> When used in a rape trial, they are strategies of domination employed in the service of one accused of domination. Thus, while these strategies may not be unique to rape trials, they have a poignancy in the rape context that is unmatched elsewhere. A woman telling a story of physical domination by one man is subjected to linguistic domination by another. In this sense, re-victimization is real, and its mechanism is linguistic.[138]

In this way, "the ordinary mechanics of cross-examination . . . , in this extraordinary context, simultaneously reflect and reaffirm men's power over women."[139]

In addition to linguistic domination, Conley and O'Barr identify two further linguistic phenomena unique to rape trials. The first is the "sexual double bind,"[140] in which the rape victim faces an impossible choice when giving testimony. If she describes herself as having been emotional before or after the rape, the lawyer may portray her as flighty, irrational, not credible, or vengeful.[141] If she describes herself as having been calm and in control at these moments, the lawyer may portray her as a logical woman who is unlikely to be dominated.[142] The second linguistic phenomenon unique to the rape trial is an attack on the basis of the victim's sexual history.[143]

In the following excerpt, Conley and O'Barr describe the phenomena of the sexual double bind and the impugning of the victim's sexual history. The transcript highlights the authors' argument that important social values about men, women, and their relationships are evident at every level of social discourse.[144] It also shows how "the law translates social values into social action."[145]

136. *Id.* at 32.

137. *Id.*

138. *Id.*

139. Conley and O'Barr, *supra* note 100, at 37.

140. *Id.* at 32.

141. *Id.*

142. *Id.*

143. *Id.* at 34.

144. *Id.* at 38.

145. *Id.*

John M. Conley & William M. O'Barr, Just Words: Law, Language, and Power 32–37 (2d ed. 2005).

The Sexual Double Bind

The double bind is the dilemma that an acquaintance rape victim finds herself in when she tries to explain her interaction with the defendant. . . . If she describes herself as having been emotional, the lawyer may play on the stereotype of the flighty woman to suggest that she is irrational and thus not credible, and perhaps now vengeful as well. If, on the other hand, she portrays herself as having been calm and in control, the lawyer may emphasize that she does *not* fit the stereotype, implying that an unusually logical woman would not have allowed herself to be dominated. When the defendant is a wealthy man like William Kennedy Smith, the calm, logical woman also becomes a target for accusations of gold-digging. The woman is thus in a double bind: she loses, whichever approach she takes . . .

Roy Black, Smith's defense lawyer, is cross-examining Patricia Bowman, the alleged victim. Black picks up on Bowman's evaluation of Smith's demeanor ("very smug") and upgrades it ("And arrogant?") in order to develop the theme of a woman scorned, perhaps driven to seek revenge by Smith's unwillingness to connect with her emotionally. Bowman falls into the trap: in denying the charge of anger, she admits to confusion . . .

> Lawyer: And he was sitting there, and I think you said, with his legs crossed?
> Witness: He had his ankle up on his knee.
> Lawyer: And you say that he was very calm at that time?
> Witness: And very smug.
> Lawyer: And arrogant? Made you madder than you were?
> Witness: It didn't make me mad. It confused me.

Elsewhere in the cross-examination, Black does the same thing in a slightly different way. Once again, he exploits Bowman's characterizations of Smith to sharpen his portrait of her as a scorned woman whose emotionally charged story is not worthy of belief. He adopts Bowman's assessment of Smith ("indifference") and upgrades it ("cold and indifferent"). She acquiesces, accepting Black's now-enhanced description of her dismay at Smith's attitude . . .

> Lawyer: He was calm and arrogant, you say?
> Witness: Yes sir.
> Lawyer: He was certainly not being very nice to you.
> Witness: It was more an indifference.
> Lawyer: He was cold and indifferent?
> Witness: Yes sir.

Patricia Bowman and other rape victims cannot win. They are either too illogical or too logical. When Bowman elsewhere characterizes portions of her interaction with Smith as calm and rational, Black pursues the topic to suggest that she had a serious interest in him. The implication, of course, is that she was a calculating pursuer rather than a helpless victim . . .

> LAWYER: He told you he was in medical school?
> WITNESS: Yes he did.
> LAWYER: Of course, that got you more interested in him, didn't it? . . .

Rape victims are not allowed to negotiate a middle course between emotion and reason. Defense lawyers push them to extremes. At one moment, the lawyer portrays the woman as so emotional that she probably consented to sex, regretted it, and then brought charges to get revenge; at the next, he depicts her as too rational and controlling to have been lured into domination by another. The woman is not permitted to be simultaneously competent and vulnerable . . . Bowman suggests that her initial feeling toward Smith was mild affection that stopped well short of sexual abandon. Black immediately challenges that possibility with negative assessments . . .

> LAWYER: Yesterday you told us that when you arrived in the parking lot in the car you kissed Will. Is that correct?
> WITNESS: I testified that when we arrived at the estate, he gave me a goodnight peck.
> . . .
> LAWYER: That's all it was?
> WITNESS: Yes sir.
> LAWYER: Nothing of any,—nothing more than that?
> WITNESS: No.

Sexual History

Rape victims are also subject to attack on the basis of their sexual history with men other than the defendants . . . Black asks Bowman a series of apparently sympathetic questions about her meeting with Smith. But he subtly connects her to "the bar scene," with all its tawdry connotations, by suggesting that Smith rescued her from it. Then, by the device of abandoning his own question in midsentence ("You were no longer—"), Black implies that Smith's arrival interrupted the unspecified bar-scene activities in which she had been engaged. The rapist is thus transformed into a missionary to fallen women . . .

> LAWYER: You had an engrossing conversation?
> WITNESS: Yes sir.
> LAWYER: You didn't have to be involved in the rest of the bar scene?
> WITNESS: Yes sir.
> LAWYER: You were happy to have found that?
> WITNESS: It was nice.
> LAWYER: You were no longer,—in fact you were with him almost exclusively?

WITNESS: I don't know . . .

It is also hard to imagine a man being subjected to this kind of cross-examination. On the one hand, imputing emotional instability to a man requires specific evidence, since it does not evoke a stereotype. On the other hand, what is to be gained by imputing a calculating, logical mindset to a man—even in matters of sexual conquest—since that is what everyone expects? The point is well illustrated by an excerpt from prosecutor Moira Lasch's cross-examination of Smith. When she accuses him of a lack of emotional involvement in the events of the evening, he simply acquiesces, and the attack goes nowhere . . .

LAWYER: So you have this conversation—, well you had this act, then you ejaculate and then you say, "Well I'm going into the water and take a swim now."
WITNESS: Yes.
LAWYER: That sounds not too romantic, Mr. Smith.
WITNESS: I don't know how to respond to that.

A final illustration of the uniqueness of rape trials comes from our own study of the Smith case. Here, Black cross-examines Bowman about her pantyhose, which she earlier testified she had removed at some point on the night of the rape . . .

LAWYER: Did you take off your pantyhose at Au Bar?
WITNESS: I don't remember doing that.
LAWYER: Did you have your pantyhose on when you left the bar?
WITNESS: I'm, I think I did.
LAWYER: Did you have your pantyhose on when you drove your car from Au Bar [with Smith as her passenger]?
WITNESS: Yes.
LAWYER: Did you have your pantyhose on when you got to the parking lot at the Kennedy home?
WITNESS: Yes.
LAWYER: Did you have your pantyhose on in the car in the, in the parking lot?
WITNESS: Yes.
LAWYER: Did you have your pantyhose on when you got out of your car?
WITNESS: I'm not sure.
LAWYER: Did you have your pantyhose on when you went into the house?
WITNESS: I'm not sure.
LAWYER: Did you have your pantyhose on in the kitchen?
WITNESS: I don't remember.
LAWYER: Did you have your pantyhose on when you walked through the house?

WITNESS: I don't remember.
LAWYER: Did you have your pantyhose on when you walked across the lawn?
WITNESS: I don't remember.
LAWYER: Did you have your pantyhose on going down the stairs?
WITNESS: I don't remember.
LAWYER: Did you have them on while you were standing on the beach?
WITNESS: I don't remember.
LAWYER: Did you have them on when you were going up the stairs?
WITNESS: I don't remember.

In this sequence, Black uses an ordinary cross-examination technique—the repetitive question form—to extraordinary effect. The form of the questions is within Black's exclusive control. The law of evidence does prohibit repetitive questioning, but Black skillfully avoids that prohibition by a subtle shift from question to question. Each question hammers home the identical point but in reference to a moment in time slightly later than that in the previous question.

In an effort to understand the effect, we have asked many of our students to analyze this testimony. The students continually focus on Black's ability to manipulate gender differences in the classification of clothing. From a male perspective, the students contend, there are two principal classes of clothing: clothes and underwear. Pantyhose constitute underwear because they are never fully exposed in public. One's underwear is exposed to the opposite sex only in circumstances of intimacy. Decent people do not lose track of their underwear when in mixed company. Patricia Bowman, by contrast, cannot remember what happened to her underwear during her evening with William Kennedy Smith. How, Black's questions imply, can a man be held responsible for his actions toward such a woman?

By contrast, the students argue, pantyhose are interstitial from a female perspective. They are underwear in the sense that they are worn beneath something else, but their removal does not always imply intimacy. Indeed, removing one's pantyhose in the dark before walking on the sandy beach is a perfectly ordinary act. From this perspective, the status of Bowman's pantyhose at various times during the evening is irrelevant to the issue of Bowman's consent to sex. Because of Black's control over the questions, however, this perspective is never expressed.

This line of questioning could occur only in the cross-examination of a rape victim. Black has identified and exploited a topic that has no male counterpart. It is meaningful only because the sexuality of a woman is at issue.

The two previous sections reveal two paradoxical failures of justice. The first section shows how the law and legal discourse deny to the average working-class American the very protection the law promises. The second failure is revealed in the way in which male-oriented hierarchies and discourse subvert the goal of justice for women who are raped, serve the interests of alleged rapists, and revictimize their victims.

The next section reveals yet a third paradox, one with even wider implications than the two previous ones.

From Paradox to Paradox to Paradox: The Rule of Law as Oppressor

In their collaborative work with the provocative title of *Plunder: When the Rule of Law is Illegal*, Laura Nader and Ugo Mattei argue that Euro-American rule of law ideology is used by wealthy Western nations to plunder the natural resources of weaker developing countries.[146] In contemporary Western society the ideology of the rule of law constitutes its dominant political discourse, although the origins of the idea of the rule of law can be traced back to the ancient civilizations of China and the Middle East. This ideology has been exported at the global level and has imposed an international normative consensus that is enforced by such international institutions as the World Bank, The International Monetary Fund (IMF) and the World Trade Organization (WTO).[147] One justification for the export is the "argument of lack" (*i.e.*, that non-Western countries are lacking in good governance).[148] By this logic, just as the use of alternative dispute resolution techniques was promoted in the United States in the name of justice, empowerment, and civilization, rule of law ideology is promoted abroad in the name of democracy, empowerment, civilization, and so on.[149] Yet the West's version of the rule of law is self-serving in that it promotes Western hegemony rather than empowerment abroad.

Among the variety of techniques that rule of law ideology uses to justify plunder is the notion of harmony, or imposed consent. Just as, say, women as consumers are coerced into internalizing beauty ideology, weaker countries are persuaded to accept Western business approaches with their attendant legal and institutional controls. But these controls have not been transplanted abroad in a literal or physical sense. Rather, the transplantation has occurred through coercive persuasion that foments the evolution in non-Western societies of a legal and political consciousness that idealizes Western ideology as superior, more rational, and more efficient than local ideology. Among the examples of such transplants are the concepts of patent and intellectual property rights, which serve to rationalize Western appropriation of natural resources belonging to other, "weaker" cultures. These and other notions form the bedrock principles of major institutions of global governance such as the World Intellectual Property Organization (WIPO), the World Trade Organization (WTO), the

146. Ugo Mattei & Laura Nader, Plunder: When the Rule of Law is Illegal (2008).

147. *Id.* at 3–4, 5, 16, 19, 30, 35–37, 50, 57–59, 68–75, 128–29, 132–33. For a study of the exploitative aspects that created the Argentinian debt crisis and economic collapse, as well as the role of Wall Street and the IMF, *see id.*, at 35–63.

148. *Id.* at 4, 65, 67, 70–75.

149. *Id.* at 1.

International Monetary Fund (IMF), and the International Bank for Reconstruction and Development (IBRD, or World Bank). These institutions, which are supported by a vast network of private transnational corporate actors such as the International Chamber of Commerce (ICC), are engaged in the private production of law (*i.e.*, private international law).[150]

The goal of the legal consciousness promoted by Western corporate interests in foreign cultures is to produce local professional elites that have internalized Western public legal discourse and can therefore provide legitimacy to hegemonic power. This hegemonic power is accepted by local elites and eventually the population at large because it is seemingly benevolent and explicitly promises "civilization, wealth, development and liberation."[151] For example, given that information is a mechanism of power, Western ideas about patent and intellectual property monopolize control of economically useful information which in turn is used to monopolize economic power.

These notions are rooted in Lockean ideas of natural rights such as the right to own property that is the fruit of one's own labor and creativity. Such Western individualistic approaches to property are, however, incompatible with certain modes of property and the basic communitarian values of many non-Western cultures. Yet they are enshrined in the structures of WIPO, through its Trade-Related Intellectual Property Agreements (TRIPS), and the WTO. For example, the concept of property among the Kayapo of Brazil is radically incompatible with its Western counterpart and therefore in conflict with Article 27 of the TRIPS agreement. This article permits a patent for any invention that is "non-obvious" (*i.e.*, altered from a natural state) and is useful and novel, and must be produced by a specific individual.[152] The Kayapos' conception of knowledge is that it is the product of nature rather than human effort; by this logic, knowledge need not necessarily be "useful." Instead, knowledge among the Kayapo is in the public domain and is passed on from one generation to the next. From these premises it follows that the Western assumption that an invention must be the product of a specific individual would be inappropriate among the Kayapo because for them knowledge is communally owned and, as such, difficult to attribute to a single person and even more so to commercialize.[153]

Ugo Mattei & Laura Nader, Plunder: When the Rule of Law is Illegal 82–86 (2008).

> Both the colonial relationship and current hegemonic globalization include a persuasive ideological dimension. Subordinates, or at least a significant portion of them, must be persuaded of the superior nature of the dominant

---

150. *Id.* at 81.

151. *Id.* at 82.

152. *Id.* at 85. Agreement on Trade Related Intellectual Property Rights, Apr. 15, 1994, Marrakesh Agreement Establishing the World Trade Organization, Annex 1C, 33 I.L.M. 1125 (1994) "TRIPS agreement"), art. 27.

153. Mattei & Nader, *supra* note 146, at 86.

order and civilization compared to their own. Without such an ideological component, oppression would be a much more costly exercise. An outright display of physical violence is not a viable long-term strategy. Soft power is much more efficient than hard power, and the establishment of the ideological apparatuses supporting its construction is a crucial aspect of any project of plunder.

While power sometimes uses outright propaganda, professionalism proves more effective in persuading the more educated sectors of the population. Particular professional elites acquire, at the international level, the influence necessary to provide legitimacy to hegemonic power. Their role, most importantly, is to target local intellectuals and public discourse in order to use the prestige of a local influential social class to narrow the costs of physical domination while maintaining foreign control and, ultimately, plunder. Such international and domestic intellectual support allows the imperial project to credibly promise to the local populace, civilization, wealth, development, and liberation. It is an ideological exercise, the province of mainstream ideologues, to render outward plunder invisible and the practices supporting it as acceptable to most because of its benevolent nature.

The function of providing legitimacy is sometimes institutionalized, as in the case of Catholic missions in colonial times. Sometimes, it is more decentralized, as in the case of a much-admired solo scholar lecturing through the world of academic invitations. The non-critical posture of such persons over their own legal and political system might itself function as a powerful ideological justification for the state of subordination because it ultimately provides conservative role models for local elites.

Programs such as the Fulbright grants for lecturing abroad, or a variety of other similar, often commendable, initiatives are examples of what we mean. In this case, to be sure, nothing forbids the traveling lecturer from being critical. Nevertheless, the process of selection and the psychology of the role, make self-critique highly unlikely. In 2005 Professor John Yoo, the author of the notorious torture brief, was Fulbright Professor at the University of Trento, in Italy. . . .

The immediate aftermath of the Cold War was opened by the invention of the world wide web protocol on the internet. It is enough to browse the internet once to see its American cultural imprint. The quantitative and qualitative advantage of US-based English language sites is yet further evidence of the very strong cultural hegemony of the United States in this network, the ultimate symbol of globalization and progress. . . . Information is today perhaps the most important source of wealth. Intellectual property, rooted as it is in an extreme Western individualistic notion of property law, is incompatible with existing modes of property and fundamental communitarian values of many societies. Western intellectual property ideas are expanded worldwide through the internet and enforced by TRIPS (trade-related aspects of intellectual property) agreements, the intellectual property "branch" of the powerful WTO. Intellectual property formalizes the disparity of wealth and power that technology yields, through granting to the global market-dominating minority an advantage seemingly impossible to overcome. The non-territorial nature of intellectual property as symbolized by the internet and the claim of universality and of objectivity of its justification is producing more institutional imperialism.

Global legitimacy of intellectual property is rooted in the notion that individual creativity deserves a prize and that exclusive property rights constitute such a prize. We are back to Locke and to natural law justifications of individual ownership, the same previously discussed line of thinking that granted legitimacy to early genocides and looting in the "vacant" Native Indian lands of North America. Nobody would farm without guarantee of exclusive property on the outcome of his/her labor. Nobody would have incentives to create if there were no intellectual property rules granting a monopoly on the benefits of his/her creativity. . . .

The general universalistic individual-centered philosophy propagated by intellectual property rights and by the institutions created to enforce it worldwide (World Intellectual Property Organizations, TRIPS), serves the needs of powerful corporate actors. Patents and copyrights are monopolies. In the name of efficiency and innovation, it promotes the notion that ideas, like every other resource, should be placed on the market to become the property of whoever is willing to pay more for them, thus increasing social wealth. This seemingly neutral justification hides the relationship between willingness to pay and capacity to do so, thus naturalizing the continuously increasing advantage of the stronger market actors. . . .

The case of the Kayapo in Brazil has been fully documented. Article 27 of the TRIPS agreement maintains that for an invention to be patented, it must be "non-obvious" (substantially altered from a natural state), useful, and novel, and it must be the product of a specific individual. The Kayapo conception of what constitutes human invention differs radically. The Kayapo consider knowledge to be a product of nature and not of human nature. Next, for the Kayapo, knowledge is not always translated into "useful products." Whereas the TRIPS agreement requires an invention not to have been known, indigenous knowledge is passed down from generation to generation. Any Kayapo can know a cure—it is in the public domain. The final criterion that it be considered the product of a specific individual would not fit the Kayapo context, for their knowledge is communal and difficult to attribute to one particular person and thus consequently more difficult to commercialize. Thus, Western intellectual property rights are not composed of values expressing the full range of human possibility but rather are composed of beliefs reflecting the interests of the Western market-dominating minority and then universalized. . . .

The Kayapo are only one example. The literature is replete with episodes of "fishing expeditions" in which Western scientists in the field observe practices or cultural expressions based on centuries-old local knowledge.

A. Hegemonic Role of Lawyers and Anthropologists

Notwithstanding the local and global disparities described in the foregoing excerpt, Western governments have funded economists, lawyers, and anthropologists to disseminate Western ideology. The argument of lack has served as one convenient rationale for this effort;[154] another is the projection and power of Western philosophy, for example, the naturalism of John Locke and the rationalism of Max Weber. We have already seen a brief explanation of Lockean naturalism; by contrast, Weber's legal orientalism contrasted Western with Eastern systems of law. The former was described by Weber's fourfold typology of formal, substantive, rational, and irrational, which in turn yields two dimensions: formal/substantive and rational/irrational. Western law is thought to have been subsumed under the ideal type of formal/rational, whereas Eastern systems are thought (in the West) to be substantively irrational. This contrast has produced the argument of lack (*i.e.*, the lack of formal, efficient, and rational law).

As the idea of *terra nullius* legitimized Western occupation of foreign lands (on the ground that they belonged to no one), usurpation of local law was legitimized through the notion of *lex nullius* (*i.e.*, foreign cultures lacked proper legal infrastructures).[155] Anthropologists have served as witting and unwitting supporters of these trends. For example, the evolutionary theories of Lewis Henry Morgan (who classified societies under an evolutionary scheme with savagery and civilization at either extreme)[156] were used by the administration of Theodore Roosevelt to dispossess and resettle American Indian populations during the late nineteenth and early twentieth centuries.[157]

Mattei and Nader refer to a case study of the Shoshone tribe by evolutionist Julian Steward,[158] whose thesis about multilinear evolution was that the degree of cultural development of any society is proportional to its ability to exploit techno-environmental factors and resources. The lowest level of sociocultural integration occurs at the family level, when each family is self-sufficient and independent of every other family. However, this integration means that no social structures can be present at the level of band, tribe, or nation. The U.S. Department of Justice harnessed Steward's thesis to claim that the Shoshone people had no institutions that could support title to land, and therefore the land of the tribe was *terra nullius*.[159] Such evolutionary ideas were also applied in Canada to expropriate lands of the Inuit, which led Mattei and Nader to conclude, "There can be no doubt that anthropological ideas have had

---

154. *See* text at note 148, *supra*.

155. Mattei & Nader, *supra* note 146, at 110.

156. *See* Chapter 1, text at notes 71–104.

157. Mattei & Nader, *supra* note 146, at 106.

158. *See* Chapter 5, text at notes 72–74, 92–96, *supra*.

159. Mattei & Nader, *supra* note 146, at 105.

a continuing influence beyond the discipline, legitimizing the premises of colonial legal ideology."[160]

Ugo Mattei and Laura Nader, Plunder—When the Rule of Law is Illegal 104–07, 110 (2008).

Following the Dawes Allotment Act of 1887, the US Congress struggled to solve claims by Indian nations for breaches of the treaties governing their surrender. Finally, in 1946, the Indian Claims Commission (ICC) was enacted to hear these cases. A progressive movement, beginning with John Collier's 1933 appointment as Superintendent of Indian Affairs, attempted to rectify outstanding legal claims. Opposition to these claims was supported on social scientific as well as legal grounds. The ICC had specified that claims could be advanced by Indian tribes, bands, and nations. Perhaps unbeknownst to the original intentions of the US Congress, there was conjured a class of North American Indians who did not fit any of the three categories listed in the ICC mandate, a society too primitive to meet the criteria of a "band," a society that could be considered unorganized. The United States Department of Justice advanced such an argument. Their expert witness was none other than the distinguished American anthropologist Julian Steward, an evolutionist building on the work of nineteenth-century lawyer-anthropologists.

The Paiute, a Great Basin Shoshone tribe, were part of a claim. The land in question dealt with some 325,000,000 acres of land acquired by the United States government without compensation or treaty agreement. The strategy of the government was to deny title to the Indian plaintiffs on the grounds that they were not organized societies, and therefore could not own lands. Julian Steward's categorization of the Shoshone corresponded precisely with the picture favored by the Department of Justice. Steward's evolutionary logic was a line of reasoning much used in colonial law under the British. This doctrine is expressed in the natural law doctrine of *terra nullius* . . . —territory unoccupied that consequently could be freely and legally appropriated by the colonizers. In this light, Steward's social evolutionary theory became a matter of legal and political significance, a theory that legitimized the denial of indigenous rights to collectively hold lands. In the case at hand, the Northern Paiutes were not considered to be an "organized" society, and seen as too primitive to belong to one of the three categories, band, tribe, or nation who could own a territory.

Steward's theories sought to connect environment with cultural development, a schema for evaluating the "level" of a specific society from simple to complex. According to Steward the lowest level of socio-cultural integration was the family level, a situation where each family is independent and self-sufficient. Stuck at the family level (not a band or a tribe, let alone a nation), the Shoshone had not achieved a level of socio-cultural integration that had institutions that could hold

160. *Id.*

title to land, a position favorable to the position advanced by the Department of Justice and consistent with the doctrine of *terra nullius*.

The reputation of Steward's project rested on the presumption that his work was scientific and objective, not ideological or interpretive. Concerns raised recently about Steward's science and objectivity emerge from knowledge that his theoretical model was developed during his stint as an expert witness for the Department of Justice over a 7-year period, suggesting that Steward's theoretical project may have been influenced by his close relationships on one side of a number of litigations. By 1950, Steward supported the view that ownership of property existed only when the form of landholding explicitly fit the characteristics of land ownership defined by American law.

According to contemporary investigations the story does not end there. Steward's position on the doctrine of *terra nullius* is argued in Canada as well. In a 1979 judgment concerning rights of the Inuit of Baker Lake, indigenous parties must demonstrate that they lived in an "organized" society in the pre-settlement period. . . .

Of course, *which* ethnologists were to gain the ears, and ultimately the money, of administrators and politicians at this time depended upon how these ethnologists thought the Indian populations should be controlled, and subsequently to which theories they subscribed. Henry Lewis Morgan's (*sic*) version of evolutionism, known as progressive (being grounded in a notion of social progress), was used to justify the continuous resettlement of Indians throughout the end of the nineteenth century and into the twentieth century by the movers and shakers of Teddy Roosevelt's time. . . .

Critical anthropologists like Frank G. Speck exposed the policies of Teddy Roosevelt, presiding over the further dismantling of Indian lands at the time, and who was speaking, as an evolutionist, of Indian nomadism. Roosevelt and his friends, perhaps legitimized (though unwillingly) by Morgan's evolutionism and later by Julian Steward, depicted the Indians as "wanderers and beggars" unattached to private property, a thin observation used to justify government plunder. The powerful evolutionists were mainstream spokesmen, and they are still with us today disguised as neo-liberals.

With the emergence of the Red Power movement in the 1960s, new economic developments on Indian reservations appeared, namely gambling and the "employment" of Native Americans as the overseers of toxic waste. Today we readily identify a fine line between coercion and informed consent, and anthropological knowledge when at the service of legalized plunder might make it even more opaque. For example, the institutional elements of federal, state, and reservation politics include the nuclear waste industry, a player that has been out of sight in ethnological reports in the past.

A number of issues appear if one considers anthropologists as providers of legitimacy and consent since Europeans came to the New World. Particular conditions in North America shaped the discipline here:

> A profound difference between the history of our discipline in Europe, on one hand, and in the Western hemisphere on the other, inheres in

> the simple fact that our subjects of study, our "primitive" peoples, were our neighbors—our ill-treated, indeed often persecuted, neighbors. In this instance, as in others, the anthropology we did and have done is conditioned by the history and social complexion of the society from whence we came....

A recent plethora of efforts to study Islam have revisited old questions regarding Muslims. Particular to this revisiting is legal orientalism and the followers of Max Weber, the father of legal orientalism. Weber's use of categories or ideal types is reminiscent of Julian Steward's evolutionism. His four-fold taxonomy of legal systems with two dimensions—formal/substantive and rational/irrational—generates four categories. Again there is hierarchy. Continental law fits into the ideal type of formal/rational, while Islamic law features "traditional prescription and arbitrary decision-making, the latter serving as a substitute for a regime of rational rules." While seemingly benign, the scholars who elaborate Weber's typology on the ground carry implications that are anything but benign. Currently, social scientists continue Weber's characterization of the capricious *qadi* (judge), using the metaphor of the bazaar to describe a world of chaos, indicating an Arab lack of appreciation for regularity and space and time. Exploring the injustice born of substantive irrationality makes Western law the evaluative standard, setting the stage for plans of US foreign policy today in Iraq and Afghanistan. American foreign policy will presumably save Eastern countries from irrationality, illegitimacy, and unchanging immortality by an imposition of "modern" Euro-American neo-liberal law. The usurpation will be legalized in this case not by *terra nullius* but by *lex nullius*. The perception that they lack something the civilized world possesses becomes a justification for invasions. And now we have the terrorism ticket. Anthropology's myopia, in spite of its real potential, is generally the guardian of conventionality born of nineteenth-century lawyer-anthropologists. The exceptions are either relegated to the margins, escape by means of abstract epistemologies, or leave the field altogether.

B. Alternative Dispute Settlement as Hegemonic Controlling Process Abroad

Western states have also imposed a coercive normative consensus abroad by promoting conciliatory models for the settlement of international disputes. Collectively known as ADR (alternative dispute resolution) and IDS (international dispute settlement), these models have been institutionalized within the World Bank and the WTO. As seen in the foregoing excerpt, in conciliatory fora the principle of equality before the law does not apply, and thus the stronger party has the advantage in a forum of privatized justice. Many international arbitral fora are run by private commercial organizations such as the London Court of International Arbitration and the International Chamber of Commerce; both of these have their own courts of arbitration, which are run by their own rules.[161]

UGO MATTEI & LAURA NADER, PLUNDER: WHEN THE RULE OF LAW IS ILLEGAL 78–80 (2008).

Mainstream thinking deems ADR to be beneficial in less developed countries that, "lacking" a high level of legal professionalism, might find it hard to properly organize a machinery of adversary adjudication. Thus, the World Bank (that actually makes mandatory the use of mediation to solve conflicts with assisted countries) promotes conciliation and mediation of disputes as a pragmatic alternative for development. ADR moreover is often presented as more "culturally sensitive" to the difference of mentality of countries "lacking" the rule of law. The Western mainstream still largely perceives non-Western legal systems as a caricature-like image of the Qadi (Islamic judge) dispensing (expediency-based) justice sitting under a tree, made famous by Max Weber and once used even by US Supreme Court Justice Felix Frankfurter. Thus ADR, with its emphasis on informality and case-specific justice, is deemed congenial to local needs, because it is closer to what is stereotyped as "oriental" mentality.

Even though such "harmony" models have little to do with American ideas of justice and having one's day in court, they are often taken for granted or deemed benign, with little attention to the fact that power disparity is even more pernicious in informal justice than it is in adjudication. We need to remember the pacification role of Christian missionaries and of their rhetoric of social harmony, under conditions of colonial domination or imperialistic conquests, in South America and Africa. There, notions of Christian resignation to a superior will of God have curtailed effective resistance, favoring plunder. Thus harmony ideology like ideologies of efficiency and the rule of law is germane to plunder.

Today, legal reforms worldwide increasingly standardize and ritualize ADRs or IDSs to fit global power strategies in a manner that *erases differences* caused by uneven power or diverse or competing cultural styles. In the process of standardizing ADR, thinking about the conflict becomes narrow and technical, and context shrinks. ADR thus becomes just another technical and professional system of justice, with its specialists and its professionals, only loosing the empowerment factor (for the weaker party) that might come from the potentially counter-hegemonic use of public courts of law. ADR thus becomes a forum of private justice where "Anglo-American law firms in international business transactions, the Uruguay Round of the GATT, and the formation of the World Trade Organization (WTO), . . . credit-rating agencies, and so forth" play a major role. The shift is from public courts to private panels, from formal adjudication to informal or negotiated justice,

161. *See generally*, ISAAK DORE, THE UNCITRAL FRAMEWORK OF ARBITRATION IN CONTEMPORARY PERSPECTIVE (1993).

part of the more generalized movement to privatize everything from prisons to social welfare institutions, thus losing the empowerment and potential counter-hegemony that sometimes comes from the adversary nature of the judicial process. It is then no surprise to find ADR clauses in most standard contracts, with banks, insurance companies, telecoms, and corporate employers eager to offer their own "private justice" to their clients.

A regime of transnational commercial law, a hegemony of neo-liberal concepts of economic relations structured very much in an American corporate style, systematically removes constitutional and institutional protections and access to law, where victims of plunder could possibly complain and maybe occasionally even win. In this arena, international arbitration and the new specialties in conflict resolution are key legal mechanisms of control. Yet, none of these happenings are standing still, and the dialectic between plunder, adjudication, and ADR is variable and in constant flux. There seems to be a trend, as any history of the WTO can attest to. . . .

Today, the power of the WTO resides in its dispute resolution panels allowing any WTO member country to challenge the domestic laws of any other member. These panels are held in secret, with no right of citizens or subnational authorities like State Attorney Generals to participate, and panel decisions are automatically adopted within no independent appeal, no written record, and selective enforcement. It is no light observation that states are conceding certain of their prerogatives to supranational entities. Even though the shifts from one type of disputing style to another are never total, that they occur at all is worth noting because it indicates how elastic models of dispute resolution, packaged as "rule of law," are.

Global reform trends seem to pursue elastic arrangements in dispute resolution to strengthen the advantage of the stronger bargaining partner. It is imperative to understand the makeup of the "soft" technologies of law such as ADR, and how such soft technologies might fit with plunder. It is, however, also important to understand that the contemporary muddy ideology of the rule of law can embrace both adjudication and ADR, sometimes in apparently contradictory ways. For example, the so-called Washington Consensus urges China to observe international patents or to create a court system to enforce business contracts, while at the same time urges Bangladesh to negotiate with India over the Ganges rather than take their complaints about water rights to the World Court.

Conclusion

The case studies by Merry, Mattei, and Nader reveal several paradoxes in the United States and its international economic relations. Merry demonstrates the paradox of legal entitlement. Resort to law by average working-class Americans is usually understood as an exercise of individual freedom, if not self-empowerment. Yet they end up in a double bind in which they not only fail to get the justice they want but also fall under the domination of the institutions of the state. This process demonstrates cultural domination because state institutions such as the courts and their branches of mediation and conciliation use their legal authority to change the frame of discourse. The typical change involves a coerced abandonment of legal solutions in favor of nonlegal ones. The litigants are thus denied the very forms of protections and remedies promised by the legal system they invoke, and the working class as a whole becomes subordinated to different normative orders manipulated by those who control the judicial system.

Because existing class hierarchies are reinforced, with their attendant social disparities, the law as thus administered is an inherently conservative mechanism that maintains the *status quo* through coercive power and ideological domination. Nor can class and social hierarchies be changed by invoking the law, because complaints against the existing social order are construed only within the frameworks established by the law, particularly its normalizing discourses of mediation, therapy, and help. The processes of cultural domination by and through law result in the encroachment by state institutions in private and intimate relations between spouses, family members, neighbors, and others.

The studies of Mattei and Nader demonstrate an equally nuanced set of paradoxes, both domestically and on the international plane. Nader's study of harmony ideology demonstrates the imposition in the United States of a culturally coerced normative consensus in law and medicine (*e.g.*, the move toward ADR, which was sanctioned by no less significant an institution than the U.S. Supreme Court). Both researchers' works show that ADR is a hegemonic normative force that operates outside and beyond the reach of the equal protection principle, even though it supposedly functions in the name of justice and civilization. In the beauty and medical industries, the case study of breast implants shows how women are culturally coerced into mutilating their bodies under the rubric of free choice.

Mattei and Nader's collaborative study demonstrates how the rule of law is a symbol used in Euro-American practices of violent extraction (*i.e.*, the plunder) of natural resources by stronger international actors that victimize weaker ones. Working within an ethnocentric configuration of institutions and belief systems inspired by, among others, John Locke and Max Weber, Western powers use rule of law ideology for colonial and imperial projects. This ideology does not depend on the use of overt force, however; rather, it provides harmony implemented through an ideological consensus that is, though persuasive, as coercive as its domestic counterpart and is legitimized by economists, lawyers, and anthropologists. It is persuasive in the sense that the rule of law is proclaimed abroad in benevolent form, promising civilization, wealth, development, and liberation.

An essential component of rule of law rhetoric is the protection of property and especially intellectual property; the latter in particular is an alien concept in many cultures. The protections of property rights, enshrined in domestic law, are exported to the legal structures of the major international economic institutions. These protections are imposed on foreign cultures on the ground not only that they promote efficiency and rationality, but also that foreign systems lack fair and efficient legal systems.

Finally, just as the various mechanisms of ADR came into vogue as controlling processes in the domestic (U.S.) economy, ADR mechanisms were integrated within the major institutions of international governance. Again the settlement of disputes occurs in secret, through a system of private justice in which the principle of equality does not operate, thereby ensuring that the stronger parties retain their bargaining power and hegemonic control of the international economy.

Presenting the Native Point of View in a Nonnative Culture: The Cultural Defense in Criminal Law

A. Introduction

Consistent with the postmodernist trend, APM is critical of metanarrative, which for our purposes is the idea of the universality of culture and its accompanying claim that, like all of reality, culture can be accurately and objectively described by language. In any case, the human condition and lived experience exists in many layers that in turn are interpreted and described through different languages. APM argues against privileging any voice or voices in such descriptions and interpretations over other voices. This argument explains APM's embrace of polyvocality—an approach that not only is inclusive but also grants equal standing to multiple voices. Rather than privileging one authoritative voice, APM encourages communication among them and the creation of polyvocal texts. Polyvocality in turn undermines the ostensible unity of ideas in metanarratives.

These concepts can be readily demonstrated in the area of criminal law, as when a native of one culture infringes on a basic normative principle of another, alien culture. As social mobility on a global scale increases exponentially, the countries of Western Europe and North America have become more and more pluralistic. They have experienced influxes of populations whose cultural traditions are often radically different from Western traditions and Euro-American legal principles. These population shifts have resulted in cultural conflict, given the host states' legitimate interest in protecting core cultural values against the countervailing interest of protecting the right of individuals to practice their own beliefs, particularly when they intend no harm. But even when no harm is intended and no harm is caused, the question remains of whether a defendant's cultural background absolves the individual from criminal responsibility for acts that would otherwise result in conviction. If not, the matter of whether cultural beliefs at least be considered as mitigating factors in deciding punishment must still be decided.

Such cultural conflicts have stimulated the growth of a new multicultural jurisprudence, as law enforcement officials of host countries grapple with the challenges of polyvocality.[162] The phenomenon of the cultural defense in criminal law illustrates how a native cultural practice is invoked as a defense in criminal proceedings in a

162. *See, e.g.*, Multicultural Jurisprudence: Comparative Perspectives on the Cultural Defense (Marie-Claire Foblets & Alison Dundes Renteln eds., 2009).

nonnative culture or how a minority voice clamors for recognition in a cultural context that otherwise denies its legitimacy.

B. A Case Study of the Cultural Defense in the United States

The case of *State of Maine v. Mohammad Kargar* is a good illustration of the foregoing issues.[163] Kargar was convicted in Maine of two counts of gross sexual assault for kissing his son's penis. Kargar, a native of Afghanistan, was part of the Mujahideen army that fought the Russian invasion of Afghanistan in the late 1970s and 1980s. At the time of his arrest, he was a refugee to the United States and had lived in this country for approximately four years. His son Rahmadan was born in the United States.[164]

A neighbor had witnessed Kargar kissing the 18-month-old boy's penis. The neighbor's mother had also previously seen a photograph, in the family photograph album, of Kargar kissing his son's penis.[165] The woman notified the police of both incidents.

Upon his arrest, Kargar not only did not deny the act in question but also asserted that kissing a young son's penis is accepted as a common practice in Afghani culture.[166] Kargar then moved for a dismissal of the case pursuant to Maine's *de minimis* statute, which in all material respects is identical to Section 2.12 of the Model Penal Code and provides that:

> The Court shall dismiss a prosecution if, having regard to the nature of the conduct charged to constitute an offense and the nature of the attendant circumstances, it finds that the defendant's conduct:
>
> (1) was within a customary license or tolerance, neither expressly negative by the person whose interest was infringed nor inconsistent with the purpose of the law defining the offense; or
> (2) did not actually cause or threaten the harm or evil sought to be prevented by the law defining the offense or did so only to an extent too trivial to warrant the condemnation of conviction; or
> (3) presents such other extenuations that it cannot reasonably be regarded as envisaged by the legislature in forbidding the offense.
>
> The Court shall not dismiss a prosecution under Subsection (3) of this Section without filing a written statement of its reasons.[167]

163. 679 A.2d 81 (Me. 1996).

164. Appellant's Brief at 4, State v. Kargar, 679 A.2d 81 (Me. 1996) (No. 7719, CUM-95-300).

165. *Kargar*, 679 A.2d at 82.

166. *Id.* at 82–83.

167. Model Penal Code §2.12.

C. The Cultural Dimensions of Kargar's Defense

Kargar submitted evidence that his conduct had not been improper or even sexual according to Islamic law. He also argued that he did not know that his act was prohibited under Maine law.[168] The evidence included statements from an expert at the Center for Middle Eastern Studies at the University of Arizona, as well as from the Director of the Afghan Mujahideen Information Bureau in New York. Both witnesses testified that the act in question is neither improper nor sexual under Islamic law.[169] Other Afghani natives testified that kissing a young son on all parts of his body is common practice in that country. An Ahman, or priest, of the Muslim community of Maine also testified as to the innocent nature of the act in Afghani culture.[170] Kargar himself testified that the penis is considered not "the holiest or the cleanest part of the body because it is from where the child urinates" and that "kissing his son there shows how much he loves his child precisely because it is not the holiest or cleanest part of his body."[171]

Other testimony was given showing that under Islamic law any sexual activity between an adult and a child is a serious crime, punishable by death.[172] Testimony was also given by investigating social workers, the guardian *ad litem*, and a psychiatrist, to the effect that if the Kargar family had suffered at all, it was due to their enforced separation following the father's arrest rather than any sexual misconduct on his part.[173]

D. The Trial Court's Ruling

The trial court rejected the defendant's motion to dismiss and found him guilty, despite also finding that he had not had a culpable state of mind or engaged in the conduct in question for purposes of sexual gratification. Nevertheless, the court held that the latter two elements (state of mind and sexual gratification) were irrelevant to the issue of guilt; the innocent nature of the act was not relevant to a *de minimis* inquiry.[174] Also irrelevant to a *de minimis* inquiry, according to the trial court, was the lack of harm to the child; indeed, harm was simply assumed.[175] Finally, the trial court dismissed culture as a relevant factor because, according to it, the legislature did not intend "a variable scale" of inquiry depending on cultural origin and because "uniformity" in the application of the law was essential.[176]

---

168. Appellant's Brief, *supra* note 164, at 11.

169. *Kargar*, 679 A.2d at 83.

170. Appellant's Brief, *supra* note 164, at 13.

171. *Kargar*, 679 A.2d at 83 n. 3.

172. *Id.* at 83.

173. Appellant's Brief, *supra* note 164, at 13.

174. *Id.* at 15.

175. *Id.*

176. *Id.*

In passing sentence, however, the court suspended the two eighteen-month prison terms, noting that any actual jail time would "send the wrong message" and that the Kargar family had already suffered enough.[177] The suspension was for a term of three years on the condition that Mohammad Kargar learn English.[178] Even though no prison time was imposed, the two-count conviction automatically exposed Kargar to deportation; he also had to register himself with the police as a sex offender with restrictions on obtaining certain licenses and privileges, such as a license to own a firearm[179] and a license to work as a private security guard.[180] Kargar appealed his conviction, challenging the trial court's denial of his motion to dismiss pursuant to the *de minimis* statute.[181]

E. The Appellate Ruling

The Supreme Judicial Court of Maine upheld the appeal and instructed the trial court to dismiss the case.[182] It began by noting that trial courts should be granted broad discretion in determining the propriety of a *de minimis* motion.[183] The court also held that the trial court had erred on a matter of law in finding Kargar's culture, lack of harm, and innocent state of mind as irrelevant to the *de minimis* inquiry.[184]

Both the Model Penal Code and the Maine statute based on it were, according to the court, designed to introduce a "desirable degree of flexibility in the administration of the law."[185] The defendant's conduct had to be evaluated "having regard to the nature of the conduct alleged and the nature of the attendant circumstances."[186] Each *de minimis* inquiry thus requires a case-specific approach.[187] The court also traced the historical origin of the *de minimis* defense in the Model Penal Code (and statutes based on it) to its English counterpart of 1879, both of which allowed acquittal when an act, although constituting a crime, did not involve "any moral turpitude."[188] In summary, the court enumerated the following broadly drawn criteria as appropriate for a *de minimis* analysis:

---

177. *Id.* at 15–16.

178. *Id.* at 1.

179. ME. REV. STAT. ANN. tit. 15 § 393 (1)(A) (West. Supp. 1997) (prohibiting the issuance of a firearm license to anyone convicted of a crime punishable by a term of one or more years in prison).

180. ME. REV. STAT. ANN. tit. 32 §9405 (1-A)(D) (West 1983).

181. *Kargar*, 679 A.2d at 82.

182. *Id.* at 86.

183. *Id.* at 83.

184. *Id.*

185. *Id.*

186. *Id.* For text *see* MODEL PENAL CODE § 2.12 *supra* note 167.

187. *Kargar*, 679 A.2d at 83.

188. *Id.* at 83–84.

> the background, experience and character of the defendant which may indicate whether he knew or ought to have known of the illegality; the knowledge of the defendant of the consequences to be incurred upon violation of the statute; the circumstances concerning the offense; the resulting harm or evil, if any, caused or threatened by the infraction; the probable impact of the violation upon the community; the seriousness of the infraction in terms of punishment, bearing in mind that punishment can be suspended; mitigating circumstances as to the offender; possible improper motives of the complainant or prosecutor; and any other data which may reveal the nature and degree of the culpability in the offense committed by the defendant.[189]

The court also rebuked the trial court for interpreting Maine's gross sexual assault law in such a way as to essentially nullify the *de minimis* provision of the statute.[190] The focus should not have been on whether the conduct in question fell within the reach of the statute that criminalized it. If it did not, there would be no need for any court to engage in a *de minimis* analysis. Instead, the focus of the trial court should have been on "whether the admittedly criminal conduct was envisioned by the Legislature when it defined the crime."[191] Had the legislature not intended a case-specific analysis, there would have been no reason to include the *de minimis* provision. Indeed, the latter provided a "safety valve for circumstances that could not have been envisioned by the Legislature."[192] Such case-specific analysis allows courts to take into account unforeseeable "extenuations" when strict application of the law would lead to "intolerable" results.[193] The trial court had failed to take into account not only such extenuations but also the possibility of intolerable results unanticipated by the legislature in Mohammad Kargar's case.[194]

The court also examined the legislative history of the gross sexual assault law and found that the law was in effect premised on sexual gratification. This element was lacking in Kargar's case because his touching was "innocent" and not sexual.[195] These and other extenuating factors (such as the threat of immediate deportation and registration as a sex offender) are explained in the unanimous judgment excerpted as follows.[196]

State of Maine v. Mohammad Kargar, 679 A.2d 81, 85–86 (Me. 1996).

---

189. *Id.* at 84.

190. *Id.*

191. *Id.*

192. *Id.*

193. *Id.*

194. *Id.*

195. *Id.* at 84–85.

196. In *State of Maine v. Ramirez*, 2005 WL 3678032 (2005), the Superior Court of Maine affirmed *Kargar* on facts that were almost identical. The Court in *Ramirez* accepted the cultural defense of a mother who was a native citizen of the Dominican Republic. Evidence was presented showing that it was accepted practice under Dominican culture for a mother to touch, caress, and kiss her son's penis. In another case, *State of Texas v. Krasniqi*, an Albanian Muslim accused of inappropriately touching

The Legislature's inability to comprehend "innocent" genital-mouth contact is highlighted by reference to another type of "sexual act," namely, "[a]ny act involving direct physical contact between the genitals . . . of one and an instrument or device manipulated by another." 17-A M.R.S.A. § 25(1)(C)(3) (Supp. 1995). The Legislature maintained the requirement that for this type of act to be criminal it must be done for the purpose of either sexual gratification or to cause bodily injury or offensive physical contact. Its stated reason for doing so was that "a legitimate concern exists for excluding 'innocent' contacts, such as for proper medical purposes or other valid reasons." L.D. 1386, Statement of Fact (112th Legis. 1995).

All of the evidence presented at the *de minimis* hearing supports the conclusion that there was nothing "sexual" about Kargar's conduct. There is no real dispute that what Kargar did is accepted practice in his culture. The testimony of every witness at the *de minimis* hearing confirmed that kissing a young son on every part of his body is considered a sign only of love and affection for the child. This is true whether the parent kisses, or as the trial court found, "engulfs" a son's penis. There is nothing sexual about this practice. In fact, the trial justice expressly recognized that if the State were required to prove a purpose of sexual gratification it "wouldn't have been able to have done so."

During its sentencing of Kargar, the court stated: "There is no sexual gratification. There is no victim impact." The court additionally recognized that the conduct for which Kargar was convicted occurred in the open, with his wife present, and noted that the photograph was displayed in the family photo album, available for all to see.[4] The court concluded its sentencing by recognizing that this case is "not at all typical [but instead is] fully the exception. . . . The conduct was unequivocally criminal, but the circumstances of that conduct and the circumstances of this defendant call for leniency." Although the court responded to this call for leniency by imposing an entirely suspended sentence, the two convictions expose Kargar to severe consequences independent of any period of incarceration, including his required registration as a sex offender pursuant to 34-A M.R.S.A. § 11003 (Supp. 1995), and the possibility of deportation pursuant to 8 U.S.C.A. § 1251(a)(2)(A)(i)(I) (West Supp. 1996). These additional consequences emphasize why the factors recognized by the court during the sentencing hearing were also relevant to the *de minimis* analysis.

Although it may be difficult for us as a society to separate Kargar's conduct from our notions of sexual abuse, that difficulty should not result in a felony conviction in this case. The State concedes that dismissing this case pursuant to the *de minimis* statute would pose little harm to the community. The State

---

his daughter was acquitted in Texas after expert testimony on Albanian culture was presented. *See* Multicultural Jurisprudence, *supra* note 162, at 65.

is concerned, however, with the potential harm caused by courts using the factors of this case to allow for even more exceptions to the criminal statutes. It argues that exceptions should be made by the Legislature, which can gather data, debate social costs and benefits, and clearly define what conduct constitutes criminal activity. The flaw in the State's position is that the Legislature has already clearly defined what conduct constitutes gross sexual assault. It has also allowed for the adjustment of the criminal statutes by courts in extraordinary cases where, for instance, the conduct cannot reasonably be regarded as envisaged by the Legislature in defining the crime.[5]

As discussed above, the Legislature removed the sexual gratification element previously contained within the definition of a sexual act because it could not envision any possible innocent contacts, "given the physical contacts described." In virtually every case the assumption that a physical touching of the mouth of an adult with the genitals of a child under the age of fourteen is inherently harmful is correct. This case, however, is the exception that proves the rule. Precisely because the Legislature did not envision the extenuating circumstances present in this case, to avoid an injustice the *de minimis* analysis set forth in section 12(1)(C) requires that Kargar's convictions be vacated.

The entry is:

Judgments vacated. Remanded to the Superior Court with instructions to enter an order granting defendant's motion to dismiss pursuant to 17-A M.R.S.A. § 12(1)(C).

All concurring.

. . .

4. Kargar's wife, Shamayel, testified during the sentencing hearing that she took the picture to send to Kargar's mother to show her how much he loved his son.

5. Application of the *de minimis* statute does not nullify the gross sexual assault statute nor does it reflect approval of Kargar's conduct. The conduct remains criminal. Kargar does not argue that he should now be permitted to practice that which is accepted in his culture. The issue is whether his past conduct under all of the circumstances justifies criminal convictions.

In the second paragraph of the excerpted opinion, the Supreme Judicial Court of Maine explicitly recognizes the cultural defense. It notes that there was no dispute that the defendant's conduct in question was "accepted practice in his culture." From this it followed that the act was "innocent" and not "sexual," as previously noted. This conclusion led to the other necessary conclusion: that no sexual gratification, and thus no victim impact, had occurred. These conclusions had to be balanced against the severe potential consequences of conviction, namely automatic deportation and registration as a sex offender.

It is interesting to ponder whether the court would have reached the same result absent the latter two consequences; we may surmise that it would have. The court's repeated reminders of the need for flexibility, the concern for moral turpitude, legislative intent regarding unanticipated cases, absence of sexual gratification, innocent nature of the act, overwhelming evidence that it was a culturally accepted practice, character as an act of love rather than abuse, lack of victim impact, explicit desire of the court to quash the conviction outright instead of using the cultural defense only as a mitigating factor in deciding punishment—all these considerations point to an acquittal even if Kargar did not have to face deportation under the law, register as a sex offender, or give up his ability to obtain a gun permit or license to work as a security guard.

Less predictable would be the outcome absent the *de minimis* statute itself. The latter gave explicit legislative authority to the court to exercise broad discretion. We may ask whether the court would have acquitted Kargar and accepted his cultural defense under these circumstances. On one hand, the drafters of § 2.12 of the Model Penal Code acknowledged that culture affects many of the factors that must be taken into account by a court engaging in a *de minimis* analysis.[197] Native cultural understandings and meanings can explain why a defendant does not know that a particular action constitutes a crime in his host country or that he does not understand the consequences of the offense. Indeed, the absence of actual knowledge that certain conduct violates the law is crucial to a *de minimis* analysis.[198] "The nature of the attendant circumstances" required by § 2.12 for consideration are also cultural in nature. The finding of absence of victim harm was thus due to the fact that the conduct in question was culturally sanctioned. It was incumbent on counsel to bring these factors to the attention of the court. Failure to do so could be seen as a violation of the right to effective counsel guaranteed by the Sixth Amendment of the U.S. Constitution.[199]

Finally, the comment to § 2.12 states that a *de minimis* analysis is triggered when "the customs that control the conduct of a particular racial or social group are at variance with those that predominate in the community that motivated the legislation in question."[200] This language is tantamount to an explicit incorporation of the cultural defense by the Model Penal Code. It therefore seems pertinent to ask whether a court would accept a cultural defense in the absence of a *de minimis* statute.

The case or rationale for its acceptance is that enculturation shapes a person's perceptions and behavior in unconscious ways,[201] meaning that he or she may be

197. *See, e.g.*, State v. Kargar, 679 A.2d 81 (Me. 1996). *See also* N. A. Wanderer and C. R. Connors, "Culture and Crime: Kargar and the Existing Framework for a Cultural Defense," 47 Buff. L. Rev. 829 at 833 (1999).

198. *Id.*

199. Alison Dundes Renteln, *The Use of Abuse of the Cultural Defense*, *in* Multicultural Jurisprudence, *supra* note 162, at 61, 67.

200. Model Penal Code §2.12 cmt. at 403.

201. Renteln, *supra* note 199, at 62.

unaware of having internalized a particular mode of being or way of life. The theoretical foundation for the cultural defense thus "hinges on the idea that individuals will think and act in accordance with patterns of culture."[202] In meting out individualized justice, taking a person's culture into account is no different from taking into consideration a person's gender, age, or mental state.[203] The constitutional foundation of the cultural defense is that it ultimately springs from the right to effective counsel, which is guaranteed by the Sixth Amendment as noted previously.[204]

By this logic, many of the ingredients that constituted the basis of the court's decision to overturn Kargar's conviction would remain unchanged—for example, the fact that the practice he had engaged in was culturally accepted, that he enacted it innocently as an individual, that it was an act of love, and that there was neither victim impact nor sexual gratification. Thus, the absence of a *de minimis* statute in the circumstances uniting *Kargar* would have had no bearing on these culturally conditioned factors.

F. The Cultural Defense as a Mitigating Factor

A *de minimis* analysis is only one vehicle through which culture mediates people's senses of guilt and, generally, of justice.[205] It is therefore arguable that both guilt and justice are concepts that have no necessary link to a *de minimis* analysis and that a court needs no express legislative grant to temper the harshness of the law to serve the ends of justice. For example, in *People v. Kimura*, a young Japanese mother attempted *oya-ko shinju* (parent-child suicide). After being shamed and humiliated by the knowledge that her husband had a mistress, she walked into the cold waters of Santa Monica Bay with her six-month-old and four-year-old children. Both children drowned, but she was rescued by passersby and charged with first degree murder, which was reduced to voluntary manslaughter in a plea bargain. In this case, the judge and the district attorney accepted psychiatric evidence that convinced them that her state of mind was less than that required for a murder conviction.[206]

Similarly, in *People v. Chen* a Chinese husband became so deranged over his wife's extramarital affair that he bludgeoned her to death with a hammer.[207] Expert testimony was provided that in Chinese culture, such conduct results in shame and loss of face for the husband. In light of the evidence that a wife's adultery makes her husband "more prone to violence"[208] in Chinese culture, the charge of second-degree

202. *Id.*

203. *Id.*

204. See *id.* at 67. *See also* text at note 199 *supra*.

205. Wanderer & Connors, *supra* note 197, at 843–44.

206. People v. Kimura, No. A-091133 (L.A. Super. Ct. 1985).

207. People v. Chen, No. 87-7774 (N.Y. Sup. Ct. 1989).

208. Taryn F. Goldstein, *Cultural Conflicts in Court: Should the American Criminal Justice System Formally Recognize a Cultural Defense?*, 99 Dick. L. Rev. 141, 165 n. 215 (1994–1995).

murder was reduced to second-degree manslaughter. Again, culture was accepted as the main force affecting the defendant's state of mind and thus indicating whether or not he was guilty;[209] Chen's counsel asserted that "the basis of the defense is the emotional strain based on cultural differences and the state of the defendant's mind." He maintained that "cultural pressures" provoked Chen into an extreme state of "diminished capacity," causing him not to have the intent necessary for the more serious charge of premeditated murder. The judge, who concurred, found that the defendant was "driven to violence by traditional Chinese values about adultery and loss of manhood."[210]

In neither *Kimura* nor *Chen* was there any express legislative grant of discretion in the form of a *de minimis* statute or in any other form. However, as seen later in this section, the court in *Chen* received erroneous cultural evidence regarding loss of face in China.[211] This error, although it may have affected the verdict in this particular case had it been discovered earlier, does not affect the point that courts can and do exercise discretion to admit cultural evidence in the absence of express legislative authority.

In addition to the five jurisdictions in the United States that have *de minimis* statutes based on the Model Penal Code, many others have enacted "interest of justice" statutes or rules of procedure that grant legislative authority to courts to dismiss prosecutions.[212] If the foregoing arguments are persuasive, interest of justice statutes are on par with *de minimis* statutes, and their absence is no bar to admitting the cultural defense. This conclusion is not shared by all commentators, however. Wanderer and Connors, for example, assert that "At least in the absence of a statute or court rule authorized by statute, allowing judicial review of a decision to prosecute or review under the common law or even constitutional precepts is narrowly proscribed, if not prohibited."[213] They do acknowledge that judicial review of prosecutions is allowed in cases of suspect classification (*i.e.*, when a prosecution is motivated by considerations of race and religion), but they decline to include culture in the category of suspect classifications for purposes of allowing judicial review of prosecutorial discretion.

---

209. Note, *The Cultural Defense in the Criminal Law*, 99 HARV. L. REV. at 1293, 1294–1300 (1986) (discussing culture, state of mind, moral blameworthiness and culpability).

210. Goldstein, *supra* note 208, at 152 (quoting Alexis Jetter, *Fear is Legacy of Wife Killing in Chinatown; Battered Asians Shocked by Husband's Probation*, NEWSDAY, November 6, 1989, at 4).

211. *See* text at note 238 *infra*.

212. *See* ALASKA R. CRIM.P. 43(c); CAL. PENAL CODE § 1385 (West 1982) (amended 1986); IDAHO R. CRIM. P. 48(a)(2); IOWA R. CRIM. P. 27(1); MINN. STAT. ANN. § 631.21 (West 1983) (current version at MINN. STAT. ANN. § 631.21 (Supp. 1999); MONT. CODE ANN. § 46-13-401; N.Y. CRIM. PROC. LAW § 210.40 (McKinney 1993); OKLA. STAT. TIT. 22, § 815 (1998); OR. REV. STAT. TIT. 14, § 135.755 (1997); UTAH R. CRIM. P. 25; VT. R. CRIM. P. 48(b)(2); WASH. REV. COD. TIT. 10, 8.3 (West 1990). New York courts, acting under an interest of justice statute, have a long history of dismissing prosecutions when moral blame is lacking or minimal: *See e..g. People v. Davis*, 286 N.Y.S.2d 396, 398–99 (N.Y. Sup. Ct. 1967) (granting a dismissal for a twenty-year-old college student found in possession of an ounce of marijuana because of his exemplary moral background and "unblemished record").

213. Wanderer and Connors, *supra* note 197, at 847.

> Even if culture were treated similarly to race for the purpose of identifying the parameters of a selective prosecution defense, the exception would not provide assistance to those seeking to advance a cultural defense to criminal prosecution. The suspect class exception to complete prosecutorial discretion is applied to ensure that prosecutors do not discriminate against minorities—that they treat minority defendants as equal to the general populace. The concern is that the prosecutor will choose to pursue a minority defendant for a crime that he or she would not prosecute were the defendant white.... In contrast, a cultural defense does not seek to prevent discrimination in the ordinary sense. Rather, such a defense seeks to have the minority treated *differently* from the majority—to have the prosecutor *forego* prosecution when the average defendant *would* be prosecuted. For this reason, those espousing a cultural defense cannot look toward conventional anti-discrimination jurisprudence as support (*sic*) their cause.
>
> Looking to affirmative action precedent for analogies provides no support for a cultural defense for similar reasons. Although affirmative action does, on one level, seek to treat minorities differently from the majority in a positive way by providing benefits unavailable to the equivalent non-minority member, such action is permitted in order to compensate for past discrimination.... Again, the focus is on leveling the playing field, not allowing for different fields for those with different backgrounds.[214]

Although it is true that the suspect classification category seeks to prevent discrimination and the cultural defense seeks differential treatment, this distinction is artificial; both are concerned with overall justice. The cultural defense may even have an *a fortiori* claim for inclusion in the category of suspect classifications because, as *Kargar* teaches, culture has a close connection to our understanding not only of justice but also of guilt. It was Kargar's valid cultural defense that led to the quashing of his conviction rather than a mere reduction of his sentence. A finding of not guilty could not be clearer. For these reasons, culture may be treated not so much as a suspect category specially crafted to serve justice but as a special and independent category dedicated to serving justice (in the same manner as suspect classifications) and for establishing guilt and/or innocence.[215] After all, there is precedent (known as Blackstone's Tenth Rule) that shows courts have authority under the common law to interpret statutes in ways that would avoid "a ludicrous result."[216] The common law rule against absurd results is another avenue through which to channel the cultural defense as a credible and principled legal argument.[217]

---

214. *Id.* at 847 n. 85.

215. *See* Nancy S. Kim, *The Cultural Defense and the Problem of Cultural Preemption: A Framework of Analysis*, 27 N.M. L. Rev. 101 at 121 et seq. (1997) (proposing a framework for testing the admissibility of the cultural defense under the Federal Rules of Evidence).

216. 1 William Blackstone, Commentaries *91.

217. Wanderer & Connors, *supra* note 197, at 849.

Furthermore, the trial judge has broad discretion regarding the admissibility of expert testimony. Cultural evidence and its admissibility may be treated in the same way and may be admitted to negate or mitigate the *mens rea* element in a criminal proceeding.[218] For example, in *People v. Wu*,[219] the defendant (a Chinese woman named Helen Wu) was convicted of second-degree murder after she strangled her son, Sidney, who had informed her that his father had a girlfriend. Her counsel argued that the act was committed because the defendant "felt trapped and, in intense emotional upheaval, strangled Sidney and then attempted to kill herself so that she could take care of Sidney in the afterlife."[220] On appeal, Wu argued that the trial court had failed to exercise its discretion properly and had committed prejudicial error by refusing to give two jury instructions requested by the defendant, one of which related to the effect her cultural background might have had on her state of mind when she strangled her son. The California appeals court upheld the appeal, stating that the defendant was entitled to have the jury instructed that it could consider evidence of the defendant's cultural background in determining the existence or nonexistence of her mental state.[221]

A less happy outcome befell the defendant in *Siripongs v. Calderon*.[222] Siripongs was a Thai national who was convicted of murder at a convenience store. Although he had participated in the robbery, he denied pulling the trigger; his presence at the scene, however, was technically sufficient for him to receive the death penalty. During the sentencing phase, when Siripongs maintained a stoic silence and showed no emotion, his attorney failed to explain that this was in accordance with a Thai cultural trait that demands stoicism under stressful and traumatic circumstances. One commentator speculated that Siripongs's stoicism may have been mistaken by the jury for a sign that he lacked remorse. Had cultural evidence been presented, the jury might have spared him the death penalty, especially if they believed that someone else had committed the murder.[223]

G. The Cultural Defense under the Bill of Rights and Balancing of Interests

Another reason that the cultural defense can stand as an independent category (on par with suspect classifications) to prevent injustice is that it can readily be woven into the web of constitutional protections under the Bill of Rights (*e.g.*, the right to due process, freedom of religion, privacy, equal protection, right to effective counsel).[224]

218. Kim, *supra* note 215, at 121.

219. People v. Wu, 286 Cal. Rptr. 868 (Ct. App. 1991).

220. *Id.* at 870.

221. *Id.* at 887.

222. Siripongs v. Calderon, 35 F.3d 1308 (9th Cir. 1994).

223. Renteln, *supra* note 199, at 67–68.

224. Wanderer & Connors, *supra* note 197, at 850 *et seq. See also*, *Awad v. Ziriax*, 754 F. Supp.2d 1298 (W.D. Okla. 2010). In 2012 the 10th Circuit Court upheld a decision that struck down a proposed

Kargar did challenge his conviction on these grounds, but the Supreme Judicial Court of Maine did not address them, given its decision to quash based on the *de minimis* statute. Nonetheless, as seen in *Kargar*, the cultural meanings and understandings of foreign communities mediate our own (Western) understandings of guilt. Kargar's lack of intent as established by his cultural defense led to the overturning of his sentence, which is another way of establishing a lack of guilt. The U.S. Supreme Court has declared that punishing acts that show no intent, and which are therefore innocent, violates the Due Process Clause of the U.S. Constitution, absent other "extraneous proof of blameworthiness or culpable mental state."[225]

Ultimately, however, establishing guilt, protecting due process rights, and promoting justice all involve balancing interests.[226] The *Kargar* case can, roughly, be seen as a balancing of individual freedom and due process interests against victim harm and harm to society in the broader sense. The concept of *de minimis*, by definition, implies a balancing test, especially when used in a penal context. As noted previously, the judge has broad discretion to take certain threshold decisions regarding the admissibility of cultural evidence, which often takes the form of expert testimony. The exercise of this discretion is itself an important element of balancing. The judge can take account of the following criteria in exercising discretion:

(1) the purpose of the cultural practice;
(2) the moral culpability associated with the cultural practice;
(3) the deterrence/educational value of prohibiting the cultural evidence; and
(4) alternative forms of sentencing.[227]

H. Limits to the Cultural Defense

One obvious difficulty raised by the cultural defense doctrine is just how far it can be pushed—in other words, how to set its limits and prevent its abuse.[228] The *Kargar* and *Turner* cases would be good starting points in establishing the minimum conditions that any cultural defense must satisfy. These should include:

(1) genuine membership of a native class
(2) motivation on the part of the defendant by a cultural belief system
(3) innocent nature of defendant's conduct

---

amendment to the Constitution of Oklahoma that would have banned courts from using Sharia law, on the ground that the amendment would violate the Establishment and Free Exercise Clauses of the First Amendment. *Awad v. Ziriax*, 670 F.3d 1111 (10th Cir. 2012).

225. Stanley v. Turner, 6 F.3d 399 (6th Cir. 1993).

226. *See Awad*, 670 F.3d at 1130 *et seq.* (discussing balancing of interests, in this case, the "compelling state interests" of Oklahoma). *See also* Goldstein, *supra* note 208, at 160–62 (discussing deterrence as an important element to be balanced against cultural factors).

227. Kim, *supra* note 215, at 133. For an expanded discussion of these criteria and rebuttal of anticipated objections thereto, *see id.*, at 133–36, and 136–38 respectively.

228. For a summary of arguments rejecting the cultural defense altogether, *see id.* at 110 *et. seq.* *See also* Renteln, *supra* note 199 at 68 et seq.

(4) uniform acceptance of such conduct by the native class of culture
(5) the absence of victim harm
(6) lack of violence
(7) lack of intent
(8) absence of culpable mental state
(9) absence of extraneous proof of blameworthiness
(10) lack of moral turpitude
(11) legislative intent regarding unanticipated cases, and, in sexual cases
(12) absence of sexual gratification

Kargar satisfied all twelve of these overlapping considerations, although, as Renteln points out, genuine membership of a native class may not always be easy to prove.[229] Similarly, *Chen* shows the difficulties of establishing the fourth condition (genuine acceptance of a practice by the native class of culture). As seen later in the section, the court was wrongly persuaded to accept that shame and loss of face are culturally conditioned responses in China.[230] Similarly, in the notorious Reddy sex smuggling case, a spurious cultural argument was advanced during plea bargaining to the effect that although sex with underage girls in the United States might be considered immoral and is certainly illegal, this is not the case in India and particularly for girls who belong to the class of Untouchables. The implication of the defense was that girls from such lower echelons of society in India can legally and morally be subjected to forced labor and sexual enslavement.[231] Although such a practice is "not widely regarded as desirable" in India, its prevalence is tolerated due to harsh economic conditions that are exploited by unscrupulous employers.[232] In any case, the *Reddy* case shows clear victim harm. It demonstrates grave violations of national and international human rights law as well as gross moral turpitude, thus violating several of the foregoing twelve conditions.

Related to the reliability of cultural evidence is the phenomenon of essentializing a culture.[233] A judge who is unfamiliar with a culture may treat it as monolithic even though it may contain many subgroups, each with its own nuanced traditions. It is therefore necessary to be attentive to cultural nuances, as well as to avoid stereotyping and improper generalizing. For example in *R v. Adesanya*, a Yoruba mother was prosecuted for assault causing bodily harm (in this case, facially scarring her children). The English judge rejected her cultural defense based on "Nigerian custom" when there is in fact no single Nigerian custom, given that Nigeria has a variety of tribal groups. Yet the judge imposed a suspended sentence, which implied that he had been influenced by the cultural defense after all.[234]

---

229. Renteln, *supra* note 199, at 70.

230. *See* text at note 238, *infra*.

231. Renteln, *supra* note 199, at 76.

232. *Id.* at 77.

233. *Id.* at 79.

234. *Id.*

Under the twelve guidelines, the cultural defense would not be available for conduct such as female genital mutilation (FGM), honor killings, homicide for loss of face, marriage by capture, and so on. Such practices, although sanctioned in certain cultures, involve violence and harm to the victims, not to mention moral turpitude in the Western sense. Not surprisingly, the decision of the court in *Chen*[235] was condemned by women's organizations and Chinese organizations as well.[236] The court's thinking was criticized as being patriarchal and archaic.[237] Indeed, a native Chinese scholar from the People's Republic argued that the cultural loss of face defense has been abolished there, that it would not be considered a "mitigating element" under Chinese law, and that Chen's conduct would be punishable in contemporary China.[238] She also warned of the dangers of using expert witnesses.[239]

The cultural defense doctrine is not only a measure of tolerance within a multicultural and pluralistic society, it is also a tool for individualized justice.[240] It is not, however, a license to unbridled freedoms that threaten core values of the host culture.[241] It is of course a truism that such core values differ from culture to culture, but at some point such relativity of values, while conceded, must of necessity engage in line drawing to prevent the destruction of the social fabric of the host culture.[242]

Many controversial cases have come before the courts of the United States and other Western countries implicating cultural defenses. These have included FGM, facial scarring of young children by parents, so-called "honor killings," marriage predicated on rape, and homicide motivated by humiliation, shame, loss of face, and so forth.[243] None of these would meet the twelve conditions. However, U.S. courts have not used a systematic approach. Sometimes they completely reject the cultural defense, at other times they partially accept it, and at still others they use the cultural defense as a mitigating factor in the sentencing phase or in plea bargaining.[244]

---

235. People v. Chen, *supra* note 207.

236. Kim, supra note 215, at 124–25.

237. Goldstein, *supra* note 208, at 165. *See also* Kim, *supra* note 215, at 121 (arguing that the *Chen* case is an example of the misuse of the cultural defense).

238. Cher Wiexia Chen, *A Critique of 'Loss of Face' Arguments in Cultural Defense Cases: A Comparative Study,* in MULTICULTURAL JURISPRUDENCE, *supra* note 162, at 247, 257–58.

239. *Id.* at 258–59.

240. Goldstein, *supra* note 208, at 157.

241. Kim, *supra* note 215, at 111 (for argument that cultural defenses should not be allowed when they reinforce subordination of women).

242. John C. Lyman, *Cultural Defense: Viable Doctrine or Wishful Thinking?*, 9 CRIM. JUST. J. 87, 111–16 (1986).

243. *See generally* MULTICULTURAL JURISPRUDENCE, *supra* note 162. This volume is an excellent collection of the cultural defense in several countries of Western Europe, North America, and elsewhere.

244. *People v. Moua*, Case No. 315972-0 (Fresno Super. Ct. 1985). *See infra* text at note 244. *See, e.g., Two Iraqi Men Face Hearing*, OMAHA WORLD-HERALD, Nov. 26, 1996, at 22; Myrna Oliver, *Immigrant Crimes Cultural Defense-A Legal Tactic*, L.A. TIMES, *Two Korean Christian Missionaries are Cleared of Murder in the Killing of Kyung-Ja Chung During Cleansing Ritual*, L.A. TIMES, April 17, 1997, at A1; Dick Polman, *When is Cultural Difference a Legal Defense? Immigrants' Native Traditions*

The practice of marriage by capture (*zij poj niam*) sanctioned in Hmong culture would not pass muster under the foregoing test. This is because in the typical case, a Hmong man's courting ritual includes the kidnapping of his prospective wife, with whom he has sexual intercourse while she is captive at his family home (the marriage is considered to have been consummated by this act).[245] It is also reported that in certain cases the Hmong woman goes willingly ("marriage by elopement") but yet protests against the sexual advances of her suitor, supposedly to prove her virtue.[246] Such questions are admittedly not always easy to decide, but ultimately it would be the burden of the prosecution to establish violence, victim harm, state of mind, and so on. For example, in the case of *People v. Moua*[247] the defendant, a Hmong immigrant in the United States, advanced the cultural defense in a marriage kidnapping case; he also argued that he was mistaken as to whether his partner had consented to sexual intercourse. This would normally have been a matter for the judge or jury as fact finders. At trial, however, his counsel did not invoke mistake of fact as a defense but entered into a plea bargain under which culture was used as a mitigating factor during the sentencing phase, whereby the defendant pled guilty only to the misdemeanor of false imprisonment.[248] Taking into account the cultural defense, the judge sentenced the defendant to ninety days in the county jail and imposed a fine of $1,000, $900 of which was to be paid as compensation to the woman he had kidnapped. But for the cultural defense, the defendant would have been charged with kidnapping and rape and could have faced a long term in state prison.[249]

A clearer example of the inadmissibility of the cultural defense would be in cases involving FGM. The procedure and its effects are described as follows:

> Female genital mutilation requires the incision and usually removal of part or all of the female external genitalia, which includes the clitoris, the clitoral prepuce, the labia majora and the labia minora. There are three common procedures with various levels of severity. A Clitoridectomy is the procedure most comparable to male circumcision. This procedure involves the removal of the clitoral prepuce, or the tip of the clitoris. Excision is the procedure whereby the entire clitoris and labia minora are removed, leaving the labia majora intact and the remainder of the vulva unsutured. Pharaonic circumcision, or infibulation, is the procedure in which the sides of the labia majora

---

Clash with U.S. Law, SEATTLE TIMES, July 12, 1989, at A1; David Talbot, *The Ballad of Hooty Croy: 'True Believer' Attorney Tony Serra Fights His Own Version of the Indian Wars—in a Courtroom*, L.A. TIMES, June 24, 1990, at 16.

245. Yaj Txooj Tsawb, *Excerpts from Pia Tus Txheej Txheem KabTshoob Key Kos (Outline of Marriage Rites)*, *in* THE HMONG WORLD 103, 105 (David Strecker, trans., James C. Scott ed., 1986).

246. Deirdre Evans-Pritchard & Alison Dundes Renteln, *The Interpretation and Distortion of Culture: A Hmong "Marriage by Capture" Case in Fresno, California*, 4 S. CAL. INTERDISC. L.J. 1, 8 (1995).

247. No. 315972-0 (Cal. Super. Ct. Feb. 17, 1985).

248. Evans-Pritchard & Renteln, *supra* note 246, at 25–27.

249. Carolyn Choi, *Application of a Cultural Defense in Criminal Proceedings*, 8 UCLA PAC. BASIN L.J. 80, 84 (1990).

> are sewn together after the clitoris and labia minora are removed. The girl's legs are then bound together from thigh to ankle for several weeks in order to allow scar tissue to form. Complete occlusion is prevented by inserting a splinter of wood, or a match stick, which preserves a small orifice through which urine and menstrual fluid can pass. It takes an infibulated woman approximately ten to fifteen minutes to urinate.[250]

Conditions of victim harm could not be clearer, not to mention that the practice offends basic human rights values including those of personal autonomy, equality, and dignity. Many countries have taken measures to outlaw FGM; currently, it is punishable in the United States under federal laws against child abuse. To date there has been no prosecution for FGM in the United States. If there were to be a prosecution, one could anticipate a cultural defense along lines similar to those in *Moua* and *Kargar*, which would attempt to negate the requisite mental state or *mens rea* for a crime. As in *Moua*, a defendant might attempt to allege mistake of fact as to victim consent or as to appreciating or fully understanding the wrongfulness of the act of FGM in light of cultural beliefs. As in *Wu*, *Adesanya*, and *Moua*, the court might be sympathetic to a diminished responsibility argument in light of a genuinely held cultural belief. However, given the gravity of the harm caused by FGM,[251] it is hard to imagine such an outcome, particularly if the court were to apply a balancing test. It is also highly unlikely that the defense would succeed under the *de minimis* analysis of *Kargar* and *Ramirez*.

250. Lori Ann Larson, *Female Genital Mutilation in the United States: Child Abuse or Constitutional Freedom?*, 17 WOMEN'S RIGHTS L. REP. 237, 238 (1996).

251. *See id.*

Epilogue

The Metaphysics of Culture II

The human mind has a deep-seated desire to know. Western philosophy from the time of the "sages" of antiquity in 600 BCE to the 21st century confirms this basic fact about the human condition. Not surprisingly, therefore, Western philosophy has continued to grapple with the fundamental question of how does the mind know. Great philosophical tracts and theories have been advanced over the centuries to explain this phenomenon, as exemplified by John Locke's *Essay Concerning Human Understanding*, David Hume's *Enquiry Concerning Human Understanding*, Immanuel Kant's *Critique of Pure Reason* and Claude Lévi-Strauss's *The Savage Mind* as well as his *Myth and Meaning*, to cite a few salient examples.

The quest of the early Ionians was initially directed at proving the hypothesis that the universe has a single material substratum, so that once identified it would explain everything (today commonly known as the search for the "theory of everything," or TOE.). However, the Ionians were content not just with explaining their material world; they hypothesized that their social, moral and cultural world could also be explained in terms of certain immutable propositions. Once identified, they too would explain "everything" one needed to know about living a fulfilling life of culture.[i]

This conflation by the Ionians of the material and social world (or the physical and metaphysical world) postulates a direct connection between physics and philosophy. Western thought has retained this dualism as its philosophical birthmark. Indeed, history lends credence to this dualism by repeatedly showing that scientific revolutions have spurred parallel paradigm shifts in social and philosophical thought. Yet the boundary between physics and metaphysics remains elusive.

Developments in quantum theory have introduced a new but related dualism, namely, the relation between consciousness in the physical universe and consciousness in our metaphysical universe of culture. Parallel to human consciousness is the idea of a cosmic normativity or "protoconsciousness" pervading the universe.[ii]

---

i. I have explained this dualism in greater detail in my Epistemological Foundations of Law (2007), Chapter 2.The dualism is also present in Chinese philosophy since at least the Zhou Dynasty (1050 B.C.E.). Originating in myth and legend it postulated Culture Hero Fu Xi who espoused a theory explaining everything from heaven to earth. It constitutes the foundation of *I Ching*, the sacred text which has served for thousands of years as a philosophical taxonomy of the universe with which human behavior has to be synchronized. For recent translations *see* David Hinton, I Ching: The Book Of Change (2015), and John Minford, I Ching (Yijing): The Book Of Change (2014). Both books are reviewed by Eliot Weinberger, *"What is the I Ching?"* New York Review of Books Feb. 25–Mar. 9 (2016) at 20.

ii. Roger Penrose, Shadows of the Mind: A Search For the Missing Science of Consciousness at 8 (1994). Penrose asserts: "Consciousness is part of our universe, so any physical theory which makes no proper place for it falls fundamentally short of providing a genuine description of the world." *Id. See also*, Robert Lanza, Biocentrism: How Life and Consciousness Are the Keys to Understanding the Nature of the Universe (2009).

There is scientific proof confirming that two entangled particles (*e.g.*, two photons of light sharing common origins and properties) instantaneously "know" each other's reactions to certain stimuli and mimic each other's behavior at opposite ends of the universe, even if only one of them is being subjected to the stimuli. Einstein had denied such a possibility, calling it "spooky."[iii]

The new dualism raises the question whether the biomolecular processes of the human brain are somehow connected to or synchronized with the structure of the universe.[iv] Do cosmic normativity and cultural normativity mimic each other? This question becomes even more urgent if the hypothetical protoconsciousness in fact pervades the universe and is not confined just in an elementary state in particles.

However, the key question that continues to elude theoretical physics is "why is there something rather than nothing?" The "something" of course is matter, our universe itself. Does it exist because of some synchronizing force (let us call it cosmic normativity or protoconsciousness) that is holding it together and is responsible for its continued existence? The existence of at least one universe is beyond doubt. In other words, there is something rather than nothing, and we as humans are trying to understand its laws of operation. Whether there is a synchronizing force of the kind mentioned above is an open question, for now. That the cultural world exists is also beyond doubt. Also beyond doubt is that the human brain has definite cognitive abilities to make sense of this universe. Even the most stalwart Cartesian skeptic must concede that this book alone is sufficient proof of this state of affairs, not to mention the hundreds of other books on different aspects of culture.

We may now briefly note other potential applications of the above dualisms in the realm of cultural normativity: Just as particle physics aims at studying the basic elementary particles of matter with a view to discovering the fundamental laws that control the make up of matter and the physical universe, the cultural scientist can try to identify the elementary principles making up the metaphysical universe of culture. If particle physics studies subatomic particles such as electrons, and how quarks combine to form protons and neutrons, the cultural scientist can also study law and symbols as the quarks of culture that combine to promote normative order in society. Beyond these elementary organizing principles of culture, the cultural scientist may, like his or her colleague in theoretical physics, take quantum leaps into other seemingly esoteric but nonetheless persuasive models of culture, explaining cultural stability and instability in emic and/or etic terms, in phenomenological terms, in terms of linguistic grammar, deep mental structure and other cognitive theories explored in this book. These studies are at bottom studies in human consciousness, and

iii. Salart, D., Baas, A., Branciard, C., Gisin, N. & Zbinden, H., *Testing the speed of 'spooky action at a distance' Nature*, 454, 861–864 (14 Aug. 2008). http://www.nature.com/nature/journal/v454/n7206/pdf/nature07121.pdf.

Geoff Brumfiel, Physicists Spooked by Quantum Weirdness Even Stranger than Previously Thought, in Nature,13 Aug. 2008. http://www.nature.com/news/2008/080813/full/news.2008.1038.html.

iv. Roger Penrose, Stuart Hameroff, Henry P. Stapp and Deepak Chopra, CONSCIOUSNESS IN THE UNIVERSE. QUANTUM PHYSICS, EVOLUTION, BRAIN & MIND (2011).

culture is the vast quantum space of man's metaphysical universe in which cultural events occur. The focus of these theories of culture is how the human brain comes to know the human behavioral world, in the same way that theoretical physics and quantum theory seek to know the behavioral world of atomic and subatomic particles.

Research in theoretical physics has led to the hypothesis that some 26% of the universe consists of "dark matter" that holds the universe together, preventing the galaxies from spinning out of control, while about 68% of the universe consists of a weaker "dark energy" that is pushing the galaxies apart, portending the eventual collapse of the universe. Kroeber's concept of "superorganic" or Durkheim's doctrines of "mechanical and organic solidarity" can be analogized to the dark forces that hold culture together, preventing social order from spinning out of control, not to mention the myriad other stabilizing normative forces studied in this book—these forces falling in the realm of consciousness rather than protoconsciousness.

Those forces that account for cultural instability and dynamic change such as Turner's concept of "structure, antistructure and communitas" or the radical anthropology of Marx, Harris and others could be viewed as accounts of the dark energy of culture.

It must be emphasized that these forces in physics as well as the notion of protoconsciousness or cosmic normativity are only hypothetical postulates; they await confirmation (or falsification) through further experimental research. This naturally raises the question of the epistemic value of the research regarding cultural normativity in this book (among others) and what further research is necessary to identify and elucidate the correlates of the forces in physics in the domain of culture.

This book has studied the latter domain. It has examined the human world in conditions of culture, without of course denying that humans simultaneously inhabit a materio-physical world. Indeed, many of the theories studied in this book demonstrate the undeniable ties between humankind's physical environment and it's metaphysical universe ("universe of signs").The works of Marx, Steward, White, Harris, Morgan, Engels and Malinowski spring immediately to mind.

This study of culture is based on two premises: first, our metaphysical world is relational; for it is impossible to imagine a culture in which there are no human relations. The second premise is that these relations are more orderly than they are chaotic, more structured than unstructured. The orderly and structured aspects of human relations flow from yet another truism about human relations; namely, that they take place within certain frameworks of understanding. A major focus of this book then has been the nature of these understandings and how they are derived. Insofar as these understandings are products of the mind, this book has entered the fray that has confounded Western philosophy from its inception: how do we know that what we know about our material and nonmaterial/sociocultural world is true?

Apart from this fundamental question of epistemology, another important focus of the book has been on the forces that bring order, structure and understanding in human relations. Herein lies the idea of normativity which we have broadly defined as anything that persuades, incites, seduces, influences, directs, restrains, controls or constrains behavior. This is the juridical dimension captured by the title "Homo Juridicus"; it includes law but goes well beyond it.

If culture is knowledge about how to structure behavior (or to the outside observer how behavior becomes structured), then how this knowledge is acquired must also be an essential component of our inquiry. Thus the deep-seated desire to know and how the mind acquires or conjures this knowledge is another fundamental theme of this book. Is this knowledge best acquired by the study of the material and techno-environmental conditions of life, as claimed by the Marxists and neo Marxist schools (studied in Chapters 4 and 5)?; or is it acquired through Lévi-Strauss's neo-structuralist methodology seeking to study the cognitive aspects and deep mental structures of the human mind, including myths (discussed in Chapter 6)?; or by the methodologies of cognitive symbolism and cognitive interpretivism (discussed in Chapters 6 and 7)?; or by studying certain allegedly universal trends of human evolution, as claimed by the cultural evolutionists and cultural relativists (studied in Chapters 1 and 2)?; or by studying the individual components of a culture taken as a functionally integrated whole, as claimed by structural functionalists such as Durkheim and Radcliffe-Brown (studied in Chapter 3)?; or is it acquired through linguistic, interpretive or hermeneutic methodologies of the kind advanced by Sapir, Geertz *et. al*, by which the ethnographer gives his or her best guess as to the meaning underlying a particular cultural behavior (studied in Chapters 2 and 7)?

These crisscrossing themes are presented in this book separately for analytical purposes only; they should not be studied in isolation but rather in terms of how they relate to and complement each other, pointing the way towards an integrated theory of culture as a whole. Thus the Marxist political critique of power has echoes in not only Foucault's study of state power (Chapter 7), but also in Nader and Todd's concepts of "controlling forces," "coercive consensus" and "harmony ideology" in domestic and international contexts (Chapters 6 and 8), in Spradley's study of the legal dynamics of proceedings in the courtroom, the experiences of the poor, the homeless, and gypsy minorities in court (Chapter 6) and the experience of the rape victim in court (Chapter 8).

A similar need for integration arises for the theme of autonomy versus determinism in culture, which surfaces in many sections of the book: from Kroeber's concept of the "superorganic" (in which the individual is dismissed as having no historical value, Chapter 3) to the opposite thesis of the cognitivists who regard the individual to be a potent agent of cultural development (Chapters 6 and 7); without ignoring the many shades of views falling between these binary opposites.

The various sections of the book dealing with the power of the mind to invent myths and symbols must be similarly linked to reveal how they give meaning, structure and coherence to life in particular cultural contexts. Thus like their Platonic counterpart, symbols of culture abound in many forms and contexts, such as rites, ceremonies, myths and rituals, as seen in the writings of Benedict, Mead and Malinowski (Chapter 3), Merry (Chapter 8), Lévi-Strauss (Chapter 6), Turner (Chapter 7), Schneider, Dolgin, Greenhouse, Berman and Kemintzer (Chapter 7). In the latter chapter we also saw how purely local symbols can transform themselves to become nationwide symbols representing the national ideology of a culture as a whole.

In sum, the overarching goal of this book is not only continued engagement with the Western philosophical project in the limited area mentioned above, but also taking a modest step toward understanding the metaphysics of culture, in the hope of inspiring further sustained research towards an integrated TOE of culture.

Index